D1705039

THE REBEL PUBLISHING HOUSE

Editing by Sambodhi Ma Prem Maneesha, S.R.N., S.C.M., R.M.N., M.M., D.Phil.M. (RIMU), Acharya; Ma Shivam Suvarna, B.Sc.

Typing by Ma Dharma Pratito, Swami Dhyan Sharan, B.Sc.

Design by Swami Deva Anugito

Cover drawing by Swami Deva Vishvasa and Ma Anand Meera, B.F.A.

Production by Swami Prem Visarjan, Ma Prem Amoha

Published by The Rebel Publishing House GmbH Cologne, West Germany

Copyright © Neo-Sannyas International

First Edition

Printing by Mohndruck, Gütersloh, West Germany

Distributed in the U.S.A. by Chidvilas, Boulder, Colorado

Distributed in Europe by The Rebel Publishing House GmbH, Cologne, West Germany

ISBN 3-89338-022-1

from the False to the Truth

◆

Answers to the Seekers of the Path

BHAGWAN
SHREE
RAJNEESH

In loving
gratitude
to Bhagwan

Rajneesh
Foundation
Australia

Special talks
for a group called
THE CHOSEN FEW
who are going to be
the messengers of
Bhagwan Shree Rajneesh
for the world at large

These discourses were given in
Lao Tzu Grove and Rajneesh Mandir,
Rajneeshpuram, Oregon, U.S.A.
in the period from April 1 – August 1, 1985

Table of Contents

DISCOURSE 1	IT ALL DEPENDS ON THE DISCIPLE	2
DISCOURSE 2	HERE WE CALL WORK, WORSHIP	12
DISCOURSE 3	MY RELIGION IS A GODLESS RELIGION	20
DISCOURSE 4	JUST DROP THE CROSS!	31
DISCOURSE 5	DISCONTENT: ANOTHER NAME FOR INFERIORITY COMPLEX	40
DISCOURSE 6	CONTENTMENT IS A STATE OF CONSCIOUSNESS	50
DISCOURSE 7	A SANNYASIN IS EXTRAORDINARILY ORDINARY	62
DISCOURSE 8	WITH ME BEGINS A NEW ERA IN ENLIGHTENMENT	73
DISCOURSE 9	BE KIND TO YOURSELF, STOP ALL THIS SEEKING	84
DISCOURSE 10	BLESSED ARE THE RICH	93
DISCOURSE 11	THAT EXPLOSION OF BLISS	105
DISCOURSE 12	DOUBT: THE METHODOLOGY OF THE SEEKER	115
DISCOURSE 13	SYMPATHY IS A DIRTY WORD	127
DISCOURSE 14	WE ARE HERE TO BE THE WHOLE	138
DISCOURSE 15	ALL PROMISES FOR TOMORROW ARE LIES	147
DISCOURSE 16	YOU HAVE TO GROW INWARDS, THAT IS YOUR EARTH	158
DISCOURSE 17	THE DEATH OF THE MIND IS THE BIRTH OF YOU	168

DISCOURSE 18	SILENCE DOES THE MIRACLE	179
DISCOURSE 19	DEEPER AND DEEPER INTO THE MYSTERIOUS, THE MIRACULOUS	190
DISCOURSE 20	ONLY AN EGOIST CAN BE HUMBLE	200
DISCOURSE 21	THE MASTER IS NOTHING BUT A SCULPTOR	211
DISCOURSE 22	YOU ARE THE ONLY HOPE!	224
DISCOURSE 23	PERSECUTION CANNOT DO ANY HARM TO YOU	236
DISCOURSE 24	GO TO YOUR BATHROOM DANCING!	248
DISCOURSE 25	SEEING THE FACT, DROP THE FICTION	258
DISCOURSE 26	ENLIGHTENMENT IS YOU COMPLETELY GONE	270
DISCOURSE 27	CHASE THE WOMAN GENTLY	281
DISCOURSE 28	DEATH NEVER HAPPENS	293
DISCOURSE 29	FREEDOM FROM BLIND BIOLOGY	305
DISCOURSE 30	EVERYBODY WANTS FREEDOM, NOBODY WANTS RESPONSIBILITY	317
DISCOURSE 31	NO RELIGIONS, NO NATIONS, NO GOVERNMENTS	329
DISCOURSE 32	GOD: THE NEED OF THE OLD MAN	340
DISCOURSE 33	YOU ARE MY FELLOW TRAVELERS	354

Introduction

The talks in this book were given between April 1st and August 1st, 1985 in Rajneeshpuram, Oregon. This was a unique season at Rajneeshpuram – a full flowering of seeds which were planted years before, in the summer of 1981, when a handful of heart-strong souls arrived at the central Oregon desert property which was to become affectionately known to the thousands of people who would come to live, work and grow there as "the Ranch."

The land was beautifully stark: an old canyon where the rivers had mostly dried, leaving their meandering stories in the lines and colors of the rock faces. But for all the beauty of these huge stone formations, of the simple animals, grasses and bushes that grew there, of the incredible star-studded night sky – it was a desert. And we came with a vision: to make the desert bloom.

At the center of this vision was a visionary – one who can see – Bhagwan Shree Rajneesh. His clear light has always beamed directly upon the secret longings of every human heart and so many came to be with Him. Together we became a wind capable of blowing down our own limiting minds. In a storm of unstoppable activity we built roads, dams, houses, cafeterias, offices, restaurants and stores. We planted crops, wildflowers, and trees.

We invited new life: ducks and swans, pheasants and quail, and two magnificent blue herons who lived by a small waterfall.

The fruits of our labors always seemed half-hidden in the continual flurry. But as the dust finally began to settle that summer of 1985, the colors of "something new" came clear. These colors were never more clear than during Bhagwan's daily drive through Rajneeshpuram's streets when He would silently greet us one by one, eye to eye.

The anticipation of such an intimate moment overflowed from each individual's inner river into a sea of music making: guitars, drums, brass horns and silver flutes flashing in the sun, tambourines with rainbows of ribbons riding on the wind. And this ocean wave of gypsies dressed in orange, red, fuchsia and purple would rise and fall joyously against a background of green – a whole spectrum of green that had slowly climbed up from the stream banks, around the rocks and over the hills. Indeed, the desert had bloomed!

But the rarest flower to open its petals in the desert that summer was the commune of a living, enlightened being. Not the organization, the hierarchical structure which drew out of some the lust for power, jealousy and paranoia which lurked just beneath their skins. Not the organization, riddled with all the pitfalls which have been fallen into throughout the history of organizations. But a master's commune: a living, breathing, changing, organic whole.

In our full flowering we were a most diverse collection of beings – East/West, young/old, straightlaced and hip – all joined together by love. Love of Him, His silence, life on this planet, each other. The visionary's vision was alive.

To read this book is to take the rare opportunity to watch a master use the powerful instrument of a commune's love to effect the deepest change in individuals; to bring about, individual by individual, a New Man on earth.

In these discourses Bhagwan explains to us why this rare seed had to be planted, its bush so carefully tended, nourished: "I was working for years individually, but then I thought, how many people can I reach? – and I was continuously traveling up to 1970. So I could go on saying things but it was not going to bring a transformation in people.

"I had to create a commune, where what I say is not just lost, but is echoed from everybody else too, from all sides and dimensions…. You have to help me in creating the New Man."

Between the pages of this book you will find the *inside* story of what happened at the Ranch. To read it with an open mind and heart is to experience the miracle of how a master, while answering a myriad of mind's questions, can enter an individual heart.

Diving into this book, it is possible to find yourself in the river which flows *From the False to the Truth*. But Bhagwan tells us no swimming is required at all; all that is needed is to allow ourselves to be cleared of that which has been piled upon us, making us dull, miserable, asleep.

"The master is nothing but a sculptor…. You come to him as a rock, but he goes on seeing in you something which you have not even imagined. He is dashing directly towards that which is your essential reality. He has to cut off pieces of rock here and there and bring you to your real shape."

While you are peering into this exotic desert flower, be prepared for His fragrance of truth to dash directly toward you. You may be surprised to find that this divine summer breeze is what you have been waiting for all along.

Ma Prem Prartho, B.A., M.A.
Poona, India
February 1988

It All Depends
On the Disciple

DISCOURSE 1, APRIL 1, 1985

Beloved Bhagwan,

Is it possible for You to be my master if I do not wish to take sannyas?

I think you do not understand the meaning of discipleship. You are asking something impossible. It is almost as if I ask you: Can you be my sannyasin if I don't want to be your master? You can see the absurdity of it. But why such a question arises in the first place has to be understood. It has to do with the whole past of humanity.

People are Christians without being Christians; people are Hindus without being Hindus. Only formally do Christians accept Jesus as their master. It is not an intimate, sincere, total relationship. It is just by birth – it is an accidental relationship. They have not chosen to be Christians. They are born in a Christian home, or in a Jewish home, and they have been conditioned to believe that Jesus is your master, Moses is your master – poor Moses knows nothing about you, neither has Jesus any idea who you are. And this is true all over the world.

Religion has nothing to do with your birth. By birth one cannot be Christian, Hindu, Mohammedan; but that's how it has been happening. Religion has been joined with birth to deceive you. The best way to deceive a person is to give him the idea that what people are seeking, he has already got. This is the most refined way of cheating.

A Christian never thinks of searching to find out what religion is, what it means to be a disciple, what it means to accept someone as your master. He has been deceived from birth to believe that he already has religion. Ready-made it has been given to him. No effort on his part has been made, no search, no seeking, no enquiry. He has a master in Jesus Christ, he has a holy book in *The Bible;* everything is supplied by tradition, family, society.

They don't leave any chance for you to enquire on your own; and the problem is, unless you enquire on your own you will never find what life is all about, what truth is, what these tremendous moments are, like when one becomes a disciple, when one finds a master…. You will never know those moments of ultimate rejoicing. You will never run in the street naked, shouting, "Eureka! I have found it!"

Archimedes was not mad. He was one of the most important scientists of his time and of all times. And if he, finding a simple thing, a scientific fact, forgets all about clothing because he was in his bathtub when he found a certain principle for which he had been looking….

When you are looking continuously in all directions, knocking on all doors, you never know which door is the right door. Archimedes was puzzled for months because the king had told him, "If you are really a scientist you should find out one thing. Somebody, another king, has presented me with a crown of gold. I want to know whether it is pure gold, or if there is some mixture in it. Is any other metal mixed in with it? And I don't want the crown to be cut. I don't want you even to touch it. You have to find the answer without spoiling the beautiful present."

For months Archimedes was troubled: how to find out? If he were allowed to cut a little piece of the crown it would have been possible to find out whether other metals were mixed in or not. When a question remains continuously with you for twenty-four hours, it takes you, by and by, close to the answer. The answer comes in a moment of relaxation. The question is a tension, but you can get the answer in relaxation only if the tension has been to its uttermost climax.

It had been so for months, and the king was asking every day. Archimedes was starting to feel embarrassed: a well known scientist cannot find such a small thing? People had started laughing at him. He could not sleep, he could not do anything – only one question…. That day, relaxing in his bathtub – which was full of water, completely full – as he sat in the tub, naturally some water flowed out to make a space for him. And something clicked in his mind. He weighed the water that had flowed out, and he found the principle. If pure gold is put in water, then a certain amount of water will come out. If some other metal is mixed in it, then a different amount of water will come out, because that certain metal will not have the same effect on water as the gold if it is pure.

Now the crown need not be destroyed; it has just to be put in water, and another piece of pure gold of the same volume can be put in water and you can see how much water comes out from both. If it is exactly the same then the crown is of pure gold; if it is not, then there is a mixture. The finding was not something great. He had not found a master, or truth; he had not realized himself. He had not entered into *nirvana*. But such a small finding…. The question is not of small or great; the question is of finding yourself. The joy comes from finding, not what you find.

If you want to have any contact with me, you will have to be ready to travel with me. It is a long journey. Much of the load that you are carrying will have to be dropped. Much of the mind which you are thinking is very valuable will prove just junk. Much of your character that you valued so much will prove nothing but forced discipline.

Archimedes jumped out of his bathtub, ran out of his bathroom, and rushed into the street shouting, "Eureka!" A crowd followed him. They thought, "We were always thinking this man is crazy, now he has gone completely crazy; naked, he is going towards the palace!"

He reached the court naked, shouting, "Eureka, I have found it!"

The king said, "It seems you must have found it. But where are your clothes?" That moment Archimedes became aware that he was naked.

The king said, "Your coming naked shows that you must have found it, because when someone finds something it is such a joy. Who cares about clothes? Who remembers about manners? You need not say anything to me; just your coming in this way has given me proof that you must have found it."

But you have not found Christianity. You have never shouted, "Eureka!" You have not found Hinduism; you have not found anything that could have driven you into the street naked, shouting. This is why such a question arises.

You have been living on borrowed things. You can borrow things but you cannot borrow experiences. You can borrow money from someone, but you cannot borrow his love experience. You cannot say, "Just give me your love experience for two days, and I will return it with interest." Love experience is not a commodity.

You are asking me, "Can you still be my master if I don't wish to be a sannyasin?" There must be many misconceptions in your mind. As if it is something that the master has to do! So if the master accepts, that's enough, you need not be a disciple, you need not be a sannyasin, you need not do anything.

That too is given by your idiotic tradition to you: Jesus is the savior, all that you need is to accept him as your savior, and that's all. The whole responsibility is his. On your part only one thing is needed: to accept him as your savior. Nothing else is needed, no transformation in you.

The reality is just the opposite: the master does nothing. It is in your becoming a disciple that the whole mystery lies. It is in your surrender of the ego that the whole search comes to an authentic point. It is in putting your mind aside.

That is what sannyas is: an authentic discipleship. It means putting your mind aside. You have lived according to your mind up to now. If that is fulfilling, then there is no need for anybody to become a sannyasin.

If you feel you are blissful with your mind, then why bother about a master? Why carry an unnecessary load? Why become tethered? It is certain that as your mind is, it is nothing but anguish; it is suffering, misery, despair. But you are not ready to become a sannyasin. That means you are not ready to put your mind aside.

Translated into reality, you are not wishing to change even a little bit – not even your clothes, what to say about your mind? You are not ready even to hang a mala with my picture around your neck, how are you going to allow me to enter into your heart?

You want me to be your master and you are keeping yourself closed in every possible way. You are saying, "Would you like to come into my house?" and you are closing the doors in my face. On the one hand you are inviting me, on the other hand you are closing your doors and windows, so I cannot enter in any way.

The relationship between a master and a disciple is one of the greatest mysteries of existence.

The master does nothing – remember it always. He is only a presence. All that is done is done by the disciple. The presence of the master is helpful, just the presence. It is immensely nourishing. His presence gives you the guarantee that what has happened to him can happen to you; otherwise where are you going to find the evidence that things like that happen? The master's only function is to give you tangible evidence.

You cannot make Jesus your master because he

has been dead for two thousand years. The relationship between a master and a disciple is a living relationship.

You don't get married to women who died two thousand years ago; otherwise, I think everybody would be marrying Cleopatra, Amrapali. Who will bother about ordinary women when you can marry Cleopatra? And Cleopatra cannot say no; she has been dead for a long time. But you are doing the same thing when you relate yourself to Jesus, Buddha, Mohammed.

You don't understand a simple thing, that relating to a master is a bigger, far bigger love relationship; it is a far more crazy love affair. It cannot happen between somebody who is living and somebody who has been dead for thousands of years; the distance is too much.

But people prefer to make Jesus, Mohammed, Lao Tzu, Zarathustra, their master, for the simple reason that the master is not present, he cannot say no. He cannot tell you, "First you have to go through a transformation."

It is a one-way affair; the other party is absent.

But I am not absent, I am present. You cannot ask such a stupid question to me.

If you don't wish to become a sannyasin – am I mad, that I should become a master to you? Why should I become a master to you? For what? You are not even wishing to be a sannyasin. You don't want to give anything, and you want to get everything. Becoming your master I will be taking on your total responsibility. And you are not even wishing to be a sannyasin – which is nothing. At least my sannyas is the simplest that has ever existed on the earth.

What is required of you? Even this seems to be too much. Then just don't be bothered with the greater things of life. Go back to your hell. You are not meant to have eyes; perhaps to remain blind is your destiny. Remain blind.

Asking such a question implies that a master is to do everything, the only thing needed is to be accepted by him, then your work is finished. Now you can go on doing all the nonsense that you have been doing. You can do it now even more without any guilt, without any fear, without any worry about the consequences, because now somebody has taken your responsibility.

Omar Khayyam, one of the great poets of Persia, said, "Don't stop me from enjoying women and wine. Don't stop me – because God is forgiving; if I do not commit sin, then what will happen to God's forgiveness? I have to commit sins just to keep God qualified, compassionate, forgiving. No sin is bigger than God's compassion. Let me commit the worst: he is there."

You see the logic of the man? It is perfectly clear. If God's very quality is to forgive, then what is the fear of sin? And how much sin can you commit? God's compassion is infinite. All your sins combined will still be finite, they cannot be infinite. If you can commit infinite sins you have become almost a God because you can do infinite things. Then there is no difference between you and God. You have infinity in your hands as much as God has.

Omar Khayyam's statement is significant because that's what all religious people are doing: they put the responsibility on somebody, and then they go on doing their thing, hoping, believing that everything will be all right in the end. They have a great savior who will stand for them before God.

Your question seems to be just throwing responsibility on me. And I am a very irresponsible person. I have never lived responsibly. From my very childhood everybody has been telling me, "Be responsible." But I have always said, "I enjoy being irresponsible so much that I don't see the point, why I should be responsible. You enjoy being responsible – be responsible. I never say to you, 'Be irresponsible.' Why do you bother about me? If my irresponsibilities are going to lead me to hell I am perfectly willing to go there, because anyway I don't want to live with your saints.

"I have lived with saints and I have lived with sinners, and I have seen that to be with sinners is far more colorful, far more pleasant, far more human. There is some song in it, some dance in it; there is laughter, there is life. To live with a saint is to live with a dead man, a corpse."

Have you ever been in a room alone with a corpse? Can you sleep? Can you eat? Can you drink? Can you laugh? The corpse will not interfere in any way, but just the presence of the corpse in the room is enough to prevent you from living. Do you see the great principles involved there? The corpse is not doing anything, and yet you cannot eat – you will feel like throwing up. You cannot sing. The corpse is not preventing you, the corpse is not going to hear it, but just the idea of singing when the corpse is there….

Saints are dead people. The more dead they are, the more they are thought to be saintly. To live with them is simply sickening. It is nauseating. They are so inhuman about everything. They themselves live mechanically, robot-like, and they won't allow anybody else to live differently. They will make you feel guilty for everything.

In Mahatma Gandhi's ashram – and he was a great saint, *mahatma* means great saint – you could not smoke. I know smoking is silly, but what is wrong in being silly? And if one enjoys it, once in a while to be silly is perfectly human. It should be acceptable. You can tell the person, "It will harm your health, your life will be reduced by five years." But if you don't want to live that long, it is perfectly good – because what are you going to do with five years more? You will smoke more!

And it is not a healthy habit; but people who don't smoke, they fall sick – and I have seen people who have been smoking continuously, chain-smokers, never falling sick. So all this is just guesswork. All that the smoker is doing is enjoying taking the smoke in and throwing it out. The smoke is warm, just like the mother's milk, and the cigarette is exactly the mother's nipple; he is again enjoying being a child.

A cigarette is just a way of enjoying one's childhood again. That's why a cigarette is so relaxing. When you are worried, tense, you start looking for a cigarette. It helps; it is human. It will look really odd to go to your mother now, and say, "I am so tense and worried…." I think cigarettes are a good substitute. Don't disturb these people; otherwise they will disturb women. Your mother may be dead – then you have to go to your wife, and she may be just mad at the idea that you have come with. She will think you are going nuts.

Cigarettes are such a simple substitute; don't disturb people. When I see you smoking I feel sorry for you, not because you are smoking but because you *have* to smoke. I think about your worries, not about your smoking; that is nothing to be bothered about. I think about your anguish, your tension. I think that there must be something eating at your heart; otherwise why should you burn yourself with smoking? I never judge your smoking, that you are doing some wrong act. I see deeper. I see *why* you are smoking.

But no saint bothers about why you are smoking. For them smoking is a sin. In Mahatma Gandhi's ashram if somebody was found to be smoking he was immediately turned out in disgrace; he had fallen. And the poor fellow was simply trying to relax. In fact his smoking was an indication that the ashram was not relaxing, that it was not a place where people could relax. Instead, it was a place where people became more tense. In fact, all the ashrams make you more tense.

It is a strange dilemma: they make you more tense, more worried. This world is not enough for them; they bring in hell and heaven and all kinds of consequences that you will have to suffer. Rather than helping you to get out of your tense mind, they make your mind more tense – and then you cannot smoke, then you cannot drink even tea or coffee; these are all prohibited because they are all relaxing.

A relaxed person may not need to smoke unless playfully, once in a while, sitting with friends, when everybody is smoking and he does not want to play the saint. I used to go to parties when I was in the university. It was a problem because the host was worried that everybody would be drinking and I might feel left out. Knowing it from many other previous experiences, I had to go to the host and say, "Don't be worried about me. You just give me Coca Cola as if I am also drinking with everybody."

But he would say, "They will think you are also drinking alcohol."

I said, "Let them think that, it is no problem. What is the problem? It simply shows I am also human. I want to participate with them, I don't want to be holier-than-thou. To me that attitude is ugly, that attitude is simply egoistic.

"I cannot drink alcohol, because I don't know what I will do after drinking. There is no problem – as far as I am concerned there is no problem, I can drink, because I don't think that even though alcohol is called spirits, it can be spiritual, or it can enter into my spirit. It will just go through my kidneys and sooner or later pass out of the body. So there is not much of a problem. I am thinking of you, because I may do something, and that may create trouble for you! So just give me Coca Cola."

Drinking Coca Cola with people – they almost all glared at me! They all said, "You are also drinking? We were worried that you would be here not drinking, and we would look like sinners."

I said, "No, I am a drunkard. You go on, you cannot compete with me" – because I could go on drinking Coca Cola as much as I wanted. But I felt happy that they were not feeling guilty. I felt that I had done something appropriate; I had been human.

Your saints are not human. Gandhi was very particular about cleanliness. He followed the same idea: cleanliness is next to God. Now for me it is a trouble – there is no God, so only cleanliness remains. Not even next to God, just the first – there is no next. But I don't come to look into your room, and into your bathroom. That seems to me evil.

But Gandhi used to do that.

He would go into your room to see that everything is as it should be. He would have a look in your bathroom to see whether it was clean or not. But this is interfering in your privacy. I can talk about cleanliness, I can praise cleanliness. I can tell you the beauty of it; but then at least I should trust you, your intelligence, your privacy, and ultimately your responsibility to yourself. I am not responsible for you.

But this is not the way of the saints up to now. They have been after their disciples almost like detectives, making the disciple feel as guilty as possible. There is some arithmetic behind it.

The more guilty they make people feel, the bigger saints they are thought to be. Their height goes on becoming higher and higher as you go on sinking lower and lower. Their whole saintliness depends on your guiltiness. And to make you feel guilty is very simple: start condemning everything that is human, that is natural.

On my path the master is only a light. You can see in that light and go wherever you want to go. The master is not somebody who is continuously following you, forcing you. He is simply a presence. In his presence you become aware of your ultimate potential. You become aware of what you can be, and what you are not. You become aware of your hypocrisy.

Sannyas is nothing but dropping your hypocrisy.

And you say to me, "I don't wish to be a sannyasin." You insist on remaining a hypocrite, a split person. Making me your master, you will be more split. You will become more guilty because you have made somebody a master and you are not a disciple to him.

It will look unkind to you that I refuse. But it is a refusal out of compassion, not out of unkindness. I refuse to be a master of anyone who is not wishing to be a disciple.

The meaning of the word 'disciple' is beautiful. It means one who is ready to learn. And there is much to be learned. Almost everything has to be learned, because whatsoever you know is not learning, it is knowledge, completely rotten knowledge. You have taken it from others; you have not searched for it, looked for it, enquired about it. It is not your own, you cannot say "Eureka!" Not for a single thing can you say "Eureka!" And a man who is ready to learn, a disciple, finds every moment like Archimedes – life goes on revealing new secrets every moment.

How can I become a master to you? You are not ready to be vulnerable to me. You are not ready to be open to me, you are not ready to listen to me, you are not ready to come along with me. You want to remain as you are, what you are, yet you want one more guarantee: you want me to become responsible so that you feel less guilty – at least you have a master. But that is not going to help.

You can have all the masters of the world – and that's the beauty of dead masters, they cannot say no. You can accept all the masters of the world, be a disciple of all the masters of the world. There are people who are following Zen, who are following Sufism, who are following Tao, anything. Neither Lao Tzu can prevent them, nor Bodhidharma can prevent them, nor Jalaluddin Rumi can prevent them. Those people are gone, just words echoing are left.

But I am yet in the flesh.

I am yet not only a word.

My word is still living.

If you want to have any contact with me, you will have to be ready to travel with me. It is a long journey. Much of the load that you are carrying will have to be dropped. Much of the mind which you are thinking is very valuable will prove just junk. Much of your character that you valued so much will prove nothing but forced discipline.

Discipline can be forced so much that it becomes unconscious. People are behaving in the right manner – are not stealing, are not harming others, not hurting others – but it is not their conscious choice.

I have heard about a retired military general…it was a case after the first world war. The general had lived his whole life in the army – and not only *his* life; his father was a general, his father's father was a general. As far back as he could remember their family had been in the army. It was in his blood. From the very beginning he was disciplined in the manners of the army.

He was retired now, the war was over. One day he was carrying a bucket full of eggs, and a man just played a joke on him; the man shouted, "Attention!" and the general stood to attention, dropping the bucket and all the eggs on the road. He was very angry; his eggs were all finished. He said, "What kind of a joke is his?"

The man said, "But can't I say 'Attention!'? It has nothing to do with you. You could have carried your bucket. I was not telling you to drop it."

The general said, "You don't understand, it has gone into my blood, into my bones. Even in the night, if somebody says, 'Attention!' I will jump out of the bed and be at attention. Only then will I realize that it is a joke – but first I will be in position."

This is discipline. Your morality, your character, are nothing but forced disciplines. They have become unconscious, and anything that is unconscious is of no value at all. Coming along with me you will have to understand that your morality is just imposed. You are an impostor pretending to be moral, not knowing even the ABC of morality. Your character is nothing.

When I applied for a professorship, they asked me for a character certificate. I said, "I cannot produce one."

The education minister said, "But why not?"

I said, "For the simple reason that I haven't found a man of character from whom I would like to have a character certificate."

He said, "You are something. You can't find a man of character?"

I said, "No, I can't find a man of character. And how can I have a character certificate from somebody to whom I cannot give a character certificate?" I knew my vice-chancellor and I told him, "I cannot take a character certificate from you because I cannot give a character certificate to you. I know you perfectly well."

I knew my head of department, who was a very loving man, who loved me. But he himself said, "I cannot give you a character certificate because I don't have any character and you know it perfectly well."

I said to the education minister, "You give me a character certificate, and I will expose you – I will just call a press conference today. You give me a character certificate and I will tell the press conference what kind of character you have."

He started perspiring. He said, "You just take your appointment later."

But I said, "What about the character certificate? – because it has to be attached to the application."

He said, "Don't be worried."

I said, "No, it is a question of principle. If everybody needs a character certificate then I will write a character certificate for myself. That's the only man I know perfectly well who has character. About anybody else it is at the most guesswork."

He said, "Do whatsoever you want, just please leave me alone. You take your order." So I wrote a character certificate for myself. He said, "But please don't sign it in your own name because I will be in trouble."

Then I said, "Whose name have I to sign?"

He said, "Anybody's name but not your own name."

So I signed it in the name of one of my professors. He said, "But you are signing with somebody else's name. I know this man, S.S. Roy; he is your professor. What are you going to tell him?"

I said, "You don't be worried. This a copy of the original, the original I will take from him." I said, "This is done everyday; the original is taken, then copies are made. This is just the reverse: the copy is given to you, the original I will make."

I went to S.S. Roy. I told him that this had hap-pened and, "This is the character certificate I have written. You give me the original."

He looked at the certificate. He said, "You should have come to me, because you have not written anything good. I would have given you a beautiful character certificate."

I said, "It was something spontaneous. That man was in a difficulty and I could not write more than this about myself. What more can I write?"

He said, "But this is not a character certificate at all, because you are saying that you are a human being – this is very ordinary. You ask me to sign it, and it says that you have all the weaknesses of human beings, that one cannot trust you, you are not reliable. Now I have to sign it," he said, "and you will show it to people."

I said, "No, I will not show it. The original I will give to you. The original you can keep in case it is needed."

He said, "Then it is okay because I don't want people to see that I have written this character certificate about you. I love you and I know you. These are not your qualities."

I said, "But when I have to write about myself, do you think I should write, 'He is the only begotten son of God'? Do you want me to be crucified? Once was enough."

Coming along with me you will have to drop almost the whole of you. Only the essential will remain, only that which you cannot drop. Even if you want to drop it you cannot. Only that will remain.

It is a great surgery in which all the cancerous growth that surrounds you has to be cut out completely. It is painful, it is hard. Just because it is so painful and so hard, I make it as light as possible, as joyous as possible. I try to make it a joke for the simple reason that the task is hard, and it is good to pass the dark night of the soul with laughter, with gossiping, with joking, with dancing, with singing. It is good to pass the dark night of the soul with joy.

What is the point of crying and weeping and

mourning and wearing the black habits of the Christian priests? The night is dark enough, why make it darker? To transform yourself, to change, is painful enough; why make it more miserable?

Once I was operated on, a little operation. I continued to joke with the doctor. He said, "You please wait. Don't make me laugh because I may do something wrong. Leave me alone. I was saying from the very beginning that you need chloroform; otherwise you will go on talking and you will disturb me. But you said local anesthesia will do. So we have given" – he was doing the operation on my finger – "so we have given you local anesthesia. But it was wrong – you don't leave us alone, you just go on joking!"

I said, "Lying down on a surgical table, is it not the right place to joke? And will it not be helpful to you to be laughing and enjoying and doing your work? Just the way a painter paints, a surgeon should do his work. Why make it sad and…. It is already painful; make it light, don't make it heavier."

Hence, my sannyas is a rejoicing. You say you are not wishing to rejoice with me. You say you are not going to laugh with me. You say you are not going to dance with me, sing with me. Then for what are you wanting me to be your master? To make you more sad? Are you not sad enough? To make you more guilty? Have not the Christian priests done enough? Do you want me to make a heavier cross? Is not Jesus' cross weighty enough for you? For what do you want me to be your master?

And to be your master or not, that has to be left to me; you are not to be concerned about it. Your whole concern should be, can you be a disciple? "How can I be a disciple?" should be your question. You are not going to be a master so why bother about the master? That is *my* business.

And I know my business perfectly well. You just leave it to me – you do your part. And if you succeed in doing your part you will not go empty-handed from my door. But first things first. You should be ready to do your part.

Becoming a sannyasin is not just changing the robe and changing the name; those are just playful things. I could have chosen any color. Blue is good, the color of the ocean. Green is good, the color of the whole of nature. I could have chosen any color.

I have chosen red for two reasons. One, because red in the East has been the color of sannyasins for centuries. I have not chosen it because it has been the color of the sannyasins, so that my sannyasins should also be part of that tradition. No, I have chosen it to sabotage that tradition, because all those sannyasins were serious people: heavy, dull, mediocre.

I wanted to bring a new breeze into the world of sannyas, and to disturb the definition of the sannyasin, which had become completely ossified. I created confusion. Now in India it is very difficult to know who is who. My sannyasins are laughing, enjoying, dancing, and the people cannot understand what is the matter because sannyasins have never done such things.

And secondly, I chose the color red because red has become associated with communism. I wanted to sabotage that idea too, that red is anybody's monopoly. Just to disturb these two I chose red. But this is just playful.

You will have to think about sannyas in its deepest meanings. It means that you have found someone whose eyes can see farther than your eyes can see, whose reach of the hand goes higher than the reach of your hand. You have found someone that you feel jealous of. You would like to have this serenity, this peace, this silence, this song. Then be prepared on *your* part.

I am ready, I have been long ready.

And don't miss the opportunity, because I will not be here forever. Today I am here, tomorrow I may not be here. So if you want in some way to use my insight, my vision, my experience, if you want to become a part of my universe, then don't miss a single moment, because nothing can be said about the next moment. I may not be here, and then your getting ready will be pointless. Now I am here, and you are not ready.

That has been happening again and again in the past. It is said the day Gautam Buddha died a man came running. Buddha had told his disciples, "This is my last meeting with you in the body. I am going to leave the body. Before I leave, if you have any more questions left" – he had been answering for forty-two years – "if anything is still left in anybody's mind, ask it, because I won't be here anymore."

The disciples were crying, weeping. What can you ask? For forty-two years Buddha had been answering even those questions which you had not asked. He had been answering questions which you had wrongly asked. But he had answered rightly. He was not only answering you, he was also creating questions for you. In forty-two years he had done everything that was possible. Now, what to ask at the last moment?

They said, "No, we are just grateful."

Buddha closed his eyes, he moved the first step inwards – that is, he moved away from the body to the mind. The second step: he moved from the mind to the heart. The third step he was just going to take, from the heart to the feeling of am-ness, *asmita*. It cannot be called "I" – it is far more refined – just am-ness. And then…the last jump into nothingness. While he was just moving in, the man came running.

He said, "But I have a question."

The disciples said, "Now don't disturb him. Where have you been? He has passed through your village at least thirty times."

He said, "I know, but sometimes there was such a crowd of customers in my shop. Sometimes I was engaged in my son's marriage; sometimes my wife was sick – and so on and so forth. I always thought, next time when he comes I will go to him. Just now I heard that he is leaving the world. What about my question?"

The people said, "You seem to be an idiot. Thirty times he passed, and thirty times you missed. And now, when he has just taken leave of us…now it cannot be done."

But Buddha came back. He opened his eyes, he said, "No, let him ask. Let him be answered because I don't want it to be known in history, for the coming generations, that a Buddha was alive and yet somebody returned from his door empty-handed. Let me do my part. If he is ready – and I can see he is ready; my death has been a shock to him and has made him ready. I am happy that even my death has helped somebody to be ready, to listen."

He answered his question. The question was not philosophical, theological, intellectual. The question was really authentic, sincerely spiritual. But that man had been missing for so many years, just because of the idea, "Tomorrow, the day after tomorrow, any time Buddha comes and goes, I can go and meet him and ask."

He asked – this was the last question to Buddha – "How can I be in a position so that whether you are in the body or not, your presence will remain available to me? What can I do?"

He had asked a real religious question. He was asking, "What can I do so that your presence remains available to me? This time I have missed – when you were in the body. But I don't want to miss forever."

Buddha gave him the instructions for meditation, *vipassana;* how to be aware of your breathing; how to be aware, silently watchful of the breath going out, coming in, going out, coming in…"so slowly, slowly you can be separate from your breathing. The moment you are separate from your breathing my presence will be available, because you are separate from your body just as I am separate from my body."

If a disciple is ready, even a dead master can be alive. If the disciple is not ready, then even a living master cannot do anything. It all depends on the disciple.

Here We Call Work, Worship

DISCOURSE 2,   APRIL 2, 1985

Beloved Bhagwan,

Is worshipping in the commune related to meditation? Why don't we have any meditation time separate from worshipping?

It has been one of the most dangerous ideas down the centuries that life can be divided into separate parts. Life is indivisible, it is an organic whole. The moment you divide it you kill it. This is one of the most fundamental things in my approach towards life: I take it as a whole.

And remember, the whole is more than the sum total of its parts.

In the world of machines, the whole is exactly the sum total of its parts; there is nothing more in it. A clock is nothing more than all its parts put in a particular arrangement; it functions. Take the parts apart, and the functioning disappears. But you can put the parts together again, and the functioning starts again. The functioning of the mechanism is not something separate.

Life is totally different from a machine. If you cut a man into different parts, life will disappear. Now you cannot put those parts together. And even if you manage somehow to put those parts together, life is not going to appear again. It categorically proves one thing, that life is *not* the sum total of its parts – it is something more, it is something plus.

And that "plus" is the real essence of your being.

But down the ages all the religions have been committing a crime: the crime of dividing the indivisible. But it was favorable to them. A divided man is a dead man, and to control the dead is the easiest thing in the world.

An undivided man is an individual. That's exactly the meaning of the word "individual" – indivisible. The individual is dangerous, he is alive. You cannot enslave him, you cannot oppress him, you cannot exploit him. You cannot do anything against his wish. His individuality gives him freedom to think, to express, to be.

Divisions can be made in very subtle ways. For example, "Religion should be separate from the state." What kind of stupidity is this? If religion is something real, something that vibrates in your being, something that you breathe, live, then wherever you are – in the church, in the office, in the marketplace, it does not matter – religion is your very breathing. It is going to be with you. Then it is going to decide every step that you take, every word that you utter, every gesture that you make.

How can you divide religion from art? A religious man painting is not in any way separate from his religious being. While painting he is going to paint religion; whatever he paints is going to be colored by his religion. The way he lives, the way he loves, the way he dances – all is going to be in his painting. The painting of a religious man, whatsoever the subject matter of the painting, will have some fragrance of religion in it; it is inevitable, there is no way to avoid it.

Sometimes you may not be able to see this, because things are very subtle. A man of meditation, silence, serenity, is going to have a different kind of dance from a man who is in anguish, tension, worry, despair. A man who is living his life totally, intensely, moment to moment, and a man who is thinking of committing suicide – both can dance, but their dances will have different qualities. The person who is thinking of committing suicide, his dance will have the shadow of death in it. It will stink of death, of a dead body. His movements will not be movements of life. The other man, who loves and lives totally and has a silent space within himself – that's what I call meditation – his dance will also have a silence surrounding it. His movements, his gestures will have a grace, a beauty, a fragrance of their own.

You cannot divide man into parts.

Your question is, "Here in our commune, there is no separate time for meditation…." It is our basic approach. We cannot have a separate time for meditation. Meditation should be spread all over your life: eating, sleeping, taking a bath, or just having a walk, or just sitting doing nothing. Meditation should be in all these actions, inactions, activities, non activities. The thread of meditation should continue underground, whatever you are working at.

A great master, Nan In, was chopping wood. The king of the country had come to see him. He had heard so much about Nan In that finally he could not resist the temptation to go and see the man. Just as he entered the monastery, near the gate was a man perspiring in the hot sun, chopping wood.

Naturally the king thought, "This man must be able to direct me to where I can find the master" – because it was a vast monastery with five hundred monks living in it. So he asked the man, who was Nan In himself, "Please forgive me for interrupting you; you are so absorbed in chopping wood, you have not even seen that I have been standing here for a few

Whatever you are doing, do it as if this is the greatest thing in the world at this juncture of time. It may be just cutting the grass, watering the road; it may be anything. Washing the floor, do it as if the whole existence depends on what you are doing, it is indispensable; without it, the whole universe will collapse.

minutes, waiting. But then I thought it is better to interrupt you because you are not going to see me of your own accord."

The man said, "I am sorry, but this is how my life is. Whatever I am doing I am doing it totally. Nothing of me remains to do anything else. Chopping wood, I am simply chopping wood. There is nobody else other than the chopper of wood. So, no need to be embarrassed. What do you want?"

He said, "I want to see the master, Nan In."

Nan In said, "You go directly into that hut and wait. The master will be coming soon."

The king went and waited there. Nan In took a shower, put on his master's robe, and came in from the back door. But the king was very puzzled, because both men looked so alike. He thought, "It is almost an impossibility. There are not two men alike in the whole world, and just in this monastery, within a few hundred yards I have seen a man exactly like this man."

Nan In said, "You wanted to see master Nan In – master Nan In is now here."

The king said, "That I will enquire about later on. First I want to know who was chopping wood at the gate."

Nan In laughed. He said, "At that time I was a chopper of wood. Now I am going to chop your head; now I am a master. We live each moment, moment to moment, but we are indivisible. The chopper was also master Nan In. If you had eyes you could have seen my involvement with the movement, my totality of action, my intensity of being.

"If you had eyes you could have seen him there; you would not have asked about master Nan In. You had already met him, but you didn't know. Now I am a chopper of heads. That's the function of a master: to make you so egoless, to make you so thoughtless that you are almost without a head, just the heart pulsating with love, with compassion. Have you come only to ask some questions? Are you really a seeker? Are you ready to lose something?"

The king was just confused, shocked, even afraid of the man. He had never been afraid of anybody, but this man was simply crazy – he was talking of chopping his head!

The king said, "You have confused me too much and I am almost falling apart. Please forgive me this time. I will come another time, because I have forgotten for what I came."

Nan In said, "You need not come again. I am going to come to you, and I will follow you wherever you go. Now you cannot escape, because I can see something really authentic in you. Yes, it is unconscious; you are not aware of it, much garbage is hiding it. You think you are a king. Even sitting before me you are still thinking *you* are a king. This is garbage – you are just a beggar. And the beggar that I am is really a king."

The king said, "I don't understand all these puzzles. Please talk to me without puzzling me."

Nan In said, "There is no puzzle in it, it is simple. I am a king because I don't need anything in the world. You are a beggar; although you have a big empire, your desires are unending. You are desiring more and more and more. The mind that goes on desiring more is the mind of a beggar. And the consciousness that is content with itself as it is, utterly content, is the consciousness of an emperor.

"Strange," he said. "You think you are a king, and you look on me as a beggar. The reality is just the opposite. Go back – and I will be coming to visit you." And Nan In followed the king continuously till he made him aware of his innermost treasure.

It is dangerous to go to a master, because then escape is almost impossible. Wherever you go – even if you go to Santa Fe – I am there. Nothing can save you. Once a master has seen within you a heart that can grow, that can expand, that can become universal, he is not going to leave you.

I don't need to go to Santa Fe. I have my own ways, far more subtle than Nan In's. I am continually there; they are talking only about me, they cannot talk about anything else. Whom are they befooling? Whether you talk for me or against me does not matter, just go on continuously talking about me. That's enough; that is going to change you.

Here, in the commune, whatever you are doing…. Here we call work, worship, for the simple reason that work is not just work, it is meditation also. That's why we call it worship. Other than this we don't have any God to worship. We have only this existence around us. So you can worship it as a gardener, you can worship it as a farmer, you can worship it as a roadmaker, you can worship any way you choose to. But whatever you are doing, you are doing with existence.

So the question is, if you are doing it lovingly, if you are doing it meditatively, and if, while you are doing it, you are nowhere else, you are just there with all of your being, nothing is missing – then work becomes worship. Work becomes worship because meditation has entered into it.

But I can understand your question, because all the religions have preached that there should be a separate time for meditation. That is just idiotic. It is as if somebody is saying there should be a separate time for breathing, that one hour in the morning you breathe and then forget about it, and for twenty-three hours you do other things. You need not be disturbed by having to breathe; you can do other things, breathing continues.

A thousand and one things continue in your body: the blood goes on circulating, the pulse goes on functioning, the heart goes on beating…. Scientists say the body of man is perhaps the greatest miracle in existence because so much is going on in it. Almost seven million living cells are continuously working within you. You are the biggest city in the world.

Seven million living beings are living in you, and they are doing all kinds of work and doing it perfectly, without any guidance and without any education, without anybody being the overseer – I mean no God as overseer. You may go on doing anything, your organic processes continue.

To me meditation is an organic process. To other religions it was not; hence, all those religions have failed. They were bound to fail. It is not an accident, it was destined; their very base was wrong. What they called meditation was nothing but some kind of thinking. The Christian was thinking of Christ, praying to God with folded hands, kneeling down. He knows neither whether God exists or not, nor whether Jesus Christ is really a messiah or just a charlatan. He knows nothing, but out of fear, out of misery, out of anguish, he is praying; and this, Christianity calls meditation.

And what is he asking God? He is asking for all those things which he is missing here in this life, which he cannot manage to create here for himself. He is asking God, "At least in the other life, give them to me; I have suffered enough." He is asking – in fact, deep down it is a complaint.

All prayers are complaints; otherwise, what have you got to pray for if there is no complaint? Every prayer simply means you are condemning God. You are saying, "You are doing it wrong. Please do it this way."

Even Jesus on the cross condemns God when he says, "Have you forsaken me?" What does he mean? One thing is certain, he means that he knows better than God. He knows that somewhere God has gone wrong. He is angry, he is complaining. He wants God to do a miracle, to prove to the world that he is his only begotten son, that he has been sent by him. He is his messenger and he has sent him for the whole world's salvation.

But from the skies no voice comes. On the clouds no angels appear with their harps, playing "Alleluia" – no sign of God anywhere. In anger Jesus shouts, "Have you forsaken me?" He is saying, "Have you betrayed me? Have you gone against your word? You have left me in this helpless situation. And I believed in you!" This is the moment to prove that God is love. This is the moment to prove that God comes to save those who trust in him. But nobody comes.

All prayers are complaints. All prayers are saying to God, "We know better than you do."

One man came to me – his wife was dying. He was a very religious man. Every day from three o'clock in the morning up to seven – for four hours – he was doing all kinds of crazy things. He had so many gods. In India they are not so miserly about gods. About everything else they are poor, but about gods they are the richest people in the world: thirty-three million gods. So everybody who is really religious has a whole roomful.

Thirty-three million of course you cannot…but a few representatives, the topmost, the bigshots, you can keep around. This man had at least sixty. Now, sixty gods, and only four hours – you can see, it was not much time. He was in such a hurry, doing a prayer to this god and rushing to another, then rushing to another, and looking at his watch continuously because in four hours he has to finish. And the fear that if he leaves any god, and the god becomes angry….

Such a religious man – and his wife was dying, and the doctors were not able to do anything. They simply said, "She has lost the will to live. Deep down she does not want to live; hence, no medicine is effective." Unless you have a will to live you lose resistance; you really want to die. Just medicines cannot do much unless a great support from your will is there.

So he came to me one day and said, "What should I do? I have done four hours of prayers each day my whole life, and still my wife is dying, and out of those sixty gods not a single one is helping. And I cry and weep."

I said, "Please answer me one question. Do you think yourself more intelligent than God?"

He said, "No. How can I think myself more intelligent than God?"

Then I said, "If God wants your wife to be freed from the body you should be happy, you should be thankful. But your prayer is against God's will. Those sixty gods that you have cannot help you in any way. You are not a religious man at all."

But he said, "I have done prayer four hours every day for years."

I said, "You can pray twenty-four hours, that too will not make any change, because your whole attitude is wrong. You are *demanding* from existence, you are not surrendering to existence."

Meditation is a surrender, it is not a demand. It is not forcing existence *your* way, it is relaxing into the way existence wants you to be. It is a let-go.

But all the religions have been doing prayers in the name of meditation. And what kind of stupid prayers! In fact any prayer that a man can do is going to be stupid. "Don't let my wife die" – do you think that is something very intelligent? If that dodo was a little bit intelligent – God was making him free, and he is praying against his own freedom.

But if you look in the scriptures you will be surprised what kind of prayers are there. In the *Vedas,* the most holy scriptures of the Hindus, the great seers…. I cannot even conceive how for centuries those people have been called great seers. They should be called the great blind men! Seers! – they were praying to God: "Please increase the milk of my cow, decrease the milk of the cow of my enemy, my neighbor. This time let rains fall only on *my* field." Great seers, great saints and sages – and these are their prayers. But what else can you ask?

The Christian asks, "Give me my daily bread." Don't you have anything else to ask? Can't you produce even your daily bread? Even that has to be provided by God? So what are you doing here? Even your daily bread is not to be created by you. Just by providing daily bread to all these millions of Christians for centuries, God must have gone bankrupt!

Nobody ever thinks of God. Just seeing his misery and anguish I declared, "There is no God!" In just a single blow I finished all his misery, all his trouble, all his anguish – past, present, future, everything;

I made it completely clean. Now, let everybody produce his own daily bread and, if you have some intelligence, a little butter will also do – but don't torture God anymore. He is not there; he has never been there.

Why should you keep a separate time for meditation? It is based on the idea of the separation of the sacred and profane. But in life there is no separation of the sacred and the profane. Life is one, so totally one that you can call something sacred if you want, you can call it profane if you want.

Christians call sex sin, and Tantra, a great Eastern philosophy, calls sex sacred, the most significant life energy – because all transformation is going to happen through that energy. Don't condemn it. There are people who are condemning sex continuously in every possible way.

You can take anything…there are Zen people in the East who say that even sipping a cup of tea in the morning can be something sacred. And they have made it sacred. If you have seen, in a Zen monastery they have a small temple for tea ceremonies, and when anybody goes to the tea ceremony he enters into a sacred space.

He leaves his shoes outside; there are special wooden sandals provided inside. Everybody is silent, because the *samovar* is boiling the tea and a beautiful music is coming out of it. It has to be listened to. People sit on their knees, just the way they sit in the temple, around the samovar. They all listen silently to the boiling noise of the tea, and they smell the fresh and rejuvenating fragrance of the tea. And absolute silence falls on them.

Then the server, who is usually a woman, comes; and in a very sacred manner she provides cups and saucers, which are all handmade. In a Zen monastery they don't use cups and saucers purchased in the market; those are produced inhumanly, mechanically, for nobody particular. They are just for the market.

In the Zen monastery they make their own cups,

their own saucers, with love, with meditation. Something of their love and meditation certainly enters into their cups and saucers and pots. And the way the woman places them before you – she places them as if she is serving a god. Christians don't even know how to move Jesus' statue from one place to another.

Then she pours the tea; just the sound of the tea being poured is listened to – no talk at all. And then people start sipping tea, enjoying it, forgetting the whole world. Just sipping tea has become sacred. It depends on *you*.

There is nothing profane in the world, nothing sacred in the world. The world is neutral. Now it depends on you what you want to make of it.

Meditation makes it sacred; then every act becomes meditative.

I am reminded of a butcher in Japan who was considered to be a great master – and he was a butcher! The whole day he was cutting animals and selling meat; that was his business. One Buddhist scholar could not believe that this man was thought to be a saint. He was simply a scholar. He went to the butcher and said, "This is something absolutely mad. Who are the people who think that you are a saint? How can a butcher be a saint?"

The butcher laughed. He answered, "Just by mixing meditation in the butchery. When I am cutting up an animal I am not angry, I am not hateful. I am full of love, I am full of compassion. I have great hope that next time he will be born in a human form; perhaps he will become a buddha. With all my blessings I am sending him on a new journey, releasing him from this prison.

"And moreover, my father was a butcher, my forefathers were butchers, and I am a poor butcher. I have never told anybody that I am a saint. If people think so, that's their business. You should go and argue with them.

"As far as I am concerned, I am absolutely content with my profession because whatever you do, the question is not what you are doing but how you are doing it. The question is not the act; the question is the consciousness with which the act is being performed. Yes, I am killing animals, but I know that they will be killed anyway. If I am not killing them, somebody else will kill them. And he will not kill them with such love, with such compassion. How can I leave this profession?

"These animals are going to be killed. If I don't kill them somebody else will kill them and he is not going to kill them with such meditation, with such love. So I would be leaving these poor animals in the hands of some butcher. I cannot do that. If I am going to be thrown into hell for being a butcher, that is acceptable. But I cannot leave these poor innocent animals in the hands of somebody who knows nothing of love."

Can you see the point of this butcher? It is very subtle. He is ready to suffer in hell if that is going to be the consequence of his actions. But he cannot leave these poor animals in the hands of somebody who will simply kill them and not even bother about what he is doing.

He said, "I am so concerned with these animals and I love them so much – I cannot leave them in somebody else's hands. Whatsoever happens to me, that I am ready to face."

I can see why the people who could understand called him a master, a saint. He never gave a sermon, he never preached anything. He was illiterate, he knew nothing of the scriptures, but he lived religion in a very irreligious situation; that's something tremendously important. He lived religion in something which is very irreligious. And yet he managed to live religiously. He must have been a great alchemist who transformed the whole act, gave it a new quality; something utterly profane and ugly became so beautiful, so graceful.

It is said that his fame spread far and wide and people started coming to see him while he was cutting up animals. Even the emperor of Japan came to see him while he was cutting because he had heard that the way he cuts, nobody has ever cut – such grace, such love, tears flowing from his eyes. And the miracle was that although human beings were not able to understand, perhaps the animals *were* able to understand.

Ordinarily when you want to kill an animal he tries to escape, but from this butcher no animal tried to escape. He hugged the animal. The animal was not bound by anything, tied with anything. He was completely free. It was as if deep down he wanted to die by this man's hand.

And the emperor asked one thing, about the knife that he used to kill the animals. The knife looked so shiny, as if it had just been sharpened. The emperor asked, "Do you sharpen your knife every day?"

He said, "No, this is the knife my father used, and his father used, and it has never been sharpened. But we know exactly the points where it has to cut the animal so there is a minimum of pain possible – through the joints where two bones meet. The knife has to go through the joint, and those two bones that meet there go on sharpening the knife. And that is the point where the animal is going to feel the minimum pain.

"For three generations we have not sharpened the knife. A butcher sharpening a knife simply means he does not know his art" – he used the word "art" – "He does not know the art and he does not know how to do it lovingly."

My commune is in meditation twenty-four hours a day; whatever you are doing, or not doing, is immaterial. Just be loving, be alert, do it with joy. Whatever you are doing, do it as if this is the greatest thing in the world at this juncture of time. It may be just cutting the grass, watering the road; it may be anything. Washing the floor, do it as if the whole existence depends on what you are doing, it is indispensable; without it, the whole universe will collapse.

When you do anything with such intensity, with such love, with such respect, as if without it the whole universe will collapse, then there is no need to have a separate time for meditation. And those who are doing meditations as separate from life are simply deceiving themselves and nobody else.

Maharishi Mahesh Yogi teaches his people, "Do transcendental meditation ten minutes in the morning, ten minutes in the evening, and that's enough." And what is his transcendental meditation? Just repeat any stupid name…go on repeating "Rama, Rama, Rama" – that is a Hindu name – or, "Ave Maria, Ave Maria, Ave Maria." Any name, in fact your own name will do – just go on repeating it. Repeat it as fast as possible because that's the whole secret of the technique.

If for ten minutes you go on repeating a single word fast enough continuously, you autohypnotize yourself. After just four or five minutes you start falling into a deliberate kind of sleep which is called hypnosis.

Yes, after ten minutes you will feel good, you will feel fresh, you will feel relaxed. So nothing is wrong with it – but it is not meditation. It is just a way of resting, having a good nap.

You can do it, but remember, it has nothing to do with meditation. It is perfectly good, healthy, psychologically and physically relaxing, but that's all it is. It has nothing to do with transcendence; it is not transcendental at all. It is not going to take you into your innermost being, it is not going to take you into some higher state of consciousness; it is not going to take you anywhere. After ten minutes you will be back where you were. You will remain the same person. You will not be transformed by it.

And unless something transforms you it is not meditation: something that makes you a new being, a new man, a new consciousness; which knows no fear, which knows no greed, which knows no hate; which knows nothing of those dark emotions, sentiments – ugly, sick, nauseating…a new consciousness, which knows only that which uplifts you, that which goes on uplifting you – there is no end to it.

Meditation brings you to a state where you are above the stars, bigger than the whole universe. That experience is what I call transformation, illumination, enlightenment.

So don't be worried that there are not separate times for you to meditate. It is not an oversight, it is done with full consideration. I don't want to give you the impression that meditation can be done separately from your life and its work.

My Religion Is
A Godless Religion

Beloved Bhagwan,

Now that God is dead, how can we quickly dispose of his remains?

God is not dead *now,* he has been dead always, so the question of disposing of his remains does not arise. God has never existed and cannot exist, for the simple reason that the whole existence is godliness. To divide God and existence, the creator and the creation, is a stupid duality.

One has to see the implications of it: God creating a world – from where? Something must have existed as a building material before God created the world. And if he can create the world like a magician then he is an idiotic magician. One can see the world as a proof. Is this the world a wise man will create? – to say nothing of a wise God.

This world shows absolutely that there is nobody behind it consciously creating it; otherwise all the nonsense that exists here should not be. God created the world at a certain time, at a certain date – according to Christians, who are the most foolish of all the religions, he created the world four thousand and four years before Jesus was born.

It must have been Monday, the first of January, or perhaps the first of April – that seems to be more appropriate.

And what did he create? In three thousand years, five thousand wars have been fought – and this is the creation of God. His highest creation is man, and the whole of humanity is on the verge of committing a global suicide. This God must be some kind of a sadist. It is better that we simply forget all about God.

In the courts, *The Bible* is presented to take oaths on. It is full of lies. In these two thousand years since Jesus, almost everything in *The Bible* has become a lie. What about Charles Darwin? What about Albert Einstein?

Sometimes I wonder: have we lost all intelligence? It would be better to provide Albert Einstein's book to take an oath on. *The Bible* is so full of obscenity, it is an insult to every court to have a *Bible* inside it. It is a contempt of court.

And wonder of wonders, you have to take an oath that you will speak only the truth! Jesus is born out of a virgin girl – I cannot take any oath on such rubbish. If a virgin girl can give birth to Jesus then everything is right; then there is no lie anywhere in the world, all is truth, you cannot lie – but this is impossible in the very nature of things.

The Old Testament says that God created the world. He created two daughters and made love to both of them. Now, the father making love to his own daughters – and this is a religious book! And this is your God! Hang him if you can find him.

And this is not only so about Christianity, it is more or less the same with all religions. No sane person can believe in God; only insane, retarded, utterly mediocre people can believe in God.

I have not found a single reason or argument given by thousands of priests of all the religions which has any validity. Still God continues to be worshipped. You have made him out of your foolishness, and you are worshipping him, praying to him. This is not the way to change the world, or man, or his consciousness.

So please don't say, "Now that God is dead." He has never been in the first place, so he cannot be dead.

I agree on many points with that madman Friedrich Nietzsche, but I don't agree on this point – that God is dead. Not that God is not dead – he has never been anywhere. Only existence is. Yes, there is a possibility of consciousness evolving, higher and higher. The moment consciousness comes to its highest peak it does not find any God there. It finds immense beauty, immense silence, absolute nothingness.

This I am saying on my own authority and through my own experience. You cannot go beyond absolute peace, silence, ecstasy. It goes on growing, but you never can go beyond it.

Hence, my religion is a godless religion.

There is no question of, no problem of disposing of the remains – there are none.

Beloved Bhagwan,

Being with You I feel so blissful and liberated, and there seems to be no end to it. You must have tricked me. What is Your secret?

I am a simple man without any secret. I am just an open book, and a book in which nothing is written. If you like to call it a secret it is your choice, but it is a very open secret.

If you want to be, learn the art of being: not to be.

Let me repeat it, because I know you are deaf. If you want really to be, the only way is to learn not to be. Disappear. Just as God disappears from existence,

Why are you seeking? You are seeking because you are not aware that you have got it already. I cannot give it to you. I can only make you aware, and for that nothing is needed but availability on my part, availability on your part. If these two availabilities are there, two opennesses, without any conditions, it clicks. Suddenly you become a mirror, and the moment you become a mirror you become a master. The same will start happening around *you*.

you have to disappear from your life. Let life flow of its own accord.

It is the simplest art in the world, to be silent. It is not a doing, it is a non-doing. How can it be difficult?

I am showing you the way of enlightenment through laziness. Nothing has to be done to attain it, because it is your nature. You have already got it. You are just so busy with outer business that you cannot see your own nature.

Deep within you is exactly the same as outside you: the beauty, the silence, the ecstasy, the blissfulness. But please, sometimes be kind to yourself: just sit down and don't do anything, either physically or mentally. Relax, not in an American way…because I have seen so many American books titled *How to Relax.* The very title says that the man knows nothing about relaxation. There is no "how."

Yes, it is okay – "How to Repair a Car"; you will have to do something. But there is no doing as such as far as relaxation is concerned. Just don't do anything. I know you will find it a little difficult in the beginning. That is not because relaxation is difficult, it is because you have become addicted to doing something. That addiction will take a little time to disappear.

Just be, and watch. Being is not doing, and watching is also not doing.

You sit silently doing nothing, witnessing whatsoever is happening. Thoughts will be moving in your mind; your body may be feeling some tension somewhere, you may have a migraine. Just be a witness. Don't be identified with it.

Watch, be a watcher on the hills, and everything else is happening in the valley.

It is a knack, not an art.

Meditation is not a science. It is not an art, it is a knack – just that way. All that you need is a little patience.

The old habits will continue; the thoughts will go on rushing. And your mind is always in a rush hour, the traffic is always jammed. Your body is not accustomed to sitting silently – you will be tossing and turning. Nothing to be worried about. Just watch that the body is tossing and turning, that the mind is whirling, is full of thoughts – consistent, inconsistent, useless – fantasies, dreams. You remain in the center, just watching.

All the religions of the world have taught people to do something: stop the process of thought, force the body into a still posture. That's what yoga is – a long practice of forcing the body to be still. But a forced body is not still. And all the prayers, concentrations, contemplations of all the religions do the same with the mind: they force it, they don't allow the thoughts to move. Yes, you have the capacity to do it. And if you persist you may be able to stop the thought process. But this is not the real thing, it is absolutely fake.

When stillness comes on its own, when silence descends without your effort, when you watch thoughts and a moment comes when thoughts start disappearing and silence starts happening, that is beautiful. The thoughts stop of their own accord if you don't identify, if you remain a witness and you don't say, "This is *my* thought."

You don't say, "This is bad, this is good," "This should be there and this should not be there…." Then you are not a watcher; you have prejudices, you have certain attitudes.

A watcher has no prejudice, he has no judgment. He simply sees like a mirror.

When you bring something in front of a mirror it reflects, simply reflects. There is no judgment that the man is ugly, that the man is beautiful, that, "Aha! What a good nose you have got." The mirror has nothing to say. Its nature is to mirror; it mirrors. This is what I call meditation: you simply mirror everything within or without.

And I guarantee you…. I can guarantee because it has happened to me and to many of my people; just watching patiently – maybe a few days will pass, maybe a few months, maybe a few years. There is no way of saying because each individual has a different collection.

You must have seen people collecting antiques, postal stamps. Everybody has a different collection; the quantity may be different, hence the time it takes will be different – but go on remaining a witness as much as you can. And this meditation needs no special time. You can wash the floor and remain silently watching yourself washing the floor.

I can move my hand unconsciously, without watching, or I can move it with full awareness. And there is a qualitative difference. When you move it unconsciously it is mechanical. When you move it with consciousness there is grace. Even in the hand, which is part of your body, you will feel silence, coolness – what to say about the mind?

With your watching and watching, slowly the rush of thoughts starts getting less and less.

Moments of silence start appearing; a thought comes, and then there is silence before another thought appears. These gaps will give you the first glimpse of meditation and the first joy that you are arriving home.

Soon the gaps will be bigger, and finally the gap is always with you. You may be doing something, the silence is there. You may not be doing anything, the silence is there. Even in sleep the silence is there.

For a meditator there are no dreams; dreams and thoughts are cousin-brothers, there is not much difference. If thoughts disappear, dreams disappear. And if for twenty-four hours a day you are surrounded by silence you will come to know what my secret is.

If you go near a lake, you start feeling cool. There is no secret in it – it is the milieu.

You go to the forest and you feel the difference in the atmosphere. You are the same but the atmosphere around you is different.

When you come closer to me…and to come closer to me you are not to walk and sit by my side.

To come closer to me is to be not a Christian, not a Hindu, not a Mohammedan, not a Buddhist, not a communist. To come close to me means that you don't cling to any ideology, you don't go on holding onto the past. To come close to me means you start living moment to moment.

Neither the past means anything to you, nor are you worried about the future. This very moment becomes the only reality. In fact it *is* the only reality. And if you can be in this moment, you can be on a faraway star but you will be close to me and you will feel a serenity, a silence, a lovingness such as you have never known.

I am not doing anything, remember, so don't be grateful to me. I am a non-doer – I am just being available. That is not much of a doing. I am available, like the trees in the forest and the lakes and the ocean, and the sun and the moon. I am availble. Now it is up to you to come close to me, or go away from me.

If you can come close to me you will start feeling things that have been unknown to you, and soon you will realize that what you are feeling close to me you can feel yourself wherever you are. That is the greatest moment of happiness for a master, when his disciple can be on his own.

You must know the meaning of being a disciple, people have forgotten; it comes from "discipline." And all the religions have corrupted the meaning of discipline; its root meaning is learning.

Coming close is learning.

What I have got, *you* have got.

I am aware of it, you are not aware of it.

Coming close to me you will learn, "My God! This has always been with me, and I have been searching all over the world, looking into the books, scriptures, seeking the teachers, becoming a member of rotten cults like Christianity, Hinduism, Mohammedanism – all dead."

Yes, when Buddha was there what is happening to you was happening to his people. But when

Buddha is gone what is left behind is mere words, containers; the content is not there. You can go on decorating the containers, but that will not help. You know perfectly well that your statues in the temples, your scriptures in the churches, are just dust of the past. It is better to be finished with them.

But why are you seeking? You are seeking because you are not aware that you have got it already. I cannot give it to you. I can only make you aware, and for that nothing is needed but availability on my part, availability on your part. If these two availabilities are there, two opennesses, without any conditions, it clicks. Suddenly you become a mirror, and the moment you become a mirror you become a master. The same will start happening around *you*.

So I don't want you always to remain disciples. That will be a shame.

In the past all the religions have tried just the opposite of what I am doing. That's why they cannot believe that this is a religion. I am changing the very definition and the foundations. Those old religions were saying that Jesus Christ is the only begotten son of God, you are not. He is special, you are ordinary. He comes with a message from God, from above. He has a speciality, he is extra-ordinary.

At the most you can be Christians, but you cannot be a Christ. Have you thought about it, that in two thousand years nobody has been a Christ again? What kind of religion is this? Just Christians! The first and the last Christ was crucified two thousand years ago; since then nothing has happened, because unless you become a Christ your Christianity is just a hypocrisy. The same is true about other religions.

Once it happened in Baghdad – Caliph Omar was the sovereign. A man was brought to him who was claiming that he had been sent by God and that he brought the latest word of God, the latest message, because Mohammed's message was thirteen hundred years old, and in thirteen hundred years a new message – better, more polished, more sophisticated – was needed. He had been sent by God.

Now, Mohammedans cannot accept anybody as a prophet after Mohammed. No religion accepts anybody else as a prophet. Christians cannot accept anybody as a Christ. Buddhists cannot accept another as a Buddha. Why? Why this similarity? There is some arithmetic behind it. A new prophet will disturb the gullible, the old believers, because he will say something new. He may say something against the *Koran, The Bible,* the *Gita;* he is bound to.

I cannot agree with Krishna, the *Gita* that he had spoken five thousand years ago. Five thousand years have not gone just as a waste; man's consciousness has risen, intelligence has become more solid. And what Krishna teaches is violence. If Krishna is right, then the third world war is perfectly okay.

I cannot give that okay to the third world war. Krishna says, "It is God's will. If he wants the war, all your pacifists can go on parading in the capitals of the world with posters against war – it will not change anything. If God wants the war then the war is going to happen." That is the message of the *Gita.* Arjuna, Krishna's chief disciple and friend, tried hard to argue.

But those arguments are all ordinary. If I had been in his place, just a single sentence from me would have been enough – there would have been no need to make such a big book. I would have said to Krishna, "This is God's will, that I am going to the Himalayas. Who are you to interpret God's will? And how can I accept it, that your interpretation is right? You say that God wants the war – I say no."

And in fact the no seems to be more rational, more loving, more meaningful, more humane. Rather than arguing with that man, Arjuna had just to say: "I have accepted your idea that whatsoever happens, happens according to God" – and then should have left for the Himalayas.

He wanted to be a sannyasin, a meditator in the Himalayas. Krishna would not have been able to stop him – just because of his own argument. Arjuna could have said, "If war is to happen, God will bring me back – but you keep quiet."

Hence Hindus would not like anybody else to be accepted as a prophet of God.

Mohammed talks nonsense. You cannot expect anything better from an uneducated man who could not write, who could not read, who had never been in any way a meditative man.

He married nine women. Now, I cannot support that, because in the world men and women are almost in equal proportions. If one man marries nine women then what about the eight men who will be left without women? Then California will be all over the world. That catastrophe I cannot allow. I would rather that California went down into the ocean with all its homosexuals, with all its perverts. It would be better, far more beneficial, and a blessing to humanity. But Mohammed marries nine women – of course; he is a messenger of God. Mohammedans he allows to marry four women – naturally; he has to keep himself higher. Mohammedans are still marrying four women.

Anyone with any intelligence can see the point: these are the people who create prostitution. They have created prostitutes, because what about the three men whose women they have married?

And can you understand a simple, biological thing? You cannot even satisfy a single woman sexually, what about four or nine? – because recent research shows that a woman is capable of multiple orgasms. A man is not capable of that. If he is young, below thirty-five, he may be able to have one orgasm. And I am saying maybe. It is not certain, because man is in such a hurry that before the orgasm can happen he is finished.

Orgasm needs a certain patience, to move with the woman, with the same pace. The woman moves slowly. By the time she comes close to her orgasm, the man has gone to sleep and is snoring. Eighty percent of women in the world have not known what orgasm is. And in a country like India, ninety-nine percent of women know nothing about orgasm.

Biologically, a man cannot satisfy four women. Then those women are going to look around the neighborhood. These religions have created all kinds of perversions: prostitution, obscenity. And if these men cannot find women, at least they can look at *Playboy* – just pictures of naked women! One feels the world has lived in an insane way. Will your hunger be satisfied by seeing beautiful dishes in a picture? Can you eat them? But that is what is happening to man's sexuality.

He looks into magazines – vulgar, obscene – of naked women. For what? – when there are equal numbers of women available, living, alive, not just photographs.

Four women to one man! But this is nothing, four or nine; Krishna had sixteen thousand women to himself! I sometimes start wondering…sixteen thousand women. Even to remember their names is difficult.

I know, because I have more than half a million sannyasins around the world; I cannot remember their names. And Krishna lived only ninety years. In ninety years how did he manage to make love to sixteen thousand women? Perhaps to one woman once in her life…and then she was abandoned. This is ugly.

That's why new prophets are not allowed by any religion – because they will look, scrutinize, see that these things are ugly.

In Baghdad this man declared, "I am the prophet of God, the latest, and I bring a more sophisticated message than Mohammed." Mohammedans could not tolerate it. Omar himself was a very cultured man…. Now you may be cultured, but your Mohammedanism is there; it goes on poisoning you. Omar sent the man to the prison, told the guards, "Don't give him food. Bind him to a pole, beat him continuously, and don't let him sleep. After seven days I will come to ask what he thinks."

After seven days he came. The man was almost dying, without food, without sleep, continuously beaten for twenty-four hours a day. Omar laughed and said, "Now have you changed your mind, or do you still think you are the last messenger of God?"

The man laughed more loudly than Omar and said, "This torture for seven days proves that I *am* the prophet of God, because when I was leaving him to take my voyage to the earth, I asked him, 'They have not behaved well with prophets in the past – what is going to happen to me?' He said, 'You will be tortured.' You have proved that I am really the prophet of God. Before this torture sometimes I used to doubt, to think that perhaps I am imagining, but now there is no question of doubt."

At that very moment, from another pole, another naked man who had been there for one month continuously being tortured, shouted, "Omar, don't listen to that idiot! I have not sent him. After Mohammed I have not sent anybody else." One month before this man had been caught declaring himself God!

These religions are just dead history. They cannot give you anything. Only a living master is capable of creating an atmosphere I call the buddhafield, the field for awakening.

And I have chosen Oregon because I could not find so many sleepy people anywhere else in the world; otherwise, who has heard of any prophet in Oregon? I thought, "Even a small place like Judea can claim Jesus, Jerusalem can claim Moses, small places like Mecca and Medina can claim Mohammed. Oregon is absolutely impotent." I thought it would be good; hence I am here.

But to wake up a sleepy man is always a difficult job. The sleepy man does not want to wake up. Sleep helps him to forget all the worries of life, the troubles of life. Sleep is a narcotic. It is a drug naturally provided by biology; otherwise you would all go mad. Six, eight hours of sleep help you to keep on dragging your life towards the grave.

Naturally Oregonians are disturbed: we are celebrating here. And what are they doing? They are collecting National Guard vehicles in Madras – as if this is an army and we are going to attack and start the third world war. We believe in love, we believe in silence. We believe that man can live in coexistence with nature, with other people.

This is the only city which has no crime, but it has been declared by the attorney general of Oregon to be illegal. This is how sleepy people behave. In their sleep the only legal city looks illegal to them! We have no crime, no prostitutes, no stealing, no drugs. *This* is our fault. For us to be peaceful, to be silent, just to be happy, they cannot tolerate. They cannot believe it, because it has never happened in their life – poor people! I really feel sorry for them.

This place is creating a New Man.

But naturally the old mind will create every difficulty, will use every means so that the New Man is not born. Why? – it hurts. Seeing a man dancing, singing, enjoying, peaceful with himself and existence hurts those people who have become accustomed to living in misery, who have become accustomed to living a life which is not living at all. They cannot tolerate you.

I have heard about a woman who was ugly, really ugly. She used to break mirrors; wherever she found a mirror she would break it immediately.

People asked, "Are you mad? Why do you break mirrors?"

She said, "These mirrors make me ugly."

Now you will be becoming mirrors amongst sleepy people. You will disturb their sleep. They are going to destroy you. And remember, you are very few – they are many.

But one thing is positively in your favor: you have something – you have a contentment. They are empty. Just kick the empty boxes as hard as you can! Perhaps they may wake up and thank you for it.

Beloved Bhagwan,

Why are only intelligent people able to realize true religion? Does the mediocre mind make it impossible to come to know oneself?

Religion is the highest luxury in the world. The idiot cannot realize it while remaining an idiot. The mediocre cannot even conceive its possibility while remaining mediocre. Only the highest intelligence can reach to that point where religion flowers.

Religion needs courage, intelligence, daring, because you are going higher and higher in the world of consciousness. The mediocre has no idea that there is anything higher than himself. The only possibility for the mediocre is that he can drop his mediocrity.

Nobody is born mediocre. People are made mediocre by the politicians, by the priests, by the education system. You think you go to the school to be made more intelligent – you are wrong. You go to the college, you to go the university, you have a masters degree, you can have a Ph.D., you can become a D.Litt. A D.Litt means that now the society has recognized that the doors for the evolution of your consciousness are completely closed. Now for you there is no way.

The whole educational system is arranged in such a way that it teaches you, trains you for memory, not for intelligence – and these two things are totally different. A very intelligent man may not have a very good memory. In fact to have a good memory means you are mediocre. A good memory simply proves you are only a computer, not even a man, so what has been fed into you you can repeat.

You can see it very easily: the people who top the universities, come first in the class, receive golden medals – where do they all disappear in the world? Their gold medals don't shine in the world. In the world you will not be able to recognize them. Educational systems train you for a good memory, so you can repeat absolutely useless things.

When was Genghis Khan born? Now what purpose does that serve? If he had not been born it would have been better. At least we can do one thing, we can remove him from our memory; he was a nightmare. When did the second world war begin? This is history, you have to memorize it. And when you memorize history – Genghis Khan, Nadir Shah, Alexander the Great, Napoleon Bonaparte, Joseph Stalin, Adolf Hitler, and other idiots who may be in the history, or who are right now making history, who soon will be part of the history....

It is better to forget these people. It would have been better if there had been no second world war. That is the only way to prevent the third world war. Forget all this nonsense that man has been doing to man.

But the whole educational system is to make you memorize. And man's mind is capable of memorizing without any limit. It has been found that that is possible because in a man's small skull there are millions of cells which memorize.

It is just like tape recording. All the books in all the libraries of the world can be memorized by a single person – that much capacity your memory has. But then you get lost in your memory, you forget what intelligence is.

Intelligence is totally different.

Intelligence is the capacity to be silent, to be awake, to be able to see the truth.

But nobody is interested in truth; in fact they are all against it, because what will happen to all these politicians around the world who are constantly lying? If truth is known they will go down the drain. You are fed with lies and you are distracted from intelligence towards memory. Memory is part of your brain, and you live your whole life in your brain.

That's why I say only intelligent people can be religious.

Just by being a Christian, going every Sunday to the church, listening to the same boring sermon.... And there is never any argument, because argument brings intelligence in.

Every religion expects you to believe; the unbeliever is condemned. And without doubt you cannot increase your intelligence. This is the trouble. All the religions are helping you to remain mediocre, stupid, by emphasizing belief: belief in God, belief in the virgin birth of Jesus Christ…. Believe, because those who believe will attain to paradise. All the religions are giving you good rewards – just believe.

Just the other day I came to know that in New York the anti-abortionists were having a conference: abortion should be no longer legal, it should become a crime. All the religions of the world agree on such points. It is very strange: they don't agree on any theological points, but on this point Hindus agree, Mohammedans agree, Christians agree, Jews agree, everybody agrees – abortion is a sin.

Mother Teresa was in the conference, speaking against abortion, and she said, "There is violence in the world because of abortion."

I could not believe it. If someone had said, "The violence in the world is because of overpopulation," that would have sounded more true. But this old woman is given a Nobel prize – for what? Everything she does is against humanity. What arguments did she place before the conference? Why does abortion create violence in the world? Because abortion means you are killing a living body, you are making people killers of their own children, that opens the door to violence. The argument looks good, but it only looks good.

At what point is the child alive? If abortion creates violence, then at what point is the child alive? At the time when the male and female living cells meet – is that the point of life? It has to be, because otherwise from where will life come? But if it is life, that means that when the living cells were male and female, when the female eggs were in a woman's body and the male cells were in a man's body – were they alive or not?

Celibacy kills more than anything else, because if a nun, a celibate nun, who is not going to produce a child at all…then all those living cells that she brings from her mother's womb…. In a woman's body cells don't grow, she brings them from birth. All those eggs waiting to be alive, waiting to be Ronald Reagan – they die without any chance.

And do you know…a man, a single man, produces in his whole life, from age fourteen up to fifty, so many living cells that that single man can populate the whole world. What to say about a celibate monk? Every single monk is killing millions of people!

From where does the violence begin? If anybody is responsible then it is Mother Teresa, the pope, their God. Why does he go on and on producing eggs and living sperms? It is time to stop. Already the world is four times more populated than it should be. If the world population can be reduced to one-fourth there will be no poverty, no violence; thousands of problems will disappear.

But Mother Teresa is given a Nobel prize because she helps orphans, opens orphanages around the world. She is creating problems; these orphans will create children. And she is against abortion, because if abortion is legal from where is she going to get the orphans? And what about the Nobel prize? This senile woman is driving people crazy.

Absolute birth control is needed at least for two decades. Absolute, I say! Not that you have to stop after two children or three children – no, that will not help.

Half the world is dying of starvation, and you will be surprised to know that the poor countries, the starving countries, produce more children, for the simple reason that they don't have any other means of passing their time. To go to the movies, money is needed; to go to a disco, money is needed. Sex is the only free entertainment.

Absolute birth control is needed.

This is the only city where no child has been born in four years.

Unless we cut the world population there is no way to avoid violence. People are hungry, people are starving, dying. When somebody is hungry he is going to steal. When somebody is dying, what does he care if he kills somebody else and gets money to survive? – because lust for life is the basis of all biological growth. A man can do anything to survive.

And secondly, if abortion becomes illegal…the pope would like to make all birth control methods illegal. If abortion is illegal, if birth control methods are illegal, can you think what will happen to this world? Everybody will be at everybody else's neck just to survive.

And it has to be remembered that birth control and abortion have given women equality, the same status as men; otherwise the woman can never be equal to man. In poor countries she is continually giving birth, a child every year. She is always pregnant. She cannot work, she cannot be financially independent. She cannot get as educated as man, she cannot be in politics; she has to take care of the children.

Birth control methods, abortion – these have made possibilities for women to be equal to men; otherwise all talk about equality is bogus, false, pseudo.

But strange…Mother Teresa is a woman, and she has there two or three dozen nuns – who are all women. She has an order of nuns, and they don't even see that not a single woman has been accepted as pope in these two thousand years. Not a single woman has been accepted as a Christ, a buddha, a prophet – no. If a woman manages somehow to get into religious matters she is called a witch.

The word is not bad, but Christians have given it a bad connotation. Literally the word "witch" means a wise woman. But when you call a woman a witch you do not mean that she is wise. These popes have been declaring women witches – not only declaring, they have been burning women alive, thousands of women. During the whole Middle Ages they were burning witches.

Who were these witches? What were they doing? They were interfering in religious matters, and man would not like any woman to enter into the hierarchy of religion; otherwise, she may become a prophet, she may become a pope, she may declare herself a Christ.

In Hinduism women are not allowed to read the scriptures. In fact there is no time for them – taking care of the house, taking care of the children…and they are continuously pregnant. This is what Mother Teresa wants. This is what your popes, your bishops want. They will create a mediocre world. They want a mediocre world, just on the survival level.

Remember one simple scientific truth, that if a plant does not get enough water, enough food, enough air, then the first thing to disappear will be the flowers. They are the most delicate. The higher a thing is, the more delicate it is, the more fragile it is. Then the leaves will start disappearing, then the branches will start disappearing. At the end there will be only roots, underground.

The same is the situation in every dimension: if you don't allow man comfort, luxury, time, he will never reach to higher peaks. He is, on the contrary, prevented from reaching towards religion.

The first thing religions say is: Believe. That is against true religion. I say to you, doubt everything, unless you discover something which you cannot doubt. I don't say to believe. I say, find out something which, even if you want to, you cannot doubt: it is there, a reality, a truth.

Go on doubting. Doubt is the method of a true religion – just as it is a method of a true science. By doubting you eliminate all that is wrong, and finally only that which is true remains in your hand. Try to doubt *it* too. But you cannot – it is *there*. And when truth is known – lived, not believed – only then do you understand what religion is.

All these religions are anti-religious. The religions that exist in the world are anti-religious. My effort is to create the first religion in the world. All these people have been preventing religion from happening; hence, they are all against me.

You will be surprised…it has never happened before – all religions are against me. They have never been against anybody all together; on this point they are in agreement. And, even more surprising, atheists are against me. They too agree with the theists on this point. Communists are against me. They don't believe in God, they don't believe in the soul, they don't believe in meditation, but they are also in agreement with people who believe in God, who believe in the soul, who believe in all kinds of things. On only one point, one single point, are they all agreed.

This has never happened; it is happening now for the simple reason that I am clearly giving you the indication.

My fingers are pointing towards the truth.

Belief is not needed, scriptures are not needed, prophets are not needed, God is not needed. A tremendous courage to doubt everything is needed. It is your doubting capacity which will sharpen your intelligence, destroy your mediocrity. But remember, with your mediocrity many other things will be destroyed which depend on mediocrity. So beware, I am a dangerous man.

If you want to be intelligent you cannot be in politics. Politics needs idiots, people who can lie, people who can go on lying, people who have double faces, people who can change their personality any moment. They don't have any individuality. If you want to be intelligent you cannot be in any politics.

If you want to be really religious you cannot be a member of any religious cult. You have to be free. You have to be individual, you have to be on your own. It will be fearful in the beginning because you have always lived in the crowd. The crowd gives you a certain coziness, warmth. You will be in the cold, alone.

If you are ready to be alone and in the cold, and ready to go in darkness in search of light, religion is yours.

Just Drop the Cross!

Beloved Bhagwan,

Rajneeshism is purely a religion of celebration, so why are so many people around the world against it?

That's why! All the religions of the world have been religions of sado-masochism. They have created a miserable world. Their whole strategy is to make you convinced that this life is a life of sin. You have been made to feel guilty for just being alive.

The biblical story will help you to understand. Adam and Eve are expelled from paradise because of a simple enquiry. And the enquiry was also initiated by the so-called God – or Godot. He told Adam and Eve not to eat the fruit of two trees: one, the tree of knowledge; the other, the tree of eternal life. One can see what kind of God this must have been.

To deprive man of wisdom, to prohibit him from tasting the beauties of eternal life, is simply ugly, inhuman – I will not call it even devilish, but it is really the devil that you have been told is God. If He were really a creator of the universe and consciousness, He would have been the first person to tell Adam and Eve to taste wisdom and to taste eternal life. He was not religious at all. You cannot find a more irreligious person than the Christian God.

Religion is nothing but a science to attain wisdom, understanding, to know what life is, and to live it in utter celebration.

And you can live life in celebration *only* if you know there is no death. If you know that it is going to be eternal, that there is no beginning and no end, only then can you live without misery. God

prohibited man from both. Without wisdom you cannot attain to religious ecstasy, and without the feeling of eternal life you cannot sing and you cannot dance.

When death is there every moment, and any moment you can be taken away…. They say, "Never ask for whom the bell tolls; it tolls for thee." You cannot be certain about the next moment. How can you enjoy, when death is so close and follows you like a shadow?

This idiot, God, prohibits man from only two trees. And they lived in the Garden of Eden where millions of trees must have existed. He is not even as intelligent as Sigmund Freud, who is not very intelligent either. Just average intelligence is needed to know that to prohibit anything is dangerous; it gives a challenge to the mind. It is not the serpent who convinced Eve to eat the fruit of knowledge, it is God himself.

By pointing out these two trees, God makes it certain that these people sooner or later will be attracted towards them. If He had not mentioned them, I don't think even up to now we would have been able to find those two trees in the immense garden of paradise. And if it was the serpent who convinced Eve, he is the first revolutionary, the first man who feels and who knows what has to be done. He is the most intelligent being in your whole *Bible* – the serpent – because he was showing the way of understanding.

Most of your misery is caused by your misunderstanding, your ignorance, your unintelligence. Most of the misery is caused because you are continuously afraid of death – and it is there walking by your side. If these two things can be removed, celebration will come on its own.

If you could be aware that there is no death, wouldn't you love to sing like birds in the morning? Wouldn't you love to dance like the peacocks of my garden? If you start understanding human problems, you cannot be miserable. I have not been miserable for so long that I cannot conceive how you go on maintaining misery, you go on nourishing it. You are really strange people. What are the causes of your misery?

You look at a beautiful woman. Naturally you are attracted, but your wife is by your side continuously watching you. She is miserable, because how can she enjoy life when she is continuously suspicious of you? You are miserable because this wretched wife is always there. You cannot even have a glimpse of a beautiful woman, you have to avoid seeing her. But a little understanding will dispel the whole thing.

It is natural, anything beautiful has to be appreciated. You have to show your wife, "Look! What a beautiful woman." And if there is understanding, the woman will understand it; there will be no jealousy, there will be no quarrel. It is human to taste different joys of life. You cannot eat the same food every day. How can you enjoy the same man or woman every day? It is asking for the impossible. Misery is bound to happen. You will become a hypocrite.

It is perfectly human once in a while to have a different dish. And if people are understanding…your wife will understand if once in a while you go with another woman; her love will be great enough to allow you that freedom.

Love always allows freedom.

Understanding *means* freedom.

And if your wife goes to some man one day, just for the weekend, you will not feel offended. After the weekend you will both be enriched. You will find your wife again, your wife will find you again. Those

This life is a gift of existence to you. You have not asked for it, you have not paid for it. You, in fact, don't deserve it. Still, existence is overflowing towards you, sharing all its joys. But you turn out to be such an idiot that when the sun is rising and the sky is full of colors – a time to dance, to sing – you are sitting in a dark church, gloomy, before a cross. My people worship, but not in a church. They worship the beauty of existence.

first days of love, those days of honeymoon will be back. And when you see that the other gives you so much freedom and so much understanding, you respect them, you feel grateful.

But all the religions have been prohibiting you from everything natural; obviously, they have made you miserable.

Your whole education system tries to create ambition in you – not understanding. Your education pushes you to become the governor, the premier, the president, whatsoever the cost. The politician cannot be happy – in spite of Jimmy Carter's phony smile. Have you seen him smiling after he was no longer president? When he was president I think he did nothing other than show his teeth to the whole world. I have heard that his wife used to close his mouth every night.

All lies – everything phony and American…all plastic. You know the phrase, "the white lie." Perhaps that's why you call your president's house the White House. It is a very suitable name, because only white lies exist there.

Man is living unnaturally. If he lives naturally then he feels guilty, because his religion, his education, his culture go on and on conditioning him: "You have to go above nature." Who can go above nature? Nature is all! – there is nothing above it. You have to be natural.

That's what my basic teaching is: be natural. Don't try to go beyond nature. That is the beginning of misery, pain. And when you are miserable, when you are in pain, you cannot tolerate anybody who is celebrating. It hurts, it humiliates you.

My people are humiliating all the religions of the world. Naturally they are against me and against you. It is your celebration that is creating the trouble. Have long, British faces. Tears are accepted, not smiles.

Have you seen Jesus Christ, in any picture, smiling? And Christianity has chosen as its symbol, the cross. Now, the people who are carrying the cross, can they celebrate? A cross is hanging on your neck – it may be a golden cross, but a cross is a cross. All Christians worshipping the cross are managing to remain miserable. They don't love Jesus Christ, they love his being crucified. Remember, Christianity was not born out of Jesus Christ's sayings – there is nothing much in them. You cannot make a religion out of them. The whole of Jesus Christ's doctrine can be condensed on a postcard.

Christianity was not born out of Jesus' teachings, it was born out of his crucifixion. Why was the cross accepted so easily? – and Christianity is now the biggest religion in the world. It suited man. It helped man in a very dangerous way. It made you aware that your misery is nothing compared to the misery of Jesus Christ. You are carrying a very small cross around your neck; Jesus had to carry a very heavy cross on his shoulders. Three times he fell on the road because of the weight of the cross. He was whipped and told to take up the cross again.

The crucified Jesus is your religion. Compared to your misery, his misery is immense. Naturally, Christianity became the biggest religion in the world, because it is the biggest philosophy of being miserable.

Jesus said, "Carry your cross on your shoulders. Everybody has to carry his cross on his shoulders." I don't see any point in it. Why carry a cross on your shoulder? Are you mad? Rather, carry a flute with you, a song, a beautiful flower – a rose I can understand. But then you will be hated by all those who have missed the joys of life. But nobody else is responsible for their missing, they themselves are responsible.

Jesus says, "Blessed are the poor." This is sheer nonsense. Wretched are the poor. But it gives solace to the millions of poor people of the world. Jesus says that those who are poor here will be able to inherit the kingdom of God. I do not understand the arithmetic. If they are going to inherit the kingdom of God, why should they be poor here? Why can't they inherit it here, now?

I say to you: the kingdom of God is yours herenow, this very moment. Just drop the cross. My religion is very simple: drop the cross. You have carried it long enough, for thousands of lives; it has almost become part of you.

So when you see someone dancing and you are crippled – crippled because of your cross, you are dying under its burden, and somebody is playing on his flute – you cannot forgive this man. He makes you aware that you have missed the train, that you are a fool. Nobody wants to accept himself as a fool – except a wise man.

The moment you accept that you are behaving foolishly, the change starts beginning.

It is your responsibility. I have never seen any miserable man for whom anybody else was responsible. It is your conditioning.

Jesus says, "The camel can pass through the eye of a needle, but not a rich man." The animals, the camels, are going to inherit the kingdom of God, remember; they will pass through the needle. But a rich man cannot pass through the gates of God. They have taught you to remain poor, they have given you all incentives to remain poor.

My religion is a religion of richness.

Why wait for tomorrow? Why wait for a lifetime, in which you cannot be certain of inheriting the kingdom of God after death, and for that, suffer your whole life here? I say to you, forget God and forget the kingdom of God. I give you here and now! Just be ready to drop your conditionings. You are not handicapped, you are not crippled. Every child is born a joy, a celebration, a dance, a song; but somewhere he loses it all. That's why all the poets of all the languages go on remembering how beautiful it was to be a child.

What was beautiful in being a child? I cannot say that, because I have been becoming more and more blissful; childhood was just the beginning. If an old man says that his childhood was paradise, that means his whole life has been a hell. He has not been growing up, he is going down. Just to grow old is not growing up.

Growing up is a totally different phenomenon. It means the last moment on the earth for you will be the most precious moment. The departure from this life will be the climax of your joy. Childhood is only a beginning.

But the religions start distorting the children from the beginning. They create guilt in them, they create unnatural ideals in them. They create their conscience in such a way that they cannot live ever happily ever. On every point they are at a crossroad, and they will choose the road that suits their conditioning.

Christians say you have been punished because Adam and Eve disobeyed God. It is impossible for me to conceive that Adam and Eve's disobedience is still keeping you miserable. And what had they done? It was sheer curiosity. And they did well. Instead of worshipping God and Jesus Christ in your churches, worship the serpent. Adam and Eve, they are the right people; they disobeyed. It was needed; otherwise there would have been no humanity. There would have been no Albert Einstein, no Bertrand Russell, no Gautam Buddha. There was no possibility. You would have been still animals, naked in the Garden of Eden.

And God immediately drove them out of the garden. I sometimes wonder what model of car he used to drive them out. It must have been a Ford, because "blessed are the poor." And strange: four-wheelers, Fords, are going in and out of God's garden, his gate, but a rich man cannot enter. Ford himself cannot enter.

If you teach people to be poor, and you bribe them to remain poor…. And the bribe is bogus – it is after death that you will have all the pleasure of life…. But if in God's garden all the pleasures of life are available, one thing is certain, that pleasures are not condemned.

If you look at the Mohammedan concept of

paradise – your word "paradise" comes from a Mohammedan word, *firdaus* – all kinds of pleasures are available. Beautiful women stuck at the age of sixteen for eternity, they don't grow up; rivers of wine – bottles are not enough…. Drink, swim, have a deep plunge into the wine; enjoy it as much as you can – and all free. This is the arrangement for the religious people.

But I cannot see how the contradiction can be resolved. Here wine is a sin. Here, to have many beautiful women is a sin, and there it becomes a virtue. Virtues are rewarded by sins – strange logic! But it was needed to keep the poor, poor.

In India I have never seen a single rich man converting to Christianity. I have seen only poor, starving, orphans being converted to Christianity. Christianity thrives on poverty, because only the poor need the consolation. Only the poor need motivation to drag their life up to the grave – beyond the grave everything is just as it should be.

When I say celebrate – because this life is a gift of existence to you…. You have not asked for it, you have not paid for it. You, in fact, don't deserve it. Still, existence is overflowing towards you, sharing all its joys. But you turn out to be such an idiot that when the sun is rising and the sky is full of colors – a time to dance, to sing – you are sitting in a dark church, gloomy, before a cross.

My people worship, but not in a church.

They worship the beauty of existence.

A bird flying, a cloud wandering in the sky, the moon, the stars… Outside you can see the whole existence is in celebration, but you have closed your eyes to it. With closed eyes you are saying, "Ave Maria, Ave Maria," and you go on saying it.

Yes, all the religions are against me because I teach celebration, because I teach joy, because I teach comfort, I teach luxury, I teach richness.

And man has the intelligence to make the whole world so luxurious that even if there are saints in heaven, they will start praying to go back to the earth. I cannot see that the saints in heaven can enjoy beautiful women, because they missed here, and this is a rehearsal, just a training period of seventy years. If for seventy years you have been repressing yourself, just by entering into heaven, what will you do with your repression? What will you do with your guilt?

The Bible was written two thousand years ago; otherwise, marijuana, LSD, hashish – everything would have been made available to the saints in paradise. Of course, here it is a crime and would have remained a crime, but for saints you have to be lenient: they have suffered so much; you have to compensate.

I don't tell you about tomorrow, I tell you only of this moment. And if you can enjoy this moment, the next moment you will be more capable of enjoying. If tomorrow ever comes, you will be ready to dance, to love.

These religions are bound to be against me, because they are not religions. I want it to be emphasized that this is the only religion. All those religions of the past were sick, pathological. If you start thinking about them, you can easily see that they were pathological. They have made the whole world sick, and they are still going on doing it. They call it "service to humanity."

Mother Teresa wrote a letter to me. Because I criticized her a few years ago, she wrote a letter to me: "I cannot understand your criticism. Service to humanity is the true religion. Don't you agree with it?" I wrote to her, "Yes, I agree. Tell all six hundred million Catholics to commit suicide. That will be a service to humanity."

The world is suffering from overpopulation – Christians should start committing suicide and serve humanity. But they go on doing just the opposite; they go on opening hospitals, they go on saving orphans. They are against birth control, they are against abortion. This is service to humanity?

Nothing can be more poisonous to humanity than

what Mother Teresa is doing.

In her letter she asked me, "Are you infallible? I believe in the infallible Jesus Christ."

I am not such a fool as to be infallible. I am an ordinary man just like you. I am very much fallible. One of my Indian sannyasins is here – his name is Falibhai. Whenever I see him I think to change his name to "Fallible-bhai."

Jesus is claiming that he is infallible – and he cannot see that Judas is going to betray him. He cannot see that going to Jerusalem during that religious festival is going to death. Only on the cross does he wake up; and he shouts at God, "Have you forsaken me?" But the skies remain silent.

Silence is so beautiful. It is good that the sky does not answer your prayers; otherwise there would be so much noise around the world. And it would be difficult – what answer is given to whom?

The sky remained silent.

Jesus asks for water because he is thirsty, it is a hot day. And you call this man infallible? He should just have carried a thermos. If he can carry the cross, why can't he carry a small thermos? When you go for a holiday – and he's going forever – a thermos is exactly the right thing to take.

Jesus is infallible, and the popes are infallible because they represent Jesus. This is a good arrangement: God is infallible, naturally his son is going to be infallible – and then you can conclude the son's representatives are going to be infallible.

One of the last popes before this pope the Polack was homosexual. It was a known fact. In fact, when he became the pope his boyfriend followed him into the Vatican. He became his secretary. Secretaries are very good – girlfriend or boyfriend, it does not matter, but secretaries are very good. Do you think this homosexual is infallible? Do you think this pope the Polack is infallible?

Just now he has been trying to convince the Jews that Christians are not anti-semitic. Why? For two thousand years they have been anti-semitic, for two thousand years they have been killing Jews. Has God changed his mind? But infallible people don't change their mind, only fallible people change their mind.

Why is he trying now? His effort is to call a conference of Jewish rabbis and Christian bishops, just to meet together and settle the thing: "We are not enemies." He has been telling bishops, "Don't say anything against Judaism." That can mean only one thing: that all the popes that have preceded him were fallible. Or, if they were infallible, then this Polack is fallible.

I am not infallible. In fact, life is a continuous change. And the conscious person goes on moving and changing with life and existence. He is like a river, moving – not like a dirty pond which only goes on becoming more and more muddy; he goes nowhere, he never changes. A river goes on flowing, changing, taking new routes.

Consciousness keeps pace with the change of life and existence.

There are many questions which remind me, "In 1972 you said this...." Forget all about it! What I am saying *now* is the truth – only for now, not for tomorrow. I will see tomorrow what is the truth. I am not a blind man. I see, and I see the existence continuously changing. But these bibles don't change, these korans don't change, these gitas don't change – they are dead books, just rubbish. These old religions don't change; they go on clinging to the past which exists no more.

Galileo was called by the pope because he wrote that the earth is round, not flat. *The Bible* says it is flat. Of course, I cannot condemn *The Bible;* it looks flat to us too. Our vision is not that vast; we cannot see the whole earth, we see only small fragments, which look flat.

When Galileo wrote that the earth is round, that it is a globe, he was forced by the pope: "You have to change it, because *The Bible* cannot be wrong. And we cannot allow one thing to be wrong, because that will create suspicion; then other things maybe are also not right. If one thing can be wrong, then everything can be wrong. *The Bible* has to be true word for word, as a whole."

Galileo must have been a man with a tremendous sense of humor. He said, "I will write whatsoever you say. If you say the world, the earth is flat, I will write it." And he wrote it, "The earth is flat – but forgive me, this is *my* statement; as far as the earth is concerned it is a globe. I cannot do anything about it. I can change my statement, but what can I do with the earth? How can I make it flat to be consistent with *The Bible?*"

1972? Don't even ask me about what I said yesterday. It is gone. What I am saying this moment is truth. And if tomorrow I see changes, I am not stubborn and I am not a fanatic, I will change; hence you will find thousands of contradictions in me. Anybody who is aware will have thousands of contradictions in his statements. Only a fanatic is consistent, he never contradicts himself. He keeps his eyes closed, he is afraid to see the truth.

Celebration is the very nature of existence.

Don't separate yourself from existence; otherwise, you will be miserable. You cannot be nourished, you cannot eat *The Bible* and the *Koran* and the *Gita.* They will not nourish your body, they will kill you. If they cannot nourish even your body, how can they nourish your consciousness?

There is only one nourishment: your roots have to be deep down in existence. There is no other nourishment. And if you are nourished…I say, "Blessed are the nourished. Blessed are those whose roots go deep into existence. They are the richest people." Richness does not mean only money. I am not against money; it is a perfectly good servant for exchanging things. But money alone is not richness.

Richness is multidimensional. It happens when you are in tune with nature, in harmony with nature; it starts happening multidimensionally. You may not be aware of what will happen to you if you destroy your conditionings of Christianity, Hinduism,

Buddhism, and simply rely on and trust in nature. If your consciousness also trusts nature just the way your body remains trusting towards nature….

You don't know what treasures you have got. Once there is nourishment you will start blossoming. You may not know that you can become a painter, you may not know you can become a dancer. You may be a Picasso, you may be a Nijinsky, you may be a Van Gogh, you may be a Rutherford. You don't know who you are. You will know only when you blossom; there is no other way to know. And blossoming happens only in harmony with nature. Your roots should go not towards any church, not towards any scripture, not towards any dead prophets, but towards the nature that is available to you.

Just be natural. Drop all sense of guilt. The guilt arises only because your conditioning says, "Don't do this" and your nature is hungry to do it. Now you are split. Your religion, your Jesuses, your Mohammeds say, "Don't do this, this is wrong." Those Ten Commandments, three thousand years old – they are still dominating you. Why are you degrading yourself? Those ten Commandments say, "Don't do this, this is sin. You will suffer in hell" – and your whole nature wants to do it.

Listen to your nature, not to your conditionings, and celebration will happen on its own accord.

Have you seen any tree miserable? Have you seen any bird miserable? They are in harmony. Fortunately they don't have priests, popes, *shankaracharyas,* imams. If the trees had popes and imams and *shankaracharyas,* then all the trees would stop flowering, would not come to fruition. They would somehow survive – only survive. Survival is not life! Survival is the minimum. You have to be overflowing, you have to be so full that you can share, and still your fullness remains full. That's what the meaning of celebration is.

But the religions are bound to be against me, because if I am heard, then there is no need for any other religion in the world. They are trying to stop my words from reaching you; otherwise, there is no hope for themselves. And they have a great investment.

In Russia I have my sannyasins – of course, underground. But I am not a serious man; only fanatics are serious. When Russian sannyasins asked me what to do about the red clothes, the mala, I said, "Forget all about them – they don't matter. They are just to provoke people." But there sannyasins will be killed, so they have to meet in basements. Still the Russian government has started torturing them. They have taken their books, they have taken their tapes that they had smuggled from the outside. And they are torturing them to make them give the names of other sannyasins.

Why does communism fear us? – because communism is also a religion. It has its own trinity: Karl Marx, Frederick Engels, V.I. Lenin – the trinity. They also have their bible: *Das Kapital.* Neither Christians read *The Bible* nor do communists read *Das Kapital.* I am the only unfortunate one who has been reading all this rubbish. Communism is an atheist religion.

All these people are going to stop my words from reaching people. That's what is happening here.

I was tremendously disappointed when I came to America. I had thought that it was a democratic country. It is not, absolutely not, because what they have been doing to my people, to me, is fascist. Democracy is just a mask; behind the democracy everything is fascist.

You will be surprised to know that one of my sannyasins, one of my oldest sannyasins, Ma Yoga Laxmi, who was the president of the Indian section of my sannyasins for almost ten years, and has been with me almost for twenty years…. She is frail, small-bodied…she has cancer. She has been operated on, much of her stomach has been removed. Still, in America – remember I am saying in America, not in the Soviet Union – she has been beaten by your naturalization services. She was not allowed to have her legal expert, she was not allowed to phone anybody. She was not allowed – but other sannyasins were waiting outside.

The officials took her first into the front part of the building. They were very sweet – just the way communists are in Russia. They tried to bribe her. They said to her, "We will give you a green card without any difficulty, we will help you in every way. And if you help us and whatsoever we say you support, we will replace Bhagwan's secretary and put you in power."

When she refused, when she said, "Whatsoever you are saying is absolute lies, and I am not power-hungry," when they found that she could not be seduced in a friendly way, they forced her – four strong people for a tiny person, fragile, the body is dying – and they took her to the back. She told them, "Please, let me have my advocate with me." They did not allow it. And at the back of the building they started beating her – of course in such a way that no medical evidence can be found. And she is so weak….

You call this democracy?

My sannyasins – the president of the international sannyas movement, the president of this commune, the head of another corporation – all these three women, and I don't know about others, whenever they come into the country or go out of the country officials take them into a dirty room, force them to be naked, and force their fingers into their vaginas under the pretext that they are searching for drugs. This you call democracy?

And doing it to three women…. Perhaps they have done it to many. Those poor women cannot say anything, just out of shame: what to say to anybody? And there is no witness; those officials will deny it flatly. These women are tortured in an ugly, inhuman way – and this is a democratic country. Sometimes I think the attorney general of Oregon must be the reincarnation of Pontius Pilate.

This is also humiliation of womankind. Not only should sannyasins fight it, all the women of America should fight it. This is simply against every woman; it is not a question only of my sannyasins. But other women will remain silent because they are Christians, they are Protestants, they are Catholics, they are Jews. People cannot see because they have so many curtains before their eyes.

Yes, religions are against me – it is natural. I am also against all of them. And remember, if Jesus could work with only twelve disciples and managed to have the biggest religion in the world, what about me?

Beloved Bhagwan,

I am happy that You are speaking again, but at the same time I'm sad too. Can You say why?

It is very simple. You are happy because I am speaking. You cannot understand my silence. To understand silence you have to be silent, and you are not. Hence you are happy that I am speaking again; you can understand words.

The problem for you is that you are sad also. That is a little bit complicated. You are sad because I may disturb you. I am a very unreliable person. In these thirty years it has happened many times; thousands of people have come to me, remained with me, and at a certain point dropped out. If I were silent they would have been still with me. I said something which they had never expected.

When I was speaking on Jesus, many Christians became sannyasins. Now when I am speaking on Jesus, only those who have guts will remain with me; otherwise they will betray me. That's why you are sad. Knowing my past, you know I don't give you, like Christians do, any catechism which remains fixed. I am continuously moving, and you may be afraid whether you will be able to move any further.

What I am saying today is nothing.

And I am not going to be silent again either. I will go on saying things, more and more dangerous, unto my last breath. Even if I lose all the sannyasins, it does not matter.

Discontent:
Another Name for
Inferiority Complex

Beloved Bhagwan,

Do You ever get sad?

Really a tough question! Yes and no. Yes, I get sad for you and for the world in which you are living. And you are not aware that you are living in the midst of a vast madhouse. You are so fast asleep, you don't know what is being done to you, to others.

The politicians make me sad because they are the ugliest animals on the earth – continuously lying to people, exploiting people, humiliating people.

Before the last election in America, the governor of Oregon had a secret meeting of all the top officials of his government. The attorney general was there, Norma Paulus was there, and everybody who means anything in the government. They did not allow the journalists inside…. And still you go on calling this a democratic country?

They were deciding about my people, but they did not allow any of my people to be present there. And the governor came out and gave a press conference in which he lied completely.

What happened inside and what he said outside are completely contradictory. In the press conference he said, "Things are normal. There is no need to be afraid, everything is in control. We are trying to calm down the Rajneeshees."

I don't know how he was trying to calm us down. He never came here, he never sent a message to us, but he was calming us down. Does he think he is a magician? And he said he was trying to keep the opposing people from getting too hot.

Inside, everything was different. Now the confidential record of the meeting has been found – he was thinking it had been burned. But in this world impossible things also happen. Now we know what happened inside the meeting; there was no question of calming anyone down, no question of creating peace. On the contrary, they were deciding how much time it would take their army to reach Rajneeshpuram to destroy it completely. They had decided to put the army on alert so any moment, within three hours, they could destroy my people.

Of course, in a way it is calming us down. If you are not here, there will be calm. It has been calm here in this place for many decades, but that calmness was death. There was only one house, and there was only one family to look after this big place. It is one hundred and twenty-six square miles – three times bigger than New York. Of course it was calm. There were no birds to sing, there were no trees to blossom. It was a dead place; we made it alive.

Now birds have started coming. Nature has a

tremendous harmony when there are so many people loving, singing, dancing. Birds have started coming to this place, flowers have started blossoming.

But it is not noisy, it is not "hot" in the governor's sense. You cannot find a cooler place in the whole world. Of course the sun is hot – that is not our fault. But the place is cool, calm, there is no disturbance. In these four years there has not been a single fight. But they want to destroy this calmness. They would love to have a dead place, the serenity of a cemetery.

There is serenity in a garden too. Do you think birds singing, flowers moving in the air, disturb anything? They make the silence deeper, meaningful.

Silence in itself is meaningless unless it has the potential for a song, unless it has something in it to blossom, something to grow.

In the meeting they decided that the army should be put on alert, and the army *was* put on alert. And they were ready, in three hours, to destroy this place, these people. Of course we would have died singing and dancing. We would have made history.

But these people make me sad – and they are in power, and they go on lying. Now what do you call it – is it not a conspiracy, to tell the people that everything is normal? Then why is the army on alert? And what crime have *we* committed that we have to be destroyed?

Just the other day the information came to me that in California, whenever there is a boxing match.... The University of California has been researching it, and they have found that whenever there is a boxing match in California, for a few days the murder rate goes thirteen percent higher than normal. And this is the murder rate – it says nothing about smaller fights, people wounded, rapes. Still boxing continues to be legal.

This place, where nobody fights, is illegal. People come close only to hug each other. This small and beautiful life is not to be wasted in fighting. That's why I say yes, sometimes it makes me sad.

A civilized man cannot be a Christian, a Jew, a Mohammedan. He cannot be an American, he cannot be an Indian. A civilized man is simply man. And if wars disappear, the world will not need priests to persuade you that "Blessed are the poor," because there will be nobody who is poor. Then the priests will not be able to distract your mind towards heaven, because we can make heaven on this very earth.

When I look around the world…we are in exactly the same economic situation as the world was in before the second world war. The American dollar was going higher and higher, and all other countries' economies were falling apart. This is the kind of atmosphere when war becomes absolutely necessary.

When I was in India the dollar was worth seven and a half rupees. Now it is worth twenty rupees – three times higher. The same is the situation in Germany, in England, in Holland – all over the world. The same was the situation before the second world war. You cannot live in an ocean of poverty, with economies failing, nations going bankrupt, people all over the world dying and starving. Sooner or later this euphoria of the American dollar will backfire; it will become an absolute necessity to start the third world war to divert people's minds.

Seventy-five percent of every nation's income goes for war preparations. People are starving and dying – and you are creating bombs. Bread is needed, not bombs. Can't you see the insanity?

Isn't there a single nation which can declare, "We are going to stop creating nuclear weapons at the risk of being defeated"? Anyway, a country like England, which has lived for three hundred years in great luxury, exploiting the whole world…. Now the empire has disappeared. England is dark, dismal; there is no hope – and still they are putting all their resources into creating nuclear weapons, knowing perfectly well that they can never again be a world power. They cannot compete with America or the Soviet Union, or even China.

When you are not going to be a world power – even with nuclear weapons you will be defeated and destroyed – then what is the point of creating those weapons? In fact it is such a beautiful situation that you can dissolve all defense measures, you can stop having a defense ministry. There is no need; you will be defeated anyway.

But what to say about England? Even India, which is dying, goes on and on creating more and more war material. They are also after nuclear weapons.

In the history of man there has never been such a beautiful moment, when some courageous nation can say, "There is no need for any defense. We are all human beings – who is going to attack us?"

And do you see the cunningness? All these defense departments are not really for defense, they are for attack. Adolf Hitler attacked the world, but he had no department for attack. It was the defense department that was attacking.

The world will be going more and more into darker spaces, ditches. But nobody is ready to listen; their minds are conditioned so deeply that they are almost deaf. They hear, but they don't listen.

I just heard that one clergyman from Europe is here. He loves me, he has been coming to all the celebrations. But because I said something about Mother Teresa, he became very upset. This makes me sad. Why did he become so upset? Can't he understand a simple thing? – that Mother Teresa is helping poverty to increase in the world, and poverty ultimately means war.

He said that his four girlfriends…. Strange, a clergyman having four girlfriends? Even I cannot afford that. And nobody is there to prevent me, I am my own master; I don't accept orders from anybody. Four girlfriends of his had been to Mother Teresa, and they all said that she is a nice woman. So what? There are millions of nice women, far nicer than Mother Teresa. And I have not said that she's not nice. Why do you get upset? Yes, she is a nice old witch. Now get upset. And pack your luggage and go back. Your love for me was of no worth.

This makes me sad. In these thirty years thousands of people have come along with me; they will go a few steps and then drop away. They had the potential, they had the courage; otherwise even to go a few steps with me towards the unknown is difficult. But after a few steps, why did they drop out? Something I said disturbed them. But they are not aware –

it is not their consciousness which is disturbed, it is their conditioning which gets upset, disturbed.

Are you going to listen to awareness or to all kinds of rubbish that rabbis, bishops, popes, mothers and fathers have forced into your head when you were very small and vulnerable?

I sometimes feel puzzled: why do you call Mother Teresa "mother," and why do you call the pope "father"? *Popa* in Italian means father. Instead of calling him pope start calling him *popa* – that sounds better. You call the pope, who has no children, "father." You call Mother Teresa, who has no children, "mother." Let these two get married. And put them on the pill, because we don't want their progeny. Enough is enough!

Existence does not make me sad. My own inner being for three decades has never felt a single moment of sadness for myself. I have completely forgotten the strategy, how to be sad. But what goes on happening around the world just brings tears to my eyes.

This world is not worth saving. Once in a while I think it will be better if the third world war happens and destroys this whole stupid humanity. Perhaps there is a time when a thing gets so rotten that it is better to burn it.

Consciousness is eternal. Even if this earth becomes without human beings, I don't see any problem in it. There are at least fifty thousand planets around the earth where life exists. Your consciousnesses will move to other planets. Nothing will be destroyed – only this ugly earth, these ugly politicians, priests; they will be finished.

This makes me sad: man on the earth has the highest quality of consciousness, and yet his behavior is barbarous. And everything that you call civilization is just a word.

Once a man asked George Bernard Shaw, "What do you think about civilization?"

He said, "It is a good thing, but it has not happened yet."

What the religions go on doing around the world makes me sad. They go on making you more and more idiotic. Their basis is faith. They force every child to be faithful, a believer, and if possible, to be a fanatic believer. You will find all kinds of fanatics around. Even if you don't want to be delivered, you don't want to be saved, they will force you to be saved.

There are Christian sects who are self-appointed saviors. Who gives you the authority to save another? And are you certain that *you* are saved? Your face, your eyes do not give any proof of it; you look angry. Even a nice man like Jesus was an angry man. Who gave him the authority to beat the money-changers in the temple of Jerusalem and throw them out?

Self-appointed judges....

Jesus wanted to save the world – he could not even save himself. And he has left an ugly heritage which goes on growing like a cancerous growth, destroying everything that can raise you to beauty, to truth, to silence, to ecstasy.

I have never seen a Christian ecstatic. Even Jesus was not ecstatic; he was burdened, and continuously having hallucinations. Now thinking oneself the only begotten son of God – do you think the man was sane? Thinking that he is the only real messenger bringing truth to humanity – do you think this man is mentally healthy? He is utterly sick, and Christians are sick.

But it is not only the Christians; the Hindus are in the same boat, the Mohammedans are in the same boat. Their names and their theologies and their scriptures are different, but the basic madness is there. They are all hallucinating.

Your religions are nothing but opium. Drugs are prohibited – and the greatest drug is your religions. They should be abandoned, completely abandoned, if we want man to get rid of hallucinations. Otherwise, people are hallucinating that soon they will reach heaven and all the angels will be there dancing and singing, "Alleluia!"

There is no heaven, and there are no angels. Heaven is a state of consciousness. It is not a place. It is not part of geography; otherwise there would be very much confusion. In India, if you ask the Hindus where hell is, they say, "Just under us, deep down." But if you make a hole from India deep down, you may enter Oregon – and *their* heaven is above. But the earth is round; everything is above, and everything from some angle, some place, is below. The Hindu's hell is your heaven, your heaven is a Hindu's hell.

You go on listening to these people, and you go on absorbing their nonsense in you. It is sheer poison. The politicians, the priests, make me sad. They are all programming your mind and changing it into a computer, a mechanism.

My work here is to deprogram you. Whether you get upset or not, I don't care. You *will* get upset, because deprogramming is upsetting. You have believed a certain thing for fifty years, sixty years, and suddenly I say that it is nonsense. You cannot accept it, because that means you have been a stupid guy. But if you have guts and intelligence, there is still time to get out of the rut.

I am, and my religion is, nothing but the science of deprogramming. And remember, don't get mixed up with the deprogrammers that exist in California. They are not deprogrammers, they are *re*programmers. If any Christian moves away from Christianity, his parents becomes paranoid; they force the person to go to those so-called deprogrammers. They don't deprogram him, they reprogram him. He was escaping from Christianity, they bring him back to Christianity. You call it deprogramming….

Deprogramming means that you are simply left without any program. You are left without any religion, you are left without any theology. You are left alone to be yourself, an individual.

People go on asking me, "How many followers do you have?" I have not a single follower in the whole world, because my whole work is to destroy following, followers, and to create courage in people

so they can stand on their own and be individuals.

It makes me sad that you are not individuals. Somebody is a Christian, somebody is a Hindu, somebody is a Mohammedan, somebody is a Buddhist. You are not individuals. You are blind followers, programmed by other blind followers.

But as far as I am concerned, there is no sadness in me. Day and night, I am in absolute bliss. That also makes me sad, that what is possible for me – an ordinary individual like me – why can't it be possible for all? I do not claim any speciality. I do not claim that I am the only begotten son of God. I do not proclaim that I am the prophet bringing a fresh message from God.

All these prophets, messengers, *avataras,* are just holy shit! Of course, it has been clinging to you so long that when I start hitting you hard so that this holy shit drops, you get upset.

I can understand, but I cannot stand it!

Beloved Bhagwan,

Please comment on this statement by J.P. Markham: "I fear the contented man. I fear him because there is no progress unless there is discontent."

I do not care whose statement this is. One thing I know, that discontent certainly makes you speedy. You go on running your whole life. You become just a vehicle that goes on moving faster and faster. But for what? I do not call it progress.

You may have all the money of the world, still you will be running after money. You may have all the knowledge, and still you will be running after more knowledge. In every dimension there is infinite space to run.

I have heard….

A man and his wife were flying in a plane; the man was piloting. The plane was going full speed, and the wife asked, "Where are we going?"

The man said, "Don't bother where – look at the speed! We are certainly going *somewhere*."

Discontent is another name for inferiority complex. Discontent means: you look around, people have this, people have that, and you don't have it – you are discontented. But just seeing that somebody has it, you become discontented, you start feeling inferior. You have to surpass it, you have to get ahead. This continuous getting ahead is called progress – it is not progress. And this kind of progress begins even before your birth.

When a man makes love to a woman, the living cells that he releases into the woman's body start running. Progress begins there, because in a single lovemaking millions of living cells are released. They must have been feeling imprisoned in the man. Whenever they get the chance they go fast – you cannot understand how fast, because they are so small you cannot see them with your eyes.

The passage between them and the female egg, in proportion to their size, is almost two miles. And their life is very short, they are almost on their deathbed, because they can live for only two days, not more than that. In those two days those tiny cells have to run two miles, with millions of competitors, and only one will reach the female egg.

Sometimes it happens, two reach at the same time – that's why twins are born. Once the female egg opens and receives a male cell, it closes, and all those millions – those progressive people – simply die. If your lovemaking is counted, you have been murdering millions of people your whole life.

And don't think that the celibate monks are not murdering. Their cells die in imprisonment – at least you give them a little freedom, a little democracy, a little chance to progress. The celibate monk, Catholic or Hindu, does not allow those poor people to get out of his body. Yoga has methods to go on preventing them from getting out of you. They go on dying within you…. You are eating, you are getting nourishment, and it is a natural process. The body goes on; the body knows no religion.

The body goes on doing its function. It is programmed by nature, not by any priest – it will go on creating new blood cells, it will go on creating new semen cells, it will go on creating everything that the body needs. But when new living semen cells are created, the old have to die and vacate the place. The new ones have come – the new generation has come and the old generation has to go. There is not much space for all of them to coexist.

When you think of progress…it starts with your lovemaking – a mad race – and where do you end? You end with a woman. Great, just great!

And then your whole life it is the same, the same story. People are running after power, people are running after money, people are running after respectability. People are running after everything you can imagine, and where do they end up? Even if you reach the last rung of the ladder – there is no such thing, just for argument's sake I am saying it – even if you reach the last rung of the ladder, what will you do then?

I remember I was driving and a dog started following my car, chasing – he was hot, really progressive, very discontented. But he was not acquainted with me. He must have chased other cars….

I stopped the car – the poor dog was huffing, his tongue was hanging out. I stopped the car and asked the dog, "What now? What do you want?"

And the way the dog looked at me…Ronald Reagan would also look the same way!

Even if you become the president of a country, or a prime minister of a country, so what? You call it progress? It is obsession with speed.

Discontent brings conflict because it brings competition. If you are running, others are also running. There is going to be competition, there is going to be cut-throat competition. Hence all these wars.

The Polack pope is reaching out to the Christians around the world with the message, "Drop your antagonism with the Jews." The Christians cannot understand. For two thousand years they have been *killing* Jews. When Adolf Hitler killed almost one million Jews in Germany, the high priest of the Christians in Germany blessed him; he had done a great religious act by removing these Jews.

For two thousand years Christians have been killing Jews because Jews killed Jesus; and nobody bothers about the fact that Jesus was a Jew, he was not a Christian – it is none of your business! If Jews want to kill another Jew, it is their internal affair. Jesus never claimed that he was a Christian. If he had claimed that he was a Christian, he would not have been crucified – then, who bothers?

Jews were upset because he was saying he was their Lord, that he was coming from God just as Moses, Abraham, Ezekiel and other prophets have come. And in a way he is higher than all those prophets, because they were only postmen, nothing much. He is the only begotten son. Naturally this Jew was going to be killed by the Jews. But they killed a *Jew,* they never killed a Christian. Christians have been killing Jews. I don't see the mathematics of it.

And how after two thousand years it happens in a Polack mind…and it is known all over the world that anything like mind does not exist in them, they are empty bottles of alcohol. If you are a cannibal and you eat a Polack, you will know what I mean. Just a little taste of a Polack and you will go unconscious!

This Polack popa is trying to create a bridge, a communication between the Christians and the Jews. Why? These things are not religious, these things are political. After the second world war they created a Jewish nation, Israel. Jews think the Americans, the British and other allies – who were all Christian – have done a great favor to them; it is not so. It was a very cunning strategy.

Israel is the holy land of the Jews, and also the holy land of the Christians. It was not in existence centuries ago, because the population was Mohammedan. There was no Israel before 1945. There used to be a nation, Palestine, which is no longer anywhere; it simply disappeared.

Christians could have taken possession of Israel, but they were aware that if they took possession of Israel, then Jews would be against them all over the world. And Israel is surrounded by Mohammedans, the whole of the Middle East is Mohammedan; Israel itself is full of Mohammedans. It would create a conflict, a war, a continuous war between Christians on the one side and Jews and Mohammedans on the other side. In fact, Mohammedanism is closer to Judaism than Christianity is; much of Mohammedanism is borrowed from Judaism.

To avoid this situation of having Jews against them…. The politicians could not do that, because if the Jews are against the Christians, then who is going to donate to their election funds? It would have been disastrous, particularly in America, because all these politicians in America are supported by Jewish money.

And it was in the hands of America, because American forces were there in Israel to hand over the country to anybody – either to Christians or to Mohammedans or to Jews. It was a Mohammedan country and it would have been right to give it back to them. But Christians are against Mohammedans for a very simple thing – that's why I say this whole world needs to be finished – a very small problem.

Mohammedans accept Jesus as a prophet of God but not as a son of God. And they are very logical about it: where is the wife? There is nobody, other than the holy ghost. And nobody knows about the holy ghost, to what sex he belongs. Is he male? Certainly Christians cannot accept that he is female, because to raise woman so high that she becomes part of the trinity, the highest in existence…the holy ghost has to be male. But that makes God a homosexual, and homosexuals don't produce children. Then Jesus' whole position becomes very strange.

Hence Mohammedans say Jesus is a prophet, a messenger of God, but not a son of God; God has no relatives. This is the only difference. And Christians and Mohammedans have been killing each other for fourteen hundred years. These things should be laughed at, not fought for.

The Americans could not give it to Mohammedans, although the country was Mohammedan, and it had been under the Mohammedans for a long time. They could not keep it for themselves, because that would mean creating two enemies: Jews and Mohammedans. They found a very political and cunning way: they gave it to the Jews.

In that way they created a bridge between Jews and Christians, a friendship; they avoided one enemy, the Jews, avoided the other enemy, the Mohammedans, and very cleverly put the Jews in such a bad situation that they will continually have to fight with the Mohammedans.

Nobody can see any end to it because the country is Mohammedan, it belongs to the Mohammedans. It was forcibly taken and given to the Jews. This gave a very good opportunity to American Christians to get more donations from Jews; and it was a very good situation: they need not kill Jews, Mohammedans will kill them. Can you see the strategy? – so beautiful, so sophisticated.

Mohammedans will kill them – they *have* been killing them – on the one hand; on the other hand, the Jews will remain dependent on Christian countries. Israel is not independent; if America stops giving support to them, they will be finished within minutes. They have to remain under American control. Israel is nothing but a slave country of the Christians. And it will have to remain a slave; otherwise Mohammedans will kill it.

American politicians have done a good job. Jews think they have been favored; that is nonsense. They have been put in such a fix that they will never be out of it. And Christians have made a great step towards absorbing them. That has been the desire of Christianity: to absorb the whole world.

This hand of friendship is a not a hand of friendship. It is a hand that wants to destroy you.

Jews are in tremendous discontent, Mohammedans are in tremendous discontent, Christians are in tremendous discontent. Whoever has said that discontent is needed for progress? Humanity has been in discontent for as far back as you can imagine. What progress has happened?

Yes, you have better roads, you have better machines, you have high technology – but you don't have a better man. And your high technology, your nuclear weapons, your so-called good roads, beautiful buildings – without a good man they are just dangerous; not only useless, very dangerous.

It is giving a naked sword into the hands of a child. Man remains retarded and he is being given nuclear weapons.

I have heard…. When Ronald Reagan became the president of America, he was on a morning walk on a beach with his favorite friend, a chimpanzee. Great progress is happening: chimpanzees are friends of presidents! One man sitting there on the beach was very much puzzled. He said, "Mr. President, sir, am I hallucinating? What is this chimpanzee doing with you?"

Reagan said, "You are not hallucinating, he is my friend."

The man said, "I am not asking you, I am asking the president. Don't interfere."

In the first world war, for the first time psychoanalysts were employed by the governments to find out the intelligent quotient – I.Q. – of the soldiers. And it was a shock: the average man's mental age is close to fourteen years. He may be seventy years old, but his mental age is not more than fourteen – it may be less.

What progress has happened? You have not been able even to keep a synchronicity between man's physical age and his psychological age, and you call your world a civilized world – where everybody is retarded?

But these retarded people are needed by the politicians, by the priests, by all the vested interests, because if a man's intelligence also grows along with his body, then he will not become just old; he will grow up. His old age will be a beautiful experience. He will be able to drop all the conditionings which have been forced upon him.

But a retarded person cannot do that. He cannot even understand anything higher. He cannot even understand Leonardo da Vinci, he cannot understand Kalidasa, he cannot understand Rabindranath Tagore, he cannot understand Lao Tzu. He can only understand third-rate newspapers – *The Oregonian*. Yes, that he can understand.

He can follow a man like Reverend Jim Jones. Only a retarded man can do that. It is not a surprise that Jim Jones' followers were all black. Of course, they are more retarded than the white people; they have lived in slavery for so long, uneducated, humiliated – they are not first-class citizens. They have not been treated as human beings. Reverend Jim Jones had not a single white man as his follower. Those who died, committed suicide in Jonestown, were retarded people.

A man of intelligence would like to love, to live, to laugh. A great opportunity has been given by existence; he would like to drink out of it to the fullest. He would like to squeeze all that life contains.

But Jim Jones convinced those fools to commit suicide. Of course Christianity has the ultimate responsibility for it, because Reverend Jim Jones was an ordained Christian priest. Of course the cross is the symbol of suicide, and the whole teaching of Christianity is not for living joyously.

If Jesus can convince retarded people in Judea that when he reaches God, soon after they will all follow him…. He never defined how long this "soon" is. Two thousand years have passed; the "soon" is still there. Jim Jones carried the logic to its very end. He said, "Why should I wait there and and you wait here? You die with me, so we all go together." He convinced those retarded people to commit suicide.

Retarded people can be convinced about anything. Retarded people are being convinced to go to Vietnam to kill innocent people who have done no wrong to them. They can be sent anywhere, can be convinced to do anything.

Japan had suicidal soldiers – a separate division. They would take an airplane full of bombs, and the pilot knew he was not going to come back, but he was dying for his country. Only retarded people can be convinced to die for a country. What is a country? Where is Palestine? And for Palestine people have been dying. Countries exist only on the map; the earth is one.

That's why I say Rajneeshpuram is not in America, not in Oregon. This whole earth is ours. Rajneeshpuram is the capital of the whole world.

We don't believe in nations. It is idiotic – what is the need of all these nations? Yes, a world government is needed, but not nations. Unless we create a world government, wars will continue because these nations will go on fighting – India with Pakistan, China with India – the war will continue somewhere or other.

The only way to stop war is not what the pacifists go on doing – carrying posters in processions. There are a few people who enjoy it; it is good exercise. And they are boiling because of discontent, so it is good in a way to shout slogans; it releases something in them. But these pacifists are not going to stop the war that is just on the horizon. Any moment, any chimpanzee can trigger it.

Tomorrow is more uncertain than it has ever been. The next moment is more uncertain than it has ever been.

Protest, protest marches, slogans – this is not going to help. These people are exactly the same retarded people, they are just on a lower rung of the ladder. I have been watching these pacifists and their processions, their shouting and their slogans. It does not give the sense of peace; these are warmongers. Perhaps they are ready to *fight* for peace.

There is only one way: nations should disappear,

they are an unnecessary burden on us. The world can easily be one, there is no need of different colors on the map. If the world dissolves the nations, whom are you going to fight? And if the world becomes a little more intelligent and drops all religious nonsense, whom are you going to fight? And if you are not going to fight, there will be no Ethiopia, there will be no poor India – because all your energy, all your money, all your resources that are going into war efforts will be freed. The whole humanity can live richly.

People ask me, "What are you doing for Ethiopia?" Whatever I am doing, I am not sending Ethiopia some bread, some butter – that is not going to help. In the first place it is never going to reach Ethiopia, it will reach the Christian missionaries. In the last year they collected fifteen million dollars in America for Ethiopia. All has disappeared, it never reached Ethiopia. The same has happened before; Ethiopia has been in trouble for four years. In the name of humanity, service, these missionaries collect the money and swallow it.

Last year when the fifteen million dollars simply disappeared, it was enquired what had happened. The Christian missionaries said they did not want to send the money to the Ethiopian government, so they found a French agency to distribute the money, food, clothes, to the starving Ethiopians. When the French agency was asked, they could not believe it; they had never heard about these missionaries.

Ethiopia will be there, more Ethiopians will be there tomorrow. Small efforts won't help. I don't believe in throwing a spoonful of sugar into the ocean to make it sweet. I am not retarded.

This Ethiopia, this India, the poor countries in the East, in Africa – this is *your* doing! First you create the problem, and then you start talking about serving humanity. Why create the problem in the first place? Dissolve all the nations if you have any love for humanity. And dissolve all the religions if you have any respect for civilization.

A civilized man cannot be a Christian, a Jew, a Mohammedan. He cannot be an American, he cannot be an Indian. A civilized man is simply man. And if wars disappear, the world will not need priests to persuade you that "Blessed are the poor," because there will be nobody who is poor. Then the priests will not be able to distract your mind towards heaven, because we can make heaven on this very earth.

If God has thrown out Adam and Eve, do tit for tat: throw him out. We will make the Garden of Eden here! Let God beg to come in.

Why should you pray and beg that you should be accepted, when we can create paradise here? But these politicians, these priests, go on diverting your energies. They are diverting science towards war. Science has now come to a point where it can make this earth so beautiful, so comfortable, so lovable that there will be no Jonestown. Nobody will want to commit suicide.

It is a discovery of scientific research that man's body has an inner capacity to go on renewing itself – of course only for seventy, eighty years, and in rich countries for a hundred years. But in some countries even up to two hundred years the body remains young. We just have to put our scientific intelligence in the service of life – up to now it has been in the service of death. Man can live forever on this earth; there is no need to search for an eternal home beyond death – that is just a consolation for you.

But if you can be as blissful as they have been depicting people in paradise, naturally you won't take any interest in their bibles, in their korans and gitas. You will not go to confess your sins, because there *is* no sin.

People just need more understanding. People need more life, more wisdom, more clarity. You don't need to be forgiven. You have not done any wrong.

You have been doing only one thing wrong: you have been following idiots. God, who does not exist, may forgive you. I cannot forgive you for that.

Contentment

Is a State

of Consciousness

DISCOURSE 6,   July 3, 1985

Beloved Bhagwan,

If discontentment does not lead to real progress, then is the contented man the alternative?

No. The religions of the world have tried to create the contented man. The contented man is really the repressed man. He has all the desires, all the ambitions, but he is repressing them. He is very disturbed inside.

So I cannot say that the contented man is the alternative. I say *contentment* is the alternative. Don't misunderstand me. The point is a little delicate.

Contentment is a state of consciousness. And when there is contentment, there is no man, no woman. There is no ego, there is no "I." There is only contentment.

It is just like when you are silent. Is there a silent man? No, there is only silence. When you are in meditation, is there a meditator? No, there is only meditation. You disappear, you have to disappear, because you *are* discontent, you *are* disturbance. You *are* anguish, anxiety, despair.

Christians say that there is only one sin God will not forgive, and that is despair. Perhaps that is the only statement I can agree with – not with the idea of God, but that despair cannot be forgiven. Despair

simply means all these things together: anxiety, anguish, discontent, frustration.

Contentment is the answer. But the religions have been trying to create a pseudo type of contentment. They tell you that if you are poor, you are blessed; be contented with it: "God must have a design behind it, and you will be rewarded soon." If there is any reward in the future, then your contentment is false. You are really suffering and waiting for the reward.

All the religions have been giving you rewards – or punishments. If you don't listen to them, you will be punished; if you don't follow them, then you are bound to go to hell. And the Christian hell is the worst, for the simple reason that you will be there for eternity. It is so illogical, so absurd, that even an idiot can understand it.

Christianity believes in only one life – that means seventy years, eighty years, a hundred years. In a hundred years can you commit so many sins that the punishment will be for eternity, forever? Even Adolf Hitler or Joseph Stalin or Mao Tse-tung – all three combined cannot manage to commit so many sins.

Bertrand Russell is right. He says, "If I count all my sins that I have committed, and also count all the sins that I wanted to commit but have not committed, even then, four or five years in hell would be enough – more than enough."

Do you know the psychological fact, that when you are in pain each moment becomes longer? Have you been at the bedside of a dying man in the night? It seems it is not going to end ever.

Time is a relative phenomenon; it changes with your psychology. In pain, despair, anguish, it moves very slowly; in utter despair it seems that the clocks have stopped. When you are happy, blissful, time moves faster. Suddenly time appears to have wings. When you are with a friend, hours pass, and it seems you have just met. When you are with your lover, your beloved, then the night becomes very short. In fact, life seems so small to a lover that seventy years look like seven days or seven hours.

Each moment in hell – Bertrand Russell is not aware of it – will be an eternity unto itself, what to say about being in hell for eternity? And what sins have you committed? Not many people are murderers, not many people are thieves, *dacoits.*

What sins are you committing? Even to call them sins is wrong. They are only mistakes – human, expected. Because you are not all-knowing, mistakes are bound to happen. Because you are not omnipotent, omniscient, omnipresent, mistakes are bound to happen. To err is human. Anybody claiming infallibility is a criminal. Perhaps that is the only sin that you can commit.

The religions have created a false contented man – false because the man is trying to be contented, waiting for the rewards in heaven, in paradise. He is repressing here. He knows this life is small, much has passed, the remainder will also pass. He has become accustomed to its pain, its suffering, its frustration, its poverty. And deep down there is great hope that soon he will be in the blissful paradise – and forever.

Have you ever considered that any pleasure, any happiness, if it continues forever, will not remain happiness anymore? Just think…kissing your woman forever. You will curse God.

Change is beautiful, it keeps you moving. But the

Life is a harmonious whole. Everything is connected with everything else. The smallest leaf of grass is connected to the farthest star, a star you cannot see. Harming a small grass flower, you are harming the whole existence, because nothing is separate. Contentment brings you insight into this wholeness. And I call only that man holy who understands this wholeness of everything.

old religions are against change, they preach permanent things. And there is nothing which is permanent except change, because anything permanent becomes dead. If you are permanently in heaven, heaven will turn into hell.

The very idea of permanence is non-existential.

Yes, the old religions have tried to create a contented man. It is a strategy to keep the poor poor, a strategy against any rebellion, revolution. It is a strategy to keep the suffering suffering; to find explanations for why he is suffering. Adam and Eve disobeyed God – that's why you are suffering. Strange logic! You have never met Adam and Eve, it is simply a myth. Have you met serpents giving sermons?

And disobedience is something very essential for every human being in becoming an individual. Not disobedience for disobedience's sake – but when you see something irrational being imposed upon you, and you go on obeying it, you are going against yourself. You are destroying your humanity, you are murdering your individuality. You are becoming a slave.

Obedience is beautiful if it is in harmony with you, with your understanding, with nature. But disobedience is also beautiful. If man had continued to disobey the politicians and the priests, we would have been in a far more beautiful, peaceful, loving world. They don't want you to disobey. They don't want you to rebel, because of their vested interests. They want you to cling to the past, because that is the only way to exploit you.

The Hindu priest goes on exploiting millions of Hindus in the name of Krishna, in the name of Rama, who cannot be said even to be religious people – there is no question of their being incarnations of God. They have committed everything that is inhuman, ugly. And still Hindus go on worshipping them, because the priest is the mediator between the worshipper and the worshipped – nobody knows whom they are worshipping. The priest knows!

The priest *pretends* to know, and imposes the idea on you that you don't know, so whatever he says has to be obeyed.

In this twentieth century, in India, if rains are not coming, then all over the country *jagnas* – fire worship – is arranged. Millions of dollars are wasted to feed the brahmins, to pay their fees, because by their ritual…which is absurd – throwing into the fire valuable food, in a poor country which is starving, and repeating mantras from ten-thousand-year-old Vedas.

Nobody understands what those mantras mean. Brahmins have been insisting that they should not be written in any language other than the original Sanskrit, because once they are translated you will laugh; they are stupid. And they have no connection with rain. They cannot persuade the clouds to come; there is no relationship at all.

There are mantras in the *Vedas*…. A brahmin is praying to God, "This year let your clouds rain only in my field, avoid the fields of my neighbors." They are praying to God, "My cows should give more milk, and the cow of my enemy should not give any milk." Great prayers! But in ancient Sanskrit, which is not understood, which has never been used as a language by people…. People have not been *allowed* to use it. It has never been a living language; it has been the monopoly of the priest.

Out of hundreds of *jagnas,* rituals, sometimes rains come, and they say, "Look! The *Vedas* are still significant, they are not outdated. Existence still listens to the prayers."

But out of hundreds of rituals, ninety percent of the time rains are not going to happen. Then they are always ready to say that something has gone wrong. Mantras have not been chanted as accurately, as exactly as they should be. Brahmins have not been fed, have not been given their fees. Something must have gone wrong in the ritual; God is not happy.

I am reminded that when I was in Poona…. Poona has seen its glorious days: ten thousand sannyasins were always there; all the hotels were packed, business was great. Although they were all against me, they never suspected that I am a very unreliable man. One day suddenly I left Poona.

I live in the moment. I don't care for the future. For me the present is enough.

Suddenly I called my secretary and told her, "I want to leave this ugly place – dirty, full of lousy people." Naturally when I left, slowly all the sannyasins left. Now Poona is in ruins.

Just by the Poona commune there was a five-star hotel, the Blue Diamond. Before we reached Poona it was on sale because they were not making money, they were losing. It was a beautiful, big building, but only fifteen percent of the rooms were ever filled. They were not even able to pay the servants, the manager. When we were there, the Blue Diamond was overfull.

They had offered it to me, they were ready to sell it as cheap as possible. But when sannyasins started coming, and we needed space and enquired, "Are you still ready to sell it?" they said, "No, not at any price."

The owner of the hotel is one of the richest men in India, Kirloskar. He was very much against me for a simple reason: his daughter is married to Morarji Desai's son, and my friendship with Morarji Desai seems to be going on for many lives. I had to tell you this, otherwise you would not have understood.

I have heard that Kirloskar himself arranged a vedic ritual – a hundred brahmins for seven days, throwing wheat, rice, milk, butter, into the fire and praying, "Bring Bhagwan back to Poona." But it is not going to happen; there is no God who can order me to go to Poona. What I have left behind, I have left behind. I go on breaking the bridges that I pass. Once is enough—the world is vast. But Poona became a world-famous name. Now all that glory has disappeared; no vedic ritual can help it.

These religions go on giving you hope. Hope is the poison; it keeps you dragging, waiting for the moment when the hope, the promise, will be fulfilled.

Christians are waiting for Christ to come back. He said to them again and again, "I will be coming soon on the clouds of glory, with a divine body, for the salvation of all those who believe in me." He has not come, and I can say to you categorically: he is not going to come again. What did you do to him when he was here? That experience is enough to prevent him – because I know if he comes back, you will crucify him again. But the hope….

Hindus are hoping, because Krishna has promised – all these prophets go on promising – Krishna has promised that whenever there is misery, whenever there is irreligiousness in the world, whenever virtue disappears, whenever things are not as they should be, "I will be coming." For five thousand years everything has been wrong – but there is no sign of his coming back. But Hindus still go on living in hope, still they go on repeating the promise of Krishna, that soon he will be coming. This keeps people unconscious of the reality. It is opium – very subtle, very psychological.

The contented man has been created by this opium: here be contented, and there you will be immensely rewarded for your contentment. Don't be bothered about the rich and the luxurious. It is just momentary; soon the rich will be suffering in hell. Don't be jealous of them and don't be competitive with them. Be contented.

India, perhaps, is the oldest country in the world; its religions are certainly the most ancient religions. But in India not a single revolution has happened, and it has been suffering for thousands of years. Starvation, poverty, sickness – it has been living in a nightmare, but with the opium of hope: that the Hindus are the privileged people of God, and this is only a momentary life. The suffering is just a test of your faith. Once you have passed through the test, all the joys of heaven are yours.

That's why I said I don't want the contented man. That is false, pseudo, sick, retarded, believing in lies.

I teach contentment. And the basic principle of contentment is to drop your ego. Don't think for a single moment, "To be or not to be." Just not to be is the rule. What have you gained by trying to be? Just for a change try not to be, and you will be amazed. The moment *you* are not, there is contentment, there is silence, there is beauty, there is bliss.

Meditation is only a methodology to make you aware that your only disease is your ego, and your only health is egolessness.

The discontented man is suffering from his ego. He is comparing his ego with others. Somebody is more beautiful than you, somebody is stronger than you. Somebody is richer than you, somebody is more powerful than you. All around there are people who have something which you don't have. You have to complete against the whole world – by any means, right or wrong, but you have to reach the top.

Sometimes I think of Edmund Hillary standing on the highest mountain, the Himalayan peak, Everest. There is not even space for two persons to stand together. And whenever I think of it, I think of poor Edmund Hillary. He must have looked silly. Now what to do? You have reached the top of the world, but what now? Jump and commit suicide.

Whatever you can attain, you will remain discontented.

Napoleon Bonaparte was not a very tall man, he was only five feet five inches. But I don't see any problem. I am five feet five inches. I have tried to figure out why he was puzzled; *I* am not puzzled. Even if I were seven feet, my feet would touch the ground. At five-five they still touch the ground, so what is the problem? But Napoleon was very much disturbed, because his soldiers were taller than him, his bodyguards were taller than him. That was giving him a continuous feeling of inferiority.

One day it happened, he was trying to put a nail in the wall to hang a picture. His hand was not reaching to the right spot, and his bodyguard said, "Sir, you need not bother about it, I can do it – I am higher than you."

Napoleon Bonaparte imprisoned that guard, and told him, "You used wrong language. You are *taller* than me, but not higher than me!" That poor guard had unconsciously used a word that touched a deep wound in Bonaparte. Bonaparte had everything, but discontent was there.

There are ordinarily two types of people in the world: the discontented and the repressed discontented. I need the third type of man to evolve: the man who has no ego; hence, he cannot be discontented.

Contentment is not something to be practiced. When discontent disappears, you find contentment has always been your nature.

Do you think a small bush is discontented because just by the side of it a tall cedar tree is standing, reaching to the stars? Do you think a small rose bush is discontented? There is no discontent in nature anywhere, except in the mind of man. It has been created by the politicians, by the priests, by the educationalists. Every child is being told to come first.

My father was a very simple man. He was not even aware – because he had eleven children – who was in which class and where. If some visitor, some guest asked him, he would have to call me and ask,

"In what class are you?" He never asked me, "Have you passed or failed?"

When I came first in the whole university, I thought, "He will be happy, I should inform him." I told him, "I have come first in the whole university."

He said, "So what! That simply means your whole university is full of stupid people; otherwise, how could you manage to come first?"

I said, "That seems to be right" – and I threw the gold medal given to me by the university into the well.

My father said, "What are you doing?"

I said, "I am simply destroying the gold medal, because I don't want to be first amongst thousands of stupid people. I am perfectly okay as I am."

He said, "But don't burn your certificates. You will need them for employment."

I said, "Okay. For employment I will need them, but the moment I leave employment, the first thing I am going to do is to burn them all" – and that's what I did.

For nine years I was a lecturer in the university. Then one day I left, because when I can share my silence, my ecstasy with millions of people, why should I waste my time with a dozen students, teaching them something which is of no use, something I am against?

I had to teach Aristotle, and I think Aristotle is one of the most criminal minds in the whole of history. But I used to say that too. I would teach Aristotle, and then I would say, "Now, what I feel about Aristotle I have to say to you."

Aristotle created a logic of duality: yes and no, and there is nothing in between; either something is or it is not. This is not true.

Life is a rainbow…all the colors.

Between yes and no there are many stages.

Life cannot be divided and cut into two separate parts. Life is an undivided rainbow – one color melting into another.

Yes and no are two ends of the same rainbow, two colors of the same rainbow. They are not opposite to each other – that is Aristotelian logic – I say they are complementary to each other.

But it was a tedious job, first to teach Aristotle and then to contradict him. And my students became confused. They complained to the vice-chancellor, "What are we going to do? This man is strange. He teaches Immanuel Kant and contradicts him, he teaches Hegel and contradicts him. How are we going to answer in our examinations?"

The vice-chancellor told me, "You are creating trouble for those poor students."

I said, "I am not creating any trouble, I am simply giving them the whole picture. Now they can choose. To give them only one side just to avoid their confusion is cheating."

Mulla Nasruddin was made a judge. The first case came before him; he heard one side and started writing the judgment. The court clerk could not believe his eyes. He whispered in Nasruddin's ear, "What are you doing? You have not even heard the other party."

Nasruddin said, "I am not going to allow myself to be confused. Right now I am perfectly clear. Why should I listen to the other party and be confused?"

I told the vice-chancellor the story of Nasruddin. I said, "Do you agree with Nasruddin?"

He said, "You are just impossible. Do whatever you want to do." But I could not manage to remain confined in a university when the whole universe was available to me; soon I left. The first thing I did was, I burned all my certificates.

I left Poona forever. Now they are praying for me. When I was there, they were trying to throw me out. Now they know all the joy and the dance and the beautiful people from all over the world no longer come there; they are coming here.

Had you ever heard about Oregon before? It never existed. It has come to life for the first time, and you have brought your joy, your meditation, your contentment.

My sannyasins are contentment, not contented *men*. My sannyasins don't care about politics. I have sometimes out of necessity to force them. Look at our poor mayor. I had to persuade him to become mayor of Rajneeshpuram. Somebody has to be mayor. If you find somebody not dancing, looking sad, you have found the mayor. Nobody is interested in politics here, nobody is on a power trip.

Contentment is a state of consciousness.

I teach contentment.

And out of contentment comes real progress.

The discontented man has created the world – ugly, disgusting. This is not progress. The repressed, so-called contented men – the monks of all the religions – what progress have they brought to the world? Yes, they have contributed something: homosexuality, lesbianism.

Homosexuality, lesbianism, are very religious

matters, because when you confine only men in a monastery, and you confine only women in a nunnery, what are they going to do with their sexuality? – which is natural, simple, not a sin. You are born out of it.

Everything in existence is sex energy. Yes, it can be transformed, it can be raised higher, but you cannot deny it. The contented man created by the religions has denied it. But your denial will not make any difference to your physiology, your chemistry, your hormones. Your body is neither Christian, nor Hindu, nor Mohammedan. That's why the same medicine works for all; otherwise there would be a Mohammedan cancer, and a Hindu cancer, and they would have different treatments for them. Your body is part of existence, it is existential.

And my philosophy is pure existentialism.

Homosexuality and lesbianism were born in monasteries. This is their contribution. AIDS is their contribution to the world – real progress! Who had heard about AIDS before? A great invention! What have they contributed to the world? Neither the discontented man nor the so-called contented man have given progress. Progress is possible only out of contentment.

Just for a moment think that there is no ego in you, that you are simply nobody, and you will feel so clean, so pure. And out of that cleanness, purity, you will start growing, growing to be what your potential is. You may become a painter, you may become a musician, you may become a poet. You may become anything – a scientist, a dancer – but it will come naturally to you. When something grows naturally in you, there is progress. And if the world can be rich with music….

I say to my people, "Don't listen to Jesus, who says everybody has to carry his cross, no." I say to you, "Everybody has to carry his guitar." Why carry a cross when guitars are available?

Just grow to your potentiality – not according to any discipline, because then you will never be yourself; not according to any dogma, because that is distracting you from yourself. Without any dogma, without any religion…can't you have a little courage just to be yourself? Part of this vast universe, nobody special…. And you are in for a great surprise.

Yes, there have been painters before: Picasso, Van Gogh, and hundreds of others. But have you ever thought that the paintings of Picasso are sick, insane? If you go on looking at a painting by Picasso, continuously for one hour sitting before it, meditating over it, then you will know what I mean. This is not a painting, it is a vomiting! That man was crazy, he vomited.

Of course, if Picasso had been a contentment, a painting would have grown; it would not have been insane and crazy. Looking at it, you would have felt a serenity descending upon you. Watching it, you would have felt peace surrounding you. But this is not possible with Picasso's paintings – he is a very discontented man.

This is not possible with George Bernard Shaw's books. You cannot find a bigger ego than George Bernard Shaw. He writes a play of fifty pages and gives it a one hundred fifty page preface. Can you think this man sane – a small play needs such a big introduction? Something is wrong with the man.

When he got the Nobel prize, one day he remained silent, made no comment. He was in the headlines of all the third-class newspapers of the world. The second day, he rejected it; he said, "I don't want to receive the Nobel prize because it is far below me! Give it to some amateur writer, a beginner. I have passed that stage long ago." Again he was in the headlines.

It was an insult to the Nobel prize committee, which is presided over by the Norwegian king or queen. From all over the world, all the royalty, all the significant, powerful, important celebrities, thousands of telegrams poured in to Bernard Shaw, saying that this was an insult to Norway, an insult to the king, an insult to the Nobel prize committee.

He waited for two or three days, made a great fuss, and finally agreed to accept it. And all these days he was in the headlines. He accepted the Nobel prize – that was a great relief for all the royalty, and all the presidents, and all the premiers. And the next moment he donated it to a society; again he was news.

For almost two weeks he maintained himself as the most important news in the world, because it was discovered that the society to which he had donated the prize was his own society – he had named it the Fabian Society – and he was the only man in the society. He was the president, and he was the secretary, and he was the membership.

Again he was in the news. And when he was asked why he did it, he said, "When you get a Nobel prize you get headlines for just one day. I managed to have myself in the headlines all over the world for two weeks. Nobody can beat me!" His ego was like a balloon which went on getting bigger and bigger.

These people cannot create real art. Their art is going to be a reflection of their mind.

Progress out of contentment will be totally different. Poetry will arise in you, just like a rosebush grows. It will give flowers to the world, and the fragrance – and without any claim for any reward, because contentment is its own reward. What more can you want than to come to fruition, to flowering? What can give you more blissfulness than just to grow into your real potential?

I do not promise anything to you. I have no theology of hell or heaven – those are all bogus, created by fools for other fools. In my vision the very contentment is the reward, the very silence is the reward, the very meditation is the reward.

And nobody can feel inferior to you. A contented man, if his contentment is of the old pattern, is going to feel either inferior or superior – which are not different, they are two sides of the same coin.

I have heard....

Three Christian monks met on a crossroad. One of them said, "I highly appreciate your monasteries, but our monastery is more scholarly than your monasteries." Remember the "more."

The second one said, "That's perhaps true, but my monastery is more ascetic. I have every respect for your monasteries" – this is all garbage, this respect, it is all phony – "but as far as asceticism is concerned, as austerities are concerned, you come nowhere close to us."

The third one said, "I also have great respect for your scholarship, for your austerities, but in humbleness we are the tops."

"In humbleness, we are the tops"! I am not talking about this kind of contented man. A real contentment will make you humble, but not the tops. Humbleness will come naturally to you. A real contentment will give you, without any effort, a respect for all that exists. It is not etiquette, it is not British; you will simply respect. How can you disrespect?

A tree, a bird on the wing, a cloud just floating, a river flowing to the ocean, a child smiling; an old man with all the experience of life; a child with all the freshness of life.... Whom can you disrespect?

How can you feel superior to anybody? Can you feel superior to a rose? Can you feel superior to a bird on the wing?

How can you feel inferior to anybody? You have all the contentment, all the serenity, all the silence. Where can that dark wound – inferiority – exist in you? You are all light.

This is the man who can bring beauty to the world – songs of silence, out of silence; really authentic poetry. This man will transform the whole nature of science. Progress will not stop, but it will have a different dimension to it.

Now the whole of science is devoted to destruction. Albert Einstein cannot be forgiven; he was the man who wrote to President Roosevelt that the atom bomb can be created, and that it is the only way to defeat the fascist forces in the world. He repented his whole life, but that repentance cannot restore Hiroshima. It cannot give life back to thousands of children, women, men, trees, in Nagasaki, in Hiroshima.

Einstein was an unconscious scientist – it was out of discontent. Basically he was a German, but unfortunately a Jew; he had to escape from Germany. He was doing the same work for Adolf Hitler. If he had remained in Germany, perhaps there would have been no Nagasaki, no Hiroshima. There may have been London, New York, Washington, Moscow, but not Nagasaki and Hiroshima.

Einstein escaped out of the fear that because he was a Jew he might get into trouble. And as a revenge against Adolf Hitler, he wrote the letter to President Roosevelt. He was not aware of what he was doing. He created the atom bomb, and he awoke only when Nagasaki and Hiroshima were finished. But it was too late.

I don't teach you repentance. Christians teach you repentance – naturally, because they don't make you alert, aware, meditative, contented. So out of your unconsciousness, out of your discontent, out of your tense mind, out of your anxiety, you are going to do something for which you will repent later. But it is always too late! It may help you to feel less guilty, but that does not change anything in existence; you have committed a crime. And Albert Einstein understood it. Before his death he was asked, "If there is another life after death, would you not like to remain a physicist?" He said, "No! I would rather be a plumber, but never again a physicist."

This kind of science will disappear. Out of peace, the whole dimension will change. Progress will not stop, but progress will be for the benefit of humanity, for the benefit of the whole existence. Science is capable, if it is in the hands of contented, meditative people, of feeding the whole earth abundantly, of creating everything that is needed – not just for survival, because survival is not life. Life has to be overflowing, it has to be luxurious. A rosebush just surviving somehow is not going to give you roses.

The earth can become abundant with everything. Science just has to be creative and not destructive. A contentment inside you will not allow you to be destructive.

If all the scientists of the world simply revolt against the politicians, the world will see a tremendous transformation. But there are very few scientists who have guts, because their guts have been destroyed by their educational system.

I am reminded of Sakharov. He was given the Nobel prize because he was the best physicist of his time. But he was a Russian. He was director of the Academy of Sciences in Russia, the highest post for a scientist – position, respect. The Russian government did not want him to receive the Nobel prize because it comes from capitalist countries, and in the Russian mind – particularly in the communist party and the people who are in power there – it is a kind of bribe, in the name of a prize.

They do the same on their own, so they know; they give the Lenin prize in capitalist countries. And by giving the Lenin prize they are bribing the person to reveal secrets. So they don't want any Russian to receive the Nobel prize, because that way he becomes sympathetic towards capitalist countries.

Sakharov is really an individual. The whole communist programming has not been able to destroy his spirit. He went against the Russian government, knowing perfectly well what had happened before to those who had not listened to the Russian government. Two other scientists had been given Nobel prizes before Sakharov. They did not listen to the government; they accepted the prize. They were not allowed to go out of the country to receive it; on the contrary, they were imprisoned, tortured – and Russia has really progressive ways of torturing.

For fifteen days those two scientists were kept awake. They were given injections so they could not fall asleep. The mind is a very delicate thing; if for two weeks continuously not a single moment of sleep is allowed, the person starts losing his rationality, sensitivity. After fifteen days he has lost all interest in science. After twenty-one days he has lost interest in his family. After thirty days he has lost all interest in himself; the mind is dismantled. And then he is brought before a court. Of course, the court judges him to be mad.

First you make him mad, and then you bring him before a court! This had happened to those two scientists, and because they were mad and dangerous, they were both exiled in Siberia. Nobody knows what happened to them.

Sakharov knew what he was doing: when he accepted the Nobel prize the same would happen to him. And he accepted the Nobel prize, and the same happened to him. He was immediately removed from his power and position. His car was taken away....

A car is a great luxury in Soviet Russia, because only very powerful people can have their own private vehicle. Everybody else has to use the public system – buses, trains.

I am against communism, because if a person is deprived of his private possessions, something of his individuality dies. His private possessions are a kind of safety around him, that keep him alive as an individual.

Sakharov's salary was cut, his car was removed, he was not allowed to go out of Russia. And then finally he was sent to Siberia. He is still alive. The best physicist of the world is simply rotting in Siberia! – and nobody bothers about it.

Just this incident of Sakharov should have been enough for all the scientists of the world – not only of Soviet Russia – to simply disconnect themselves from their governments. And if the politicians are so interested in fighting, they can have wrestling matches and you can enjoy it. They can have boxing matches, and you can enjoy it. If those fools insist on fighting, perfectly good. The Soviet prime minister wrestles with Ronald Reagan – enjoy it, there is no harm. But these people should not be given power to destroy the whole humanity.

My people cannot in any way create anything that will be harmful. They can create only something which will be a joy to see. They have created this small commune which has become a nightmare to the politicians of America.

We are not doing anything except making this land, which has remained barren for years, green again. We are dancing, singing, meditating, farming, gardening. We are not doing any harm to anybody. Even deer understand it, but the attorney general of Oregon cannot understand it. You can see in the evening, deer moving on the road without any fear. You go on honking your horn and the deer does not care. He knows these people are not destructive.

My own peacocks in my garden make me come here late sometimes. They will not move from the road, they will walk just ahead of me. When I go back, they are all ready just in front of my porch, dancing. I have to stop the car and wait till they decide to give way to me. They know perfectly well nobody is going to harm them.

Deer have come, birds have come. Even the poor juniper has become a rich tree. When I came here these junipers were just dying, somehow managing at a survival level. The juniper is a very strong-willed tree. Where nothing else can exist, the juniper can. But no birds to sing, no people....

You have to understand: this existence is a cosmos, it is a deep harmony. When people moved here, suddenly birds started coming, deer started coming. Even junipers understood the presence of my people. They are far greener, far thicker, far bigger than they were when I came here.

There is a deep connectedness in life. You cannot live without trees, trees cannot live without you. When you inhale, you need oxygen; when you exhale, you exhale carbon dioxide. The tree does just the opposite: when it inhales, it takes in carbon dioxide; when it exhales, it exhales oxygen.

Life is a harmonious whole. Everything is connected with everything else. The smallest leaf of grass is connected to the farthest star, a star you cannot see. Harming a small grass flower, you are harming the whole existence, because nothing is separate.

Contentment brings you insight into this wholeness. And I call only that man holy who understands this wholeness of everything. I call that man holy who can understand that sex and silence are not separate, that sex and meditation are not separate. Nothing is separate. Everything is woven into everything else. All colors are mixing with each other.

I have an idea – I'm just waiting for the right time. I would like my sannyasins to wear rainbow clothes. But I have to wait a little and keep you in red clothes for two reasons: one, to shock the fools outside; and two, so that I can recognize you easily. But before I leave this world, you will be in rainbow clothes.

Beloved Bhagwan,

In the last few days, as I listen to You, it seems You are trying to be a martyr. Are You?

I am not even a Christian – why should I like to be a martyr? The word looks beautiful, but the reality is that those who would like to be martyrs are suicidal.

Jesus was suicidal; he was trying in every way to be crucified. He was not even courageous enough just to shoot himself. Why unnecessarily make other people responsible for your crucifixion? If Jesus had shot himself, the Jews would have lived in peace without any trouble. But he forced the Jews to do it.

It is to Sigmund Freud's credit that he discovered a suicidal instinct in man. It was always accepted that man has a deep lust for life; he wants to live and live, and live forever. But in existence nothing exists without its opposite. That was the discovery of Sigmund Freud, and it is absolutely right – with the life instinct there is a death instinct. There is not a single man on the earth who has not at least once thought of committing suicide. From where does that idea come?

But a man who is contented has all the bliss that is possible. Both the instincts simply disappear. He has no desire to go on living; he has no desire to destroy himself by his own hands or by other people's. For him this moment is all. Whatever happens in the next moment is welcome.

I have no desire to be a martyr, but if somebody kills me, what can I do? It will be absolutely their responsibility. As far as Jesus is concerned, Jews are not absolutely responsible. Ninety percent of the responsibility is Jesus' himself. If Mansoor is killed by the Mohammedans, even more – ninety-nine percent of the responsibility is al-Hillaj Mansoor's.

If Gandhi is shot, one hundred percent of the responsibility is his, because before his death he is reported to have said many times, "Now I don't want to live. It will be a mercy if God takes me away from this body, because I have become absolutely useless."

Strange…. To think in terms of use is ugly. Neither do you have to use anybody – because to use somebody is to exploit them – nor do you have to allow anybody to use you. That is your birthright.

Gandhi wanted to die, and he was praying for death. That makes one thing very clear. When Nathuram Godse shot him….

It is good that Nathuram has "Ram" in his name: Ram was Gandhi's God.

Nathu is meaningless. In India, if a couple finds that their children die and don't survive, then something has to be done. So when a new child is born, either his nose is pierced – a hole is made so a ring of gold can be put through – or his ears are pierced and rings of gold are put in. *Nathu* means nose, so if the nose is pierced, Ram becomes *Nathuram*. If the ears are pierced, Ram becomes *Kunchiberam* – *kun* means ears. In fact he was just a "Ram" with a pierced nose – Gandhi's God.

And when Gandhi was shot, he put his hands together, looking at Nathuram Godse, and the words he uttered were, "Hey, Ram." He was waiting for it; that's why I say one hundred percent. And he rejoiced – he wanted to die, because his ideology was no longer listened to. Nobody was ready to follow his suggestions.

The country had become free. Gandhi was needed when the country was under slavery, under British rule, because he controlled the masses. The superstitious Indians cannot be controlled by logic, by reason. They can only be controlled by their emotions, sentimentality, superstitions, religiousness, and all kinds of rubbish.

Gandhi was an expert in rubbish.

I have no desire to live the next moment, or to die the next moment. I have known and experienced everything that is possible. If existence allows me one moment more, I will create a little more disturbance in people. If existence feels that I am no more needed, it is perfectly good to go into eternal sleep. To me, death is not going to be a death, because I am not going to be reborn.

You are reborn if you have committed mistakes, and if you feel guilty. Albert Einstein must have been reborn, and of course, as a plumber, because the last desire becomes the seed for your future life.

I have no desire. My death will not be a death.

In India we make a difference. When an ordinary man dies, it is death. When someone who has attained enlightenment dies, it is *samadhi,* it is not death. And the word "samadhi" is immensely significant. Samadhi means: one who has attained the ultimate harmony with existence.

A Sannyasin Is Extraordinarily Ordinary

DISCOURSE 7, July 4, 1985

Beloved Bhagwan,

I can't conceive of You ever being unenlightened. Did You really become enlightened only thirty-two years ago?

Neither can I conceive it. This is one of the very fundamental things in the nature of enlightenment. Once you are enlightened, you are in a very strange situation – trying to conceive how you could manage to remain unenlightened for so many lives. It is a tremendous work, it needs great effort. Misery, jealousy, competitiveness – all that is ugly is needed to remain unenlightened.

Enlightenment itself is simple, it is natural. Unenlightenment is your creation.

Enlightenment is a gift from existence. So it is up to you how long you want to remain unenlightened. Any moment you can drop unenlightenment. Never ask how to become enlightened, because nobody can become enlightened. Everybody is born enlightened. Just ask, "How can we drop all those props that are keeping us unenlightened?"

There is a beautiful story in Gautam Buddha's life. Again and again he has told it....

In one of his past lives he met an enlightened being. Out of respect he touched his feet. But he was surprised – in return the enlightened man touched his feet. Buddha could not believe his eyes. He said, "What are you doing? I am an unenlightened man, ignorant. I have not experienced truth. I have not yet been able to love, to be compassionate. My laughter is still phony, my heart is full of discontent. Why have you touched my feet?"

And the enlightened being laughed. He said, "Don't be worried. As far as I am concerned, you are as enlightened as I am."

From your side, that is your problem – I don't see any of you here as unenlightened, it is impossible. Enlightenment is your very center, your very being. But you have been conditioned, programmed to remain unenlightened. All your religions are responsible for it. They don't want you to become enlightened, because an enlightened man cannot be a Christian, a Hindu, a Mohammedan. From his state of consciousness, all these theologies, religions, are sheer nonsense – fictions created by ignorant people for other ignorant people.

Never ask how to be enlightened. You can ask how to remain unenlightened, that is relevant. If you want to be enlightened, you *are* this very moment. Nobody is preventing you except yourself.

And you are making so much hard, arduous effort to become enlightened. That is one of the ways to remain unenlightened. The very effort keeps you troubled; and each effort is going to fail, because what you are already you cannot become.

Just see the difference between these two simple words: being and becoming. Enlightenment is being – you cannot become it. Becoming is a process somewhere in the future after long journeys, doing all kinds of stupid things – yoga postures, Christian prayers, fasts, remaining celibate, entering into a monastery forever, you will not come out of it....

There are monasteries where you enter but unless you are thrown out you cannot get out; only your dead body comes out some day. I have heard about such a monastery. It was famous for two things: one, for one thousand years no woman had entered into the monastery – it was prohibited. Even a six-month-old baby girl was not allowed.

When I heard about it I thought, were monks living in the monastery, or monsters? A six-month-old baby is not allowed in! You can conceive the mind of those people who are living inside.

And second, it was famous in that silence was the rule. Only after seven years – once, after seven years – if you wanted to say something to the abbot, you could say it, and then for seven years again silence.

One man became a monk. For seven years he suffered, because the mattress was missing, he was sleeping on a bare floor. It was hard, it was cold, but he had to wait for seven years to say, "I need a mattress."

Seven years, by and by, passed – they must have looked to that man almost like seven centuries. And he was so happy when he went to the abbot and said, "Master, I have a complaint to make. In the room you have allotted me, there is no mattress. And for seven years I have been prohibited from speaking."

The abbot said, "Okay, a mattress will be provided immediately. You go back."

A mattress was provided. But the cell in which the monk was living was very small, and the door was very small, and the mattress was big. So while they were bringing the mattress in, the door fell out

Never ask how to be enlightened. You can ask how to remain unenlightened, that is relevant. If you want to be enlightened, you *are* this very moment. Nobody is preventing you except yourself. And you are making so much hard, arduous effort to become enlightened. That is one of the ways to remain unenlightened. The very effort keeps you troubled; and each effort is going to fail, because what you are already you cannot become.

and the window's glass was broken. Somehow they forced that big mattress into the small room. For seven years the poor man again suffered – from rain, wind, snow, because there was no door and the window was broken. In fact, he started thinking that the first seven years were far more beautiful: "I was an idiot to make that complaint!"

Again after seven years he went to the abbot. And the abbot said, "Again?"

The man said, "I have to say something, I am compelled to say it: the mattress that was provided was bigger than my cell, and the people, the other monks who brought it, somehow forced it in. I could not say no – I could not speak. They broke the door, they broke the window, and you can conceive – for seven years I have been living in wind, in rain, in snow. I was not thinking that I would be able to survive, but somehow by God's grace I am here again. Please put the door back and mend the window."

This was too much. The abbot became angry, and he said, "In all these fourteen years you have done nothing but complain, complain, complain! This is not a way to be religious. You simply get lost!"

Enlightenment is not something to be achieved. It is not an achievement, it is not a goal far away that you have to journey to. It is not a pilgrimage at all. The more you seek and search for enlightenment, the more you will miss it, and the more miserable you will be.

Enlightenment is a very simple understanding. So once you stop all efforts to be enlightened and just remain at ease with yourself, totally accepting yourself as you are…. That's how existence meant you to be. Don't try to improve upon existence, you cannot do that. Relax, be existential, not religious. And suddenly you are amazed, "My God! I have always been enlightened."

Your question is right. After enlightenment everybody is amazed – and *knows* that he has always been enlightened.

Thirty-two years ago I awoke from the night-mare of making a continuous effort to attain enlightenment. I simply dropped all efforts to be enlightened. I simply accepted myself as I am – good or bad. I simply stopped judging myself. And a miracle happened: with judgment disappearing, with ambition to become enlightened disappearing, it was as if I came out of a nightmare fully awake. And when I saw myself as enlightened, I saw the whole existence as enlightened.

You are part of a tremendous blissfulness, but you are keeping yourself closed. You go on doing something against nature, against existence. You have been taught that to be natural is something wrong; you feel guilty when you are natural. You feel happy when you repress your nature, when you become phony, a hypocrite. All religions have been doing only one thing for thousands of years: making people hypocrites.

I want you to drop all that crap, and just be yourself – with no effort to go anywhere, because you are already there, this very moment.

I know about a man who is present amongst you, his name begins with "T." Forgive me, I cannot tell you his full name. I know his tent number, but I cannot tell you the tent number.

He has come here to assassinate me.

I cannot tell you his name and his tent number, because I don't want to interfere in anybody's life. If he wants to assassinate me, and can have a moment of joy – I have had enough, so let him have the joy.

But I would like him to wait at least for the 6th of July, because I have a date with death. Whenever I die, I will die on the 6th of July. The year does not matter, but the 6th of July matters. I want it permanently to be the Master's day. So, Mr. T., only this much favor you have to do for me.

He is trying to find ways, proper situations, spaces, places, from where he can assassinate me, and he is in much trouble. I am perfectly willing – after enlightenment what is there? All is fulfilled. I will be of every help to him. He could have approached me and asked, "How to assassinate you?" and I could have given him exactly the right information. I could have left my bedroom door open in the night... because I don't want that man to suffer. After assassinating me, my sannyasins will not leave him to himself. He will be killed immediately, and I am against violence. But that is the trouble he is facing: everywhere there are thousands of sannyasins – he will be caught.

I cannot even do what Jesus did on the cross. He prayed to God. There is no God, so I cannot pray. And he said to God, "Please forgive these people because they know not what they are doing."

That too, I cannot say, because Mr. T. knows exactly what he is doing or planning to do. He just does not know how to do it. He seems to be an amateur. I feel sorry for him; perhaps he will not be able to do what he has come here for. I cannot interfere with him, I cannot interfere with my sannyasins. And my sannyasins also have guns. I don't interfere with anybody.

I have always been enlightened, but just thirty-two years ago I recognized it, just thirty-two years ago I became aware of it.

And the same is going to happen to you too.

Whenever you become awakened, you are in for a great surprise.

Beloved Bhagwan,

Women have a better feeling for others than men do. How come there have been no great masters among them so far?

It is a very delicate question, and a little difficult too – about women everything is difficult – but I will try my best.

First, you never ask why no man in the whole history of existence has been pregnant, why he has not given birth to a child. You simply know that biologically he has no womb. He can make many women pregnant. This has to be understood; that's why there have been religions which allow four wives to a man, but no religion allows four husbands to a woman, for the simple reason that a man can make many women pregnant. But once a woman is pregnant, then you can bring Muhammed Ali the Great – even he cannot do anything; for nine months the woman is booked.

I know women have a much more feeling heart, are more loving, are more open, are more receptive. But these are the qualities of a disciple, not of a master. The disciple has to be open, receptive, vulnerable, loving, feeling. The only thing the disciple has to drop is his mind, not his heart. His mind is a constant disturbance. It goes on creating skepticism, and a disciple cannot be a skeptic.

The woman can be a prefect disciple, but cannot be a perfect master. Now, I am not responsible for it, I am simply saying what the fact is. And you can see it with your own eyes.

I have more women disciples around the world than men, and I can trust women more than men. I have given every responsible job in all the communes around the world to women, not to men. You must be surprised, because man has better reasoning, is more rational, is more authoritative, is more interested in being higher and higher in a hierarchy. The woman is not interested in hierarchy. Her interest in life is not through reasoning, but through feeling. Logic is not her world – love is her world.

To be a master is a very strange job. You have to convince people about the heart by argument and reason, rationality, philosophy; you have to use the mind as a servant for the heart. The master's work is to take your mind away from you, so that your whole energy moves into your heart.

It is from the heart that we are connected with existence, it is not from the mind. Nobody can go directly from mind to existence.

Mind can create science, but it cannot create poetry, it cannot create paintings, it cannot create sculpture. And it is impossible for the mind to go into the dimension of religion. If the mind tries to go into the dimension of religion it creates theology, not religion.

The word "theology" has to be understood: *theo* means God, *logy* is logic – logic about God. Mind is capable of creating logic about God, arguments about God. God is not there, but through your argumentation, your reasoning, you can create a hypothetical God. All gods of all religions are hypotheses, and hypotheses which are absolutely unnecessary – not only unnecessary but dangerous, because if you get caught up in those hypothetical gods you are not going to ever find the authentic truth.

Heart knows no argument; it feels. And existence has to be felt. Even when a man feels existence, he feels through the heart. But the heart cannot convince anybody.

The man has a tremendous capacity for logic and reason. Once he has found reality, enlightenment, through his heart, he can use the mind to spread the fragrance that he has found. The woman cannot do it. That's why there have been not only no *great* masters, there have been *no* masters who were women. Even the famous religious women saints were disciples.

Saint Teresa – I don't mean Mother Teresa – Saint Meera, Saint Lalla…these three women were absolutely *capable* of becoming great masters, but they could not. They became enlightened, but they remained devotees.

And there is nothing great in being a master; it is just a technical thing. The real thing is to realize your potential and your flowering.

Your question is like: "Why in history has a woman never been a husband?" What can I do? A woman has to be a wife, and there is no suggestion that the husband is higher than the wife. In fact, just the opposite is the case.

I have never come across any husband who is not henpecked. If you don't want to become henpecked, then be a freelance lover, then never get married. Marriage simply means you have surrendered your freedom, your individuality – everything. Yes, when you go out of the house you go like a lion, roaring. But when you come back to the house you come like a rat, trembling. It is a strange thing.

This is a factual story I am going to tell you. Akbar, a great Mogul emperor in India – perhaps the greatest Mogul who has ruled India – was very curious about everything. One day he asked his council of wise people – he had collected nine of the most famous wise men around himself in his court – he asked them, "Can you find a husband who is not henpecked?"

Only one remained silent. He was the most wise; his name was Birbal. The other eight said, "Yes, we can find many husbands, what to say about one?"

Akbar looked at Birbal and he said, "You have not raised your hand."

He said, "I cannot, because even you are a henpecked husband. You are a great emperor of a vast subcontinent, and I know the moment you enter your harem, you are nobody; the woman rules over you. These eight people don't know the reality. First they should think about themselves. I would like to ask these eight people, 'Are you henpecked or not?' As far as I am concerned, I am. When *I* cannot remain free, I don't believe these people are free. They have not pondered over it. But give them a chance – if they can find one, it will be a revelation."

Those eight wise men went to New Delhi, the capital of India, to look for a man who was not henpecked. Akbar gave them two horses, beautiful horses from Kabul, one pure white and one pure black. And he said, "Whoever you find that is not henpecked, you can give one of these two beautiful horses as a reward from me."

They were really precious. In those days horses were something of a treasure; to have a beautiful, strong horse was a great joy. Now there are no more horses; there are cars which have horsepower.

Those eight wise men went around the capital, and they were getting frustrated again and again, because they could not find one. The condition was: "If you say you are not henpecked, and it is proved not right, you will be hanged. If it is proved right, one of these two horses will be your reward." There was nobody courageous enough to take the risk.

Only one man they found, who was a very strong man – seven feet tall, a great wrestler, a champion wrestler. He was sitting outside his house in the garden. His body was something to see; so solid that if he hit a man just with his fist, he could kill him. He looked like a man made of steel.

They thought, "Perhaps this man is the man we are searching for." They asked him, "Are you henpecked?"

He said, "If you repeat it again, I will kill all of you. Me henpecked? Are you mad?"

They looked inside the house. A very small woman, very thin, was cooking food. The eight men said to the strong man, "Just to find out the facts – which horse would you like as a reward, the black or the white?"

And the man turned back and asked his wife, "Muna's mother" – that is the way in India it is done. You cannot take the name of the husband or the wife. The wife says, "Muna's father," the husband says, "Muna's mother." Muna is just like Tom, Dick, Harry. He asked, "Muna's mother, should I take the white horse or the black?"

Muna's mother said, "If you take the black horse, I will give you hell! Take the white one."

And he told the wise people, "I would like to take the white one."

They said, "You come with us – you don't get either. You will be hanged!"

In the house, within the boundaries of the house, the woman has tremendous power. But she is not interested in the outside world. Women's natures are different. A woman can become a great disciple, but

for a woman to become a master is almost impossible. But there is no question of somebody being higher.

The master is not higher than the disciple. The master is simply trying to awaken you. The moment you are awakened there is no master and no disciple. It is just out of gratitude that the disciple remains a disciple – just out of gratitude. But there is no difference; they have known the same reality. They have become what nature wanted them to become, they have blossomed.

So don't feel depressed that women have not been great masters – they have been great disciples.

Man finds it difficult to become a disciple. In fact, man should worry about it, because to become a disciple is the real thing – and the beginning. And to come to the perfection of being a disciple is the end.

A man passes through a very difficult phase. He cannot become a disciple, or can become one only in a wishy-washy way, always ready to quit. And without becoming a disciple, there is no question of becoming a master. Yes, once in a while it happens that a man becomes a master without becoming a disciple. But for that immense patience, a certain stubbornness, is needed.

I don't have any master. In my previous lives I never had any master. I have lived with many masters, I have known many masters, but I could not manage to become a disciple. That is why I am so late; otherwise, Jesus would not have preceded me. But it was simply difficult for me to be a disciple. I remained searching, and searching on my own. Yes, it took many many lives to arrive where I have always been.

I have never been initiated by anyone. I am not a sannyasin. I am really outside of any crowd, and that's the way I have always been. It was a long, arduous journey to find that there is nothing to find.

Women are far more fortunate, because the beginning is in their hand, and the beginning is almost half the achievement. That I can see myself.

This was the basic reason why women could not

become great masters. But there is no need to feel sad. They became great disciples – which is far more fortunate, because to begin from the beginning is easier than to begin from the end.

Beloved Bhagwan,

We have been studying this community for a few years. What do You think are the most important things to observe and understand? How can outsiders have a better understanding of what it is like to be a sannyasin? How can we show what is special about sannyasins?

It is not one question, there are many questions in it. First, this is not a community, it is a commune – and there is a vast difference between the two.

Christianity is a community, Hinduism is a community. A community is a closed phenomenon. This is a commune, it is an open reality. Anybody can enter – *anybody*. I have not made any qualifications to be fulfilled before you become a sannyasin. And any moment you want to leave, it is absolutely acceptable; you are not condemned. You are received with love, and if you want to leave, you are given a good-bye with love. It is a very important thing to understand.

In existence nothing is closed, everything is open. In existence there is no noun to be found, everything is a verb. It is our language which has made great trouble.

You call a tree a tree, a river a river, but you are not aware that the tree is constantly growing; it is not dead, it is alive. In a better language it would be "treeing," because it is growing. For a river a better word would be "rivering," because it is flowing. Everything is a verb, always moving, growing, expanding, changing.

A community is a dead thing. A commune is alive, growing, expanding, open – people coming in, going out.

I am not offended when somebody leaves the commune; it is not my business. I never try to convert anybody to become a sannyasin. It was his desire to be a sannyasin, it is his desire to leave it. You cannot blame me. I remain completely a witness, like a mirror; things go on passing. When they are in front of the mirror, the mirror reflects them. When they go out, the mirror remains silent. It is not angry, it is not feeling that something has to be condemned.

But the people who have left the commune – they are not many – they only *think* they have left the commune, because I have not left them. Wherever they are, they are talking against me – here they were talking for me. In fact, here they may have forgotten me, may have taken me for granted; once they leave the commune, I am with them twenty-four hours a day. Whether you talk in favor of me or against me, you belong to me. Once a sannyasin you are always a sannyasin. You can drop the clothes, you can throw the mala, but you don't know; it is impossible to be anything else again, you will remain a sannyasin.

In fact, that is the trouble for those few people who have left – mostly they are men; if a woman has left, she has left because of the man she loved. These people who have left the commune cannot mix with the outside world. If you have left me, forget all about me! They cannot forget me. Don't forgive me, but please forget me! They cannot mix with the outside world, because I have deprogrammed them. When they are in church listening to an idiotic sermon, they will remember me, and they will be in favor of me inside their hearts.

So what do these people do? They start creating a small group. In America, in Santa Fe, there are a dozen sannyasins who have left. Now, why are they all in Santa Fe? That is my commune! They are just stupid people – why waste time on a man with whom you are no longer, from your side, in communion? Why waste your time? Those twelve people there in Santa Fe are continuously talking about me, against me.

Do you understand the psychological phenomenon? They cannot get rid of me. If they are not in favor of me, then they are against me, but they cannot get rid of me.

And why have they gathered together? Because in the outside world, who is going to listen to them talking against me – people who don't know me? And they have gathered also because they cannot mix with the outside world. They cannot be again Christians and Hindus and Mohammedans and Buddhists. They were Rajneeshees, now they are anti-Rajneeshees. It makes no difference at all: they are my people. And in existence everything has its opposite as a complementary. These people are complementary Rajneeshees.

A commune is a flowing phenomenon, a rivering, a treeing, a flowering. It is not a noun. So please don't call my commune a community, it is not a community. A community is closed. A community depends on belief. A commune depends on communion. Here people are meeting heart to heart.

You have asked, "How to explain sannyas, sannyasins, this commune, to the outsiders?"

It is not possible. They will think you are crazy. The only way is to somehow trick them into coming here. It is something to be experienced, not explained. It is not a theory, it is something existent.

Just think of a country where no flowers grow. Can you explain to those people what a flower is? They will laugh, they will say, "You must have hallucinated, you must have gone crazy. Trees never give flowers." They will not understand the word "flower." You will have to take them to where flowers exist. They can see with their own eyes, and they can smell with their own nostrils.

I lived in India in a place, Jabalpur, for at least twenty years. Just thirteen miles outside Jabalpur is one of the most beautiful spots – perhaps the most beautiful in the whole world, something that seems to be not of this world. A great river, Narmada, flows between two mountains there. The mountains are not ordinary mountains, they are marble mountains. Just think of a white, marble mountain…for two miles on both sides, two marble mountains. The river flows just in between, and in the full moon night the mountains are reflected.

I tried my best to explain to one of my teachers in the university who loved me very much – Dr. S.K. Saxena. He had been a professor in America, in Hawaii, around the world; he was one of the foremost authorities on Indian philosophy. I tried hard to explain to him, but he said, "I have seen the whole world – you cannot convince me. You have not seen the whole world, you cannot convince me that there is a spot which is the most beautiful in the whole world. I know the whole world, you have not traveled anywhere."

I said, "It is not a question of comparison. The moment you see the place…. You cannot conceive that anything can be more beautiful."

I tortured him continuously. Finally he agreed, "Okay, I am coming with you."

On a full moon night I took him there. For thirteen miles he was continually saying, "I don't see anything here." I remained silent. He said, "You are very articulate, very vocal. This is the first time I am seeing you silent, and I am continually saying that I don't see anything." But I remained silent. He said, "What has happened?"

I said, "You just wait" – because those thirteen miles are ordinary. Beautiful road, surrounded with beautiful trees, but nothing special. I took him in a boat. For almost half a mile the mountains are not marble. He asked, "Is this the place?"

I said, "Just wait. When the place comes I will not need to tell you, 'This is it.'" After half a mile, suddenly you enter into those marble rocks and the river, the deep river. I remained silent.

He said, "I am sorry. *This* is it." He had tears in his eyes, because he had not listened to me for two years. He said to me, "I might have died without seeing this place."

As we went deeper the place became just something other-worldly, almost a dreamland. He said to me – he is a very logical man – he said, "Take the boat close to the rocks. I want to touch them and see whether they are there, or I am hallucinating, or you have given me some drug."

I had to take the boat close to the mountains. He touched them, he kissed them, and he said, "You need not go around the world to find the most beautiful place. This is it."

This is my answer to you. Don't try to explain to anybody. This is an experience – or, in my language, an experiencing; the word "experience" again is dead. It is a continuous experiencing. Come again after one month and you will see the commune's new colors, new faces, new dances, new songs. I am not a consistent man, neither are my people. I am consistent only as far as inconsistency is concerned. Whenever you come you will find an alive, breathing commune – new flowers, new dances, new songs.

You have to bring those people. If you tell them that this is a religion, they will think it must be like Christianity. And you know the inside of a church – gloomy, reminds you of death, a cross in front of you…. If you talk to a Christian, his experience of a church will come and disturb your explanation. What can you say? He will not believe that this is possible – a godless, a religionless religion? A religion that has no holy book? – because I call all holy books, holy shit!

There are far better books than your holy books. Don't waste your time with reading *The Bible,* the *Gita,* the *Koran.* It is better to give the time to Dostoyevsky, Tolstoy, Chekhov, Gorky; you will be immensely enriched by these people. Don't be bothered with the Old Testament when I am giving you the Last Testament – unless you are an antique collector, that is a different matter.

Truth is always fresh. It remains fresh only when it finds a master to speak it. You can write notes. Remember, those notes will not have the same quality,

the same fragrance, the same truth – although the words will be the same as I am speaking.

Do you know that no master ever wrote a book in the whole history of humanity? Can it be just a coincidence? No, it is not a coincidence. No master ever wrote a single book, for the simple reason that the moment the word is written it is dead, it is a corpse. The word has to be alive. It has to come from the heart, it has to beat. Only then can it reach to your heart.

Only heart can commune with heart.

Bring those people here. There is no other way of explaining what is happening; otherwise, you will become a laughingstock. This is a very dangerous game. Truth cannot be explained, it cannot be described. But truth can be tasted.

I remember, a missionary had gone to the cannibals in Africa. He was the first Christian missionary who had dared to go to the cannibals to convert them to Christianity.

Cannibals are the most difficult people to convert. They have not even dropped eating man, they have eaten their own people. In the beginning – the beginning of this century – there were thousands of cannibals in Africa. There are only three hundred left, because if you cannot get your food from outside, you eat your children, you eat your old men – what else to do? Their number goes on decreasing; they will disappear. Perhaps the last cannibal will have to eat himself.

But the missionary was a fanatic. And just the way Jesus believed that God would save him from the cross, a miracle would happen…. And nothing happened. It was such a disappointment to thousands of people who had come to see the miracle. It was a greater disappointment to Jesus himself.

He looked again and again upwards – as if God is sitting on the roof of Rajneesh Mandir. He called, prayed – no answer, no miracle. Not even an angel playing on the harp, coming down on a cloud – nothing stirred. Slowly people started going away, thinking that it was just a waste of time, the whole day wasted in the heat.

This Christian bishop was also just as fanatical as Jesus Christ. He said, "The Lord is with me. What can the cannibals do to me?" But the cannibals did what they wanted to do. It is strange, this God of yours is very strange. He was not with the priest, he was with the cannibals; he was not with Jesus Christ, he was with Barabbas.

When Pontius Pilate asked…. It was a ritual that if the people demanded it, then one person could be freed from being crucified. Three persons were being crucified that day. One was Jesus Christ, who was utterly innocent, simple – more exactly, a simpleton. Pontius Pilate was thinking that people would ask for Jesus, because the other two were confirmed criminals; Barabbas had committed many murders. And the people asked for Barabbas to be released!

God's miracle was happening to Barabbas, not to Jesus – and not just one time. Because Barabbas was accustomed to murder, he did not care about crucifixion or anything, so even though he was forgiven…. In fact, Barabbas was resurrected, not Jesus Christ. From the cross he was brought down; *he* was reborn, not Jesus Christ. God! Perhaps *this* was the miracle!

Within three months Barabbas was caught again, because he had murdered, in three months, three people. But the law was, once a man is given freedom from the death sentence by the Roman emperor, then he can never be crucified again. So now they could not crucify him for his murders; they had to find a substitute. They sent him to Sicily to work in a coal mine for his whole life. And you will be surprised: the coal mine collapsed, all other prisoners – there were thousands – died, and Barabbas was saved!

And you think Jesus is saved? And these fanatic Christians are trying to save others.

A miracle *did* happen: thousands of people died and Barabbas was the only one who was saved. Even the emperor of Rome was impressed; twice the man had been saved. Barabbas was called to Rome for the annual festival, where they brought their criminals to fight with lions. And you will not believe me: Barabbas was again saved. He killed the lion!

Even the emperor called him close and touched him; he seemed to be the very representative of God. He gave him not only freedom but first-class citizenship – because slaves are second-class people, and Barabbas was a slave, sentenced for his whole life. The emperor freed him.

This God seems to be crazy. This whole idea is nothing but imagination, projection.

The fanatical missionary was caught immediately by the cannibals. He said to them, "Have you ever tasted Christianity?"

They said, "Wait. Just within an hour…. Look at that pot." There was a pot, a big pot boiling.

The missionary could not understand. He said, "What do you mean?"

They said, "We will put you in that boiling pot and make a soup of you, and then we will taste Christianity for the first time. Everybody is so eager to taste Christianity."

I think those barbarians were right: religion is something to be tasted, not explained. Bring those people here. We are not barbarians, we are vegetarians. Only in this milieu can you help your friends to understand what sannyas is all about, and what this commune is.

You are asking me if there is something special about a sannyasin that you can tell to your people. Yes, there is. A sannyasin is extraordinarily ordinary. He has no claims to any superiority. Not only in regard to human beings, he is in tune with trees and birds and rivers and clouds, and he claims no superiority even to animals and trees and rocks. We are all part of one cosmos. But please don't try logically, rationally to explain this to them.

This is not a theology that I am giving to you.

This is a taste, this is an experiencing.

This is love, not logic.

But why are you concerned to explain to those outsiders? As far as I can tell, you are still not a sannyasin, because a sannyasin would not ask such a question. If you really want to help people to understand the tremendous phenomenon that is happening here, the first step should be: become a sannyasin. Of course, you will be thought mad. So what? In a mad world, to be thought mad means you are the only sane person.

Become sane. That is the meaning of becoming a sannyasin.

Advice is the only thing in the world which everybody gives and nobody takes.

You can ask me a question, but you cannot ask for advice; I am not that foolish. I will never give you any advice, because who am I to give you advice? You are unique, every individual is unique. My advice will be my experience. That may distract you from your own life, that may take you away from your own being. I have never advised anyone.

Yes, you can ask a question. The answer that I give only has to be understood, it has not to be accepted on my authority. You have to be just a listener to it, without any prejudice. My answer, listened to without any prejudice, will become a totally different thing in you; it will be molded molded by your being.

Then it is no longer mine; it is yours.

That's the function of a master – not to create followers, but to create masters.

I am not saying anything to be believed. I am saying, just give me a little understanding, try to understand what I am saying to you. Listen – and it will take a different shape, a different form, a different aura within you. It will not be the same that was said, because words are empty.

When the words are in my heart they are full. The moment they leave my lips, the content is left behind; only the container reaches you. But if you allow the container to enter you, it will reach your heart – because it is coming from the heart – and your heart will fill it with its own content. Then it is yours, it has nothing to do with me.

You cannot blame me; whatever happens to you, it is your responsibility. I just like talking – I don't take any responsibility. Why should I take anybody's responsibility? I like talking, you like listening – good! So far, so good.

But understand the whole alchemy of listening: listening rightly, you will have your own understanding flowering. You will not be dependent on me, you will not be my follower. You will be yourself.

You are asking for advice. I don't give any advice. And I say to you, don't ask anyone for advice either. You ask advice only because you are not courageous enough to experience on your own. The moment you ask for advice, you become a slave. And if you follow it, you have committed suicide.

I don't want you to commit suicide. I want you to grow higher and higher into life, into love, into light.

With Me Begins
A New Era
In Enlightenment

DISCOURSE 8,   July 5, 1985

Beloved Bhagwan,

Why haven't other enlightened masters told the truth about God, Jesus, heaven and hell?

The phenomenon of enlightenment is very rare. It should not be so, because everyone is born enlightened and then enters into a dark tunnel of religions, cultures, civilizations, education. Enlightened you are born, unenlightened you die. That's why I say it should not be so rare.

It should be just the contrary; most of the people should be enlightened, to find unenlightened people should be difficult. But that's not what has been happening down the ages.

The society is not interested in enlightened people. They are dangerous, contagious. They cannot be enslaved – and all societies want people to be enslaved, exploited, oppressed.

The enlightened person is rebellious, against all that man has been doing to other human beings. That's why all the societies from the very beginning start closing the doors and the windows from where any light can enter the child. They will start making him a Christian. Now, no Christian can be enlightened. He will have to drop his Christianity before he becomes enlightened.

The same is true about Hinduism, Mohammedanism, Buddhism, communism, fascism.

The enlightened person has no "ism." He need not be concerned with any ideology. He has his own eyes open, he can see; he need not think. Only a blind man thinks about where the door is to get out, where the road is to move on. Only a blind man waits for someone to help him to cross the road. Only a blind man needs a guide, a master; if you have eyes, you cross the road yourself, you find the door yourself. In fact, there is no question of finding: you don't even think about it, you *see* it.

Please understand the difference between seeing and thinking. Thinking is a very poor substitute for seeing. If you have not seen a lotus flower, howsoever you think about it, you will not be able to figure out what a lotus flower is. The moment you see it, thinking stops. There is nothing to think about; the thing itself is in front of you. And a lotus flower is so beautiful that it is bound to stop your thinking process at least for a second. Only in that second will you experience the beauty, the grandeur, the godliness of the flower.

The world is divided into civilizations, societies, cultures. They all do the same thing to the visitors coming into the world, the new people – the children. Mankind has committed the greatest crime against its own children. The children are dependent on you, they think you know all – and you know perfectly well that you know nothing.

The children are very curious about each and every thing. They are continuously asking, their enquiry is constant. You try to shut them up – not because their questions are irrelevant, but because you don't have answers. And you know perfectly well that by the time they reach your age, they will understand the situation – and they will do the same with their own children.

This goes on and on, generation to generation; hence very rarely have there been enlightened people.

Of the people who are known as enlightened, at least eighty percent are just bogus. How can they criticize God, Jesus, heaven and hell? In fact, they are accepted as enlightened because they accept Jesus as the son of God. They are accepted as enlightened because they go on telling people they have seen God, met God, talked with him; he has sent messages through them to you. How can they criticize God? That is their foundation. How can they criticize heaven and hell? Their whole enlightenment, saintliness, wisdom, depends on these fictions. Destroying them, they will destroy themselves.

Hence, eighty percent of your so-called enlightened people are more unenlightened than you are. But it is a strange world. The blind go on leading other blind. Of course, finally they all fall in a ditch someway or other. But the other blind far away in the line don't know that the leader and the close followers have fallen in a ditch and disappeared.

I cannot accept anything that is not my own experience. I have enquired without any investment. I do not want to be worshipped; hence, I am not dependent on you. I do not want to become a God to you; hence I am absolutely free to say what is the truth.

Eighty percent of enlightened people have been either Christians or Hindus or Mohammedans or Buddhists. To me this is something of a fundamental

Be alert, be conscious. Don't go against nature. Don't try to swim against the current, go with the river. Be in a let-go. Accept anything that arises naturally in you. And you will not need any repentance, any prayer, any God.

contradiction. A man is enlightened and is still a Mohammedan? Then what is the difference between blind people and enlightened people? At least he should renounce Mohammedanism, Hinduism, Christianity. He should simply say, "I am myself. I am not a sheep, and I don't need any shepherd. I am a man of my own consciousness, and I have a light of my own. I don't need *The Bible* to guide me, or the *Vedas* to be my vision. I have my own vision."

An enlightened person cannot belong to any religion. He belongs to existence. So you can cut off eighty percent of your enlightened people without any difficulty.

Ten percent of enlightened people remain silent. You never come to know about them, for the simple reason that you cannot understand silence. And to be enlightened is one thing; to give it an expression is totally different. And unless the enlightened person starts expressing his vision, his experience, his realization, how are you going to know about him?

Why do ten percent choose to remain silent? It is because to be articulate is a different quality, it does not come in the same parcel as enlightenment. You don't expect an enlightened man to be a painter necessarily. You don't expect him to be a poet necessarily. Why should you expect that he will be able to be articulate with words? And it is a very difficult job. Perhaps the hardest job in the world is to tell you about something you know nothing about.

Even Gautam Buddha remained silent for seven days after his enlightenment, thinking, "What is the point? First, I cannot say what I have seen; there are no words for it. Words are impotent and the experience is so immense, so vast...

"Words are so small, they are for day-to-day use. They are not made by enlightened people, they are made by blind people living in darkness. Those words have connotations of ignorance. Now, to express light through those words is almost impossible."

"Secondly," Buddha thought, "even if I speak, manage somehow to deliver the message, who is

going to listen?"

People are interested in money, in power, in politics, in becoming bigger and bigger, higher and higher compared to others. Who is really interested in enlightenment? It is just an accident if you come across a man who is enlightened and get infected. The thing is contagious, and there is no way of preventing it – and no antidote.

So Buddha said, "Even if I speak, people are not going to listen. Perhaps they may hear, but hearing and listening are totally different things."

When I am speaking even buffaloes are hearing, donkeys are hearing, but they are not listening. Hearing is a simple thing; you have ears, that's all, nothing else is needed. The buffalo will go on chewing the grass – and you will go on talking about enlightenment. And man is not much different; in fact he is worse, because the buffalo at least has no rush of thoughts in her mind. She is a simple being, just chewing grass, enjoying the morning sun, the cool air – tremendously happy.

Have you seen any buffalo laughing? You must think that buffaloes don't laugh because they are in tremendous misery. You are wrong. You laugh because you are in tremendous misery. You need the laughter just to keep you going.

Jews have the most beautiful jokes in the world, because they have suffered the most in world. Strange...I have been searching my whole life for a single Indian joke – I have not found one.

They have lived peacefully. India has never invaded any country, has never been aggressive, violent, has had no desire to become bigger and bigger, huge; India has never been imperialistic. It has been invaded by many people, and for two thousand years it has been a slave country under Hunas, Turks, Moguls, British people, Portuguese people, French, you just say the name – and India has been invaded by everybody.

And why did such a vast country, almost a continent, yield so easily? They were not interested in fighting. Small groups of people...what is England? – not bigger than a district in India. What is its population? If all the Indians had pissed simultaneously, England would have drowned. No atom bombs would be needed!

I have heard that when for the first time the Americans reached the moon, walked on the moon, they were surprised: a few Indians were sitting there. They could not believe their eyes! They were singing their *bhajanas* – "Hare Krishna, Hare Rama." The Americans thought, "My God! We have been putting so much energy, science, money into reaching the moon – how have these idiots managed?"

They asked the Indians. The Indians said, "It is not difficult. We just started standing upon each other's shoulders, and finally we reached."

India is a huge and vast country. Eight hundred million people...eighty hundred million people...no... You guess how many! They can reach the moon without any trouble, just standing upon each other. And small groups of Turks and Moguls defeated them!

This is not history; actually India has never been defeated by anybody. India simply allowed anybody to invade – they welcomed them! The country was peaceful, there was enough food, enough space – what did it matter if a few more people were absorbed? There was so much to be shared. These peaceful people, without any desire to be aggressive, remained slaves for two thousand years, for the simple reason that they were not interested in fighting.

Are you interested in meditation, in enlightenment? You have heard the word, but listening to the word "enlightenment," does anything stir in your heart?

Buddha thought, "Whom am I going to teach? In the first place teaching is difficult. In the second place to find a disciple is difficult." And he thought, "Even if I can manage to convey something of my experience, and I can also find some disciples who cannot only hear, but listen too...."

Listening means hearing without thinking.

The prerequisite for listening is that you put your mind aside, so you are just a pure space. It does not mean believing; you need not believe what you listen to. But unless you listen, how can you decide whether it is true or untrue? And a fundamental law of life is: if you listen without thinking, you will be able to see whether it is true or not. There will not be any need for you to think logically, to balance this way and that, to argue for and against.

Arguing does not help. Can a blind man argue whether light exists or not? And you have eyes – have you ever argued whether light exists or not? Seeing is enough – you know! In the same way, listening is enough. An immediate understanding arises.

For seven days Buddha pondered over the matter, and decided that it was useless. And the final day, when he decided not to speak, his thought was, "Many masters have existed, and what has happened? People go on living the same way, doing everything the same way." In fact, things go on becoming worse. If there had been no Mohammed, thousands of wars would have been avoided. If there had been no Jesus Christ, the world would be much more at ease and at peace – because Christians have been killing, Mohammedans have been killing.

Buddha's insight was that first, to bring the experience down to the level of language evolved by blind people, some kind of braille-ish language is needed. Then to find disciples, then to teach them to hear rightly – that is, to listen....

"And if a man is capable of all this," Buddha thought, "even without me, sooner or later he will become enlightened. It may take a little more time, but that does not matter in the eternity of time."

The story is beautiful.... In Buddhism it is said that gods came, after waiting seven days for Buddha to speak. In Buddhism there is no God, but there are gods. And gods are not creators of the world. They are just people like you who have earned so much virtue in their past life that they are given a holiday period in paradise. As they spend their virtue, they have to come back to the earth again, back into the misery, the suffering. Yes, they enjoyed the weekend in heaven…. Those people are called gods in Buddhism.

The gods became very much afraid, because they were waiting for Buddha to speak. If they can understand Buddha, then there will be no need for them to end the weekend. If they can understand him and become enlightened, then there is no need to come back into the world of suffering, misery, pain, anguish, anxiety – gods are not superior to enlightened people in Buddhism.

So seven gods, representing all the other gods, came down on the seventh day when Buddha had decided not to speak, and persuaded him, "All your arguments are right, but there may be just a few people who are on the margin, just on the borderline, a little push and they may jump into a new existence. And we have waited for a man of enlightenment for thousands of years; now you have become enlightened and you are not going to speak! One enlightened man in thousands of years, and he is not going to speak, he is not going to be of any help to anybody."

I am telling this story to make it clear to you that ten percent of buddhas, enlightened people – that is the meaning of *buddha* – have remained silent.

They have achieved, they have known, they have arrived home, and the experience and the ecstasy is so tremendous – who has time, or energy, or inclination to go back on the county roads to find disciples?

Nine percent of buddhas have spoken, but they have not criticized Jesus, God, heaven, hell, or anything, for the simple reason that they were aware of the fact that it is very difficult to attract people to your vision, and if you start hitting them…. A Christian comes and you speak against Jesus – rather than changing the man's enquiry into a deep intimacy, you create an enemy.

Only one percent of enlightened people have tried that. And I am the one percent – because I am not interested in any bullshit. I am not interested in increasing my numbers, I am not a politician. I don't care a bit about more and more people becoming sannyasins.

There are six hundred million Catholics. So what? – just labels. I don't want to put a label on you.

And I want to say that the ninety-nine percent of enlightened people in the past – whether they have spoken, remained silent, or were bogus themselves – have failed.

A new humanity has to emerge.

It has to begin with a new kind of enlightened man; there is no other way. The new enlightened man heralds the beginning of a new history, a New Man, a new hope, a new future.

I will criticize everything that hinders, that prevents you from knowing your self-nature. I will hit you hard. If you escape, that is your problem. If you are strong enough, and you go on being with me, soon it will be possible to drop all the crap – Christian, Hindu, Mohammedan…crap is crap; it is very sticky.

And forgive me, because I have to bring you to that purity in which you were born – in that beautiful, utter nudity, when you were just yourself; nobody had manipulated you, you were innocent.

All the cultures and religions have used your innocence, have treated it as ignorance. It was not ignorance; it was not knowledge either. To be ignorant you have to be a little knowledgeable – of course, in a wrong way, upside down. The innocent person is totally different from the knowledgeable and the ignorant. The child is innocent, not ignorant.

I want to offer you back your innocence. But much garbage has to be moved out of the way. You are carrying all kinds of rubbish around with you; you have become identified with it – that's why I have to use hammers!

I will expose the bogus enlightened people. I will criticize those who remained silent – they were not people of compassion. Even if nobody listens to you, it does not mean that you can excuse yourself. If the sun rises and no flower blooms, do you think the sun will stop rising? "What is the point? No bird sings, no flower blossoms" – no, the sun will go on rising.

To me, to experience the ultimate automatically brings a tremendous urge to share it. If you reject it, that is your problem. Passing by a rosebush with beautiful fragrance, if you close your nostrils, hold your nose with your hand, what can the rose do? But it does not mean that roses should stop blossoming. A rose blossoms out of its own realization. If somebody is thrilled by its fragrance, good. If nobody even comes around it there is no harm, the rose has done its work.

I cannot forgive those people who remained silent. Even if they were not articulate, they should have tried at least. If they could attain to the ultimate they were people of great intelligence, they could devise methods and ways. Listening to me, you know I go on devising methods for meditation.

In fact, there is no method for meditation. All the methods that I use are for a different purpose: to prepare you for meditation. Those methods are not meditation themselves, they simply prepare you, they bring you to the very bank of the river and leave you there. Now it is up to you to jump and have the joy of the running water and the coolness and the swim, or to remain stuck on the bank like a lamppost. That is up to you.

But I cannot forgive those people who remained silent. They were selfish, utterly selfish, more selfish than those people who go on accumulating power, money, and all kinds of things of the world. They are nothing, because what they are accumulating is junk. But the man who has known enlightenment and keeps it to himself, he cannot be forgiven. I am going to condemn those people.

And the people who have spoken – the nine percent – I have to show you how many of them are only using borrowed knowledge. I don't think Jesus is enlightened, he is simply quoting the Old Testament. Here and there he tries to improve on it, but it is not his own experience. He is trying to prove to his people that he is the only begotten son of God.

Just the other day I was talking about Barabbas to you. When I put Jesus Christ and Barabbas side by side, I think Barabbas looks…he was a son of a bitch, but he looks as if he is the only begotten son of God: three times he returned from death. Jesus does not look enlightened.

An enlightened person cannot claim such egoistic things – that he is the only begotten son of God, that he is the messenger, the latest messenger, that his word is law, that those who follow him, their paradise is guaranteed and those who are not going to follow him…. At the day of judgment, the last judgment, he will sort out people. His people will go to paradise and the remaining ones will fall into the abysmal darkness of hell.

Sometimes I have been wondering: on the last judgment day, how many people will be there? The whole history…billions, trillions and trillions. Perhaps mathematics hasn't a number for them.

Mathematics was born in India. Only in Indian mathematics are there numbers which can manage even the last judgment day. No other language has words for such large numbers. The largest number in Indian mathematics is *mahashankh*. *Shankh* means that which can be measured, counted. *Mahashankh* means not countable.

Mahashankh people will be there on the last judgment day. And remember, half of them will be women…chattering, fighting. It is going to be a very difficult day, because a man may have been a husband to millions of women, a woman may have been a wife to millions of men – so many lives! There is going to be so much shouting and fighting – I don't think God will be able to manage judgment. And Jesus Christ says he will sort out his people. Forget it, boy, it is impossible!

And Jesus was not a great mathematician either.

He must have used his fingers to count, because he was an uneducated man. Uneducated people count on their fingers.

That's why in every language ten digits are the basic digits, because there are ten fingers; mathematics was born out of counting on the fingers. There are only that many real numbers; other numbers are just additions and repetitions of those ten, again and again.

I don't see any statement of Jesus which proves enlightenment. He talks about prayer, but not about meditation – and without meditation there is no way towards enlightenment. Prayer is a childish thing. You don't know God. To whom are you praying? You don't know the language that God understands. In what language are you praying?

I don't think that God could understand all the languages. Three hundred languages exist just on this earth, and there are fifty thousand planets where life exists, so there will be millions of languages. God must have gone crazy by now – listening to all these prayers, and consulting the dictionaries….

And how can you pray when you don't know God? It is mad! Your God is a belief. Jesus has given you a system of beliefs, he has given you a faith.

An enlightened man gives you a *science,* not a faith. Belief or faith means you simply have to accept something without knowing it. A man of integrity will simply reject it. He will say, "Unless I know it, how can I trust?" All the religions ask you to believe, and you have never enquired what belief means.

Belief means preventing you from enquiry into truth. You already believe there is a God – then there is no need to enquire. Science has progressed because it is not based on beliefs. All religions are retarded. There has been no progress in any religion – cannot be, you have cut the very roots.

Faith is not needed, but an enquiring mind. But no religion supports enquiry; they are afraid of it. If they have the truth, why should they be afraid of enquiry? They don't have the truth. They have invented a God. They may say, "God created man in his own image" – the reality is just the opposite: man has been creating God in his own image. That's why there are so may gods around the world.

A Hindu God cannot have a Jewish nose, that is inconceivable. A Mohammedan God cannot be conceived by the Jainas. A Mohammedan God says, "Convert people to Mohammedanism by the strength of the sword." Mohammedanism is not argumentative, it knows nothing of logic or rationality; it believes in the sword. Its argument is the sword.

Now, somebody puts a sword on your neck, and says, "Either be converted to Mohammedanism or be ready to die" – because Mohammedanism believes even if you kill a person because he was resisting conversion to Mohammedanism, you will both be rewarded.

You will be rewarded because you tried your hardest – certainly you did! And the other will also be rewarded because if he had been left to live without being converted to Mohammedanism, he might have committed many sins and would have suffered in hell. Now he is dead, and the dead don't commit sins. You have released that man from the opportunity to fall into hell. And if you die fighting, you will reach paradise.

Jainism cannot conceive of such a God, such a religion. Their religion says that even if you kill an ant, you will suffer in hell. Now, I don't see that anybody can be anywhere else than in hell. Whatsoever you do, you will be killing millions of live things every day! Your whole body system continuously goes on changing: dead cells are thrown out of the body, new cells go on coming in. According to Jainism, just to live is to commit a sin.

To breathe is to commit a sin, because your breath exhaled is hot, and in the air there are millions of small living cells moving around you. That much heat is enough to kill them. Even to breathe is enough to send you to hell. You are not killing anybody knowingly.

The Jaina prophet, Mahavira, slept in the night

only on one side. He would not change sides, because if you change sides you will be killing more small living beings. Just remaining exactly in one posture the whole night.... I cannot conceive of him being enlightened. Just think, even in the night you cannot relax. Just keeping one posture the whole night, can you relax? Such an unrelaxed man cannot be called enlightened.

I am going to tell you the truth.

If it hurts, that is your problem.

And I am not asking anything from you – that's why I don't care whether it hurts you or not. I am not the only begotten son of God, so I don't depend on you. I don't claim to be the messenger of God, I don't claim to be a prophet; all these people are unknowingly becoming dependent on you. They are becoming slaves to you. If all the Jews leave Moses, his prophethood is gone. Who is going to call him a prophet? If all the Christians drop Jesus completely, who is going to make him the only begotten son of God?

I don't depend on anybody, I am simply myself. For that I don't need anybody's consent, belief, faith. I don't need anybody to nourish my ego.

And anybody who is trying to be nourished by others, particularly for his ego, is not enlightened.

The enlightened man has no ego at all. He is simply without any "I." I have to use the word, but there is no corresponding reality in me. The word "I" is just a linguistic device – it has no reality.

Whether you listen to me or not makes no difference. I am not saying believe in me, because what I know you can know; there is no need for any belief. All beliefs are anti-religious, anti-spiritual. All belief systems have to be dropped, only then can man be at peace. These belief systems are keeping you fighting each other, destroying each other. They don't give you even a chance to discover yourself.

Getting rid of all belief systems is liberation. For that liberation I am criticizing people like Jesus or Mohammed or Mahavira, and I am criticizing their strategies to exploit you: heaven and hell. Through heaven they create fear in you, and greed. Through hell the same thing, fear and greed. Fear and greed are poisons, but they are saying, "Those who believe and believe totally...."

They are asking something impossible. That's why you are all tense, because you cannot manage it. How can you believe, and believe totally, something you know nothing about? They are not even saying to you, "Believe only hypothetically." They are asking you, "Believe totally." How can you believe? Deep down you know you don't know. Deep down you are repressing your disbelief.

All believers are underground unbelievers. Underground, all Christians are continuously suffering, because by their belief they have created a division, a split in their being. The belief says Jesus is born out of a virgin girl! And they believe it, out of the greed for heaven – for enjoying the beauties of heaven for eternity – and the fear of falling into the depths of hell. And the Christian hell is the worst – avoid it! If you want to fall into hell, fall into any other, because every other hell has a time limit; the Christian hell is for eternity.

These religions are living on your fear and greed. I have to destroy your fear and your greed, because they are preventing you from seeing your reality, seeing your eternal being, your immortality. I have to go on hitting on the head of your so-called God, because if God is there then man can never be liberated. God is another name of eternal imprisonment.

If God can create, just out of his whim – because there seems to be no excuse for creating the world.... Why did he create the world? And just four thousand and four years before Jesus Christ was born? What was he doing before that? For eternity, going backwards, he has not done anything. What prompted him to create the world four thousand and four years before Jesus was born?

No explanation is given by Christian theologians, because there is no explanation. If they give any explanation, that means God can be forced to do something. If they say that God created the world because he loved to create, where was this love to create for the whole eternity? And suddenly one day...? There must be some reason. No Christian theologian in two thousand years has been able to say what prompted God to create the world – and *this* world.

And if God is whimsical – that is the only possibility; he is whimsical, eccentric, a little off the track; in short, just a nut – if he created this world, why did he create heaven and hell? If he enjoyed creating, he could have created you without all that which can lead you to hell. If he can create this whole immense world, can't he create a man without sex, without anger, without jealousy, without greed, without fear, without death? He seems to be a very cruel type of God, very unkind.

And then he creates the priests who preach to you, "Be celibate." Some great conspiracy is going on. God creates you as a sexual being, and his priest – who is infallible, the pope – teaches you to remain celibate. Have you ever asked, "Is the pope against God?" He must be, because God creates love in you, God creates anger in you, and the pope says you have to drop all this. To whom are you going to listen? To God? Or to this Polack pope? And this is the situation of all religions.

I am telling you, listen to nature and just be natural. Sex is beautiful because it is natural. And a tremendous transformation happens when you accept your naturalness. When you accept everything that you are, there is a transformation, because a new thing has arisen in you: acceptance – which all the priests of all the religions have been destroying.

They destroy your acceptance of yourself, they create guilt in you. That is something of an ultimate crime – to create guilt. And the easiest way is to teach you to go against your own nature.

You cannot go against nature.

Who will go against it?

You *are* nature.

So all these monasteries of Hindus and Mohammedans and Buddhists are full of hypocrites; there is not a single man worthy of any respect. And these religions have created all kinds of perversions in the world. When you suppress your sex, it starts flowing in unnatural ways. You cannot stop nature, it will find some other way. If you keep men and women apart you will be responsible for creating homosexuality.

When I was a lecturer in the university, the first thing I did.... In India the girls and the boys cannot sit together in the class. The girls sit on one side, the boys sit on the other side, and a space is left between them. The first day I entered the university I said, "Get mixed up."

They were very much puzzled, nervous. They said, "But we have been told to remain separate."

I said, "This is *my* class, and nature has not told you to be separate. Nature has managed in every way to bring you closer. I am not against nature – just get mixed up.

"And you know, when a girl is not pinched by a boy, how much she suffers. I don't want any suffering here. You can sit mixed up, you can hold hands. I want you to be relaxed, because then you can hear me better; otherwise I am wasting my time here. You are throwing your letters to the girls and girls are throwing letters to you – I cannot tolerate this nonsense."

Of course, the vice-chancellor was very disturbed when he came to know. He called me and asked, "What are you doing?"

I said, "I want you just to remember your own student days."

He said, "But what has that to do with it?"

I said, "It has everything to do with it. Were you not hankering to be closer to the girls? Tell me the truth!"

He said, "You just go and do whatever you want."

It is absolutely natural that boys will write letters and follow girls, and girls will try to escape. This is just a natural game. The girl does not want to escape! You just stop chasing her and she will start chasing you.

That is continuously happening in my commune. No man is chasing women, the women are chasing men, because the number of men is less, and the number of women is more. And it is perfectly natural – the girl escaping from the boy is simply becoming more attractive to him, becoming a challenge to him.

You will never be interested in a woman who is chasing you, if you are a man, because she is not a challenge. Man loves challenge; it is a hide-and-seek game. But it is natural, and whatever is natural is virtue; whatever is unnatural is criminal.

And I can say all these things to you because I don't claim any extraordinariness about myself. I am a simple, ordinary, natural human being. Perhaps this is the first time any enlightened man has had the courage to say that he is just ordinary, simple, natural.

If you understand me, what I am saying.... I am saying, with me begins a new era in enlightenment.

Beloved Bhagwan,

There are many questions I want to ask You, and I feel the answers within me too. But the answers that I feel do not help me. Why is it so?

Because they are not answers! Are you stupid or something? If they don't help you, and the question remains, you have some nerve to call them answers. Forget those answers, they are not.

The moment you find the answer to your question, the question dissolves, the problem disappears. This is the criterion to judge whether it was an answer or not.

But the man who has asked the question must be very egoistic. He says, "I have many questions that I want to ask; I have my own answers but they don't help." They will never help. Please ask your questions.

And you cannot have many questions either. That is an exaggeration. These are the ways of the ego: "I have many questions, and I also have all the answers."

But the ego is just like a balloon.

If you go on filling it with air, there comes a moment when it bursts. Today, that moment has come.

Beloved Bhagwan,

I am happy to be free from any God, and to be living more and more on my own authority. But now I cannot imagine what enlightenment is all about. Isn't it just another God?

It seems to be the same stupid man. How do you know that there is no God – because I have said it? But when did I say to you, "Believe in me"?

You must be enjoying great egoism: "I am free of God." You are not free even of your ego, how can you be free of God? How do you manage to know that there is no God?

One can know this only after enlightenment, because then the whole existence is crystal-clear, open; life is there, but there is no God anywhere.

Because you started with a belief – hearing me say again and again that there is no God – you felt good, because if there is no God then you are free to do anything. When I am saying there is no God, I am not freeing you from responsibility. In fact, when there is no God you become totally responsible for every act. If there is a God you can commit a sin and then just go and confess to the priest, and you are forgiven. But if there is no God, nobody can forgive you; you will have to undo what you have done. Your responsibility is tremendous. You cannot pray for any help – no help will be coming.

The religions have kept man in this idiotic situation because on the one hand they say, "Don't do this" – and they know perfectly well you will do it, it is natural. Then they give you the medicine for it: you can confess. Or you can go to a holy river and take a dip in it and all your sins will be washed away. Or chant a mantra every day, do transcendental meditation – which is neither transcendental nor meditation – and you will always be clean, forgiven.

God is looking after you, he is holding your hand in his hand. All this has kept you crippled; you have not been able to walk on your own feet. And you have not been able to see what you are doing, why you are doing it. Is it right? Is it confirmed by your consciousness, your awareness?

A man of awareness never repents, because a man of awareness does only things that can done with full consciousness. But Jesus goes on telling Christians, "Repent! Repent! The day of judgment is coming soon." He does not teach people a life of non-repentance – and that's what I teach you.

Be alert, be conscious. Don't go against nature. Don't try to swim against the current, go with the river. Be in a let-go. Accept anything that arises naturally in you. And you will not need any repentance, any prayer, any God.

You say you are freed from God and you are enjoying it. You are enjoying only a licentiousness; it is not freedom. Freedom is responsibility.

A slave need not be responsible, his master is responsible. In fact, I say to all the religions of the world, "You need not be worried. When you face God tell him, 'It is *you* who created us in this way, with these instincts. We are not responsible. Why should we repent, and why should we pray? You should repent for this creation, and you should ask forgiveness from us. This is a day of judgment!'"

But you don't know that there is no God. You are not freed from God, you just have another belief. And I go on saying to you: Don't believe in me!

I am not creating a faith.

I am giving you a science.

Enquire, search – and find. If you had found that there is no God, then your question would not be there: "What about enlightenment?" That would have happened before. You could not have asked, "Is not enlightenment another God?" because you would have known yourself that enlightenment is not a god, but it is absolute godliness.

And remember the difference: God is a person, godliness is a quality.

Godliness is the fragrance of the man who has attained enlightenment.

Beloved Bhagwan,

I have heard You say that Jesus was not a healer, yet my personal experience is that You are. Can You comment? Also, is this a religious matter?

You must be kidding! Me, a healer? I am suffering from so many sicknesses myself – and I touch myself so many times in the day! The diabetes remains, my asthma remains. Just because of your holy scriptures that I have been reading for forty years continuously…they have destroyed my eyes. And I have found nothing in them – sheer garbage, to be burned.

Godliness is a totally different thing.

You cannot worship it, you cannot pray to it.

It is not the beginning of your religion, it is the very end, the flowering. It is a quality of the man of enlightenment.

Be Kind To Yourself, Stop All This Seeking

DISCOURSE 9,   July 7, 1985

Beloved Bhagwan,

It has been my understanding that the meditator and the lover have different paths. The other day we heard your beautiful explanation of the path of meditation. Is this path different from that of the lover? If so, how to tell which path to choose?

There is no path – either of meditation or of love – because a path leads to some goal. There is no goal in life. What you are searching and seeking is already present within you.

So the first thing to be understood is: there is no path to truth. There has never been, there is no possibility of there ever being – for the simple reason that every path leads you somewhere else, farther and farther away from yourself. If you are going somewhere a path is needed, but you are not going anywhere. You have gone so long already, so far already, from yourself. You have to drop all paths altogether. Drop the path and it is there.

Jesus says, "Seek, and ye shall find." I say unto you: Stop seeking and you have found it. Jesus says, "Ask, and it shall be given." Nonsense! Who is there to give it to you? And a truth that is given can be taken away any moment. It is worth nothing; it is against the dignity of human individuality. And why ask anybody?

Stop asking, begging, praying; you are just being stupid. You *are it*! In each of your breaths it is here – I will not say "there." There is no distance between you and the truth. I say unto you, stop asking, begging, praying, and you will be surprised that it was the asking, begging and praying that was preventing you from finding it.

Jesus says, "Knock, and the doors shall be opened unto you." The doors are already open! Where are you going to knock? And if you manage to knock, you must be knocking your head against some wall. The doors have never been closed.

And that is the beauty of existence: it is always open, available – just for you to take. Existence will not respond to your questions; it responds only to your silence. And knocking is making noise, beware of it.

Can't you see a simple thing? You are alive, and life is truth. And out of this life many flowers blossom; out of this life grows love, out of this life grows laughter. You are not to seek life. You have been seeking it for millions and millions of years. It is time: be kind to yourself, stop all this seeking. The moment a person stops seeking, asking, knocking, he is where he always wanted to be.

Jesus was a carpenter, so the word "knocking"

comes very easily to him. I cannot say that because I know the door is open. Your *eyes* are closed. Are you going to knock on your eyes? Then you will go blind.

Just see, the door is open.

And you are not outside, you are inside.

All the religions have been teaching you that you are outside the kingdom of God. You are not, you *are* the kingdom of God, you are in it.

Whatsoever the biblical story says, that God threw Adam and Eve out of paradise, I categorically contradict it. He cannot throw out Adam and Eve, because there is no place outside paradise. This whole existence is paradise – infinite in every direction. Where can you be thrown? Wherever you will be, you will be in; you cannot be out. There is no "out" in existence, all is in.

You say this is your understanding, that there are two paths, the paths of love and meditation. Understanding knows only one. It is misunderstanding that knows the two and the many. It is not your understanding that I have been speaking on the path of meditation. These are simply words. Call it love, call it meditation, or invent your own word, because all words are invented. The words don't mean anything; they mean what you want them to mean.

You have not understood what I have been saying to you. I have been saying to you, "Drop all effort and you will be full of meditativeness." And meditativeness cannot be anything other than love. When you are full of meditativeness, it means you are at the very center of your being. The experiencing of the very center of your being starts blossoming into love, into laughter, into a song, into a dance.

Just remain at your center. And when I say remain at your center, I am saying that you have not moved from it; you are only dreaming that you have moved. Renounce only one thing in life.... I do not tell you to renounce the world, to renounce the family, to renounce the wealth, no; all this is nonsense. Religion is not renouncing, religion is rejoicing.

Rejoice in the world, rejoice in your family;

Stop asking, begging, praying; you are just being stupid. You *are it*! In each of your breaths it is here – I will not say "there." There is no distance between you and the truth. I say unto you, stop asking, begging, praying, and you will be surprised that it was the asking, begging and praying that was preventing you from finding it.

rejoice in all that is available to you. Rejoice simply because so much has been given by nature to you. And in this rejoicing can you think of hatred, of anger, of negativity, of any dark holes? When you are at your very center, everything is light, everything is love, everything is as it should be. You are not to do anything. This is the most difficult thing, to stop doing anything.

Have you not seen a dead body floating in the water? When you are alive, if you don't know swimming you will go down into the water till you die. Strange, the dead body knows some secret which you have forgotten. You cannot drown a dead body. Not that the dead body knows swimming; the dead body has stopped doing everything, swimming included. And suddenly a miracle: the dead body is floating on the water.

People who drown get drowned not by the water. It is a scientific truth that just as the earth has gravitation – it pulls things downwards…water is just the opposite. Its law is not gravitation, its law is levitation; it raises things up. That's why in water you feel light; in water you can lift a big rock very easily. The same rock you may not be able to lift outside the water, because the water – the levitation – is helping you. The person drowns not because he does not know swimming; he drowns because he makes so much effort to remain above water. That very effort exhausts him.

If you don't know swimming, and by chance you fall into water, just get drowned without any effort. Just go immediately to the very bottom, and you will be lifted up by the water itself. Swimming is absolutely unnecessary.

A Japanese scientist has been working on swimming. He started teaching six-month-old babies swimming – must be mad! But he succeeded, because six-month-old babies don't make much effort. Then he went even to three-month-old babies; they were even more successful, they simply floated. They don't know how to swim, how to make an effort to survive.

They don't take water as the enemy who is going to drown you, they are utterly innocent – and for a simple reason: they have a trust. In their mother's womb they were swimming in water for nine months – not swimming, just floating.

That Japanese scientist is convinced, and I think his conviction is going to prove right, that even a just-born baby can be left in water and he will float. He has been floating for nine months.

Going to your center is just like that. You have been at your center, not only for nine months, but perhaps for nine million lives. But you go on making hectic efforts in all directions – searching, seeking, becoming Christian, becoming Hindu, reading the *Vedas* and *The Bible* and the *Koran*. Naturally you prove to be a crackpot; you are going to end up insane.

So please don't say that you have the understanding – you don't have it. Yes, you have a misunderstanding.

I have not been talking about any path. I have been talking about pathlessness. Meditation is my word for pathlessness. I have not called it love, because then there is more possibility of your misunderstanding. I know your love. You will immediately translate my word into your kind of love – which is not love at all. It may be chemistry, it may be hormones, it may be physiology, it may be biology, but not love.

You are attracted to a woman or to a man; you think you are in love. You are unaware of the fact that it is your hormones, your chemistry, your biology. Just very easily your hormones can be changed, and all your love for the woman will disappear. Your chemistry can be changed, and a man can become a woman, a woman can become a man. The difference between a man and woman is not much.

It is very simple. It is just like your pocket: pull it out, it becomes man; push it back into its place, it becomes woman. No other difference. Your sexuality is hanging out; their sexuality is hanging in. And you call it love?

Have you seen animals making love? You must have seen them. Do you remember? – when they are making love they don't look happy. They are not so foolish. They look as if they have been forced to make love. Their faces show a certain kind of despair: "What is this all about? Why am I being forced?" Look at two dogs making love – both in great trouble.

It is not different for man either. It is this fact that makes people want to love each other in darkness. It is good: you don't see the face of your woman, what is happening to her; she is going into convulsions. The woman cannot see your face, because your face has turned into a monster. Next time you are making love, just see the truth of what I am saying. And you are not the one who is doing it – something is forcing you to do it. It is something surrounding you, but it is not you; it is your body, your biology.

I know about one spider – they also make love; in this world it seems everybody makes love – and while the male spider on top of the female spider is just coming to orgasm, is trembling, the female spider starts eating him. By the time his orgasm is finished, he is also finished. Great love! And they are doing the same thing you are doing.

That's why married men and women cannot live together in peace – their love does not allow them to live in peace. Soon they become prisoners for each other, torturers for each other. It is because of this fact that I have not used the word "love" for this pathlessness.

But once you are at your center, that means you are no longer your biology, you are no longer your physiology, you are no longer your hormones. You are just pure awareness, a witness, a small light, a flame inside, of consciousness. Meditation seems to be a better word, because you are not acquainted with it. But you can call it love if you are alert enough not to get mixed up.

Out of meditation, there is a fragrance which is not chemical, which is not like passing through a hospital. That fragrance is love. It is not directed towards some particular address, it is not directed to some person. Do you think when a flower opens up and sends its fragrance to the winds, that fragrance is directed to some person? No, it is just overflowing. Anybody passing by can enjoy it. I say, *anybody* passing by can be overwhelmed by it. True love is just like that.

Whenever I use the word "love," this is my meaning: it is a fragrance of the flower of meditation, unaddressed. It is not a relationship. Yes, it may relate if somebody happens to be there. If nobody happens to be there, there is no despair; the flower is enjoying its overflowing energy, it is blessed. It has given its treasure to the whole existence.

Yes, it is relating in a way, but it is relating to the whole. It is not that it will keep its fragrance and wait for the person whom it loves. That's what you have been doing, because you don't know the authentic quality of love. You are making it a relationship.

Somebody attracts you; there can be any reason for that attraction. Mostly – perhaps one hundred percent, not mostly – the woman you are attracted to has something in her eyes, in the color of her hair, in her way of talking, in her voice, in her gestures, the way she walks…something in her resembles your mother. You are always in love with your mother, and your whole life you are seeking another mother. Of course, you are going to be frustrated.

All lovers are frustrated, except those who never manage to get married. For example, Laila and Majnu – the society did not allow them. Shiri and Fariad – their families came in. They were never frustrated, they remained lovers their whole life. They lived loving the other person, they died loving the other person. But if you come together…. They were prevented from coming together. If you come together you are going to find that this woman is not your mother.

Now, it is a very complicated phenomenon. You cannot get married to your actual mother, or your actual father, but that's what your biology is seeking. It never finds it. People go on changing their lovers, and each lover frustrates more, because by and by they start becoming aware that this search is never going to end. You can have all the women of the world or all the men of the world; still you will not be contented. In fact, you will be the most frustrated human being ever, because you have known all the women – now there is no hope.

All the old societies insist on monogamy. They are trying to prevent you from getting too frustrated. In India you will not find so much frustration as you will find in America; it is just out of the question. You are married to a woman – this life is finished. If you want to search for another, then wait for another incarnation, but in this life there is no chance. People get settled, not out of joy, it is a compromise – what else to do?

But in California you can never get settled. There are other women around you, other men around you. Perhaps if this woman has failed, there must be some woman who is born just for you; it is only a question of finding her. The poets have given you that idea that every man is born for a certain woman. And when they meet for the first time, lovers usually say, "We are made for each other."

Nobody is made for each other, and it will not take long to discover that you were wrong. As your honeymoon ends, you know perfectly well, one thing is certain: you were not made for each other. No woman can be exactly like your mother, no man can be exactly like your father. In this world, everything is unique; you cannot find the same person again. But every small girl loves her father, every small boy loves his mother.

In a way it seems natural, but this is one of the basic causes of human misery. Later on, what are you going to do? That first imprint of his mother in a vulnerable child's mind is going to haunt him for his whole life. Yes, fragments he may find here and there: the color of the hair, the color of the eyes, the sound of the voice. But a fragment is not the whole, and you are searching for the whole.

This is not love. This is biology intending to propagate; it is a strategy, a trick. Just think of one thing: if there is no joy in making love, no attraction in making love, no desire for making love, will you fall in love with somebody? Then I think that, just like a death sentence, in the courts they will give a "love sentence": "You get married and suffer, this is your punishment."

But whether courts do it or not, it has been happening for millennia. Since man has come into existence it must have been going on. No court is needed to give you a love sentence, you have given it to yourself. That's why I avoid the word "love"; it has very ugly connotations.

If you try to understand, then there is a totally different kind of love. But that happens only when you have found your center. Finding the center is easy. Just not doing anything to find it is difficult.

It is difficult to convince you that enlightenment is a moment when you are not doing anything – the doer is absent. That's why I call myself the lazy man's guide for enlightenment. It is not work, it is play, relaxation.

Beloved Bhagwan,

I'm afraid that the world is going to end before I get enlightened. What can I do?

You seem to be very much in a hurry. If you understand me, there is no problem – right now you can become enlightened. At least right now the world has not ended. There are thousands of people in the world trying for enlightenment, but their very trying is the barrier. It postpones enlightenment.

For ninety years J. Krishnamurti has been working, first upon himself, then upon others. And now he is getting immensely frustrated. Nobody is to be blamed, he himself has made it a difficult job. He is obsessed with reading detective novels; he has made the search for enlightenment a very sensational, puzzling, difficult detective story. My Krishnamurti Lake is doing far better: just the other day somebody became enlightened there.

You are asking me, "The world is going to end, what am I supposed to do?" Have I to answer you? Can't you understand? Krishnamurti Lake is not far away.

Krishnamurti himself will not help you. He has been just on the border of enlightenment. One step more…but that one step is missing. And the reason is that he was forced to become enlightened. For twenty-five years in his early life…. The theosophical idiots found him. He was nine years old, the son of a poor, very poor father; the mother had died, he had one brother. The father was in much difficulty. He was just a small clerk in some office; to look after these two children, and do the work – it was becoming maddening.

So when the Theosophists told him they would like to adopt his two children – one was Nityananda and the other was Krishnamurti – he happily handed over the children to Annie Besant, knowing that at least they would be taken care of, given a good education. The theosophical movement in those days was the top movement of the world. Very important, significant, powerful people had become involved in it.

The Theosophists started making these two poor boys enlightened – it had never been done before…so much hammering that Nityananda died. My feeling is that the Theosophists were responsible for his death. They tortured these two boys as much as possible: wake up in the morning at three o'clock; go to the river, take a cold bath, then chant mantras…spiritual teaching that went on deep into the night. Both escaped them finally, because it was absolutely inhuman – Nityananda in one way, Krishnamurti in another. Nityananda died – he must have been of a weaker constitution. Krishnamurti survived.

The Theosophists were going to declare Krishnamurti the world teacher. When he was twenty-five they gathered in Holland to declare him the world teacher, with great hope: "The man who can deliver the whole world from misery has arrived. He is the Christ, he is the Buddha; he contains all the hopes of the past humanity."

Krishnamurti stood up to declare himself to be the world teacher, but on the contrary, he simply said, "I am nobody's teacher. I am fed up with teachers! And just forgive me, I am not *jagadguru,* the world teacher. And I dissolve this whole organization that you have created around me." A special organization called The Star of the East, a branch of the Theosophical Society, was created for Krishnamurti. He dissolved the organization. The people were simply shocked; they had worked so hard to make him enlightened, and this man freaked out at the crucial moment.

Since then he has been going around the earth alone. But those twenty-five years are still heavy on him; that's why he cannot take that one step. He is not freed from those dead Theosophists. They are long dead, the movement has almost disappeared, but what happened in those twenty-five years in the beginning is holding him back.

Remember always: love is an attachment; hate is a bigger attachment, far more solid. Compassion is very delicate, but cruelty is very hard.

He is still fighting with the ghosts of the Theosophists. All his life he has been fighting and fighting with those ghosts – who are dead, there is no need to fight with them. One should be simply free of them, but being free means you don't hate them. Hate imprisons you.

He has become so afraid of the master and disciple phenomenon…. It is his experience – I can forgive him, I can understand him. What happened to him through his masters was so ugly that he has been teaching everybody that you don't need any master.

This is a contradiction. If they don't need any master, why are you bothering them? Who are you? You have assumed, unknowingly, the role of a master, of a teacher. What have you been doing for ninety years? – teaching people: Beware of teachers! If the people had really understood you, they would have left you, because, "What is the need? Why should we listen to you? This is what a teacher and a student, a master and a disciple do." The master knows, the disciple does not know. The master imparts his knowledge to the disciples.

Krishnamurti has been doing that, and I am amazed how blind people are. They don't say to him, "Shut up! If we don't need any master, then who are you to bother us? For ninety years you have been bothering people, and not a single person has become enlightened out of this whole effort."

He has created a different kind of effort: "Don't make effort, don't accept any master, don't be open to any teaching." All kinds of egoists have surrounded him for all these years, because the egoist feels great that he need not be open, he need not listen, he need not be concerned about masters and teachers; he is enough unto himself.

It is true, you *are* enough unto yourself, but you don't know it! Somebody has to hammer it on your head. But things can backfire. That's what has happened in Krishnamurti's case: a man of tremendous intelligence, fighting with ghosts, and continuing teaching, telling people there is no master, telling people, "You are enough unto yourself" – this can be misunderstood.

You are enough unto yourself if you relax and settle in your being; otherwise you are the greatest enemy of yourself. If you go on making an effort to become enlightened…. And man is so strange: if you tell him that no effort is needed, he starts making "no effort"!

Krishnamurti has never criticized any individual by name. Although he has criticized principles, doctrines, he has not criticized Gautam Buddha, Jesus Christ, Moses, Mohammed. Just the other day I received the information that he has criticized me. This is great! He has always pretended that it is not worth his while to criticize Jesus, Mohammed, Mahavira; it is something below him. That attitude is ugly.

But he could not restrain himself about me, for the simple reason that I have told my sannyasins, "Wherever he is, just go and sit in the front line." And you ask me why I have chosen red clothes for you?

The color red has something mysterious about it – just show a red flag to a bull and you will know. You can show a blue flag, nothing will happen; a green flag, nothing will happen. But show a red flag to a bull and he will rush towards you to kill you. Krishnamurti must have been a bull in his past life. The moment he sees my red people he forgets all his philosophy, he starts immediately criticizing me. But this is the first time he has used my name.

And what criticism has he given? – very childish. He has said against me that I am convincing people that enlightenment is their sheer inheritance, it is a gift of existence – just as life is a gift. I have always respected Krishnamurti, his intelligence, his courage to dissolve a great organization. But I cannot help it, I have to say the truth to you: he is just on the borderline, he is not yet enlightened. He can be any moment.

You should not be afraid of the third world war. For you there is enough time. But he is ninety; for him there is not much time. He should come to Krishnamurti Lake and get enlightened!

Beloved Bhagwan,

I'm confused hearing You say there is no God. There have been many beautiful moments in my life when I feel something moving through me which I know is not me.

I used to call it God, now I call it godliness. But I still don't like hearing that there is no God. Can you ease my confusion?

Baby, my whole work is to confuse you! Unless you are utterly confused, you are not going to drop your knowledgeability. What do you mean when you ask me to "ease your confusion"?

In other words, you want certain, settled knowledgeability. You want to convince yourself that you *know* it. I cannot commit that crime. You do *not* know it.

So first I have to remove all your knowledge – which is bogus anyway. You have not earned it, you don't deserve it. It has not grown within you, it is all rubbish that you have collected from books, from people.

I am going to confuse you more and more. And look, what is your confusion? You say that there have been moments in your life which you used to call God – you cannot deceive me. I know you may have experienced a few beautiful moments; everybody experiences a few beautiful moments of well-being, of great uplift.

Seeing a sunset, suddenly you are silent. Or listening to the tidal waves of the ocean shattering on the rocks on the shore, suddenly you feel almost a nobody before this vast existence. Looking into the sky and the stars you may have had certain moments, and you may have called them God. Don't make God so cheap. I am raising God higher than he has ever been.

The Jewish God says, "I am a jealous God. I am a very angry God. I am not nice, I am not your uncle." Jesus tried to raise the Jewish God, and that was his crime. He said, "God is love." Now, this is very contradictory. The Jewish God says, "I am jealous, I am angry, I am not nice," and Jesus makes him a goody-goody: "God is love."

This man Jesus should be removed before he destroys their certainty that God is jealous, angry. You *have* to be afraid of him, because that will keep you on the right path. If God is love, then who bothers what is right and what is wrong? A loving God cannot punish you in hell for eternity.

But Jesus on the one hand says, "God is love," and on the other hand – he is a Jew after all – the eternal hell remains. He cannot see a simple fact, that if God is love then eternal hell should be removed – because you need not be afraid of love. Love gives you freedom to be yourself; sandwiched between heaven and hell you cannot have any freedom, any individuality.

I am trying to raise God. When I say there is no God, I mean there is no person as God, there is no personality as God.

You have to understand clearly that personality is something false. The word "personality" comes from the Greek *persona* – *persona* means a mask; in Greek drama the actors used to have a mask. You know *sona* means sound; a sound coming through a mask was called *persona*. You cannot see who is behind the mask; hence the actor has a *personality*. And if you all have personalities, you are all actors – you are not being authentic, sincerely yourself. Personality and individuality don't mean the same thing.

I am taking the personality of God away. I don't want him to be an actor – you have so many in Hollywood. Strange, that the place is called "Hollywood"…all gods, personalities, great personalities. I don't want God to be a Hollywood actor. I am trying to destroy his mask, and once the personality drops what is left is godliness. That is the true individuality of existence.

I will not say, "God is love," because that still keeps God as a person. On the contrary, I say, "Love is God." You can forget all about God. If you can understand love, that's enough religion; more than that is not needed.

I use the word "godliness" and you are confused, because those moments…have you seen anybody in those moments that you can call God? You have not seen anybody in those moments, because there is nobody. You were using a wrong word, I am correcting you. Those moments you can call moments of godliness. I am changing God from a quantity to a quality.

God is a quantity; godliness is a quality. And you are confused by it? Just a hangover. Shake yourself well – slap yourself and shake yourself – and all confusion will disappear.

Beloved Bhagwan,

Where is this moment? I keep losing it.

Here!
You ask me, "Where is this moment?" Your question implies it must be somewhere else. You have already lost it.

It is always here!

Don't try to find where it is, because while you are finding where it is, you are losing it. You are missing the train continuously.

Time knows no tenses: past, present, future, no – absolutely no!

Time knows only one tense, and that is *now*.

It is always now.

But your mind can carry the past and destroy the beauty of the now.

Your mind can project the future, and can lose the precious moment.

Please, start relaxing here and now.

This is the taste of it.

Blessed

Are the Rich

DISCOURSE 10,   July 8, 1985

Beloved Bhagwan,

Clergyman Olds Grandlund from Sweden has asked You a question. The question has many questions, so I have separated them. He says, "Beloved Bhagwan, I have made you sad, but still I don't like you talking bullshit about Mother Teresa."

Jesus!...Jesus used to teach his disciples, particularly the two fishermen who became his first disciples, how to catch men instead of catching fish. I teach my people how to catch clergymen, instead of catching simply men and women. This is going to be a great feast. We are not cannibals, otherwise we would have tasted Christianity, but still, some vegetable salad can be made.

I have heard a small story.... In a school the teacher was telling the little boys and girls how God created the world, man, woman, and how he created these two sexes in trees, in birds, in animals. And when she was telling all this – that there are two sexes, man and woman – a small boy stood up. He said, "No! There are three sexes: man, woman and clergyman." It is a totally different species.

I have read his letter – it is so long, many questions in it. Start asking them one by one.

I mean that You have fallen down in the same pit, hollow, like other great masters and leaders, to tell bullshit about others.

First, he was sad because I criticized Mother Teresa. Mother Teresa wrote to me saying that she prays for me every day, and asks God to forgive me. Now, this is an absolute trespass.

I wrote her back, "Who are you to pray for me? – and to a God who does not exist at all. And even if he existed, you have no right to pray for me! I don't want any interference in my life, in my ways of thinking. This is violating the freedom of the individual. You stop praying to God – at least for me. I am perfectly happy, and my happiness is based on knowing that there is no God, that man is free."

God was a monopolist, a fascist, an imperialist; he dominated everything. If God is there, there is no possibility of freedom; you are just puppets in his hand. He wants to create you – he creates you; he wants to destroy you – he destroys you. There is no court of appeal against him. He is the final and absolute authority. Christianity is an anti-democratic religion. And all the religions who believe in God are fascist. They have accepted slavery.

The clergyman...I don't know how to address him, Mr. Clergyman or Mrs. Clergyman – because his sex is neither. So please forgive me, I will just use the address, "Clergyman."

These people are strange – so programmed, so conditioned that they cannot listen to the truth. I have no enmity with Mother Teresa. But if she writes to me that she prays to God to forgive me.... I have not committed any sin, I have not committed any crime – why should I be forgiven? And I have not given her my power of attorney to pray for me. And if I say this, you are disturbed that I criticized Mother Teresa.

This clergyman was leaving yesterday; he had packed, he was so angry. But then he decided to write all these questions, and decided to listen to what I am going to say. I think after today it will be difficult for him to remain one more day.

Mother Teresa has many orphanages in India. Why in India? Why not in Christian countries? A simple fact.... Those orphans in India she collects from the streets – urchins – and then converts them to Catholicism. It is a politics of numbers. In each of her orphanages there are hundreds of orphans who are being taught Christianity – Catholicism more particularly.

Those orphans are born either of Hindus or Mohammedans; none of them belong to Christianity. But to increase the numbers of Catholics in the world – because numbers mean power – she feeds them, clothes them, provides medical facilities; hence even stupid Hindus and Mohammedans think she is a saint. She is a sheer, dirty politician.

One man with his wife, from America, went to Mother Teresa to adopt a child, because they were childless and the doctors had said that there was no possibility – physiologically they could not have a child; it would be better to adopt one. Mother Teresa said, "You can choose. We have beautiful boys, girls – seven hundred." But she forgot to ask what their religion was. She assumed they must be Catholics; only Catholics come there.

And as she remembered she had not asked their religion, she asked them. They said, "We are Protestant Christians." Now there was a great silence. She said, "Excuse me. Right now we don't have one orphan to give you." Just a moment before there were seven hundred orphans; now there is not even a single one.

And the man and the woman, the couple, were

> I do not care at all what people think about me. I am not dependent on them. If I hanker for respectability, then certainly I will not say anything that may destroy my respectability. I am going to say exactly what is the truth to me. If it brings me notoriety – it *has* brought me notoriety in these thirty years – I enjoy it.

neither Mohammedan, nor Buddhist, nor Hindu. They were Christians – but they were not Catholic Christian, they were Protestant Christian. They wrote a letter to the newspapers describing the whole story, and saying, "This is strange. We were turned away, we were not taken in. We had no idea that those children are only provided for adoption by Catholics."

When I wrote to her, asking, "What is this nonsense? What is going on?" she tried to convince me that what she had done was right. She said, "Yes, there were orphans, but because they had been brought up according to Catholicism, they would not fit into a Protestant family."

Cannot I be allowed to ask her, "Why in the first place have they been brought up according to Catholicism? They were not born Catholics. If you want to teach them religion, then the Hindu orphans should be taught according to Hinduism. If they are Mohammedan, they should be taught Mohammedanism.

"And what a poor argument! You can convert a fully grownup Hindu, who has lived his whole life as a Hindu, into a Catholic, and there is no problem. But those small children who have been taught the Catholic catechism cannot be accepted in a Protestant family which is Christian? There is not much difference between Protestantism and Catholicism. So where is the problem?" She stopped writing to me.

And if I say these things publicly, this poor clergyman is offended. He wanted to leave.

Read the first question again.

I have made you sad, but still I don't like you talking bullshit about Mother Teresa.

I like it! And I am going to talk as much bullshit as possible. And what is wrong with bullshit? It is divine. And all this bullshit will fall on the clergyman, remember. He will not be able to find his way back to the church.

What do I care whether you like it or not? I am not here to convert you, convince you. And I am not talking to a single religion. Here are people from all religions, from all countries, all ideologies.

And if my talking against Mother Teresa hurts you, it is your problem. It is not hurting anyone else. And why does it hurt? You should ponder over it. Why does it make you sad? It is your programmed mind. And my effort is simply deprogramming. So whenever I deprogram a Hindu he will also think I am talking bullshit.

You should rather contemplate why it hurts you. *You* are not Mother Teresa. And whatever I am saying, I am giving you absolutely valid arguments. If you were really hurt, sad, you should have given arguments in favor of Mother Teresa. You have not given a single argument in your long letter. You don't have any! You cannot deny what I am saying, that's what makes you sad. Try to deny it, accept my challenge. It will help you. Whatever I say, I say with full conviction, and I give you my argument, why I am saying it.

To trespass somebody's garden is illegal, to trespass somebody's house is illegal. And she is trespassing my *being* – praying for me, giving me no answer. This is her answer – praying for me, to a God in whom I don't believe.

Please try to find something in favor of Mother Teresa.

He says, "I love Jesus more than anyone."

He also says – you have forgotten – that I have fallen in the same hollow pit as other great masters and leaders. I am neither a great master nor a great leader.

I am a simple, ordinary man. I don't want to be categorized with all those fools.

Being simple and ordinary has one beauty: you cannot fall. To fall, one thing is absolutely necessary, that you should be high, great, on the top of the world.

I do not belong to that category. I live a simple, human life, with all its weaknesses, frailties, mistakes. I cannot fall, there is nowhere to fall. If you want to fall, first go up a ladder. I have been walking my whole life on the plain ground.

This is strange. First you make me a great master, a great leader, just to make me fall from there. I know enough logic…. From the roots I cut things. I don't claim to be great.

Only people who are suffering from an inferiority complex claim to be great masters, great leaders of men. I don't have any inferiority complex. I don't want to be superior to anybody in the world. Whatsoever I am, I am tremendously happy and at ease with it. So please show me how I can fall. An infallible pope may fall, but I am fallible, and not a pope. But I cannot fall in his pit.

And why does he say I have fallen in a pit? — because I am "talking bullshit about Mother Teresa." Yes, there is a mistake. I should talk cow dung about Mother Teresa. Bullshit is male; cow dung is female — and she is very old, dried cow dung.

And I can say these things because I don't want any respectability from anyone. The clergyman will be in a difficulty because he has dealt with people whom you can exploit by the simple strategy of giving them respectability. When you give respectability to somebody, he becomes afraid to say anything that may destroy his respectability.

I do not care at all what people think about me. I am not dependent on them. If I hanker for respectability, then certainly I will not say anything that may destroy my respectability.

I am going to say exactly what is the truth to me. If it brings me notoriety — it *has* brought me notoriety in these thirty years — I enjoy it.

He says, "You tell about joy, love, life, celebration, freedom, et cetera. My question just now is, can you feel it in your own life — repeatedly showing yourself in Rolls Royces and feminine clothes, saying, repeating words about Jesus Christ, Mother Teresa et cetera, having bodyguards — any freedom, celebration, joy?"

It really amazes me to know that clothes also have genitals! This clergyman is saying that some clothes are female and some clothes are male. Mr. Clergyman, are you nuts? Clothes are either comfortable or not comfortable. I use what is comfortable to me.

In fact, just on the way coming here I enquired about the clergyman to my secretary: "Has he got a beard and a mustache?"

She said, "No."

I said, "That is feminine."

Why have you cut your beard and your mustache, which God has created in you? That's what so many men have done. Just think of a woman with a big beard and mustache. And it is not only a mustache and beard….

As I have told you, Christianity is the worst of all religions — I never say anything without supporting it with valid reasons. Before the communist revolution in Russia, there was a big Christian sect — Russia was one of the most orthodox Christian countries. The most famous and the most respected Christians were those who used to cut off their genitals. Every year men would cut off their genitals, women would cut off their breasts.

Whatsoever wrong communism has done in Russia, at least one thing good they have done: they have stopped these idiots doing such an utterly insane thing. And this gave those Christians respectability; they became saints.

I looked at my dress and I could not find that it is feminine; it is comfortable, it is beautiful. I am not a soldier who has to be in clothes so tight that just his tight clothes make him kill somebody, so tight he just wants to get out of the clothes.

I am a lazy person. My clothes are nothing — just a loose robe. Without any effort I can take it off, put it on. And strange, that a clergyman should indicate to me that this is feminine.

I am reminded…I lived for a few months in a place called Raipur in India; I was a lecturer at Raipur University. Just near my house two trucks collided and killed somebody who was crushed so badly that it was impossible to recognize who it was.

Somebody came running to me and asked me, "What can be done now? A woman has been crushed, and she has died."

I went there. I said, "Why do you say this is a woman?"

It was a Mohammedan area where I lived. Mohammedan women wear a black mask over their face and a black robe over their whole body. You cannot see a Mohammedan woman's body. She can see through small holes in front of her eyes. So they thought that this must be a Mohammedan woman. It was a man – not a man, a Christian clergyman in his black habit.

I wonder why Christian clergymen call their dresses habits, *black* habits.

And why have they chosen the black color when there are so many beautiful colors? In fact, black is not a color at all. Black is an absence of all colors.

If you see a rainbow, there are two colors you will not find there: black and white. White is a combination of all the seven colors of the rainbow; it is the richest color. Seven colors meeting and merging create the white. And black is not a color, it is the absence of all seven colors. That's why down the centuries, around the world, death has been conceived as black – because it is the absence of life, the absence of everything.

Why have Christians chosen the black robe as their habit? They are not messengers of God on the earth, they are the messengers of death! Their black robe indicates their intention. They are all Reverend Jim Joneses; they want to turn this whole earth into a Jonestown.

He is talking about my clothes. I use all the colors. The rainbow is my love. I want finally to give all my sannyasins rainbow dresses. I am waiting for the right time. First I want you, through your red dress, to be identified: that you are not part of any old, rotten religion, that you don't belong to the blind society that surrounds you, that you are asserting your individuality.

You may have wondered why I don't use red – because I don't want you to be my imitators. I don't want anybody to say, "Why do you imitate Bhagwan?" My seamstresses – Gayan, Veena, Arpita, Ashu – I have told them to avoid red as far as possible in my clothes.

I don't want you to imitate me. I don't want you in any way to lose your individuality.

The red color is just to shock the outsiders. The color red has some mysterious quality. Nobody can ignore it; it just hits the eyes. Go in a red robe anywhere in the world, and everybody will look at you. Even if you pass people, they will stop and look again: what is the matter with this man?

Do you know the meaning of the word "respect"? It is not honor, it means seeing again – respect. The red color creates great respect.

He asks further, "Aren't you speaking in one way and living in another way? I feel much more free, joyful than you, your sannyasins — yes, everyone in Rajneeshpuram. When I see you, I see a prisoner imprisoned in your own prison."

Great! Then why are you here? If you think you are more happy than me, more blissful than me, more free than me, then what are you doing here? Why have you been coming here year after year, each celebration? Are you crazy?

I don't go anywhere. There is nothing anywhere which can make me happier.

And what criterion are you using? When you say that you are more blissful than me, there must be some criterion, some way to decide who is more blissful. A blissful person does not go in search of bliss – and you are here in search of bliss. Why are you listening to me, wasting your time?

You must be miserable. You want to get rid of that misery.

And still you address me as "Beloved Bhagwan." You don't know the meaning of "Bhagwan," it seems. It means the blessed one. There is no possibility of being more blissful then the blessed one. Perhaps your addressing me as "Beloved Bhagwan" is just Christian hypocrisy.

And you call me "Beloved." On what grounds? A man who is talking bullshit – are you in love with bullshit? A man who is talking against Mother Teresa and Jesus – are you in some way against Mother Teresa and Jesus but afraid to say so, because it will go against your vested interest? You are a clergyman – that is your job; you are getting money for it, respect for it. I am not getting anything, no salary, no money. I don't have a single cent with me. I don't have even pockets in my robe.

Twenty years ago I told my tailors to drop the pocket. It is unnecessary, because I don't have anything to put in the pocket. And for twenty years I have lived without any money. You cannot find a single man in the world who has lived twenty years without money. I have not even touched money for twenty years – not that I am against money. I have not seen a dollar yet, although for years I have been in America. And I don't think there is any possibility for me to see a dollar before I die.

You talk about Rolls Royces. I don't own them. And why do you ask about Mother Teresa, Jesus Christ, Rolls Royces? Is there some connection? There is bound to be in your mind. You seem to be jealous, utterly jealous. I don't own any Rolls Royces. Those Rolls Royces are owned by my sannyasins; out of their love they provide a Rolls Royce for me for one hour every day. I don't even know which Rolls Royce they are going to bring today, it is up to them.

And why have they chosen Rolls Royces for me, just for one hour? Because my back is bad. They tried all other cars; only the Rolls Royce seat suits my back. Now what can I do? It is the fault of the Rolls Royce people. And anyway, I am a man of very simple taste. I am utterly satisfied with anything which is the best.

But why should a clergyman be concerned? Poor fellow, he needs a four-wheeler Ford.

It is a good strategy for me to move in Rolls Royces – and not just one. I would like the clergyman to burn even more – there are ninety Rolls Royces. And it is not the end! My sannyasins are trying to have at least three hundred and sixty-five Rolls Royces, so only once in a year, for one hour, do I get the same Rolls Royce. And I know they will be able to manage, because I am not a poor man's savior. I am the rich man's savior.

So many people are saving poor people, nobody is looking after the rich. They are completely ignored. This is inhuman. There are thousands of saints looking after the welfare of the poor. I am the only one – and I am not even a saint – who is looking after the welfare of the rich.

I will manage, if there is any heaven anywhere – I know there is none, but just for the argument's sake…. If there is any heaven anywhere, then a camel may pass through the eye of a needle, but not a poor man through the gates of heaven.

A poor man in heaven will look out of place. Only the people who have lived in luxury will be able to become part of paradise. They are already disciplined to luxury. If you have never tasted wine and you enter the Mohammedan paradise, where water is not available and you have to drink only wine, what will happen to you?

If you have been celibate, as this clergyman must be pretending – because all celibacy is pretension, you cannot go against nature…. And foolishly he has himself admitted that he has four girlfriends. To his congregation he must be a celibate man, and behind the curtains he has four girlfriends. Are you a Mohammedan, by the way? A poor man…you cannot think of his misery when he finds himself in paradise, with everybody singing, "Alleluia! Alleluia!" and doing nothing, because there is nothing to do.

I teach my people the art of non-doing – that is the preparation for paradise. I teach my people to sing, "Alleluia" – that is the preparation for paradise.

A poor man will be simply in a foreign land in paradise; he will not be able to make any connection with the situation that has been depicted as paradise. Rivers of wine, beautiful girls who always remain young…and the whole work is just to go on playing on your harp and singing.

I have heard…once it happened to a poor man. The poor man was a porter in Munich in Germany, drinking as much beer as possible, speaking language which is not included in dictionaries, fighting for any excuse – just ready to fight. By some mistake, he entered paradise when he died. It must have been a mistake – even angels of death are not infallible. Somebody else was wanted, but they took him there.

He was so miserable there! He had been a porter on the station, and he was very happy – the whole day working and then drinking, and then finding some woman. And doing everything…. In paradise there was nothing. Beer was not available. The women who were available were so beautiful he was afraid even to approach them. He had known only prostitutes, poor prostitutes; he had never known those beautiful prostitutes of paradise.

He was handed a harp and told, "Sit on a cloud and just say, 'Alleluia, alleluia.'"

He said, "This is a strange place. I was far better in my station, doing my job, waiting for the evening to go to the pub, then searching for a woman. This is a strange place. Sit on a cloud?"

He had never played on a harp, he had not even seen a harp in his life. He was so angry, but what else to do? – he started making an effort to play on a harp. It was not music, he knew nothing of music. He wanted to punch somebody on the nose. He was looking all around for this so-called God to ask, "What nonsense is this?"

In paradise you don't sleep at all. It is always day,

it is always light. And he was habituated to using his language, so although he used to sing, "Alleluia, alleluia," in between he would say, "Fuck you all!" and again, "Alleluia, alleluia."

It was reported to the guard that this man is dangerous. He says loudly, 'Alleluia! Alleluia!' and in between he inserts, 'Fuck you all!' He was sent back to Munich. He was so happy you cannot conceive.

I said to you I am not a saint. To me the word "saint" is more obscene than "Fuck you all," because fucking is natural. Everybody is doing it – even the clergyman. What everybody is doing, how can it be obscene? When the whole of nature is doing it, how can it be obscene? When even your God was doing it, what is obscene in it?

But the word "saint" is obscene. You may not be aware of where it comes from. It comes from "sanction" – the pope gives the sanction to somebody, and makes him a saint. This is simply absurd. Who can make me a saint? I don't accept anybody's authority. And a pope giving the sanction – then sainthood becomes something like a certificate.

It happened to Joan of Arc; Christians burned her alive. Christians have committed so many sins in the world that if there is any hell, it will be full of Christians: clergymen, bishops, archbishops, popes, Jesus Christ.

Burning living people, and particularly women – it seems to be a certain psychological revenge, because the priests of Christian communities were prohibited from any relationship with a woman. They were really enraged. They wanted to do something to hurt the woman, because the woman was very attractive. Remember, whenever you are attracted to somebody immensely, you also feel to destroy that person or that thing. Why? – because your being attracted to it makes you a slave.

That's why men and women cannot live together harmoniously. Both are attracted to each other, and both are destructive to each other. All these husbands and wives are continuously fighting, nagging, harming each other in every possible way. The reason is, they are attracted to each other. They cannot leave each other, and they cannot live together. They are in a fix.

The priest, the clergyman, is in an even more difficult situation. The woman attracts – attracts him more than anybody else, because others have some experience of woman and he has none. He would like somehow to force the woman to be destroyed, because deep in his heart is not Jesus Christ – it is Mary Magdalene. He goes on repressing Mary Magdalene by repeating some stupid prayer. But he knows perfectly well she is there, so he wants to destroy the woman.

In the Middle Ages, Christians burned thousands of innocent women – they just had to find an excuse. And the excuse was that the women were in a conspiracy with the devil.

Christians have been taught that the woman has been an agent of the devil from the days of Adam and Eve. The serpent did not approach Adam, he approached Eve. Since then the woman has been somehow in connection with the devil. In the Middle Ages the Christians accused thousands of women of having sexual relationships with the devil: "They are witches, and they are dangerous to the society. They should be burned."

They declared Joan of Arc also a witch. Of course she is one of the most significant persons who has ever walked on this earth. Single-handedly she fought for the freedom of her country, and attained freedom for her country. Certainly it gave the clue to the clergymen that she must be deriving all her power from the devil; otherwise a fragile woman, a young woman – how can she be so powerful? This was the reward that they gave to her: they condemned her as a witch and burned her alive. This was the judgment of an infallible pope.

After three hundred years another infallible pope reconsidered the case – because people were not agreeing with it. It was such an ugly act in the name of God. You rewarded the woman who brought freedom to the country by burning her alive? To keep these people on the side of the church, after three hundred years another infallible pope – remember the word "infallible" – declared that she is a saint.

Nobody asks, if both the popes were infallible…. Then it seems to be impossible – how are you going to manage? One declares her a witch to be burned alive; another declares, after three hundred years, that she is a saint. Her bones were dug out from her grave and worshipped.

Many nuns were burned alive, many priests and monks were burned alive, but ninety percent of those who were burned alive were women. Even nuns – they were forced to confess, they were tortured to confess that they had had intercourse with the devil. Can you see how the mind becomes perverted when you go against nature? And they were tortured so much that they had to confess.

The same tactics have been used by Adolf Hitler and Joseph Stalin, but the whole credit goes to Christianity. Torture a person – there is a limit, and then the person thinks, that there is no point in being tortured and again and again with the same question. It is better to accept it and be finished with it.

They were tortured and asked, "Have you had any intercourse with the devil?" Now nobody today can even imagine that there is a devil and women are having intercourse with him. Of course because the devil is a man – and he is not a homosexual – that's why women were tortured. And they were told, "You have to confess the reality." Finally they confessed; and their confessions are very significant to remember. Mr. Clergyman, please remember what those nuns confessed.

After the confession they were burned, because they had admitted, they had confessed that they had had intercourse many times with the devil. But what was the proof? And Christian priests have been giving them proof: the proof was that the woman said that the devil has a forked prick, so that he can enter the woman's body from both holes. Great holy people! And the women – thousands in number – confessed. They were nuns. And they were burned.

Now the devil has disappeared completely. After Sigmund Freud, he thought it was better to leave this earth. The few men – monks – who were burned, were burned because they were making sexual approaches or contacts with nuns. You call this a religion?

And if these clergymen, priests, reach heaven, where beautiful men, beautiful women, are all living in absolute freedom, with no fear of sin, with no guilt…. I have not come across a single reference that in heaven there are churches, and there are clergymen, and there are congregations. All that stupidity happens only on this poor earth.

All the priests of all the religions are looking after the poor, exploiting them, exploiting their poverty to convert them to their religion.

I am taking care of the rich. Blessed are the rich, for theirs is the kingdom of God. And of course, in heaven you will get a Rolls Royce. Anything less than that would be a humiliation of paradise, of your God himself. What do you think – which car does your God use? I think it must be a Rolls Royce.

Why is this clergyman so worried about it? It is my problem. If I have to suffer for being in a Rolls Royce and go to hell, I am perfectly happy. In fact I don't want to go to your heaven, because the best people of the earth will be found in hell, if it is there.

Where will you find Gautam Buddha? He denied God; he must be in hell. Where will you find Mahavira? He denied God; he must be in hell. Where will you find all your great painters, singers, dancers, poets, musicians? They cannot enter heaven.

They have committed so much sin in the eyes of the Christian priests, they must be in hell. You will find all the geniuses in hell – if there is any hell. Of course, there is none.

This priest, this clergyman, must have forgotten my watches, thinking that the letter is becoming too long. But what is the problem? There are a few people who write to me, but they don't know at all about my watches. This is the cheapest watch in the world. These are not diamonds, these are stones, ordinary stones. It is made by my own sannyasins, it is not a Piaget. My own sannyasins, Ajito and Bodhi, out of their love make watches for me.

And I love everything beautiful. Look at this watch! I don't make any difference between a beautiful diamond or a beautiful stone. The criterion is beauty. Yes, a few of my sannyasins allow me to use real diamond watches. I have no objection.

In Jainism, which is one of the most ancient religions of the world, in their heaven, mountains are made of diamonds, gold, silver. If in your heaven you can have mountains of diamonds, can't I have a small watch? This seems to be absolutely consistent. Be rich, be luxurious, be comfortable, because whatever you are here, wherever you go you will be able to adjust to more luxury, to a higher standard of living.

Don't listen to these idiot clergymen. If you live in a poor way…. And that's what all the religions teach – live in poverty; if you are not poor you will miss everything after life. I can't see the logic. Here you practice poverty….

What did Gandhi invent to prevent the mosquitoes? He cannot allow them to be killed by Flit, because he is a non-violent man, he believes in nonviolence. Mosquitoes are not to be killed, and a mosquito net is also not good, because it is a luxury. I cannot conceive, a mosquito net is a luxury? So he told his disciples: "Before you go to sleep, put kerosene oil on your face, on your hands, or any part of your body that is exposed." Kerosene oil….

Mahatma Gandhi's son, Ramdas, used to be my friend. I asked Ramdas, "If even mosquitoes have enough sensibility not to come close to a person who is painted with kerosene oil – it stinks, even a mosquito is not ready, even though he may die without food – what about the man? How can he sleep with this smell?" But those who did that were great saints.

You will be surprised to know – particularly this clergyman – that in Mahatma Gandhi's ashram there was a man, Professor Bhonsali, who lived for six years eating only bullshit. And he was worshipped like a god. He had done a great act of austerity – just eating bullshit for six months.

This clergyman should try. At least for six days, eat bullshit, and you will forget all your Mother Teresas and all your Jesuses. And then you will remember me!

He further states, "Bhagwan, you have given me pieces of hell and heaven here in Rajneeshpuram."

On one thing I can agree with you: I may have given you pieces of hell, that is my business. The other part I cannot agree with.

I cannot give you pieces of heaven, you must have been hallucinating.

I know what is actually the case. Whenever I said something which was in agreement with his conditioned mind, he felt euphoric. It was not me, it was your conditioned mind feeling nourished, supported. Those were the pieces of heaven.

And whenever I said something which gave you an electric shock, of course those were the pieces of hell. You cannot hallucinate and imagine shocks, electric shocks – that's why I must have given them to you. You are hallucinating, imagining, projecting heaven. So whenever I say something which falls in tune with your conditioning, you feel great. You feel great that you are right, that your religion is right, that your *Bible* is right.

You are certain that your religion is right. You are looking for certainty, for guarantee. And strange – you are more blissful than me, and you are asking for my authority? I have never asked for anybody's authority, I have never asked for anybody's support. I have simply lived on my own. I don't belong to any religion, I don't belong to any philosophy.

It simply shows that whenever your belief system is supported, you will feel good, great; and whenever hammered, you will feel bad. But in fact, those moments that you feel I have given you of heaven are poisonous, because they are making you cling more tightly to your conditioning.

The moments that you call "of hell" are the real thing. Only those moments, if you are courageous enough, if you have guts – which is very rare in clergymen, because why should a man who has guts become a clergyman? – if you have any guts, then forget all those moments of heaven, and remember those moments of hell. They are going to help you.

My work is surgical. I have to cut so much crap which is clinging to you, and you are clinging to it. It hurts, I know. It hurts. You can forgive me for hurting you – but don't forget that this hurting is being caused by your clinging.

If you really listen to me, and you see that something is so and drop it instantly, you will not feel any pieces of hell, moments of hell. And the moment you drop all that is painful to part with, a new phenomenon will happen to you. The moments of hell disappearing will make you able to see that your moments of heaven are only hallucination. You have been drugged from your very childhood. All religions are nothing but opium. And if you can drop both, you will be free for the first time.

You are saying that you are more free than me, you are more free than my sannyasins in Rajneeshpuram. Don't befool yourself. You say that I live in a prison. I don't live in a prison. Yes, I live in my room almost the whole day. But the reason why I live there is because the world outside has nothing more to offer to me. And the world inside me is so rich, so overflowingly rich, that I need not go looking outside. Yes, roses are beautiful, but inside me I have seen bigger, more alive, more fragrant roses blooming. Now, what do you suppose I should do?

I am the freest man in the whole history of humanity. It is out of my freedom that I am inside my room. Nobody is preventing me. On the contrary, my personal physicians, Devaraj and Shunyo; my caretaker, Vivek; my secretary – they are all trying to get me somehow to go out.

I am trying here for you to go in!

Yes, there are guards around me, because I am not a suicidal person. I am not as suicidal as your Jesus Christ was. He had absolute knowledge that that day he was going to be caught. What was the need for him to go to Jerusalem, unless he was attracted towards death? He had a very great death instinct in him. I don't have any suicidal instinct in me. Both things disappeared together: the desire for eternal life and the desire to commit suicide. They are two sides of the same coin. I threw away that coin thirty-two years ago.

Those guards around me are not placed by me but by my people. You have to remember that I must be the most fortunate person to have so many intelligent people around me. Just look at who Jesus had: fishermen, farmers, woodcutters, carpenters. He had only one man, Judas, who was a little literate and a little intelligent; otherwise, those so-called apostles needed adult education.

I am here to share myself with you. I have no concern with the moment that has passed, and I have no concern for the moment that is coming. But my people would certainly like me to be with them as long as possible.

It is their arrangement. Not only have they arranged the guards, they have arranged every medical facility in my house, every surgical facility in my house. Any moment, if anything happens, they don't want to lose time taking me to Portland or to Bend or to Redmond. And I never interfere with anybody. If this is their joy, they should do it.

Who am I to interfere? If somebody wants to kill me, I will not interfere even in that. But if somebody wants to save me, do you want me to interfere in it? And these guards have done no harm to anybody in four years. They are just standing there as a precaution. And it is not me who is responsible for them

standing there. But my people are free to do anything they want to do for me.

It would have been beautiful if Jesus had also had some intelligent people around him. Only Judas was a little intelligent, and he betrayed. Perhaps he did well, because he must have seen this suicidal instinct in Jesus. He must have seen that Jesus wanted to be a martyr, he was not going to listen to anybody. He wanted to be on the cross, because by his teachings he had not been able to convert the Jews to Christianity. He was hoping, perhaps, that what he had not been able to do, his martyrdom, his crucifixion may do. And he was right – it happened.

There is no Christianity in the world; it is only "crossianity." The cross made a great impact, aroused sympathy towards him, just as my Roll Royces and my watches arouse in you jealousy, my clothes create jealousy. But if I was hanging on a cross, then this clergyman would have been at my feet praying to God.

It is strange but true, that you are sympathetic to misery, to poverty, to sickness, to death.

Have you ever thought what it means? You are never sympathetic with somebody who is blissful, happy, joyous, dancing, singing, has no worry at all, no tension. Have you felt any sympathy with that man? Have you gone to that man and said, "I have great sympathy for you"? You would look foolish. He does not need your sympathy in the first place. In the second place, his being in a blissful state creates jealousy in you, not sympathy.

The crucifixion of Jesus created great sympathy, and out of that sympathy was born this whole cancer of Christianity.

I am not asking for your sympathy; otherwise I would be carrying my cross on my shoulders. I do not care, because to ask for your sympathy simply means that I am empty within, that I want to fill that empty hollowness through your sympathy, your love, your compassion. No.

Why do people get angry with me? Why do they

become arrogant, aggressive towards me?

The reason is simple.

I am so blissful that only great jealousy starts burning in their hearts.

You have never loved anybody who is going higher and higher in his happiness.

If your house is on fire, even your enemies will come to sympathize with you, even those who were not on talking terms with you.

But if you make a beautiful marble palace, even your friends will disappear.

The jealousy…. That jealousy is all over the letter of the clergyman.

Finally he says, "Blessings."

Please forgive me, I cannot accept it. I have so much blessedness in me, I am just blissed-out. What am I going to do with a poor man's blessings? And what blessings can you give to me? You don't have them in the first place to give. This is simply egoistic stupidity. You should have asked for my blessings. I have them and I can give them to you, or to anybody. In fact, I am simply throwing them to everybody!

Please forgive me, this clergyman destroyed your whole morning.

That Explosion
Of Bliss

Beloved Bhagwan,

J. Krishnamurti has criticized You and said that You are a self-appointed master. What do You have to say?

It seems that J. Krishnamurti has finally become senile. It is time too, he is ninety years old. What he has said is absurd. Who was appointed before me? Was Gautam Buddha an appointed master? Was Moses an appointed master? Was Jesus appointed by somebody? There are things which blossom on their own. It is not a government bureaucracy, where you are appointed. And if a master is appointed by somebody else, he can be dis-appointed any moment. Nobody can dis-appoint me.

It is not a criticism of me, it is a criticism of himself. He is the only man in the whole history of humanity who was appointed by others as a world teacher. And it is very strange – the people who appointed him as a world teacher were themselves ignorant. They were waiting for the world teacher to make them awake. These sleeping and snoring Theosophists appointed J. Krishnamurti as the world teacher.

It is good that he refused. He refused the organization, he refused the idea of being a world teacher. But his refusal seems only superficial, he has remained a teacher all his life. What has he been doing for almost a century? – teaching. But where is the appointment order?

To know oneself is not something that anybody else can do for you. And more particularly, how can sleeping people help the one who is awake? They are dreaming; in their sleep they can only dream. Do you expect these sleeping people to appoint the awakened one? That would be hilarious.

Yes, nobody has appointed me. On that point he is not absolutely wrong. But there is another point also, which is a little delicate. I say nobody has appointed me, including myself. I am not a "self-appointed master." Whenever there is a master, he is recognized, not appointed.

When the rose flowers, you don't make it flower, but you can recognize the fragrance. Even in your sleep you can feel that the night is over and the sun has arisen. You are just hanging between sleep and waking. You may take time to wake up, but somewhere deep down in you, you know it is time to wake up.

I am not appointed by anybody – to be appointed is an insult. And I am not appointed by myself, because what is the need? – I *know* it.

The word "master" in the world of spirituality has a totally different meaning. It is not the same as a schoolmaster. A master in the spiritual sense is one who has mastery over himself, who does not function unconsciously, whose every act – even the smallest gesture – is conscious, alert. He may not have a single disciple – it doesn't matter.

Do you see the point? The word "master" creates

the idea of the disciple, the follower. How can there be a master without a disciple, a follower? But in the spiritual sense of the word, "master" means mastery of oneself. It has no relationship with any following; it does not depend on the crowd. A master can be just alone.

I had started alone, and then slowly people started joining my caravan. I was really surprised – I am still surprised. Surprised, because how did these people recognize the fragrance, the flowering of self-mastery? They are not awake, but one thing is certain: they are not asleep either. Just the early morning hours…. You know, everybody knows, that you are awake and still pretending to sleep. You would have loved to sleep, but what to do?

I have never said that I am a master. It is something others have to understand. I am not like Jesus who goes on proclaiming himself to be the messenger of God, the only begotten son of God, and all that crap. Of course, it is Christian crap. I am not like Mohammed, who says, "I am the messenger of God, and the last messenger. After me there is going to be no change in the message." Did God die fourteen hundred years ago, when Mohammed declared, "I am the last prophet"?

I do not claim anything, and I am criticized for things which I have never claimed. I am not a prophet, I am not a messiah, I am not a messenger from any God – because there is no God. Yes, I am an alert, conscious, ordinary man.

The whole beauty is that I have not proclaimed anything, and still you have heard it. I have not said it, and you have understood it. I have not knocked on your doors, I have not tried to convince you about anything. I have never bothered about any respectability. I have just lived in my own way, according to my own consciousness.

I don't claim that you are my followers. All followers are blind – only the blind need to follow. Without any claim on my side, millions of people around the world have come closer and closer to me.

Your mind is somehow very stubborn about changing, because change brings difficulties. Change brings new things, and you have to begin again and again and again. But be courageous. If you are not courageous you are already dead. Just to go on breathing is not enough to be alive. I define life as a constant change, and the capacity to go with it wherever it leads you. If you have that courage, truth is not far away.

It is a miracle.

I don't count Jesus as a man of miracles. Whatever are called his miracles are invented by the Christians. Secondly, even if he had done those miracles, they are third-rate. Making bread out of stones…. If this is true, there should not have been any Ethiopia. Half of the world would not be dying. If he can change a stone into bread, then why not change the whole Himalayas into a big bread? The secret is the same.

He turns water into wine. And I am always amazed – from Christian pulpits this is declared to be a great miracle. This is a crime! What about Jesus turning water into hashish, marijuana, LSD? He would be behind bars! Do you think wine is not of the same category? In fact, it is worse. LSD is far superior and less harmful.

Yes, if he had turned wine into water, I would call it a miracle, and not illegal either. But I say to you, he has not done any of these things, because if he had done these things – healing the people who are sick, making the blind see, the lame walk, the dead come back to life again – just average intelligence is needed to see it: if a man had done all these things, do you think the Jews would have asked that he be crucified?

If a man had done the miracle of raising the dead Lazarus back to life, the whole of Judea would have fallen at his feet. That seems to be absolutely natural. You can think yourself – if you see somebody raising dead people to life, what are you going to do, crucify this man?

And how can you crucify a man who raises dead people to life? You may have crucified him, but the man could have turned the crucifixion into anything he wanted. The cross may have become a golden throne. If stones can become bread, water can become wine, what is so impossible? The cross becomes a golden throne…. That did not happen. Jesus could not save himself.

I do not claim anything. I am just like you. But

what can I do? If you feel some fragrance arising out of my being, and you start moving towards me from faraway lands – in spite of all the difficulties – then I must say *you* are doing miracles. I am only a witness to what is happening.

It is time for J. Krishnamurti to shut up completely.

Beloved Bhagwan,

You have said that all Your words of the past are not important. So what are all Your books for?

Jesus! I have never said that my books of the past are not important! But you may have *heard* that. What I had said is that to me truth is not something unchanging. Anything unchanging is dead.

Truth is alive, breathing, moving. So when I am saying something to you now, don't be bothered about the past – what I said twenty years before. And I say to you, if I am still here tomorrow, the truth will have become more potent, deeper, higher. My books of the past are not unimportant.

I am just like a tree. When it comes to blossom, do you think now the roots are unimportant, the trunk is no longer needed, the leaves are unnecessary, because the tree has blossomed, the flowers have come? No, you don't say that. You know perfectly well that those flowers are intrinsically connected with the hidden roots in the earth. It is all one process. The flowers cannot exist without the leaves, without the branches, without the trunk, without the roots. But when flowers are there, don't be bothered to compare them with the roots. Then you will find great contradictions, inconsistencies.

There are. What is consistent between the roots and the flower? What is consistent between the branches and the leaves and the flower? The leaves may be green and the flower is red – so contradictory, so inconsistent! The roots are ugly, the flower is so beautiful – what is consistent? But when the flowers are there, you know perfectly well that those roots underground are the base. The trunk, the branches are moving – a movement towards the flowers, the leaves. They all help the flower.

I have lived in many places, but I don't own any house. I am a houseless wanderer. I have always been a guest of somebody. But wherever I have been, I have created beautiful gardens.

In one place the land was big. It was impossible for just me alone to make the whole land green. I searched for a gardener, the best – because less than that does not satisfy me. This gardener was receiving awards every year, because every year there was a competition to see who brings the biggest flowers, the most beautiful. From the whole province people were participating, but this old man, a poor gardener, had been getting the first prize for years. I asked him, "Would you love to be with me and be my gardener?"

He had never lived in such a big bungalow – he was a poor man. He was very happy, he had never had such a big piece of land. And I said, "All the facilities will be provided, you don't be worried. Whatever salary you want, you just say. It is up to you to decide."

A poor man, he said, "Thirty rupees per month would be enough."

I said, "No. Thirty rupees for a man who creates so much beauty? Sixty will be okay." He could not believe me, he thought I was mad – and perhaps he was right.

Sixty rupees in those days was a great salary; the headmaster of a school or the head clerk of a big government office was getting it. And I was alone in the big bungalow.

I said, "You take as many rooms of this bungalow as you want – free of charge. I am a guest, I don't pay anything; you are my guest, there is no problem. And every facility that you need for the garden will be provided. Go and find out, purchase all beautiful plants, flowers, trees, and make this barren land…."

It had remained barren for many years, because somehow the rumor spread that the house was haunted. The owner could not sell it. Who is going to purchase a haunted house? The owner was very nervous when he offered it to me – he loved me. And I said, "That's perfectly…that is a beautiful building" – it was Victorian architecture – "I would love it."

He thought perhaps I didn't know that the house was haunted. He said, "But one thing I have to say to you – I don't want to keep you in the dark – the house has been empty for years, and nobody purchases it, nobody rents it, because the whole city know the house is haunted."

I said, "That's great! In such a big house, to live alone does not feel good. If a few ghosts are there, it will be good company."

The gardener brought all kinds of plants and flowers, and he started working, because in the next competition he had to bring the greatest rose flowers. But what did he do? On each rosebush he went on cutting the buds. He would leave only one bud and cut all the other buds.

When I came to know of it, I said, "What are you doing?"

He said, "This is the only way to bring the biggest flowers, because then all the juices of the tree start moving into one flower to make it blossom. If there are many flowers, then the juices are divided."

I said, "You forget about your annual exhibition. From now onwards I will give you the award for not cutting a single bud! It is not important that the rose should be big, it is enough that it is a rose. And you are being murderous."

I wanted to make it clear to you that the roses are there, but the juice is flowing from the roots.

Whatever I have said in these thirty years – and I have been speaking continuously, except for those few years when I was silent – every single word is important, because they are all interconnected.

You may find contradictions, you may find

inconsistencies. Don't be afraid; life is full of contradictions, full of inconsistencies. And I don't know any other god than life itself.

I have never said that my books of the past are not important. But this goes on happening: I say one thing, you hear something else. I have said only that what I am saying now is the highest flower on the tree that I have been growing for thirty years. So if you have to decide, decide on this moment's statement, and don't be bothered about inconsistencies, contradictions.

And I have also said, remember this for tomorrow also. Tomorrow this day will be old, gone. Newer flowers will be blossoming. Be always in the present, and you will be always right. And don't be afraid when tomorrow you find an even better thing. Then don't cling to the yesterday. It was beautiful, but it was beautiful *yesterday*.

It makes a very important implication clear.

Why do people worship dead saints, prophets, messiahs? They are very convenient; because they are dead you can rest assured that they are not going to change their statements. While they are alive you are always trembling – the man may say something else tomorrow.

It is your incapacity to change, incapacity to remain a flow, that makes you worship Jesus Christ when I am here! But Jesus Christ is convenient – you can be certain about him. Not only that, you can read whatsoever you want to read in his statements; he is not going to say to you, "This is not what I said."

All these theologians of different religions around the world, what are they doing? They are making you more and more comfortable with the religion you are addicted to. Yes, I use the word "addiction," because all religions are nothing but drugs. The theologians go on polishing, making the statements more suitable to you. This you cannot expect here.

I don't say anything considering *you,* I say it because it is true! If it hurts you, I am helpless. If it does not suit you, disturbs you, it is your problem; I have nothing to do with it. My concern is to remain flowing with existence, life, truth. And whatever existence wants to speak through me, I will speak.

I never hesitate to contradict myself, because who am I to interfere? It was a life force that said that, the same life force is saying *this*. There must be some inner connection which you cannot see.

My books of the past are important, because they will be a test for you – whether you can grow with me or you have stopped long ago.

It happened…a beautiful man, George Gurdjieff, had a great disciple, P.D. Ouspensky. Nobody knew about Gurdjieff, but the whole world know about Ouspensky, because Ouspensky was one of the best mathematicians the world has ever known. Gurdjieff was a Caucasian…who cares about the Caucasus? He was uneducated, but a tremendous man, really terrific.

Ouspensky was in search of truth. He roamed around the world, he was in India. He was searching for someone in whose eyes he could see that the man knows. He was not looking for beautiful words, theorems – all that he himself was capable of doing. And he searched all over India and Tibet and could not find a man who was a living truth. He found great scholars, he found famous religious leaders, but that was not his search.

Ouspensky was really an authentic seeker. He was searching for a man who was an embodiment of truth, who is not repeating words of some sages who died thousands of years ago, a man who could say, "This is so." Whether religious scriptures agree with it or not does not matter. If they agree, good for them; if they don't agree, they are wrong. And strangely enough, he found Gurdjieff in the same town, in the same cafe where he used to go every day after his university classes. He found him in Moscow. Life is very mysterious.

Gurdjieff was just sitting there. And the moment Ouspensky entered and looked at the man – just like a flash, he knew, "This is the man I have been searching for." There was that aura, there was that light, there was on that face something unknown, mysterious. He fell in deep love with Gurdjieff. But Gurdjieff was just as strange a man as I am. He was not an ordinary scholar; he was not talking about what others have discovered, he was saying only that which he had come to know.

Ouspensky lived with Gurdjieff for many years. Then the first world war came, and Gurdjieff had to escape from Russia; Ouspensky also had to escape. Ouspensky was welcome anywhere, any university would be proud of having him.

He had written a book which has become almost the most important book about not only mathematics, but about life and all its problems. He had written a book called *Tertium Organum* – the third canon of knowledge. And in the beginning of the book he writes that the first organum was written by Aristotle. Aristotle has a book named *Organum* – knowledge, wisdom. And the second book was written by Bacon, *Novum Organum* – the new wisdom. Both are very significant persons in the history of thought. Aristotle is the father of all the logic that the West knows, and Bacon is the father of all the sciences that have developed in the West.

Ouspensky said, "I am writing *Tertium Organum,* the third canon of wisdom, and I declare that the third canon existed even before the first." And it was not out of any egoism – I have gone through all the three canons – it was a simple statement of fact. Ouspensky has transcended Aristotle and Bacon both. The book caused a great stir in the whole world. London University invited him, because Russia was no longer a safe place; the first world war and the communist revolution were going on together.

Gurdjieff was hiding in a very faraway part of Russia, Tiflis. It was almost another planet from London. And he asked Ouspensky to drop everything and come back to Tiflis. Ouspensky loved the man so much, he dropped his job, he dropped his work. He had opened a school in which he was teaching Gurdjieff's message. He closed the school and went into a dangerous country where life was not safe. He arrived in Tiflis, and the moment he entered Gurdjieff's room, Gurdjieff said, "Good, you have arrived. Now go back and resume your work."

This was too much. Even Ouspensky, a man of such integrity, could not stand it. But Gurdjieff's methods, devices were such. This was a moment of test, a test of trust. Ouspensky failed in that moment. He thought Gurdjieff was simply insane: "I wasted everything that I had arranged, traveled in a country where any moment I could have been killed – and he does not even say, 'Sit down, rest.' He says, 'Good that you have come. Now just go back and resume your work.'"

He went back. Gurdjieff had impressed him immensely, so what did he do? He dropped Gurdjieff, but he could not drop the Gurdjieff with whom he had lived for years, or his teachings. A strange phenomenon happened. For him Gurdjieff was divided into two parts. He continued to teach only that part of Gurdjieff that was in tune with his logical mind. Beyond that, Gurdjieff was his enemy.

Gurdjieff lived long, longer than Ouspensky. Ouspensky continued to teach Gurdjieff's teachings, but those were the old teachings up to the point where Ouspensky dropped out of the fold of Gurdjieff.

It is difficult to be with a living message, because the message goes on moving in tune with existence. It does not bother about you. You have to keep yourself running with the message, you have to forget all about what was said in the past. The new, the latest, is always the right. And it does not mean that what has preceded it was not important. Without it this new phenomenon would not have been there at all.

In my thirty years' life of talking from my heart to people, thousands have come and gone. They still love me, but only up to the point when they departed. After that they say, "Something has gone wrong."

Just the other day I heard about Amitabh – one of my sannyasins, very much loved and respected by the commune. He just dropped sannyas a few months ago and he is telling people, "Bhagwan was right up to the moment I left. Now he has fallen from his enlightenment." Great idea! Nobody has ever heard that anybody can fall from enlightenment. Amitabh has all the credit for finding something new.

But it is absolutely idiotic – there is no way to fall from enlightenment. Once you have known, there is no way to become ignorant again. It is very difficult from ignorance to move towards wisdom. It is very difficult – but only difficult, not impossible. To come back down from wisdom to ignorance is impossible. It is just not the law of life.

People, thousands of people, have walked along with me, but they go only so far and stop. They were not coming along with me; they were really finding nourishment for their own rubbish, knowledge. The moment they found that I was saying something that went against their knowledge, their religion, their party line, their ideology, they stopped.

They departed.

If you ask them, they will say, "Yes, there was a time when Bhagwan was right. He is no longer right." But this is natural. Only a person who has immense capacity to change, to go on and on, can find the truth of life. And once you have found it there is no way to lose it, because you find it in the very innermost being of yourself. You *are* it! How can you drop it somewhere? How can you forget about it?

But the disciple who stops at a certain point certainly has to console himself, that "Up to this point Bhagwan was right. After that, he has gone wrong." He does not know that right is not a static thing, it is a growing phenomenon.

You are very comfortable with Jesus – and he was born a Jew, he lived as a Jew, he died as a Jew. He never heard the word "Christian." He was unaware even of the word "Christ," because the word "Christ" is Greek. He knew only one language,

Aramaic; he was not even acquainted with Hebrew. Aramaic was a local language of ordinary people; Hebrew was the language of the priests, of the high-class people. Aramaic is just a common form of Hebrew. In Hebrew and Aramaic there is no word like "Christ," the word is "messiah."

His own people, the Jews, could not accept Jesus as a messiah, because he was saying things that were disturbing them. His common way of talking was, "It has been told to you in the past, an eye for an eye. But I say unto you, if somebody slaps you on one cheek, give him the other cheek also." He was contradicting the old prophets. This was not acceptable to his people.

Jesus alive was crucified. Dead, he has the biggest following in the world. This is a miracle. When he was living, nobody wanted to be associated with him. Dead, even those who are not Christians, like Mahatma Gandhi, Hazrat Mohammed – one is a Hindu, another is a Mohammedan – are ready to accept him as a prophet. It is easier now. He has stopped; you can manage to go up to the stoppage.

With me you will find it difficult – until I die. And don't hope that I am going to die soon. I am going to disturb you as much as possible. If you can manage to live with a living message, and if you have the guts to go on changing with the living message, you are blessed. Many will come around me, but only a few will remain. Yes, after my death many more will come, and everybody will remain!

Your mind is somehow very stubborn about changing, because change brings difficulties. Change brings new things, and you have to begin again and again and again. But be courageous. If you are not courageous you are already dead. Just to go on breathing is not enough to be alive. I define life as a constant change, and the capacity to go with it wherever it leads you. If you have that courage, truth is not far away. Only the courage is missing.

You are asking me, that I have said that my old books are not important…. You want to divide me in two parts – my old books, and my present message to you – so that you can choose. I will not allow you such a convenient way.

My old books are immensely important. Unless you understand them, you will not be able to understand me. But remember, it is a constant flow and change, so don't be bothered with inconsistencies, contradictions.

If you go on, soon you will be able to find the truth. And once the truth is revealed, all contradictions and inconsistencies dissolve. Then you can see, crystal-clear, that it is a single message from the roots to the flower. It is a single organism.

Beloved Bhagwan,

A few months back You said, "If this is bad land use, then your land use laws are bogus, and they should be burned." Walden Kirsch, KGW Television Channel 8 News, has said, "The Oregon Supreme Court ruled this morning that Rajneeshpuram is indeed a legal city. This is extremely important to the people who created the city for their comfortable existence, and to practice their religion, Rajneeshism." What do you have to say about it?

I do not care what the Supreme Court decides. This is the only legal city in the whole world. There is no crime here, no rape, no theft, no murder. Even in the middle of the night any woman can go anywhere in the darkness without any fear. It is not a question – whether this city is legal or not.

I have known many cities. People are living there side by side, but they are not together. Those cities are just like a crowd, not a living organism.

This city is a totally new phenomenon. It is a living organism. People are not just a crowd here; they have chosen to be part, a living part of the whole. There are no families in this city, this whole city is a family! You cannot find this phenomenon anywhere else. Families are small units keeping themselves separate from other families, fighting with their neighbors – you know.

Jesus had two things to say: "Love your enemy as you love yourself." That is not great, many have said it, but the second thing is really great. He said, "Love your neighbor just as you love yourself." And that is very difficult to do. Have you ever heard of neighbors loving each other? Not only ordinary neighbors, but great leaders, religious masters – they too cannot stand the neighbor.

I have heard.... A rabbi and a Christian bishop lived in one neighborhood. Their houses were opposite each other, and they were continuously hating, being jealous, competing about everything.

The bishop purchased a Buick car; that almost caused a heart attack in the rabbi. In the morning the bishop was pouring water on the Buick. The rabbi could not contain himself. He asked, "What are you doing?"

The bishop said, "I am doing a baptism. The car is being transformed into a Christian car." This was more trouble. The rabbi could not sleep. Somehow he managed, and the next day purchased a Cadillac.

Now it was the turn of the bishop to get a heart attack.

And in the morning the rabbi started to cut the exhaust pipe with big garden scissors. The bishop could not believe what was going on. He said, "What is the matter? What are you doing?"

The rabbi said, "I am doing a circumcision – now the car is really Jewish."

This is the only place where you will find people from all over the world – different races, different colors, different languages – becoming one family. We don't have any neighbor, so we don't need Jesus' advice to love your neighbor – we don't have any.

But it is good that the Supreme Court proved itself, proved that there is still hope of democracy in America, that there is a possibility of some fairness. The Supreme Court's decision is very decisive and very historic in the sense that against all the bigots, against all the politicians, against all the pressures, they still remained true to the law. The decision must rejoice you, for the simple reason that it shows we are not in the Soviet Union.

America should think over this decision, and try to remain democratic whatsoever the consequences, because this is the only country that holds any hope for humanity.

Rajneeshpuram was legal – it would have remained legal even without the decision of the Supreme Court. We were going to fight to the very end, because it is not only a question of a small commune; it is a question of the very spirituality of this nation.

Politicians are nothing but pollution. As a democracy becomes purer and purer, more and more does the pressure of the politicians become insignificant. Democracy comes to its uttermost flowering when politicians disappear completely.

Our fight will continue, because those cunning politicians who were trying to destroy this city – just because we want to live in our own way, and we want to think in our own way, and we want not to be led by those idiots – they will go on trying other ways to harass you. But nobody can harass my people, because to harass somebody two parties are needed: one who harasses and one who becomes harassed. We are not going to become harassed. We have nothing to lose, nothing to fear – who fears dead people? Their cities are nothing but cemeteries, *legal* cemeteries!

I must thank the Supreme Court on behalf of all of you, that it has saved so many innocent people from getting utterly disappointed.

Now we can grow – because in my vision, I have always seen the commune consisting of at least 100,000 sannyasins. And it is going to happen! No evil politicians can stop it happening. We are going to make this place, which was just a desert, green, full of rejoicings, songs and dances. I want Rajneeshpuram to become the Garden of Eden.

You will see God one day – if there is any God –
knocking on your doors: "Please let me come in!"

Beloved Bhagwan,

What is beyond rebellion, beyond aloneness, beyond meditation?

You!
Next question.

Beloved Bhagwan,

What is a good sannyasin?

I have never come across one, because it is a contradiction. A good sannyasin – what do you mean? Can there be a bad sannyasin too? To be a sannyasin is to be goodness itself.

Okay.

Beloved Bhagwan,

If enlightenment means to be beyond all dualities, not choosing, then why are You against wars, politics and other stupidities of mankind?

Yes, enlightenment means choicelessness – but you are not enlightened yet. For me there is no choice. If the third world war comes, I will be just the same as I am. If the whole world is destroyed, it won't change anything in me – neither my bliss, nor my peace, nor my love.

But for you…. Because you are not enlightened, I have been talking against wars, against superstitions, against stupidities. I am not speaking to myself – do you think I am crazy? – I am talking to *you*. And for you there is at every step a choice. Till you come to the moment of enlightenment and choicelessness, you will have to choose; before that there is no other way.

It is just as a blind man carries a stick in his hand, groping for his way. But if his eyes are cured, will he still grope with the stick? He will throw the stick away.

Whatever I am saying to you is just giving you a stick till you are ready to open your eyes. Then, throw the stick. Then there is nothing good, nothing bad. Then whatever the enlightened person does is right. And there is no question of choice, because he can *see*. He does not choose.

Choice implies thinking. He does not think, he simply sees his way and moves on it.

My work is arduous. I have to speak from a point to you, who are almost on another planet; the distance is vast. Remove the distance. Of course I am not going to move close to you.

The thirsty goes to the well, not vice versa.

I am here, available. If you are thirsty, move closer to me. And soon you will know that light, that insight, that explosion of bliss in which there is no choice.

Enlightenment is choicelessness.

But don't misunderstand me. Before that, you will have to move very cautiously, choosing the right against the wrong, choosing the truer so that you can reach to the ultimate truth.

Doubt:
The Methodology
Of the Seeker

DISCOURSE 12,   July 10, 1985

Beloved Bhagwan,

I have heard Swami Prem Anam say about the discourses that they are boring, he does not get anything from them; that discourses are a waste of time, and he prefers workers' darshan.
Could You please comment?

Anam is a confirmed creep. But what he is saying has much truth in it – not because the discourses are boring, but because he is not here. Physically he is here, but his mind is roaming all over the place. Perhaps he may be hearing, but he is not listening to me.

These discourses are my heart. I am opening myself to you, revealing to you finally and exactly what I am. But there are people like Anam who are not interested in this revelation. Then the thing appears boring. But I am puzzled – if it is boring you, who is forcing you to be here? Are you sitting here to torture yourself? I am not at all interested whether you are here or not. If the discourses are boring, then you must be enjoying your boredom. And boredom is not in the discourses, because you are the only one who is bored.

Look at these people! Raise your hands, those who are not bored – both hands!

Anam, have you seen these hands? You are a bored person, utterly bored. You don't have the patience even to understand what I am saying. Are you British by chance?

I have heard that whenever a joke is told, the French understand it immediately. Their laughter is an immediate response. The British laugh twice: first, when they hear the joke – not that they have understood the joke, but just to be polite, not to offend you in any way. And the second time, in the middle of the night they laugh again: they have got it.

The Germans never laugh. And the Jews…if you tell a joke to a Jew, he will not laugh, he will say to you, "This joke is very old, and moreover you are telling it all wrong!" It is the same joke, but different people are reacting differently.

What I am saying is the same for all of you, but everybody is interpreting it in his own way. Most of you are rejoiced, your hearts are open to me. Your ears are not only hearing; behind your ears you are silently listening to me. How can you be bored? But Anam is bored. The whole credit goes to himself, I am not responsible for it. And why does he go on dragging himself here every day – to be bored? Perhaps he is some kind of masochist, he *wants* to be bored.

The question is significant, because I am the first

person in the whole history of human consciousness whose people are allowed to have a hearty laugh in the temple. Otherwise in temples, churches, *mandirs,* you go with a long face, looking very serious. This mandir does not belong to those traditional temples and churches and synagogues. This is a place of rejoicing, and if you are unable to rejoice, don't come. Do something else, don't waste your time.

You are saying your time is wasted, Anam. Your whole life is wasted. What have you done? Your whole life – just have a look backwards – has been a wastage. What flowers have blossomed in you? It is really your whole life, dry, dull, boring, which has made you incapable of enjoying. And if you are not coming here, how are you going to use your time so that it is not wasted? What are you going to do?

Here there is a chance that perhaps you may awake one day and start growing. Then the time will not be wasted. Of course, in your sleep you may have thought it was wasted, but when you wake up you will be grateful.

But don't come here. And remember always, I am a very unreliable man, as unreliable as nature, particularly here in Rajneeshpuram – the weather changes so quickly. If you feel bored, it is not unimaginable for me to just leave this podium forever. But remember, all these people will suffer because of you.

I said just the other day that I am not going to be silent, but that was the other day. If anybody is bored, I am not interested in boring anybody, I can just now stop speaking forever. But it looks very undemocratic to me, that just because of one idiot, my whole people around the world will miss my word.

So you have to decide, Anam. If you come here, get in tune with me, with what I am saying; otherwise, there is no need to come here. Our commune is a family of totally free individuals. You have decided on your own to be part of it. You can leave not only the Mandir you can leave the commune, and we will rejoice.

And you are saying you enjoyed in the past years

God is not to be discovered in a test-tube, God has to be searched for. Of course when you begin to search you will have to doubt thousands of things until you arrive at a point where your doubt disappears. Suddenly you are face to face with reality. You will be amazed: you will not find a God, and at the same time you cannot deny that you have found something, something which is even higher than God. I call it godliness.

the silent satsang with the sannyasins. I am amazed at people's stupidity. You cannot remain silent for two minutes! We had satsang on the sixth, and I got so fed up with your insensitivity that I have dropped it forever. In the future there will be no silent satsang in the morning…because we were playing music and then there would be a gap – just a little gap of two minutes. We would do the humming and then there would be a gap of two minutes.

Devaraj was quoting some words from my past expressions to remind you of what I am saying.

I have been sowing the seeds for a long time. You cannot see in the seed the flower. He was quoting the seeds to make it clear to you that those same seeds have come to a flowering, and they are going to flower more and more. After his quotation there was again two minutes' silence.

And what were you doing, Anam, in those silent periods? I saw people coughing all over the place. That coughing is absolutely psychological. Why are you not coughing now? I will speak for two hours and you will not cough a single time. And in those two minutes of silence, not one person, but everybody was coughing. Coughing has something to do with your psychology. One man coughs, and it is infectious, suddenly you realize that your throat is also ready.

While the music was there, you were engaged with the music. While you were humming, you were engaged in humming. The most difficult parts were those few moments of silence. Either you were coughing all over the place – suddenly the Mandir became Koran Grove – or you were laughing, which was disrespectful to the Mandir, to the commune. After music, after humming, an intelligent person will fall into a deeper silence; that is the purpose of that music. But no, you start laughing. The reason is, you cannot stand to be in silence for two minutes.

And now, Anam, you are asking for silent *satsang*. And I know you more than you know yourself. You may think yourself a wise guy, but you are simply crazy. You think you are a therapist – *you* need therapy.

And there may be a few other creeps who have crept into the commune. It is good if they get lost forever. A single rotten fish will spread its rottenness to other fish in the pond. And people in this commune are so close to each other, so intimate with each other, that anything contagious affects not only one person, it affects the whole commune.

That's why I don't call it an organization. It is not, it is an organism, just as your body is an organism, not an organization.

If your body were an organization, scientists would have been immensely happy, because then if you had a fracture in your leg, the whole leg could be unscrewed – you would just have to go to the workshop and they could screw on a new leg. If your head was going cuckoo, you could go the workshop and they could change it. But man is not a mechanism put together, man is an organism. Everything in man is connected with everything else; the whole body is functioning in tremendous harmony.

This commune is an organism.

I don't want any bored person here. You will be immensely benefited – become a Catholic priest, then your boredom will pay you. Here, you will just look out of place.

And I am not saying this only to Anam…. I had given you the name Anam – *anam* means anonymous, nameless – because when I gave you sannyas I could see in your eyes that you were not an organism functioning in beautiful silent harmony: you are a cuckoo. But I give sannyas to anybody – even to cuckoos, hoping against hope that perhaps just through your being near me a miracle may happen.

And when I am talking to you, do you understand the process of talking in deep love and intimacy? Perhaps you are not aware. You love a person – you want to touch the person, hug the person, kiss the person. Why do you do all these things? To get as close to the person as possible. I cannot hug millions of people. Before they have stopped hugging me, I will be dead. Kissing to me is unhygienic.

I can touch you only with my words. It is a touching experience, far superior to the ways you know of touching each other. A word is a bridge. If you allow yourself to become part of the communion, you cannot be bored; you will be in immense rejoicing, you will be blissful.

But nobody can force you to be blissful. Why get miserable sitting here? Do something that makes you happy. And I don't know what makes you happy. If my words cannot make you happy, then take it for granted that at least in this life you are not going to be happy.

It is a great art to be blissful.

One has to learn it.

Become more and more organic.

And when I am speaking, *I* am speaking; *you* are silent. The moment I stop speaking, you start yakety-yak, yakety-yak; your mind starts going round and round. You are not listening to me, Anam, that's why you feel bored. You are bored with yourself. In not listening to me, you are simply listening to your own mind, and you know your mind perfectly well. If you are listening to me, then your mind stops. Then who can be bored? And how?

I have heard about a man who was sitting in a chair in a waiting room on the railway station. Many other people were also waiting in the waiting room. They all became interested in this man, because what he was doing appeared very strange. Sometimes he would smile for no reason at all. Sometimes he would burst into laughter. Sometimes he would throw away something which was not there, but his hands, his face, expressed the idea that he wanted to get rid of something. He was saying, "No, no" – not in words, in gestures.

The whole waiting room fell into silence. What was this man doing? And he looked rich, well-dressed, educated. Finally one man got up to ask him, "What are you doing? – because we are getting more

and more curious. Now it is too much; and the train is late – we will have to watch you for at least two hours more. It is becoming mysterious."

The man said, "There is nothing mysterious. I was just telling jokes to myself. And whenever I came across an old joke, I threw it away – I have heard it so many times. When something really juicy comes into my mind, there is a smile. Sometimes just a smile is not enough, the joke is so wonderful that I burst out into laughter. But all this I am doing to myself. How are you concerned? You do your work."

Anam, if you are bored, you are doing it to yourself. Please stop doing it.

What I am saying to you is of the utmost importance, because it is a way of touching, but more subtle and sophisticated. A word comes out of my heart, travels to you, and if you are available, reaches exactly into your heart. Neither holding hands can do it, nor even kissing can do it – even French kissing! Not even making love can do it. Making love is a also a way of getting close, so close that you are in each other. But what a communion can do, even lovemaking cannot do.

Genitals meeting is not a great meeting. It is the lowest form of meeting – even buffaloes are doing it. Only man is capable, at the highest sophisticated level, of touching your very heart.

And if you cannot understand my words, forget forever the idea that you will be able to understand my silence. Even while I am speaking, it is there. I am not an orator, I am not a speaker. That's why, speaking a word, just in the middle of the sentence I will stop, will give a gap; in that gap I am trying to reach you through silence.

Don't just listen to my words, listen also to the gaps. And any orator will think that I am strange; this is not the way to speak. But I am not interested in speaking, I am trying to contact you in thousands of ways.

My talk is full of silence. If you sort it out, in two hours you will certainly find for half an hour I have

118

been silent. And it is a far deeper silence, because the word makes you listen to me, and then comes the silent period. In that silent period you are waiting for me to complete the sentence.

And this cannot be *done* — I never *do* a thing — it is a happening. I cannot speak in another way, because my purpose will be fulfilled only by words followed by wordlessness.

Anam, I love you as I love everybody. Just think of it — I go on throwing flowers on you, and you go on throwing mud on me? My own people saying to me that my talk is boring?

My talk is so full of silence. Listen to both, and it is easier. After a big storm there is a deep silence following it. This is the law of nature: day follows night, life is followed by death, word follows wordlessness. On both sides…. Then it is not a discourse, not oratory; it is a way of reaching you, touching you at the very innermost center of your being.

But if you are still bored, then just get up and get out, and get lost.

Beloved Bhagwan,

You say a skeptic cannot be a disciple, and on the other hand, that You never want us to stop doubting. Please explain the difference between skepticism and doubt.

There is a great difference between doubt and skepticism. Not only is there a difference, they are diametrically opposite to each other.

Skepticism is already a religion, a belief, a conclusion; it is a negative type of conclusion. The skeptic has no philosophy of his own to contribute; all he does is argue against anybody else's ideology. But don't ask about his ideology, he has none. He has become a big no, he has become negativity. He does not believe in anything — but this is also a belief.

For example, he does not believe in God. We call him an unbeliever, but it is not right to say that he does not believe in God; he believes that there is no God. It is a belief. Because it is negative you are confused. The theist believes in God; the skeptic does not believe in God, but he is not a seeker, he is not creative, he is not positive. He is not searching for the truth.

In ancient Greece there was a school, before Socrates, called the Sophists. They were skeptical people. They had nothing to offer, and they had everything, every argument, every weapon to destroy.

It is very easy to say no.

To say yes is very difficult.

You can say no to anything. If somebody says, "Look at the beautiful sunset," you can say, "I can see the sun is setting, but I don't see that there is anything beautiful. Prove to me what beauty is. How can you dare to call this sunset beautiful? Unless you define beauty, you cannot call anything beautiful."

And beauty has escaped definition. For thousands of years people have tried to define beauty, to define truth, to define love, but no effort has succeeded, for the simple reason that these things are experiences; you cannot explain them. But if you want to explain them *away* there is no difficulty.

The skeptic has already settled in his "no" attitude towards everything. The man is not different from any other believer; they have all settled. None of them is on the way to seek.

Now you can understand the difference and the diametrical opposition between doubt and skepticism. Doubt is not a conclusion, doubt is the beginning of a journey, a pilgrimage. The skeptic has arrived and found as an answer, no — to everything, everything that cannot be placed in front of him, on the table, so he can dissect it.

Karl Marx has said, "Unless I can see God in a test-tube, in a scientific lab, being dissected, I am not going to believe in him."

God is not to be discovered in a test-tube, God has to be searched for. Of course when you begin to search you will have to doubt thousands of things until you arrive at a point where your doubt disappears. Suddenly you are face to face with reality. You will be amazed: you will not find a God, and at the same time you cannot deny that you have found something, something which is even higher than God. I call it godliness.

Doubt is the methodology of the seeker. Doubt sharpens your intelligence. It is a challenge. You are neither saying yes, nor are you saying no. You are saying only one thing, "I am ignorant, and I am not going to trust unless I have experienced, whatsoever the case, unless I arrive at something which is indubitable – howsoever I make the effort to doubt it, my doubt goes on failing."

The reality is so vast, overwhelming, so tangible, so real, that even this so-called real world, compared to that reality, looks like a dream.

Doubt is something of tremendous significance. Only those who have doubted to the very end have found what truth is, what love is, what silence is, what beauty is. Skepticism finds nothing. It is utterly empty, but it makes much noise. Empty drums make much noise. And you cannot argue with a skeptic because he will go on saying no to anything, to any value which you cannot place as an object before him.

But doubt – of course, it is a long way and a hard way – goes on eliminating all that is not true. Ultimately only that which is true remains. And nobody can deny truth when one is facing it, experiencing it. Out of that experience comes yes: "Yes, Bhagwan, yes."

It is not a belief. You have searched, gone into great anxiety, anguish, despair. There were many moments when you wanted to stop, because it looked as if the journey was endless. It is not. There is an end; you just have to keep yourself going.

Doubt is surgical – it goes on cutting all that is absurd. But finally the real remains, unclouded. Doubt removes the clouds.

The skeptic says no to the sun because it is clouded; he cannot see the sun. He comes immediately to the conclusion that there is no sun, no light. The doubter removes all the clouds, cuts his way through the clouds. Not that he believes that there is something behind them – there may be nothing – but he has to know whatever is behind the clouds. And everybody who has gone far has ended with truth. It needs guts.

The skeptic is a poor man, just like the theists, just like all the so-called religious people in the world. Skepticism is a negative side, it is a negative religion. There is no difference between a skeptic and a believer; they both agree that there is no need for search. One believes there is a sun behind the clouds, another believes there is nothing behind the clouds. But nobody is ready to take the long journey, to pass through all kinds of nightmares, and to reach behind the clouds. Few have reached.

I teach you doubt, I don't teach you skepticism. And remember, doubt is not skepticism; it is search, it is seeking.

Before Socrates, this school of skeptical people was called Sophism. They were traveling teachers, wandering teachers. They used to take a big fee, much money, to make you a sophist. A sophist is one who can take any side, he does not care for truth. If you pay him good money, he will be on your side. Or, if the opposite side pays him big money, he will be on the opposite side. As far as he is concerned he knows nothing, but he knows the art of argumentation.

I have heard…. In a small church in a small town, the priest was very much disturbed by an old man. But the old man was the richest man in his congregation. He had donated much – in fact he had built the church. He was paying the salary of the priest, of course. He used to sit just in the front row in front of the priest, but he was old and always went to sleep. The sleep was not disturbing to the priest, but he snored – and really loud. The priest was disturbed because the old man was disturbing the whole congregation, and the congregation was disturbed because he was disturbing everybody's sleep!

Finally the congregation said to the priest, "Something has to be done. This old man disturbs you – just in front somebody snoring, and loudly. And this old man disturbs our sleep also."

People in Christian countries remain awake late on Saturday night because tomorrow is Sunday, they can rest. And early in the morning they have to go to church. Perhaps they have not slept the whole night – and church is the best place to sleep.

So they said, "We come early in the morning just to have a good nap, and this idiot wakes everybody. Rather than listening to your sermon, we listen to his snoring – so please do something!"

The priest thought. The old man used to come with one of his grandsons, a small boy; he used to sit by his side. The priest thought, "Perhaps the boy can be bribed."

He talked to the boy and he said, "I will give you one dollar every Sunday if you go on waking the old man. Just with your hand go on hitting him so he remains awake. The moment he snores you start hitting. I will give you one dollar."

The boy said, "Good. There is no problem, I will not let him sleep anymore."

And the next Sunday was beautiful. Everybody slept. The priest repeated the same sermon that he had been…he had three or four sermons ready. And the boy went on hitting the old man with his hand.

The old man said, "What nonsense! What are you doing continually?"

The boy laughed, but he did not allow the old man to sleep or snore.

Outside, the old man asked, "What is the matter? You disturbed my whole morning. You have to tell me."

The boy said, "It is a question of business. The priest has given me one dollar to keep you awake, because you snore."

The old man said, "Don't be worried; if it is business, I will give you two dollars. Just don't disturb me the coming Sunday."

The next Sunday came, and the priest was puzzled. He looked at the boy many times, blinked at the boy that the old man had started snoring, but the boy sat silently smiling. Nobody could sleep. Somehow the priest finished the sermon, took the boy aside and asked, "What happened? Don't you want the dollar?"

He said, "What can I do? It is a question of business."

The priest asked, "What business?"

He said, "The old man has promised to give me two dollars. Now it is up to you."

Of course the poor priest knew that he could not win in competition with that old man. If he gave three dollars – which was too much for a poor priest – the old man would give four. He was bound to lose completely by this strategy. The boy was not interested – he was not interested in the priest, he was not interested in the congregation, he was not interested in the old man. It was a sheer question of business.

That was the attitude of the sophists. Even kings used to send their sons, who were going to become kings of their country someday, to the sophists to learn the art, so that whatever the case is, you can always manage to win it. There is no question of right and wrong for a sophist; the question is whose argument is stronger.

But it happened…a young man came to a very famous sophist teacher. The young man was very rich, and the sophist teacher asked for an enormous amount of money. The young man said, "Don't be worried, whatever you ask I will give, but on one condition. Half of the money I will pay now and half of the money I will pay to you when I have been victorious in some argument with somebody. That will be the test of whether you have been really teaching me or just exploiting."

It was understandable, and the old sophist teacher knew that there was no problem. "You are going to win against anybody. I am the greatest sophist in the whole of Greece, don't be worried."

Half the money was paid. After two years the young man was perfectly trained in the art of argumentation; from any side he was able to win. If he chose to support theism he was able to win, if he wanted to support atheism he was able to win. He now had the knack of how to present a case and how to argue about it.

The teacher said, "Now your education is finished. Bring the other half of my money that you had promised."

The man said, "But I have not yet been a winner. You will have to wait, that was the condition." And the young man proved far smarter than the great sophist. He never argued with anybody. Whatever you said, he would say yes. But he would never enter into any argument, so the question of winning never arose.

One year passed, two years passed – but the old sophist was not going to be cheated in this way. This young man was trying to be really too much.

The old man filed a case in the court against the young man, that he had promised to give him half of the money when his education was over and he had not given it. The idea of the great teacher was really marvelous. He thought, "If the court decides, 'You will receive half the money only when he wins a case', I am defeated, the young man has won his first victory." So he planned that outside the court he would say, "Now you have won your first victory, give me half the money."

But he never got that money, he got defeated in the court.

He had thought of the other possibility: if he won the case – although there was no possibility, but he was a great arguer – if he won the case, then too, he would tell the young man, "You are going against the court's decision, you have to pay the money." But he had not thought about it – that the young man was his own student, and knew all his tactics.

The young man argued perfectly, and in fact the case was clearly stronger on his side: "Until I win my first argument, I will not pay the other half." The teacher was not interested in winning the case. He said, "It is certainly true that this was the condition." He accepted it before the court, hoping that out of the court he would say, "Now...."

He lost the case, the young man won the case, and after the court on the steps he took hold of the young man and said, "Boy, now you have won your argument, give me my money."

The young man said, "I am your student – you cannot deceive me. I cannot go against the court's decision; that would be contempt of court. And if you insist, come back inside the court and ask before the magistrate."

This sophistry has continued down the ages; it has taken many names – now it is called skepticism. The skeptic has no ideology, so you cannot defeat him.

He never proposes anything. If he never proposes anything, how can you defeat him? He has no belief system. He is in a far stronger position. You have a belief system; he can find loopholes in it and defeat you. The skeptic is bound to win against anybody who has a system of beliefs.

The skeptic gains nothing but only these futile argumentations and victories. And the more he becomes articulate in arguments, the more he is unaware that life is not to argue, life is not to say no, because no means death. And just wasting your life destroying other people's arguments, what are you going to gain?

You wasted your whole life.

I am not teaching you skepticism, I am teaching you the art of doubt.

Doubt does not say that it is not so.

The doubt simply says, "I am ignorant. I have not experienced it yet; hence, I will continue to doubt till I achieve the authentic, the real. Then I will be all yes – but not before that."

The man of doubt, only the man of doubt, some day becomes the man of truth.

If yes and no are complementary, and the smallest blade of grass is needed as much as the most distant star, what can You say about the negative resistance of the Oregonians to Your vision? How are we to understand it?

I welcome it. The antagonism of the Oregonians is our strength. Their antagonism is a blessing to us. They may be thinking otherwise, but they don't know how the law of life functions. The more they try to destroy us, the more indestructible this commune will be, because when you had to face opposition, for the first time you bring your intelligence to its highest peak. When you see that so much negativity is around you – you are just a small island and all around is the ocean of Oregonians – it gives you an opportunity to rise to the moment, to face it.

It is a well-known fact that even the greatest scientists use only fifteen percent of their intelligence. The average person uses only seven percent of his potential. What is the difference between the ordinary, average person and the scientists? Why does the scientist rise to fifteen percent? Because he has taken upon himself a challenge to find the truth about something.

He will be opposed by those dogmatic people who have already come to a conclusion. They will say, "There is no need for you to work on it. We know the answer, it is in *The Bible;* just read *The Bible.* One book is enough. It is the holy book; God has given everything that is needed to be known."

But people like Copernicus, Galileo, Columbus, go against *The Bible.*

The Bible says the earth is flat. It *looks* flat. Science has to rise above the average man's idea that whatever you see is right. In all the languages there are proverbs which say, "Don't believe in hearing, believe in seeing."

If you look around you, the earth is flat, because our vision through the eyes in not vast enough, and we are standing on the earth. There is no horizon; it is your limited capacity of vision. When you start losing your eyesight, the horizon comes closer to you; when you become blind, there is no horizon. When you are young, you see the beauty of the horizon. The horizon depends on your eyes, it has nothing to do with the earth.

The earth is vast, and man is so tiny and his eyes cannot see so far.

But the scientist tries to find whether there is some place where the earth and the sky meet. He doubts your knowledge of the past, he doubts your scriptures. He wants to know it for himself; only then can he be sure.

He goes on and on and on, and finds that the horizon is an illusion. There is no place where earth and heaven meet.

These scientists first started logically, rationally, to find out what kind of earth is possible, and they decided that it is a globe, not a flat piece of land. It was hypothetical. Columbus experimented on this hypothesis. He was thought to be a madman. But never be afraid – even a madman will find somebody more mad to help.

In thirty years, this has been my experience.

I am a madman, but I have never been without friends.

They are certainly madder than me.

The queen of Spain supported Columbus. She said, "What is the harm? I have enough money, he has enough argument. Let him have a chance, let him go for for a journey around the earth. If the earth is a globe, then finally he will come back to the same place from where he started." It is simple logic: if you move in a circle, you will come back to the same place.

"And if the earth is flat, we are not responsible; he is insisting. If the earth is flat, then his ship will finally fall down at the edge of the earth. That is his responsibility, if he goes to hell. For me, it will be just a little loss of money – that does not matter."

Then it was a question of finding at least ninety people – three ships were to go, because nobody was clear how long it would take to come back. So much food, clothes for every season, enough people to take these three big ships.

The queen said, "Don't be worried, money can purchase anything," and she purchased ninety people. They were all Christians; they thought that the earth was flat, but she was giving so much money that they thought, even if the ship fell into utter darkness, they would be leaving enough money for their family, at least for three generations – which they could not manage to earn being there. They could not even manage enough food, enough clothes, shelter. So ninety people were ready and they sailed off.

The horizon was there, but again and again it changed its place. Two months and twenty-seven days had passed, and there was the horizon still at the same distance. This proved perfectly that the horizon is an illusion. It is the limitation of our eyesight and our position standing on the earth. You can see the sun is round, you can see the moon is round because you are so far away that you can see the whole thing. But standing on the earth itself you cannot see the whole earth.

Columbus was immensely happy. But they had taken enough food for only three months. Those ninety people – they were not scientists, they had not come to prove anything; they were just there for money. With their *Bibles* they still believed that the earth was flat and that Columbus was mad. But they had got so much money, who cared whether he was mad or not?

But after two months and twenty-seven days, they became nervous. They were almost having nervous breakdowns: "What is going to happen now? Even if Columbus is right and *The Bible* is wrong and we are not going to fall off a flat earth, after three days the food will be finished. We will be dying, starving; and that looks far uglier than sudden death.

We will die gradually."

So they all gathered – when Columbus was going to sleep – on one ship in the night, and they thought that the only sane course now was, "We have tried to persuade Columbus to let us go back. He is not a man who goes back, he goes only forward. Now we have come to the dangerous point – in three days the food will be finished. So the only way is, to throw Columbus into the ocean, get rid of him. Let him swim and find out the truth – why should we lose our lives? – and we will go back."

Columbus, seeing that all ninety people had gathered on one ship – he was just going to sleep, but he was not asleep – he also went there. Hiding, he listened to their decision that he was going to be thrown into the ocean tomorrow. These fools *would* do it, and he was almost helpless – a single man against ninety people. He came out of hiding, went into the meeting – they were very shocked.

He said, "There is no need to be shocked. Your decision is perfectly practical. I just want to make a suggestion. It took us two months and twenty-seven days to reach this place. Do you think in three days you will be back home?" Even those fools could understand; the logic was simple. "You cannot go back in three days. But there is a possibility that in three days we may reach India if we go on and on" – because that was the idea. One route was open to India; going around Africa and reaching India – that route was open. They had been been moving in the opposite direction.

But they thought, "If we cannot reach Spain, at least we will reach India." That was the last known place; between Spain and India was the whole known world. Columbus' argument was so solid that they decided to go on.

That's how you are going on with me.

You cannot go back!

We have already broken the bridge. The day you took sannyas, the bridge collapsed. Now you can only go forward.

And I say to you, just as Columbus reached America in three days…. He could not reach India. America was not in his mind; it was unknown, a new land, but he thought he had reached India. That's why the aboriginal Americans are called Red Indians. It was Columbus who called them Indians.

In three days' time they saw green leaves floating in the ocean, birds flying in the sky. And he said to his men, "Now don't be afraid. You can see the birds; trees are not very far, you can see the leaves floating in the ocean. The land is not so far, we will reach it in three days. Or even if we have to fast for a few days, we are going to reach." And strange, within three days they landed.

The scientist is not skeptical; he has doubts about the outside world. The truly religious person doubts about the inside world. Both arrive. The point is that you should go on and on till you arrive, because you may stop just one step before.

Columbus gave them a challenge: "In three days you cannot return. I will allow you, you can go; I will swim, you need not throw me. I will jump into the ocean myself, I will try to reach without you – but remember, all you ninety are going to die, and a cowardly death. Be a little brave, face the situation; come along with me. The earth is round. We have seen in these past days that there is no horizon – we are bound to reach land."

This was a great challenge to their manliness, to their guts, and they agreed with Columbus; otherwise there would have been no America. It was Columbus who doubted *The Bible*. It was Galileo who doubted *The Bible*.

We are surrounded by fanatical Christians. In America, Oregon is perhaps one of the most backward, fanatical, unprogressive states. I have chosen it knowingly, because here is the challenge. And you need a challenge so that you can become sharp – and you can see it happening.

We have in our commune the most intelligent group possible. Just in the law department of the commune there are four hundred sannyasins. There is no firm anywhere in the world which has four hundred legal experts. And there is nothing to lose, we have everything to gain; just remain courageous. And in four years' time they have not been able to make a dent. A small commune has already taken two cities of Oregon. Wait, more cities will be following! Feel strong – you are, just you have to remember it. And their opposition goes on hitting you, helping you to remember.

And because we are fighting for truth, there may be some small battles in which we are defeated, but the ultimate victory is ours – and it is the ultimate victory that counts. Even the greatest warriors have lost a few small battles. That does not matter. The decision, the judgment of the Supreme Court yesterday, is a victory; it is not a small thing.

The whole of Oregon, except for a few intelligent people, is against this commune – for no reason at all. We have not harmed them, we don't intend to harm anybody. We are so absorbed in ourselves, we don't care whether Oregon is there or has disappeared!

The Supreme Court must have been under great pressure, but they proved that truth cannot be defeated by any pressure – political lies, religious fanaticism, just the animal heritage of being afraid of the new, of the unknown. But the judges could see through all this.

There is a group in Oregon, "One Thousand Friends of Oregon" – they were fighting against us.

Now, if they have any dignity they should start calling themselves "One Thousand Enemies of Oregon."

The Supreme Court and its judges have to be appreciated. They put aside their Christianity, they put aside the fact that they are Oregonians, they put aside all kinds of rumors and gossip against us, and they tried to see the truth. And it was not a single judge – it was the whole Supreme Court panel. And the decision was not from one man, it was a unanimous decision of the whole Court.

Truth may take a little time for its recognition, but finally it *has* to be recognized, for the simple reason that it is true.

Now, can you believe…. A city exists here, thousands of people are living here – and for many years it had been a wasteland. And it is not a small piece of property, it is one hundred and twenty-six square miles. It is three times bigger than New York, two times bigger than San Francisco. And this is the only city that has supporters all over the world; otherwise, cities don't have supporters. It has millions of supporters, sympathizers, lovers.

In Oregon itself there are thousands of Oregonians who have every sympathy for you and your commune. But they are afraid of their neighbors, their community. We receive hundred of letters of support, but they don't want their names to be made public. So it is not that the whole of Oregon is against you, it is only the mob – which has no intelligence.

Let them be against us. Their being in opposition is going to help us in every possible way. It is not only going to help us, it is going to help democratic values. Our presence here is going to transform the state of Oregon – because truth is a wildfire. Once recognized, it is going to burn all opposition. And it is not only Oregon that I am interested in – it is too small for my interest – we have to awaken the whole of America, so that democracy is not just a word but becomes a reality.

The last words of George Gurdjieff were very strange, inconceivable, but they were addressed to you. Dying, he opened his eyes and said, "Bravo, America!" Nobody was expecting it. They were thinking he would give some spiritual guidance departing from the world. And look at him – he says,

"Bravo, America"! But he was not addressing them, he was addressing you, he was addressing me. He was able to have a vision; he was one of the enlightened masters of this century.

America is certainly the very hope for the whole world, but not the way it is now. Its hypocrisy has to be exposed, and it has to be made aware: you are not fighting against Soviet Russia, you are fighting against fascism, nazism, all the anti-democratic values. You are fighting for individual freedom. Your fight is not just a war against the Soviet Union, your fight is far more valuable.

We are fighting for the New Man to be born, and the New Man can be born only in the new world.

America is the latest discovery of humanity; that's why it is called the New World.

Old countries have traditions, conventions; their past is heavy. it is very difficult for them to get rid of it. America has no past – three hundred years is not much of a past. India has been there, according to Hindu scholars, for ninety thousand years. India can say she has a past – ninety thousand years! It is very difficult in India to make a man free from the programming that has been going on for ninety thousand years. It is easier in America to deprogram people because they don't have much – only three hundred years.

We have to deprogram America from dirty politics, from fanatic religions, from all kinds of hypocrisy.

It is not a coincidence that suddenly we have landed here. In nature, in existence, nothing happens accidentally. We have to do something really great for humanity's sake.

Gurdjieff was right: Bravo, America!

Sympathy
Is a Dirty Word

DISCOURSE 13,   July 11, 1985

Beloved Bhagwan,

Yesterday, the whole day I saw many sannyasins give sympathy to Swami Prem Anam after Your discourse. Could You please comment?

Sympathy is not compassion; it is just the opposite. Sympathy is a kind of exploitation of the other person. When you sympathize with somebody, you are higher, better, and the other is lower, falling, degraded. Your ego gets immense satisfaction out of sympathy. But this is how the unconscious mind functions. You don't know exactly what you are doing.

These sannyasins who sympathized with Anam must have been the same people who had raised their hands here against him. Now, this is strange. You raise your hands against him, and then you start feeling a little guilty. When you see him, you want to compensate for the guilt, so you hug him. And it is an enjoyable moment for you, because the other is in need of your sympathy. You are the giver, the other is the beggar.

If a few of you did it to Anam, it was ugly, inhuman, against the dignity of an individual. You should have given him your compassion. In the dictionaries they mean the same, but not in actual life.

Compassion means making the other aware that he is going astray, that what he has done is not good. You are not putting him down, you are trying to raise him up. You are not saying, "You are alright as you are," you are making it clear: "Something is wrong in your attitude, and being your friend, being part of the commune, it is our duty to draw your attention to it, so that you can drop that attitude."

Nobody is right or wrong, only attitudes. And attitudes can be dropped, changed. If you were really compassionate you would have made it *more* clear to him again and again, all over the commune, wherever he went. It should have been emphasized, "Your attitude is wrong, and you are capable of dropping the attitude. We are in total support of you, we love you, that's why we want you to drop the attitude."

Why did I waste my time on Anam? Do you think I was criticizing him? Do you think I was saying anything against him? Then you have missed the point. I love the person, but he can be even more lovable. I love the person, that's why I pointed out to him that his attitude will hinder his growth. Yes, it looks a little hard. But only love can be hard, because only love can change you.

Your sympathy was phony, because here you were raising your hands, and with those same hands you were hugging Anam. Either your raising the hands was phony, or hugging Anam was phony. You should not have double faces, that here you show one mask before me, and when you meet Anam you show another mask. Stop this stupid game, because in this game you are the loser, a person who is not integrated, who is not *one*.

127

Circumstances may change, but an integrated person remains centered. You can kill him, but you cannot make him a hypocrite. Anam gave a good chance to you. I knew it when you were raising your hands – I knew how many hands were going to hug Anam. Don't try to be so split. If you don't want to raise your hands against him, don't; raise them against me – but be true to yourself. If you are really in favor of Anam, then there is no need to be in favor of me. If you are in favor of Anam, then you should stand with him. That is the integrated person and his fragrance.

Remember, whomsoever I love I am going to be hard with. I love you all – any day the hammer can fall on your heads. And I want others to remember to remind you, "Bhagwan loved you so much; otherwise why should he bother about you? He loved you, that's why he picked up a wrong attitude in you – to purify you, to make you more in tune with the commune, with the way of life that we are living here." You will not start doing something that goes against me, my love.

The master is hardest on the best disciple – who cares about the third-rate? I am reminded of a beautiful true story. In India, just in this century, there was a world-famous painter, Nandalal Bose. He learned painting from his teacher who was world-famous. The teacher was none other than the father of Rabindranath Tagore, who won the Nobel prize for his poetry.

One day Nandalal painted a beautiful picture of Krishna playing on the flute. Whatever may be wrong in Krishna, one thing has to be appreciated – that he has chosen the flute as his symbol, rather than the cross. The flute reminds you of love, life, songs. The flute reminds you of the beauties and the wonders and the mysteries of life. It is a very life-oriented symbol. The cross is a death-oriented symbol.

Hence, around Krishna there is always dance; he is playing on the flute, and his female lovers are dancing around him. Many things are wrong in Krishna's

You come to me just like a rock, with no face of your own, with no being of your own, with no centering, no grounding, no integrity, no individuality. I have to cut much; perhaps the major part that is hanging around you has to be cut. It hurts, because you have been under the illusion that it is you. But when you come to see – if you go on hanging around me – one day, when all that is not part of you is eliminated and your reality is revealed to you and to others too, you will feel grateful.

philosophy, but I cannot say that his celebration is wrong, that his dance is wrong, that his flute is not the right symbol.

Have you ever heard of apostles dancing around Jesus, and Jesus playing the flute? That is inconceivable. His whole attitude is death-oriented. Just the other day I said to you that his own disciple – who was the most intelligent amongst all of his disciples, perhaps more intelligent than Jesus himself…. When he saw that Jesus was bent upon dying, Judas went ahead of him, just like a Jew: "He is going to die, he cannot be prevented; crucifixion seems to be his goal – why not do some business in between?" For thirty silver pieces Judas sold Jesus to the enemies.

It is just Jewish – nothing was wrong with Judas. He was an intelligent man, he used the opportunity. In other circumstances, can you sell a dead human body for thirty silver pieces? And thirty silver pieces two thousand years ago was a great amount of money. Red Indians sold New York for exactly thirty silver pieces to the foreigners who had invaded it. It was a good price. But Judas loved Jesus. Don't be surprised – he loved Jesus, he tried to prevent him, but when he saw the impossibility, just like a good Jew, he earned some money.

But when Jesus was crucified, Judas could not forgive himself. Then repentance overcame him and he started feeling guilty. And do you know, within twenty-four hours he committed suicide. Judas is condemned all over the world by the Christians. Nobody looks into that man's suicide – why did he commit suicide? He loved Jesus so much, he wanted him to turn back, not to move towards Jerusalem where nothing but the cross was waiting for him.

Jesus did not listen to Judas, and Judas started feeling bad – he should have made more effort, he should have persuaded him. If it was needed, he should even have dragged him away from the cross. On the contrary, he simply proved a Jew, he made a business of it: he sold his own master. The guilt was so much that he committed suicide. The suicide was just to compensate for what he had done.

Nandalal Bose made a beautiful picture of Krishna playing on his flute, beautiful girls dancing around him. When he came to show it to his master – Rabindranath was present there – the master looked at the painting and said, "Nandalal, this kind of third-class painting is not expected from you." He threw the painting out of the house, and said to Nandalal, "In Bengal, on the birthday ceremony of Krishna, thousands of people paint Krishna's picture. They are sold very cheap."

In Bengal there are many painters who paint only Krishna. They are called *patias,* because on a plate – *patia* and "plate" you can understand are the same – on a plate of wood, either they carve or they paint. But those patias, those painters, remain anonymous; nobody comes to know about them. They are not thought to be great painters. Just by the side of the road in Calcutta you can find them, selling pictures, paintings, carvings, for almost nothing. They are poor.

The master said to Nandalal, "Listen, your painting is not even equal to the paintings of the patias. Go to the patias and learn how to paint Krishna." This was so hard. Nandalal touched the feet of the master and disappeared. For three years he was moving from one patia to another patia learning the art, how to paint.

Rabindranath could not tolerate this. He said to his father, "If you want to know the truth, the truth is that his painting is better than the paintings that you have made of Krishna. And your behavior is just insane!"

The master laughed, and he said, "Rabindranath, I have to be very hard on Nandalal. He is my best disciple, and he has much more capacity. Yes, I know you are right – his painting is far better than my own paintings, but he has yet much potential. If I had praised his painting, that potential would have remained just a potential. I want to bring him to his utmost flowering." And there were tears in the eyes of the master; he said, "The job of a master is not easy, and it is not easy even to understand."

After three years Nandalal appeared with a new painting of Krishna. The master was thrilled. He said, "Now I can say to you, your first painting was also great, better than my paintings – but this is superb! Now nobody can transcend this painting. Now I am contented. You had potential, but a challenge had to be given to you."

Man's potential blossoms only when there are challenges.

I said a few things about Anam. I know he has great potential, and he is wasting his potential in stupid things. And you sympathized with him! Do you want him to remain the same as he is? It is not compassion that you gave him. You were not friends while you were hugging him, you were enemies. You should have told him, "You have behaved wrongly – this is not the way to communicate with a master. You are not making bridges with the master, you are making walls. We have great love for you, but no sympathy for your attitude."

And if he had heard, from thousands of sannyasins, the same thing – do you think something was not going to happen to him? I hit him hard, and you hugged him hard and destroyed my whole effort. Receiving your sympathy, he must have felt great, that everybody is favorable to him. You have supported his wrong attitude, not him. I was working on him, destroying his attitude; you did just the opposite.

Growth is not child's play, it is a very conscious effort. And you all have to be supportive to the person's innermost being, but never support any wrong attitude. Supporting the wrong attitude you are poisoning him, and enjoying your ego. It is a double-edged sword: you are killing him and you are killing yourself too.

You have to learn very clearly that if you support any wrong attitude, sympathize with it, that means you are also carrying something alike in you. Secondly, you are exploiting the man's situation, and becoming holier-than-thou. Thirdly, you are pumping more air into the balloon of your ego. You are destroying both yourself and the other person.

I am also very destructive, but my destruction is devoted to creation. I am going to destroy so many things in you that unless you are courageous enough, alert, aware of the fact that my destruction is of all that which is wrong in you…. I am doing exactly what a sculptor does.

Michelangelo can perhaps be said to be one of the best sculptors of the whole history. He has made statues of Jesus so beautiful, so alive…even Jesus was not so alive nor so beautiful. The case is otherwise; there are ancient scriptures describing Jesus as an ugly man. Perhaps it may be an exaggeration by his enemies, but there must be some truth in it. At the best, he was just homely.

But Michelangelo has created such beautiful statues…. One of his statues of Jesus a few years ago was destroyed by an atheist. It was in St. Peter's Cathedral in the Vatican. Nobody had ever thought that it had to be guarded! It was available for everybody to see. Just to be close to that statue was an experience – but one atheist destroyed it.

He was caught. Because he had destroyed one of the most beautiful things that man has created, he was asked, "Why have you destroyed it?"

He said, "I am against God, I am against Jesus, I am against religion. That statue, although just a piece of marble, was creating in many people something which can only be called religiousness."

And do you know how Michelangelo found that piece of marble, that big rock? It was lying in front of a shop which had sold marble for years. Nobody had asked for it. Just to create a space in his shop, the shopkeeper moved the rock to the other side of the road, and it was lying there.

One day Michelangelo, passing along that road, saw the rock. He enquired of the shopkeeper, "To whom does it belong?"

The shopkeeper said, "Do you want it?"

Michelangelo said, "Yes, absolutely."

He said, "Take it – without any charge. I want to get rid of it." And out of that ugly marble rock, which no artist had even looked at…and it was given to Michelangelo free, so some space would be created for other rocks. It was a big rock, and out of that rock Michelangelo created this statue, which was destroyed three or four years ago.

When the statue was completed, he asked the shopkeeper to come and see. The shopkeeper could not believe his eyes. He said, "You are a magician. What have you made out of that rock?"

The answer of Michelangelo is worth remembering. He said, "I have not created Jesus out of that rock. He was already there; I have only taken away unnecessary parts that were hiding him. Only the unnecessary has been removed, and the real which was lying within is now available to you. I have not created the rock, I have only destroyed those parts which were hindering the reality of the rock from your vision."

That's my work. You come to me just like a rock, with no face of your own, with no being of your own, with no centering, no grounding, no integrity, no individuality. I have to cut much; perhaps the major part that is hanging around you has to be cut.

It hurts, because you have been under the illusion that it is you. But when you come to see – if you go on hanging around me – one day, when all that is not part of you is eliminated and your reality is revealed to you and to others too, you will feel grateful. And then you will understand why I hit so hard.

I am chiseling, hammering all that is ugly in you, all that has been given to you by your society, by your culture, by your civilization. I want to discover in you your original face.

So whenever I hammer on somebody, nobody is to show sympathy. Be a little more compassionate. Sympathy is a dirty word; be a little more compassionate. Help the man to understand that whatever I have said is creative, is to bring out his nature, his purity. And if you all go on making the man aware, there is a possibility that he will start thinking, "If so many people are saying it, there must be something in it."

But your sympathy destroyed…you washed out all that I had done. So when you see Anam again, take your sympathy back and tell him clearly, "That sympathy was bogus, unconscious, and what has been said is not against you" – what purpose have I to be against anybody? – "it was for your growth. We were wrong to sympathize with you. Our sympathy will strengthen your attitude, because you will think if so many people are with you, you must be right." So change it. Make it clear to him, "We were wrong to sympathize, and you were wrong in your attitude."

I was working for years individually, but then I thought, how many people can I reach? – and I was continuously traveling up to 1970. So I could go on saying things, but it was not going to bring a transformation in people.

I had to create a commune, where whatever I say is not just lost, but is echoed from everybody else too, from all sides and dimensions. And the person finds himself thinking, "So many people, friends, lovers, cannot be wrong."

You have to help me in creating the New Man.

Beloved Bhagwan,

Whatever the question, Your answer seems to be the same. How long will this go on before we understand?

As long as you wish. As far as I am concerned, this very moment it can happen. It is not a question of time, it is a question of intense understanding.

It is true: whatever the question, my answer is the same, because there are not many questions, they are just phrased in different ways.

But the question also is one: you don't know who you are. You are absolutely in darkness – unaware of your glory, your divinity, your beauty, your truth. All the questions differ only in phrasing. Naturally, I have to phrase my answers also according to your question.

Somebody has counted through my books and found that I have answered ten thousand questions. My answer is one. I have not answered ten thousand questions, and I have not given you ten thousand answers. Your question is one, but you have asked it in ten thousand ways. My answer is one; just not to spoil the game I have answered you in ten thousand ways, hoping that perhaps, sometime, in a certain moment of silence, in a certain way, you may catch hold of the one answer.

How long you are going to miss, that depends on you. You have to receive it. I cannot give it to you, you have to take it.

Gurdjieff's disciples were very puzzled about his statements. One of his statements which has been puzzling his disciples – there are still a few disciples of Gurdjieff in the world – was, "Unless you are capable of stealing the truth from the master, you will never get it."

There is nothing puzzling about it. I am saying "You have to take it" just not to puzzle you. In fact, you have to steal it. It is just in front of you. The doors are open, nobody is guarding it, but you are keeping your eyes closed. It all depends on you. Open your eyes and see the light. Turn your back towards darkness, turn your face towards light. But you are standing just in the opposite way: facing a darkness that centuries have made denser and denser, darker and darker.

If you go on looking at this darkness of millions of years, you are bound to think you are blind. And what is the point of opening your eyes, even if you are not blind? It is better to keep your eyes closed and dream of some beautiful things.

What is the point of looking into the abysmal darkness? – and that is what your Christianity is, your Hinduism is, your Mohammedanism is.

All the cultures and all the civilizations have been created to destroy the individual in you, and to create phony personality in you, and make you so much attached to the phony personality that you start thinking, "This is my individuality."

I have to hammer hard on your personality. It is going to hurt, but there is no other way. If you want not to be hammered, drop the personality yourself. Who is Anam? – just a personality. Who are you? – whatever people have said about you.

Women are known all over the world for continually looking in the mirror. The more idiotic of them carry a mirror in their bag too. What do they go on seeing in a mirror? The mirror cannot reflect your individuality – for that you need a master.

The mirror can only reflect your personality; it cannot reflect your being, your center, but only your circumference.

And women go on looking again and again. Once is enough – but how to be certain? Somewhere deep down you know perfectly well that that which is mirrored is not you, but you want to be convinced that it is you. And you go on decorating your personality – your hairdo, your lipstick. It is very strange.

To have red lips out of health is totally different to just painting them with lipstick. Who are you going to deceive? You cannot deceive even yourself. And this is not only true of children and young people; I see old women, who should have been in their graves by now, still painting their lips, putting on false eyelashes.

Your personality is your creation. The society gives you all the incentives to create it, because phony people can be enslaved. Phony people can be Americans, Indians, Arabians, Chinese. Phony people will go to the church, to the mosque, to the synagogue.

The real individual finds his synagogue, his mosque, his temple, inside himself. He need not go anywhere. Whenever he wants to have a taste of that indefinable phenomenon, he just goes in. And just to be there is enough religion. More than that is not needed.

There is your silence, there is your peace.

There is your blessing, there is your ecstasy.

There is your love – the whole treasure, the whole kingdom of God.

Hammering on your personality, I am trying to turn your attention from the personality towards the individuality. So please remember, whenever I hit somebody's head, you are not to sympathize; you are not to put ointment on his head. And the person who gets the hit should feel grateful that he has been chosen, that he has been thought worthy, that he deserved a hit from the master. So whatever you have done with Anam, you have to undo. Anam has to be brought to his real, beautiful being.

And I had to create a commune, because alone, how many people can I hit? And their skulls are so thick that small hits once in a while don't matter. Here, you are thousands of sannyasins. Whatever I am doing, you all have to take part in it, you all have to help me.

I would like you to be completely free from personality, because that means you are free from religion, you are free from culture, you are free from civilization, you are free from nationality, you are free from other kinds of ideologies. They are all part of your personality. Your individuality is just pure ecstasy.

So this should never happen again. And those who have hugged Anam should say to him, "Give it back – and we are sorry that we did something wrong to you. We love you, but we cannot love your stupidity, we cannot love your insanity."

Then only will the commune become a real organism, functioning in tune. Then only can there be a strange and new music, an unknown fragrance surrounding you and this holy land. This land is the same everywhere. It is the people who live on the land, who by their living meditatively, joyously, lovingly, consciously, not only transform themselves, they

transform the whole atmosphere.

Jerusalem is not the holy land; perhaps once it was. Mecca and Medina are no longer holy lands; perhaps once they were. Bodh Gaya is no longer a holy land. It was once, but twenty-five centuries have passed since Buddha meditated, lived with his disciples in Bodh Gaya; it was a holy land.

If you remove the barrier of the personality, holiness suddenly explodes.

Beloved Bhagwan,

Something is happening in my heart. It pounds when You are near. It is happening to many of us.
What is happening?

This is the happening for which I am here, you are here. It has no name. Call it just "happening." It is immensely beautiful. When your heart starts pounding, that means your heart is close to my heart.

It is a sign to you that the mind is left far behind, that you are no longer thinking but feeling, that you are no longer doing anything; it is *happening*. In the beginning you may get scared because it is so new. You may think something is going wrong – why is my heart pounding? – but only in the beginning. Just allow it, don't try to stop it. Enjoy it, rejoice in it. This is communion, heart to heart.

There comes a moment when your heart pounds, beats in exactly the same rhythm, in the same frequency as my heart. Immediately there is a meeting. And that meeting brings transformation.

The master cannot do anything. He can only create certain devices in which the happening becomes possible. This commune is a device; otherwise there was no need for it. You were living somewhere, everybody was doing something. To take you out of your houses, your families, your cities – what is the purpose? The purpose is that if so many hearts start beating in the same rhythm and frequency, others whose hearts are not beating but whose heads are circling may catch the fire. It simply jumps like wildfire from one tree to another tree.

I know a few people are in tune with me. That makes it easier for others to be tuned in with me. All these hearts together become a tremendous force. If five thousand people can be in one rhythm, in one frequency, they may create such great energy that it will start spreading around the world.

That's why I have created communes in so many countries. I want all those communes to be exactly like this place, because I will not be there.

The governments are making it impossible for me to go anywhere.

In India it was happening, just a very strange thing: in Poona the people were exploiting my sannyasins. For those seven years I was there, prices of everything had gone up ten times – only in Poona! A house that was available for twenty thousand dollars was not available even for one hundred thousand dollars. And seven thousand sannyasins were almost always there, and at moments there were ten thousand, fifteen thousand. All the hotels were full, overfull. People were renting houses, giving enormous amounts of money. They were becoming paying guests, giving enormous amounts of money.

So on the one hand the Hindu chauvinist mind was against me, because whatever I am doing goes absolutely against any kind of chauvinistic attitude – Hindu, Mohammedan or Christian – and on the other hand they were very happy that I was there. They were pressurizing the government of the state that I should not be given any land in the state; I should be living in Poona. Poona knew if I moved to some other place, all the beauty, the joy, the money – particularly the money – would disappear.

The Maharashtra government was preventing my moving from Poona. They found a way to prevent me. They would not say – politicians are cunning, they would not say, "You cannot go out of Poona"; that is against freedom. They continued to say, "You can find a place and you can go there," but in that place they would create trouble so that people in that place would start being aggressive and protesting that I should not be allowed to be given any land close to them.

The Maharashtra government was enjoying, and greatly, because they have never seen so many tourists coming to Bombay airport. Now my secretary has just been there; you cannot find any tourists. And poor countries like India have much investment in tourism. So the Maharashtra government was forcing the central government, saying, "You should not give any place to Bhagwan, because Maharashtra does not want to lose its tourism."

The central government was being wishy-washy, always saying "We are giving you this land and that land." It went on for seven years continually. They would not allow us to purchase more houses in Poona either, because they were afraid that if thousands of people who belong to me started living in Poona, they would take it over. And certainly, it would have happened.

Even the Poona ashram was not in the name of the Foundation. We paid prices ten times more than anybody else, yet the government did not put those houses in our name. It was a very strange situation: we were paying the taxes, we were paying the electricity bills – and the houses were not in our name! We had given the money to the previous owners, but the houses remained in the name of those owners.

They were afraid that if a great commune happened, Poona's whole character, its whole atmosphere, would change. And they were afraid of that. Poona is a very Hindu-minded city. It is a strange coincidence that the man who killed Mahatma Gandhi was from Poona, and the man who attempted to kill me was also from Poona. This is strange, because both these people belonged to the same political party. I have always been against Gandhism, but the political party that killed Gandhi…the same people tried to kill me. I am not a Gandhian, I am absolutely and totally against Gandhi and his ideology.

But the moment the knife was thrown at me, I could see the hesitancy in the minds of Poona people. On the one hand they wanted to exploit all these people; on the other hand they were afraid these people would destroy their so-called culture – which is already dead. There is nothing to destroy; the dead culture just has to be dragged to the crematorium.

The man who threw the knife must have been of the same dual mind. The whole of Poona was of the same dual mind: they could neither allow me to move out, nor could they allow me to grow vast. He threw the knife, and the knife fell nearabout twelve feet away from me. I was surprised! One can miss the target, but not by twelve feet.

It shows something in the psychology of the man. He represented the whole Poona-Hindu mind. He wanted to kill me, and yet he wanted me to remain there. So he did both things together: to satisfy himself and the Poona people he threw the knife, but it fell twelve feet away from me.

I cannot go to another country, they have taken precautions. In Germany, they have put a lawsuit against me – I have never been in Germany! They have filed a case in the court to prevent my coming; if I go to Germany I will be arrested, and I will not be able to leave Germany till the litigation is over.

It is natural: the creation of a new milieu for growing individuals is bound to be opposed by everybody in the world. But there is nothing to be worried about. In fact, their opposition keeps us growing stronger and stronger. But they don't know that. They are not intelligent enough to know either.

Politicians are always mediocre, because to be in politics you don't need any qualifications except that you can be cunning, a hypocrite, expert in lying. And these things are not taught in any university, you don't get any degrees in them. Politics is the only job where no qualification is needed. In fact, an intelligent person will not degrade himself by getting into politics. He can do far more and better things; why

should he be sitting foolishly in a parliament, arguing about trivia?

For months, what do these people in the parliaments and the assemblies go on doing? It is just a kind of insane chattering club. About small things they go on arguing. The whole world is on fire, and they go on talking about land use laws. The attorney general of Oregon, the governor or Oregon, the "One Thousand Enemies of Oregon" – they are trying to prove that if Rajneeshpuram becomes a legal city it will go against land use laws. Can you think…are these people sane?

This land has not been used for many decades: no use is perfectly good use! We have made this land productive, and we are going to make it more and more productive; this is misuse, it is against land use laws. The Oregon Supreme Court has proved to be saner.

Anybody can see a simple thing, that we have made a wasteland a beautiful oasis; they should be grateful to us. But the fear is that if this commune becomes a great power, it is going to create a wildfire all around. And they cannot ignore us.

Nobody can ignore us.

But before they woke up to the fact, we had already made the commune, the city was incorporated. Now there is no way of going back. And my people are always going forward. We are going to make this place – for the first time – a real holy land.

Beloved Bhagwan,

Do You make decisions? Or do things just happen around You? Can You give some examples?

I have never done anything in my life. Even my shoes…Vivek puts them on my feet. You can't conceive of a more lazy man than me. You must be thinking, why do I cross one leg over the other and never change it? It is sheer laziness, it is not some yoga posture. I don't even put the watch on my wrist; that is Vivek's job. She puts it on me, she chooses.

I have never done anything in my life, but millions of things have gone on happening around me. I cannot take the credit for those happenings.

Existence is not an act, a creation by a god; existence is an autonomous happening. Nobody is behind the curtain pulling the strings, sending messengers, holy books; there is nobody. Existence functions as an autonomous happening.

That day, thirty-two years ago, I became aware of the fact that even my birth was a happening. I have not had anything to do with it. In fact, nobody had asked me, "Do you want to be born?"

My breathing goes on happening – it is wrong to say that I am breathing. You are not breathing; otherwise you would have been dead long ago, because what will you do in the night? When you are asleep, the breathing will stop; or sometimes even in the day you may forget, and you are finished.

I trust in existence – I am part of it.

And the moment I became aware that if stars go on moving without any mover behind them, if this whole vast existence is possible without any doer…. I am just a small, tiny part of this whole existence, why should I bother doing anything? Let things happen. And so much has happened that sometimes even I start wondering whether it has happened or somebody has done it.

But I have been continuously aware – aware that I am not going to do anything, because the ego is the doer. If you don't do anything, the ego disappears; doing is nourishing the ego. Shifting from doing to happening, you have dissolved the ego. In doing you can fail, but in happening there is no way of failing. Whatsoever happens is right.

So nobody can make me depressed, nobody can make me disappointed, because in the first place I am not trying to do something.

Do you think that when I speak I move my hands? No, my gestures are just a happening, there is no doer behind them. My gestures are not the gestures of a Christian missionary.

I used to go to visit…. In Jabalpur there was Asia's biggest training center for Christian missionaries, Leonard Theological College. Thousands of people were being trained to become missionaries. I used to go – the principal was my friend, but that was just an excuse – I used to go there to see how stupid people can be.

The professors were teaching the students how to speak – when you have to speak slowly, when you have to shout loudly – and when you are speaking what gestures are suitable: when you have to raise your hand, when you have to hit the desk to make a point. I was simply amazed. These are actors, these are not missionaries; they are being trained.

I don't know how to speak; you cannot find a more amateur speaker in the world. I don't know what I am going to say the next moment. My hands move on their own. In fact, the hands are extensions of your brain; your right hand is connected with your left brain, your left hand is connected with your right brain. They are in tune with my brain, so whatever gesture is there, it is not my doing. And the brain is a mechanism, it is not me.

What I am going to say, I don't know; I simply allow it to be said. That's why it is so easy for me to go on speaking for years – there is no problem. These are no prepared speeches.

Just the other day Vivek was very amazed…. In the morning, after my bath and taking my breakfast, which is nothing much, just a glass of juice…. I am always in such a beautiful relaxed state that although I have slept the whole night – that was also beautiful – after my bath I can fall asleep again. I have to come here, so I have to leave at eight-fifteen. Vivek came and she saw me fast asleep. She woke me up, and she said, "It is now eight-twenty. Your secretary is waiting outside, and you are sleeping!" So just out of sleep I come here and start. But there is no doing in my life.

You all have come to me, I have not called you.

Just think, your coming to me was a happening. Your being here with me is nothing like doing. Anybody who is here with effort is not going to remain here long. Only those who are here simply as a happening are going to be with me forever. And to me, each moment is an eternity unto itself.

If you are with me without any effort, without any doing on your part, you have fallen in tune with me, because I am just happening. If you are also in the mood of happening, suddenly there is no duality between me and you. Two happenings are not two; a thousand happenings are not a thousand. If all the sannyasins here are here without any effort and are just enjoying whatever is happening, then we are one soul.

Why does one have to make an effort? – because deep down one does not want to be here, that's why one has to make an effort to be here. How long can you repress your going away, and why waste your time in repressing? If that is your destiny to go away, go away with joy, with all my blessings.

If it is a happening to you, then there is no question ever of saying, "Be here with all my blessings." You will know it without my saying it. I will be overflowing in you, you will be reaching me. And this will be an absolutely invisible phenomenon.

We are Here
To Be the Whole

DISCOURSE 14, July 12, 1985

Beloved Bhagwan,

Can You imagine Yourself being a Rajneeshee and living in a commune?

It is impossible. I am simply an individual who belongs to no religion, to no caste, to no cult, to no nation. And I cannot belong to anybody, for the simple reason that I am completely content with myself. The desire to belong arises because you feel empty. In a crowd of any kind – political, religious – you forget your emptiness; the crowd fills you.

It is impossible also because I am no longer seeking, searching for anything – existence has opened all its doors to me. I cannot even say that I belong to existence, because I am just part of it. If you are not part of it, then in some way you create a relationship, a belonging.

When a flower blossoms, I blossom with it.

When the sun rises, I rise with it.

The ego in me, which keeps people separate, is no longer there. I am dissolved – who can belong? I am not there. My body is part of nature, my being is part of the whole. I am not a separate entity.

When you are a separate entity, there is fear. The universe is vast, the problems are immense. You would like a family to belong to, a community, a society, a culture, a religion. Alone you cannot face the vast emptiness surrounding you. Alone you are so small in comparison to the expanding universe –

great fear arises.

But when you start belonging to a big crowd, the fear is diluted. So people belong to the family, they belong to a society, they belong to a culture, they belong to a church. And if even that is not fulfilling, then they create Rotary clubs, Lions Clubs, the "One Thousand Enemies of "Oregon." The bigger the crowd, the bigger you start imagining yourself to be. If you are a Catholic, you know there are six hundred million Catholics – you become huge.

I have no fear, because the one that could have fear has disappeared long ago. Even here, you are Rajneeshees, I am not. In fact, in my whole life I have never belonged to anything. I have been just a guest everywhere – even here I am simply a guest. Even my guesthouse is not within the boundaries of Rajneeshpuram.

I am just an outsider, but to be an outsider and contented, fearless…because death cannot destroy me, there is nothing to be destroyed. My death has already happened thirty-two years ago; this is my posthumous existence. Any moment the body can fall apart, and I will be part of the whole. And remember, being part of the whole is not the same as being part of a machine, an organization. The words are the same, but in reality, to be part of the whole means to *be* the whole. There is no other way.

To be part of any kind of mechanism is not to be the whole mechanism. In your machines, cars, you can change a part because the part is really apart –

you can take it out and put in another part. It was not the whole machine.

But to be part of the whole is totally different. You are irreplaceable. The stars are within you, just as you are within the universe. The universe is within you; there is no demarcation line.

And this is my whole message to you:

Dissolve, be in a state of let-go.

Then there is no death, then there is no fear. Then you are not alone, the whole universe is within you.

Anybody who is awakened to the truth becomes an outsider to all kinds of collectivities. Gautam Buddha is not a Buddhist, Mahavira is not a Jaina, Jesus is not a Christian. There have been very few individuals in history who were part of the whole.

Nothing less than that will do. Everything else is just a poor substitute.

When I can have a friendship with the flowers and the trees and the birds and the stars, when I can love the smallest blade of grass and the biggest star – because they are mine and I am theirs – then what is the need to belong to a small, tiny group?

I am making every effort so that you dissolve, so that you start melting into the whole, so that slowly, slowly you forget yourself and only remember the reality that surrounds you. Just as a dewdrop falls from the lotus leaf into the lake and becomes one with the lake, thirty-two years ago my dewdrop slipped from the lotus leaf into the lake of wholeness.

I am no more. Whatever I say to you is the voice of the whole; hence, I am not worried about respectability or notoriousness. I am not worried about anything, because the worrier is not there. I am not even responsible. I have dropped myself into the whole; now the responsibility is of the whole. This is exactly the case with everyone, but you have to remember it. You have forgotten – you have been *made* to forget it.

In this commune slowly, slowly merge, melt, if the universe seems too vast and scares you. The

A commune is only a small experiment, a kind of rehearsal where you can dissolve without any fear. Once you know how to dissolve, melt, you have known all; the same has to be done with the whole. And the paradoxical phenomenon is, when you dissolve in the whole, the whole dissolves in you.

purpose of the commune is to give you an opportunity that does not scare you. Melt! Don't be a *part* of this commune, become the whole commune. Each individual in this commune is the whole commune.

This will give you a glimpse of dissolving, and if with such a small commune dissolving brings such great blessings, you will know the secret, from where it is coming. Then why remain stuck? You know the key – you can open the doors of the whole universe for yourself.

A commune is only a small experiment, a kind of rehearsal where you can dissolve without any fear. Once you know how to dissolve, melt, you have known all; the same has to be done with the whole. And the paradoxical phenomenon is, when you dissolve in the whole, the whole dissolves in you. You don't lose anything; you gain the whole universe! Perhaps you lose your chains, bondages, you lose your small, cozy, egoistic existence. But when you have the whole existence melting in you, who cares for small things?

So this is the only university. The other universities are teaching you to become strong egos. They are not universities, because the university should teach you to become one with the universe. That is the meaning of the word "university." I don't know what kind of idiots go on creating language. They create a university to strengthen your ego; they are against the universe.

In my way of seeing, they should call all the universities of the world – Oxford, Cambridge, Harvard, all the universities of the world – they should stop calling them universities; they are *multiversities*. There is nothing like unity with existence; they are making you more and more solid, crystallized, separate from everybody.

This university is exactly what the word means. We are not here to be part, we are here to be the whole. And when you can be the whole, it will be sheer stupidity to remain a part.

I don't belong to anything, because to belong means separation. I am *in* everything, and everything is in me.

Beloved Bhagwan,

Why haven't people from Africa come to You? Most of the people who come are white-skinned. To me, what You say is for everyone. Are the others afraid of You?

It is true, what I say is for everyone. But everyone is not ready for it.

We have become accustomed to dividing the world into East and West. It has to be changed – we should start conceiving of the world as divided into North and South. East and West is not a true division, because the eastern people and the western people are all different shades of whiteness. They come from the same root, the same race – the Aryans. Their languages can prove it very easily.

All the languages of East and West are sister languages; their roots are derived from a single source, Sanskrit. The words may have taken different shapes, changes – a little bit here, a little bit there – but if you are careful you can figure out what has happened to each word.

Just think of a few words of East and West, and you will see they are not separate people. You call man's first beginning, Adam. Arabians call him Dum, Indians call him Admi. Do you see any difference?

Sometimes words take such a turn that suddenly you cannot see they are one. The first woman, you call Eve. In many languages she is called Eve. In Arabic she is called Hava. Now "Hava" and "Eve" seem to be two different words; they are not. "Eve" and "Hava" may seem very different, but if you go through all the intermediate steps: Eve, Eva, Hava – just one link, and you know this is the same language.

This is not true about South and North; their languages are not connected at all. They are totally different evolutions happening on the earth.

Gautam Buddha, Mahavira, Mohammed, Moses, Jesus – they are all born in the northern regions. All the religions are born in the North; there is nothing comparable in the South. All the scientists are born in the North; there is nothing comparable in the South.

The South is living at least five thousand years behind. They are still living in the world of magic – science is very far away. Even your so-called religions have not evolved there. If in the South there are Christians it is because you have converted them, bribed them with education, food, better clothing, better possibilities to rise higher on the ladder of prestige, power, respectability.

In the South there are Mohammedans; they have also been converted – at the point of the sword. Mohammedanism in a way is very straight and direct. Why go in roundabout ways: teaching, feeding, giving clothes, education, sending people to learn in England, in France, in America – too long a route. They take a shortcut. They just put their sword on your neck, and they say, "Decide. You can live only as a Mohammedan, so choose between Mohammedanism and death." It is not a question of choosing between two religions, it is a question of choosing between Mohammedanism and death. And naturally, one chooses Mohammedanism.

You are asking me why people from Africa are not coming to me. Now, what can I do? You should go to Africa and ask those people!

But I can see why they are not coming. There is a gap of five thousand years between you and them. I am saying, "between you and them" – the gap between *me* and them is immeasurable, you cannot calculate it. Even the northern white people find a great gap between me and them – what to say about the poor black people of southern Africa? They are still worshipping the magician, they still believe in superstitions which were prevalent all over the world in the past. They are still groping in the dark.

The southern hemisphere needs to be transformed. But it is so difficult even to transform the northern people, who have been thinking for thousands of years, have created great philosophies, theologies, religions. You cannot name a single person from southern Africa who can be compared to Socrates, Plato, Aristotle. You cannot, because it has not happened. There has been no Kant, no Hegel, no Feuerbach. There has been no Martin Heidegger, Jaspers, Jean-Paul Sartre. And to understand me, you need this whole background.

It will look strange to you, that what I am criticizing continually and destroying continually is a basic need as a background to understand me.

I cannot criticize Jesus to a southern African. What does it mean to him? Jesus has nothing to do with him. I cannot criticize Aristotle, he has never heard the name. So I can go on criticizing Aristotle, it is not going to make any dent; it is not his heritage. That's why they are not coming.

But if you blossom, and your fragrance spreads, it will not be far in the future that even the Africans will be able to walk along with you. Right now, it is almost impossible. Your problems are different from their problems; your background is different from their background; otherwise, there is not much difference. As human beings there is no difference except the color.

The black people of South Africa are a little richer in color than the white people, because they have something more that you don't have. They have a certain color pigment – not very valuable, maybe one-third of a dollar; that color pigment in their bodies is the only thing they have more than you. And it is an absolute necessity there – the sun is so burning hot that unless the body is black, it will not be able to survive.

In India, I know…. India is something in between: the skin is not as white as German nordics, but it is not as black as southern Africans, because India's climate does not need that pigment which prevents sunrays from entering into the body.

India was under British rule for two hundred

years. For the people who had come from England, it was a suffering; India was too hot. Delhi is one of the hottest places in India, and that was the capital. So the British government made another capital in Simla, in the Himalayas; it was the summer capital. As the summer came, all the British people would move to Simla – the whole capital. They could not even survive in New Delhi. The moment India became independent, Simla was no longer a summer capital; the Indian skin can take the heat of Delhi.

So the only difference is of a little color pigment. Scientifically, I think it would be possible to inject you with the pigment and you would become black; or to find some way to take out the black pigment from the African, and he would be as white as you are – or even more, because he would be fresh. But then he could not survive in Africa, or he would have to make different arrangements to survive. Except for the color there is no difference, they are human beings just like you. But they have evolved in a different way from the North.

The North – particularly India – has created almost all the best religions. Compared to Jainism and Buddhism, Christianity and Mohammedanism look very childish. The reason was, India was affluent, rich; there was no poverty as it exists now. Twenty-five centuries ago India was known all over the world as a golden bird. It attracted all kinds of thieves to exploit that gold. Those who came – Moguls, Turks, Mongols, Hunas, Portuguese, French, English – they were all thieves in search of the riches that were available in India.

India never attacked anybody – there was no reason. A rich man never goes to steal in a poor man's hut, that is absolutely absurd. If the poor man goes to the rich man's house to steal, it is absolutely logical. India never attacked any country; it was attacked by almost everybody. In twenty-five centuries they exploited everything India had. They were parasites; they have left India almost in a the situation of a skeleton. But in those good old days, India created the best philosophers.

Yes, even now, when the West is so rich, affluent, its philosophers cannot compare with the Indian philosophers of two, three thousand years ago – Nagarjuna, Shankara, Nimbark. Even today Sartre, Jaspers, Russell, have much to learn from these people. The country was so satisfied physically that it started groping for some spiritual nourishment.

Mohammed was a poor man, illiterate; so was Jesus a poor man, illiterate. Buddha was not a poor man and illiterate. He was a prince, the only son of his father; soon he was going to be crowned. He was educated in the best possible way, he was acquainted with all the wisdom available. His intelligence was sharpened in every possible way…because in India, philosophy has developed differently than it has developed in Europe.

It was developed not by writing philosophic treatises, it was developed by wandering philosophers arguing all over the country, debating, discussing, winning. And the rule of the game was that whoever wins in an argument becomes the master of the person who is defeated. And the defeated person – not in any sadness, but with great joy – surrenders to the master, because the question is not who is winning, the question is: What is true? And if this man has a better insight into truth, then there is no reason to be sad and sorrowful that you are defeated. You have found a better mind.

Indian philosophers moving all over the country, arguing, sharpened the mind of the whole nation. They were not just sitting in their rooms and writing books, like Immanuel Kant or Wilhelm Hegel. That cannot give you that sharpness.

I know it from my own experience. For thirty years I was traveling in India – arguing, fighting, challenging. I know that under that challenge, argument, your capacity, which ordinarily remains dormant, becomes active. Your intelligence, under the pressure of challenge, functions perfectly. It is a question of life and death.

The southern hemisphere is lagging behind – poor, uneducated. And the gap is big – five thousand years at least. That's why it is very difficult for them to commune with me.

Even negroes in America who have been here for two hundred years, three hundred years…. They go on writing questions to me, "You criticize Christianity, but you never talk about the religions of southern Africa." There is no religion there – and I am not fighting magic, I am not a magician. Red Indians of America go on writing questions to me, "What about *our* religion?" You don't have any. What you have is so primitive that I am not going to waste my time on it.

It is so difficult to convince the white races of the world. They are the most progressive, yet to convince them to drop all programs and conditionings is so difficult. And even if a man drops them, listens to my argument, understands the argument, that understanding mostly remains intellectual. And the question is: how am I going to reach your heart?

The Christian clergyman was from Sweden. He was under great pressure and trouble in Sweden because he was spreading my message there. He was giving my books to people he thought would understand. He created a great stir in Sweden – all the Christian churches condemned him and his congregation, saying that he was trying to destroy Christianity.

He continued to fight; in newspapers, on television, on radio, he was arguing. But coming here this year, he fell flat on the ground and forgot that he was giving my message to the Christians – because he had never heard me speak against Christianity. He was thinking that what I am saying…. I commented on Jesus and the Christians were surprised. I received so many letters from Christian clergymen around the world: "The way you have explained the words of Jesus, we had never thought…we never knew that Jesus was such a great philosopher, and that what he said has so many implications."

Now they all know: I was simply speaking for myself, my own ideas, using Jesus' name – for a simple reason. I have done that with Hindus, with Mohammedans, with Christians – because from where else to get my congregation? So first I spoke on Jesus, choosing only those parts which I can support. Now I have my own people, and I don't care a bit. Now I am going to tell you the whole truth!

Hearing the whole truth, that clergyman freaked out. I can understand his trouble. Now he will be torn apart in Sweden, because the Swedish orthodox Christians will be against him, and he cannot any longer go on propagating my word. And if he stops propagating my word, then the people who have come to him because of me will be against him. I have put him in a real fix. Now it is a question of either/or; he has to choose. That's why he said, "You have given me moments of heaven and moments of hell."

First I give everybody moments of heaven. When I see that you are getting in tune with me, then I give you the moments of hell, because I have to destroy all the garbage that centuries have poured upon you. Unless you are completely free from all prejudices, you cannot open your heart to me. And I am not interested in your head; I am searching for your heart, because real religiousness is not a matter of the head.

Science is a matter of the head, it has nothing to do with the heart. Religion is a matter absolutely concerned with your heart. Unless your heart starts beating with me, in tune, nothing is held back, you are totally and utterly harmonious with me…only then can I bring you to the vision where this whole universe is yours.

Then you know there is no death, everything is eternal; nothing dies, things only change forms.

Then you know the universe is not static; it is moving, alive, breathing. It is not standing still, it is progressing every moment.

First, if you fall into a harmonious pace with me, then I am going to throw you into a bigger harmony, the biggest, so that you can move with the stars, with the trees, with the rivers, with the oceans. Then only will you know what it is to be blessed.

I feel sorry for southern Africa, but what can I do? They will not listen to me. Even you are hearing me and not listening to me. And I am a very pragmatic, existential man. I am not a Don Quixote. But if I can transform the vision of millions of white people, there is a possibility that those millions of people will create enough energy, enough power to transform even those who are so backward.

I cannot go anywhere – no country will allow me in. Secondly, I cannot go anywhere because America will not allow me back in. They are holding my green card and hoping that somehow, someday I may go out of the country for some reason. Then they won't allow me any entry again.

Boys, forget all that. Green card or no green card, I am going to be here, because I know where I can have people who understand me. They will carry the fragrance.

I have come to a new arrangement. I cannot go, but I have communes in Europe, in Japan, in Australia. I am starting a new program: we will be exchanging sannyasins for three months from one commune to another commune. Thirty sannyasins from Germany will be coming here; thirty sannyasins from here will be going to Germany. These thirty people going from here will take my fragrance there, and those thirty people living for three months here will catch fire!

Politicians think they are very intelligent – I can manage without going anywhere. From all over the world now, there will be exchange programs. Sannyasins who are now in tune with me will be going there. In fact, I am going there within those thirty sannyasins! And the thirty that will be coming here, I will enter in their hearts too. And this exchange program from commune to commune around the world will create, in fact, one single commune around the world.

We will be the first to dissolve the idea of boundaries. In Germany, or in Holland, or in England, or in Italy – anywhere – they will feel part of Rajneeshpuram, and they will not miss me at all. But about Africa, we will have to wait a little.

Beloved Bhagwan,

What is the relationship between truth and lies? Some of Gurdjieff's disciples questioned him about things he had said that they understood as lies. He replied that for most people the truth could be understood only in terms of a lie. Is that the truth?

Absolutely true.
Who can know it better than me?
There are problems in expressing truth. First, when you experience it, there is no word, there is no language. The mind is put aside. You experience it in such a profound silence that to give it in the form of words to others already makes it a lie. And a great master knows which lies can bring you nearer to him.

You cannot understand truth, that is certain, because truth is not something to be understood; it has to be experienced. The master's work is not to make you understand what is true. His work is to create a situation in which you can see the truth.

And if he speaks the truth right now, you will not be able to bear the shock of it. So he has to go very slowly. He will lie, because you can understand only lies. Unconscious people, blind people – they have lived on lies for centuries, they can understand a lie. But the master's lie is a strategy.

When I commented on Jesus before, in five volumes of books, I was lying. Jesus has not the meaning that I was putting into his words. But to bring Christians closer, that was the only way. I was speaking on Buddha, on Mahavira, on Krishna, because that was the only way.

Truth cannot be said in the first place; and if you try, people will simply escape from you. You have to think about the people first, what is possible for them to absorb. And then slowly slowly they can absorb more and more. A time comes when you can start turning their vision towards the truth.

It is a great and arduous job to take away your diseases from you; you are clinging to them. I have to gain your confidence first. You are a Christian or a Hindu or a Jew, you are clinging hard to your religion – and I want you to drop it. The only possible way is to tell you that whatsoever you are carrying is not crap, it is Christianity, it is great! That helps you to come closer to me.

The moment I see you have come so close and so far, and the return is not possible, then I start hitting you. And then you will not feel hurt, you will rejoice that I have taken so much trouble in lying to you. That's the way you catch men in your net. Once you are caught by me, once I see the certainty in your eyes that whatsoever happens you are going to be with me, when I have made absolutely certain that if you have to leave Jesus for me you will; that if it is a question of Krishna and me, and you have to choose, there is no uncertainty, you are going to choose me....

Gurdjieff is right. He had a tremendously clear insight into the human mind. Perhaps in this century he was the most significant figure. And when he says, "The master has to use lies to bring you to the truth," he is absolutely right, because that's what I have been doing my whole life.

It is always a risky game. First talking to you about Jesus, his enlightenment – and he was not enlightened. First giving beautiful meanings to his words – which he was incapable of giving to those words. Once you become certain that I am in tune with Jesus, you have fallen in the trap.

I don't care about Jesus, Buddha or Mohammed. I care about *you!*

And I will do everything that can make you alert, aware, conscious of the reality within you and without you.

Beloved Bhagwan,

The words "negative" and "negativity" are often used in this commune. What do they really mean? They seem to refer to any doubt or question about the organization of the commune.

No, they don't mean what you are thinking. They don't mean that any questioning, any doubt, is negativity. I am teaching you doubting, questioning. How can my commune call you negative? Negative, negativity have a totally different meaning.

There are people who can only see the dark side; they are addicted to seeing the dark side. These addicted people are negative people. It is impossible for them to see the lighted side of anything.

Doubt, question, but don't become a negative being. A negative being cannot see anything right. A negative person cannot see anything beautiful; everything is dark, ugly, hopeless. A negative person is always in despair. Doubt is not despair, it is enquiry. Questioning is man's birthright. Question as much as you can. Doubt, and don't repress it, bring it forth.

Doubt and questioning are positive qualities. You are saying, "I want to understand more clearly before I move, hence the question. The question is not against the commune, the question is for the commune, so that I can do better. If I go on keeping this doubt in me, I cannot commune with other people totally. Let me be freed from this doubt, this question."

Why do I go on answering you? For what? Just so that your questions drop, they don't become a barrier; your doubts drop, they don't become a barrier, and you are light, you can fly...because doubts and enquiries repressed make you heavy. When all doubts are dispersed and all questions are answered, you start growing wings; you can fly, you are light.

But a negative person is a totally different phenomenon. He is determined to remain negative. He is determined to see only the black side. They say,

"Every black cloud has a silver lining." The negative person will say, "Every silver lining is surrounded by a black cloud."

I am reminded of a beautiful story. In a monastery, two monks were walking in the garden, and they both were in the same trouble. They were allowed to smoke outside the monastery, but they were not allowed to smoke inside the monastery. Most of the time they were inside the monastery, and they were chainsmokers; it was really a torture.

They enquired, "Why are we not allowed to smoke in the monastery?"

And the answer came from the abbot, "The monastery is a place of prayer. You cannot be allowed anything that spoils the pure, divine atmosphere in the monastery. It is not a movie hall."

But just this much was not going to help; they were addicted to their smoking. They said, "We should try one time more – separately, not in the congregation."

The next day one monk was sitting in the garden joyously smoking. The other monk came and was very angry, he could not believe it. He said, "What are you doing? Have you asked the abbot?"

He said, "Yes, and he allowed me."

The other said, "This is simply injustice. I also asked him, and he said no!"

The man who was smoking smiled and he said, "I know why he said no to you and yes to me. I approached with positivity, you approached with negativity. Your negativity became a 'no' in the heart of the abbot. My positivity became a 'yes' in the heart of the same abbot. Please tell me what you asked, and things will be clear."

The man who was angry said, "I asked, 'Can I smoke while praying?' And the abbot said, 'No! Absolutely no.'"

The one who was smoking said, "I also asked him. I asked him, 'Can I pray while I am smoking?' And he said, 'Yes! Absolutely yes!'"

All Promises
For Tomorrow
Are Lies

DISCOURSE 15,   July 13, 1985

Beloved Bhagwan,

It disturbs me when You don't seem to bother about facts.

You must be crazy! Why should it disturb you if it does not disturb me? It is true I have no respect for facts, for the simple reason that the fact is not the truth. The fact is our opinion about the truth. And what opinion can *you* have? – unconscious, blind, conditioned by centuries of rubbish. Why should I pay any respect to all this nonsense?

Something was a fact yesterday, today it is not. It was a fact for Jesus, Moses, Abraham, that the sun goes around the earth. It is no longer a fact, it is just the opposite: the earth goes around the sun. So why should you be disturbed? As man progresses and becomes more intelligent, has more scientific methods to probe into reality, facts go on changing every day.

I have immense respect for truth, because truth is not man's opinion. Truth is a revelation. You are not, when the truth is there.

You cannot *make* an opinion about the truth. You can experience it, you can taste it, you can be it, but you cannot have an opinion about it, because the moment truth faces you, you are no more. The ego that used to make opinions simply disappears, just as when you bring light into a dark room the darkness disappears. In fact it was never there it was only the absence of light. The moment the light is present, how can the light and the darkness exist together?

And your opinion is simply a barrier in finding the truth. You somehow have got the idea that fact and truth are synonymous; they are not. Sometimes the fiction is more true than the fact. Just look at the three hundred years' growth of science. Everything has changed. Aristotle's logic was a great discovery, accepted by all for almost a thousand years. Now it is just garbage. Non-Aristotelian logic has taken its place; someday it will also be in the garbage.

Man's truth – what he calls fact – has no validity. It is the blind man's idea of light. Why should I have any respect for it? And the most amazing part is: why are you disturbed? The psychology of it is very clear. When I don't pay any respect to the so-called facts, your knowledgeable mind gets disturbed. You want me to be infallible, you want me to be the greatest master in the world. Not that you are interested in me, your interest is in being the disciple of the greatest master in the world. Your desire is to belong to a master who is always respectful of facts.

Remember, in many different contexts this will happen to you. I have said again and again, I am a fallible, ordinary man. And to be a disciple of a fallible, ordinary man is disturbing. But that simply shows your ego and its longing. You would like to make me a God, because then you become also God's disciple. Then there is a direct communication line between God and you.

Forgive me, I am not God, and there is no one who is, no one who has ever been. It is your psychology that has created the prophets, the messiahs, the *avataras*. They fulfilled your desire. And naturally, it was good business: they became messiahs, and you became the special apostles of the messiah.

Unless man drops this stupid psychology, it is very difficult to get rid of messiahs, prophets, great masters, because you are so insistent on being a great disciple. How can you be a great disciple if the master is fallible?

I am trying in every way to destroy your psychology, which has dominated humanity for centuries. It has made you almost unintelligent, but the balloon of your ego goes on becoming bigger and bigger. You, your individuality, your consciousness, go on diminishing in the same proportion.

What do you want? Should I say things which satisfy you? Or should I say things as they are, whether they satisfy you or hurt you? It is your responsibility, it is not my concern. Listening to your question, I said, "Aha! Back to zero again!" Are you ever going to grow or not?

The geometric philosophy of Euclid dominated for centuries; no one ever objected. Just within a hundred years the whole Euclidean geometry has become a fiction; a non-Euclidean geometry has taken its place. I say to you, the non-Euclidean geometry is also a fiction. It is not going to remain there forever as a fact. Nothing that man creates out of his sleep can become the eternal truth.

To know the eternal truth, man has to disappear completely. He is the hindrance.

I am going to continue hammering your psychological slavery. I am not concerned about facts, I am concerned with your freedom. You have to be freed from all that is not your experience. And

Marriage creates the need to get rid of each other, because it means freedom is taken away – and freedom is the highest value in human life. Make all the couples free, and you will be surprised, this very world becomes paradise.

remember, your experience is not yours, it is only experiencing. I have immense respect for experiencing. The facts, at the most, may be useful in the ordinary world of objects, but they have no basis in reality.

Experiencing may not be of any use in the outside world – perhaps it may create trouble for you, but flowers will start showering on you, your being will be contented. You will feel an absolute certainty that you have come home.

Beloved Bhagwan,

Lately I have not felt blissful, but have been having many doubts and questions. Am I missing the point of what is happening here?

Yes, you were missing the point when you were feeling blissful. Now you are getting it! All that blissfulness was just bullshit; you projected it. Now you are disturbed: that blissfulness has disappeared and doubts, enquiries, questions are arising. And I say, this is what should happen to everybody.

If your blissfulness was existential, true, then there would have been no way for doubts to arise. It was a hallucination. You were on a honeymoon trip, and now the honeymoon is finished. You are back home unpacking the same suitcases which just seven days before you were packing with such great joy. And now, look in the mirror and see your face again. What happened to that bliss? What happened to that expectation? What happened to your sweet dreams?

A dream is a dream, whether it is sweet or bitter, and sooner or later you have to drop it; you cannot carry it forever. Only truth can remain with you forever. That's why I say feel blessed, not blissful, that for the first time your intelligence has started functioning, that some kind of awakening is happening, that the morning is very close by. Those questions, enquiries, doubts, are of immense value; your blissfulness was not worth a penny. I say so because

these doubts, these enquiries, these questions, are the beginning of the pilgrimage to truth.

I am against drugs for this reason – because the drugs can give you a false blissfulness, and can stop you questioning, enquiring, doubting. Even a man like Aldous Huxley fell into the same ditch. When he took LSD he thought, "This is what Buddha was experiencing, Kabir was experiencing, and all the great masters of the world were experiencing." He thought, "We have found, for the first time, the shortcut to paradise." But within hours the effect of the LSD disappears, and you are back again, the same man, the same miserable creature. LSD has not transformed you.

Any hallucination – either created by drugs, or created by programming your mind, or created by your hidden desires of being great – is a hindrance to realizing the truth.

Let me repeat: now you are in the right state of mind. It is painful, bitter, but this is the nature of existence. Truth in the beginning is bitter, in the end, tremendously sweet – and sweet forever. The untruth is very sweet in the beginning, but ultimately leads you into hellfire. And then it is too late to come back to your original state and start again. Very few people have that courage.

Friedrich Nietzsche, although a madman, had many beautiful flashes of light, love, truth. He says man passes through three stages of consciousness. The first stage he calls the camel, the second stage the lion, and the third stage – the ultimate – the child. He has chosen strange names for these stages.

You are all camels, the ugliest animal on the earth! – nothing is straight. Have you ever ridden on a camel? Then you will know. I have suffered much, because in India in the desert of Rajasthan, the camel is the only way to go from one place to another. Sitting on a camel for a few hours, one starts believing that hell is real.

The second stage Nietzsche calls the lion…a strange coincidence, because Buddha used to call his words "the lion's roar." The lion is one of the most beautiful animals on the earth; strong, and capable of being alone. The lion doesn't live like a sheep, in crowds. He lives alone, without fear. He is ready to take any risk.

You have to become a lion to be alone. That does not mean that you have to leave your family, your friends, your society, your commune – no. You can be alone in the crowd, there is no problem. In fact, you *are* alone. The crowd may be big – you can forget your aloneness in the crowd, but forgetting makes no difference. Here, you are thousands of sannyasins…. Just become a little alert, and you will find you are alone. I am talking to each of you separately. Nobody can talk to a crowd.

And the third stage Nietzsche calls the child. He has chosen a beautiful name for the third stage – the newborn baby, fresh, no ego, no desire to be somebody special in the world, no programmed mind, no conditioning. He is neither Christian nor American, neither Hindu nor Indian; he is simply himself. And there is utter silence in his being. He has not yet read all kinds of things – which are useless, but they clutter your mind; a moment comes when you are just a junkyard. The child's consciousness is just a mirror. It reflects whatsoever comes in front of it.

The child does not know names. Do you think if you bring a red roseflower before the child he will be thinking in his mind, "This is a red rose, a very beautiful flower"? No, he will be *seeing* the flower, as you never have. The fragrance will be reaching him as it cannot reach you because there are so many barriers. He does not know the name of the color, of the flower. He does not know that it is beautiful. As far as his mind is concerned, it is silent, but he experiences the flower in its totality. Words are not needed.

A rose is a rose is a rose.

Names and labels are not needed.

What is needed is clarity, innocence.

The third stage, the ultimate stage , Nietzsche calls the child. And that's what I am trying to do: to make you a child again – fresh, uncluttered, with no ideology, so that you can encounter existence directly. But if you want to experience it directly, you will have to cut out all that prevents you from experiencing directly. Doubt is a great instrument, questioning is of tremendous help, because without them there is no enquiry.

Remember that doubt, enquiry, questions, are not negative. They are a search for the positive. They become negative only when you get stuck with them, when you make your doubt your belief – then they are negative. When your enquiry becomes an addiction, and you forget completely what you are enquiring for, then you are in bad shape. Otherwise, it is a blessing that your hallucinations are over.

What has actually been happening with my people in these thirty years? I have been in contact with thousands. I was speaking on Mahavira – only the followers of Mahavira felt blissful. I was speaking on Jesus – Christians felt blissful, because they thought I was supporting their ego, their programmed mind, their Christianity, their Jesus. So this has been happening again and again. First, to gain your confidence, I say beautiful things about Jesus, Mohammed, Buddha. The moment I see that now it is time – you cannot go back, you have come too close to me – then I start speaking the truth.

It hurts, but this hurting is healthy. It hurts because it uncovers your wound. A covered wound you may forget, but it is there and growing, and may become a cancer. Open it to the air, to the sun, to the moon, to existence. The whole existence is a healing force. If it can give you life, can't it heal small wounds created by your parents, your teachers, your politicians? It is a very small job for existence. You just have to open your wounds. And in the beginning it will hurt.

You are asking me, "Am I missing the point?" No, sir! This is the point, you are getting it. Now it is up to you: you can escape and hide again in your illusory blissfulness, or you can give a lion's roar and take the quantum leap into reality, knowing perfectly well it is going to hurt.

But that is not the end. It hurts only because of your clinging to your past blissfulness. Once your past blissfulness is dropped, understood as a dream, the hurting disappears, the despair disappears. On the contrary, for the first time you have risen as a man; you are no longer an animal. For the first time the night is over and the sun has risen. And you have learned a great secret.

Go on using that secret, and the third state of consciousness is not far away. It is within your reach. The lion's roar breaks you away from your past, and joins you with your future.

To become a child again is the greatest joy, and the greatest achievement, because it gives you innocence, freedom, clarity to see things as they are.

I am reminded of a story I have loved always. A great king conquered almost all the known world of his time, and then there was frustration – what to do next? He had everything, and he was stuck. The old habit, the old greed of gaining more and more – and now he found suddenly that now there was no more. His whole life's training was for more and more and more, and now he had everything, there was nothing more.

He was very sad. His wives, his advisors, all tried to cheer him up, but he said, "It is futile. Unless I have something more to conquer, what is the point of living any longer?"

Then a very cunning priest – in fact, I should not say both the words together, because the priest means the cunning – appeared in the court. And he said, "Don't be worried, I have heard about your anguish – there is still much more. For example," he said, "I can bring you divine clothes from God, which have never come to the earth. You will be the first man, and perhaps the last to have them."

There was silence, there was doubt. But the king said, "What can he do?" He asked, "What is going to be the cost?"

The priest said, "Then forget all about it. One who asks the cost is not worthy of receiving them. They are priceless. But just to satisfy your enquiry I will say that a few billion dollars will be needed."

The king said, "There is one condition. You will remain in one of my palaces, guarded inside, and do whatsoever ritual, prayer you want to do. And the moment you bring the clothes here, the money will be delivered."

The man said, "There is no problem; as far as I am concerned it is perfectly good. But I will have to deliver the money when I get those clothes from God – and I am a poor priest, you have to give me money now. And I will remain in your palace. Keep all the doors closed, keep the palace fully surrounded by your military, so that you can feel comfortable. And the moment I bring the clothes, I will knock on the door; then the guards have to take me to the place where you live."

After three days he knocked on the door. Nobody believed it, everybody was thinking that he seemed to be either very cunning or just insane. Who has ever heard of the clothes of God coming to the earth? But they all waited. The king could not even sleep, he was so thrilled. He was again blissful: a new horizon to be achieved, a new dimension opening – and for the first time! These moments were historic.

After three days the man came with a beautiful box to the court of the king. He put the box down and said to the king, "God was very pleased, because you are the bravest man ever. He has sent the divine clothes. Just two things have to be remembered. One, the clothes are invisible, just like God. Secondly, you have to take *your* clothes off. Give me your cap and I will give you the divine cap; put it on your head.

"Just as I was coming I said to God, 'This is a little hard, that the clothes will be invisible.' God said, 'I will make one exception: the man who is truly born out of his own father – one who is not a bastard – will be able to see them.' This is a special concession."

The box was opened. The king looked into it: it was empty – of course, the clothes were invisible. His intimates in the court looked into the box, and they all started cheering and clapping, and they said, "What beauty!"

The king thought, "Strange! Now if I say that the box is empty I will be condemned by my own people. They will say that I am not the son of my father, that my mother was flirting with somebody else. It is better to keep quiet and save my prestige." He also said, "Great! You have done something impossible."

All the people in the court saw that the box was empty, but the same question was in their minds: "All the others are seeing them, only I am not; something is wrong with me. It is better to keep silent – not only silent, but to praise the clothes more than the others, to prove that I am the son of my own father."

If things had stopped there, the king would have been happy. But the man was really a priest. He took the clothes out one by one and gave those invisible clothes to the king to wear, and he acted as if he was putting a new robe on him. At the end it became difficult, because he asked about the underwear.

The king hesitated. He knew that there was nothing, that he was standing almost naked, only the underwear was left. But now it was too late. If he said, "You cheat! You have taken so much money," that wouldn't be right because the whole court was dancing with joy: "You look so beautiful, just like God!"

The poor king had to part with his underwear too. Now he was standing completely naked. And the priest said, "Because the clothes from paradise have come for the first time on the earth, the whole capital is standing outside the palace; they want to see their king in divine clothes."

Again the king thought, "What to do? If I say no, it is too late." He had to say yes. On a beautiful chariot the naked king was standing, and the crowd lined the road on both sides – millions of people shouting, dancing, clapping, saying to each other, "This is the greatest moment in our lives! We have not seen God, but we have seen his clothes. This is not a small thing." And they were all seeing that the king was standing naked, but they had heard the condition – that only those who are born out of their own fathers will be able to see the clothes.

So everybody was seeing them, except a little child who had come with his father. Sitting on his father's shoulder, he said, "Daddy, the king is naked!" The father simply said, "Shut up, you idiot! When you become my age you will not see the king naked. You don't understand anything. And if you say it again, I will beat you! Keep your mouth closed."

But the child said, "It is strange! Everybody is seeing the clothes except me." Only the child was seeing the truth, and the crowd was pretending to see. And if you pretend anything long enough, it starts becoming a fact to you, you start believing in it. But it is poisoning your whole potentiality.

Forget all those blissful moments that you had felt before here. Now I am in a hurry, and I am going to open all your wounds. So only those who have the courage of a lion will remain my sannyasins. The camels have already left for Santa Fe!

And if you are courageous enough, like a lion, your beautiful childhood innocence is not far away. It is yours just to take. Be thankful to your doubts, your enquiries, your questions. They will lead you to the truth.

Beloved Bhagwan,

Why is it so difficult for men and women to be friends? It seems so ordinary, and turns out to be almost impossible. Either there is an ugly compromise – like man and wife – or else passion that eventually turns into hate. Why is there always ugliness between men and women?

It is very simple to understand. Marriage is the ugliest institution invented by man. It is not natural; it has been invented so that you can monopolize a woman. You have been treating women as if they were a piece of land, or some currency notes. You have reduced the woman to a thing.

Remember that if you reduce any human being to a thing – unaware, unconscious – you are also being reduced to the same status; otherwise, you will not be able to communicate. If you can talk with a chair, you must be a chair.

Marriage is against nature.

You can be certain only of this moment that is in your hands. All promises for tomorrow are lies – and marriage is a promise for your whole life, that you will remain together, that you will love each other, that you will respect each other till your last breath.

And these priests, who are the inventors of many ugly things, say to you that marriages are made in heaven. Nothing is made in heaven; there *is* no heaven.

If you listen to nature, your problems, your questions will simply evaporate. The problem is: biologically man is attracted to woman, women are attracted to men, but that attraction cannot remain the same forever. You are attracted to something which is a challenge to get. You see a beautiful man, a beautiful woman; you are attracted. Nothing is wrong in it. You feel your heart beating faster. You would like to be with this woman or man, and the attraction is so tremendous that in that moment you think you would like to live with this woman forever.

Lovers don't deceive each other, they are saying the truth–but that truth belongs to the moment. When lovers say to each other, "I cannot live without you," it is not that he is deceiving or she is deceiving, they mean it. But they don't know the nature of life. Tomorrow this same woman will not look so beautiful. As days pass, the man and the woman both will feel that they are imprisoned.

They have know each other's geography completely. First it was an unknown territory to be discovered, now there is nothing to be discovered. And to go on repeating the same words and the same acts looks mechanical, ugly. That's why passion turns into hate. The woman hates you, because you are going to do the same thing again. To prevent you, the moment the husband enters the house she goes to bed, she has a headache. She wants somehow not to get into the same rut. And the man is flirting with his secretary in the office; now *she* is an unknown territory.

To me, it is all nature. What is unnatural is binding people in the name of religion, in the name of God, for their whole life.

In a better, more intelligent world, people will love, but will not make any contracts. It is not a business! They will understand each other, and they will understand the changing flux of life. They will be true to each other. The moment the man feels that now his beloved holds no joy for him, he will say that the time has come to part. There is no need for marriage, there is no need for divorce. Then friendship will be possible.

You ask me why friendship is not possible between men and women…. Friendship is not possible between the jailer and the imprisoned. Friendship is possible between equal human beings, totally free from all bondage of society, culture, civilization, only living true to their authentic nature.

It is not an insult to the woman to say, "Honey, the honeymoon is over." It is not an insult to the man if the woman says, "Now things cannot be beautiful. The wind that has blown is no longer there. The season has changed, it is no longer spring between us; no flowers blossom, no fragrance arises. It is time to part." And because there is no legal bondage of marriage, there is no question of any divorce.

It is ugly that the court and the law and the state interfere in your private life – you have to ask their permission. Who are they? It is a question between two individuals, their private affair.

There will be only friends – no husbands, no

wives. Of course, if there is only friendship, passion will never turn into hate. The moment you feel passion disappearing, you will say good-bye, and it will be understood. Even if it hurts, nothing can be done about it – it is the way of life.

But man has created societies, cultures, civilizations, rules, regulations, and made the whole humanity unnatural. That's why men and women cannot be friends. And men and women either become husbands and wives – which is something absolutely ugly; they start owning each other....

People are not things, you cannot have ownership. If I feel your wife is beautiful, and approach her, you are angry, you are ready to fight because I am approaching your property. No wife is anybody's property, no husband is anybody's property. What kind of world have you created? People are reduced to properties; then there is jealousy, hatred.

You yourself know that you are attracted to the neighbor's wife; naturally, you can guess about your wife too. Your wife knows perfectly well she is attracted to somebody else, but she cannot approach that person because of the husband: he is standing there with a gun! Love is bound to turn into hate, and for the whole life the hate goes on accumulating. And out of this hatred do you think beautiful children are going to be born? They are not born out of love, but out of duty. It is the wife's duty to allow you to use her.

To tell the truth, there is no difference between wives and prostitutes.

The difference is just like the difference between having your own car or going in a taxi.

You go to a prostitute – it is for a few hours, it is beautiful. After a few hours it is finished; you have paid the woman. And now there are male prostitutes also, particularly in California; California seems to be not part of this world. A few hours of relationship is purchased, and when you pay the woman or the man, everything is goody-goody. You will not recognize each other the next day when you meet on the street; there is no need, there has been no contract. You will not even say hello, not even "Hi." There is no need.

A prostitute is purchased only for a few hours; wives are a long-term affair, it is economical. Royal families are not allowed to marry outside royal blood: status, money, power.... Nobody can love anybody in such circumstances, where the relationship is financial.

The woman is dependent on you because you earn. And for centuries men have not allowed women to be educated, to be in business, to have jobs, for the simple reason that if the woman has her own financial status, her own bank account, you cannot reduce her to a thing. She has to be dependent on you. And do you think anybody who has to be dependent on you will love you?

Every woman wants to kill the husband. It is another matter that she does not kill him – because if she kills him, what will she do? She is not educated, she has no experience of the society, she has no way of earning. The husband – every husband, I don't make any exceptions – wants to get rid of the woman. But he cannot get rid of her. There are children, and he himself has promised the woman thousands of times that he loves her.

When he goes to his job he kisses the woman; there is no love in it, just skeletons touching each other. Nobody is present.

Man has created a society in which friendship between man and woman is impossible.

I would like my people to remember – even though you have to follow the laws of the society; otherwise they will imprison you and punish you and kill you...but remember, friendship is so valuable that whatsoever the consequence, remain friends even with your wife, even with your husband, and allow absolute and total freedom to each other.

I don't see any problem. If I love a woman, and one day she says that she has fallen in love with somebody else and feels very happy, I will be happy. I love her, and I would like her to be happy – where is the problem? I will help her in every way so that she can be more happy. If she can be more happy with somebody else, what hurts me?

It is your ego that hurts: she has found somebody else who is better than you. It is not a question of better, it may be just your chauffeur – it is just a question of a little change. And if you give full freedom to each other, perhaps you can remain together for your whole life, or for the whole eternity, because there is no need to get rid of each other.

Marriage creates the need to get rid of each other, because it means freedom is taken away – and freedom is the highest value in human life. Make all the couples free, and you will be surprised, this very world becomes paradise.

There are other problems. You have children – what to do with children? My answer is that children should not belong to their parents, they should belong to the commune. Then there is no problem. The parents can meet the children, they can invite the children, they can be friends with their children; and yet the children are not dependent on them, they belong to the commune. And it will destroy many psychological problems.

If a boy knows only his mother, the mother's personality becomes an imprint on him. Now, his whole life he will be trying to find a woman who is like his mother – and he will never find such a woman. A girl will never find another man who is exactly a copy of her father. Then you cannot be satisfied with any woman, any man.

But if the children belong to the commune, they will come in contact with so many uncles and so many aunts – they will not carry a single picture in their minds. They will have a vague idea of womanhood or manhood, and to that idea, many people of the commune will have contributed; it will be multidimensional. There is a possibility of finding somebody, because you only have a *vague* idea. You can find somebody, and that person will make your vague idea solid, a reality. Right now you have a solid idea

within you, and you meet a vague person. Sooner or later there is disappointment.

And children belonging to the commune will learn much, will be more friendly, will be more available to all kinds of influences. They will be richer. A child being brought up by a couple is very poor. He does not know that there are millions of people with different minds, different kinds of beauty. If a child moves in the commune, naturally he will be far richer. And he will have known so much before he decides to be with someone that there is a possibility of a long friendship.

What happens now? You see a girl on the beach and you fall in love. You know nothing about the girl, you know only her make-up. Tomorrow morning when you get up and the make-up is gone, you will say, "My God! What have I done? This is not the woman I married, this is someone else!" But you cannot go against your word either. And if you do, then the government is there, the courts are there to put you back into your right place. This is a very ugly situation, sick.

People should be given freedom to know each other, to know as many people as possible, because each person is so unique, there is no question of comparison. Let the child drink from many sources, and he will have some insight into who is going to be the right person to live with.

Nobody will fall in love; everybody will decide consciously that "This is the one." He has known so many people, he understands that this is the one who has those characteristics, those qualities that he has loved. And then too it is only going to be a friendship. There is no fear; if tomorrow things change there is no harm.

The society should not live in a routine way, in a fixed way – static, dormant – it should be a moving flux. One woman can give you a certain kind of joy, another woman can give you another kind of joy. A third woman will be a surprise. So why remain poor? – just because Jesus has said, "Blessed are the poor"?

Be richer in every dimension, and keep yourself open and available. And whoever you are with, let the other person understand clearly that "It is freedom between us, not a marriage license. Out of freedom we meet, with no promises for the future – because who knows the future?"

When I was a student in the university in my final master's course, one girl was very much interested in me. She was a beautiful girl, but my interest was not in women at that time. I was crazy in search of God!

After the examinations, when she was leaving the university…. She had waited – I knew it – she had waited and waited for me to approach her. That is the usual way, that the man approaches the woman; it is graceful for the woman not to approach the man. Strange idea…I don't understand. Whoever approaches, it is graceful. If fact, whoever initiates is courageous.

When we were leaving the university she said, "Now there is no chance." She took me aside and said, "For two years continuously I have been waiting. Can't we be together for our whole lives? I love you."

I said, "If you love me, then please leave me alone. I also love you, that's why I am leaving you alone – because I know what has been happening in the name of love. People are becoming imprisoned, chained; they lose all their joy, life becomes a drag. So this is my parting advice to you," I said, "Never try to cling to a person for your whole life."

If two persons are willingly together today, it is more than enough. If tomorrow again they feel like being together, good. If they don't, it is their personal affair; nobody has to interfere.

Up to now, the problem of the children has always been raised. My answer is that children should belong to the commune. They can go to their parents, whether their parents are together or separate. And they should learn from their parents that love is no slavery, it is freedom. And they should move in the commune, tasting, enjoying different qualities of different people.

So by the time they decide, their decision will be not just a foolish type of "falling in love"; it will be a very considered, contemplated, meditated phenomenon. There is a possibility they may remain together for their whole lives. In fact, if there is freedom, there is more possibility; more people will remain together.

If marriage disappears, divorce disappears automatically. This is a by-product of marriage. Nobody takes note of the simple fact: why for centuries have there been prostitutes? Who created them? Who is responsible for these poor women? It is the institution of marriage.

You are bored with your wife; just for a change you go to a woman who is not going to be a bondage – because one is enough, two will be too much. It is just a temporary, few hours' meeting. You can keep yourself lovely for a few hours, loving for a few hours. She can keep herself lovely and loving for a few hours. And moreover, she has been paid for it.

Around the world millions of women are reduced to selling their bodies. Who has done it? Your political leaders, your religious leaders. I consider these people criminals. And not ordinary criminals, because for centuries the whole humanity has been suffering because of these few idiots.

But you have to start with yourself, there is no other way. If you love somebody, then freedom should be the connecting link between you. And if you see your woman tomorrow hugging somebody else, there is no need to be jealous. She is being enriched, she is tasting a little newness – just the way you go sometimes to a Chinese restaurant! It is good. You will come back to your own food, but the Chinese restaurant has helped you; you may relish your own food more.

But after a few days, again – that's how the mind is – you are moving towards an Italian restaurant …spaghetti. I cannot even tolerate somebody eating spaghetti in front of me! But that is my problem.

Life is so simple and so beautiful, just one thing is missing: freedom. If your wife is being with some other people, soon she will come back to you enriched, with new insight. And she will find something in you she had never found before. And meanwhile, you need not just sit down in your chair and beat your head.

You also gain experience, so that by the time your woman is back you are also new. You have also been to the Chinese restaurant.

Life should be a joy, a rejoicing.

And then only can there be friendship between men and women; otherwise, they are going to remain intimate enemies.

You Have to Grow Inwards, That is Your Earth

DISCOURSE 16, July 14, 1985

Beloved Bhagwan,

The growth movement has been called the "new narcissism" by many, due to its emphasis on assertiveness and valuing one's own personal ego. How does Your way differ?

There *is* no way. It is impossible to have a way, because you are already there. You have never left home. This whole search for the way is driving you crazy; you cannot find it because you are already there. Wherever you go, you will go against your being, farther and farther away. You have gone already too far.

It is time to drop the idea of the way. Life is not a becoming, not some kind of process. It is being.

You cannot ask me how my way differs from the growth movement, because I have no way. I am not teaching you a way – really, I am taking you away from all the ways.

But the question has some significance. The growth movement was egoistic. It was the assertion of the ego repressed for centuries. Just by being assertive and egoistic you don't start growing. Or worse, you start growing in a wrong way.

My movement is not egoistic. I am not here to make your ego more and more strong – it is already too strong. My movement is towards egolessness.

That's where I depart from the growth movement. And no one can grow by strengthening the ego. He will remain just an imaginary being; he will not come to know his authentic reality.

The ego is not you, it is a pretender. People need it because they don't know who they are, and it is really difficult to live without having some idea of who you are; hence the ego comes into existence. It is make-believe; it is constructed by you so that you don't feel the vacuum, so that somehow you can manage to drag yourself to your grave.

I want you to drop the ego and then see: you will be vast, there will be no limit to you. That is growth. To become a tiny, pygmy ego is not growth, it is just the opposite.

The growth movement should not be called a growth movement at all. It is selling phony commodities to you; it is really cutting your very roots. And if you become satisfied with the ego you will never search, seek, for your self, because you will continue to believe, "This ego is me."

In Japan, for centuries it has been thought to be an art: great gardeners have been cutting the roots of trees. The tree is placed in a pot which has no bottom, so whenever the roots start growing, they just have to take up the pot and cut the roots. There are four-hundred-year-old trees only six inches high. I cannot conceive that this is art – this is murder. And those poor trees cannot say anything. If you don't allow their roots to grow deeper into the earth, they will not grow higher into the heavens, towards the stars. The deeper their roots, the higher will be their growth.

The same is true about man. Nature functions in an absolutely harmonious way. There are not many ways that nature grows. It may be a tree, a bird, a man – it doesn't matter, the principle, the law of growth remains the same: Let your roots go deeper.

Of course, a tree is standing, does not move – it has no legs. There *are* a few trees in Africa which, out of sheer necessity, have had to move. The jungles in Africa are so thick, and the trees are so big that there is no chance for new trees to grow; the sun never reaches them. It is just a sheer question of life and death. And they start moving out of crowded spaces to find some place where they can also have the sun, the air, the moon, the earth. In Africa there are walking trees; they walk in their own way, and are very intelligent.

Forget the idea that man is the only intelligent being on the earth. Yes, just as a tree is different from your body, it is different from your intelligence. But it has its own kind of intelligence. It has been found that the trees which move always move in the direction where more water is available, more sun is available, more air is available, more space is available. How do they know which direction to move, which path to take? And they never make any mistake.

They are not like Moses, who wandered for forty years with the poor Jews dying in the desert, finding Israel, the holy land promised to him by God himself. Forty years in the desert? Almost two-thirds of the Jews died on the way before they reached the place. I certainly say that it has nothing holy about it. But Moses was also tired and old. His people were almost finished, and the remaining ones were getting angry with him. They had lost all trust in him. He did not know where he was going. And in a desert it is very

While I am here, I am pouring myself into you. And I am grateful that you are allowing it to happen. Who bothers about the future? There is nobody in me who can care about the future. If existence can find me as a vehicle, I can remain assured that it can find thousands of people to be its vehicle. I am simply giving you a little opportunity to become vehicles of the whole.

difficult to find a path; there are no roads, no paths.

But these trees are far more intelligent than Moses. They don't wander here and there, they simply rush exactly to the point where they can survive, grow. In a few places where water pipelines are close by, they don't bother to go to a faraway place where they can find a river or a pond. They are very progressive, more progressive than Mahatma Gandhi.

They drop the idea of going to the river, which their parents have always followed. They don't care a bit about the past and the tradition; they rush towards the pipeline. And they are strong enough to break steel pipelines; they put their roots into the pipeline. Can you call these trees unintelligent? They have a different kind of intelligence.

But growth is possible only if you go deeper into your roots. You are not a tree; hence, you are not to grow your roots into the earth – that will be sheer death. You have to grow inwards. That is your earth. There you have to spread your roots, because there is your nourishment: your water, your sun, your air, your being.

Once you have found the center of your consciousness, growth happens of its own accord. It has not to be done, you have not to grow. It is just as when the tree gets nourishment, it starts growing: fresh leaves and flowers and branches suddenly start appearing.

The growth movement was not a growth movement. It started, of course, in California. Any nonsense…if you find it, and you want to trace where it started from, you have to go to California. It started in Esalen.

One of the directors of Esalen came to me, because he had become fed up. No growth was happening – and he was the director, so what about the poor fellows he was directing? He became a sannyasin here in America, and after one year he came to see me.

And this is one of my experiences: these people who become accustomed to leading others, who become accustomed to the attitude that "I know, and you do not; therefore, follow me"…. This director was directing the whole show in Esalen for many years. How many people he destroyed I don't know, but he must have destroyed a lot. Reading my books…. First his young daughter became my sannyasin, because she was still unpolluted. She became my messenger in Esalen, she turned many Esalen people to sannyas. It was she who insisted that her father come to me, and he came.

To read my books, to listen to my tapes, is one thing. But to come to me and look eye to eye – it is very difficult.

The man's name was Dick, and he proved a dick! Just within a few days he escaped without telling anybody. We looked for him – where had he gone? From Esalen I received his letter saying, "Yours is too dangerous a place." He must have been thinking that growth is without risk, growth is just a game, a gimmick. Perhaps you have to read something, do a few stupid groups, and within a few weeks you are grown-up.

Growth is simple on the one hand – the simplest thing – and on the other hand the most difficult thing, almost impossible. The reason why it is so, is: it is simple if you have guts. It is so simple that nothing has to be done, you just have to become a little more ingoing, directed towards your inner reality. Just as you see things with open eyes, you have to close your eyes and see what is there.

It is so simple.

It becomes dangerous because you have to lose many things. You have to lose all your past, your knowledgeability, your so-called growth. You have to lose everything that you have accumulated around you. It is all junk! If you cling to it, growth becomes impossible.

That man ran away from me. He still reads my books, he still listens to my tapes, but now I am so close, he has no courage to come back – because there in Esalen he is the director, and here he has to be nobody.

Esalen is almost dead, it has seen its days of glory. People have deserted it – only a few people once in a while go there – because they could see the point: that in becoming egoistic they are creating a more miserable life for themselves. What is the point of growing up? – misery, agony, jealousy, competitiveness, violence…because if you are assertive, violence is not very far away from you. It is just behind you like a shadow; your assertiveness can become violence any moment. And with a strong ego it is bound to become your very way of life.

I am not trying here to polish your egoistic mind. I am trying to demolish, not polish. I am trying to help camels to become lions! Of course, it is difficult for a camel to become a lion, but it is not impossible, because I have made many camels into lions.

And once you become a lion, I have nothing to do. Your very lionhood will make you a child: simple, innocent, clean, pure, holy. That is growth. You have found the roots. And those roots are not just yours. You cannot claim, "These are *my* roots," because your ego is no longer there to claim it. You have found the universal source of roots. You know now, perfectly well, that it is the same existence that blossoms in the rose, in the lotus, that moves the stars.

It is the same universe that is your energy too. You are not apart from existence, you are part of it. And the moment you realize that you are part of this beautiful universe, a great ecstasy surrounds you twenty-four hours a day.

So there is not only a difference between the so-called growth movement and what is happening here, they are diametrically opposite. The so-called growth movement is preventing people from growing. It consists only of camels. We are not interested in keeping you in the lowest grade of consciousness – camels, ugly. Nothing is straight in a camel; you cannot find a single straight line. Everything is as it should not be.

The lion has a beauty, tremendous beauty. If you have seen any statue, or a photograph or a drawing of the face of that great lion, Bodhidharma, you will be surprised looking at his eyes. Those eyes look so ferocious. The man was not like that, he was one of the most beautiful men who has walked on the earth. It is symbolic: those are the eyes of a lion.

It is a well-known fact that when the lion kills some animal, his method is hypnotism. He simply looks into the eyes of the animal, and the animal becomes hypnotized, stuck, frozen. He cannot escape, he cannot *move*. Trembling, he stands before the lion. The lion just has to keep hold of his eyes; through the eyes he prevents him from escaping. You will see in Bodhidharma's eyes the same flare, the same flame.

Many people escape from me. Their whole lives they will escape; now this becomes their growth. They waste their lives just escaping, and they can't see a simple fact, that they are just cowards. There was an opportunity to go through a transformation. Of course something has to be dropped, something has to be burned, something has to be completely forgotten; only then do you allow transformation to take place.

The master's work is to transform camels into lions. Then things take their own course: the lion becomes a child without any effort. The lion has found the roots.

The child is going to blossom into his being.

Here, the sannyasins have to drop everything – and dropping everything you have saved yourself; otherwise you are going to be drowned in all the mud that you have accumulated. Your parents, your teachers, your priests, your culture, religion, society – they are all pouring mud on you. And it is a very sticky mud, you become glued to it.

The decision to become a sannyasin is a very great, momentous decision, because from that point you will have to leave everything that you thought was yours, and you will have to move into a new dimension where nothing belongs to you. On the contrary, you belong to the whole.

Do you see the difference? When you say, "This

belongs to me," this is the language of the ego. And when you say, "I belong to the universe," this is the language of egolessness. Then you are in a total let-go. If you belong to the universe, then it is the universe who is going to take care of you.

I am saying it from my own experience. For thirty-two years I have been the poorest richest man in the world. And I don't have anything that belongs to me, nothing belongs to me, but the phenomenon of belonging to the universe has created harmony out of a great contradiction. As far as belongings are concerned, I am the poorest man you can find. Even a beggar has something which belongs to him.

I used to go to the university to teach. An old beggar was always there. The railway station was just in between my house and the university; the old beggar was always begging at the railway station, and he knew when I would be passing. He would come to the road and stand there. One day I was surprised – a young man was standing there, a young beggar. I said, "What happened to the old man?"

He said, "I got married to his daughter, and he has given me his place as the dowry. This is the best place in our profession! The railway station – so many new people coming and going – the university, so many people coming and going…there is nothing comparable to it."

So I said, "What happened to him?"

He said, "Now he has moved to another spot." The city had two stations, so he had moved to another station. And he was a very strong fellow; he must have thrown out the beggar who was thinking that that station belonged to him.

Nothing belongs to anybody, but even beggars are richer than me. Because I am not there, how can anything belong to me? And the moment I disappeared, my consciousness became part of the whole. I lost everything and I gained everything; hence I say, I am the poorest and the richest man. In these thirty-two years I have lived like a king, and I have not earned a single cent. The universe takes care. The universe is benevolent.

You *are* this universe's children. Just become a child, and your eyes will be able to see the point. And from that moment, growth goes on happening; you go on and on. And there are no borders to existence. There are no borders to your growth either.

Beloved Bhagwan,

You have just been saying that the words of the master become mere words after the master is gone. What will happen after You are gone?

Do you think my words are not already dead for you? First, think of that. The master is there, his words are there, but are those words alive for you? If they are alive for you, don't be worried. You know the secret.

It is not the words. The master can be there and the words can be dead. So why can't it happen the other way around? – the master is dead, but the words are still alive. It all depends on you. It is not a question of the master's life or death, but how you relate to those words.

Yes, it is simpler when the master is there, only in one way. Because those words are spoken, they carry some flavor of the master's heart. They carry a few beats of the master's heart towards you. It is simple in this way. But on the other hand, when the master is alive, perhaps the words will never become alive to you, because you start taking the master for granted. Then the words are dead.

It happened in the second world war that Adolf Hitler declared that he was going to destroy the Tower of London. Millions of people rushed towards the tower – they had passed the tower thousands of times in their lives, but had never taken the trouble to see it. People come from all over the world to see the Tower of London, but Londoners take it for granted. The moment Hitler said he was going to destroy it, suddenly those people who had lived their whole lives in London became aware that the Tower of London could not be taken for granted anymore. They rushed to see it before this madman, Adolf Hitler, destroyed it.

The master is alive – but the disciple can take him for granted. You can take me for granted. Then those words are already dead, because your aliveness is not available. If you are capable of being alert, alive, responsive, it makes no difference: the master may be dead, but his words will go on resounding in you. Even the written words, which are dead, can become alive in you; you just have to open your heart.

The question is not of the master's life and death, the question basically is of your response.

So don't be worried about when I am gone. Those who are missing me now will be missing me then too – no loss. Those who are living my message now, they will go on living it. And if they go on living it, they cannot help but spread it. I am not depending on books – all the religions have depended on books – I am depending on *you*!

George Gurdjieff used to say – very sadly, of course – that if even two hundred people are enlightened, they can make the whole world full of light, full of life. Just two hundred people can transform the whole character of humanity. He could not manage it, but what he said is true.

I am going to manage it! I will not leave you unless I have made enough people enlightened so that they can make the whole world afire, alive. I am depending on you, not on any books. Those books may be helpful in some way to bring people to you, but my word will be throbbing in your heart; only then can you help anybody who comes to you.

And it is so simple. I have more than half a million sannyasins in the world, and more than one million people who are just on the borderline – a little push and they will be sannyasins. One million more who are lovers but cannot drop their camelhood....

On this big a scale, a worldwide scale, nobody has worked before. Gautam Buddha remained confined to the small state of Bihar in India – not even the whole of India. India has thirty states; Buddha remained confined to one space, one state.

He did great work, but it was impossible to transform the whole quality of consciousness on the earth. The same is true about Jesus, Moses – anybody who has been trying.

For a simple reason I have been able to contact millions of people around the world: I am not confined to any tradition. I am not burdened by the past, I am completely weightless. So anybody who is burdened – and who is not burdened? – becomes interested in me, particularly the young people who are fed up with all the nonsense that is being taught in the churches and the synagogues, in the temples, in the mosques.

All these people, these churches, synagogues and mosques, are trying to bridge the gap. You have heard the phrase "generation gap." Between you and the church, between you and the synagogue, there is not just a generation gap, there is a gap of hundreds of generations. And in trying to bridge it, they are proving themselves buffoons, because truth never compromises. It cannot – with whom will it compromise? Compromising truth means compromising with lies.

And all these people have become afraid that young people are no longer interested; they don't come to the synagogue, they don't come to the church, so something should be done that can attract young people. Their whole business is going down.

I have heard about three rabbis.... And by the way, don't let me drift. Whenever I come across the word "rabbi" I immediately associate it with rubbish. These three rabbis were meeting, discussing, talking about great things. One rabbi said, "My synagogue is the most modern, because we allow people to smoke in the synagogue. There is no harm in it."

The second rabbi said, "This is nothing, my synagogue is even more modern: we even allow people to make love in the synagogue. What is wrong with it?"

The third rabbi said, "This is nothing. My synagogue is the most avant-garde."

The two rabbis said, "Just tell us what you have done."

He said, "My synagogue remains closed for Jewish holidays!"

They are trying hard, but it is just foolishness. They cannot catch hold of the new spirit of man.

I don't give you any tradition.

I don't give you any scripture.

I don't give you any discipline.

Those are all non-essentials. I simply concentrate my whole work on making you more conscious. Consciousness is the key to transform the whole of humanity.

And yes, Gurdjieff *is* right: if even two hundred people are aflame, enlightened, the whole world will become enlightened, because these two hundred torches can give fire to millions of people. Those people are also carrying torches, but without any fire. They have everything, just the fire is missing. And when fire passes from one torch to another, the first torch is not losing anything at all.

The enlightened consciousness is an infinite reservoir: it can give to you and yet it remains the same. Its quantity does not decrease, because it is not a question of quantity at all; it is a question of quality. Qualities can be shared without losing anything.

You can love as many people as you want – that does not mean one day you will go bankrupt, and you will have to declare, "Now I have no love." You cannot go bankrupt as far as love is concerned. Yes, you can go bankrupt as far as money is concerned. Money is a quantity; love is a quality. What to say of enlightened consciousness? It is the highest quality possible; there is nothing higher than that.

Don't be afraid, worried that if I am gone, then what will happen to my words. I will not be gone before I have sown the seeds of those words in you.

They are not mine! They are nobody's. They are coming out of existence itself – I am simply a vehicle. *You* can become a vehicle. Everybody is capable of becoming a vehicle. Hence, I am not depending on old strategies; they have all failed. I am depending on living human beings.

And that is the only way to save humanity without becoming a savior, to save humanity without creating in them greed for heaven and fear of hell. The only way to save humanity is to give them some taste of what it means to be enlightened, a little fragrance, so they can feel the invisible.

And I am absolutely certain, utterly happy, that I have got the right people: people who are going to be my books, my temples, my synagogues. This is the reason I call this the first religion, because it depends on living human beings, not on dead holy scriptures, traditions, beliefs.

I am giving you the taste of my being, and preparing you to do the same, on your part, to others. It all depends on you, whether my words will remain living or will die. As far as I am concerned, I do not care.

While I am here, I am pouring myself into you. And I am grateful that you are allowing it to happen. Who bothers about the future? There is nobody in me who can care about the future. If existence can find me as a vehicle, I can remain assured that it can find thousands of people to be its vehicle.

I am simply giving you a little opportunity to become vehicles of the whole.

Beloved Bhagwan,

I am British, miserable, unenlightened, and an ex-sann-yasin. Is there anything else left for me to achieve?

No, sir! You have done everything. You have done really more than is possible. Now the only thing left for you is Krishnamurti Lake.

If You depart on the 6th of July of any year, are we all going with You?

No, nobody is going with me. I am not Reverend Jim Jones, I am not even a Christian. The day I go, your responsibility to live becomes greater – to live me, to become me. All around the world all the communes have to understand it.

It is very easy to die with me. It is so easy that it is against my sannyasins' dignity. I will not give you such any easy job. You have to *live*! And when I am not there, you have to live more consciously, more carefully – because who is going to spread me all over the world?

Remember, dying is a very easy thing; it happens in a single moment. Living is the real challenge. My leaving the body will be a challenge for you, that now that I have left one body, I can be in *all* of your bodies; that now I am not speaking from one mouth, I can speak from millions of mouths.

Christians have been cowards, not accepting the responsibility of Jonestown. They have created a religion which is death-oriented. My religion is life-oriented, I do not believe in death. In fact, there is no death. Nothing dies, it only transmigrates into new forms.

The enlightened person does not enter another life circle; he has nothing left to learn. The world is just a school. If you go on committing mistakes in unconsciousness, existence will give you millions of chances to come back again and again until you get awakened and drop your mistakes. That will be your last embodiment.

I am not going to be reborn in a body, because that would be just idiotic. When I can live in the bodies of millions of my sannyasins, what is the point of again getting caged in one body? In fact, the enlightened consciousness simply spreads into all those who are available and open. It becomes universal.

You are not going with me, but I am coming within you!

Beloved Bhagwan,

You speak of reincarnation. I have not experienced it, and I don't want to believe in anything I don't experience. What to do?

Who is asking you to believe in reincarnation? And why are you concerned to do something about it? There must be some lingering belief. If you don't believe in reincarnation, that is the full stop. Why bother about what to do?

Don't believe in reincarnation! Just live this incarnation, and you will come to experience that reincarnation is not theory, it is a reality. Just live this incarnation. Do you believe in *this* incarnation, or not? Reincarnation is either in the past or in the future, but you are here, alive. Life is throbbing in you.

I know reincarnation is a truth. But I am not saying that you should believe it because I say so.

Never believe anybody else's experience; that is a hindrance. I can only say to you, just live this incarnation. That will open doors and you will be able to see backwards, you will be able to see forwards. And then it is up to you to believe in it or not. How can you disbelieve it then? But before that.... Let it become an experience.

All the religions are based on belief systems. I am giving you absolute freedom to enquire, to doubt, because that is the only way to experience on your own. And unless you experience on your own, there is no value at all in believing.

You love me. Naturally, if I say reincarnation is a truth, out of your love you may believe in me. Out of your love, how can you conceive that I may be telling something untruthful to you? You trust me.

And this trust has been exploited for million of years, this love has been exploited by every religion. I am not going to exploit in any way. About whatsoever I have known I can open my heart to you, but remember not to fall in the trap of believing. Love is good, trust is good – but belief is poison. If you really love me, if you really trust me, then make every effort to experience what I am saying to you. I want enquirers, people who are capable of doubt, who are capable of asking questions.

All the religions have repressed people's questions, their doubts, their enquiries. They say, "Don't bring in all these things. We *know*. For you, all that is left is to believe." That's why you see the whole humanity in such a miserable, dark, dismal ignorance. The responsibility goes to the religions.

Your love, I respect. For your trust, I am grateful. But these beautiful things should not be used as a strategy to make you a believer. I want you to be a knower. If you love me and trust me, then go on enquiring, searching, seeking. Till you have found, never believe. And I can say it with such certainty, because I know that if you enquire you will find it; it is there!

The other religions have been telling you to believe, because they are not certain that it is there. It is because of their own doubt that they are repressing your doubts. They are afraid that if you start doubting and asking and enquiring, you may not find any God, any reincarnation, any truth. Then their whole business – and it is the biggest business in the world – will simply disappear.

As far as I am concerned, not a single word from me has to be believed, but to be experienced. And I am giving you the method, *how* to experience it.

Become more meditative. Reincarnation and God, heaven and hell, do not matter. What matters is your becoming alert. Meditation awakens you, gives you eyes – and then whatever you see, you cannot deny.

As far as I am concerned, reincarnation is a truth, because in existence nothing dies. Even the physicist will say, about the objective world, that nothing dies.

You can destroy Hiroshima and Nagasaki – so much power science has given to chimpanzee politicians – but you cannot destroy a single drop of water.

You cannot destroy. Physicists have become aware of this impossibility. Whatever you do, only the form changes. You destroy a single dewdrop, and there is hydrogen and oxygen; they were its components. You cannot destroy hydrogen or oxygen. If you try, then from molecules you come to atoms. If you destroy the atom, you come to electrons. We don't know right now if we can destroy the electron. Either you cannot destroy it – it is the ultimate objective constituent of reality – or if you can destroy it, then you will find something else. But nothing can be destroyed in the objective world.

The same is true about the world of consciousness, of life. There is no death. Death is only a change from one form into another form, and ultimately from form to formlessness. And that is the goal – because every form is a kind of imprisonment. Unless you become formless, you cannot get rid of misery, jealousy, anger, hatred, greed, fear, because these are concerned with your form.

But when you are formless, there is nothing that can harm you, there is nothing that you can lose any more, there is nothing that can be added to you. You have come to the ultimate realization.

Only Gautam Buddha has given the right word for this experience. In English it is difficult to translate it, because languages develop only after experience. It is just arbitrarily that I am calling it "enlightenment." But it is very arbitrary; it does not really give you the sense that Buddha's word gives. He calls it *nirvana*.

I can explain the word to you. *Nirvana* means ceasing to be. Strange…ceasing to be. I could have used that word, but that would make you afraid. Already people are so much afraid of me – I, who have never done any harm to anybody.

Not to be is nirvana. That does not mean that you are no more; it simply means you are no longer an entity, embodied. Yes, in that sense you are no more, but that is the way – not to be is the way to be all. The dewdrop drops into the ocean. You can say it has died, but those who know will say it has become oceanic. Now it is the whole ocean.

Existence is alive at every stage. Nothing is dead. Even a stone – which you think seems to be completely dead – is not dead. So many living electrons are running so fast inside it that you cannot see them, but they are all living beings. Their bodies are so small that nobody has seen them; we don't even have any scientific instrument to see the electron, it is only guesswork. We can see the effect; hence we think there must be a cause. The cause has not been seen, only the effect has been seen. But the electron is as alive as you are.

The whole existence is synonymous with life.

Here nothing dies. Death is an impossibility.

Yes, things change from one form to another form till they become mature enough that they need not go to school again. Then they move into a formless life, then they become one with the ocean itself.

The Death
Of the Mind
Is the Birth of You

DISCOURSE 17, July 15, 1985

Beloved Bhagwan,

For the last six years I've lived in Your communes. You are here, all my friends are here; everything I love and value is here. And yet, I often think of leaving. What's wrong?

That's what is wrong. You have all your friends here, all that you love, all that you have aspired to. When one comes to a point of having all, a great desire to escape from it arises – for the simple reason that the mind wants more and more and more.

If all is available, the mind starts feeling restless; it has nothing to do.

It is a strange fact that poor countries and their people are more satisfied and contented, compared to the rich countries and their people, because the poor can hope and hopes keep them going. If you reach the final rung of the ladder, you are suddenly at a loss; you cannot hope anymore, there is nothing to hope for.

The mind and its functioning has to be understood; the continuous desire for more has to be understood. It is very sick.

One should start looking into one's desire to leave when everything is available. Who is prompting this desire? The mind wants more, and there is no more anymore. The mind is bound to create turmoil

in you to escape. And the dichotomy is that on the other hand you see, "All is available here. Where am I going to be and what am I going to gain by going there?" It is sheer stupidity. But this mind comes from the monkeys and *is* stupid.

You have to learn not to be identified with the mind. You have to be just a watcher, and see all the buffoonery that the mind goes on doing around you. Don't applaud, don't support, don't negate – just watch. Take no action against the mind because that is also part of the mind. Only one thing in you is the door, and that is witnessing, because it is not part of the mind. It is simple to understand: if you can witness your mind, certainly you are not the mind. Anything that you can see in front of you, you are not.

This is the whole simple and open secret of meditation. Whatever the monkey within you is doing, watch, with no judgment, because any judgment is either going to be for or against; you have become party to the foolishness of the mind. Neither for or against, just remain watchful of what is happening and this desire to leave will disappear, because you will be able to see that what you wanted is here. So where are you going? And this mind will be with you wherever you go, and it will not allow you any rest.

The mind always wants to go on and on, because that is its very lifeblood. Stopping, even for a single moment, the mind dies. And the death of the mind is the birth of you. While the mind has power over you, you are not born yet.

All the great masters in the East were either kings, or princes who were going to become kings. Buddha, Mahavira, Parshvanatha, Bahubali – what happened to these people? Not a single poor man in the whole history of the East has become a great master, for the simple reason that he still has hope.

Hope is your opium. It keeps you going. It is just there, you have to stretch your hand a little bit more. It is hanging just before you: a little effort and it will be yours. It is not going to be so; it will always go on hanging just there. It will not be too far because that may create the idea, "Perhaps I cannot manage to go that far. I don't have the strength. The journey is very long." So your hope is not very far away, just close enough so that it would be foolish not to get it. By the time you get it, it is still there in some different form.

That's why religions in the East – particularly in India – have a flavor that religions which are not born there don't have. In India, three religions have existed for thousands of years: Jainism is the oldest, then Hinduism, then Buddhism. Jainas have twenty-four *tirthankaras,* the great masters. But strangely enough, all twenty-four came from royal families. Either they were already kings or they were going to be kings sooner or later. And they escaped – they had everything, just at their fingertips they had the whole world. That was the problem; they had to escape.

In Buddhism there is a strange story – but worth understanding, because it is the story of each of you. When Buddha was born, the great astrologers said to the king, "We are afraid, but you have to be made aware of it: this newborn baby is either going to become a *chakravartin*" – a *chakravartin* means one who rules over the whole world – "or he is going to become a beggar who owns nothing." ...two extremes.

The king was old and this was his only son, born in his old age. He asked the astrologers how to prevent him from becoming a beggar and renouncing

Every hope is against existence. Every prayer is against existence. You are asking for something that existence has not given to you. You are trying to get something that existence is not willing to give you. Perhaps you don't deserve it. I don't teach you hope, because to teach hope means that following the hope, just like a shadow, will be hopelessness. I teach you to enjoy whatsoever *is*.

the world. Those astrologers had no idea of mind and psychology. Astrologers may have ideas about far-away stars, whose light takes millions of light years to reach the earth…. And what a foolishness, that man thinks his fate, his destiny, is determined by all these millions of stars so far away!

There is a reason why astrology has remained significant: it gives you great satisfaction that the whole universe is interested in you. Even the faraway stars are trying their best to do something to you; you are not an ordinary person, you are not nothing. Those faraway stars are not even aware of you, cannot be, but your ego feels tremendous satisfaction.

Astrologers have been exploiting this since the very beginning of man. Of course, they exploit you, you have to pay for it, but it seems worth paying them; they are giving you a big ego. You are bigger, far more important, than the biggest star in the sky. They are all just revolving around you!

But those poor astrologers were not even as intelligent as Sigmund Freud. They told the king, "If you want him not to renounce the world, then a few arrangements have to be made."

In India there are three clear-cut seasons in the year. Since the atomic explosions around the world, that has changed; otherwise, every year on the same day the rains will begin, and on the same day they will stop. On the same day the winter comes, and after four months on the same day it stops. For centuries it has been absolutely certain. Now it is not so, but in Buddha's time it was certain.

Buddha's father made three palaces, one for each season. For summer, a palace in the hill station: cool, beautiful, green. Every care was taken that Buddha would never become disappointed with the world. For winter, a warm and cozy atmosphere was made in the palace.

The astrologers told the king, "From the very beginning let him be surrounded with beautiful girls, so by the time he becomes a young man he has all the beautiful girls of the land."

They even went into details: that he should not see any old man, because in his seeing an old man the question could arise in him, "Is this the destiny for everyone?" Never allow him to see a dead body. Keep him absolutely unaware of the realities of life, keep him in a dreamland. Their argument was, when he has everything, why should he renounce?

The greatest physician of the country was looking after him. Even the gardeners in the king's garden were told that Buddha should not see a flower withering away or a leaf turning pale. In the night everything that indicates death had to be removed. He should see only beautiful flowers which are always young. He should see only green leaves which are always green.

And this the king could manage. He managed it – and his management backfired. Those idiotic astrologers had no idea of a simple fact: that if you give a man everything and keep him unaware of all that is ugly around, soon he is going to be fed up with it. Soon he will start thinking, "Is this all? Then tomorrow is going to be the same, and the day after tomorrow is going to be the same. What is the point?" He will become bored.

And that's what happened. Buddha became bored with unchanging beautiful women, unchanging beautiful flowers. How long can your mind keep silent? The astrologers were the reason why Buddha renounced the kingdom. If he had been allowed to live just the ordinary life of every man, perhaps there would have been no Buddha.

In a way, the idiotic astrologers unknowingly did a great service to humanity.

The story is beautiful. There used to be an annual festival in the capital, and the prince who was going to be king used to inaugurate it, declare it open. It lasted for a few weeks – all kinds of things, all kinds of athletic games, shows. Buddha was going to inaugurate this youth festival in his twenty-ninth year.

On the way every care was taken – but existence has its ways to reach you. You cannot remain completely closed in a grave, unless you are dead. If you are alive, there are bound to be loopholes from where existence will enter and make you aware of the reality. The astrologers and the kings could not be more intelligent than existence itself.

Every care was taken that on the way from the palace to the festival stadium, no old men should be seen, no dead bodies should be carried – nothing that could create a questioning in Buddha. But you cannot avoid reality for long. As the chariot was going towards the festival grounds, Buddha saw an old man. The old man was deaf and he had not heard that today he was not to pass on this road, he was to remain in the house or go somewhere else. He was deaf, he could not hear it, so just as usual he came out of his house; he was going to purchase something from the market.

Buddha, for the first time in twenty-nine years, saw an old man just on the borderline of death. He asked his charioteer, "What is the matter? What has happened to this man? I have never seen anything like this!"

The charioteer loved Buddha just as his own son. He could not lie. He said, "Although it is going against the orders of your father, I cannot lie to you. You have been prevented from seeing people getting old. Everybody gets old – I will get old. This is the way of life."

Buddha immediately asked, "Am I also going to be old one day just like this man?"

The charioteer said, "I have to say the truth to you: I would like that this should not happen to you, but it is the law of nature; nothing can be done. Just as from childhood you have become a young man, from youth you will become one day old too."

And then, just then, somebody died. Now you cannot prevent death. You cannot order death, "You are not to happen on this road, you can happen anywhere else." Death is not in your hands. Somebody died, people were crying, and the dead body was there.

Buddha asked, "What has happened? Why are people crying?" He had never seen anybody crying, he had never seen anybody with tears; he had never seen anybody dead. He asked, "What has happened to this man? He is not even breathing!"

The charioteer said, "This is the second stage. First you saw the old man. Soon death will come to him too. It has come to this man."

Buddha asked, "Am I also going to die one day?"

The charioteer – afraid of the king, but he must have been a man of some integrity – said, "Truth is truth, nobody can deny it. Your father the king is going to die, I am going to die, you are going to die. Death begins the day you are born. After birth there is no way to escape death."

And just then they passed a sannyasin. Astrologers had said to the king, "Your son should not be allowed any contact with sannyasins, because those are the people who have renounced everything. Those are the people who teach that this world is illusion, that all your desires are going to lead you nowhere, that you are simply wasting your life, and death is coming close by every moment. Sannyasins have to be avoided." And for twenty-nine years Buddha had no notion that there are people who are trying to find something which is beyond life and death.

This red-clothed sannyasin looked very strange to him – just as when you move into the world outside the commune *you* look strange to people. They are living a life of dreams. You suddenly come, and you shock them! Questions, enquiries: "What has happened to you? Why are you wearing a red robe?"

And a man who has not seen a sannyasin his whole life, for twenty-nine years, is bound to be more enquiring. He said, "And what about this man? I have seen people, but nobody wears a loose robe like this, with a begging bowl in his hand. What kind of man is he?"

The charioteer said, "This man has understood that beauty is going to turn into ugliness, that youth is going to turn into old age, that life is going to turn into death, and he is trying to find, 'Is there something eternal? Is there something which is not affected by youth, by old age, by death, by disease?' He is a sannyasin, he has renounced the ordinary world. He is a seeker of truth."

They were just reaching the stadium. Buddha said to the charioteer, "Turn back – I am not going to the youth festival. If youth is finally going to become old age, disease, death, and if this is going to happen to me, then I have lost twenty-nine years uselessly. I have lived in dreams. I am no longer young, and I am no longer interested in being the prince. Tonight I am going to renounce this world and be a seeker of truth."

What the astrologers had thought looked like common sense…but common sense is superficial. They could not think a simple thing: that you cannot keep a man for his whole life unaware of reality. It is better to let him know from the very beginning; otherwise it will come as a big explosion in his life. And that's what happened.

That very night Buddha escaped from the palace where everything was available.

In India, all these three religions' great masters come from royalty. That's why there is a great difference, almost unbridgeable, between Christianity and Buddhism, between Mohammedanism and Jainism. The difference comes because Jesus is not a prince. He comes from a poor family, he is the son of a poor carpenter, Joseph. He knows all, nothing is hidden from him. His religion is going to be the poor man's religion. No wonder all around the world poor people go on turning into Christians.

In India, I have traveled continually trying to find a single rich man who became a Christian, and I have not found one. Those who become Christians are orphans, beggars, starving people. Of course they cannot understand Buddhism because Buddha does not turn stones into bread, and that's what they want. Buddha does not change water into wine; on the contrary, he prohibits you because any alcoholic drug is going to destroy your meditativeness. He is not going to raise a dead man from the grave and bring him back to life. What is the point – he will go again. Why give him trouble?

Do you know what happened to Lazarus?

Even if Jesus raised him from the dead – which is nonsense…. For the argument's sake if we accept that yes, he was raised from death back to life, then what happened to him? Where is Lazarus? He will have to die again so what is the point? Maybe a few years more of misery and poverty, sickness, anxiety and anguish – and you call it a miracle? And again he will be back in the grave. At least in the grave he will be without anxiety, without poverty, without sickness, and without any fear of death. It has already happened, now it cannot happen again. Jesus really was unkind if he *did* raise Lazarus from death.

Buddha would not do it. It is not a miracle, it is foolishness. A similar case happened in Buddha's life: a young child died; the father had died, and the woman was living only for this child. That young child was her whole life and her only hope; otherwise, there was nothing for her to live for. And the child died. She was almost on the verge of going crazy. She wouldn't allow people to take the child to the crematorium. She was hugging the child in the hope that perhaps he might start breathing again. She was ready to give her life if the child could live.

The people said, "This is not possible, it is against the law of nature." But she was in such misery, she could not listen to anybody. Then somebody said, "The best way is, let us take this woman to Gautam Buddha who, just by chance, is in the village."

This appealed to the woman. A man like Gautam Buddha can do anything, and this is a small miracle – nothing much – that the child starts breathing again. She went, crying and weeping, put the child's dead body at the feet of Buddha, and asked him, "You are a great master, you know the secrets of life and death, and I have come with great hope. Make my child alive again."

Buddha said, "That I will do, but you have to fulfill a condition before I do it."

She said, "I am ready to fulfill any condition. I am ready to give my life, but let my child live."

Buddha said, "No, the condition you have to fulfill is very simple. You just go around the village and find a few mustard seeds from a house where death has never happened."

She was in such despair, she went from one house to another. And those people said, "We can give you as many mustard seeds as you want, but those mustard seeds will not help you. Not only one, but many have died in our family; perhaps thousands have died."

By the evening, a great awakening had happened to the woman. She had gone through the whole village, and the same reply…. They were all ready to help her but they said, "These mustard seeds won't help. Buddha has made it clear to you, 'Bring the mustard seeds from a family where nobody has ever died.'"

By the evening, when she returned, she was a totally different woman. She was not the same woman who had come in the morning. She had become absolutely aware that death is a reality of life – it cannot be changed. And what is the point? "Even if my child lives for a few years, he will have to die again. In the first place it is not possible; in the second place, even if it were possible, it is pointless."

Now there were no more tears in her eyes, she was very quiet, serene. A tremendous understanding had come to her: that she was asking for the impossible. She dropped that desire. She came and fell at Buddha's feet.

Buddha said, "Where are the mustard seeds? I have been waiting the whole day."

The woman instead of crying, laughed. She said, "You played a good joke. Forget all about the child, what is gone is gone. Now I have come to be initiated and to become a sannyasin. The way you have found the truth which never dies, I also want to find. I am

no longer concerned with the child or anybody else. My concern is now, how to find the truth which never dies, which is life itself."

Buddha said, "Forgive me that I had to ask you for something I knew was impossible. But it was a simple device to bring you to your senses, and it worked."

I call *this* a miracle. Lazarus being raised from the grave is not a miracle; it is just a bogus story created by the Christians to make their master appear as the greatest master in the world, who can do such miracles, who can walk on water. Nobody can walk on water. I find it difficult even to walk on the ground! Do you want me to walk on water? I will become enlightened again!

One very rich, super-rich Jew was visiting Jerusalem in the holy land, Israel, and he was going around seeing all the places. He saw Lake Galilee where Jesus used to walk on water. He did not believe it – he was a Jew, he was not a Christian. But he told the boatman that he would like to go around the lake – it is a really beautiful place.

The boatman was a Christian. He had no idea that this man is a Jew because Israel is a holy land for Christians too, and Christians are coming daily to the boatman to take them around the lake where Jesus walked. This water is no longer ordinary water; this lake is no longer an ordinary lake. Jesus walking on it has made it something holy, something divine.

But he could not see that the man was a Jew, not a Christian…only Christians used to come there. One thing he could see: that he was American, rich – he has come in a big limousine. So he raised his price. Ordinarily he was asking only one dollar to go all around the lake; he asked for twenty dollars.

The Jew said, "My God, twenty dollars! Now I know why Jesus used to walk on water – for the first time I have discovered the truth. From where would that poor guy get twenty dollars? Of course he had to walk on water! I am not going to walk on water, and I am not going to give you twenty dollars either!"

Christianity and Mohammedanism are the two religions born outside of India. Mohammed was also a very poor man, uneducated, just capable of somehow managing two meals a day. He was a shepherd – not metaphorically, as Jesus goes on calling himself the shepherd and you the sheep. Mohammed was actually a shepherd; that was his job.

Mohammedanism and Christianity are the two religions created by poor people. They don't have that elegance, that delicacy, that flavor, that comes from meditation. They don't have even the word "meditation" in their vocabulary. They are the religions of prayer.

Prayer makes you a beggar; meditation makes you a master. Prayer is a degradation: you are humiliating yourself, falling on your knees, folding your hands towards the sky, knowing nothing of what you are doing. And what do you ask in your prayer? "Give us more wealth, give us more life, give us more health." What else can you ask?

And religion is not for those who ask. Religion is for those who give. But to give in the first place you have to have. You have to experience the life that is flowing in you; you have to experience the consciousness that you are. Then suddenly you are no longer a beggar and prayer becomes absolutely absurd. There is no one to whom the prayer can be addressed, and there is no need – even if someone is there – because meditation opens the doors to your own treasures.

Unless you are in a meditative state, this mind of yours will go on being a beggar. You may have everything, but the mind wants more. That is what I mean by being a beggar: always wanting more, more, more…. And there is no end to it.

Meditation does not desire for anything. There is no idea of more. Meditation simply wants to know, "What is in me? If I can discover my own center, I have discovered the center of all" – because the center of you is not only the center of *you*.

On the circumference we are different, but at the center…there is only one center, it is universal. It is at the center that I and you and everybody meet and become one.

It is easy to understand your desire, that you have everything here – but that is the trouble. What do you want? – that things should be taken away from you so you can start again and not feel stuck? No, more and more will be given to you. And that is creating a dichotomy, because on the other hand, you would not like to lose what you have got. That is the schizophrenic nature of the mind.

All minds are schizophrenic. Mind as such is sick. Mind creates a split in you: you would like to have all this, all that is available here, so you cannot go away. And you have everything that you wanted available to you, and the mind wants more. You have to decide and choose between mind and meditation. Mind is a beggar, and meditation is a master.

Become master of your own self. And I would like you to become more and more rich in every dimension, because I accept life in its totality. I would like my commune to be the richest, to be the most intelligent, to be in the best of health. I would like my commune to change into paradise. But that is possible only if you drop this crazy mind which goes on asking for more. And it is only a question of simply understanding and shifting your energies from the mind to the witnessing consciousness. Don't be identified with the mind, because you are *not* it, you are the witness.

Without knowing it, your question itself makes it clear that you are a witness. You are witnessing that you have everything here, there is no need to go anywhere – and anyway you cannot go. This is your home, these people are your people. You cannot find so much love and life and laughter anywhere in the world. So you cannot go. But once in a while the mind will create the disturbance and say, "Here you are just stuck. Nothing is happening."

I am answering the question because it happens to many people, and they go on writing to me, "What to do? I would just like to go in the outside world for a few days, the mind is going crazy. I don't want to miss anything, and I know I am not going to get anything there, but what to do with the mind? It says, 'Just go for a three week holiday. Go to the beach.'"

And during all those three weeks on the beach, your mind will say, "What are you doing here? You are an idiot! All that was beautiful, lovable, you have left behind."

In fact, we are constantly enjoying a holiday. Where can you go? If there is anything missing here, we are able to create it, to bring it here. Rather than you going to the beach, we can bring the beach here! And that will be far better, because one person going on a holiday…you will miss your friends, and you will miss this great family.

And you will find you are just an outsider there. You will not be able to mix with the people outside the commune. You have changed so much that you and they are living in two different worlds. They will not be able to understand you, nor will you be able to understand them.

Drop the mind. Move towards the witness. Then you will be immensely attuned with the milieu here. If anything is missing, so many intelligent people can create it. And we have to create something that the whole world feels jealous of!

Beloved Bhagwan,

On my way from the City of Rajneesh to Rajneeshpuram, I saw many signs along the road which are against You. The last one, just before the turn to Rajneeshpuram, said, "All you who enter here shall give up hope." Is there really anything to hope for?

Those fanatic Christians are writing all these things, but they don't know that these things are not against me. They have written what I am teaching you! You are entering here; there is no hope, no hope even of getting out from here!

Those idiots who have written that will be thinking that this will stop you entering Rajneeshpuram. In fact it is an invitation, because hope brings hopelessness, sure and certain. All hopelessness in man exists because he hopes.

You have heard the proverb: Man proposes and God disposes. There is no God who disposes. Man certainly proposes, and hopes that it will be fulfilled. Nature has no obligation to fulfill your desires, crazy demands. Existence is available only for those who have dropped hope, because every hope is against existence.

Do you see the point? Every hope is against existence. Every prayer is against existence. You are asking for something that existence has not given to you. You are trying to get something that existence is not willing to give you. Perhaps you don't deserve it.

I don't teach you hope, because to teach hope means that following the hope, just like a shadow, with be hopelessness.

I teach you to enjoy whatsoever *is.*

Hope is always in the future, and you are always in the present. How can there be a bridge between the hope and you? Existence is here, hope is there – the bridge is not possible. Every hope is going to be frustrated. If you enjoy being frustrated, if you love to be hopeless, then you can hope as much as you like.

If you want to be blissful, to be blessed, then all hopes have to be dropped. Just visualize for a single moment that you don't have any hope. Immediately you can see hopelessness also disappears.

It is a very significant question. If you ask for the meaning of life you will feel meaninglessness. Jean-Paul Sartre feels life is meaningless. Life is neither meaningless nor meaningful, life simply is. But if you try to find some meaning in it, naturally that meaning is not there. You are the creator of your meaninglessness. And then despair, anguish….

Life simply is. Enjoy it! Why hope? When life is

here, you are wasting your life and time in hoping, and then one day you will find those hopes cannot be fulfilled. Then you will suffer hopelessness. This is all your own creation: hope, hopelessness; meaning, meaninglessness.

I don't have any hope. That does not mean hopelessness. Hopelessness is the other side of hope. Throw away the coin of hope and the hopelessness is thrown away too. You cannot save one – you cannot have a one-sided coin – the other side will be there. You can go on deceiving yourself, but for how long? And whom are you kidding? Just wasting your life....

People have been asking me, "What is the meaning of life?" Now, if I say there is no meaning, they feel sad. It is not life that is making them sad, it is their stupid question – "What is the meaning of life?" – that is creating the sadness.

I don't ask for the meaning. Why should there be any meaning? What is the meaning of a roseflower? But it blossoms, releases its fragrance. What is its hope? Is the roseflower hoping that somebody will come and say, "How beautiful!" That somebody will pass by and say, "What fragrance!" No, the rose-flower even flowers in a place where nobody passes by, nobody sees it, nobody feels it.

In the Himalayas there is a place, a valley, which is called the Valley of the Gods, for the simple reason that it is impossible to go deep down into that valley – steep hills surround it. But in that valley where nobody goes – there is no way to go, no path, and it is so deep that you can only see it from the hilltop – in that valley there have been growing for millennia, beautiful flowers. I have seen it. I think there must be many flowers which are not even known to us, which are not even named by the scientists.

The valley is completely just flowers and flowers. For whom are they blossoming? For whom are they waiting? What is their hope? There is no hope, there is no desire. They are not waiting for somebody, they are simply enjoying themselves blossoming to their completion. They are enjoying the sun, they are enjoying the hills, they are enjoying the other flowers blossoming all around. They are enjoying the moon in the night, and the stars in the night. But remember, there is no meaning and there is no hope.

Destroy all hope in you and you will never be hopeless, you will never feel hopelessness. Drop the enquiry into the meaning of life and you will never feel it is meaningless. I am not saying that you will start feeling it is meaningful, no. You will be freed completely from meaning and meaninglessness, from hope and hopelessness. And there is no need for them. You can just enjoy.

And the whole existence is enjoying except man. Something is crazy about man. The trees must be laughing at you; the rocks must be thinking, "What has happened to you? Why this sadness?" The birds must be thinking, "This whole humanity has gone mad." And it *has* gone mad.

Sanity is to enjoy the moment. Whatever it brings to you, relish, rejoice. I teach you the moment and its joys, and I want you to completely drop dreaming about hopes. Your dreams about hopes have helped you to be exploited by the priests. They give you the hope; they say, "This life is hopeless, but there is a life beyond the grave."

Strange…everything is beyond the grave and nobody comes back from the grave to say, "Yes, the priests are right." Not a single man has come back from the grave to say, "These priests are perfectly right: all that you are hoping for, desiring for, is abundantly available in the kingdom of God – but that kingdom of God is beyond the grave."

My kingdom of godliness is here, now, this very moment. Who cares about tomorrow?

Only people who are living in despair cling to hope. That hope keeps them dragging on: "If it is not happening today, it will happen tomorrow; it is just a question of a little more waiting." But you are waiting for Godot, who is never going to come.

In fact, existence is pouring on you all its treasures this very moment, but you are not here! You are digging in the future, and the future is only a projection of your mind.

Those who cannot think of the future start thinking of the past. Old people are afraid: death is coming, tomorrow is death! And their whole life and its experience has raised many doubts in them: who knows whether after death all that you wanted will be available? There is not a single eyewitness. The old man starts being afraid of death. He turns his eyes towards the past which he has lived – he starts remembering the beautiful days of youth, the wonderful days of childhood.

And I tell you, he is inventing it. When he was a child, he was as miserable as anything. When he was a young man, he was burdened with all kinds of miseries and problems. Now that death is coming near, he cannot look forward – there is only the darkness of the grave. He turns his back towards the grave and starts looking at the past, which he has not lived, which he has missed! A strange phenomenon…when you are a child you are wanting to grow up and become a young person because young people are enjoying so much.

I used to go for a morning walk, and there was a post office nearby. I knew the postmaster, I knew his family. One day, early in the morning – it must have been five o'clock, it was still dark – I saw a small boy with a mustache passing by my side. I could not believe that a small boy…I ran after him and caught hold of him, and he said, "Please don't tell my father."

But I said, "What are you doing?"

He said, "Whenever I see somebody with a mustache, I feel so bad that I don't have any mustache. I have purchased this, but don't tell my father. I enjoy it very much."

I said, "What else do you enjoy? I will not tell your father."

He said, "Promise?"

I said, "Promise."

He took out a pack of cigarettes. He said, "I enjoy cigarettes, although I start coughing and the taste is bad. But what to do? One has to enjoy. So many people smoking…. And I am waiting to come of age, but it is coming so slowly."

In old age this boy will remember, "Wonderful were the days of my childhood," and that will be simply imagination.

All that is real is here.

Whether you are a child, or a young man, a young woman, or an old man, or on your deathbed, all that is to be experienced is here. And here is the only time, and the only place. There is no "there" anywhere, past or future. There is no "then" past or future. It is always here, now.

Just the other day I received a letter from a sannyasin – of course he is from California. He is a man but he wants to wear the clothes of a woman. He says he enjoys it so much but he is afraid that somebody will find out. So, closing his doors, he puts on women's clothes. He was asking me, "Is it okay? And can I move in the commune in women's clothes?"

No woman is enjoying her clothes, and this guy is enjoying women's clothes! I receive letters from women saying that they want to change their sex, they want to become men. What can you say to these fools? Can't you see the men all around you? And it is happening in the world: men are changing their sex, becoming women; women are changing their sex and becoming men. What could be the cause of this?

You cannot enjoy whatsoever you are, wherever you are. You are always thinking that the other guy is smarter, that men are enjoying, that women are enjoying. You are all in the same ship – and nobody is enjoying. And of course, once you have changed your sex from a man and become a woman, you cannot say that now you are not enjoying it; that would look very stupid. You went through such a process – painful operations, plastic surgery – and now to say that it was useless would not be right. You brag that you are enjoying, that it has been a great experience.

I cannot conceive that a man becoming a woman

or a woman becoming a man can be a great experience. It is bragging. You have done something stupid; now to accept the stupidity of it is embarrassing, it is better now to go on pretending. But I know… People who have changed their sex have written to me that there is nothing great in it, it is the same, you just change one place for another place. But you are the same, because you are not your body, you are not your mind. You are consciousness, and no plastic surgery can change your consciousness – your consciousness will remain the same.

The only way to become blissful is to raise your consciousness from its dormant position. It is fast asleep, because you have never bothered about it. You are searching all over the world, leaving only one spot that is deep within you, and the key is there.

My whole effort in creating communes all around the world is to make you aware of this tremendous gift of existence, these flowers that are showering continuously on you. But your eyes are focused somewhere else.

You are closed to the present; that is the only misery, the only hell. Be open to the moment; that is the only heaven and the only blessed state.

Silence

Does the Miracle

DISCOURSE 18,   July 16, 1985

Beloved Bhagwan,

Are these illusions of God and ego one and the same?

Yes. The moment ego is found illusory, immediately God also disappears. Ego is an imaginary center in individuals, and God is the imaginary center of the whole universe. They are related to each other, dependent on each other. Neither God can exist without ego in you, nor can ego exist without God there above, in heaven. God is the ego of the whole.

It is not a coincidence that all the religions emphasize both together – God and you. They try to make your ego more and more – at least in appearance – a reality. To make the ego they have all kinds of disciplines: you have to do this, you have not to do this – because the ego cannot exist when you are not doing anything.

It is just as if you have a torch of fire in your hand; if you go on moving it round and round fast enough, you will see a circle of fire – which does not exist. It is illusory, you just cannot see the gaps. It is just a single fire, a flame, but moved fast it becomes a circle. That circle is simply not there. Stop moving your hand and the circle disappears.

All the religions go on teaching you, "Do something – fast, exercises, prayers; go to churches, mosques, synagogues. Read the holy scripture every day." These are all methods to create the ego in you.

The torch goes on moving and goes on creating the illusory circle.

And when you start feeling that you have a center in you, it becomes very easy for you to believe that there must be a center to the whole. If each individual is moving on a center, then the whole existence must be moving on a center, and that center is God. Ego strengthened in you creates the belief, the faith in God, and makes it look very logical.

What I am doing here is just the opposite. I want you first to learn moments of non-doing, moments when you simply *are,* not doing anything – the torch has stopped moving in a circle – and you are amazed. The moment you are silent, not doing anything at all, suddenly, in a strange, mysterious way, the old you has disappeared, evaporated, and a new feeling of being arises.

The ego is separate from others, has to be. It has its own territory. The bigger the territory, the bigger ego you can have. If you become the president of America, of course your ego becomes millions of times bigger. You have much money, and you go on and on accumulating money – that feeds the illusion; your territory, your power, goes on increasing.

I want you to know a state of utter nothingness.

That is your reality.

The child is not born with an ego. Ego is being taught by the society, religion, culture. You must have watched little babies: they don't say, "I am hungry." If the baby's name is Bob, he says, "Bob is

179

hungry. Bob wants to go to the toilet." He has no sense of "I." He indicates himself also in the third person. Bob is something that people call him, so he also calls himself Bob. But a day will come…as he grows you will start teaching him that this is not right. "Bob is the name for others to call you; you have to stop calling yourself Bob. You are a separate personality, you have to learn to call yourself 'I'."

The day Bob becomes "I," he loses the reality of being and falls into the dark abysmal pit of an hallucination. Once he calls himself "I" there is a totally different energy functioning. Now the "I" wants to grow, it wants to become big; it wants this, it wants that. It wants to rise higher and higher in the world of hierarchies. It wants a bigger territorial imperative.

If somebody has a bigger "I" than you, it creates an inferiority complex in you. You make every effort to be superior-than-thou, holier-than-thou, bigger-than-thou. Now your whole life is dedicated to one stupid thing – which does not exist in the first place. You are on a dream path. You will go on moving, making your "I" bigger, and bigger. And it creates almost all your problems.

Even Alexander the Great had immense problems. The "I" within him wanted to be the world conqueror, and he had almost conquered the world. I say almost for two reasons. In his time, half of the world was not known, America was not known. Secondly, he entered India, but he could not conquer India; he returned from the boundaries.

He was not very old, he was just thirty-three. But in these thirty-three years he had been simply fighting, fighting, fighting. He had become sick, bored with the fight, killing, murder, blood. He wanted to go back home and rest, and even that was not fulfilled. He could not reach his home in Athens. He died just one day before he was supposed to reach Athens; Athens was only twenty-four hours away.

But his whole life's experience – growing richer, bigger, more and more powerful, and then also feeling an utter helplessness, not even capable of

What I call meditation is nothing but a great decision on your part to have a few moments at least when you are not doing anything – not even thinking anything, because that is also an act. You simply *are*. In that simple existence you will find no ego inside you, and it will bring such clarity. Because all the turmoil of the ego is no longer there, your vision takes wings, you can see that God is nothing but the ego of the whole universe.

postponing his death for twenty-four hours…. And he had promised his mother that once he had conquered the world he would come and put the whole world at her feet as a gift. No son had done that for any mother before, so it was something absolutely unique that he was going to do.

But he felt helpless, surrounded by the best physicians. They all said, "You cannot survive. This twenty-four hour journey…you will die. It is better to rest here, perhaps there is a chance. But don't move. We don't see much chance even for resting – you are drowning. You are getting closer and closer, not to your home, but to your death; not to your home, but to your grave.

"And we cannot help. We can cure sicknesses, we cannot cure death. And this is not sickness. You are almost like a spent cartridge. In thirty-three years you have spent all your life energy in fighting this nation, that nation. You have wasted your life. It is not sickness, it is simply that your life energy is spent, and spent uselessly."

Alexander was a very intelligent man. He was a disciple of the great logician and philosopher, Aristotle; Aristotle was his private tutor. He died before reaching the capital. Before his death he told his commander in chief, "This is my last wish, and this has to be fulfilled." What was his last wish? A very strange wish. The wish was, "When you carry my coffin to the grave, you have to keep both my hands hanging out of the coffin."

The commander in chief asked, "What kind of wish is this? Hands are always kept inside the coffin. Nobody has ever heard of a coffin being carried to the grave with the hands hanging out!"

Alexander said, "I don't have much breath to explain to you, but in short, I want to show to the world that I am going with empty hands. I was thinking I was becoming bigger and bigger, richer and richer, but in fact, I was becoming poorer and poorer. When I was born I had come into the world with my fists closed, as if I was holding something

within my fists. Now at the moment of death, I cannot go with my fists closed."

To keep your fists closed you need life, some energy. No dead man has been able to keep his hands closed. Who will close them? A dead man is no longer there, all energy is gone – the hands open of their own accord.

"Let everybody know that Alexander the Great is dying with his hands empty, just a beggar."

But I don't see that anybody has learned from those empty hands, because people after Alexander have continued to do the same in different ways.

Man's ego is the source of all his problems, all the wars, all the conflicts, all the jealousies, fear, depression. Feeling oneself as a failure, continuously comparing with others makes everybody hurt – and hurt tremendously, because you can't have *everything*. Somebody is more beautiful than you, that hurts; somebody has more money that you, that hurts; somebody is more knowledgeable than you, that hurts. Millions of things are there to hurt you, but you don't know, it is not those things that are hurting you, because they don't hurt *me*. They are hurting you because of your ego.

Ego is constantly trembling with fear, knowing perfectly well that it is an artifact, an artificial device created by the society to keep you running, chasing shadows. The politicians are happy, they want you to go on running. This game of the ego, reaching higher and higher, is politics. The priest is happy, you go on asking for his blessings.

One of my friends was a cabinet minister in Indira Gandhi's time. When his election was coming near, he was very much afraid whether he was going to win again or not. And now, being a cabinet minister, he was hoping someday to become the prime minister. And to lose the election and again be just nobody was very painful.

He came to me. He said, "I have never asked anything from you, but this time, you bless me. I want to win this election. There is every possibility that I will go higher in the cabinet. Perhaps I may become the deputy prime minister."

I said, "You have come to the wrong place" – because in India people go to the saints for blessings. I said, "You have come to the wrong place. If I really give you a blessing, you will fail utterly in your election."

He said, "What do you mean? What kind of blessing is this?"

I said, "Your becoming a cabinet minister, a deputy prime minister, or even a prime minister, is not really a blessing to you. You are going in an hallucinatory direction. My blessing will bring you back to your reality."

In India, many couples, when they got married, used to come for my blessing. And Vivek used to tell them, "Don't ask for his blessing, because his blessing means divorce" – because she had seen, year by year, whoever had asked for my blessing was finished, asking for my blessing was the end of the relationship. But they could not understand it.

They had come to ask the blessing that for their lives they remain devoted to each other, that their love goes on growing, their love should not know any end, it should be endless.

But this is illusory. Everything that is born, dies. And the more beautiful a thing is, the more delicate it is. Love is a beautiful flower; it withers very easily. Yes, a relationship you can carry – that is legal, social – but it will be a burden when the love between you has stopped flowing. You will torture each other in every possible way.

My blessing can be that you enjoy the moment to the fullest, and if in the next moment you feel the bridge has collapsed, then say good-bye to each other – at least in a friendly, compassionate way.

The ego and all its games…marriage is its game, money is its game, power is its game. All the games are the games of ego. The society up to now has remained playing games; it is an ongoing Olympics all over the world. Everybody is fighting his way upwards, and everybody else is pulling his legs down, because at the Everest peak there is not enough space for you all to stand.

It is a cut-throat competition. And it becomes so important to you, that you forget completely that this ego was planted in you by the society, by the teachers. From the kindergarten to the university, what are they doing? – strengthening your ego. More and more degrees go on being added to your name, and you start feeling bigger and bigger and bigger.

Ego is the greatest lie – which you have accepted as a truth. But all vested interests are very much in favor of it, because if everybody becomes aware of egolessness, this whole Olympics going on around the world will simply come to a standstill. Nobody will want to climb Everest, they will enjoy wherever they are. They will be rejoicing.

The ego keeps you waiting: tomorrow when you succeed, you will rejoice. Today, of course, you have to suffer, you have to sacrifice. If you want to succeed tomorrow, today you have to sacrifice. You have to deserve success, and for that you are doing every kind of gymnastics. And it is only a question of a little time to suffer, and then there is rejoicing. But that tomorrow never comes. It has never come.

Tomorrow simply means that which never comes. It is postponing living. It is a beautiful strategy to keep you suffering. Politicians want you to suffer, priests want you to suffer, your educational system wants you to suffer. They all teach you that sacrifice is great: Sacrifice – only then will you be able to find something to rejoice in; sacrifice is the way.

I say it categorically, No! Sacrifice is the invention of the cunning people. There is no need to sacrifice anything because all that you need to rejoice is already here within you.

But the ego cannot rejoice in the present. It cannot *exist* in the present; it exists only in the future, in the past – that which is not. The past is no more, the future is not yet; both are non-existential.

Ego can exist only with the non-existential,

because it itself is non-existent.

In the present, pure moment you will find no ego in you – simply a silent joy, a silent and pure nothingness.

But the priest is afraid: if you come to know this nothingness, you will know immediately there is no God, because if you can exist without any crystallized center, why cannot the whole existence exist the same way?

God is nothing but your ego multiplied by everybody else's ego. God is the biggest ego in the world. God is the greatest hallucination man has suffered, and is still suffering. If you want your ego, then you have to keep your belief in God intact. They remain together, they go together.

Many questions have come to me, asking why I insistently destroy people's belief and faith in God. It is pure arithmetic: without destroying God I cannot help you to destroy your ego. If there is no God and existence can remain flowing, moving, growing, expanding; nobody is controlling it, nobody is maintaining it, it is autonomous....

That's what I mean when I say there is no God. I am saying existence is autonomous. Trees are growing of their own accord, birds are flying of their own accord, the sun is rising of its own accord. And it is beautiful that nobody is behind this beautiful existence, turning it into a puppeteer's show. That's what the religions teach – all the religions without exception – that you are only a puppet. With God there, you cannot be anything more than a puppet. The strings are in his hand.

They have a proverb in India that not even a leaf moves without God's permission. Nothing happens without God's permission, so this whole existence is a permanent slavery. And it is very strange, the same people who say, "Not even a leaf moves without his support...." Then how do people commit murder? Then how do people commit rape? Then how do people become thieves? If not even a leaf moves without him, the murderer is not responsible, the rapist is not responsible. If anybody is responsible, it is the puppeteer.

But strange…you will be punished for an act over which you have no control. You will be thrown into hell because God managed to make a murderer of you. It is God who manages Genghis Khan, Tamerlane, Nadir Shah, Joseph Stalin, Adolf Hitler, Mussolini. It is God. If one million Jews are killed by Adolf Hitler, religions have no guts to say the truth: that it is God who is pulling the strings of Adolf Hitler – the poor puppet – and he is killing people.

Religions want you to be responsible for your acts on the one hand, and on the other hand, God has created you, and everything that is in you is created by God.

I have asked many saints, "How do you reconcile this contradiction?" and I have never received any answer. They said, "It is beyond human comprehension." You can comprehend God, that he created the world. You can comprehend that a particular sin will throw you into hell, another particular act will take you to heaven. You can comprehend everything else….

I have seen in India, in temples, there are maps hanging which show where hell is, where heaven is, where God lives, his house. These idiots who made these maps didn't know anything about America, because those maps were made thousands of years ago. Even now they are hanging – without America! They knew about heaven and hell, and they didn't know anything about this very earth on which they were living.

Your ego is just an idea implanted in your mind. It is poisonous. Your ego keeps driving you madder and madder.

What I call meditation is nothing but a great decision on your part to have a few moments at least when you are not doing anything – not even thinking anything, because that is also an act. You simply *are*. In that simple existence you will find no ego inside you, and it will bring such clarity. Because all the turmoil of the ego is no longer there, your vision takes wings, you can see that God is nothing but the ego of the whole universe.

If you can exist, breathe, be, and there is no sense of "I," it makes clear to you that there is no need for any God, that there is no need for this slavery under which we have all lived for millennia, that you are not a puppet, that you are an individual.

And nobody is responsible for your acts, remember. That is very significant.

Why did people decide to remain slaves for so long? Why did they continue to believe in God, repressing their doubts and queries? – for the simple reason that the presence of God makes you irresponsible. He is the all-knower, he is everywhere; you are just to follow his commandments.

And there are people like Moses who say that they have seen God, heard him, and they bring stone tablets with commandments written on them. They say, "This is God's own handwriting." Of course, he knew only Hebrew, that's why he wrote the commandments in Hebrew. And he gave his commandments to Moses because the Jews are his chosen people.

This fiction that Moses created is responsible for all the miseries Jews have suffered all through history. If you carry the idea that you are the chosen people of God, then naturally you are superior to everybody. As a by-product you are making everybody your enemy. And the Jews are still carrying the same idea. God has been used by priests and prophets and messiahs to keep you deluded, deceived. But why did you accept all kinds of nonsense? There is a reason: it relieves you of all responsibility.

When you are with me, I make you responsible for every act. And if there is no God, and you are a free individual, naturally you have to be very alert and awake, because there is no one protecting you from on high. Even Jesus was under that delusion. On the cross he was crying, "God, my Lord! Have you forsaken me?" He was thinking that God was

behind him; that was giving him an illusory strength and power. His authority was because he was God's messenger.

Jesus was fully convinced that on the cross God was going to come down and prove to the whole world that Jesus was his only begotten son; and those who were crucifying him would suffer in hell for eternity, and those who were with him would be raised in glory to heaven, to enjoy it forever.

These deluded people are your messiahs. These people need psychiatric treatment! Instead of putting them in a madhouse, you have been worshipping them. Why? The same reason: they relieve you of a great thing – responsibility. They take your responsibility on their own shoulders; and of course, they have a direct communication line with God.

I want you to be silent, meditative, searching inside yourself, looking…is anyone there? And you will be surprised – there is no one, just pure existence, autonomous. There is no entity in you. You are part and parcel of the whole existence. You are connected to the trees and to the rivers and to the ocean in a thousand and one ways – visible, invisible. You are not separate.

Can you remain alive without breathing? Perhaps for a few seconds you can manage, because you have a certain storage of oxygen in your lungs. So it is not a big deal that you can keep your nose closed and you can dive in water for a few seconds. But soon you start feeling suffocated; a little more and you will be finished. What are you doing when you close your nose? You are disconnecting yourself from the atmosphere, the air, that surrounds you. It is invisible, but it is very tangible. You can feel it with your hand. You are constantly taking it in, sending it out. It is there.

Eighty percent of your body is water – and not just water, but sea water. That's why you are constantly in need, not only of ordinary water, you have to have sea water. That's why salt is one of the most necessary things in the world. In your body, inside, it is exactly the same combination of salt water and other chemicals as in sea water.

When you go to the beach, why do you feel a sudden joy? The salty breeze, the vast ocean. the waves…. Why do you suddenly feel more alive? Because you are part of it. Eighty percent of you is part of the ocean! There is a certain need for your body, once in a while, to be close to the ocean so you can renew your love affair with it.

Why do you feel good looking at the green trees? When you go to a lush, green forest something in you starts dancing. The cool breeze, the green color surrounding you…. Do you know that trees are constantly supplying you with oxygen, that you are constantly supplying carbon dioxide to the trees, that you are not separate – you are connected by very invisible bridges.

On the full moon night, you can see the ocean is affected: its waves are bigger, as if it wants to touch the moon. Something in the ocean is stirred by the full moon. It is now an established scientific fact that your great oceans – the Pacific, the Atlantic, the Indian ocean – all your great oceans are really the places from where the earth was removed to make the moon.

In the beginning the earth was not solid, and when something is not solid and is moving, spinning, it will throw off a few parts of itself automatically because they are loose, they are not solid. The earth has thrown off millions of its parts. When you see a star falling in the night, it is not a star, it is just some part of the earth that has been floating beyond the gravitation of the earth and has come back into the area of gravitation. Two hundred miles around the earth is its area of magnetism. Every night thousands of those stones enter, and this has been going on for millions of years. Still they are not exhausted.

The biggest part thrown off by the earth, was the moon. Of course, if such a big part drops out, it leaves big holes on the earth. These holes became oceans, water collected in them. On the full moon night something in the earth remembers, something in the ocean stirs. They are still in communication.

And you must remember that on the full moon night you also feel very good. Poets for centuries have been writing poetry about the full moon. Singers have been singing, musicians have been playing on their instruments to the glory of the full moon. Why does this full moon attract you? Because you are also eighty percent ocean.

More people go mad on the full moon night than any other night. More people commit suicide on the full moon night than any other night. More people have become enlightened on the full moon night than any other night. It cannot be just coincidence – for millions of years the same thing….

Gautam Buddha was born on a full moon night; he became enlightened on a full moon night – the same full moon, the same month. And he died on the same full moon night, the same month. He must have been really in deep communication with the moon. It is not visible; everything need not be visible.

We are connected with the whole universe. The moment your ego disappears, this connection with the whole becomes absolutely certain. There is no need to worship – you are then worshipping yourself. There is no need to pray. To whom are you praying? Then what is left for you is to rejoice, to enjoy all the gifts of existence. They are your inheritance! They belong to you, you belong to them.

There will be a totally different humanity if all the egos disappear. This whole earth will become a disco – Zorba the Buddha. People will be dancing, singing, enjoying. And there is so much to enjoy that who bothers about having a big post in the government? A few idiots may do that, but nobody will be jealous of them. And if you are not jealous of them, their joy at holding the big post of the president or the prime minister will be finished. Nobody cares! Ronald Reagan passes by and you don't even say "Hi."

Sooner or later those idiots will also come to

their senses. What has happened? Nobody is recognizing them, nobody is bothering who they are. And everybody is so blissful.

Ego disappearing, God disappears. Ego disappearing, hope disappears, despair disappears. Ego disappearing, there is no hell, no heaven. Ego disappearing, you become part of the universe, as you really *are*.

To me, this is enlightenment, this is liberation. Nobody can do it on your behalf. That's why I say people like Jesus are talking nonsense – that they have come to save others, they are saviors.

And it is not only Jesus, all the religions have their own buffoons.

Nobody can do it for you, you will have to do it for yourself, you will have to take the responsibility. Whatever the society has forcibly implanted in you, you have to undo it.

Silence does the miracle. That's why I say, yes, absolutely yes: your ego and God are not separate. God is the ego of the whole; your ego is the ego of the part. And the vested interests would like you to continue carrying the ego, because if the ego disappears, God disappears. All churches, all temples, mosques, *gurudwaras,* will have to be turned into discos where people come to dance and sing and play. That will be true religion.

Beloved Bhagwan,

Why is it that we want approval?

It is simple: from the very beginning a child is told what is right, what is wrong. He is never given freedom to choose on his own. He is taught principles; he is not allowed to enquire and to find out himself. And of course, whenever he does anything on his own, he is disapproved of by the family, by the society, by the school, by everybody. He becomes shaky. Just to do anything on your own is not accepted by the society. You need approval for everything.

When I was a small child, as far back as I can remember, I could not understand it. I said, "It is my life, I am going to live it. You have lived *your* life. Why should you impose things upon me?"

There used to be an annual fair a few miles away from my town. I went there without asking my family. For three days I enjoyed the place. It was by the side of a very big and beautiful river, and there were so many magicians and dancers and dramas…. Those three days just passed so quickly.

When I came back home, everybody was angry. My father asked me, "If you wanted to go to the fair, why didn't you ask?"

I said, "Because I wanted to go. If you are honest enough, tell me: if I had asked would you have said yes? Just be honest, at least once." And I looked into his eyes. For a moment there was silence. I said, "Your silence has said much."

He said, "Perhaps you are right; I would not have allowed you to go there because there is gambling, prostitutes, and all kinds of ugly things. I would not have allowed you to go there."

So I said, "Things are clear. I wanted to go – that's why I did not ask. And from now on," I told him, "remember, whatever I want to do I will not ask you. Whatever I don't want to do, perhaps I may ask you, because I am always contrary."

I wanted to cross the river – in the rainy season it becomes so big, it is a mountainous river. In summer it shrinks and becomes small. In rainy seasons, suddenly it becomes vast.

I wanted to swim. I went – it was risky. When I came back home…because it took me six hours to go to the other side. You cannot swim straight in a mountainous river; the water is going down so forcefully that you can reach to the other shore only three, four miles down. Then four miles you have to walk – not four miles, you have to walk eight miles. And then again you can swim back to the place from where you had started. They thought I must have drowned because by the time I reached home they were all searching with boats, looking for my dead body.

I said, "What are you doing?"

They said, "We could not believe that you would do it. You should have asked!"

I said, "I wanted to do it. Whether I die or remain alive does not matter. Whatever *I* want to do, I am ready to pay for it; it is my responsibility. I am not to be dominated, I am not a puppet."

I had to struggle constantly with my family – and they were all well-wishers. I had to fight constantly with my teachers, with my professors, with my vice-chancellors – and they were all well-wishers. Their intention was not bad, they wanted to help me. But to everybody I made it absolutely clear all through my life that I didn't want to be helped, because that creates dependence.

One of my professors – he is now retired, so I can say the truth...Professor S.S. Roy retired as head of the department of philosophy in Allahabad University. He was my professor, and he was very much concerned; he loved me, he wanted me to become somebody. And I told him, "I am not going to become somebody, I don't have that desire. I want to become nobody."

He said, "Don't talk like that. The examinations are coming, and I know you don't have any textbooks."

I never purchased any textbooks. I purchased thousands of books – in my library when I left India, there were one hundred fifty thousand books of rare value – but I never purchased a single textbook.

He knew it. Just when the examinations were to begin, he called me. "Tomorrow morning," he said, "your examinations are to begin, and this is the questionnaire that you have to answer. So please sit with me and answer me, because I want to know.... I have set these questions, this paper has been made by me, so you answer me, one by one, so that I am certain that you will not fail – at least in my paper. It will be a shame if you fail in my paper."

I said, "You don't be worried." I took that questionnaire and just threw it out the window, tearing it into pieces.

He said, "What are you doing?"

I said, "I am going to answer the questions. Whether I pass or fail does not matter. What matters is that I do not want to be dependent – that will keep me burdened my whole life. You love me, I can understand it, but your love is not very much if it cannot understand what I have done. I have not seen those questions; I want to see them tomorrow morning in the examination hall. And finally those copies will be coming to you; then you can see my answers."

He said, "I gave you the whole paper – which is illegal, criminal; I risked my prestige for you. But I should have known before, because I know the type of a person you are. I can understand," he said, "you don't want to be obliged."

I said, "That's true. Neither do I want to be obliged, nor do I want to oblige anybody else in the world. Everybody should be on his own, choose his way. I would rather go to hell, but not losing my freedom, than to heaven, being directed by somebody else."

You are asking why we go on seeking the approval of others. It is because you are uncertain of yourself. You have been brought up in such a way that uncertainty has become your very second nature. Somebody with authority, power, prestige, approves of you, then you feel good, then you know that you must be right. You cannot decide on your own, because from the very childhood whatever you did on your own was found wrong and you were punished for it. That child is still there; just your body has grown. But your mind is somewhere in your childhood, still seeking approval.

Someday you have to stop it. The day you stop it, you start growing. If you don't stop it you will remain a child even when you are dying – a hundred years old and you will still be a child.

Even while dying you will need approval.

At the death moment, when it is coming close, immediately the priest is called, the bishop comes, the *maulvi* is called, the pundit comes; and they start giving you great advice for the future life. They won't allow you even to die freely. They have not allowed you in your life to live freely, how can they allow you to die freely?

In fact, you also would not like to die freely, because you don't know; now you are entering into an unknown dimension. You need someone who knows, who can give you courage, who can say, "Don't be worried, only the body dies; your soul will still remain." If you are a Hindu the advice will be different, but the basic thing is the same – that you cannot die in freedom.

Sometimes it happens, a person suddenly dies. The person is dead; by sheer accident he died in freedom without any priest around. But these priests of all the religions are really the jailers of your consciousness. The person has died but the ritual will be done. If you are Hindu, the mantras of the *Vedas* will be recited – and the man is no more! Water from the holy Ganges will be poured in the mouth of the corpse, because Hindus believe that the water of the holy Ganges takes you into heaven.

They have this fiction that the Ganges is really a river of heaven. One great ascetic, Baghirath, prayed to God, did all kinds of austerities possible, tortured himself as much you can imagine, and prayed, "I will continue my austerities until you send the Ganges to the earth." And he succeeded: the Ganges came down from heaven to the earth. That's why its water is heavenly, it is pure.

If you drink it before death it will take you to heaven. So in every Hindu family they preserve the Ganges water. Who knows? – any time somebody can die. It is good if he drinks it before he dies.

If by accident he misses, then no harm – you can drop a little water into his mouth, hoping that he will go to heaven. Even after death you are not going to allow freedom.

Freedom comes as a by-product of meditation.

Once you start knowing your inner being, you have then the insight of what has to be done and what has not to be done. And it comes from your own still, small voice. It can be heard only in silence. For the first time you start moving in freedom, living in freedom. And remember, the slave – particularly the psychological slave – cannot know of any rejoicing, any blessing. He wants approval. Approval of whom?

I asked my father, my teachers, my professors, "Are you certain what you are saying is right? – because in the world there are so many cultures, so many religions, and they are all certain and they are all contradicting each other. They cannot all be true. They all can be *false,* but they cannot all be true. And how to decide who is right? Perhaps one is right, but how to decide?"

And I have never received an answer that satisfied me. Then I told them, "Then let me alone. You yourself are uncertain. You start quoting the *Vedas, The Bible,* the *Koran;* you are seeking approval. But what are the grounds for the certainty that Mohammed was not mad?"

A very simple person can see that these things that Mohammed is saying cannot be right. Mohammed says every man can have four wives. Now, in the world there are not four times more women than men, they are equal. Nature keeps the balance. If one man marries four wives, he takes away three men's right to be married. Now three persons have to remain celibate their whole life; they have been forced to remain celibate. They are bound to become perverts; they will find some way to express their sexuality. I don't see that Mohammed is saying anything which makes sense.

Hindus say that when the husband dies, the wife has to jump into the funeral pyre of her husband; then only does she prove that she was sincere towards her husband. For thousands of years, millions of women had to jump alive into the funeral pyre of a husband who had done nothing except beat them and make them pregnant continuously. And they were treated just like cattle.

She should rejoice that that dodo is dead. On the contrary, she is forced…. And they had made arrangements, because alive…just think of yourself jumping into the fire – you will try to come out of it. So there were brahmin priests around the fire with burning torches to push her back. And so much purified butter was poured into the funeral pyre that there was smoke surrounding the whole area, so nobody could see what the priests were doing.

In the second circle, there was another group of priests who were chanting the *Vedas* so loudly that the poor woman's screams would be lost. Yes, you can find the authority for this in the Hindu scriptures, but the very thing is ugly, inhuman. And whoever has written that was not a man of sanity. He was a male chauvinist; he was not interested in human values.

If the woman refused…and a few women were courageous enough to refuse, they didn't want to die. Yes, they loved their husband, but that does not mean that they had to die with the husband. They loved him, but they were not going to commit suicide. These women were treated very badly. They could not marry again. Manu, the greatest Hindu authority on all kinds of things, says they cannot marry again.

Strange – a man can marry again, and a man is not asked to jump into the funeral pyre of his wife. Anybody can see the point, that this is simply fascist on the part of men. This Manu is not a man of truth, a man of silence, a man of wisdom. You will be surprised, Manu's book is five thousand years old. Even Hindus who believe in it feel a little bit ashamed because there are many things in it which make them feel ashamed.

But Friedrich Nietzsche – who was the philosophical source of Adolf Hitler's fascism – respects Manu as he respects nobody else. Adolf Hitler declared Manu one of the most significant authorities as far as morality is concerned. And these are not Hindus. You can see the relationship: these are fascists, and Manu approves of all kinds of fascism.

The Hindu widow remains alive in a very ugly way – if she chooses to remain alive. Her hair is cut so that she does not look beautiful. She cannot use any ornaments, because the man for whom she was supposed to look beautiful is dead. She cannot use any colored clothes, only white. All her hair, which is one of the most beautiful parts of a woman – is shaved. That hair gives a certain individuality to each woman.

She cannot use any cosmetics, she cannot use any ornaments. Even the cheapest glass bangles have to be broken. She has to hit her hands on the earth, on the wall, on the stone, to break the glass bangles. It brings blood to her hands. She cannot go in any place where celebration is happening. She cannot participate in any marriage, she cannot participate in any festival.

She has to remain isolated, and she has to be treated just like a servant.

She does all kinds of things like a servant – utterly degraded, deprived of her humanity. You cannot see such humiliation anywhere. It would have been far better to have jumped into the fire – within minutes things would have ended. Now this woman has to suffer perhaps fifty years, sixty years. She will be just a living corpse.

If you ask the professor, as I used to ask, "What do you say?" – because Hindus believe Manu is a *maharishi,* a great seer. And I say, "He must be the greatest blind man ever! Seer, my foot! This is the law that he has given to the Hindus. You go on finding approval in scriptures – and you don't know who wrote those scriptures, what kind of people they were."

Neither any man can be the source of approval, nor can any scripture be the source of approval. You have to listen to your own inner voice, and move accordingly.

That's the way of the sannyasin.

Deeper and Deeper into the Mysterious, the Miraculous

DISCOURSE 19, July 17, 1985

Beloved Bhagwan,

Outside, then inside — beauty, utter beauty. Is there more?

There is no end to it.
There is infinitely more.
You cannot exhaust it.

But one condition has to be remembered: You should not ask for it. You should not seek it, because it comes on its own. It is not a desire from your side. Desire kills it.

It is the abundance of existence that simply goes on flowing towards you if you are available.

Just remain available, and there will be more and more and more. But from your mind, the idea of getting more has to be dropped entirely. The moment you ask for more there will be less. If you become too ambitious, there is every possibility you will lose it completely.

So it is a slightly delicate matter. You keep your doors and windows open and enjoy whatsoever happens. And so much happens that you cannot conceive more is possible, but when more happens you will be surprised. And this more goes on happening. But remember the word "happening." It is nothing like an effort, a plan, a project on your part. You have to be just an empty receiver.

Just as water flows downwards towards the ocean, beauty, truth, love — all that is valuable in existence — flow towards a person who is nobody.

Beloved Bhagwan,

I wish there was only You and no commune. I feel wings when I see You, but aggressive and helpless in connection with the commune. And this makes me feel unhappy and ashamed. Everything You say is so clear to me, and yet I have the feeling that I don't understand You at all. What is the matter with me?

Much is the matter with you.
There are half a million sannyasins around the world. Everybody wants the same thing you are asking, that he should possess me totally, that there should be nobody else who shares me. But please, think of me too. Just you and me.... Are you bent upon boring me to death? And remember, this is the desire of every sannyasin. You have to understand it. Why this fear and helplessness with the commune?

The commune is nothing but my expanded being. If you really love me, you will automatically love the commune. If you are feeling beautiful winds blowing when I am with you, then in the commune you will feel even more, because I am there in many forms. I have lost my personality completely. I am just an opening. Whoever enters into me also becomes part of the infinite.

If you are somehow fearful and detest the commune, that simply means you have not yet come close to me – not at all. You say you feel you understand me clearly, every word that I utter, you understand it, and yet you have the feeling that you don't understand me at all. Your second part is right, you don't understand me at all. You only understand the words that I speak. And the words that I speak are just simple, ordinary, day-to-day use words. Anybody can understand those words. I am not a scholar, I am not a theologian. I am not crazy enough to be esoteric.

I am speaking to you – not even giving a discourse. It is just a heart-to-heart talk. Words you understand – that gives you the misconception. To understand my words is not the real thing. There is something more between the words, between the lines, in the moments when I suddenly pause in the middle of a sentence. If you understand those pauses, those moments of silence, those gaps between two words, no dictionary is needed. No dictionary can manage to explain those gaps, those intervals.

That wordlessness is my real message.

I am using words only to create wordlessness as a contrast. Forget everything that I have told you, but remember all those moments when I was silent. It is a strange way of speaking – nobody speaks that way. But when I stop, you are also in a stop…waiting, awaiting what I am going to say. Catch those wordless moments. I am there, and you will find yourself also there.

The Bible says, "In the beginning there was the word." This is sheer stupidity. In the beginning – if there was any beginning – there was wordlessness. *The Bible* says, "And the word was with God." What kind of reasoning is this? First you say, "In the beginning there was only the word." Then from where does this God come? And *The Bible* says not only this,

It is the abundance of existence that simply goes on flowering towards you if you are available. Just remain available, and there will be more and more and more. But from your mind, the idea of getting more has to be dropped entirely. The moment you ask for more there will be less. If you become too ambitious, there is every possibility you will lose it completely.

it says, "The word was with God and the word was God." It is just the opposite of reality.

In the beginning there was wordlessness – and there was no God with wordlessness. And the question of God being one with wordlessness is absolutely stupid, because "god" itself is a word and nothing else.

That silence was not only in the beginning; it is in the middle too, it is in the end too. It is always. It surrounds you twenty-four hours a day. But the difficulty is, not only a single word but millions of words are with you. They make a very thick wall between you and existence. You are encaged in words – Christian, Hindu, Mohammedan, Buddhist. The sermons in the churches, in the synagogues, are just words.

I am not giving you a sermon, I am simply creating a device, using two words to make you aware of the pause in between; only then will you understand. And it is not a question of understanding *me,* understanding is simply understanding.

When you bring a lighted torch into a dark room, it shows you the whole room, all that is there: the paintings on the walls, the furniture, the floor, the ceiling. Understanding is a quality in you. It has not to be connected with me. It is not linear, it is multidimensional. The moment you understand, the whole existence is an open book for you. Then all the mystifications of the religions disappear. Remember, I am saying "mystifications," I am not saying the "mysteries."

In fact, when all the mystifications of the religions disappear and you suddenly find yourself just in a moment of understanding, life is an open book, but tremendously mysterious. When mystifications are no longer there, then there is mystery. Then each moment of your life is a mystery, and every moment of your life goes on leading you deeper and deeper into the mysterious, the miraculous.

All the religions have committed a great crime against humanity. They have tried to explain to you what is not explainable. In their effort to explain to you the mystery of life, they have really explained it away. By inventing a God they destroyed the mystery of creativity. They created a God as creator; they continually conditioned you that existence is the creation. But existence is not schizophrenic, it is not split in two – the creator and the creation – it is simply creativity.

Hence I say to you that sometimes poets, singers, dancers, have come very close to the mystery – but I don't recall any saint, theologian, philosopher having come close to the mystery of existence. In fact, their whole attempt is to demystify existence. They are trying to put before you a certain dogma which explains everything and leaves nothing for you. Those are mere words, empty, ugly.

I don't want to give you words; you are already burdened too much.

I want to take all words from you.

And I am using words for a very strange reason – because if you have a thorn in your foot, you have to use another thorn to take it out.

I am destroying your words by my words, and giving you a chance continuously to listen to the pauses, the silent moments.

You are right that you feel you understand my words – anybody can do that. I don't use big words, I don't use any jargon. And you are also right that the feeling arises that you don't understand me at all. You will have to choose. Either you go on understanding my words and become a great pundit, a scholar…and a scholar is farthest away from existence. You may become very knowledgeable, but your knowledge is just an effort to cover up your ignorance.

But if you choose the silent periods, then suddenly all the mysteries of life become available to you – not as explanations; you don't get reality as an answer, you get it as an experience. And with that mystery you also become a mystery.

This is not ignorance, this is innocence.

You become the child.

I have attempted suicide a number of times, and I feel really attracted to death. This disturbs me, but at the same time gives me joy. Will You say something about it?

This is great! One can commit suicide only once, and you have attempted many times – and you are still alive. Those attempts were not true, they were all bogus, and you knew it even then.

I have heard…. Mulla Nasruddin wanted to commit suicide. Being a man of great cleverness, he made all the arrangements, left no loopholes. Perhaps nobody else had attempted suicide in that way.

He went on top of a hill, taking a pistol with him. Just underneath the hill, deep down, was a river, very dangerous, deep, and surrounded by all kinds of rocks. On the hill there was a tree – he had also brought a rope. Not to take any chances, he figured out all the possible things so that suicide was absolutely certain. He also carried with him a big container full of kerosene oil.

He hanged himself from the tree, but because he was going to do many more things, he could not take his feet from the earth – because then how was he going to do other things? So he was hanging from the tree and standing on the earth. Then he poured kerosene oil over himself; he had brought a lighter too. He created a fire, the kerosene oil was burning all around him. But he was not a man to take any chances, so he also shot a bullet into his head. But the bullet cut the rope, he fell down into the river, and the river water destroyed the fire!

Desperately, he was coming back home when I met him. I asked, "You are still alive after all that arrangement?"

He said, "What to do? I know how to swim!" Everything failed!

You say you have attempted suicide many times. One thing is certain: you don't want to commit suicide, you want to play with the idea. And you feel also that there is fear about death and there is also a certain joy. This is not only your situation. It is a very common human phenomenon.

Life is a torture, a burden; it is anguish. One wants to get rid of it. To get rid of it means getting rid of all the anguish, the despair, the hopelessness, the meaninglessness – this wife, this husband, these kids, this job. Hence there is an attraction towards death, because death will put an end to all your misery. But it will also put an end to you – that creates fear.

You really want to live, and live forever, but you want to live in paradise. And you are living in a hell! You want to get rid of the hell, you don't want to get rid of yourself. And I want to emphasize that you are your own hell. So suicide is attractive from one side in that it will put an end to all your miseries, but on the other hand there is a great fear: it will finish you too.

Isn't there some way that the miseries can be finished and you can live more intensely?

I also teach you that a certain suicide can help you – the suicide of the ego, not of you. Let the ego die, and then see that with it all problems disappear. You are left full of joy, blessedness, and each moment goes on opening new doors to new mysteries. Each moment becomes a moment of discovery – and it is an unending process.

You have attempted so many times to commit suicide. This time you commit suicide *my* style. And anyway, you have failed so much that you must have become very much of an expert in failing. And deep down you don't want to die because you are afraid of death – which is natural. Why should one put an end to one's life when life has not even been lived? You have not even tasted it, you have not explored the multidimensional beauties, joys and blessings of life.

Naturally you are afraid. But still you go on attempting it, because you don't know how to get rid of all the miseries. Suicide seems to be the simplest way. You are in a split: half of your mind says, "Commit suicide and be finished with all this nonsense –

enough is enough." The other part tries to sabotage your effort, because the other part wants to live. You have not lived yet.

Suicide is not going to help. Only more life, more abundant life, is going to help. So this time kill the ego, and see the miracle happen. With the ego gone, there is no misery, no anguish, and no need to commit suicide. With the ego gone, all the doors that were closed by the ego suddenly open and you are available to the sun, to the moon, to the stars.

And it is easier, because to kill the ego you don't need a pistol, kerosene oil, a rope to hang the ego, fire to burn the ego, and if everything fails, then a deep mountainous river underneath to finish the ego. You don't need any of these things, because the ego is only a creation of the society, of the religions, of the culture. It does not exist in fact. You have only to look deeply into it; it is a shadow. You have to look into it, and it is not there.

Meditation is simply a method of looking into what this ego is. And whoever has ever looked in has not found it. Without any exception, throughout the history of man, whoever has looked inwards has not come across any ego.

This is the suicide of the ego. Nothing has to be done, just a little turning in. And once you know it is not there, then all the sufferings that you were carrying because of a non-existential ego disappear. They cannot have any nourishment anymore. All these things have been created in your mind by conditioning, by programming; that's what the society has done to you.

We have lived the whole of history in an ugly way.

One of my professors did not agree with me, that something can be created by other people when it is not there at all. So I said, "I will show it to you."

I was very much loved by the man; his wife was also very loving towards me. I went to his wife and told her, "Tomorrow morning when the professor gets up, you have to pretend that you are shocked, and say to him, 'What has happened to you? When you went to bed you were perfectly okay; now your face is looking pale. Are you sick or something?'"

The next morning the professor simply denied it. He said, "What nonsense are you talking? I am perfectly okay."

I had told his gardener, "When he comes into the garden, you simply say, 'My God! What has happened to you? You cannot walk, you are wobbling. Something is wrong with you. Just go inside and rest and I will go and call the doctor.'"

And I had said to both these people, "Whatsoever he says, exactly in his own words, you write it down. I will collect those notes."

To the gardener he said, "Yes, it seems something is wrong. Perhaps I should rest, I should not go to the university. But I don't see any need to call the doctor." He was perfectly healthy and there was no problem, so finally he decided that at least for half an hour or an hour he would go to the university.

On the way I had said to many people whom I trusted…. On the way there was the postmaster. I told him, "Even if you are busy, don't miss: when the professor passes by you shout at him, 'What are you doing? Where are you going? Are you mad? Your body is absolutely sick! You come into my house, rest. I will call the doctor.'" I collected all these notes. The professor said, "Yes, since last night I have this feeling that something is going wrong. I am not exactly sure what is going wrong, but something *is* wrong. I feel a certain trembling inside, a fear, as if I am not going to last long."

His house and the university philosophy department were almost one mile apart, and he had always walked – but that day, in the middle, he stopped another professor's car and told him, "I don't think I will be able to reach the university department."

The university was on a hilly place, up and down. From his house it was an uphill task to reach the department; the department was on the top of the hill and his house was in the valley.

He said, "I am huffing, huffing…my body is

trembling. I think there is fever, and there is much more which I cannot figure out." So he wanted a lift.

And the professor who had passed him was sent by me: "Just when he is in a very bad situation, you stop your car and ask, 'What is the matter?'" In the car he said, "You should not have come, you should have called the doctor. Your eyes look as if they have lost all luster. Your face looks dry, faded; you look like a faded painting. Just in one night! Had you a heart attack in the night? It must have been serious."

And he said, "It seems that I had a heart attack and I was not aware because I was asleep, but now I know. All the symptoms are showing that my life is at the very end."

When he entered the university department, the peon who used to sit in front of the department.... I had told him, "When he comes, you simply jump and hold him."

He said, "But he will be very angry. And what kind of thing are you asking? You have never asked anything before."

I said, "We are doing an experiment – me and the professor. Don't interfere, you simply do what I say. You just hold him and tell him, 'You are going to fall.'" He did that and the professor thanked him. And the peon had no need to tell him that he was going to fall; the professor said himself, "If you had not been here I would have fallen."

Inside the department I was waiting for him. I said, "Jesus! You look like a ghost! What calamity has happened to you?" I took hold of him, put him in a reclining chair.

And he said, "Just one thing I want to tell you. My children are small" – he had only two children – "my wife is young, inexperienced. I don't have any family; my father is dead, my mother is dead. I don't know anybody who can take care of them when I am gone. I can think only of you."

I said, "You don't be worried. I will take care of your children, your wife – better than you are doing. But before you decide to leave the world, I have to

show you a few notes."

He said, "A few...what notes?"

I said, "I will have to go and collect them."

He said, "From whom?"

I said, "From your wife, from the gardener, from the postmaster, from the professor who drove you here, from the peon who saved you from falling."

He said, "But how do you know?"

I said, "It was all planned. And you say that man cannot be deceived by something nonexistential?"

I went down, collected all the notes, and I showed him them one by one. And I said, "Look how you are getting caught up. To your wife you absolutely denied there was anything wrong. To the gardener you said 'Perhaps something is wrong.' But it was 'perhaps,' you were not certain yet. But the idea was getting in. To the postmaster you said, 'Yes, something must have happened. From the very evening I was feeling bad, sick, apprehensive.'

"With the professor in the car you accepted that you must have had a heart attack while you were asleep. You were feeling so weak" – and he was a strong man – "that you could not conceive yourself walking uphill to the department. And to the peon who jumped and took hold of you, you said, 'I am grateful to you. I was just going to fail, to collapse.' Now this is a simple idea," I told him, "that has been implanted in you."

Now do you see the point? This man can even die, you just have to keep on going. I was only proving a point on which he was not agreeing, so this was only an argument – I did not want him to die. Otherwise, I would have talked to the doctor and had him say to him, "Your days are finished, so whatever you want to do – write your will or anything – do it quickly. It is not something that I can help with, your heart is simply finished; any moment it is going to stop." I could have killed that man just by an idea.

Seeing the notes, immediately he was back, perfectly healthy. He walked down the hill laughing, and told the peon, "You should not listen to this man, he is dangerous. He almost killed me!" He told the other professor, "This is not right, that you suggested to me that I must have had a heart attack." He told the postmaster, "You are my neighbor, and is this right, to push me towards death?"

He was very angry with his wife. He said, "I can think that he persuaded other people – he has everybody impressed by him – but I cannot believe that my own wife deceived me, listened to him. We were in an argument; it was a question of my prestige, and you destroyed it!" But the wife said, "You should be grateful to him. He has given proof that man can be programmed for something which does not exist at all."

You think you are a Christian? It is just an idea implanted in you. Do you think there is a God? An idea implanted in you. Do you think there is a heaven and hell? It is nothing but programming. You are all programmed.

My work with you is to deprogram you. And I am showing you all the notes – day after day, continuously – that these are the things that have made you almost dull, stupid, even attracted towards suicide, towards death. My religion is unique in this way: all the religions of the past have programmed people; I deprogram you, and then I leave you alone, to yourself.

People have been asking me, "What is your religion? What is your philosophy? Can't you give us something like a Christian catechism so we can understand that these are your principles?"

I have none, because that will be programming you again. When a Hindu becomes a Christian, what happens? The Christians deprogram him as a Hindu, and *reprogram* him as a Christian. There is no difference. From one ditch he has fallen into another ditch. Perhaps the newness of it may keep him happy for a few days, but soon he will start looking for another ditch. Now he is addicted to ditches! And in this way he is simply digging his own grave. That is the final ditch into which he will fall.

I deprogram you, and I don't give you any other program. I leave you alone, empty, just a zero. In that zero, the ego disappears and all the blessings start showering on you.

Beloved Bhagwan,

Sometimes during discourse my vision becomes unfocused. I see You change: with other faces, other clothes, and other bodily gestures. It's a strange feeling. Do You have anything to say?

It is nothing. It is not a strange phenomenon, it is just the Oregonian sun and its heat.

You should simply go to Pythagoras – you need medical treatment. And of course, I am not a medicine man. First, get medical treatment, and when you start seeing me the way everybody else is seeing me, then if you have any question I can help.

Beloved Bhagwan,

Do You see experiments on human life, such as artificial birth and the exchange of hearts and brains, as an advance, or as an action against nature?

It all depends who is going to do it. If the politicians are going to do it, or the so-called religions are going to do it, then it is against nature. They cannot do anything natural, they are against nature. But if it is being done by an international academy of scientists – I say *international* academy of scientists – it can be a tremendous, progressive step, and it will not be against nature. It will be nature's growth.

But it all depends on who is doing it. The experiments themselves are neutral. No experiment has any vested interest, it is neutral. You can use poison to kill you; the same poison can be used by medical people to save you. It all depends who is doing it.

For example, the discovery of atomic energy was a step of tremendously great progress, a quantum leap. We had found a key to transform the earth into paradise – so much energy in such a small atom. And they are in everything…just in a dewdrop there are millions of atoms. Any atom, if it is exploded, releases so much energy that you can make the whole earth live in luxury. Or you can create Hiroshima and Nagasaki – thousands of people dead within seconds.

But because atomic energy, after its invention, went into the hands of the politicians, it became a servant of death. Now there are even more advanced nuclear weapons which can destroy the whole earth. The already existing weapons are enough to destroy this earth seven hundred times. One simply wonders why nations are going to develop more and more nuclear power. Seven hundred times destroying the earth is not enough? In fact, you can destroy the earth only once.

But scientific progress falls into the hands of the politicians because only they can provide enough finance to make these discoveries possible. The scientists of the whole world should think it over: their genius is being used by idiots! The scientists should disconnect themselves from any nation – whether it is the Soviet Union or America. They should create an international academy of sciences. And it is not difficult. If all the scientists of the world are together, finances can be made available, and these discoveries can help man tremendously.

The international academy of scientists can be in this international city. We can give them land, and every possible support. But they should be the decisive factors in what is going to happen through their experiments. And it is time the scientists should recognize their great responsibility. If a third world war happens then the scientists will be the greatest criminals, because they supplied all kinds of inventions to the politicians.

Science should not be the monopoly of any nation, any country. The whole idea is stupid. How can science be monopolized? And every country is trying to monopolize the scientists, keep their inventions secret. This is against humanity, against nature, against existence. Whatever a genius discovers should be in the service of the whole.

You are asking whether discoveries like changing human hearts or human brains are progressive steps. They are of great importance to bring a new humanity on the earth. If Einstein's body is no longer capable of living, do you think it would not be good if his whole brain is transplanted into a young, healthy man? The new man will become an Einstein, because all the genius of Einstein is transplanted to a younger body. This way bodies may go on changing, but we can keep the genius of Albert Einstein growing for centuries. And if a man in a seventy-year life can give so much, you can imagine if his brain continues for centuries how much benefit it will be for humanity, for the whole universe.

This is really a wastage: the container gets rotten, and you throw the content also. The body is only a container. If the container has become dirty, old, unusable, change the container, but don't throw away the content. The genius mind can live for eternity in different bodies; that is nothing against nature.

Your heart, if it starts failing, and if you are of immense value to humanity…what is the fear of exchanging the heart? Somebody may be dying from cancer, but his heart is perfectly healthy; that heart can be planted in a man who is talented, a genius, and is healthy, but whose heart is not strong. This is simple; there is nothing in it against nature.

But with politicians and the power in their hands, of course every advance has gone against nature. Everything that human genius has discovered, invented, finally is in the service of death. So are the priests. Now science is no longer a child, that it has to depend on others. Science is now grown-up enough, it is adult. Just a little courage….

I give the invitation to all the scientists of the world; we have the place, we have intelligent people here to help you in every possible way. And if you want to make an international academy here, we are capable of managing finances for you.

It will be a great revolution in the history of man. The whole power will be in the hands of the scientists, who have never done any harm to anybody. And once all the power is in the hands of the scientists, politicians will fade away of their own accord. They have been exploiting scientists for their own purposes, and to be exploited by anybody is not an act of dignity.

The scientists should recognize their dignity, they should recognize their individuality. They should recognize that they have been exploited down the ages by the priests and the politicians. Now it is time to declare that science is going to stand on its own feet. This will be a great freedom.

Then all these experiments, such as laboratory babies, will be of a different caliber, because you can arrange what kind of genius you want. Up to now it has been just accidental, and because it has been accidental, ninety-nine percent of the people have nothing to contribute. They contribute only problems to the world.

Now, what has Ethiopia contributed to the world? What have the poor countries contributed to the world – or even the rich countries? Except problems, wars, there is no contribution on their part.

But if you can give birth to a child in a scientific lab…. It is possible, there is no problem in it. The male semen and the woman's egg can meet in a tube. There is no need to go on in the old bullock-cart way. We can look and we can have the whole picture of what this child is going to be. If we want more poets, we can create more poets. If we want more musicians, we can create more musicians. And we can create only geniuses; there is no need for mediocre people – they have had their day.

We can give the child strength, long life. We can make sure that he never becomes sick, that he will never become old. It is just a question of managing and finding the right egg and the right male contribution to the egg. What we have been doing is just utterly unintelligent.

And this will free man also from guilt, possessiveness, jealousy, because you will not be producing children. Sex, for the first time, will be simply fun! Children will be produced in the lab. They will belong to all. And because you are not going to produce children in the old way – it should be illegal and criminal to do so, you will be behind bars if you do it – then many problems of your life will be simply dissolved.

Why is the man so insistent…? Throughout the ages the insistence has remained there: he wants to be certain that the child born out of his wife's womb is his. Why? Who are *you* anyway? It is a question of property, because your child will become the inheritor of all that you have accumulated. You want to be certain that it is your child, not your neighbor's child.

Women have been kept almost imprisoned, for the simple fear that if they start mixing with people it will be difficult to decide whose child it is. Only the mother will know, or even she may not know.

Once production of life goes into the hands of science, sex will be transformed. Then you are not jealous, then you are not a monopolist, then monogamy is absurd. Then sex is just fun, the way you enjoy tennis. And you don't bother that the partners should remain monogamous – two bodies enjoying each other…. And there will be no fear that the wife may get pregnant and there will be problems, financial and other.

Sex will no longer be a problem for the world population; it will no longer be a problem for the priest. In fact, if children are produced in the scientific lab, many of the troubles of the world will dissolve. And we can create the best people: beautiful, healthy, capable of living as long as we want. Old age is not necessary – a man can remain young, healthy, without sickness.

All these hospitals and so many people, so much money involved…. Do you know? America spends more money on laxatives than on education. Great idea! Who cares about education? The question is laxatives!

But the basic thing should be remembered. Scientists have to be courageous enough and declare that they don't belong to any nation, to any religion, that whatsoever they will be doing will be for the whole humanity. And I don't see that there is anything impossible in it.

I am absolutely for those progressive inventions which can make man happier, live longer, be younger, healthier, and which make his life more of a play, fun, and less of a torturous journey from the cradle to the grave.

Only an Egoist
Can be Humble

DISCOURSE 20,   July 18, 1985

Beloved Bhagwan,

If You are only a fallible, ordinary man, and not a great master, why are we called "The Chosen Few" who are going to be messengers of Rajneeshism for the world at large? Doesn't this fulfill our egos?

I have no ifs and buts in my philosophy of life. It is not a question of "if." I am not a great master but an ordinary, fallible man – it is the truth.

And to be chosen by an ordinary, fallible man – I cannot conceive how it can fulfill your ego. If you were chosen by a great master, then certainly your egos would be fulfilled. But in your being chosen by an ordinary, fallible man, your egos will be completely destroyed. The fallible man will most probably choose the wrong person. The ordinary man is bound to choose ordinary people. It is impossible for you to feel extraordinary.

I want you to realize a simple thing: in existence there is nothing higher, nothing lower. There are no separate entities to be compared – it is one existence. And to be part of it you cannot remain extraordinary. You are dividing yourself from the beautiful ordinariness of existence.

The people who have called themselves the great masters, prophets, messiahs, are simply egoistic. Naturally, these people attracted other egoistic people.

Jesus declares he is the only begotten son of God.

He chooses his twelve apostles – all idiots, but their egos are tremendously fulfilled. Chosen by the only begotten son of God, they become extraordinary in their minds. The moment Jesus was departing, the last night, do you know what the disciples were asking him? They were not concerned that tomorrow he is going to be crucified, they did not ask a single question about that. They did not ask, "What can we do to prevent it?" Not a single one of them said, "I am ready to be crucified in your place."

What they asked is simply disgusting. They asked, "Lord, when you reach paradise, of course you will be sitting at the right hand of God the father. Please tell us, what will be our positions? Who will be next to you?"

Do you think these people are sane, sensible, reasonable? These people are madly egoistic. They are with Jesus not because they love him but because they are going to use Jesus as a ladder to reach paradise, to the highest possible post there. Of course, they allow Jesus to be at the right hand of God, but who will be next to him? – and then? – all twelve apostles.... I do not see any love, any gratitude. They have not come for that.

They were attracted by Jesus' proclamation that he is the messenger, the prophet, the son. And a fisherman is asking, "What will be my place in paradise?" A fisherman has no place in this world. He is trying to console himself; he is trying to believe that Jesus *is* the son of God, because on that belief depends his ego. Without Jesus being the only begotten son of God, he is only a fisherman. But if Jesus is the son of God, and the fisherman is by his side, naturally he becomes extraordinary, the most superior person possible. He has bypassed all the rabbis, all the saints, all the prophets, all the priests.

This is the inner functioning of their mind.

You can be with me only if you don't have such idiotic ideas about yourself. To me, being a fisherman is far better than being a stupid apostle. And who cares about God? He is not even a fisherman, he is not even a carpenter – who cares to be on his right side or left side? In the first place he does not exist, so there is no left, no right.

You can be with me for a simple reason only.

They were doing business. They were all Jews, and it was a good bargain. Just to hang around this crazy man and then to gain all the glories of heaven – it was a good bargain!

With me, you have only to lose; you cannot gain anything. You are in a game where you can only be a loser. You will have to lose your ego, you will have to lose your jealousy, you will have to lose your fear. You will have to lose all kinds of crap that you are filled with. You will have to be empty – and emptiness cannot claim the ego. There is no place in emptiness, in nothingness, for the ego. You can be with me, not for anything that is going to be profitable in the future; you can be here only for this moment.

I do not promise you anything. All your prophets and messiahs and avataras have been *lying* – because all their promises are simple lies and nothing else. They have been befooling you, cheating you, exploiting you, knowing your weakness. This is your weakness: the ego. Anybody can exploit you, he just has to make your ego a little bigger.

In India, we have a proverb, "In time of need one has to call a donkey 'Daddy.'" Knowing perfectly well that he is a donkey, in time of need you have to call him Daddy. Of course the donkey feels great. It is

The ultimate law is to be innocent, simple, incorruptible, trusting in life and existence and just floating with the river – not fighting against the current, but going with the river wherever it is going, just being in a let-go. The moment you are in an absolute let-go, the ultimate law of life is clear to you. It is let-go, totally – no conflict with existence, a merger, a communion.

a mutual phenomenon: you are calling him Daddy for your profit, and he is readily available because nobody has ever called him Daddy. Everybody has been, up to now, calling him donkey.

I was expelled from one of my colleges. I have been expelled many times, but this time it was very difficult for me to get into another college. The city I was living in had almost twenty colleges, but now everybody was aware that it was better not to let me in, because I made expulsion difficult, almost impossible. And the trouble was that I was always right! All their expulsions were absolutely wrong, and they accepted it.

The principles told me, "We are sorry, and we know that you are right, but what can we do? It is difficult, we are in a great fix." Once, a professor who had been in the college for thirty years, one of the most important professors of the college, known all over India, had written a letter: "Either this student should not remain in the college, or accept my resignation. We both cannot be in the college together."

The principal told me, "I know, I understand your argument. It is absolutely valid" – because the professor was teaching logic and not allowing me to argue!

"What kind of professor is he?" I asked him. "Particularly in the subject of logic, argumentation is absolutely appropriate. He is not teaching me love, he is teaching me logic. And if I find loopholes in his logic, what is wrong in it? He should correct himself."

The principal said, "I understand. He is behaving arrogantly, knowing that we cannot lose him. He is one of our best, most well-known professors; he attracts students to the college. He knows that I can be blackmailed, and he is blackmailing me; but I am sorry, I have to expel you."

No college was ready to accept me because the same was going to happen everywhere; it had happened in a few other colleges before. But I have my own way of doing things. I went to one principal who

was thought to be a crackpot. And why was he thought to be a crackpot? Because in the early morning from five to seven he was praying to the mother goddess Kali. He himself was a big man, black, ugly, and he was a devotee of the mother Kali – *kali* means black. And the pictures or the statues of mother Kali are really unbelievable. Who is going to worship this woman?

She has in one of her hands a freshly-cut head of a man, blood dripping, and in another hand, a sword ready for anybody she comes across. And she is dancing on the chest of her husband! Twelve skulls of human beings make her garland. She is ferocious, blood-thirsty. She seems to be more representative of death than life.

He was a devotee of the goddess Kali and he got almost in a frenzy…. When he prayed, he would pray so loudly – and his voice was not musical. The whole neighborhood was tortured. Nobody could sleep in the morning when it is so beautiful to turn over and go to sleep again. You would go on tossing and turning, and he would shout his prayers and dance.

I reached his home – I did not go to the college, to his office – I reached his home at four o'clock early in the morning. He was just coming out of his bathroom. He said, "Why have you come here?"

I said, "I wanted to meet you in your temple, not in that ordinary principal's office. Here you are your reality. There you are nothing but a principal. There are millions of principals in the country, but there is not a single other devotee of your caliber. I wanted to meet you and see you at your best."

He smiled, he put his hand on my hand. He said, "You are the first person to recognize me. Nobody recognizes what I am doing. All the neighbors are against me, all the professors are against me, all the students are against me."

I said, "It will be a great privilege for me if I can sit and just watch your devotion, your dance, your musical singing." And that day he did his best! After he was finished, I told him, "You have converted me:

I have become a devotee of the mother goddess Kali. Now I will see you in the office."

He said, "There is no need. I know you have been expelled – and a person like you with such great insight! You need not bother; you are admitted to the college. You need not apply for it. You are my most respected student."

And he kept his word: he permitted me in his college, he gave me a scholarship. And whenever there was any occasion – and he used to find occasions to torture the professors and the students by his long, boring speeches – he would always mention me. He would say, "Perhaps nobody else is understanding me, but I am certain that there is one person" – and I was always sitting in front – "who understands me, and that is enough."

You cannot be close to me when I say I am an ordinary man. And it is not "if." Don't try to deceive yourself, baby. I am really an ordinary man. Unless you are also ordinary, there is no possibility of communion between me and you. If you are extraordinary you will be so high, above the roof of the Mandir. If you are also simple and ordinary, you will understand the beauty, the grace, the innocence of it. Your ego will disappear.

But because of your "if" the whole problem has arisen in your mind. Deep down you want to believe that I am extraordinary. You may be arguing within yourself that I am just being humble in saying that I am ordinary. I am not a humble man. Only an egoist can be humble. Humbleness is just the ego standing on its head. I don't have any ego – how can I be humble? There is no way.

You must be arguing within yourself that this is my way of teaching you humility, simplicity, egolessness, but I am not ordinary. Please, don't deceive yourself. I am just as ordinary as you are, with all the weaknesses, with all the frailties. This is to be emphasized continuously because you will tend to forget it. And why am I emphasizing it? So that you can see a very significant point: if an ordinary man – who is just like you – can be enlightened, then there is no problem for you either. You can also be enlightened.

All the religions of the world have created a totally different situation. Krishna, the Hindu god, is an incarnation of God himself. You can listen to him, you can appreciate him, you can worship him, but you cannot imagine that you can become another Krishna! He is not an ordinary mortal, he comes from on high – you cannot even imagine the height from where he comes. You are ordinary creatures of the earth. He has come to give you a message, he has come to save you; he is your savior.

You know yourself perfectly well – how can you imagine yourself a savior? You know your weaknesses – you cannot drop smoking, how can you be a savior?

If you want me to prove my ordinariness…. There are a few difficulties; otherwise I would start smoking. It is just that I am allergic. That means you are in a far better position than me. I cannot smoke, I will immediately start coughing and will have an asthma attack. You are in a far better position. I can start doing everything that you do – I am just lazy. You have to tolerate me. But my point has to be understood completely, without any ifs and buts.

I belong to you.

I am part of you.

My place is amidst you.

That will destroy your egoistic trips and numbers. It will give you a great rejoicing that one need not be an incarnation of God to be enlightened; one need not be a special messenger of God, like Mohammed, to be enlightened. One need not be in direct communication, with a private line to God, and still you can be enlightened.

The ego is the barrier. I am exposing my whole heart to you. I was not born out of a virgin mother, I was born just as you were born. I was not born while my mother was standing, she was lying down just as your mother was lying down.

When Buddha was born, his mother was standing, and he dropped onto the earth, standing. I have

203

never done anything like that. Not only did he drop from the womb standing, he walked seven feet, seven steps – symbolic, esoteric. The number seven is very esoteric. And on his last step, he stood there – just born, standing, walking – he stood there and declared to the whole universe, "I am the most supreme enlightened being!"

Now, I have not done anything like that. Even if I had been told to do it, I would have refused. It looks so foolish. Now, how can you imagine yourself walking side by side with Buddha? Impossible, he is superhuman – you are an ordinary creature.

Mohammed died, but in a special way. He is no ordinary man, he is the last prophet of God. After him there is not going to be any prophet. He closed the door because he has given the final message. Now there are going to be no further additions, impressions, no editing, nothing has to be added. He has given the essential and basic and the most profound, final message to the world. He cannot die in an ordinary way.

When he died, he flew with his horse upwards. People saw him going beyond the clouds, and then he disappeared. Even the horse went with him. It was no ordinary horse, it was Prophet Hazrat Mohammed's horse. You cannot even compare yourself with Mohammed's horse – you are just a donkey!

These people were pure egoists, creating stories about themselves, and then their followers went on and on creating more and more stories to make their prophet higher than other prophets. Over the centuries, so many extraordinary miracles have accumulated around these prophets – that impresses people. Becoming a Catholic, you become special.

But to be with me you have to become ordinary, you have to come down to the earth. You have to be human. And the moment you understand humanity, its frailty, its weaknesses, you will understand other human beings more clearly. You will not be so unkind if somebody commits a mistake; you know it is human. If somebody goes wrong, you will not be too

hard. You will say, "So what? I am also prone to go that way." If somebody drinks alcohol, smokes cigars, plays cards….

Prophets are not allowed to do such things. Prophets are not allowed to do natural things even. Mahavira, the Jaina prophet, is not allowed to perspire. I am very much worried about the man, because perspiration is a natural device to keep your temperature exactly the same, normal. If perspiration stops, Mahavira will explode into flames; his temperature will go higher and higher.

Perspiration is a natural way to keep the heat from entering you. You perspire, and the sunrays are prevented by your perspiration. The sunrays become engaged – they are foolish – they become engaged in evaporating the perspiration. They forget you, they leave you alone, and your temperature remains the same.

You have holes all over your body: seven million small holes, with glands ready to perspire any moment. If Mahavira never perspired, I can think only of one thing – that we should forget the idea that *we* have invented plastic. Mahavira's body must have been a plastic body; only a plastic body cannot perspire.

Plastic is very stubborn. Now the scientists of the whole world are worried: so much plastic is being thrown into the ocean, into the rivers, into the earth, and there is no way for plastic to dissolve into earth or into water. It is accumulating there because it is not a natural product.

If a tree falls down, soon it will disappear into its basic elements: the water will move into the water, the earth will move into the earth, the air will be released into the air, and the tree will disappear. But plastic is not going to disappear; it is going to remain there, preventing natural cycles of rejuvenation. And each year there is more and more plastic, because it is cheap. You need not keep it: you use the content and throw the container; it has no value.

Mahavira's body does not perspire. What about

other things? He does not urinate…because a man who does not perspire, do you think he will urinate? What happens to the water that he drinks? His bladder must be getting bigger and bigger and bigger – at bursting point. Any moment he can create a flood! He does not defecate. Now, he must be unique, the only person in the whole history – past, present, future – at the top of the line of those who are constipated. You cannot defeat him.

One man has tried. The greatest length known to humanity is…one man in England – of course, it has to be in England – remained constipated for eight months. This is the longest period. Only an Englishman can manage that. But what about Mahavira? – for eighty-two years!

All this nonsense, all these lies are invented for a simple reason: to humiliate you, to make you feel unworthy, to make you feel guilty, to create an inferiority complex in you. And if an inferiority complex is created in you, you start going towards something which is superior. You want to become the president of the country, you want to have all the wealth of the world, you want in every direction and dimension to be something special and higher. From inferiority to superiority is the journey of the ego.

I want you to understand that you are perfectly okay as you are. Just relax in your simple ordinariness. Don't try to change it. Don't try any discipline to improve yourself. Just relax and accept.

If the sun accepts you…. Do you think presidents get more suntan than you? Do you think trees look greener to the presidents than to you? Do you think the world is in any way different to the kings and the queens than to you? If this existence accepts you, then who is the priest to condemn you? He is against nature, against existence. And because of his continuous condemnation of your ordinariness, he goes on destroying you.

I respect you, not because you don't perspire. I respect you, not because you were born of a virgin girl. I respect you, not because you were born standing, walked seven steps and declared, "I am the most enlightened man ever!" I respect you because you are simple, ordinary, vulnerable, fallible.

If existence is ready to accept you, who I am not to accept you? All the religions have been rejecting you. And it is a strange phenomenon: they go on condemning you, rejecting you, humiliating you – and you go on falling at their feet, worshipping them.

You need not worship me, you need not fall at my feet. You need not in any way think of yourself as my followers. You are my fellow travelers.

As long as it suits you to be with me, be with me. The moment you feel it is time to depart on some crossroad, then go to Santa Fe. I have nothing against Santa Fe. Santa Fe is my commune – just a few camels have gathered there.

Beloved Bhagwan,

Would You speak about the significance of the gachchhamis? How can we keep them fresh and alive and prevent them from becoming like the meaningless, stereotyped rituals practiced in other religions?

It depends on you, not on the *gachchhamis*. If you are alive, if you are full of love, if you are as curious as a child – wondering about everything in life – if you are alive, flowing, then whatever you do will remain alive. You are trying to throw the responsibility on the gachchhamis.

Please remember: everything, if you do it as a duty, will be dead. Everything, if you do it out of love, will be alive – you are pouring yourself into it.

When you wake up in the morning do you say, "Shit! Again?" Then your day is going to be what you want: it is going to be shit. But if you wake up in the morning, just the way a child opens his eyes for the first time, looks all around: such an immensely beautiful world – so many colors, so many birds singing, the sun and the moon and the stars…and the people, each individual and unique. The child makes everything alive.

See a child trying to catch a butterfly – those colors of the butterfly, the beauty of it! He is running. Most probably he will not be able to catch it, because butterflies are clever enough. They will sit and create the desire in the child, that now is the moment; and as he reaches close by, again they are on the wing. But the child is enchanted with flowers, with seashells, with anything! Colored stones on the beach….

In my childhood, my mother had to take all kinds of things from my pockets. Now I have no pockets, then I used to have four: two on the side, two in the front – and long pockets. I harassed the tailor, "The pockets have to be as long as possible."

He said, "But that looks odd. And your father says something else to me, 'Don't listen to him.' And it is not beautiful to have that long a pocket, four pockets. And what do you do with those pockets?"

I said, "There are so many things to collect in the world – beautiful stones by the riverside. It is so challenging."

My mother had to empty my pockets before I went to sleep, because otherwise all those stones would be on the bed and I would not be able to sleep. But she had to keep them, because in the morning the first thing I would ask was, "Where have all those stones gone?" I had piles of stones, seashells; and collecting all these things I was more happy than King Midas must have been.

Midas had the blessing of gods. He had been praying for it; so remember always, sometimes prayers just by accident come true. He was praying that the power should be given to him that whatever he touches becomes gold. And then he was caught. He was the most miserable man the world has known.

He would touch his food and it would become gold. Even his own children would not come close to him, because he had touched one of his boys; he was standing there – a golden statue of course, but dead.

The people of his court escaped. His own wife was not ready to sleep with him – not even in the same room, because who knows? In sleep he may touch you, and you are finished!

That man was deserted by everybody, and he was surrounded with nothing but gold. His palace was gold, his streets were gold, the trees of his garden were gold. It was all gold, and Midas was the most poor man in the world. Not a single friend; even his own wife and children finally escaped. He died in utter misery and starvation, because water he could not drink, food he could not eat. Whatever he touched immediately became gold. He had to carry the great weight of his clothes – because they all became gold. Now he understood what he had asked for. This was a golden poverty, golden death. But it was not alive.

Remember that: it depends on you, it is your touch that keeps things alive or dead.

The gachchhamis have to be understood. The first thing: they are not prayers, because there is no God to whom you can pray. The gachchhamis are your decision. And because you are so asleep, you have to go on reminding yourself.

The first is, *Buddham sharanam gachchhami:* I go to the feet of the awakened one. It does not say, "I go to the feet of Jesus, Mohammed, Mahavira, Gautam Buddha" – no.

Buddham is not Gautam Buddha. Gautam Buddha's original name was Gautam Siddharth. When he became awakened, then Siddharth was dropped and the world has know him since then as Gautam Buddha. "Buddha" is nobody's property. It simply means the sleep is over, you are no longer dreaming, no longer hallucinating; you are simply awake.

Reminding yourself, "I go to the feet of the awakened one," is not worshipping, because the awakened one is not any person in particular. There are no feet of the awakened one. It simply says, and reminds you, that you are surrendered to the fact of awakening, that this is your decision, this is your commitment.

The second line of the *gachchhamis* is, *Sangham sharanam gachchhami:* I go to the feet of the commune of the awakened one. Why? Because the awakened one is no longer an individual. He becomes spread over all those people who love him.

My commune is me. So anybody who tries to divide – he loves me but he does not love my commune – has not understood it at all. And he does *not* love me – he is befooling himself. If he loves me, then it is natural that he will love those who love me. The commune is all those people who are seeking and searching to be awakened. At least one decision they have made, that they love the awakened one and they would like to have the same quality to their consciousness. Howsoever long the journey may be, they are determined to reach the goal.

In the commune there will be all kinds of people: a few will be camels, a few will be lions, a few may have become children. It is a good hit for your ego. To go to the feet of the awakened one may again create from the back door the same ego. But to go to the feet of the commune, where there are camels…. Sometimes you will touch the feet of the camel. Sometimes the lion will roar at you when you are trying to touch his feet; he may make a breakfast of you. And the child….

No culture, no society, no religion, has respected the child. Every culture is trying to make the child behave in the ways of the old people because they know what is right; how can a child know what is right? A child has to be trained, nurtured. He is thought by all the civilizations of the world to be a savage, a primitive. He has to be cultured, he has to be made civilized. They are all cutting and pruning the child and trying to make him a good citizen.

The old man has been respected by all the cultures, all the religions, all the societies. Why? Just because he has lived seventy years, eighty years, ninety years? All old people become cunning. Naturally their experience of life makes them cunning. The more cunning you are, the more successful you will be. They all become suspicious, mistrusting, because the more you trust, the more you will be exploited. You have to continually go on mistrusting everybody, so nobody can manage to exploit you.

The old man has learned that life is a struggle, a struggle to survive. It is a continuous war against the whole world. Everybody is at your neck – before he cuts your neck, you have to cut his. There is no time, you cannot wait; you have to be the first to cut, to destroy the other. And this old man has been respected by everybody.

I am telling you, respect the child, because the child is innocent, trusting, loving, enjoying the small things of life. He has no desire to rise higher on any ladder of success. He is utterly contented – you have not yet poisoned him. Your educational system has not yet put his mind on the way of ambition. The child has no ambition. And the awakened one regains his childhood.

The awakened one comes back to a greater childhood, to a greater innocence. The child's innocence was not his achievement, he was simply ignorant of the ways of the world; but the awakened one has passed through the whole life's experience, the whole expanse of good, bad – and still, by becoming awake, he has dropped it.

The child was going to be corrupted sooner or later. The awakened one cannot be corrupted. The child's innocence was really ignorance. The awakened one's innocence is not ignorance, it is his wisdom. But it is a circle, complete. As a child he started, moved around the world and its experiences – miseries, sufferings, anxieties, anguishes – and has come back to the same point again. The circle is complete, he has become a child again.

So in the commune there will be many camels – the new arrivals are bound to be camels, some old stubborn guys are going to be camels. There will be lions who have dropped their camelhood. And there will be a few children – innocent.

To go to the feet of the commune simply means to destroy your ego completely. It is so easy to go to the feet of the awakened one; it is more difficult to go to the feet of the commune. More difficult, because your ego will hurt; but more important, because that ego has to be destroyed.

And the third gachchhami sutra is: I go to the feet of the ultimate law of the awakened one.

The ultimate law is just to be silent, utterly at ease, without any condemnation of any part of your being – a total acceptance.

I have been asked hundreds of times…. One day a woman came and said, "You have given sannyas to my husband. Do you know that he is a drunkard? Have you told him to stop drinking?"

I said, "Why should I tell him to stop drinking?"

She said, "But what kind of a sannyasin is he?"

I said, "Anybody who comes to me is bound to have weaknesses, frailties. I have no condemnation. You think your husband has not told this to me? This was the first thing. With tears he has told me, 'Please let me tell you that I am a drunkard. I have tried my hardest to stop drinking before I came to you for sannyas, but it is impossible. In this life it is not possible for me to stop drinking.'"

So I said, "Let me take a chance. If you refuse, it is perfectly okay."

He said, "But if you give me sannyas knowing perfectly well that I am a drunkard, then…. You know better."

I said to the woman, "Your husband has exposed himself – that is simplicity. He was not hiding anything. And there is nothing to be worried about. Sannyas is the beginning of transformation. It does not ask you…. All the religions have asked you first to fulfill certain conditions and then you can be a sannyasin.

"I am a totally different kind of man. My approach is utterly different. I say become a sannyasin without any conditions and sannyas will transform you slowly, slowly, and will bring into existence all those qualities that other religions were asking before sannyas. Before sannyas, those qualities are not possible.

"If I say to this man, 'First you stop drinking alcohol completely, only then can I give you sannyas,' he will not be able to . He has tried his whole life – and the more you fail again and again, the more you know that it is completely useless to try. You know you are going to fail. I don't make any conditions.

"I have given sannyas to your husband. Don't be worried, because my sannyas is not renouncing the wife or the children or the house or the business of the world. I am bringing a totally new conception of sannyas into the world.

"This request for sannyas is only the decision of a sleeping man. Perhaps in a moment when the sleep is not so thick, and he is just on the borderline from where he can be awakened…. You know in sleep sometimes you are fast asleep, in a deep sleep; and sometimes the sleep is thin – you can even hear voices, people talking, vehicles moving on the road. You are still asleep, but very superficially. In these superficial moments of sleep a person hears about sannyas, and the alchemy of it, and the transformation that is possible through it.

"I give sannyas without any conditions. This is enough, that the man has asked to become a sannyasin. He is far better than those who don't drink, than those who don't smoke, than those who don't gamble. He is far more courageous, and far more simple."

After a few days the man came and said, "You have created a trouble for me" – because in India if people see a sannyasin they simply fall at his feet. A sannyasin passing by, you have to touch his feet. He has done something that you also desire to do but are not strong enough to do – he has done it.

But those people were not aware that he is my sannyasin. And I had chosen the red color particularly for that purpose, because in India that has been for centuries the color of the sannyasin.

The drunkard said, "I am now really in a difficulty – people touching my feet, and I am a drunkard, a third-rate man! Now I have to do something. This is just too heavy for me, that a brahmin is touching my feet! And I cannot go to the pub, because in this dress if I go to the pub…. I tried first not to go, but the temptation was too much. So one day I went there, and even the manager of the pub touched my feet. He said, 'You have become a sannyasin? It is a miracle!' I had gone to ask for alcohol, but I said that I had just come to see the old friends, and came back home without any drink! Now what am I to do?"

I said, "Now it is your business. My business is finished. You asked for sannyas – I gave you sannyas. Now, you have to work it out."

He said, "You are dangerous! You trapped me: you said there are no conditions."

I said, "There *are* no conditions."

"But," he said, "all the conditions are coming in. Even my wife has stopped sleeping with me" – because no woman in India will sleep with a sannyasin; that is thought to be a sin. He said, "My wife used to quarrel with me continuously. Once in a while when I was too drunk and people carried me home, she had even beaten me. Now she touches my feet every morning. And I think, 'My God! I have lost my wife. And Bhagwan was saying you are not to renounce, but this is renunciation. I have not done anything – she has renounced me!'

"My children had never paid any respect to me. They all were against me, they were in favor of their mother. They thought that I was destroying the whole family, their future, their education, because I was wasting the money that I earned on alcohol. Now before going to school, they all touch my feet, they ask for my blessing. And just the other day a man got married in my neighborhood and the couple came to ask for my blessings. That was too much!"

I said, "Now, you try whatever you can" – and he did try. It became clear to him that in his whole life nobody had respected him, nobody had accepted him as a human being, nobody had thought that he was intelligent. Now it is difficult to go back. He has to go forward whatsoever the troubles, whatsoever the consequences.

And he turned out to be not only a lion, but a child too. He is a poor man, but somehow he managed this festival to come here. I enquired how he managed. He sold his house, he sold his land. He arranged for some other sannyasin to give the guarantee bank balance because he had no bank balance. And there is no need for him to go back, because all that he had he has sold. His children are grown-up and he had come here with his wife. He is now old.

He said, "At least once more I wanted to see you, because time is fleeing fast. I am old enough – seventy-five – any day I may be gone. But I didn't want to leave this world before I had seen you once more, so I have risked everything."

I was surprised because the wife was also a sannyasin; I had given sannyas only to him. I asked, "What happened to your wife?"

He said, "I have given sannyas to her."

The ultimate law is to be innocent, simple, incorruptible, trusting in life and existence and just floating with the river – not fighting against the current, but going with the river wherever it is going, just being in a let-go. The moment you are in an absolute let-go, the ultimate law of life is clear to you. It is let-go, totally – no conflict with existence, a merger, a communion.

The gachchhamis are not a prayer; this is simply your determination. But because you are asleep, asleep in different stages – somebody asleep in the stage of the camel, somebody asleep in the stage of the lion…. And there are more stages in between. These three are just to make it convenient for you to understand, because between the camel and the lion there will be many steps; it is a growth. Between the lion and the child there will be many steps; it is a growth. It is your whole program of sannyas.

The gachchhamis are a continuous reminder. But whether they will become dead, stereotyped or not, is not in my hands. It is up to you. You have to keep them alive, and the only way to keep them alive is to live, yourself, more abundantly, more intensely, more totally.

Your intensity, your totality will give more life to the gachchhamis. Your each single remembrance of the gachchhamis will be a step forward towards the ultimate law, when you are born again, when the child in you is back.

The world had taken it away, but now you have found your lost childhood.

Now nobody can take it away.

The Master
Is Nothing but
A Sculptor

DISCOURSE 21,   July 19, 1985

Beloved Bhagwan,

When I read Your books I have felt great love for You. Now that I am here I feel less love. Sitting in discourse I feel more back pain than love. And lately I've been feeling a lot of fear, even hatred, of You. I feel unsure of You, especially when You talk about "my sannyasins."
It seems that You expect the total yes, which I have always fought against. I've seen many loving, awake people here who feel differently, and that helps me, but it will not last when I have gone.

I am wondering how to address you: Mr. Camel, Mrs. Camel, or Miss Camel? Perhaps the last is the best: you have been missing continuously.

You say when you were reading my books you loved me extremely. That is dangerous, because your love is carrying, just as a shadow to it, hatred. Extreme love is going to be followed by extreme hatred. So what is happening to you is simply natural. It shows the quality of your love: you don't know what love is.

It is easy to love me reading my books, because books are dead. I am not. It is easy to love the books because you can interpret what is said in the book according to your mind. You can manage to read only that which strengthens your ego, and bypass that which destroys your ego. Books have never been known to make anyone enlightened. What can books do? You are the master of the book; it is in your hands to manipulate it in any way you want.

So if you want to continue loving me extremely, please don't come near me. Then I am almost dead for you; those books are far more valuable to you, they support you. You choose to hear, to read only that which is in tune with your mind – and your mind is the problem. Your mind has to be hammered. All your defenses have to be destroyed. And when you come to me you are taking a risk. If you really come to me, you will return a totally different man, with no ego, no defenses.

Against whom are you creating defenses? We are one with existence. That oneness proves that there are not any real egos; all are phony. Coming close to me you will become aware that your ego is phony, that your defenses are just useless – they cannot prevent me from reaching you. And the moment I start entering you, there is great disturbance; hence you feel fear. Love disappears, fear comes in.

Miss Camel, you missed.

When there is fear, that is only a passage from love to hatred. You never fear a person you love; you cannot fear a person you love.

You are absolutely open, vulnerable, without any

defenses to the person you love. That's the meaning of trust. And if your love cannot create that trust it is just something phony; you are living with an idea but not with reality.

The ego is not you. And to discover yourself, the ego has to be completely destroyed. That's the only way. The master is nothing but a sculptor.

Michelangelo was asked by a shopkeeper, "In this ugly rock, a marble rock, which had been lying there for almost a decade.... First I used to keep it in my shop, but nobody bothered about it. In fact, everybody laughed at me: 'What can be made of this?' Finally I threw it on the other side of the road. How did you manage to see something in this rock?"

Do you know what Michelangelo said? He said, "Jesus called me from the rock, and asked me, 'Please, free me from this rock. I am encaged.' I saw Jesus clearly in the rock. Just a little hammering is needed – a few chips here, a few chips there – and Jesus can be discovered."

Exactly that is the work of a master. You come to him as a rock, but he goes on seeing in you something which you have not even imagined. He is dashing directly towards that which is your essential reality. He has to cut off pieces of rock here and there, and bring you to your real shape.

Books cannot do that. You have purchased those books; you cannot purchase me. You can manage to do anything to those books you want.

I never liked in my whole life to read a book from a library or from somebody else, for the simple reason that people go on doing nasty things to books. They will underline, they will make notes on the margin. You can do anything to a book; the book cannot say, "What are you doing to me?" A secondhand book is one of the most ugly phenomena in the world.

The book is absolutely in your hands. I am not in your hands; on the contrary, you are in my hands. That creates fear, that creates a trembling inside. That makes you alert that you are coming to a

Your innocence is not an ordinary thing, it is something immensely valuable. In your innocence you will be able to see that in the contradictory statements of the master there is no contradiction, that there is a hidden connection between them, that in fact they are not contradictions but part of each other – complementaries, not contradictions.

dangerous place – one step more and you may be gone, and then you will never be able to find yourself again.

The real work of the master is really murder: murder of that which you are not. The master takes away all that which is not really there, and strangely, gives you that which you have always been.

Fear is natural, it is a good sign. And when you fear someone, hatred arises – a natural consequence, a simple, logical process. The person is trying to destroy you. He is changing, transforming the way you think you are. He is killing what you think is most valuable in you. Hatred, extreme hatred…you began with extreme love, and you end up with extreme hate.

But you have to understand the whole process. This happens to everybody. People who come to me either come through reading my books or listening to their friends talk about me. They come here with a certain image of me, certain expectations of me. They don't come clean, clear. And when they come here and they don't find their expectations fulfilled, great hatred arises. But this is in a way natural to the state of sleep. Nothing is wrong with it; you just have to understand the process and you will be free of it.

You meet people who have gone a little ahead of you – and that's one of the reasons for creating a commune. The gap between me and you may be too big, and you may not be able to just take a jump over the gap. The commune gives you a chance to jump in installments.

You meet somebody who is no longer a camel. He may not yet have become a lion, but certainly he is no longer a camel; he is in the process of transformation. That gives you courage that if the camel dies that does not mean your death. And in fact, with the death of the camel begins the birth of the lion.

You meet somebody whose lion is starting to roar, to declare to the whole world its freedom, courage, fearlessness. By chance you may come across a person who is just in the process of changing from a lion to a child. To see that is a miracle! The ferocious lion, the dangerous lion is turning into an innocent child. It gives you the hope that if it is possible for somebody else, it is possible for you too. And you may come across, by chance, the person who has become a child. That will give you immense trust, confidence – also a challenge.

You are meeting people here, you say, and listening to them you feel clarity, but you are afraid that when you are gone that clarity will be gone also. Remember, if you feel this clarity is going to be lost when you are gone from here, then it is not clarity; you are simply hypnotized. Not that somebody is hypnotizing you – people here in the commune are living their lives, nobody is interested in hypnotizing anybody else. Who has time?

This life is so short – to love, to live, to be – it is so short for a man who is seeking and searching for his inner truth. It is so long for those who are simply dragging, waiting deep down for death to come and release them.

All the religions are death-oriented. They are focused beyond death, they are turning their followers' eyes beyond death. They are saying to them, "Don't be bothered with life. Somehow manage to remain alive till the grave; don't fall before you reach the grave. Just on the minimum level, remain alive." That is not life, but vegetating.

If your clarity is authentic and not just the influence of a person who is a lion or a child, then it will remain with you – not only remain, it will grow. So be very alert not to be impressed, not to be influenced – those are poisons. They will give you false illusions of clarity, enlightenment.

I have a disciple in Germany who had become enlightened many times. But the trouble was, whenever he came back to see me, his enlightenment would disappear.

He was very angry. He said, "Whenever I am back in Germany I become enlightened, and I feel very grateful to you. Just to pay my respects, I come here and my enlightenment is finished!"

The enlightenment that sannyasin was having was his autohypnosis. You can hypnotize yourself. Reading my books you can say, "This is the truth, and this is the truth I have always known. I had just forgotten it. The book has brought it back to me." But this bookish enlightenment is not the true thing. You will have to face the master.

Meetings with camels will be very comfortable, because they are just like you. They are not strangers; you can understand their language, they can understand your language. You can see beauty in them, they can see beauty in you.

Meeting with the lion is a little difficult, but after all, a lion is also an animal. There is a certain connection between the camel and the lion. The gap is not very big, you can take the jump. But at least you will be very much impressed – even if you remain a camel, you will be very much impressed. These lions become prophets and messiahs to you, because you know that you are a camel and only a lion can save you.

And when the lion roars, you know he has power. You are getting hypnotized, but this hypnosis is of no use; it is a kind of intoxication. When you go back home to meet your family of camels there, you may start doubting whether you have really seen camels turning into lions. Your logical mind will say it is absurd: how can a camel become a lion? There is no way from being a camel to become a lion. Lions are born out of other lions, they are not born out of camels.

It is because of this logical training of the mind that Hindus don't believe in converting anybody, Jews don't believe in converting anybody. In fact, for centuries Hindus have kept their doors closed. They say a Hindu has to be born from other Hindus.

There is no way that a Mohammedan can become a Hindu; it is simply impossible that a Christian can become a Hindu. In fact, even within the Hindu fold there are four castes; nobody can move from one caste to another. A sudra is born a sudra, and he will die a sudra – he cannot become a brahmin. A warrior, a *chhatriya,* is destined to remain a *chhatriya* – he cannot become a brahmin. The brahmin is the highest caste. Brahmins are born, not converted.

Jews also, for centuries, have believed that they are the chosen people of God. Now, it is up to God to make somebody a Jew. How can you convert anybody? – it is not within your power. And you are a superior race. Now, how can you change a man belonging to an inferior race? You cannot change his blood, you cannot change his bones, you cannot change his marrow, you cannot change his soul.

These are the two most ancient religions. Both have denied conversion. New religions, of course – Christianity, Mohammedanism, Buddhism – *have* to convert people; otherwise, from where are they going to get numbers, congregations? If a Buddhist is only to be born from Buddhists, where are the Buddhists? Conversion is the idea of new religions to expand their empires.

Back home you will start thinking perhaps you hallucinated here, perhaps you were hypnotized: you saw things which don't happen in the natural course of things. Camels are born camels and die camels. So you start suspecting, doubting; your clarity is gone.

And it is impossible for a lion to become a child. Perhaps a camel may manage – camels are cunning and clever, very political and diplomatic. The camel may go through plastic surgery, he may go to Leeladhar and let himself be transformed into a lion. But even plastic surgery will not be able to make a child out of a lion. This is a bigger gap.

Animals – camel and lion both, howsoever different in shape – were animals, they belonged to the same category. But the child is not an animal. The jump is from animal to human being – and not an ordinary human being, but innocent, awakened, pure of heart, full of trust. No plastic surgery can do that, so you must have dreamed it.

Back home amidst camels and their scholars and

their logicians, you will feel yourself stupid even to say that you have seen lions, that you have seen the child being born as a transformation of the lion. Nobody is going to believe you, they will think you have gone nuts.

The gap between the camel and the lion is not very big, but the gap between the lion and the child is very big. And unless you are a child you cannot love a master. Now comes the biggest gap, because to love a master you will need certain qualities in you.

What happens in ordinary love? Try to understand. You fall in love with a man or a woman. The qualities are in the woman with whom you have fallen in love: she is beautiful, she is young, she is juicy. You are falling in love without thinking at all about yourself, that you are not beautiful, that you are not young, that you are a completely dry bone, there is no juice. No, when you fall in love you are completely focused on the object of love, you are not thinking about yourself. This is the ordinary love which is going to change any moment into hate.

The love I have been talking about is the love where the whole structure is just the opposite of your love. You don't fall in love with a master because the master has charisma, because the master has some influence, he catches hold of your heart; or because he is convincing – whatsoever he says seems absolutely right. No, if this is the way, it is not going to last long.

The love I am talking about means you have to think of *your* qualities. Are you as innocent as a child, as trusting as a child, as open as a child, as silent as a child? If your love arises out of your child, your innocence, then whether the master lives or dies will not make any difference. Whether the master says this or contradicts that will not affect your love. The master may be contradicting himself continually. That will not affect your love because it was not dependent on the master's statements.

Your innocence is not an ordinary thing, it is something immensely valuable. In your innocence

you will be able to see that in the contradictory statements of the master there is no contradiction, that there is a hidden connection between them, that in fact they are not contradictions but part of each other – complementaries, not contradictions.

Can light exist without darkness? Can darkness exist without light? Can man exist without woman or vice versa? Can life exist without death or vice versa? These are not contradictions, these are complementaries. They are two sides of the same coin, they are always together.

Only very mediocre minds are consistent. Idiots are absolutely consistent, they never contradict; in fact they never say anything, so there is nothing to contradict. Their whole life is a simple consistency: they remain idiotic, they keep their quality of idiocy just the same. From the cradle to the grave they are the most consistent people in the world, nothing changes in them. They are really dead; they don't have any intelligence.

The more intelligent a person is, the more he has to contradict himself, because each moment his vision is growing, each moment his insight is deepening, each moment brings new facts, new truths. And he is not a coward who closes his eyes to that which is opening up in front of him. And he is under no obligation to the past – that which he had said in his childhood he has to repeat when he is a young man, when he is old, to remain consistent.

Intelligence is such a growing, expanding phenomenon, and each small truth discovered changes the whole map. You cannot go on keeping the old intact; the old has to be dropped and the new has to be accepted. Do you know, all the religions insist that that which is old is gold. The older it is, the golder it is. Each religion tries to stretch its oldness as far back as possible.

When Christians came in contact with Hinduism they felt very inferior, because the Christian religion says God created the world four thousand and four years before Jesus was born – there is no past beyond that. In fact, you can go back only to Jesus Christ; you cannot even go beyond him, because beyond him is Judaism. Christianity is only two thousand years old. In India Christians came across scriptures ten thousand years old. They were simply confused – what to make of it?

They had tried their best to bring everything within six thousand years. That's why they go on insisting that the Hindu religion is five thousand years old. But the evidence is not in their favor. They may go on teaching that to the Christians – who are already convinced, there is no need to bring evidence before them – but all the evidence shows that Hinduism is at least ninety thousand years old.

In the most ancient Hindu scripture, the *Rigveda,* there is a description of a configuration of stars which, according to the astronomers, really did happen ninety thousand years ago. And since then that certain configuration of stars has not happened again. And it is described in full detail; the *Rigveda* is certainly ninety thousand years old – it may be older, but that much is certain. In no other scripture of the world is that configuration described, because they all were latecomers.

But Hinduism finds it difficult to prove that it is older than Jainism, because the Jainas' first master, Adinatha, is referred to with great respect in the *Rigveda.* Now, contemporaries are never referred to with such respect – contemporaries are criticized.

Jesus was crucified by Jews, and now the great rabbis and the pope are trying to come together and forget the past. The pope has informed all his congregations around the world, "We have to drop this anti-Jewish attitude that we have carried for two thousand years unnecessarily. One Jew, the high priest, was responsible. For his responsibility you cannot make all the generations that follow responsible."

Now, Jews are also willing – there is no problem, Jesus is no longer a disturbance. But to the contemporary Jews he was a nuisance. No contemporary Jewish scripture even mentions the name of Jesus. There is no information about his crucifixion. It was such a big event, killing an innocent man, who may have been a little bit out of his mind, but that is not a crime. Everybody has the birthright to go out of his mind, there is no problem in it.

If Jesus needed anything, he needed sympathy; he needed treatment, not crucifixion.

But the contemporary Jews were very much disturbed, because he was proclaiming himself the messiah the Jews had been waiting for. "I am the one," he said, "for whom you have waited so long. Now I have come to save you all." A carpenter's son, uneducated, coming from a small village, Bethlehem…. They have seen him cutting wood, chopping wood, working with his father in his small workshop making benches and chairs, and suddenly…has this boy gone mad? He has become the messiah who is going to deliver everybody from all their sins!

Jainas say, "If Adinatha is so respectfully mentioned in the *Rigveda* even though he was against the brahmins, against the brahmin religion…. How can the *Rigveda* mention his name with such respect?" The logic seems to be significant. They are saying that Adinatha must have preceded the *Rigveda* by a few centuries, and by that time he was no longer a contemporary. Now his name can be mentioned with respect, he cannot do any harm. Jainism also does not believe in converting anybody. A Jaina is born a Jaina; you cannot become a Jaina.

Everybody is trying to take their religion as far back as possible. Why? What is the argument behind it? The older the religion is, the truer. But new religions like Mohammedanism, which is only fourteen hundred years old, and Sikhism, which is only five hundred years old, are in great trouble. They have also been trying to find something against all these old religions which prove their truth by their age – as if religion is like wine; the older it is, the better.

Mohammedans say the latest religion in the world is Mohammedanism. And of course, when man was primitive, God gave the *Rigveda* to the world, because people could not understand more than that. Its age only proves that it was given to primitives, aboriginals who were just coming out of the trees and trying to learn to walk on the ground. Naturally, God could not give them the ultimate truth; nobody would have understood it.

Now is the time, they say. Now means fourteen hundred years ago, when God decided man was grown-up enough, and he sent his *last* messenger – because now there will be no need to improve upon it; he has given his final judgment.

Mohammedanism, Sikhism try to prove…. Sikhism says, "Even Mohammedanism is old. We are only five hundred years old. There must have been some confusion because God has sent the latest message now with Nanak, the founder of Sikhism."

That message too, is now five hundred years old. Do you want me to say that I bring you the last message? I am not going to say it. I am not going to be in the company of all these fools who have been trying somehow to make their religion look bigger, higher, truer.

I say to you that I am not bringing anybody's message – because there *is* nobody! I want you to understand that I am simply trying to share my experience with you. It is always fresh, always young; it is always in the now, in the here. That is a fundamental quality of truth.

And I'm not saying that after me there will be nobody who will experience it. On the contrary, I am saying to you that if you understand me, there are going to be millions of people after me who will go on and on and on discovering more and more. Even if they have to contradict me, don't bother about it – let them contradict. Who am I? I am not closing the doors. I am not putting a lock on the door and taking the keys with me.

My house is without doors.

It is open from everywhere – and I want it to remain always open.

Naturally, people who will be coming will make new arrangements of the furniture in the house. They may plan a new architecture for the house, they may make new plans for the garden. I leave it to them, but the process will be the same.

This is a great jump, from the child to the master. The child is innocent, full of love. He falls in love with a master because something in his innocence, in his lovingness, in his openness, resounds with the heartbeat of the master. He in fact does not go into a relationship with the master, he becomes one with the master; hence it is a great jump. You are completely disappearing. But don't be worried, the master has disappeared long before you, and in disappearing he has found himself.

If you are courageous enough to disappear in the master, you will find yourself for the first time. Then you can move amongst camels – in fact, you can ride on them. You can play with lions, you can commune with children. You can commune with flowers, with rivers, with mountains. Now there is no barrier for you. Now you are as big as the whole universe.

P.D. Ouspensky, in his great contribution to humanity, *Tertium Organum*…. I have come across more books perhaps than anybody else in the whole world, but *Tertium Organum* has a beauty that no other book has. Your bibles and gitas and korans and talmuds, all are far behind.

In *Tertium Organum* Ouspensky states one thing which is tremendously beautiful for you to understand. He says, "In ordinary mathematics" – and he was one of the greatest mathematicians of this century – "in ordinary mathematics, the part is smaller than the whole, the whole is bigger than the part. It would be absurd in ordinary mathematics to say that the part is equal to the whole." And this is coming from a mathematician. He says, "But I have discovered a new mathematics, a higher mathematics, where the part is equal to the whole – not only that, sometimes bigger than the whole."

It looks mysterious, not logical – certainly against

Aristotle. But I say to you, he is talking about the mathematics of consciousness. When you dissolve, you don't become just a part of the whole, you *become* the whole. And there is every possibility that you go on growing and become bigger than the whole, because growth is the ultimate law of life.

It will be difficult logically to understand it. It is something to be experienced. Since the moment I found the ego evaporating from me, I have not felt *part* of the universe, but the universe itself. And yes, I have found many moments when I am bigger than the universe — because I can see the stars moving within me, the sunrise happening within me, all the flowers blossoming within me.

But don't believe in it because I am saying it. Take the jump from the child to the master.

Miss Camel, it is time: you should stop missing!

Beloved Bhagwan,

Why am I so afraid of being free?

Everybody is. Freedom is a great risk. People talk about freedom, but nobody really wants to be free. It is pure talk. Everybody wants to be dependent, everybody wants somebody else to take the responsibility. In freedom you are responsible for every act, every thought, every movement. You cannot dump anything on anybody else.

Just watch a Freudian psychiatrist, psychoanalyst. The patient is lying down on a couch, the psychoanalyst is sitting behind so the patient cannot see him. He is sitting behind the couch; he can see the patient, but the patient cannot see him. Some psychoanalysts use curtains so that the patient feels he need not keep his secrets to himself.

And what happens — in all psychoanalysis sessions all over the world, what is happening? The patient goes on dumping everything either on the mother — mostly on the mother — or on the father.

But he is not taking any responsibility upon himself. He is trying to prove that he is absolutely innocent; everybody else is at fault and driving him to do things that he never wanted to do in the first place.

Perhaps there is some truth in it, that's how it is happening: mothers are driving their children …mothers are trying to make their daughters real ladies — British ladies! American won't do.

In fact, in America the lady has disappeared. In California there are only women, no ladies. The father is trying to make his son a real man, a gentleman. So there is some truth in it.

But when you are grown-up and you see the whole scene, what has happened, you can simply drop it — just like that! But you don't want to, because then you will be responsible. If right now you do something wrong, you can always point towards somebody who is responsible for it.

Everybody is afraid of freedom. That's why all around the world, layers of slaveries exist in you. Every person is a multiple slave. He is a slave to the parents, he is a slave to the religion, he is a slave to the state, he is a slave to the neighbors — all kinds of slaveries which are not visible.

When I was a student in the university, I had a roommate with me for the whole year, and I had never thought that something was wrong with his speech. Then his father came to meet him and he started stuttering. I was amazed; I said, "What is the matter with you? Since your father has come you have been stuttering, you cannot speak the way you have always been speaking."

He said, "From my very childhood he has been teaching me how to speak, what to speak, what not to speak, whom to speak to, when to speak. He confused me so much that I lost my own sensibility, and stuttering started." He said, "I was amazed myself when I came to the university: leaving the house behind, my stuttering disappeared. And whenever I go to my house and to my family and to my town, the stuttering starts again."

I asked him, "When you go to the temple and pray to the father, God, what happens?"

He said, "The same thing, stuttering comes in. Just the word 'father' is enough – any father-figure."

When he was called for something by the vice-chancellor of the university, I went with him. He asked me, "Why are you coming?"

I said, "You don't be worried. I will be just outside the room waiting for you."

"But," he said, "there is no need."

I said, "I will explain it to you afterwards."

And inside the room of the vice-chancellor, he was stuttering. I had to enter without asking permission. Both were shocked. He was shocked because he was stuttering. The vice-chancellor was shocked also: "Don't you know that you have to ask permission? And I am talking to somebody."

I said, "The situation was such that I had to come in suddenly. I wanted to catch him stuttering before you for two reasons: I want to make it clear to him that it is not that something is wrong in him. Any father-figure, any authoritative figure causes his stuttering. And you are the highest authority in the university, so I wanted you also to know: please come down, don't make poor students stutter; you are not a big daddy. That's why I had to come in without asking, and suddenly. And I have caught you both red-handed. You are being authoritative, and that is ugly. You are imposing something on the poor student, who is already burdened with his daddy."

The vice-chancellor said, "Perhaps you are right – I *was* shouting at him. I will never do such a thing to anybody again; I don't want my students to stutter. When he started stuttering I was puzzled, 'What is the matter? Perhaps this is his habit.'"

I said, "It is not his habit. He has been living with me for the whole year, and he has not stuttered a single time. But when his father came, immediately things changed. Since then I have been watching: in the temple when he prays to God the father, he stutters. I wanted to see what happens between you and him. He is stuttering – you must have been behaving authoritatively. There is no need. You have to be more human, you have to be more friendly, you have to be more loving. You are not his father."

Now this student came out with me, and he said, "My father is responsible."

I said, "No, you are a coward. Every father is trying to improve upon the son, because the son is going to take his place sooner or later. That does not mean that the whole humanity is stuttering. You are a weakling, and you are avoiding that responsibility. Just accept that you have been a coward; otherwise, what is so great in your father? I have seen him. In fact, you are taller than your father. If you wrestled with him you would win, because he is getting old and you are in your prime, healthy and young.

"And that old, small man makes you stutter! Still you throw the responsibility on him. This is slavery, mental slavery. But it gives you a relief that you are not the cause of it."

Who is forcing you to go to the church, to the temple, to the synagogue? Yes, when you were a child you were taken, but now? Still you are continuing the old routine. And if you are forced to explain, you will say, "It was my father who dragged me to the synagogue. It was my Jewish mom who dragged me to this or that."

You don't see it as a slavery. It *is* a slavery. You have not been fighting against it. Yes, I know, small children are dependent on the parents, and the parents take every advantage of your dependence. They know you cannot rebel, they know you cannot go anywhere else.

I figured out in my very childhood what makes them so authoritative: "Perhaps they think I cannot rebel. Perhaps they think I cannot get food if I go against them. Perhaps they think I will be lost in this vast world without their protection." So I had to do all these things; only then would they understand that authority was not going to work with me. I made it clear to my father, "One thing is absolutely certain: if you want me to do something, please don't say it authoritatively."

He said, "Then in what way has it to be said?"

I said, "You have to ask me, 'Will you please do it?'"

He said, "This seems to be too much. I have to ask my own son, 'Will you please do it?'"

I said, "You will have to say this. If you say to me 'Go and do it!' I am the last person to do it. I would prefer to die hungry, but I will not do it. And if you ask me, 'Will you please do it?' I can even climb Everest – there is no problem. I am doing it, it has not been forced upon me. I don't want to live like a slave in my life."

One day my father was not at home. My uncle told me, "Lately I have been seeing that you come in at any time of the night. You have to be back home before nine o'clock" – because in India nine o'clock is really night. It is not evening; the sun-sets at six, and then suddenly everything becomes dark.

I said, "You don't know the contract between me and my father. You can be certain I will never enter the house unless nine o'clock has passed."

He had no children; he was just married and he was very cocky. In fact, the Indian word for uncle is *Kaka* – and he was trying to be the master of his wife. He said, "I repeat it again. If you don't come before nine, then I am not going to open the door."

I said, "That is settled. I will remain outside the door the whole night, but I am not going to accept authority in any way." And that's what happened. He was thinking that in one hour, two hours, I would drop the idea of remaining for the whole cold night outside.

In fact he became worried. My father was not in the town, and if I became sick or something happened to me… The night was really cold and it was getting colder. And he could not sleep either, because he was waiting for me to knock. Finally, nearabout twelve, he opened the door and he said, "Forgive me, just come in. Don't create trouble for me."

I said, "I am not creating trouble for anybody. I am simply keeping myself trouble-free."

In the school, in the college, I always loved to be a little mischievous. I felt those students who were not mischievous to be just dull and dead. So I would do something…. Just sitting in the class I might start what you do in *darshan* or *satsang* – I might start "Om-m-m-m" with closed mouth. Now "Om" is a religious, sacred word to the Hindus. Nobody can say that this is wrong to do; but in the class when the teacher was teaching, and he was writing on the board and his back was towards us….

He turned suddenly, looked all around – everybody was silent – and he asked, "Who was making this sound of Om?"

And I would always stand up. I would say, "I did it. It is a sacred sound."

He said, "I know, but in a class when I am teaching you something…."

I said, "You cannot teach anything higher than Om! And why are you getting so freaked out? You should have continued your work. Om would have remained in the background; it is not a problem."

He would drag me to the principal – it was almost an everyday ritual. The principal would say, "So you have come. Can't you leave these professors at ease even for a single day?"

I said, "Today I was doing such a spiritual thing. And I could have remained silent when he asked who had done it. I know perfectly well that nobody in my class can point his finger towards me, because they all know that I will create trouble for them, they are perfectly aware of it. There was no way for him to find out. I stood up myself. In fact, he should be respectful towards me: I did it, I accept it."

Many professors have asked me, "Why…? You are such a nice guy in every possible way, we cannot find a better student. But once in a while, what goes on? You start doing something which is unexpected."

I said, "It is not unexpected, at least as far as I am

concerned. It is absolutely prepared."

"But why do you do it?" they would ask.

I would say, "For a single reason, that I don't want to become a slave in any way. I want to keep my freedom intact whatsoever the cost. If I feel like chanting 'Om', then I don't care what happens to me. I chanted it, and I have not harmed anybody; I have simply saved my freedom. And I take the whole responsibility for it!"

In the school, the headmaster stopped even asking why I had been brought, because it was an everyday affair – sometimes twice a day – that I would be brought to the headmaster. In the beginning he used to enquire, "What has he done? What happened?" – this and that. After a few days he stopped enquiring, he simply gave me the punishment.

He would say, "Go around the whole building seven times."

I would say, "Yes, that's okay, but I will go nine times – not less than that."

He said, "Are you mad? This is a punishment, we are not rewarding you!"

I said, "That is my way of changing the quality of the punishment. I am enjoying it – the wind is cool, the trees are beautiful. Why seven? At least I cannot accept *your* order. I will go nine times; then I am free of your authority, I am doing it on my own, and I'm enjoying it! And you should remember that to be authoritative is ugly – you have to understand me, why I did it. You don't care to understand. You simply listen to the teacher, you don't even give a chance for me to explain."

That day he said, "Okay, what do you have to say? You were keeping your hand on a boy's shoulder in the class. In the classroom some discipline has to be maintained, and you know it. The classroom is not some place of entertainment – a park, a cinema hall. There you can walk with your hands on someone's shoulders, but not in the class."

I said, "I walked in the class with my hand on another student's shoulder simply to make this teacher freak out – because in the class he continually says smoking is bad, and I have caught him red-handed, smoking. Now this man should apologize to the whole class, because he was lying to them when he said, 'Don't smoke.' He himself smokes. He says to the students, 'Don't go to the movies,' and one day when I was entering the movie house for the second show, he was coming out from the first show.

"When I asked, 'What are you doing here?' He said, 'I am your teacher, you are not my teacher. You have no right to ask what I am doing here.' Is this a human way of behaving? I deny all kinds of authoritativeness. And still he goes on telling the students, 'Don't go to the movies, don't waste your time. Don't destroy your eyes' – this and that. And he is a regular visitor to the movie house."

The movie house belonged to one of my friends' father, so I had told the friend, "Keep me informed how often he comes to the movie." He was a regular visitor, and a chain-smoker outside the class.

"I had to do something so that he can bring me to you, and I can expose his reality. Now what do you say? Should I do nine rounds around the school or he? As far as I am concerned, we both can go together, it is perfectly good."

Since that day, that headmaster stopped punishing me. He would always ask, "Why? What was the reason?" And he was always satisfied with the reason. In fact, teachers stopped sending me to the headmaster, because there they found themselves guilty of doing something wrong. By and by, they stopped preventing me from doing anything, because if I am doing something, that means there must be much more to it – what can a teacher do?

My headmaster changed and a new headmaster came into the school. And the first day I went, he took his cane and he said, "I am a strict man, and from the very first day I make it known to the school that I am going to beat you badly."

I said, "You can do it – but can you see, just there on the other side of the road is the police station. And corporal punishment is illegal – you start beating me and you will be behind bars! The court is not far away, and I am a great friend of an old advocate who is the best advocate in the town. And I have told him that this is going to happen: 'I have heard about this man, that he beats students.' And he has promised me, 'Let him do it – you come immediately to me and we will file a suit against him in the court.' So I have made my position clear to you. Now, start beating."

His cane fell from his hand. He said, "Are you a student or some government agency?"

I said, "I am a simple student, but I don't want any authoritativeness over me. If I do anything wrong, I am ready for any punishment. But just punishing me to prove your authority? I am the last one to accept it."

"And I was not wrong – the teacher has brought me to you…. It is revengeful, because the other headmaster had stopped punishing me. Rather, he had started telling the teachers, 'It was not right on your part.' And today I have not done anything. Just when the teacher called me, I was sitting on the bench with my legs on top of it. I don't see that it is a crime, I was simply relaxed. In fact, children should be provided with chairs which are comfortable, with foot-rests so they can relax."

When you are relaxed you can understand things more easily. But in Indian schools the benches are hard – it is just a copy of British benches; in British schools the benches are hard. You have to sit on those hard benches for six hours and it starts hurting.

"Something is wrong with you people. You are not teaching us but torturing us, and under torture no teaching is possible. So I want to know what wrong I have committed. Have I given a wrong answer to his question? No, I was just keeping my feet on top of the table. These are *my* feet. If I drag his feet and put them on the table, you can punish me. But if you think this is a crime, you start punishing me, and I will see you in the court."

One has to understand one thing: What can happen? At the most, death can happen. Remember a simple maxim: Hope for the best, and wait for the worst. Then nobody in this life can disappoint you. Nobody can make you a slave, physically or psychologically.

A Hindu is a slave, a Christian is a slave, a Mohammedan – all these religions are psychological slaveries, because they give you consolation that if you follow and believe and have faith, then nothing wrong is going to happen to you. They give you all kinds of strategies to remain dependent. They teach you prayer – prayer is just begging.

I don't teach you any prayer. To whom are you praying? You have not even asked the people who have taught you prayer. Kneeling down on your church floor, you are humiliating yourself. I am not for egoist assertion, but neither am I for humiliation to be accepted as humility, humbleness. I want you to be simple, without any ego and without any humbleness – straightforward, clear.

And freedom is such a great value – perhaps the greatest value in life. It cannot be lost for anything. Even if death is the consequence – I would rather accept death than accept anything that goes against my freedom.

India was under the British Raj for almost three hundred years. My whole family was in the freedom movement; they all have been in jails. I was too young, but I was continually arguing with my father, with my uncles, "Don't blame Britain for your slavery. Such a vast country, almost a continent, cannot be made a slave by a small country like England. Somewhere deep down you are afraid of being free, somewhere deep down you are ready to accept slavery. And still you go on throwing the responsibility on Britain. But you have been a slave before too" – India has been in slavery for two thousand years. Masters changed, slavery remained.

"It is such a simple thing to see that if anybody wanted to make you a slave, you became a slave, as if you were just waiting for it, for somebody to invade you, somebody to come and enslave you."

I told my family, "I don't accept the idea of Mahatma Gandhi, that Britain is responsible for India's slavery. India itself is responsible for its slavery; otherwise, just in a single hour, all the British people can be thrown into the ocean. India just has to understand that freedom is our birthright. How many Britishers are there? Not many."

Is your mental slavery somebody else's responsibility? No. You don't want to be responsible for your own acts, you don't want to be responsible for your way of life; that's why you are afraid of being free. Drop this fear. This fear is worse than anything that can happen to anybody.

I teach you responsibility. But remember, don't misunderstand me, because all around you people are using the word "responsibility" with an absolutely different meaning – in fact, diametrically opposite to the meaning I see in the word responsibility.

They say, "Be responsible to your parents." That is not responsibility, that is slavery. They say, "Be responsible to your church, to your religion, to your faith." That is not responsibility, that is slavery. They say, "Be responsible to your nation." That is not responsibility. These are all beautiful words to cover up an ugly fact: slavery.

When I use the word "responsibility," I use it the way it should be used. Responsibility means that whatever you do, it is your response. If I ask you, "Does God exist?" and you say, "Yes, because it is written in *The Bible*," your answer is not a responsible answer. It is out of your Christian slavery.

But if you say, "I don't know. I have never come across God yet," this is your response. You are not repeating some catechism – Hindu, Mohammedan, Buddhist, Christian, Jewish – no. You are facing the question directly and responding to it. Responding on your own is the meaning of responsibility.

Freedom brings responsibility. Responsibility helps you to become more and more free. And only a person who knows the taste of freedom, who knows the beauty of responsibility, is worthy of calling himself a human being; otherwise, you are camels and nothing more.

You Are
The Only Hope!

DISCOURSE 22,   July 20, 1985

Beloved Bhagwan,

Are You a messiah, a prophet, or a reincarnation of God?

I have never expected that one of my sannyasins would ask such a bullshit question!

I am simply myself. I am not a messiah, because there is no God to send messengers to the world. Moreover, I don't want to be crucified. To prove that you are a messiah of God, crucifixion is absolutely necessary. Not that I am afraid of death, but I would like a comfortable, luxurious death. Not carrying the cross on my own shoulders, not even on your shoulders – the cross will be carried on a Rolls Royce limousine.

I am not a prophet either. I don't know what is going to happen in the next moment. I don't know even what I am going to say in the next moment. The future does not exist for me. That's exactly the meaning of the future: that which does not exist. And the prophet is one who prophesies, predicts. This is the most cunning business in the whole world.

And how can I be an incarnation of God? God is invented by those people who want to be incarnations of God. Their God is phony – American, plastic. And all those prophets, messiahs and messengers of God, incarnations of God, what have they done to the world?

Look…in five thousand years, all these people have turned the earth into a big madhouse. What kinds of things have they been telling you to do? What kind of belief systems have they imposed upon you? They have humiliated you, degraded you, turned you into a subhuman species. All these messiahs, prophets, gods – they have made life impossible, love impossible, laughter impossible. They have made the whole earth a big graveyard.

And they have all been fighting with each other. Millions of people have been killed because of these few criminals. Somebody is a Christian – that means he is conditioned by the ideology of Jesus Christ. That man, Jesus, was a crackpot! He was trying to save the whole world; he could not save himself. He was telling people things which are absurd.

He was telling the people, "Blessed are the poor." As a corollary he must have said, "Blessed are the ugly, blessed are the blind, blessed are the deaf, blessed are the crippled." All the blessed people are in the hospitals. The most blessed of all are in Ethiopia. There is going to be a tremendous fight on the day of judgment to decide who is the most poor – because of course, if the poor are the blessed, then the poorest is the Blessed One.

Forget it! No American can enter paradise. Nobody who has at least two meals every day can enter paradise. You are all going to be defeated by Ethiopians, by Indians. The western world has no hope!

But why did Jesus say, "Blessed are the poor"? He himself was poor, uneducated, uncultured. There was no way for him to rise higher in any hierarchy, to become richer, affluent, to have all the joys and comforts of life. It was not possible for him, he was not capable of it – and he saw millions of other people in the same boat. It was a self-consolation: Blessed are the poor. I wonder why he did not say, "Blessed are the poor carpenters"? He consoled himself, he consoled the poor people.

Do you know who was attracted to his teachings? – not a single man who was rich, educated, who was living life joyously. He attracted miserable people, poor people, starving people – and even they did not come in multitudes.

Those who came to Jesus, you can count on your fingers. But they were feeling great – this man has opened a door for their egos. This man is the only begotten son of God; they had to believe it, because unless they believed that he is the only begotten son of God, then what about his promises about paradise? They believed in him – not truly; they simply wanted a consolation, sympathy, and a hope that some day they will take revenge on the rich, on those who are enjoying life and its beauties.

Of course, it was not possible even for Jesus to give them those blessings here, now. They had to wait for death to come. Everything he promises is after death. You can see the strategy. Nobody comes back and says what there is after death.

You can see the strategy. You can befool people: just keep them drugged about the future life after death. And those poor people, of course, wanted to live blissfully. They had failed here; now comes this man – a carpenter, Joseph's son – and gives them a great hope, a promise.

But all those twelve apostles were simply idiots. Not a single one of them had enough intelligence to wonder what was happening. Jesus turns stones into bread, why can't he turn all the mountains into great loaves of bread? He knows the secret, and once you know a secret, it is only a questions of using it on a bigger scale. There would have been nobody poor.

He changes water into wine – why not change all

Nuclear weapons can be destroyed by a laughing, smiling, dancing humanity. But as humanity is now, there is no hope. You are the only hope! So don't keep your joy to yourself, spread it, make it available to anybody. Don't even think whether he is introduced to you or not. Don't be British, be human!

the oceans into wine? Nobody will feel thirsty ever again. He raises dead people from their graves. But why only one person? Why only Lazarus? In Jesus' lifetime, many people must have died; he should have raised all of them. And if he can raise a person who has been dead for four years, he can raise a person who has been dead for four thousand years – Moses, Abraham, Ezekiel. He could have raised all the prophets, at least, back to life. But all these are stories invented to prove that this man is no ordinary man: he is a messiah, he has extraordinary powers.

I don't claim any powers, extraordinary or ordinary. I am a simple human being. I don't want to put myself on a high pedestal and condemn you all for your sins, curse you all for your sins, and bless only those few who have faith in me.

The same is true about other messengers of God, incarnations of God. For example, Krishna is a Hindu incarnation of God – not a partial incarnation, God has come in his wholeness on the earth to save it. Strange, nobody seems to be saved.

In fact, Krishna was the cause of destroying the very backbone of India, because he forced his disciple and friend, Arjuna, into a war.

Five thousand years ago that war happened. The whole responsibility goes to Krishna – because Arjuna, the warrior, seeing millions of people, started thinking, "What is the point of it all? – killing all these people just to sit on a golden throne? There will not even be people to see that you are sitting on a golden throne. What is the point?"

Arjuna was far more intelligent than your incarnation of God, Krishna. Arjuna said, "This war seems to be absolutely meaningless. I am going to the Himalayas to meditate. Let my cousin-brothers rule, but at least there will be life. I am not going to take this great responsibility of killing so many people for my own glory, to become Arjuna the Great."

But Krishna is very clever, very cunning. He goes on arguing, convincing, persuading Arjuna. And finally he says to Arjuna, "You don't understand that God *wants* this war, because without him not even a leaf in a tree moves. You are not responsible if people are killed; it is God's will."

And when you bring God in and relieve people of their responsibility, it becomes difficult to refuse. I would have certainly refused it, but Arjuna had a conditioned mind. Krishna says, "God's *will*!…the war has to happen whether you participate or not. By not participating you will fall in the eyes of God. The war will happen." His actual words are, "You see these millions of warriors on both the sides gathered, alive? In fact, they are just waiting to die. They are dead, you are not killing them. You cannot do anything on your own; you are just a puppet in the hands of God."

God is the greatest lie that these people have been teaching. And in the name of God you can convince people to do any stupid thing.

If I had been in the place of Arjuna I would have said, "Perfectly okay, I am going to the Himalayas. How can I go to the Himalayas if God is not willing me to go there? Let him kill these people through other puppets."

It was so simple. But Krishna goes on forcing him: "You are born in a warrior family, you are a warrior by nature, from your very birth. This will be dropping out. It will be ugly, shameful to you and to your whole family and to your forefathers. Don't be a coward! Prove your mettle – the opportunity has come!" And he forced Arjuna into a war, which is called *Mahabharata,* the Great Indian War. It must have been something like the third world war which is looming on the horizon. And there are so many Arjunas; only one Krishna is needed to convince some Arjuna to start it, to be the pioneer.

It must have been of tremendous proportions, because since that war, India has never been able to regain its strength. It has been going down and down; it lost courage, it lost the joy of life. It became too concerned about death. Any religion which is concerned too much about death is fundamentally wrong. And all the religions are death-oriented.

Hence I say, all these messiahs, prophets, incarnations of God are simply clever, cunning politicians. They have destroyed humanity, they have poisoned you in every possible way. Whatsoever you enjoy is a sin, and whatsoever you suffer is virtue. Look at their logic! They have made you all into sado-masochists. You cannot recognize it, because all around you are the same kind of people. Just in names they differ – Christians, Hindus, Mohammedans, Buddhists – but fundamentally what they have done, and are doing, is exactly the same.

If you relish life, you are condemned. If you renounce life, you are respected. If you enjoy the beautiful treasures that existence makes available to you, you are going into the abysmal depth and darkness of hell. But if you torture yourself…you stand on your head in the hot sun of Oregon doing yoga exercises – which are nothing but inventions of somebody who must have been a masochist – torturing yourself. You fast; the longer you fast, the more spiritual you become.

I don't see any connection between food and spirituality, between hunger and spirituality. And if hunger is spiritual, rejoice about Ethiopia! Those people are becoming holier and holier every day. Strange that the missionaries – the pope, Mother Teresa, and their kind – are appealing that "Ethiopia should be saved; people are starving, people are hungry, people are dying in thousands." This is contradictory.

Ethiopia today is the most holy land in the whole world. And if thousands are dying, they will be entering paradise; they are the poorest people in the world. Christians, particularly Catholics, should rejoice all over the world that Ethiopia has become the real holy land – it is no longer Israel. But they are asking for help, for food, for people to come and save these dying, hungry people. For what? to convert them to Catholicism?

These religious leaders need the world to remain poor; otherwise they are out of a job. Mother Teresa receives the Nobel prize because she takes care of orphans. Orphans are absolutely needed; otherwise Mother Teresa loses her Nobel prize. It is necessary to create more orphans so more Mother Teresas can be there. They become respectable, they receive prizes, honorary degrees. They are welcomed all over the world, they are thought to be great saints.

And to create more orphans, birth control methods should not be used. Abortion should be illegal, criminal. If birth control methods are used, and abortion is legal, then from where can you get the orphans? Those orphans give business to the priests, to the pope. And those orphans are your power, because you will convert them to your religion. It is a simple politics of numbers.

I would say: if you don't want poor and hungry people, starving people and dying people, and countries like Ethiopia, then you have to get rid of all your messiahs, your prophets, your incarnations of God, because they are basically, originally responsible for all this misery, suffering, pain.

No, I absolutely deny having any kind of relationship with these people. I am a simple human being, just the way you are. I am not special in any way.

This is something momentous and historical that is happening here, because never before have people gathered around an ordinary, simple man who has no extraordinary powers, who has no miracles to his credit, who does not walk on water…. Really, I find it difficult even to walk on earth. I am bobbily, almost a drunkard! Somehow I manage.

The day humanity is completely finished with these exploiters in the name of religion, this very earth can become a paradise. There is no need to wait for death. What has death to do with paradise? Paradise is the way you live. Paradise has something to do with life, not with death.

If you don't listen to these people, just simple reasoning will show you that this much population on the earth is impossible – we have already crossed the borderline. Starvation is natural; nature is trying to keep the balance, and you don't allow nature to keep the balance because you need more Catholics!

Why are people dying in poor countries? In the first place, why are those countries poor? – because poverty has been praised, poverty has been explained away by beautiful theologies.

Hindus say you are poor because in your past life you committed great sins. It seems to be a very delayed result. The cause was in some past life far away, and the effect comes now. You put your hand in the fire and wait for the next life for it to get burned! Cause and effect are connected; the cause is nothing but unmanifested effect. You cannot put them so far apart, and you cannot put death in between than. But Hindus have been doing that, Jainas have been doing that, Buddhists have been doing that.

You give beautiful explanations to the poor, you give them respectability. Mahatma Gandhi used to call the most poor people in India *harijanas*, the people of God. If to be poor, to be condemned by the whole society…because Hindus don't even touch them, they are called untouchables.

You will be surprised, they don't touch these people because they are so degraded; they don't even allow their shadows to touch them. If an untouchable passes by and his shadow touches your body, you have to take a bath immediately to cleanse yourself – you have been polluted.

And Gandhi calls them the people of God! If poverty, humiliation, oppression, exploitation, make you people of God, then why should one try to become rich? Because in the kingdom of God, even a camel can pass through the eye of a needle, but not a rich man. Strange, camels are holier than a rich man. Only the poor can enter there.

If that is the truth, then let this whole world be poor, suffering, starving, dying. What is the need of serving the poor, giving them food, hospitals, schools? What is the need? You are destroying their license to heaven!

No, I don't belong to this company. I absolutely disconnect myself from all the religions of the world that have existed before, because I say to you, they were not religions. They were cunning strategies of clever people to exploit you, to keep you in your ugly situation, your disgusting state. These religions have not allowed you to make the earth the Garden of Eden. I don't have a God above the roof of Rajneesh Mandir, so I cannot ask him, "Father, forgive these messiahs and prophets and incarnations of you, because they do not know what they are doing!"

I cannot pray in this way for two reasons: one, there is no God above the roof – maybe some electrician working…. Secondly, I cannot say that these prophets and messiahs and incarnations of God do not know what they are doing. They *do* know! They are perfectly aware of what they are doing. They are cheating you, they are keeping you repressed; they are forcing you to remain attached to the past, to the dead traditions, conventions, beliefs which have no evidence. They are preventing you from rebelling against this whole nonsense!

To me, the truly religious person is a rebel, and his religion will be rebellion against this state of affairs. I don't want you to become faithful, I want you to doubt intensely all that you have been taught to believe.

I don't say, "Remain contented as you are because contentment is a great virtue." Contentment *is* a great virtue, but these people are using the word very cunningly. The real contentment comes only when you are utterly happy, rejoicing, when you are so full of joy that you want to dance and you want to sing, and you want to share – because you have so much that if you don't share it will become a heavy burden on you. Then there is contentment.

But these people have been telling you, "Remain contented as you are." They are agents of politicians, they are agents of the status quo. They have not allowed you to think of passing through a great revolution so that we can have a better earth, a better humanity. They are not concerned with humanity at all.

No, I am not a messiah. And it is very difficult too, to become a messiah. First you have to be given birth to by a virgin girl – and who wants to be a bastard? Strange things are expected of you … Mahavira does not perspire – I cannot manage that. Mahavira remains naked. There is nothing wrong in remaining naked, particularly in a hot country like India, but in winter when it becomes so cold, I don't see any point. Yes, when the sun is there and it is hot, it is perfectly good to be nude – even in your office, sitting and working nude should be thought rational. But in winter when things are getting frozen, to remain naked…I cannot do it.

Naturally, I cannot enter in this club of messiahs, prophets and incarnations of God. But I am not sorry for that. I am immensely happy that I was not born from a virgin girl; I am happy that I am the son of my own father, not of somebody who is on the roof. I see utter ugliness in all these people. But they have made it philosophical, and it is all garbage, simply shit! But you can wrap around it beautiful philosophy, theology, and it becomes a commodity of great price.

I am not with them, I am against them. And I am against them *totally,* because I never do anything partially. If an enlightened man – one who is alert, awake, conscious of reality – can do things like Krishna or Mohammed or Jesus did, then I don't want even to be enlightened anymore.

Mohammed married nine wives. It is criminal – the wives are not human beings, they are just cattle. But Mohammed is nothing compared to Krishna, who had sixteen thousand wives. And these were not women who had fallen in love with him; otherwise, I have no objection to it. These women were already married to somebody else. They were hijacked, forcibly taken away from their children, from their husbands, from their families.

Sixteen thousand women? But a perfect incarnation of God cannot just have one wife like an ordinary man! I don't think that he could have even remembered the names of sixteen thousand women. And I don't know whether those sixteen thousand women made love to Krishna. If it happened, he must have been the most spent man in the whole world.

Even one woman is more powerful than man as far as her capacity to have sexual orgasm is concerned. A woman can have multiple sexual orgasms. A man is very poor in comparison, he can have only one – that too is not necessarily an orgasm, because for the orgasm to happen you need a little time, a little foreplay. You need to not be looking at your watch while making love.

But everybody is in such a hurry, without knowing where they are going. You are only concerned whether you are going with the topmost speed or not. Within seconds, the man's love is finished. He turns to the other side and goes to sleep and starts snoring, and leaves the wife weeping and crying, because it has not even started and the man is finished.

Sixteen thousand women? – a sure way to commit suicide. No, I cannot do that. And don't think that this must be simply mythological, it is not. It is a historical fact.

I used to think it must be just mythological, but when I went to Hyderabad, a Mohammedan state in India, the Nizam of Hyderabad – the king of Hyderabad state – had five hundred wives in the twentieth century! I told the Nizam, "It is good I came here, met you and came to know about your five hundred wives. Now I can believe in Krishna and his sixteen thousand."

Sixteen thousand are only thirty-two times more. And if it can happen in the twentieth century, then five thousand years ago you can think anything is possible. Man is still so superstitious; how much more superstitious must he have been five thousand years ago. But this was a certificate…because it is written in the Hindu scriptures, "When God comes on the earth, he will have sixteen thousand wives." The scripture has to be fulfilled; only then will you be recognized by people as the complete incarnation of God.

Because Rama, another incarnation of God, had only one wife, he is thought to be a partial incarnation – just a little bit of God in him. Strange, I think…is it the quantity of women that is used as a criterion of how much godliness is in you? Then I don't want this type of godliness. The woman is not a measurement. The woman is just like you.

Have you ever thought about the word "woman"? It simply means a man with a womb. She has something more than you. If it is to be decided who is more, then the woman is more: she is a man with womb. And a womb is not an ordinary thing; it is something of immense value, because all life comes out of the womb.

Man has always felt inferior to woman. Because he has felt inferior to woman, he has tried in every way to repress woman and make himself superior. It is a simple logic: only the inferior man wants to be superior. The superior is already superior, there is no question of wanting it.

Unless man frees woman completely from all bondage – religious, political, social – he will never get rid of his own inferiority complex.

The freedom of woman is going to be the freedom of man too. It is not only woman's liberation, it is a double-edged liberation. And science has given you all the means to be liberated now. The greatest revolution in human history, after the discovery of fire, was the pill. That makes you equal, unafraid of getting pregnant, unafraid of becoming dependent. And sex loses all the stupid ideas around it; it becomes simple, fun – neither sin nor virtue, but simply fun.

I am the beginning of a totally new religious consciousness. Please don't connect me with the past. It is not even worth remembering. It will a great blessing to humanity if we burn all the past histories, destroy the whole past, and give man a fresh beginning, unburdened. Make him again Adam and Eve, so that he can start from scratch – a new man, a new civilization, a new culture.

Beloved Bhagwan,

What is Your business? What are you doing here?

My God! My business?
I am busy without business.
I have heard…. One Sunday morning a hippie-type young man with long hair entered the biggest church of New York. It was very early; the people of the congregation had not started to come, but the bishop was there. Looking at this man, he asked, "Who are you? And what is your business to be here?" The hippie-type person laughed, and he said, "Can't you recognize me? I am Jesus Christ."

And of course, Jesus Christ must have looked like a hippie – there *is* a similarity. Perhaps he was the first hippie. It is no coincidence that hippies go on turning into Jesus freaks; they have found the way.

The bishop got a little puzzled because he had never imagined in his life that Jesus Christ is going to appear in his church one morning. Now, how is he supposed to behave? He immediately had a long phone call with the pope. He said, "I am puzzled, confused, I don't know what to do. A man here says he is Jesus Christ. And he says that he had promised to come back, and he has come back. What am I supposed to do?"

The pope was puzzled. For a moment there was silence, and then the pope said, "The most I can think of is, look busy. Who knows, he may be the Lord. Just look busy. And by the way, inform the police."

I don't even look busy. I am just doing nothing, and spreading this infectious at-ease to everybody. My whole message is: Sitting silently, doing nothing, and the grass grows by itself. You cannot call it a business. But in the world you have to give some name – then I can call it a great show business.

In fact, from my very childhood I wanted to create a big circus. And it has happened; I am running the biggest circus around the world!

I take life nonseriously.

It is a circus, it is a carnival.

Rejoice!

When Jesus says rejoice, those words do not sound right on his lips. Just look at his face – so British, so long, as if he has always been on the cross, crucified. He is so serious that there exists not a single description or any picture or any statue in which he is smiling or laughing. He was a serious businessman.

I am utterly nonserious. I don't care whether this circus continues or stops; it does not matter. To me, what matters is this moment. This pause between me and you is the bridge.

I am not saying don't work, I am saying transform your work into worship. Transform whatsoever you are doing into art, into music. Let it be a dance, not a burden and a duty. Let it be love, not marriage. Marriage is a serious affair; business people do it, with all the business considerations – financial, educational, social status. These are the considerations for marriage.

Love can even fall in love with a wild flower. Love is not serious, it is sincere; it is truer than anything in life. But all other religions have been doing business, great business, and doing it seriously. All their so-called missionaries are nothing but salesmen. In their theological colleges they are taught for six years nothing but salesmanship.

I am reminded of one person, Erhard, who created a little stir called EST. In the beginning the word "EST" meant Erhard Seminar Training. But later on, he found out from somebody that in the Latin language, *est* means "is." Then the meaning changed, he dropped the old meaning: he started talking about "is-ness."

But before he started EST he was a salesman of dictionaries and encyclopedias. That is one of the most difficult jobs, to sell encyclopedias. Who wants encyclopedias? And even those who have them, they keep them just so that their drawing room looks a little literate; nobody turns the pages of the encyclopedia. And they are costly: thirty volumes, thirty-two volumes, thirty-six volumes – they cost a fortune.

This man selling encyclopedias was successful. He thought, "Even if I go on selling encyclopedias my whole life, how much am I going to get?" He gave it a little serious thinking, and he said, "If I can sell encyclopedias, why not do the real serious business of religion? Why not give people something which doesn't exist – growth. Growth is just an American name for God."

People are fed up with God; enough is enough. They don't want to think about God. But growth? – they immediately become interested. Just two weekends for two hundred and fifty dollars or so, and growth happens to you. In fact he left all other competitors far behind. Esalen started dying because the people were going to Erhard.

And you must know that Erhard is not his real name. The name sounds German. Whenever you want something to sound solid, real, a German name is good; it is just like steel. He is a Jew. He must have thought, "Who is going to get this commodity of growth from a Jew?" From the very beginning they will become suspicious, doubtful. A Jew selling growth? Jews have been selling all kinds of things, but about religion they have been failures. They missed the biggest business when they crucified Jesus. They repent; they don't say it to anybody, but they know they missed the greatest business.

Nobody is going to purchase growth or such phony ideas from a Jew. He changed his name into a German name – solid, it makes sense. Then this man started teaching people other things.

Once the business started moving he started bringing new commodities in: relationship, friendship, and all kinds of "ships."

He had escaped from his own home, leaving his wife and children, old father, old mother – who were all dependent on him. And he is teaching other people how to relate, how to make your love flower, how to be an authentic individual. But now everything has become known about him, and EST has died.

If you become aware of all the religions and what they have done to man, there will be no need to kill them. Just a kick, a good kick, and the pope is gone. They are already dead, they just need a kick; they will fall down of their own accord.

You can call *that* my business.

Beloved Bhagwan,

What do You say about the third world war? Is it going to happen or not? What should we do to prevent it?

Don't do anything to prevent it, because this humanity that you see around the earth is not worth anything. A good third world war will at least clean this planet of human garbage: cathedrals, temples, mosques, White Houses where only lies are manufactured. Perhaps that's why it is called the White House – because we know the phrase "white lie." Lies are always white; they have to be painted white.

All these politicians, with no awareness, no love, and with all the nuclear weapons in their hands…. The world right now contains so many nuclear and atomic weapons that this poor humanity can be killed seven hundred times – although that is not needed, once is more than enough. And they go on piling them up.

But I am not a pessimist. I am saying it to you just to emphasize the fact that it is not a question of the third world war, it is a question of a change in human consciousness. You cannot prevent the third world war with the same mind as human beings have today

– and there is no need either. But human consciousness can be changed.

You can become the beginning of a new mankind. And the very newness of your consciousness will be contagious. If sannyasins go on growing around the world as they are growing, there is every possibility there will be no third world war. My sannyasins are not politicians. My sannyasins have no political aspirations; only idiots have those kind of aspirations – chimpanzees and others.

My sannyasins are learning to live right now, intensely, totally, burning the torch of life from both ends together. If you can make the people around the world dance and sing and celebrate…. You may not see the connection between the third world war and what I am saying, but there is a great connection.

The third world war is possible only if humanity feels suicidal, if people lose all interest in life and become so frustrated that they don't want to live – for what? For Ronald Reagan to become the president? For Ethiopia, so that thousands will die every day? For India, which goes on producing children? The Indian woman is continuously pregnant. Half of India is starving; soon it will be a second Ethiopia, far bigger. If you cannot manage Ethiopia, it is impossible to manage India. And the same is going to happen to other third world countries.

What is there to save? – your football matches? the Olympics? What is there in people's lives? They are living empty, hollow lives. In fact, the third world war is coming closer and closer because people are feeling more and more hollow, without any meaning. They will certainly be happy that the whole world is finished. But if we can create a little joy in people's lives, a little silence, so that what they think of as hollowness is no longer hollowness; it is serenity, it is silence, it is emptiness, but intensely full, overflowing with joy….

I don't have any dogma, any creed, any cult to spread. I want you to be carriers of joy – in small things. Life does not consist of big things.

Alexander the Great is just a fool. You have another fool in America – Muhammed Ali the Greatest. There is nothing big in life, because nothing is small either. There is no question of thinking in terms of great, not great. There is no need to think in terms of mundane, spiritual; materialistic, spiritualistic. All these divisions are false. Life is one single whole. It is material, and at the same time it is spiritual. It is mundane, and at the same time the holiest thing possible.

If you can become the carriers of my at-ease – that is just the word I have invented against dis-ease – if you can do this…. And it is not much, just rejoice in small things: a cup of tea…sipping it, feel blessed, because who knows? tomorrow morning you may not be there, the third world war may have happened. When you go to sleep, say goodbye to the stars and to the universe, because who knows at what time Ronald Reagan may go berserk. When you wake up in the morning, greet it. Greet the sun, greet it the way the birds are greeting it with their songs, greet it the way flowers are greeting it by releasing their fragrance.

Dance! Don't be bothered that you will be thought crazy. Once you are my sannyasins you *are* crazy. And craziness gives such great freedom that the so-called sane people cannot even understand. You can dance for no reason at all. You can laugh although no joke has been told to you. You can do anything, because you are a recognized crazy man.

Why have I given you this red uniform? So it will be recognized: "This man is crazy. He talks to himself, he laughs when there is nothing to laugh at. Watching the sunset, we have seen tears of joy flowing from his eyes."

I gave you the mala with my picture to be certain; I don't want to take any chances. I want you to be recognized in the world as the craziest people around. And slowly you will be surprised: the people who call you crazy will become curious. They also want to laugh, but their mouths are tightly closed by the society. They also want to dance, but their culture does not allow it, or allows it only in certain situations, certain occasions.

In my childhood I was very much interested in going to the crematorium. Anybody dying in the city…I was always going. Whether I knew the man or not was not the point. My father asked me, "Are you crazy? That man was a beggar. Why did you go with him and waste your time?"

I said, "I have become immensely rich going with the people carrying a dead body to the crematorium. I have seen many things which I would not have seen. I have seen that the body they are carrying, and the people who are carrying it, both are dead. It was a shock in the beginning.

"And I have seen these people…. The body is on the funeral pyre, and they are sitting around it far away – because the fire creates so much heat, particularly in India – talking about film actresses. Somebody is looking at *Playboy* others are gossiping about people who are not present there, telling all kinds of lies, but nobody is concerned with the person who has died. In fact, whatever they are doing is an effort to create a barrier between them and the burning body. Nobody is thinking that one day their body will be on the funeral pyre and people will be reading *Playboy*. They don't want to see it; it is escapism."

One of my teachers died. He was a funny man, very fat, and he used to have a very ancient type of turban – very big, maybe thirty-six feet long or more. Thirty-six feet is normal for the old, ancient turban. His face was also such that you could not remain looking at him without smiling. And he was my Sanskrit teacher.

He was a simple man – in fact a simpleton. We had been playing all kinds of tricks on him, and he was never able to find out who had done it; he never punished anybody. We had been really hard on him. He would fall from the chair, because we had managed to cut the legs of the chair before he came. He would fall from the chair, his turban would fall all over the class, and there would be great laughter. But he would start putting his turban back on and writing on the board again, not getting disturbed. He was really a nice fellow.

He died. We used to call him Bhole Baba. That was not his name. *Baba* is simply used for grandfather, a respectful word. *Bhole* means a simpleton, so innocent that anybody can deceive him. I have completely forgotten his name, because we never used his name; we always used Bhole Baba. I have been trying to figure out what was his real name, but I cannot find it anywhere in my mind.

When I went to his house with my father, his wife came running from inside the house, fell on the chest of that poor fellow, and said, "Oh, my Bhole Baba!" I could not contain my laughter. My father tried telling me, "Keep quiet!"

I said, "The more I try to keep quiet, the more it is becoming difficult. I cannot contain it; let me laugh!" But everybody was shocked: somebody is dead, and you are laughing so loudly. I said, "Please, don't be shocked. If you knew the whole thing as I do, you would all be laughing."

And I told the whole thing, that he was always getting irritated by being called Bhole Baba. And we used to write on the blackboard every day, "Welcome, Bhole Baba." And the first thing he would do was, he would erase it. And now the poor man was dead and his own wife…

When I told them this, everybody started laughing. And the wife also became silent and said, "It is really strange for me to call him Bhole Baba, because I used to tell that boy not to call him Bhole Baba, that it is not his name."

And who was the boy? Mostly I was the boy who always going past his house, would knock on the door and say, "Is Bhole Baba inside?" And the wife knew me. With the door closed she would say, "No, he is not inside" – he was always inside – "but remember, don't call him Bhole Baba! If you stop calling him Bhole Baba, I can open the door and you can

find him inside." Perhaps continually hammering, "Bhole Baba, Bhole Baba," then at the moment of death….

Of course, a Hindu wife is not supposed to say her husband's name. She cannot, that is thought to be disrespectful – just the male chauvinistic mind. The man can call her by her name, but the woman cannot call her husband by his name. So perhaps…there was no time to figure out what to say; Bhole Baba came in handy.

But even the wife started laughing, thinking that this was really hilarious. "My whole life I have been telling you and other boys who are your friends… who you have been telling that whenever they pass the door, they should knock and enquire, 'Is Bhole Baba inside?'"

The death became a laughter. But back home, my father said, "I am not going to take you to another death, another cremation – not with me, at least. What you have done is not right."

I said, "Everybody laughed – even the wife who was crying, started laughing. You should all be grateful to me that I made even death nonserious, fun, a joke."

If my people go on being nonserious, laughing, dancing, singing, not finding any reason for it – *life* is enough reason for it – we can make the whole world aflame with laughter. Nuclear weapons can be destroyed by a laughing, smiling, dancing humanity. But as humanity is now, there is no hope.

You are the only hope! So don't keep your joy to yourself, spread it, make it available to anybody. Don't even think whether he is introduced to you or not. Don't be British, be human! These are the only two kinds in the world.

The third world war can be completely stopped – should be stopped. But it is not going to be stopped by the pacifists and their processions and their screaming and shouting for peace. They are not the people to stop it. They are really showing by shouting and screaming that they are not peaceful men. They may be pacifists, but they are ready to fight for it!

I am not a pacifist, I am at peace.

I have never participated in any protest of any kind. I have never been a part of any organization of any kind, and I would like you not to be pacifists, but peaceful, radiating your silence around you. It is invisible but it stirs hearts. Radiate your love – not even to your wife, which is the most difficult thing, so I am leaving it for later stages. Radiate your love – not even to your neighbors, that is too difficult. Radiate to strangers.

Start radiating your being to a tree. Hug it. Have you ever hugged a tree? If you have not hugged a tree you have missed something of grandeur. If in a silent, deep, peaceful moment you hug a tree, you will find it is not a one-sided hug; the tree is responding. And the response is so tangible, that the tree is happy. Dance, and the tree will also rejoice with you; it may become greener, may bring more flowers.

Have you not watched this happening to this desert, this Big Muddy Ranch? When I came here it was really a sad place: no flowers anywhere, no trees except the juniper. The juniper seems to be German. And those junipers were also very few, not thick, somehow surviving like human beings, at the minimum. Now, after just four years of our being here – and we have not done anything to those junipers – they are greener, thicker, bigger. You can feel their joy.

We have changed the desert into an oasis. And soon the whole Muddy Ranch will be green. Your laughter is nourishment even to the trees. There were no birds when I came here, not a single bird. Now birds have started coming. Life is such an organic whole.

In my garden there must be nearabout eighty peacocks. Near my house we have made a small river out of rainwater. There are beautiful swans.... Your joy, your love, your peace does something without your knowing to everything that is around you.

So I cannot say, "Go and become pacifists. Take the flags and the banners and go to Washington or to Moscow and scream against nuclear weapons." Nobody is going to hear you. Those politicians are deaf; those politicians are just dodos. That is not going to help. But doing something totally different, which has nothing to do with the third world war.... That's why I said, "Please don't try to prevent it," because that would be directly making an effort to prevent the third world war. You cannot do it; things have gone too far.

The third world war is the conclusion of all the religions and the politicians and all the cultures of the past. It is a logical conclusion. It is only a question of time – and the time, too, is not so much. Things are moving. The way they are moving, before this century ends, the world will be finished.

But you *can* help the world to continue. I am not concerned with the war directly, I am concerned with something else, some other energy as an antidote. Be meditative, be loving, be silent, be sharing – and spread your craziness.

Soon the same people will start doubting their sanity; you just have to go on spreading your craziness. It takes a little time to hammer the fact, but the so-called sane people will not be incapable of seeing. What is the point of being sane if you cannot love, you cannot dance, you cannot sing, you cannot even whistle? What is the point of being sane? They will say, "Let this sanity go to hell, or to Oregon, but we are no longer going to be sane. We are going to be human, alive, thriving, so full of life that it starts touching others and everyone."

And you know it by your experience. What I am saying is not giving you a belief, it is your experience too. Just don't be miserly and hoard it.

Remember the law of existence: the more you give, the more you get.

Persecution
Cannot Do
Any Harm to You

DISCOURSE 23, July 21, 1985

Beloved Bhagwan,

The way You walk, it seems as if You are drunk. What is the truth?

Man, I *am* drunk! But not drunk with ordinary alcohol, marijuana, hashish, opium, LSD. I grow my own marijuana within me. No government can interfere with it. My source of drunkenness is my silence, my love, my centeredness, my rootedness in myself. Yes, I walk like a drunkard because I *am* a drunkard. You have observed truly.

Once you know the inner serenity, a gap between you and your body arises, a gap between you and your mind arises. That creates my bobbily walking. Nothing can be done about it. It is not a medical question, it is natural to anyone who is enlightened.

Mostly enlightened people die immediately after enlightenment, for the simply reason that they cannot manage any connection with their body and mind. It is very rare that somebody goes on living after enlightenment. But one has to compromise.

That bobbiling is the compromise.

Beloved Bhagwan,

Most people, rightly or wrongly, equate democracy with the freedom to choose their politicians, yet You seem to envisage a country which is both democratic and pollution-free, because you see politicians as pollution. How is this possible?

Just the very existence of nations, countries dividing humanity into stupid parts, is the whole game of the politician. And this I call pollution. It is poison to humanity. That's why you don't see really authentically alive people in the world.

You are asking, "People generally understand democracy to mean the freedom to choose politicians." Do you see the idiotic understanding of the people? It is choosing between poisons. The bottles contain the same poison – on one is written "Democratic," on another is written "Republican."

Politicians have been befooling you. They have managed the whole strategy in such a way that you never become aware what is happening. You choose one kind of poison for five years; for those five years you have to suffer that poison. After five years you are fed up with this kind of poison. You change to another bottle – Republican, Liberal, Democratic, Communist, Socialist. They are all available in all shapes and sizes, whatsoever suits you. But you will fall in the same ditch. Maybe there are minor differences between poisons, but poison is poison.

I do not see democracy as the freedom to choose between the politicians. To me, democracy means there are no longer any politicians around. You individually choose somebody you feel is the right person; there are no political parties. In a real democracy, political parties cannot exist; there is no reason why they should exist. People are intelligent enough to choose on their own. The politician need not go and convince the people, "I am the right person and the other is wrong." And the other is also doing the same, and the poor people in their utter confusion somehow choose somebody.

I have never voted in my life, for the simple reason that all those politicians and political parties are basically the same. They want to exploit you, oppress you. And it is a good strategy that after five years when you get fed up with one party, you can choose another.

People's memory is not very strong. So for five years it is the Republican party sucking you, doing everything that is wrong, deceiving you and the whole world. After five years, it is the Democratic party doing the same thing behind a different label. And when for five years the Democratic party is ruling, you get fed up with them, and you forget completely that those Republicans had done the same before. Five years is enough time for people to forget. And you go on moving between two parties.

There may be more parties in other countries, but basically two parties are in a deep conspiracy against the people: "Five years we exploit them, then we will give you five years to exploit them. And again we will come back."

In a real democracy what is the need of political parties? The real need is to make people more alert, more intelligent, so they can choose individually, not impressed by propaganda.

And what small things impress you! Why was Nixon defeated by Kennedy? You will be surprised and shocked, because it will prove to you how idiotic you are: It was the television that made the whole dif-

Just be a little courageous. And to suffer for freedom is not suffering, it is a joy. To suffer for individuality is not painful; it is a pleasure, because you are moving towards a blissful state. Just a little courageousness – I don't ask you for great courage. Just a little courage, and the world can be free of politics and pollution.

ference. On television, the supporters, the advisors of Nixon, had insisted that he wear dark clothes "so your figure comes out clearly, strongly, because millions of people will never see you in person; they will only see you on the television."

Nixon did not listen to them. He came in a gray suit, and that decided his defeat. Kennedy came in a dark, black suit. When they were together you saw that Nixon looked gray, weak, while Kennedy looked clear, strong.

Television has changed almost the whole political phenomenon. Before television, you were coming in contact with the real person. Now when you come in contact with a person, experts have decided his hairstyle, make-up, the color of his clothes. They have taught him how to walk, how to stand, how to look exactly into the eyes of the people; what to say, how to say it, when to make a gesture with his hand; when to almost shout, and when to almost whisper. Now it is in the hands of the experts to program him.

Nixon was not ready for it, and I think any man who has any sense of integrity will not agree to all this nonsense. He is not an actor. But Kennedy followed the advice of the advisors. He came on the television very strong, very clear, standing the way a strong person stands, speaking the way a strong person speaks. He was chosen. It has nothing to do with politics – just two poison bottles, but one has a beautiful container, more modern. The other is an old container, out-of-date.

Nixon looked lousy on the television. That decided his fate, and also made him learn that television has changed the whole situation. The next time he came like an actor, played his role well, and was chosen. And he proved to you that he was a poison.

It is very strange, nobody assassinated Nixon. Kennedy was assassinated. Then his brother, another Kennedy, was assassinated because he was also fighting to become the president of the country. And now the third brother, the last brother, is being threatened: if he tries to become the president, he will be gone the same way the two others have gone. You call this country democratic?

Yes, in the constitution it may be written that everybody has the right to run for any office, but the third Kennedy is being threatened, and he knows that the people who are threatening him mean business. His mother is very old – ninety years old; he had to listen to her. She has suffered her whole life. She has lost two of her sons and she does not want to lose the last one; otherwise the whole family tree will be destroyed. She has taken a promise from the third Kennedy that while she is living he will not run for president.

Is this politics or mafia? Is this democracy? It is not. The only difference between a communist country like Russia, and America, is superficial. In Russia, one party rules forever. In America, they give you a chance to choose which political party you want to be exploited by. But what is the difference? – you are going to be exploited. The exploiters go on changing, but the exploitation remains the same. What does it matter? One party exploits you forever, or two parties make a pact and in rotation they exploit you? But your exploitation is the same.

My concept of democracy is people deciding on their own, without any political propaganda from anybody. Choose the candidates you like. In fact, the candidate approaching the people and asking, "Please choose me," is ugly, disgusting. If he is of any worth, people should reach him and ask him, "Please take this responsibility for us. We want you to be in the parliament."

Then a different quality of people will be coming into the assemblies and the parliament, people who will not have any political leadership of the party, its program. They will be free individuals acting out of their intelligence. They can choose the president, the prime minister – anybody. And they will be deciding on every issue according to themselves. People have given them immense respect by sending them to the government; they cannot be exploiters.

A real democracy will choose the wise people. They are all around. But remember, a man of wisdom is not going to beg you for a vote. He is not going to kiss your children and shake hands with you. He is not going to act on the television screen so that he appears to be the way you would like your president to be.

The wise man is not interested – in fact, he will not be inclined to be dragged into this mess. You will have to persuade him. The whole scene changes – not the politician persuading you, but you persuading someone to represent you. More fresh blood will be coming into the government.

And secondly, democracy can exist only if the countries are dissolved. With so many countries preparing to fight with each other continuously, of course you choose the most cunning politician you can, because he will be safer. You want him to be smarter, more cunning than the Soviet premier. The same is the situation in every country.

The wise people remain out of politics. It is so dirty, stinkingly dirty. And it will remain dirty till nations dissolve and we have one world where there is no question of any war, no question of preparing for war.

You can divide history in two parts: one, when people are really fighting, killing, burning people – innocent people who have not done anything wrong to you. In fact, you don't know whom you are killing. Or the second part of history, when you are preparing for the next war. Of course, a little time is needed between two wars, and if the wars are going to be world wars, then at least ten or fifteen years' gap is needed.

Now we are on the verge of a third world war. Albert Einstein was asked once, "Can you say something about the third world war?" He said, "No, but I can say something about the fourth world war."

The questioner was simply surprised. He said, "If you cannot say anything about the third, what can you say about the fourth?"

He said, "The fourth is not going to happen."

The third world war is going to finish all living beings: men, birds, animals, trees – anything that is alive it is going to be destroyed completely. And your politicians are preparing for it.

The world needs to be free from politicians, only then can it be free from pollution.

What is the need for nations? Why can't we have the right to move freely around the earth? This is our earth! Now I have been here for four years, and I am still a tourist. It seems I am going to die as a tourist. The government agencies who are responsible for deciding are in a difficulty. If they say no to me, I am going to fight the courts up to the Supreme Court. That will give me enough time – almost twenty years. So they are afraid to say no. Yes, of course, they cannot say. So they are in a dilemma, just waiting for some miracle to happen. But I am not a miracle man!

But who are these men to decide? They are also foreigners, America is not their country. Perhaps they came four generations ago and I came a little later, just four years ago. But they are invaders – I am not an invader. I have come to the country as a friend.

Man should have a birthright of free movement around the earth, and one day a birthright to move around the stars. We have to dissolve all the boundaries and all the nonsense that exists because of these boundaries. Anybody who divides man, for any excuse, is unforgivable. Black and white…. And what about me? – neither black nor white.

In India, we have a beautiful joke…. When God created man – of course he was an amateur, he had never created before – so when he put the man made of mud into the oven, he pulled Him out a little too soon. These are the white men, uncooked. And it is natural – because he saw that this is an uncooked man, next time he waited a little longer, went to the other extreme, and when he pulled the man out, he found a Negro. He said, "This is going to be a difficult job." So he decided on a time exactly in the middle. That's why there are people like me neither uncooked nor cooked too much.

But what difference does color make? What difference does sex make? Why should woman be treated differently than man?

In China, for centuries it was thought that the woman has no soul. Great thinkers! Great discoverers! They have not bothered about themselves, whether they have any soul or not, but they decided unanimously that the woman has none. She is a thing to be possessed. Therefore, for centuries in China if a husband killed the wife it was not murder, it was not something against the law. You could not drag the man to the court as a murderer, because the idea was that the woman was a thing. If you destroy your chair it is your business, if you want to put your house on fire, it is your house. The wife belongs to you, you can do anything to the wife.

And they did everything to the woman. From her very childhood the Chinese girl was given iron shoes, so that her feet remained very small. That was their idea of beauty. In fact, they crippled the woman. Of course, her body want on growing, but her feet remained small. They thought they looked very dainty – they were simply out of proportion. The feet should grow in proportion to the body, because they have to take the whole load of the body. It was difficult for the Chinese woman to dance or to walk properly.

All kinds of ugly things around the world…just because one is man, another is woman. And what is the difference between a Christian and a Jew and a Hindu and a Mohammedan? Just their conditionings are different; otherwise, they are exactly the same people. But they have been labeled by their conditioning as Jews, as Christians, as Mohammedans. You are not a thing. You should refuse to be labeled.

Man has to rebel against all these stupidities, because stupidities have divided the world. And divided, naturally everybody is afraid of everybody else. Your neighbor starts doing gymnastics; you get paranoid. Why is this man trying to become stronger? – you join a gymnastics course immediately. Seeing you – that you are going for a gymnastics program, you have joined the gym – the neighbor becomes afraid. He starts making better efforts, because it is going to be a tough fight.

And this is happening around the world. In Pakistan they have American soldiers. Now, it is absolutely natural for India to invite Soviet soldiers. The American politicians say, "Expel Soviet soldiers from India, remove them; then we will remove the American soldiers from Pakistan." But who is going to remove them first? Both say, "You remove them first, because we don't want to take the risk." Nobody is removing soldiers, nobody wants to remove them.

If you look clearly, the way I see…. Because I am nobody; I don't belong to any nation, I don't belong to any religion, I don't belong to any political party. I am simply an individual, the way existence created me. I have kept myself absolutely uninfluenced by any idiotic ideology – religious, political, social, financial. And the miracle is that because I am not burdened with all these glasses on my eyes, and curtains before me, I can see clearly.

The world can be a paradise any moment it decides! It will just have to drop a little crap: Christian, Hindu, Mohammedan, American, Russian. Politicians will not help you to do it, they will hinder you from doing it. Priests will not help you to do it, they will hinder you from doing it. All their greatness – the president of America, the premier of the Soviet Union, the infallible pope in the Vatican…what will happen to these people?

If you drop all your conditionings, and if you remove all the lines from the map, you burn all your identity cards, your passports, your visas, and you start moving around the world absolutely freely – it is *our* world – what will happen to these idiots who are sitting on your head? They will create every difficulty.

But the time has come to face the fact; otherwise,

you are on the very verge of a total global war which will destroy everybody. Before that happens, get free of all poisons – nations, politicians, priests, religions – and the world will be pollution-free.

It is not the ordinary pollution that exists in L.A.; that is nothing. That too exists because of vested interests. A car can be created which does not pollute the air, but what will happen to all the manufacturers of hundreds of cars around the world? Their factories will go bankrupt. Right now they are billionaires; they will be beggars immediately.

You may not know that many inventions which are going to help humanity are prevented; their copyright is purchased by somebody whose vested interest will be interfered with. And the poor scientist, if he gets enough money, how can he refuse? There are hundreds of inventions which have been prevented. Money has been paid, and humanity goes on suffering.

Man has to declare his freedom. It is not a question of a nation being free, it is a question of every individual on the earth being free from all the jargon that the past has left within you.

The cars pollute the air but the politicians and the priests pollute your very soul.

The air can be cleaned, the cars can be changed. If man is capable of reaching to the moon…I don't see why the scientists who can reach to the moon cannot make a fountain pen which does not leak! It seems simply absurd.

Man has come to a maturity, and now decisions have to be made by free individuals – not Americans, not Russians, not Indians. We can make this earth pollution-free, outwardly and inwardly.

That's my message to my sannyasins: First, be free, and then let others taste your freedom and the joy it brings with it. It is not a difficult job at all. People are waiting for some savior to come and deliver them from all this misery. The savior is not going to come, but half of their waiting is right: they are waiting to be transformed. If they go on waiting for the savior they are waiting for Godot, who has never come, who will never come. They have to drop this idea that tomorrow somebody is going to come and deliver them from their suffering, misery. No, it is not going to happen.

You have to become the savior of yourself.

I teach selfishness, because to me to be selfish is not wrong, it is natural. Everybody should be selfish, self-centered, not waiting for anybody's help. Declare your freedom individually.

And that's my movement. You are here, not as a society, not as a community, you are here as an individual. There is nothing higher than an individual and his freedom.

Just be a little courageous. And to suffer for freedom is not suffering, it is a joy. To suffer for individuality is not painful; it is a pleasure, because you are moving towards a blissful state. Just a little courageousness – I don't ask you for great courage. Just a little courage, and the world can be free of politics and pollution. The world can be free of fights, murder, massacre, burning people alive….

If you look at history, it is so ugly. In my university, one day I went into the history department. I was looking around and getting introduced to all the subjects, so I could choose. And that was my last day too, because immediately I was fighting with my professor. I told him, "If this is history that you are teaching, then don't poison people's minds. It is better they forget all about the past. Don't go on pouring rubbish into their heads, because then there will be no space for the present and no space for the future." There is no need of history. All history is bunk!

It can happen in a single moment of understanding. That is the only miracle I know. All other miracles are inventions or gullible people, of stupid followers, of cunning scholars. But one miracle is part of nature.

If you see something clearly, then don't wait for the next moment. Do it right now, drop all nonsense. And you will see the birth of a new man in you.

I heard You say that Moses was responsible for the persecution of the Jews, because he created the concept of the chosen people. What's the difference between the Jews and us? I know the difference between Moses and You, but what about the phenomenon of a rising anger and hate in the outside society?

Are we, or You, responsible for our persecution?

Baby, you don't know the difference between me and Moses. If you had that much intelligence there would have been no question at all. What do you know about Moses? And what do you know about me? What difference do you know?

Moses was a politician, not a prophet. He was taking his people from slavery to find a new land where they could live without slavery. But to convince slaves that you can be free is difficult; hence, he invented all kinds of incentives: "It is God's wish," and, "I have spoken with God face to face, and he has said to me that the Jews are the chosen people, my people."

Strange, God's people were slaves for centuries, making pyramids in Egypt. What was this God doing all the time? His chosen people were being murdered mercilessly, continuously beaten. It is now a well established fact that the pyramids are made of such big stones that unless there were better cranes than we have, there was no possibility of lifting them. How did they manage to move those big stones, going higher and higher into the sky?

They were not managed by cranes, they were managed by "God's chosen people," followed by the Egyptians with their whips, on their horses, continuously whipping the people who were carrying the stone. And when somebody has to choose between death and life, he is ready to do anything. What was God doing all this time before Moses? It seems that the post reaches God after thousands of years – a very inefficient postal service. It must be managed by Indians – so lousy, so lazy....

I lived in Jabalpur for many years. Katni is a small place eighty miles away from Jabalpur. One letter came from Katni to Jabalpur in thirty-six years! Even if the envelope had walked, it would have come long before. By the time it reached Jabalpur, the man to whom the letter was written was dead. So it was returned to the sender, but by that time the sender was dead! But the postal service between God's chosen people and God seems to be even more lousy.

There is nothing in this whole idea of the chosen people of God. Everybody is chosen; otherwise you would not be here. Everybody – not only man, but animals and birds and trees – is chosen by existence; otherwise, there is no reason why they should be there. They are, because existence wants them, *needs* them.

Moses bluffed those poor slaves. And it is very easy. When you say to a poor man, "You will be rewarded immensely after death, it is just a question of a few years. Be patient and these rich people who are enjoying here only for a few days will suffer in hell for eternity," he does not argue, it is so consoling.

When Moses said to the Jews, "You are the chosen people of God," they accepted it without any argument. I have not heard anybody arguing with Moses: "On what grounds are you saying we are the chosen people of God? Then why did we suffer for thousands of years? Why were our women raped by the Egyptians? Why were our people killed by the Egyptians? And why has God given only one work to His chosen people?" – to carry huge stones, almost an inhuman job. If this is what it means to be chosen by God, they should have refused: "We don't want to be chosen. Now choose somebody else!"

But poor people – slaves, hungry, starving – don't argue; they want consolation. They were immensely happy. They did not ask, "What evidence do you have that you encountered God? Was there any eyewitness? What proof have you got that these ten commandments that you are bringing from God are written by God and not by you? because they are in Hebrew. Is Hebrew also the chosen language of God, amongst three hundred languages in the world?"

Nobody argued. In such a position nobody argues; people simply swallow it with relish. They followed Moses out of Egypt – but soon they became worried, because their leader seemed to be as lost as they were, in the vast desert of the Middle East. But leaders have to go on pretending that they know what they are doing: "You simply believe us, you follow us."

It took Moses forty years to reach a place, Israel – which is not much of a place. If he had encountered God himself, if he had had that clarity of consciousness, he should have moved just in the opposite direction, towards Kashmir – which can be called a paradise on earth. But Israel and the whole surrounding area is just desert. If he had had any insight and the extraordinary powers of a prophet, he would have chosen the countries which have oil – Israel has no oil. Then perhaps Jews would have been the richest people in the world, just as Saudi Arabians are today. And Saudi Arabia he had bypassed.

What do you know about Moses? He was lying, purely lying to his people, pretending that he knew where the holy land was. And why did he stop at Israel? Had he found the holy land? No, but he was getting old, his people were dying of starvation, dehydration – no water, no food. Only one-third of the people survived; two-thirds had already died in this search for the holy land.

And the one-third that survived were almost of a different generation. There was a great gap between these people and Moses. These were small children when the journey started, the search for the holy land. They had no idea of the slavery of Egypt, they had no idea what had been happening to their race for centuries, they had no idea whether this Moses had really encountered God or was just a pretender.

The new generation and the generation gap begins with Moses and the Jews. You will be surprised to know that Moses felt so frustrated that he himself escaped from Jerusalem. Of course, he found an excuse. He said, "One of our tribes is lost somewhere in the desert, and I have to find them."

It was true. A few of the Jews, seeing the situation, had turned in the other direction – that is natural logic: "If this direction goes on and on into desert, perhaps going in the opposite direction we may find good land." And these are the people who live in Kashmir now. They are Jewish, forcibly converted by Mohammedans to follow Mohammedanism. Moses finally reached Kashmir. He was very ancient at that time; he could not live much longer, and he died in Kashmir in India.

A great coincidence: Moses died in India, Jesus died in India, Buddha died in India, Mahavira died in India, Krishna died in India. The founders of almost all the great religions of the world were either born in India or at least managed to die in India. Just to disconnect myself from all that rotten lot, I left India. It was not in my hands not to be born there, but it is in my hands to be assassinated in Oregon.

What do you know about Moses? And what do you know about me? You know nothing, so please be clear about it. Yes, your question is relevant. Moses is responsible for the persecution of Jews down the centuries, because he declared them to be, and convinced them that they are, the chosen people of God, that they are born higher than anybody else; all human beings are lower than them, they are a superior race. Or course, the implication is clear: they are here to rule, not to be ruled. They are here to dominate the whole world, and not to be dominated.

This idea made them fanatics, and naturally, anybody claiming superiority over everybody else creates persecution. They have been persecuted down the ages; they are still being persecuted. Moses is responsible. He implanted that idea, and these poor people have carried that idea for three thousand years. It is very difficult for them to drop it. The

Jewish nose keeps itself higher than that of anybody else.

You are asking me: if my people are going to be persecuted, who is going to be responsible – I or they? My whole effort is that whatsoever I am doing I am responsible for. If I am persecuted and assassinated, I am responsible for it. But if you are persecuted and assassinated, remember, it is your responsibility, not mine. Why in the first place did you join me? I will not allow you to shirk away from your responsibility. I will not take your responsibility on myself.

I am responsible for whatsoever I am doing, and whatsoever happens to me. You are responsible individually – because I don't believe in any collectivity. Every individual has to accept his responsibility for whatsoever he is doing, whatsoever happens to him.

I had started alone. Then people started coming by and by, and my caravan started becoming bigger and bigger, and now it is all around the earth. But those people I respect. They have joined me on their own decision; I have not persuaded anybody.

I have not given you any promises of a holy land. I have not given you any incentives after death. I have not given you any guarantee that if you are with me, soon you will be with God. I don't give you promissory notes, and I don't take any responsibility on your behalf, because I respect you. If I take the responsibility on myself, then you are slaves; then I am the leader and you are the led.

No, I am not the leader, and you are not the led. We are fellow travelers. You are not behind me but by my side – just together with me. I am not higher than you, I am just one amongst you. I don't claim any superiority, extraordinary power, and all kinds of nonsense which Jesus, Moses, Mohammed, Krishna, Buddha, Mahavira, all are to be condemned for. Do you see the point? To make you responsible for your life is to give you freedom.

A few of the sannyasins – for trivia, absurd reasons – have left the caravan. I am not at all angry with them. They had joined; it was their responsibility. They have left; it is their responsibility. If they want to come back, it will be their responsibility.

Every single sannyasin is responsible, remember. You cannot dump your responsibility on me. I am simply taking my own doings, sayings, happenings on myself. If you feel that because of me you are persecuted, drop sannyas. Why should you be persecuted for me? Who am I?

But if your sannyas is your love affair with me, then take the responsibility: be persecuted. And persecution cannot do any harm to you, for the simple reason that we are not fanatics, we are not dogmatic. My people are open, vulnerable, available.

Some Jesus freaks come on the county road to save my people. They take real trouble coming down to save my people, and nobody listens to them. Or, if sometimes somebody stands there, he simply laughs and walks away. This is a new experience for those people. Either people start arguing with them or agreeing with them. They know those two kinds: arguing, agreeing.

This is a different kind of species: they listen, they laugh and go on their way. The reason is obvious: you cannot save somebody who is already saved. Saving somebody twice is not possible – that's why they simply laugh at the whole absurdity of the idea. But remember, I have not saved you. I am very clear about it: if you are saved, you are your own savior, and persecution cannot destroy you.

Persecution is going to happen; it is already happening. But you are intelligent people; you can fight the persecution through legal means in the courts, in the Supreme Court. I have given you no dogma, nobody can criticize you – and I have made you capable of criticizing everybody else in the world. So what can persecution do to you? Anybody who comes to persecute you is going to become a sannyasin! Let them come.

They are very much afraid even to visit the commune. They are continuously talking about the commune, they are continuously talking about me – knowing nothing, just gathering things from gossips. But their interest is clear. Why don't they come here? They don't have guts – particularly the Americans don't have any guts. It happens when you are rich enough and you have all the comforts of life: you start losing guts because you become afraid – anything can take you away from your comforts and your television.

And there are rumors about me that I am hypnotizing people. When I used to go driving on the highways, sometimes I was stopped by a police car, but the police officer would not look directly into my eyes – afraid of getting hypnotized!

Nobody is hypnotizing anybody here. In fact, we have a program of dehypnosis, which exists nowhere else in the world. We are teaching our people how to dehypnotize themselves – because the society has hypnotized you already. What is your Christianity? What is your being American? What is the reason for your being a Hindu?

Society starts hypnotizing you when you are a child and you don't know what is happening. By the time you are adult, you are already full of bullshit. Now you go on carrying that bullshit as treasure. You are afraid if you lose this bullshit, you will find emptiness within – something is better than nothing.

And you have become accustomed to the smell of the bullshit; perhaps not only accustomed, but enchanted.

I have heard about a fisherman's wife who used to come from her village to the nearby, bigger town, to sell fish. One day after selling the fish, when she was returning back home, she met one woman, a childhood friend. The woman said, "We have just moved to this town and it will be a great joy if you spend the night with us, and in the morning you can go." The house was beautiful, with a big garden around it, beautiful flowers and their fragrance. The woman's friend did everything to please the guest. She put roses around her bed – the whole room was full of rose fragrance. But the woman was tossing and turning; she could not sleep.

Finally, the host asked the guest, "What is the matter? Is there some problem? Is something uncomfortable? As far as I see, I have made everything as comfortable as possible. But tell me, because I don't want you to remain awake the whole night."

The woman was a little ashamed in answering the host. She said, "Please forgive me. Just give me back the clothes and the bucket in which I had brought the fish; unless I smell fishes I cannot sleep. And please remove these roses, they are such a disturbance."

The roses were removed, her bucket and clothes were given back to her. She kept the bucket by her side, made the clothes damp with water, put those clothes on her face – and then she was fast asleep, snoring. Fish have a disgusting smell, but not to the fisherman. He knows nothing better than the smell of fish.

It is difficult for you to drop everything that the past has given to you and just be free. And then you will see that everything you do, and everything that is being done to you is your responsibility. You will never dump things on others – that is childish; that is the way of the retarded.

Just the other day in the World Press Conference, I could not communicate with only two people, they were from Africa. The first one could not manage to say what he wanted to ask me. Somehow it was figured out what he was asking. He was asking why Africans don't come to me. Now, is it my responsibility? Is it my business, my concern why Africans don't come to me? Ask the Africans!

They know only the smell of fish; roses are not going to satisfy them. And I am offering roses to you, so only those who can understand the fragrance of roses can be here with me. I am offering you the best everything.

The people who can understand Mozart's music or Wagner's music, the people who can understand Leonardo da Vinci, Michelangelo, the people who can understand the beautiful poetry of Rabindranath, Kahlil Gibran, the people who can understand Tolstoy, Dostoyevsky, Turgenev, Chekhov, Gorky, and can find the beauty, the truth in these people – they can understand me. Then there is a possibility of communication. I was not wanting to be rude to the poor African, but this is the truth, the naked truth.

It was happening in India too. We had become an island; people from all over the world were coming there – except the Indians. Strange, but not really: Indians cannot understand anything which is so superior, so delicate. In two thousand years of slavery, they have forgotten all. In two thousand years of slavery, they have learned only how to polish the boots of the British, of the Moguls. Now these boot-shiners cannot communicate with me. Yes, they can hear what I say, but they will not understand it.

This happened with the second African. He asked the question, and he was looking all over the place. I was answering his question in front of him, and he was not looking at me. Poverty, no education...Africa is far behind. The gap is big.

When I was answering his question, he was looking all around, finding himself in an awkward situation, because what I was saying was beyond his grasp. And the moment I stopped answering the first question, he immediately came up with a second question. Perhaps while I was answering his first question he was thinking and preparing the second question. He was not listening to me, because the second question was not connected with the first question at all. The second question was not connected with my answer at all.

If he had listened to me, he would have asked something in response to my answer. But he must have crammed two questions, and he must have been trying to keep remembering what he was going to ask next. And he did not want to be disturbed by my answer! If he gets interested in my answer, he may forget the second question. Now, what can I do if Africans don't come? It is *their* responsibility.

Scientists now have agreed on the fact that man was born in Africa. Naturally, Africa has the biggest chimpanzees, monkeys; only those chimpanzees and monkeys can turn into men. Indian monkeys are too small, they won't do. Man was born in Africa – but why is Africa so backward? It is not only that their skin is black – because black skin has its own beauty, as white skin has its own beauty. More important is that they are living in darkness, in a total, black night. What has happened?

The intelligent people.... If man was born in Africa, the intelligent people left Africa thousands of years ago, because it was not a land worth living in. And the intelligent man is always searching for something better, so the man of intelligence left Africa. Only the retarded who were still very close to the chimpanzees remained there.

I am not condemning, I have all compassion for them. I would like them to come up and be equal to the whole humanity. But what can I do except tell it to them? They have to take the responsibility on their own shoulders. And the backward people are the last to accept responsibility.

Your question makes you a confirmed retarded person. Drop thinking such questions. Without responsibility you are not a real human being. Come of age, grow up. And remember always, growing old is not growing up. Even donkeys grow old, but they don't grow up. Only man has the prerogative, the privilege of growing up. Become more conscious, more alert, more meditative, more silent, and you will see what I am saying.

Everybody is responsible for himself.

Beloved Bhagwan,

Since You have been speaking again this time, many of us feel that You are taking us into another phase of Your work. Is this true?

Absolutely true. I had to give a three year gap and remain silent for so many reasons.

One of the reasons relevant to your question is that I had been speaking on Jesus, on Krishna, on Buddha, on Mahavira. I was speaking on all other traditions of religion: Hassidism, Zen, Sufism. I had spoken on almost all important people who had contributed something to human consciousness: Lao Tzu, Chuang Tzu, Lieh Tzu, Bodhidharma, Bokuju, Socrates, Pythagoras, Zarathustra, Kabir, Shankara, Dadu, Milarepa, Marpa, Nagarjuna, Vasubandhu. I covered almost the whole world. Wherever I found a man who has contributed to human consciousness, whether it was Greece – Heraclitus, Diogenes, Dionysius – or it was Tibet, or it was China, or it was Arabia, it did not matter to me.

I was speaking on these people for a certain reason, a simple device. I had no people of my own. I had to throw my net far and wide. When I spoke on Jesus, Christians were happy, immensely happy; they started coming to me. Even priests, bishops, became sannyasins.

And I was laughing all the time inside, that what I was saying was my own, it had nothing to do with Jesus; Jesus was just an excuse. I used his words, but put my meaning into them. And those people were thinking, "We have never understood Jesus rightly, we were thinking something else." In fact, they were right; I was changing the wine, keeping the bottle.

And when I had enough people who were capable of listening to me directly, and I didn't have to drop things which are ugly in Jesus, ugly in Mahavira, ugly in Mohammed…because in the beginning I was not in the position to offend these people. To offend these people in the beginning would have been a disaster: you would not have been here, I would not have been here.

So I used those devices, and then I stopped speaking just to give a gap – so that those who are only interested in me because I speak on Jesus will leave. Those who think that I am supporting Hinduism by speaking on the *Gita* will leave – because silence is not a discourse on the *Gita*.

This was a beautiful experience. A few people left, just enough to be counted on your fingers. But more than half a million people are now ready to listen to *me*. Now I don't care. I can call Jesus just what he is: a crackpot. I can call Mahavira just exactly what he is: a masochist. Now I know that you can understand me.

It was a preparatory period. I was not thinking that I was going to catch so many fish, but truth has its own mysterious ways. I have with me, with great love, trust, friendliness, more than half a million sannyasins.

But that is not the whole number who are getting close to me. There are at least two million people who are in great sympathy with what I am saying, but they don't yet have courage enough to come out and declare, "I have dropped the past and I am ready for the present."

And there are at least one million people who are just fifty-fifty: they read my books, they go to church too. I know that if they go on continuing to read my books – particularly now that I am creating the new *Bible* and *The Last Testament*…. You have heard about the Old Testament and the New Testament; I am creating *The Last Testament*. If they go on reading what I am saying now, things will be settled. Either they will burn my books and take shelter in a church, or they will burn the Old Testament and the New Testament and be my people.

Right now they are in a split. But I don't see how any intelligent person can choose – if he understands me – anything two thousand years old, three thousand years old, five thousand years old, unless he is a junk collector.

Yes, it is totally a new phase, because I have found my people and now I can open my heart totally. Now all the cards are open on the table!

I have nothing to hide from you, because I know your love will be able to understand it.

Go to Your Bathroom Dancing!

DISCOURSE 24, July 22, 1985

Beloved Bhagwan,

When You said that You are not celibate, I was shocked. I guess I thought You had transcended sex. Why did this disturb me?

I was also shocked, because I was thinking you all would be shocked and only one camel got the shock. But his question is meaningful.

You were shocked, Mr. Camel, because you had certain expectations of me. It is strange – I don't expect anything from you, and you go on expecting how I should be, what I should do, what I should not. I am giving you total freedom, and you want me to be a prisoner of your expectations?

You were shocked because of the long, ancient tradition of a very surprising phenomenon: masters have been imposing their ideas on their disciples; in return the disciples were imposing their ideas on the masters. And it was not that the master was really a master – because he followed his own followers, he fulfilled their expectations.

If he does not fulfill their expectations all his respectability is gone, the followers will disperse. In fact, the same people who had respected him like a god will treat him like a dog. He will be condemned and cursed. And your old so-called masters were not courageous enough to remain free. What could they give you? They were imprisoned by you.

You both were doing the same thing. The follower was fulfilling the master's ideas; otherwise he would be condemned – that is clear. The other thing is a little more subtle: the followers had certain criteria, expectations, and their so-called masters – they don't deserve even to be called "so-called" masters – were fulfilling their expectations for centuries; it was a mutual slavery. That's why you were shocked. It has nothing to do with my celibacy or my love. It has something to do with your rotten mind.

Who are you to expect anything from me?

We have no contract, no bargain.

You are here out of your own freedom, I am here out of my own freedom. Freedom is the only bridge between us. I don't expect *anything* from you, still, what stupidity…you expect anything from me? I should follow your idea of enlightenment? Are you enlightened? An enlightened man should follow the idea of the unenlightened, how he has to behave?

Do you see the absurdity of it? But the follower's ego is fulfilled: his master is celibate, his master is this, that….

Every religion has created different kinds of expectations. The Jaina master has to remain naked, only then will Jainas recognize him as enlightened. I don't see any relationship between nakedness and enlightenment. Do you see any relationship?

The Buddhists will not allow Gautam Buddha to touch a woman, to hold her hand and have a little dance with her, because the enlightened man does not touch a woman. In fact, he is expected not even to see a woman. The Buddhist master walks looking only four feet ahead of him, so that his eyes are glued to the earth. At the most he may be able to see the feet of a woman, but not the face.

The Hindus have their expectation. The Hindu master is not supposed even to sit on the place where a woman has been sitting before. Even that part of the earth has become dangerous, because the woman has left her vibrations there, and those vibrations can destroy his celibacy.

All these people were fulfilling the desires of their followers. I don't care a bit what you expect; that is your problem. I am going to shatter all your expectations of me. I am totally a free man. I don't care even about whether you think me enlightened or not. I *am,* why should I care?

When I became enlightened I also had the idea, which has been there for centuries, that after enlightenment one transcends sex. So for a few days I waited for the transcendence. It was not coming; on the contrary, the grass was greener. The women were more beautiful than ever before, because my eyes were clear.

It has been traditionally understood that if an enlightened man makes love to a woman, his enlightenment is finished. So I was a little hesitant. But then I thought that if enlightenment is such a weak thing, it is not worth having. How can making love to a woman destroy enlightenment? And if it does destroy it, that means the love between a man and a woman is a far bigger, stronger and more vital force than your bogus so-called enlightenment.

And I am always attracted towards the unknown, untried, unexplored. I said to myself, "For five thousand years the enlightened people have perpetuated the idea. I have to experiment and to see." And I have loved many women – my enlightenment has not changed. I have created a historical event!

In the future, no enlightened man should be expected to be celibate. I have risked much. But in a way, after enlightenment something *is* transcended –

If you ask me, I will say my philosophy is both hands open before you. I am not going to keep anything private, anything secret. For the first time, an enlightened man is trusting the people who love him. But I would not like to be loved by you according to your conceptions, your conditions. I don't need that kind of love, it is poisonous. I would like you to learn to be open to me the way I am open to you.

it is not sex, but sexuality. After enlightenment I have not been able to look into the eyes of any woman with sexuality.

It is nothing on my part, I cannot take the credit for it. The whole experience of enlightenment has changed many things. Even making love to a woman is now totally different, absolutely different, has no connection with the love when I was unenlightened. It was not love, it was just a biological, chemical, hormonal attraction. It was just a kind of slavery; it was a need, and you were possessed by the need. That need has disappeared. Now making love to a woman is just pure fun – and I have never heard that after enlightenment fun is transcended.

In fact, only after enlightenment can you love. Before that you were just animals, camels. Have you seen two animals making love? Watch carefully – you will be surprised. They both look so sad, so depressed. A clear perception is there that they are feeling the bondage of biology, they are feeling the slavery of biology. Animals don't enjoy making love. They *have* to do it; it is something that they cannot avoid – they are not conscious enough. When the season comes, they have to mate.

Man, even though unenlightened, has changed one thing: there is no season for mating for him, the whole year he is free to love. A certain freedom has come to humanity which is not available to the animals.

It is very strange to see animals: for one month or two months they become attracted to each other and then for ten months they are celibate; for ten months they remain enlightened! Just for two months those poor guys, under the impact of biological forces, have to make love. It is almost as if somebody is holding a gun behind you and telling you to make love. The biological gun is not visible, but it is very powerful. How can you enjoy? How can you be blissful?

No animal is happy making love. Only man has risen a little higher, and that height has made him capable of being freed from one thing: the biological

period of mating. But still, it is biology that goes on forcing him to make love all the year round.

In the East, people make love only in the night. In the West, they have a little more intelligence, they make love early in the morning – of course they also make love in the night. The western mind has grown a little more towards freedom. Why make love in darkness? The reason was always because making love was a kind of enforcement, and the faces of the lovers looked distorted. It was better not to see the faces of each other. Not to spoil the game, the darkness was good. Under the blanket of darkness they could manage to believe that everything was going right.

It needed a little more intelligence to ask why you should remain bounded by the night. Animals are bounded by a certain period in the year. Man's intelligence freed him for the whole year.

In the East they are bound to make love in the night, silently – nobody should know about it. In the West, intelligence has grown a little better. Why in the night only? In fact, a man who is tired after the whole day's work, worries, tensions, anxieties – what kind of love is he going to make? His love is more or less like a sleeping pill. It gives him good sleep, it gives him relaxation. The whole day he was so burdened that his heart was not functioning normally. Making love, he loses energy; the heart starts cooling down, calming down.

Now it is a medically-established fact that people who make love never have heart attacks. The longer in their life they go on making love, the more powerful, relaxed their heart remains. Have you heard, in the millions of years of the past, that anybody has died while he was making love?

People have died in every kind of situation. People have died eating, people have died sleeping, people have died working, people have died walking, people have died talking, but strange – people have never died making love. It establishes something: that love is a relaxation. It is good for sleep and good for your heart, but after a tiring day it cannot be much of a joy. Just a last thing to do somehow, quickly, and then turn your back and go to sleep – a kind of duty.

Morning, perhaps, is the best time to make love. Energies are fresh, you are rested, there is no anxiety burdening you, it is the beginning of the day. And to make love in the beginning should be considered something auspicious, holy; you cannot begin the day religiously without making love. But still you are in a biological bondage.

After enlightenment, love is no longer a need. In that way there is a transcendence. Love becomes just like any game: playing cards, playing tennis…. I have loved many women, and I am the first enlightened person in the world who is being absolutely truthful to you. You could have never found out whether I am celibate or not. I thought, although I have not said I am celibate, you would consider me a celibate. I have not participated in this lying positively, but negatively I am responsible. And now I am not going to hide anything from you.

Once Gautam Buddha's most intimate disciple, Ananda, asked him, "Bhagwan, can you tell me the essential quality of your philosophy in a very short statement?"

Buddha said, "My philosophy is like a fist; it is a secret. I have not told you everything. The most precious is hidden."

If you ask me, I will say my philosophy is both hands open before you. I am not going to keep anything private, anything secret. For the first time, an enlightened man is trusting the people who love him. But I would not like to be loved by you according to your conceptions, your conditions. I don't need that kind of love, it is poisonous. I would like you to learn to be open to me the way I am open to you.

I am not a fist, but an open hand – and not only one hand, but both hands. And if you can love me still, then that love will be meaningful.

It is a strange phenomenon that you have never considered. Why do you want the enlightened man, your master, to be naked, to be celibate, to be eating one time only in a day, sleeping on a hard bed, not allowing women any closeness, eating only certain things?

If you see Gautam Buddha drinking even a Coca Cola, you will not anymore consider him enlightened – he has not even transcended Coca Cola. I don't drink Coca Cola, but I love it. I cannot drink it because of my physicians; Devaraj is after me, Shunyo is after me. I cannot drink Coca Cola, I had to transcend it. But it is not enlightenment that helped me to transcend it, it is diabetes!

Your old religious leaders were captives of your expectations. I am nobody's prisoner. And I feel very light, because I am not burdened. I can say to you everything; there is nothing being withheld. All your masters were withholding things from you. I do not consider them authentic, open, sincere. Even to their own disciples they were not true.

If enlightenment does not make you transcend hunger, thirst, urination, then why should it make you transcend your sex? Sex is part of your whole being, it is not something separate. You eat, you drink, you exercise. Your body has nothing to do with your enlightenment; the body will go on functioning in the same way. It will create blood, it will create semen. How can enlightenment make you transcend sex? You will have to stop eating, you will have to stop drinking. In fact, you will have to stop breathing; only then will there be a transcendence – in your death.

Sex is a natural phenomenon. Yes, it takes fourteen years to make your sexual energy mature. And if you enjoy it blissfully, without any condemnation, without any Christ standing between you and your beloved….

I think this is very disgusting of these enlightened people – always poking their nose into your affairs, always watching you from the keyhole, what you are doing. And naturally, because they go on watching you from the keyhole, you also go on watching them even more carefully, because you may be following a wrong man. You have to be certain that his is a twenty-four carat enlightenment.

It fulfills your ego that you are a follower of an enlightened master. That's why, Mr. Camel, you got shocked. I am sorry for you. You are a fellow traveler of a simple, natural, authentic, open person. You are not my followers, because to make you my followers I would have to follow you! Then I would have to keep continuously alert that something is not found out by you.

Celibacy is unnatural – at least, up to the age of forty-two. Between fourteen years and forty-two, celibacy is absolutely unnatural, and if you force yourself to remain a celibate, you will become just a pervert. Your sexual energy will find ways. It is very simple….

How long can you keep your bladder full? Sooner or later either you have to rush towards the toilet or the bladder will drop any idea of your support and will start functioning on its own. Semen is a similar phenomenon. It is manufactured in you, by your food, by your breathing, by your exercise, by your very living. How long can you hold it? And holding it is such a painful job! That's why you see your saints so sad.

It is natural, if your bladder is full and you are afraid that, "Now I am coming near the boundary when there will be no control…." Semen is a natural by-product of your life. Yes, after enlightenment there is a tremendous change. To me, that is transcendence. That does not mean you stop making love. That simply means it is no longer a need, you are no longer a slave to it. Just, in moments when you want to play with the energy that you have, you can make love. And if the other person is also of the same quality, or even is moving in the same direction, your love will become meditation.

All other religions have forced you to become perverts. In your monasteries there is masturbation but no meditation. And I want to say the thing as it is:

Transcendence simply means slavery is transcended. Now I am not making any love to anybody, for the simple reason that I am no longer healthy, my body is fragile. It is not ready to play tennis! It is nothing spiritual – if I get my health back again, which I have wasted for you….

Just think of me for thirty years continuously wandering in India, and in return getting stones, shoes and knives thrown at me. And you don't know Indian railways, waiting rooms, you don't know the way Indians live. It is unhygienic, ugly, but they are accustomed to it. I had suffered for those thirty years as much – perhaps more – than Jesus suffered on the cross. To be on the cross is a question only of a few hours. To be assassinated is even quicker. But to be a wandering master in India is no joke.

I was the healthiest person you could find. Before I started these journeys, knowing perfectly well my health was going to be destroyed…. I had to eat all kinds of food, and in India the food pattern changes just within a few miles. I had to live with dirt, uncleanliness, and I had to be ready for all these rewards – stones, shoes, knives being thrown at me. And India is a vast country, almost a continent – I was always on the train.

There are places which take forty-eight hours to reach by the train. And airplanes reach only to a few capital cities. If you want to reach the people you have to go in a train. And if you want to enter the very central parts of the country, you have to use even worse trains. Of course, I went on and on destroying my health, knowing perfectly well what I was doing.

But what I had found I wanted at any cost – at the cost of my life – to share with a few people, to make them afire. My body may die in the effort, but I have made a few other bodies lighted with the same flame, and they will go on spreading the fire around the earth.

People used to say to me, "Your body is like a marble statue." It was. My weight was one hundred and ninety pounds, and it was not fatness – I have never been fat. It was immensely solid, like a rock. I was never sick, I was unaware what it means to be sick. But as my body went on deteriorating, I became aware what headache is, what migraine is, what stomach upset is, what finally became my diabetes and my asthma. Now I am only one hundred and thirty-one pounds, down from one hundred and ninety.

Now I don't have any energy for any game. Whatsoever energy I have got, I want it to be devoted to you and to my people around the world. I want to say so many things to you, and life is so short – one cannot be certain even of tomorrow. But I am determined that death will have to wait till I have fulfilled my task, because it is no longer *my* task; I have disappeared long ago. Now it is existence meeting you, existence trying to reach you. I am only a vehicle.

But one fact I have proved absolutely and forever – that making love does not destroy enlightenment. On the contrary, it makes it richer, more beautiful – new flowers in it, new colors in it, new fragrances in it, new laughter, new smiles.

The whole idea that the enlightened man cannot make love is absolutely wrong.

But you got shocked because of your expectation. You are unenlightened, you don't know enlightenment. First, to become enlightened is so arduous – the camel changing into the lion, the lion changing into the child. And when you have passed this whole long track, you are not courageous enough to do something that may spoil the whole pilgrimage.

But, forgive me, I am a different type of man. When I became enlightened, I wanted to test it in every fire: if it passes through all fire tests, then only is it real. Otherwise, I was hallucinating, I was just imagining that I had become enlightened. And I can say to you now that I have done everything that no enlightened person is expected to do – even things in which I was not interested at all, but just to test that I was not hallucinating....

After my enlightenment I smoked my first cigarette. I had never had any interest in doing such a silly thing. When you can breathe fresh air and exhale, why should you pollute it with smoke, with dangerous nicotine? But I did smoke, for almost one month. It was difficult, I was coughing; it was a hard thing to do.

I used to live with one of my friends. He was puzzled; he said, "You are mad! You were never interested in cigarettes, and now you are smoking continually."

Coughing, tears coming to my eyes, I said, "I have to see whether the cigarette is stronger than the enlightenment. I have to give it a chance."

I have done everything after enlightenment which has been thought would destroy enlightenment. And I tell you now that nothing can destroy enlightenment, because enlightenment is not just an experience, it is a transformation. It is not that it happens once and you see the light, and then the whole of your life you remember with joy that vision, that opening of the window to existence. It is not like that. Enlightenment transforms you. You are totally a new man.

But of course, if I start smoking here while I am speaking to you, many camels are going to be shocked. But I am an unreliable man, I live moment to moment. If it happens to me, tomorrow you will see a table by my side with the best cigarettes in the world – what is it? Five-Five-Five? – and a bottle of champagne, and my Gudia, one of the most beautiful girls I have come across, pouring champagne into the glass for me. I can do that, it is just a question of the idea arising in me. Then nobody can prevent me.

I have found freedom in dropping being respectable. Respectability is a social strategy to keep you imprisoned. Around the world there are so many rumors.... I don't care a bit. Sometimes I have been told by my friends and lovers, "Why don't you contradict them? These are absolutely absurd, they destroy your respectability with people."

I said, "I don't want to be respected by anyone, because if he respects me he will expect me to remain respectable" – and that I cannot promise. It is better to be notorious, because it gives you immense freedom. I am a notorious man.

Jesus, Mohammed, Mahavira, Buddha, Lao Tzu – none of them was courageous enough to drop the desire for respectability.

People go on condemning me. The moment I come to know that they are condemning me for a certain thing, then I go on doing the same thing on a bigger scale. I had only one Rolls Royce. They started condemning me, so I told my secretary, "Arrange for two."

In India it was very difficult, because the Rolls Royce after 1965 became a banned item, it could not enter the country. I was the only man who managed to have two Rolls Royces enter the country.

When I came to America, I said to my secretary, "Now there is no limit." I had seven, and they were condemning me – a spiritual man, an enlightened person, having seven Rolls Royces when people are dying of starvation? Now I have ninety. Now they don't condemn me. They know that if they continue condemning me, I will go on having more and more Rolls Royces until they are satisfied.

I have my own individuality. I don't need anybody's respect, because I am so full there is no space for anything else. And it has been a tremendous experience to be so notorious and yet to be loved by millions of people. That gives a great hope, that even an ordinary man can be loved; you need not to be extraordinary to be loved.

How much love I have received! I don't think anybody before me has received so much love. And certainly I have received more hostility, anger, condemnation than anybody else. I am richest man in the world – I receive everything!

Love I have received – nobody can come even close to me. Hatred I have received – nobody can come close to me. And just for a single, simple thing: that I dropped the idea of respectability.

If you ask me, my enlightenment made me transcend only one thing, and that is the opinion of others. That is their business. They cannot disturb my sleep by their opinions. And I don't have to be concerned about what they are thinking. I am living absolutely alone, but utterly fulfilled.

You ask me why you were shocked – because you are still a camel. The lions were not shocked. They must have roared! They must have found a synchronicity between me and themselves. They must have been rejoiced and danced: "Our master is not celibate, so we need not be unnecessarily depressed that we are not celibate."

Those who have reached the stage of being a child, they must have enjoyed knowing that at least in this whole world there is one man who can say everything truly without taking an oath that, "Whatever I say, I will say only the truth."

I am not one who has taken an oath to speak the truth. I simply want you to understand what a beauty it is to be truthful, authentic, just the way you are. I have put my heart in front of you. Now it is up to you whether to be shocked, or to rejoice. It will depend on your mind. But you cannot influence me; nobody in my whole life has influenced me. Anybody who has tried has found that he was forcing me to do just the opposite. Slowly, slowly people dropped the idea.

In India, Jainas were a great majority of my lovers, but the day I spoke on sex that majority – camels – simply disappeared. Yes, a few remained, a few of them are even here. They proved to be lions; they could see and connect themselves with my truth.

There were many Gandhians – until the day I spoke against Gandhi and said that he was the most cunning politician, not only of this century but of the whole history, that all his religion was mumbo-jumbo; it was a curtain to dominate the whole country. And although he was saying that he was in search of truth, he was continually lying, just like a politician. He was saying that when the country becomes free, all the armies will be dissolved; there will be no military, there will be no weapons, because a nonviolent country has no need of such things. One American author, Louis Fisher, asked him, "If you dissolve all the armies and the military, and you don't have any weapons, and somebody attacks you, what will you do?"

He said, "We will welcome them. We will say to them, 'There is no need for any bloodshed. If you want to live here in this country, come, be our guests. You are welcome.'"

But this was before freedom came to India. When India became independent, everything changed. The army was not dissolved, but increased. The military was not dissolved – now India has one of the biggest military forces. Weapons were not dissolved. India has atomic plants and is now making every effort to have nuclear weapons – at the cost of half of the country dying, without food! India is exporting wheat to other countries, because the politicians need money to make a nuclear plant. And these are all Gandhians.

When Gandhi was alive, after independence, Pakistan attacked one part of Kashmir. India had to fight with the invaders, and you cannot believe that Gandhi blessed the first fighter planes to go and destroy Pakistanis – who were Indians just a few days before! Where had his nonviolence gone? He was blessing fighting planes, sending them to destroy the same people for whom he had been fighting for freedom his whole life.

When I said that his nonviolence was a political strategy....

It was clear that to fight against the British government with weapons was impossible. From where are you going to get all those weapons against the empire? – perhaps the biggest empire that has existed ever. It was said that the sun never sets on the British empire. It was true: if it sets in one country, it rises in another, but as far as the whole British empire is concerned, it never sets. This was the biggest empire of

man's history. Against this empire how can you fight?

And not only can you not fight, you don't have the means to fight. You don't have even men to fight – Indians are so lousy, so cowardly, so superstitious, and so faithful to the idea that nothing happens without God's will. "It is God's will that Britain is ruling our country. To fight against Britain and its empire is to fight against God's will." That was the Indian conditioning.

Naturally Gandhi invented a new strategy – nonviolence, which was always respected by the Indians as the most significant religious quality. But his nonviolence was not that of a religious man.

I am nonviolent. You see the guards around me with weapons...and now they are being criticized. Remember, that criticism will create more and more guards and more and more weapons. But I know that those weapons are just toys. Against nuclear powers, you are carrying a small gun. I know it, I know it makes no sense, but the gun is not the point! And I have not arranged those guards either. I don't know even who my guards are, what their names are.

It is you, the people who love me – a person who never fulfills any of your expectations – you are worried about my life. It is your love; otherwise those guards are just of no use. Just a bomb will finish...it can become another Nagasaki, Hiroshima. But I am nonviolent.

People have been asking me, if I am nonviolent then why are these weapons here? Those weapons are your love, and I respect your love, knowingly perfectly well those weapons are toys. But I know the person who is carrying the weapon is carrying it out of love. There is no other reason. I cannot tell him to throw the weapon, because that would be an insult to his love. I cannot insult love, I have tremendous respect for love.

You have to come out of your shock; otherwise the bridge between me and you will be broken.

Remember perfectly, I am not going to change in

any way. If change has to come, it has to come to you and your mind, because it is your disturbance, your shock. It is your problem – take the responsibility for it. See the simple fact that you were carrying some expectations – that means some chains for me. It is time: throw those chains.

I am an absolutely free man. There is no bondage for me. I can do anything, you just have to suggest it to me!

Beloved Bhagwan,

I love Your vision, but whenever I listen to You speaking about the future of the world, I feel like politicians and priests are too powerful and too deeply asleep for our songs and our laughter to turn the world around.
Is this skepticism?

It is not skepticism – for that a little more intelligence is needed. It is simply stupidity.
I also know that the powers of the politicians and the priests are so vast. What can our laughter, our song, our dances, our love, do against these big powers?

I have to tell you one thing, that if an atom of hydrogen gas can release so much energy that it becomes the hydrogen bomb, a hundred times more powerful than the bomb that destroyed Hiroshima or Nagasaki, why do you think that authentic love – which is the most precious thing in the world – that a real rejoicing, that a total laughter when you are not laughing but you are laughter, that a dance in which the dancer disappears cannot release a totally different kind of energy?

All these priests and politicians have the energy derived from matter. I am trying to tell you that if material energy can be so big, spiritual energy can be a million or billion times bigger.

It just has not been tried, ever. This is a good opportunity.

Remember, the word "opportunist" has been used always in a condemnatory sense. I want it to be freed from that association. A really intelligent person is always an opportunist. To me, an opportunist means one who takes the challenge of the opportunity and risks himself.

What are we going to lose? If my sannyasins all around the world go on spreading songs and dances and love, these politicians will look stupid. Right now, they cannot be much bothered with the humanity that is there. If it is destroyed, so what? – it is not worth anything. But if we can make the earth blossom with new people, the politicians will have heart attacks. The very idea of destroying *these* people, *this* earth, will become inconceivable.

And the man of laughter, the man who can dance in tune with the wind and the sun and the moon, is far more powerful than any nuclear weapon can be, because his is life energy. They are playing with dead matter. If dead matter can release so much energy, a living being…it is inconceivable how much energy he can release.

We can create of this whole world a celebration.

And I tell you, your politicians will commit suicide, because they will be the only sad people, they will be the only ones who are unfit. And I don't think, howsoever idiotic they are, they can think of destroying the laughter, the songs, the beauty of love, the innocence of a child, and the authenticity of enlightened people.

Just take the challenge of the time. They are going to destroy you anyway – why not celebrate before they do it? Let them create death for the whole earth. But what are we going to lose? We will die laughing, dancing, singing. We are not going to be like Hiroshima or Nagasaki.

In the first place, it is impossible. If we really work for the New Man to go on spreading like wildfire, it is impossible for them to destroy this earth. Even their conscience – which is not much – will not allow them to destroy this beautiful garden of people.

And the laughter is not American or Soviet, it is not Indian or English. Rejoicing has no nations. Songs, dances, and disappearing into your dances and your songs, don't belong to any religion.

The New Man will declare this whole earth his own. Politicians will simply fall by the way. They will not be able to figure out what to do with these people. They know how to deal with the sad slaves – slaves of theologies, political ideologies, they know how to deal with them.

My effort is to create a man that they simply have never seen. They will simply stagger and fall wherever they are. And I don't see that a world full of flowers and fragrance can be destroyed. But just for argument's sake, even if it is destroyed, that is the best way to go away from this earth to some other planet – dancing, singing, rejoicing. Yes, they can destroy your body, but they cannot destroy your spirit. And I am trying to create a man who has spirit, ecstasy.

You can ride upon your ecstasy to other planets; rockets are not needed. And remember, only bodies die, the soul within you is immortal. No nuclear weapons can destroy it. You have something indestructible in you; you just have to become aware of it, and you have to make others aware of it.

I am not concerned about the future. I am concerned with you, with people who have been given a chance of drinking the wine of life, squeezing the whole juice of it every moment. The future makes no sense to me, but it is going to come whether it makes sense to me or not.

And I am not worried about myself. I died thirty-two years ago, and the one who is speaking to you is beyond any nuclear weapon. I would like you also to be beyond nuclear weapons. And these are the methods: the laughter, the joy, love, rejoicing, making your life a beautiful garden.

The last moment of your life is very decisive. Nothing is more decisive in your whole life. The last moment of your life…if it is a dance, you will join other dancers on some other planet. If it is love, you will join some planet where love is no longer sin, where love is religion.

So what I am saying to you is double-edged. On the one hand it can stop the third world war; on the other hand it can take you to the right place amongst right people. Whatever happens in the future is not my concern. My concern is with this moment, because the next moment may be the last moment on the earth.

Remember this: when you go to sleep, say goodbye to life with great gratitude. It has given you so much – never forget it. I don't say to you, go to sleep praying to Jesus Christ on your knees, or Gautam Buddha or some other guy. I say to you, go to your sleep with a thankful heart for all that life has given to you: all the laughter, all the loves, all the beautiful flowers, the songs of the birds, the colorful rainbows, the amazing sunsets, sunrises. It has given you so much that if there is not going to be tomorrow you have not missed anything.

Let there be no tomorrow; you are already fulfilled. And if by chance you wake up again tomorrow morning, don't start with any mantra-chanting or prayer – these are all irreligious ways. Again, start the day with gratitude, love, joy.

People say that you should not get out of the bed with the wrong leg, wrong foot, because then you spoil your whole day. As for as I know, legs have nothing to do with your day. I would like you, when you get up, to get up with laughter. Any leg will do, but go to your bathroom dancing!

Seeing the Fact, Drop the Fiction

DISCOURSE 25, July 23, 1985

Beloved Bhagwan,

All our lives we have been forced to learn grace, beauty, etiquette. But now, when You are teaching us genuine grace and beauty, a lot of us are so insensitive to graciousness and aesthetics that even coming close to You, in the presence of You, we continue the resentments of forced grace, beauty, etiquette, etc. We behave without respect, love, dignity towards our beloved master — You, Bhagwan. Please say something to our thick brains so we do not miss out on the graceful experience.

It is almost natural that when you drop any conditioning there is a gap between the dropping of the conditioning and the beginning of the genuine, the natural, the spontaneous in you. That gap happens easily.

From your very childhood you have been told to be respectful. You were not able even to see why you should respect this man. You had no reason to respect the man, but you were forced. You were dependent, you were too small to fight against it. That resentment is always underneath your respect. Just a little scratching and your resentment will come up, because it is as old as your respect, etiquette, grace. Each time you have been trained for these things, resentment has been created in you side by side, just like a shadow.

These are not things to be taught, these are qualities to be caught. And when they are caught there is no resentment; when they are caught they are spontaneous, natural. You don't have to do them, they happen of their own accord. But this has not been the case up to now. For millions of years you have lived with a duality, a thick layer of resentment — which is deeper, more underground — and a thin layer of forced grace, sensitivity, aesthetics, respect, love.

The basic thing, the fundamental thing is to understand that when you drop your grace — the learned one; when you drop love — the learned one, remember also to drop the resentment. That too is learned. You have learned it on your own, against all those people who had power over you. If you don't drop it then I can go on telling you, "Be naturally graceful," and you will think, "It is good, there is no need to make any effort to be graceful." Your thin layer will disappear — but where will the resentment go?

That resentment will become your behavior. Instead of respect, you will start disrespecting anybody and everybody. Instead of the arousal of a natural love…the bogus love has gone, now you have only hate. That's why societies and cultures are afraid. They are trembling always because they are depending on something which is not natural.

But you have to understand that when you drop the learned thing, the conditioned thing, don't forget to drop with it the resentment that had come with it; otherwise, you will become ungraceful, and to be ungraceful is ugly. You will become disrespectful and to be disrespectful is not human. It is falling below the human.

You have got this whole beautiful existence. You don't deserve it; nobody deserves it. You had not even asked for it. You have suddenly found yourself amidst these beautiful millions of stars, the flowers, the birds. And if you are disrespectful, you will be blind to all that commands respect, you will turn your back to all that which commands respect.

It does not demand. It does not say to you, Respect me, I am your father. But silently have you not felt sometimes the flowers, without saying a word, are commanding your respect, your love, your grace? And the same applies to other human beings.

We are all strangers to each other. We come into the world alone, and if you are not graceful, not loving, not sensitive, you will find yourself in a state of loneliness, abandoned. Who cares about such a person? That will strengthen your resentment even more, and will make you more and more ugly.

The basic fault has been made by the society, the culture, the religion. Nothing can be done about it, except one thing, of which you are capable: seeing the fact, drop the fiction. But always remember that behind the fiction you have been always carrying antagonism to it.

From my very childhood I was wild. My whole family was trying to make me cultured, graceful, respectful, but they failed. Fortunately, they failed. I had decided one thing: that if something is natural, it will come on its own. There is no need to learn it, to rehearse it.

In India, there are joint families. In one family there may be fifty people, sixty people. Every old person in the family has to be respected. And I know that this old guy needs to be beaten, rather than respected; there is no reason why I should respect him. Just because of his age? But then, I don't see any relationship between respect and age. There are trees four thousand years old, there are animals who live longer than man.

I invite all the sannyasins of the world: slowly start moving to the closest commune. You will find a great rhythm between yourself and others. You will find for the first time a loving, compassionate, rejoicing group of people, who do not expect anything from you, but who are always ready to share with you whatever they have got.

Nietzsche has described these three stages: the camel, the lion, the child. He has taken only the evolutionary part and described these three stages. He has forgotten that there are exactly the same stages below the camel – the camel is not the lowest animal in the world. Of course, considering Charles Darwin and his theory of evolution, I say the monkey is below the camel; otherwise there would be no man.

Nietzsche is not talking about the actual camel, he is talking about man – that he can be a camel. And if man is born out of monkeys, then certainly the monkey will be a lower stage than the camel. And you can easily recognize amongst yourselves how monkeyish is your behavior. That destroys your grace, that destroys your serenity.

Below the monkey is certainly the donkey, who is absolutely thick. You cannot teach a donkey any tricks. Have you seen any circus where donkeys are doing something? – impossible. Elephants are there, horses are there, monkeys are there, but everybody has forgotten about the donkey – such an important personality, more famous than the monkey and the camel.

Donkeys are absolutely stubborn – no intelligence; you cannot teach them anything. You can go on loading the donkey with your holy scriptures; he will carry the weight, but will never understand the meaning. And of course, below the donkey there is only the Yankee. And you all know about the Yankee; there is nothing to be said about the Yankee. You have to start from the Yankee – at least become a donkey.

The Yankee is absolutely phony. The donkey is at least authentically real. He may not listen to you, but he follows his nature, his instinct, without any interference from anybody.

In my village there were many donkeys – of course, in every place there are many donkeys – and I loved to ride on donkeys. In India, that is not right. In other countries, for example in Judea, Jesus was riding on the donkey always, it was acceptable. But in India, the donkey is thought to be the worst kind of animal – they don't know about the Yankee. After even just touching the donkey you have to take a bath.

I became enchanted with the donkeys. Why should the poor animal be abandoned? I started finding donkeys in the night, and I would ride on them. And I was amazed to know that it is wrong, the idea that the donkey is without intelligence.

If you ride on the donkey, he will never move in the middle of the road. He will go to the sides and move so close to the walls of the houses that your whole leg is almost crushed. It is very difficult to keep him in the middle. Right or left – either he is a rightist or a leftist, but never has the donkey listened to the advice of Gautam Buddha, that exactly in the middle is the right path.

And then I recognized that they are intelligent people. To get rid of me – he has no weapons, but he has found a way. If I see my leg being rubbed against a stone wall, I am bound to jump off and leave the donkey to himself.

I was trying all the donkeys of the town. Slowly, slowly they became really acquainted with me, and then I could see even a deeper layer of intelligence. They became aware even of my footsteps in some miraculous way. The donkey may be fifty feet, a hundred feet away, and I would move very slowly, very cautiously so that he did not become aware that I was coming – but he immediately would start running. He knew my steps, he felt in some way my presence.

Other people would be just passing by him and he was not worried. And I was a hundred feet away, taking every care not to disturb the poor fellow, but he would start escaping. He knew who was coming, he knew what my purpose was. He knew there was going to be trouble, because when I saw that these donkeys are cunning, not so dumb as people think, I started to take them into the fields where there were no walls. Then the donkey, of course, was at a loss. What to do? Whether he was rightist or leftist, it did not matter; there were no walls.

Because I started taking them to the the fields outside the town, they became very sensitive about my presence. Even donkeys have a certain intelligence.

Camels, howsoever ugly they look, are very gentlemanly. And in the deserts they are very friendly – to the point that if you are dying of thirst, they are ready to sacrifice themselves. When in the desert a camel is killed – because he keeps a reservoir of water inside himself....

I have heard from people who own caravans of camels that when you kill a camel in the desert the camel makes no resistance, he simply allows you to kill him. He is perfectly aware that this is the moment to be of some service to you. In some unknown way he feels you have been thirsty for days and you cannot survive unless he gives you his water reservoir.

A camel can move in the desert for six weeks without any trouble, needing no water. That much water he keeps within himself for emergency purposes. I could not believe it, that he does not resist being killed. I enquired, "If you kill a camel where there is no emergency or any danger to your life, does the camel resist?"

They said, "You say resist? He will kill you! He knows that there is no need for him to be sacrificed; this is simple murder." And a camel is a big animal, huge, of great power, he can simply crush you under his feet, no weapons are needed. But deep in the desert, lost in the desert, he does not resist. That is something really to be understood.

The camel is graceful to the point that he can sacrifice himself. He is respectful and loving, so much so, that he is ready to die so that you can live. He puts your life above his. He is not egocentric.

And in man you will find all these animals. I am not talking about the real monkeys, donkeys, camels, lions, the child, so don't get confused. The real child

is so nasty that even after enlightenment I cannot sleep in the same room as a small child. The whole night he will disturb you. In the day he sleeps perfectly well, but as the night comes – of course, his sleep is over, now he is ready to torture you. He finds excuses: "I want to go to the toilet. I am thirsty. I am hungry. I am feeling too cold, I need one blanket more."

So when I am talking about these stages, I am talking symbolically. To me, when I say the child it simply means innocence, simplicity, no desire for any power, no hankering to dominate anybody, and a tremendous beauty.

Have you seen any child who is ugly? All children are beautiful. But what happens to all these beautiful children when they grow up? They all disappear. They start becoming cunning, cruel, diplomatic, political. They lose their innocence, they lose their grace, they lose their beauty.

Amongst you, all kinds of these people are there. And it is not that you can define somebody as the camel. In fact, in each person they are all mixed up. Each person has all these qualities, from the Yankee to the child.

The society is afraid that if you are left alone.... You will turn into a Yankee, a monkey – at the most a donkey, or perhaps if you are fortunate enough, a camel. But beyond that your parents, your civilization is afraid. You cannot be left alone; you have to be trained, and their training has proved poisonous. With all good intentions they have destroyed your spontaneity. With all their well-wishings, they have made you a hypocrite.

I am all for naturalness.

The question is significant, because when you listen to me say that I am all for naturalness, you immediately drop what you always wanted to drop. But you don't become natural. You have forgotten the resentment. By dropping your etiquette, by dropping your grace, by dropping your cultivated beauty, by dropping your make-up, you are not simply going to become natural. There is something more between your phony self and your real self: your resentment. And you have thick layers of resentment, because for your whole life you have resented.

And the resentment was yours. The grace was imposed by others – it is easy to drop it, you always wanted to drop it – but the resentment was yours. It is closer to you, it is more difficult to drop it. But unless you drop your grace, cultivated beauty – just make-up; unless you drop your nice etiquette – behavior which is just diplomatic – unless with all this that has been forced upon you, you remember to drop the resentment…because now there is no need for resentment.

You are getting free of all those things which were the causes of your resentment. You can easily get rid of things that have been forced upon you, but the things that arose within you – there comes the real problem. You have to drop your resentment. If you cannot drop it, the natural flow of your energies will not be available.

It has been happening in all of history: many people have dropped the forced values. Just a few years back you had hippies all around – they had dropped the forced etiquette, the forced niceness, the forced cleanliness. They had been told, "Cleanliness is next to God, only God is above cleanliness." They were forced to take baths, they were forced to do this, that. They were forced to go to the school, to the college. They dropped all that, but they did not drop the resentment.

Hippies did not flower into beautiful human beings. Their resentment burned them. They went just to the opposite pole; they stopped taking baths. Dirtiness became next to God, uncleanliness became a value. The more unclean, the more dirty you were, the greater you were considered to be by other hippies who were not so courageous as you were. Once in a while they took a bath, once in a while they cleaned themselves. It created guilt in them. Just see the phenomenon!

Many hippies have visited me. I felt really sorry for them. They were going on a right path, but somewhere the path turned to the polar opposite. Their resentment was so strong that they started doing exactly the opposite of what they were taught to do. They dropped out of schools, out of colleges, out of universities, because it was not their own choice.

But do you know what happened to the hippies? You don't find them. After the age thirty-five they come back to the society, become again what they have been taught. Their long hair disappears, their beards disappear, their mustaches disappear. All the hippies who have reached nearabout the age of forty are now perfectly accepted gentlemen in the society. They are good businessmen, good salesmen, successful.

This was bound to happen. You cannot live in resentment for long; it is a fire, it will burn you. So you don't find old hippies – seventy years old. You don't find old hippies. In fact, that should have been the case: as a hippie gets older, he should become even hippier. But something happens by the time they start crossing the borderline of thirty-five.

There was a day when hippies declared, "We do not believe anybody who is more than thirty years old." There was a truth in it. But you cannot stop your age at thirty. It isn't like a clock that you can stop at any moment; it goes on growing whether you are a hippie or not. And by the time they are close to thirty-five, the exact middle point in life – after thirty-five they will start declining, their energies will start getting lower and lower – they become afraid. How are they going to live?

Then suddenly they want to be married, to have a stable life, to have some profession, some job, some money. Old age is coming close – they don't want to die on the streets. It was perfectly good when they were young, they had energy enough. That energy has been burned by their resentment.

They thought they were being revolutionaries; they were not, they were simply reactionaries. They were reacting to their parents, to their society, to their education. Reaction is not revolution, revolution needs much more meditative understanding. Then you don't go to the other pole, the other extreme; then you remain just exactly in the middle. And only in the middle will your natural being show. But there will be a gap. Before the natural starts flowing in you, you will have to get rid of all the hindrances to it.

I can understand your question. You say, "It hurts to see sannyasins becoming disrespectful." But the commune has to be patient with any sannyasin who is disrespectful, ungraceful, behaves in a cruel way, talks just to hurt you. The commune has to be patient: that person is going through a great change. Patience and help – both are needed for him.

Even if he is not respectful to you, you all have to be respectful to him. He needs it – this is the moment. He may not be very loving to you, or may be even hateful to you. He is sick, he needs all your compassion.

And that's the function of the commune. If five thousand people go on pouring their love on the person who replies with hatred, how long is he going to survive? He behaves disrespectfully, and five thousand people don't take any note of his disrespectfulness; they go on being respectful to the person. Soon he will drop his resentment.

These are not the people who had forced him to do certain things against his will. These are a totally different kind of people: you disrespect them, still they smile and are loving and respectful to you. They are not your parents, they are not your teachers. They are not your old rotten society.

My communes are harbingers of a new man, a new world.

But you have to be very aware, because if somebody is disrespectful towards you, it is a little difficult to be respectful to him. But be respectful out of love for humanity, out of compassion for your brothers and sisters, and understanding the fact that that man is not being disrespectful to you – he is being disrespectful to his parents, to his teachers, to the priest. You are just an excuse. It is just a coincidence that he has found you; otherwise, he would have been disrespectful to somebody else.

Don't take it personally. Living in a commune, remember you are not personalities. Certainly you are individuals, but don't take anything personally. The person is sick, he needs hospitalization. He needs more love than anybody else, he needs more warmth than anybody else. This is the way the commune becomes the crucible of transformation.

The sannyasins who are living outside the communes don't have this opportunity. If they can manage to be in the commune, they should be in the commune, because there you have the possibility of dropping all garbage, all your resentment, and becoming your natural self again. There you can find your original face again.

But there may be thousands of sannyasins who cannot manage for hundreds of reasons to be in a commune. For them I would suggest, if you cannot be a permanent resident in a commune, at least every year make it a point – six weeks, eight weeks, twelve weeks – to be in the commune. Learn the flavor of the New Man. Then perhaps even in the outside, old, rotten and dead society you may be able to protect yourself from their rottenness.

Just the other day one journalist had asked me, "Cannot your commune and the neighbors live in coexistence?" I simply said, "No!" I don't think he will be able to understand my no, there is every possibility he will misinterpret it. But my no has tremendous implications in it.

It means…he was asking, "Can you sleep in the same room in coexistence with a corpse?" It will be difficult to sleep if the corpse is also sleeping by the side on the double bed. You may have loved the corpse before, but now that you know it is a corpse you will be in a nightmare, waiting for the morning, to get out of this room.

I said no, because the old society and the New Man cannot coexist. The old, the dead will have to give way for the new, for the fresh.

We are not hostile towards them, for the simple reason that we are the new, and the victory is ours! They are hostile; deep down in their unconscious they understand that they're dying and you are living, that they are getting more and more rotten and you are getting more and more juicy. They *are* hostile. It is natural, because they have to empty the space for the New Man to take over.

Somebody else had asked me, "Do you intend to take over Oregon?"

I said, "No. Oregon is too small a thing. I would love to take over the whole world."

I am saying it on behalf of the new. I am saying it on behalf of the sun that is rising on the horizon. And it is not just a coincidence that I come from the East. In the West the sun is always going down, it is always sunset. The sunset represents death; the sunrise is the beginning of a new life.

It is not a coincidence that all that is great, beautiful, truthful, has arisen out of the East. India could not produce Adolf Hitler, Joseph Stalin, Benito Mussolini – just inconceivable! India could produce Gautam Buddha, Bodhidharma, Nagarjuna. We are not separate from existence, we are very deeply connected. The countries of sunrise have given the best to humanity.

India has never invaded any country. Such a big country could have produced the biggest empire in the world. If England can do it – which is just equal to a district of India, not even a state – why could India not create a great empire? On the other hand, the greatest emperor in India – and of course the greatest emperor in the whole history of man – Ashoka, renounced his empire. Not only did he renounce his empire, he sent his son and daughter as messengers of peace to different countries.

His daughter, Sanghamitra, went to Ceylon. Now Ceylon is Buddhist – then Ceylon was thought to be one of the most violent parts of the world. To convert Ceylon, Ashoka sends his beautiful only daughter? He understood human psychology: only something beautiful, something with freshness can help those barbarians then in Ceylon. It was a risk, but worth taking.

Those who are not living in my communes, start making efforts to move towards the communes. And nothing is impossible if you want to do it. What can prevent you? What is there left in the old society? Why are you hanging around there? You are being just as stupid as dogs are.

You give a dog a dry bone and he will start chewing it, and will enjoy it very much. Nothing comes out of the dry bone, there is no juice in it. But the dry bone makes wounds in his mouth and blood starts coming out of those wounds. He sucks his own blood, thinking it is coming from the dry bone.

Don't be foolish! The society outside is just a dry bone; you will be sucking your own blood. And they will all be hostile to you. They will try in every possible way to destroy your newness.

And remember, a new plant is very fragile – you just have to put a rock on top of it and it will disappear. And those people have big rocks – the church, the state. They will use all kinds of means. My sannyasins have been removed from colleges as teachers, from schools, from universities, for no reason – just because they are sannyasins. Strange – you don't remove anybody because he is a Christian, you don't remove anybody because he is a Hindu. Why are you afraid of the sannyasin?

Their attitude makes me feel proud of the sannyasins. They are afraid of you. The whole university may have hundreds of professors, but just a single sannyasin and they are afraid. They know that this single man is more powerful because he is new. The future belongs to him, not to them. To them belongs the past, which is just a burden.

But if you are removed from your job you will find it difficult to survive. Your family will be against you. From everywhere you will find antagonism. My sannyasins have been beaten on the streets. They had done no harm to anybody, but just because they were sannyasins they were beaten. Their malas have been taken.

There is no need to torture yourselves with those who are already dying. There is no need to cling to the family, to the society. Perhaps you may be helpful if you change yourself, move to the commune, and once in a while visit the family, the friends, and let them see what has happened to you, what is happening to you. That is the only way to help them.

Parents have written to me, "We were afraid that when our sons or our daughters became sannyasins we had lost them forever. But we want to be forgiven by you, because when this time my daughter came back home, for the first time we could relate heart to heart. There was no need to say much, she was just holding my hand and it was enough." Something transpired between the sannyasin daughter and the old father. She would not have been able to do it if she had remained with those old people. A certain gap is needed.

You need to live in the commune to catch the fire, to become aflame. Then once in a while, certainly go.

We are not interested in converting those dead people, because what is the point? We will have to celebrate every night in the crematorium; that will be too much unnecessary work. We are not interested in converting those people, but we are certainly interested that those whose days are gone should understand that they need not feel sorry; a better man, a better woman is going to take their place. They can go without any complaint. They can leave life joyously, because the people who are going to take over will be able to manage better than they have ever done.

For thousands of years, the politician and the priest, in a deep conspiracy, have been in power. But what have they done to you? What have they done to

the world? Monkeys remain monkeys, donkeys remain donkeys, camels remain camels – no transformation in human beings.

It is not their fault. A camel cannot see that there is anything better than a camel. It is just short-sightedness. And you cannot put glasses on the camel – have you seen a camel with glasses? He will stumble, fall down on the earth, he will not be able to make any sense of what is happening to his eyes. The monkeys cannot see beyond themselves.

Those old people, even if they can understand a simple thing, that sannyasins are going to create a better earth, which they themselves have failed to do…. And they had enough time – thousands of years – and they have not been able to create love, beauty, grace. All that they have been able to do is just train you, and force you into being phony.

I invite all the sannyasins of the world: slowly start moving to the closest commune. You will find a great rhythm between yourself and others. You will find for the first time a loving, compassionate, rejoicing group of people, who do not expect anything from you, but who are always ready to share with you whatever they have got.

Then once in a while go to the old society just to show them that you have started flowering, just to make them aware that they need not be worried about you. You have found the holy land, Israel. And we are creating many Israels around the earth.

Before true love arises in you there will be a time gap. The time gap can be made smaller if you are living with other sannyasins. If you are really immersed in the commune, the gap can completely disappear. The moment you drop the false values imposed upon you, resentment also will disappear.

And remember, when your resentment disappears, then for the first time you will be able to be loving towards your father, towards your mother, towards your brothers, sisters, towards your teachers – because you will have the understanding that whatsoever they did, there was no bad intention behind it.

They were simply doing to you what was done to them by their teachers, by their parents. You will have a deep compassion for them. You will have a new feeling arising in you, of love – and of sadness too, because those people have missed.

The day you can feel sad that your father and your mother have missed life, do you think you will be still angry against them? You will feel great love. Just go once in a while and share your love, share your song, share your dance. They will be surprised, and you will be surprised also. They will be surprised that this boy who has always been a troublemaker in the family has become so peaceful, so serene, just a silent lake full of lotus flowers.

And you will be surprised that they are not treating you the way they used to treat you. In fact, you will see that they want to understand what has happened to you. You look so beautiful, you look a totally new being – what has happened? They would like to know, and they would desire, if it is possible, for them also to be in the same space you are in.

But if sannyasins go on living for small things – the salary, the position, the power in the old rotten society – there is every possibility…. Those dead corpses are many, too many, and you will be very alone. And when death is stinking all around you, there is every possibility you will become accustomed to it, just the way others are accustomed to think this is the only fragrance in the world – the stinking death, the sick, slave mind, souls chained by the past, hearts burdened with mountains that are millions of years old. It is very difficult for you to save yourself where everything is just a grave.

Why live in a graveyard? Even if you are paid as a watchman for the graveyard, forget about that pay. Of course, you are great there – the only living being, and everybody is dead. You are almost a king – the watchman in a graveyard is almost a king. His whole empire…nobody can go against him, nobody can move against him. He is whole and sole authority; he can do anything to anybody. He can change their names, he can change their gravestones.

But please, don't enjoy such stupidities. Life is very valuable and very short. Move to the communes. Make new communes. If old communes are too big and cannot take you in, create new communes. These oases around the earth – which is completely a desert – will become the womb for the New Man to be born.

And don't be worried in the commune by people who start behaving…because they always wanted to rebel against anything that has been forced upon them. If they start behaving a little wrongly, don't be hard on them. Your hardness will not help them. Be soft, loving. Your love will cleanse them, and a natural growth of all that makes you the privileged beings in existence will arise of its own accord.

We don't teach any discipline. People ask me, "You don't teach any discipline – then how can five thousand people go on living together?" There is no need to teach discipline. All that is needed is that everybody should feel loved, respected, dignified – whatever he is doing.

In our commune whether you are the vice-chancellor of the university or just a driver makes no difference. These are functional things. One is serving the commune as a vice-chancellor, another is serving the commune as a driver. Both are necessary. Both are exactly dignified human beings.

Don't be worried about a few people being disrespectful towards me, because I have never come across a sannyasin who is disrespectful towards me. Perhaps I am blind, perhaps I don't understand the language of disrespect? No, I am not blind. No, I do understand every kind of language.

But when I am respectful to you, how can you manage to be disrespectful to me? It is just impossible. If I love you so much, how can you manage not to love me? And I am not *expecting* it. I love you because I cannot do anything else, and I am grateful to you that you don't refuse my love. That's enough for me.

But this is bound to stir your heart – a new

dimension opening. Your father was giving you gifts because you respected him; your mother was very favorable to you because you loved her. Between me and you there is nothing other than love.

It is happening for the first time in the history of man that a master declares himself as ordinary as you are, that a master wants to be just one amongst you. There is no desire in me to be holier than you, higher than you, better than you. How can you manage to disrespect me? If you can manage, manage. If you can manage to hate me, do it. Perhaps I deserve it. Perhaps that is the only way for you to get rid of the hate.

Even the person who hates me relates with me emotionally, just like the person who loves me. They both are relating to me: one positively, one negatively. And this is such a small job, for me to change the negative into the positive. I can do it any day, so I never feel in a hurry and jump upon you to change; I wait. I wait for the change to come on its own, otherwise, something of resentment will remain – a thin layer maybe, somewhere.

So as far as I am concerned, be absolutely sure I have no complaint against any sannyasin – even against those sannyasins who have left sannyas. My love to them remains the same, my hope for them remains the same. I know perfectly well, sooner or later, they will have to come back, because they cannot exist with the dead, old society. Once they have tasted the juices of a living, new commune, they cannot mix with the old society. Where are they going to go? Santa Fe?

It is so simple, you can understand…. Those few sannyasins who have left me have all gathered in Santa Fe. Now I have to take care of two communes: your commune and the commune of the camels in Santa Fe. But those camels are going to come back home sooner or later. You should not have any resentment for those who have left. Freedom to me is the highest value; there is nothing higher than that.

Out of freedom you have joined my caravan.

Out of freedom, some day you feel to depart.

I bless you exactly the same on both occasions. When you become a sannyasin I bless you, and when you drop sannyas I bless you – because sannyas does not matter. What matters is the respect, the dignity of a human being, and I cannot in any way hurt your dignity.

Beloved Bhagwan,

You have about four hundred thousand sannyasins around the world. Nobody ever reached that many people before. Is there any limit to the number of Your disciples?

First, correct your numbers. I don't have four hundred thousand sannyasins. I have almost double that number: eight hundred thousand sannyasins. And there is no limit – we are going to take the whole earth! There is no limit. And this takeover is not political. Politicians should not be worried about it. This takeover is far deeper, far more significant; it is spiritual.

The reason why nobody before me in his lifetime has been able to reach so many people is simple: he was not open to all. He had a certain prejudice, a certain ideology, a certain program that he wanted to impose upon you. He could reach only those people who were ready for that kind of program.

I don't have any program. I am available to all. Whether you are a Jew, or a Hindu, or a Mohammedan, or a Christian, or a communist does not make any difference, because I don't have any program to enforce upon you. My work is just the opposite: I am deprogramming you.

So if you are a communist, my work is the same – I deprogram the communist, he is no longer communist. If you are a Jew, I deprogram the Jew – the process is the same, you are no longer a Jew. If you are a German, I deprogram you. It is a little hard, but on the other hand, when the deprogramming succeeds, the German proves to be the most reliable. He takes a little time, resists, but when he gives way he gives way totally.

Whoever comes to me, I don't give him any discipline that he has to live by: don't smoke cigarettes, don't drink alcohol, don't look at somebody else's wife with desire.

I don't know…how can you look at a beautiful woman without desire? It is insulting to the woman, it is against her human dignity.

A woman, a beautiful woman, should be desired. The more she is desired, the more people look at her with desire, the more beautiful she becomes, the more contented she becomes.

I don't see that anything that all old, stupid religions have been telling you will prevent you from reaching God. In the first place there is no God to reach, so don't be worried about it. You are not going anywhere – to any God, to any paradise.

Secondly, I have not experienced that anything – alcohol, cigars, gambling, love affairs – anything that all the religions have been prohibiting can prevent your becoming enlightened. You can perfectly become enlightened, there is no need to sit under a bo tree.

You can become enlightened with a Havana cigar, resting in your chair by the side of Patanjali lake, naked – there is no problem in it. How can a Havana cigar prevent enlightenment? I don't see the arithmetic of it. It may perhaps help, but it cannot prevent.

It may help you to relax. It may help you just to be in the moment – naked, by the side of Patanjali Lake, enjoying the fresh air. A little champagne, may help you to be more meditative, because it will help you to get rid of other worries: that you have a wife, a nagging wife, that you have a husband who is just an idiot. Just a little champagne will take you away from all these ideas.

That's why I have been able to reach eight hundred thousand people around the world. And these are the sannyasins. There are millions more who are just on the borderline; any moment they can become sannyasins. There are many more who may never become sannyasins, but feel that they are cowards, feel that this is the right thing to do. Perhaps in their next life they may become sannyasins.

We are going to take over the world in a spiritual sense. We are not interested in taking over governments, nations. We are interested in destroying nations, governments – there is no need of all this paraphernalia! What is the need of a president? Yes, if there are nations, then presidents are needed, premiers are needed, commanders in chief are needed, an army is needed, nuclear weapons are needed.

I don't see that these things are needed to make humanity happier, more comfortable, more lovable, more dignified, more free. I don't see how these things can help; they have not helped for thousands of years. It is time that we take over the whole world spiritually, and dissolve all kinds of nonsense that have been torturing man, stopping his growth.

The world can live in so much peace, serenity…. My effort, in short, is not to take you to paradise, but to bring the paradise to you on *this* earth. It can be done, because I have done it for myself.

I don't think paradise can give anything more to me. In fact, I don't want to go to paradise – if there is any paradise – because I don't want to associate with those dead, ugly saints, ascetics, of all the religions. They will be there.

If…it is only an "if," there is no heaven, no hell, but if there is a hell I would like to go there, because there I will find all the juicy people of the world, not dead bones, dry. I will find there Maupassant, Tolstoy, Byron, Van Gogh, Lautrec, Rabindranath, Nijinsky – the list is infinite. All the poets, all the musicians, all the dancers, all the lovers, all those who are creative will be in hell because they were not religious people. They were not ascetics, they enjoyed life to the fullest.

Now, you cannot think of Byron in heaven.

England had to expel him – do you think paradise will accept him? England had to expel him because he was a woman's man. All the so-called ladies completely forgot that they were ladies. Byron was so beautiful, so charming, that any woman would have fallen in love with him, and hundreds of women did fall in love with him.

It is said that husbands became so much afraid – and you can imagine British husbands! – that if Byron entered a restaurant, husbands would take the hands of their wives and rush out from the other door. Finally they could not stand him anymore, he was creating so much nuisance. And he was doing nothing, he was just a loving being, non-possessive.

They expelled him. The day he was expelled, even the ladies from the royalty were there to give him a send-off – thousands of women. Now, this man cannot enter heaven, that much is certain. And I would like to meet Byron; I see a potential sannyasin in him.

Of course, I will be doing the same work in hell. If I can do this work on this earth, which is far worse than any hell, why can't I do this work in hell? It will be easier there, because there is a better quality of people – intelligent people, creative people. They are just waiting for me to come.

The moment you allow me to go, I will be with them. That is the company I would like to be associated with.

Enlightenment is You Completely Gone

Beloved Bhagwan,

Seeing that everyone wants so much to be enlightened, isn't it also true that we are all scared too? What is the fear that prevents us from relaxing into our own self?

There are many fears, not one.

First, if you want to be enlightened, you have to die a psychological death. You have to be reborn as a new spiritual being, and you don't know anything about spirituality. All that you know about yourself is your mind, centered around the ego.

It is a very strange phenomenon, that you are identified with something which you are not, and you have forgotten that which you are, have always been, will always be. There is no way to be anything else. Your being belongs to the existential. But there are layers and layers of conditioning – of parents, of teachers, of priests, of politicians. Between you, the real you, and you, the unreal you, there is a great line of people.

And naturally, you loved your parents, they loved you. Whatsoever they have done to you is absolutely unconscious, it was not intentional. They never wanted you to be a hypocrite, but they have made you a hypocrite. I never suspect their intentions. Their intentions were to make you something great, but they are as unconscious as you are. Their parents have given them their unconsciousness as an inheritance; and this has been going on since Adam and Eve. Every generation goes on loading the coming generation with all kinds of rubbish, stupidity, superstitions.

But don't be angry with them. You have heard about "the angry young man." The angry young man is an idiot. Anger is not going to solve anything; it is going to make everything more difficult and more complicated. Your parents, your teachers, your neighbors don't deserve anger; they deserve compassion. They could not do anything else. With all good wishes they have destroyed you, just the way their parents had destroyed them.

And if you don't become enlightened you are going to destroy your children. For their own sake, you are going to give them all kinds of crap.

You have been told you are a Christian, you are a Hindu, you are a Mohammedan. You came into the world as a *tabula rasa;* nothing was written on you. Your parents engraved on you and made you a Christian and forced the idea of Christianity on you, and they used your fear, your greed to implement it. You were made afraid of hell, you were made greedy for heaven. And of course, they wanted you not to fall into the ways of sin, but to follow the royal road of virtue.

Nothing was wrong in their intentions; their intentions are not in question. What is in question is that they were not conscious, that the seeds they were sowing in you were seeds of poison. No well-wishing, no good intentions are going to change those seeds. And once they have got roots in you it becomes more and more difficult to get rid of them, because you are identified with the tree of poisons.

It is difficult for a Christian to put Christianity aside. He will feel he is doing something like a betrayal. Putting aside Christianity he will feel he is betraying Jesus Christ. He is not betraying anyone. He is simply trying to get out of the mess of conditioning that all kinds of people have put upon him.

My grandmother – my mother's mother – was a tremendously beautiful woman. She loved me so much that I was more in touch with her than with my own mother. I used to come to my mother's house to eat twice a day, and then I went to the school. But every night I was in my grandmother's house. She lived in the same town; when her husband died, she moved there. She was alone, there was no other child – my mother was her only child.

But she was of an independent character. Everybody tried to persuade her to live with my father's family, but she said, "That is not possible. Not that I don't love you and don't want to live with you, but I want to be utterly independent, on my own."

So she lived just a few houses away, so that my father and my mother could take care in any emergency – she was old. But I was sleeping every night at her house. She had all blessings for me.

One day when I was carrying her spiritual book of Jainism, it fell. She immediately fell on the earth and put her head at the imaginary feet of the religious book. I asked her, "What are you doing? A book is a book – religious or unreligious, it doesn't matter. It is printed on the same kind of paper, with the same kind of ink, with the same kind of words."

She was old, but very understanding. She said, "Perhaps you are right, but my whole life is involved. The religious book falling on the ground is not a good sign; we have to ask its forgiveness. It has to be on our heads, not at our feet."

I used to argue with her. I said, "The book is dead. Whether you put it on your head or you stand

Don't make enlightenment a desire; otherwise you will go on missing. What I suggest to you is, forget about enlightenment. It has nothing to do with you, you will never see it; it happens when *you* are not. When you have peeled the onion completely, when your ego evaporates, it is there. But you cannot say, "I have become enlightened." The "I" is no more there – enlightenment is there.

on it, it will not know the difference."

She was shocked, and at the same time she said, "What you are saying, I can see the point of it, but now it is too late. I am so old – now to start living from scratch, now to start thinking again from the very beginning is a great task. And it is not only a question of this book; so much is involved in it – my attitude towards the religion, my attitude towards the priests, the monks, my attitude towards my parents.

"I got this mind as an inheritance, and it is all that I have. You can destroy it, but then I will feel empty. And when death is coming closer and I can hear the footsteps of death louder and louder, my son, it is too late. I don't want to die empty."

This is the fear. You are afraid of dropping any conditioning because that conditioning is giving you a certain personality. But you are not aware of that, so you are not worried about it. Your personality has taken the place of your individuality. And to throw away your personality – which means all your past, the whole of it; there is no question of choice....

It is not a question that there are bad parts in it, throw them; and there are good parts in it, preserve them. Your whole past is imposed by others on you, so whether it is good or bad does not matter. The significant thing to remember is that it is not your discovery, it is all borrowed; it is secondhand, thirdhand – perhaps through millions of hands it has passed. It is really dirty. You have to get rid of it in its totality.

There will be a gap when you will feel completely lost. You used to know yourself, who you were. There will come a gap when you will not know who you are, but that is a beautiful experience, because your innocence is back again. You are born again; it is a rebirth. Now you can start discovering.

The whole territory is new, you have never been here before. You were kept going round and round on the circumference of your existence. It is adventurous, it is a great challenge. Fear arises. Fear arises because what you think you are is certainly in your hands. And the individuality I am talking about, you don't have in your hands. You don't know what you are going to discover, or whether there is anything to discover or not.

There is a proverb in many languages...similar proverbs: "Half a loaf of bread in the hand is better than the full loaf far away." And I am asking you to drop the half loaf for something that is so far away from you right now. Fear is natural. It is nothing to be worried about, it just has to be understood.

One fundamental law of life: you were as alive – perhaps more alive – in your mother's womb, but you were not a Christian. You had not yet heard of Jesus Christ, you were not carrying a Bible, you were not clinging to a cross. You had no idea what your name is, you had no ambition to become the president of America, to be the richest man in the world. You had no ambitions. Ambitions are extensions of your ego: the bigger the ambition, the bigger ego you are searching for.

At birth you were simply there. So one thing is certain, that whatever you have gained after your birth is not really a gain, it is a loss. On each step you have been losing the real and getting cluttered with the unreal, losing the precious and getting attached to some junk.

It is a question of understanding that even if you drop your whole past you are not going to die, because you were alive for nine months in your mother's womb perfectly well. In fact, scientists say that during the nine months in the mother's womb the child grows more, faster, than he will grow in his whole life of seventy years. He passes through so many phases; he passes through almost all the phases humanity has passed through. At a certain moment he looks like a monkey in the mother's womb. Earlier than that, he looks like a fish.

It is now almost an agreed idea that man was born in the ocean as a fish, millions of years ago. All those millions of years, the child passes through in days. From the fish to the monkey is a long way; from the monkey to man is also not a short way.

In nine months he moves exactly, step by step, as the whole humanity has moved. He repeats the whole history. So it is absolutely clear that the way he grows in the mother's womb…the speed is phenomenal. He will not grow that fast in a lifetime of seventy years. In fact, in those seventy years he will simply grow old. He will become less and less alive. In those seventy years he is moving towards his grave. He is not growing up, he is going down – down the drain. So there is no need to be afraid of being reborn.

I can assure you only of one thing: there is no question of belief. You can see the point yourself, that without being a Christian, without being a Jew, without being a Hindu, without being a communist, you were perfectly alive and kicking.

In that innocence you have known the most wonderful experience ever.

Sigmund Freud has many beautiful insights. One of his insights is that everybody on the earth has some idea of a paradise. There is no culture, no civilization in the past, in the present, which has not had some kind of idea about a paradise. From where does this idea come?

Sigmund Freud's insight is that this idea comes from the womb of the mother. Those nine months were of tremendous comfort, of absolute luxury. You had no responsibility, no burden on your head; you had no duty. You were not doing anything at all except living – and living alone! You were so full of life that there was no need for someone else to fulfill you.

Those nine months in the mother's womb you have forgotten consciously, but your unconscious remembers them. In deep hypnosis you can be made to remember that experience. That unconscious experience of the most beautiful life for nine months is the reason that people are searching for a paradise – the paradise they have lost.

That is the basic root of the story of Adam and Eve being thrown out of the garden of God. That story is not a historical truth, but it has a psychological insight. And around the world, in every religion, there is something similar to it: that there was a day when you lost contact with all that is beautiful, glorious. The story is simply symbolic. The child leaving the womb of the mother is really being thrown out of the Garden of Eden.

Now begins a tedious journey – from the very beginning, painful. As he opens his eyes…. His eyes are very delicate: for nine months he has lived in darkness. There was no need for him to open his eyes, or even if he had opened them there was nothing to see. Now he opens his eyes – glaring lights; he starts being hurt. In the mother's womb he was not breathing for himself, it was the mother who was breathing for him. Even that much responsibility was not placed on him, that he has to breath for himself.

Thrown out of that beautiful space, he gets his first experience of the world. The doctor hangs him upside down, and hits him on his buttocks. A strange reception! And the child has no idea what is going to happen now. He is so small, everybody is so big. And this Nazi behavior of the doctors…. Something better can be found. It is barbarous – of course it is done with all good intentions.

The doctor does it for two reasons. One, he hangs him upside down so any mucus that is inside his breathing passage comes out. Because he has not been breathing in his mother's womb, there is mucus filling the tube that he has to use now. But in a scientific age we can find a better way to take the mucus out; it should not be done the way it is done. We have vacuum cleaners. Can't we manage some vacuum cleaner for the poor child that takes out the mucus?

And secondly, as the child is born, the cord that joins him with his mother's womb is immediately cut. It is a shock, the greatest shock of your life, to be cut from your life source. You will have many shocks in the future, life will give you many troubles; but the child – who has known no shock, no trouble – is really hurt. It is almost murderous to cut the cord that joins him with the mother.

But the doctor does it with all good intentions – because if the cord is not cut the child may not learn how to breathe. But that is not a fact; the doctors have been in an unnecessary hurry. If the child is left on the mother's belly – he was inside the belly for nine months – if he is left again on the mother's belly…just two minutes are needed. But to the doctor even two minutes seem to be too long. And he has to deliver many other children; it is simply his profession.

Just after two minutes, resting on his mother's belly, the child starts breathing on his own. A little patience….but who is patient? And after the child has started breathing on his own, then you can cut the cord and it will not be a shock. He has become an individual on his own.

The child should be given birth to in a very dim light – soft, soothing. And as soon as the child is able to breathe on his own, the first thing should be to put him in a hot water tub because he has been, in his mother's womb, floating in warm water that is constituted of exactly the same chemicals as sea water.

So man has come millions of years away from his first ancestors who were born in the ocean, but basically nothing has changed. Every child is born in the ocean even now. And women who have known pregnancy will be aware that when they are pregnant, suddenly they start hankering to eat salty things, because the child needs water as salty as the ocean.

So just a small, warm, salt-water bath, and the child will not feel shocked, will not feel expelled. The story of Adam and Eve will become absurd. The child will feel welcomed, entering a vast world of exploration. He will feel freedom from a confined space. And that kind of child will not be desirous of any paradise; his *life* will be a paradise. He will not hanker for and desire something after death because he lost something at birth which can be attained again only after death.

Why do your religions say that paradise is after death? It is simple – because your paradise was before birth. It is appealing, logical.

I want you to remember that you have existed for nine months with great energy, growing tremendously – with such speed that in nine months you passed through millions of years. And you had no political ideology, you had no religious theology. You had not even a name. Nameless, religionless, without politics you have existed. So there is no need to fear.

I can only make it clear to you that there is no need to fear. You can drop all that has been added to you after birth, still you will be living – not only living, but living abundantly. You need not wait for death. You can give death to your personality *now,* and be reborn.

That's exactly what enlightenment is: the personality dies and the individuality which was repressed by the personality starts growing, flowering.

But your question raises one more question. Listening to me, or reading about the idea of enlightenment, you start being greedy for it. That's where you miss from the very beginning. You say, "I want to be enlightened." Wanting is a barrier. Who is this "I" that wants to be enlightened?

This "I" is your very ego, which is preventing you from being enlightened. Now this "I" which was trying to become a great leader of men, the richest person in the world, the most powerful president – of America or the Soviet Union – the same "I" gets a new idea to become even bigger than all these presidents and all these rich people – enlightenment. The ego says, "Great! I want to be enlightened." The ego cannot be enlightened, just as darkness can not become light.

Listening to me, or getting the idea from somewhere else, remember: you cannot *want* to be enlightened. You *can* be enlightened, but you cannot want it, you cannot desire it. It is not some commodity that you can purchase. It is not some country that you can invade. It is not there – outside – that you can approach and find it. Enlightenment is the name of an inner experience in which both are involved: death of the personality and rebirth of the individuality.

The people in the monasteries around the world are desiring to be enlightened, to be awakened, to be liberated – so many words for the same experience. But they are just being stupid. They are, in fact, by desiring enlightenment, making enlightenment a commodity in the market.

Enlightenment is not something to be desired.

Then what has one to do? One has to understand one's personality, layer by layer. Forget all about enlightenment, it has nothing to do with you. One thing is certain: you cannot be enlightened. Begin with what you are.

Just as one peels an onion, peel your personality, layer by layer. Go on throwing those layers. New layers will be there, but finally a moment comes when the onion disappears and there is only emptiness in your hands. That moment is the moment of enlightenment. You cannot desire it, because desire adds another layer to your onion – and a far more dangerous layer than any other layer.

Becoming a president is not such a big thing, any idiot can do it. In fact, idiots are doing it all around the world. Who else is interested in becoming a president or a prime minister? I have never seen any man of wisdom trying to become the president, the premier.

Have you observed a strange fact, that in the past there have been a few kings who became enlightened? Ashoka in India became enlightened. He was one of the greatest emperors in the world – in fact, India has never been that big since him. Parts of India went on being invaded, becoming new countries. Today India is only one-third of what it was in Ashoka's empire.

There have been other emperors in China, in Japan, in Greece who have become enlightened. An emperor is not one who has desired to become an emperor. Just as somebody is born a beggar, he is born an emperor. He takes it for granted; it does not become a layer of greed around his onion.

But we have never heard of any president, any prime minister becoming enlightened. It sounds strange, but the reason is clear. Presidents are not born, they have to struggle for it, they have to lie and promise – knowing perfectly well that these promises cannot be fulfilled. They have to be diplomatic, they can't say what they want. They go on saying things, and they are never going to do them. The politician has to be very cunning.

No politician has been known to become enlightened, for the simple reason that in a democratic world, where monarchy has disappeared, to be the head of the state is one of the greatest desires of the ego. But the desire for enlightenment is the ultimate desire; you cannot desire anything bigger than that. You have asked for the ultimate bliss, you have asked for the ultimate existential wisdom.

Don't make enlightenment a desire; otherwise you will go on missing. What I suggest to you is, forget about enlightenment. It has nothing to do with you, you will never see it; it happens when *you* are not. When you have peeled the onion completely, when your ego evaporates, it is there. But you cannot say, "I have become enlightened." The "I" is no more there – enlightenment is there.

The fear is natural, because you have to drop your whole personality, and that's all you have got right now. You don't know there is something behind it. You want to gain more, and I am saying to you to lose everything that makes *you*. That's the fear. If you listen to the fear, then there is no hope.

But in fact, what have you got? Anxiety, anguish, boredom, despair, failure – thousands of complexes. This is your whole treasure. Just look at it! What is the fear in dropping this treasury, in getting rid of your anxiety, throwing away your boredom?

But things are really complicated. Why are you bored? And why can't you get rid of it? There must be some vested interest in it. You are bored with your wife or your husband. Every wife and every husband are bound to come to a point when they are fed up with each other, bored. But there is a complication. You cannot just say goodbye to your wife. You have got children, you both love them, you don't want to leave those children. There is going to be a fight in a court over who is to have the children; both can't have them.

You have a certain prestige in the society. People think you are one of the model couples because they see you always showing love to each other. When you leave for the office you kiss your wife, when you come from the office you kiss your wife – as a ritual. Neither you mean anything nor she means anything, and you both know it. And while you are kissing your wife you are saying within yourself, "To hell with all this!"

But the people don't hear what you are saying within yourself. They just see. "Thirty years of marriage, and still they are so loving, as if on their car the board is still hanging: Just married. Their honeymoon seems to be becoming longer and longer – thirty years of honeymoon!" There is no end to it. When you go in the society you pretend; you have to keep people's idea of you as the best couple. These are your investments.

Perhaps you are rich because you married a rich woman. If you drop her you will be a beggar again; you don't want to do that. Perhaps you got a good employment because of your wife's good looks – it is a very strange world – or your wife's relations, influence. You may lose the job if you drop your wife.

So how to drop the boredom? – the boredom is connected with so many investments. It needs courage, great courage. And I would like to say to you that it is better to be a beggar but without boredom, far better than to be an emperor and bored, because boredom is spiritual begging. And it never comes alone. If you are bored there will be despair, there will be anxiety, a continuous tension in the mind: What to do? You have to go on living with a woman or a man you would like to kill – and you have to kiss them.

To drop boredom means to take a revolutionary step, whatever the cost; you are not going to drag through your life as a bored man, because what is the point of living? And you will see all around the world, everybody is bored. Somebody is bored with his work, his job. He never wanted to be a doctor, but his parents forced him to be a doctor because it is respectable, profit-making. You make the profit, you get the respect, and still you are called a great public servant, because you are serving humanity. It is really great!

Your parents forced you to become a doctor. You hate it, you never wanted it; you wanted to become a painter. But nobody listened to you, they said, "You are crazy. If you want to be a painter you will die as a beggar on the street. Forget all about this nonsense. When one is young all kinds of romantic ideas come into the mind. Cool down, boy. We also have seen younger days, and we have also dreamed of great things, but now we know that all those romantic ideas are just a passing phase. If we allow you to become a painter, you will never forgive us! We cannot allow you to be a painter."

You want to be a musician, a dancer, a sculptor, but nobody is going to support you. You wanted to be a dancer and you have become a businessman; you are bored with it. You really want one day to hang yourself from a tree and be finished with it all. But that too you cannot do because there is so much to do – you have to fill in your tax return forms, and the tax department is after you…. You don't have time to hang yourself.

So many things are unfinished around you. First you have to finish everything, then go and hang yourself. But things will always remain unfinished. And the idea of hanging yourself gives a little relaxation, gives a certain pleasure that whatsoever the situation, there is always one exit: you can always hang yourself. So what is the hurry? And who knows?

Tomorrow things may change, you may find the right woman.

There is no right woman, no right man, nobody has ever found one. But the fantasy of finding the right man, the right woman…. Every couple, when they fall in love for the first time, think they are made for each other: this is the woman he has dreamed of always. This is what the man, the woman, has been always thinking of, desiring. But by the time the honeymoon is over you know you are caught with a wrong person; you are not made for each other.

But you go on fantasizing, "Perhaps some other woman?" – because the world is so full of women, so full of men. This time you missed, *next* time….

One of my friends got married three times. It is difficult in India to get a divorce. Almost his whole life was wasted; women were the trouble. The law is not easy, but somehow he managed, because in India you can somehow manage everything. All that is needed is money, and he had money. You can bribe everybody. It is a national tradition and not new, very ancient.

Indians have been bribing God, so what do they care about bribing a clerk or a judge? When the Indian goes to the temple and says to his god, "If I win this lottery, I will present you with sweets worth five rupees" or "I will give a feast to eleven brahmins," what is this? And the lottery is one million rupees; with five rupees he is trying to get one million rupees! And for centuries Indians have been bribing God; it is their heritage. Nobody feels bad about it.

You can give a bribe to anybody – neither you feel bad about it nor he feels bad about it, because he is doing you work. It is almost payment for the work. And he is doing work which is far costlier than the bribe you are giving him. You manage everything. You can murder, and you will be released respectfully by the court; all that you need is money.

So one goes on thinking that tomorrow may be different. My friend changed wives three times, and he was always telling me, "This time I am not going to fall for a woman like the one I am getting rid of. She is a real bitch!"

And I told him, "You will always fall in love with a real bitch."

He said, "This is strange. You go on insisting, and the wonder is that you are always right! The next woman proved as bitchy as the first, the third woman proved as bitchy as the others. How do you predict?"

I said, "I don't predict, I am not an astrologer. I simply know you; what kind of woman will be appealing to you, that I know. Why had you fallen for the first woman? Have you thought, analyzed, what qualities of that woman have attracted you? And who is going to find the second woman for you? You will, again, and you will again be attracted to the same things.

"You have not changed, your attractions have not changed. You have never bothered that you are responsible for having chosen that woman. That's why three times you have got the same kind of commodity…again and again and again. It is not a question of divorce, it is not a question of changing women; it is a question of changing your mind."

But people always try to dump things on others. You are in anxiety because your children are becoming hippies. Your girl is taking dope, your boy is doing everything that is wrong – long hair, beard, drugs, and he has dropped out of the university. You are in anxiety: What is going to happen? You are dumping your anxiety on the girl, on the boy, on the wife – anybody will do.

Do you think if your boy was going perfectly straight, your girl was not getting pregnant before marriage, if they were not on drugs do you think you would have been without anxiety? I know many people whose daughters are following whatsoever they say, whose sons are doing their education the way the parents want – still they have anxiety over something else. They will find some other object to become worried about.

If you have children you are worried about your

children. If you don't have children you are worried why God has not given you children. It seems to be really a zoo of all kinds of animals, this world of ours.

Dropping the layers of your ego means that you are ready to commit a psychological suicide. I call it sannyas just to give it a good name, because if I call it suicide you will be more frightened. You have come here to be enlightened, not to commit suicide. But the reality is that unless you commit suicide there is no enlightenment. People want enlightenment, and they don't want to drop anything, to lose anything.

The day I said, "Before I leave the world I would like to give my sannyasins rainbow-colored robes, there should be no need by that time for my sannyasins to wear red clothes" – immediately, the next day, people started reaching the commune's office, saying, "We want sannyas, but we are not going to use red clothes, nor are we going to use the mala. Give us sannyas. Bhagwan has said already that the red clothes or the mala are not sannyas."

My secretary came to me and asked, "What to do? You go on creating trouble for us. In the first place, from where are we to get rainbow dresses? And people are understanding according to their mind. They are understanding that all the colors of the rainbow can be used – somebody in red, somebody in blue, somebody in green – the commune will be using all the colors. They have not understood what you were saying." I was absolutely clear, but you managed to understand what you wanted.

I received a few letters: "We are thinking of taking sannyas, but your idea of a rainbow-colored dress made us frightened, because in the past only buffoons, jokers in the circus, have used rainbow dresses. We don't want to become laughingstocks. Red is perfectly good."

I told my secretary, "Tell these people, 'Then why are you waiting, if red is perfectly good?'" It became good in comparison to the rainbow robe. It is not good in comparison to ordinary clothes that people wear, because in red clothes you will immediately attract attention, discrimination. People will not feel at ease with you. They will be hostile to you.

I have asked my sannyasins to be in red clothes, with the mala, with the locket of my picture, just to see whether you can gather a little courage or not. If even this much courage is not possible then you cannot commit suicide, you cannot drop your ego.

You want enlightenment as you are. Now, that is impossible. You will have to chop out many things which have become almost identical with yourself. And that's what I am doing continuously – hitting, hammering, shocking you. And I will go on doing everything possible that can shock you, hurt you, wound you because I want you to become aware that it is your ego that gets wounded, it is your ego that gets hurt.

Just the other day I was saying I am going to start smoking Havana cigars while delivering the religious, spiritual discourse. Now many camels will start moving towards Santa Fe. "What kind of a master smokes Havana cigars?" Do you think you are going away because of my Havana cigars? No. It hurts your ego. You wanted a master nobody can say anything against. You wanted to be a disciple of a great master who has extraordinary powers, who changes water into wine.

I also do miracles – I change wine into water. So if you see me drinking champagne, don't be worried. The moment I touch it, it is water. But champagne by my side, and the camels will get troubled, will start looking at the map – where is Santa Fe? All the camels are going towards Santa Fe.

It is not my champagne, it is not my Havana cigars, it is not anything to do with me – it is your ego. This is a great conspiracy that has been going on between the disciples and the so-called masters all through history. The disciple feels his ego fulfilled because he has found the right master, who does not smoke Havana cigars, does not drink champagne. Both are controlling each other.

The master cannot do anything against the expectations of the disciples, because then he will lose disciples, and with fewer disciples you are a smaller master. It is a question of numbers; with more disciples you are a bigger master. A great number of disciples, and you are the greatest master in the world.

So he cannot lose camels; even if the camels never change, he is not going to do anything that will make the numbers become less. It is a politics of numbers. And, of course, because he fasts, he can force his disciples to fast.

I cannot. I do not fast. In fact, I cannot go to sleep in the night unless I have eaten Indian sweets – against my doctors' advice. I have told them, "It is your business to figure it out. Diabetes I give to you, you figure it out." But I cannot go to sleep…. My grandmother used to keep the sweets that I liked by my bedside, because in the middle of the night I might wake up. Then to go to sleep again needs sweets; otherwise I cannot.

You want a master who fulfills your ego, but you don't know – the man who fulfills your ego, who is in tune with your expectations, is your enemy; he is not your master. The sooner you get rid of such a man, the better. But no, if a master goes on a fast for twenty-one days every year he will gather many people around him who will say, "This is the man. It is worth being a disciple of this man." And what has he done? He has just been hungry, starving, for twenty-one days.

Why don't you go to Ethiopia? You will find great masters who are fasting unto death – not twenty-one days, because nobody dies after twenty-one days of fasting. It takes ninety days for a man to die by fasting.

But you are not aware of the conspiracy. The man who fasts for twenty-one days becomes authoritative, more powerful than you. He demands that you at least fast for three days, and you cannot say to him that he is asking too much. He is fasting for twenty-one days, and he asks you only to fast for three days. He is perfectly authorized to ask it. He is celibate, he asks you to be celibate. He eats only one time a day, he demands you also eat one time a day.

Do you see the mutual conspiracy? You feel you are the disciple of a great master – of course you are a great disciple as a consequence: a simple arithmetic. Great masters have only great disciples, but those masters are fulfilling their egos, and they are fulfilling your egos. No transformation is possible in such a conspiracy.

I don't give you any discipline. I don't command you to do certain things and not to do certain things, for the simple reason…who am I? I have no authority over you.

I look at you as my friends. If you think about me as your master, that is your generosity. But it is not required by me. This way I remain free from your expectations, and I keep you free from my expectations. In this way I am not trying to fulfill my ego, and I am trying in every possible way to destroy your ego the way I destroyed mine.

It is a difficult task. Fear is bound to be there, but to act according to your fear is to degrade yourself even from camelhood. You become a monkey, or a donkey, or finally a Yankee. Perhaps you are there already, at the stage called Yankee.

I will accept you at any stage. I will not demand that you become something else, something more, something bigger, something holier, something spiritual. No, all those are games of the same ego we want to get rid of.

Don't follow your fear instinct, because that is going to make you a coward. It degrades your humanity. It is a humiliation imposed by yourself. Whenever you see some fear, go against it! A simple criterion: whenever you see there is fear, go against it and you will be always moving, growing, expanding, coming closer to the moment when ego simply drops – because its whole functioning is through fear. And the absence of the ego is enlightenment; it is not something plus.

Enlightenment is not something plus added to you. Enlightenment is you completely gone.

It is minus phenomenon; you are no longer there. It does not happen to *you*, it happens when you are no longer hindering it, when you are not. That's why I call enlightenment a psychological suicide.

Chase the Woman Gently

DISCOURSE 27,   July 25, 1985

Beloved Bhagwan,

I have noticed that the women here are becoming juicier and more active, while we men are becoming lazier and lazier. Would you comment?

The women is not the weaker sex, as it has been said by man for centuries. The woman is the stronger sex. She is *made* weaker. For centuries upon centuries she has been conditioned; she has been told she needs a protector.

The Indian scripture of Manu, which has dominated the Hindu mind for five thousand years and still dominates it, says that when the woman is a child she should be dependent on the parents, protected by the parents. When she is young, she should be dependent on the husband and protected by the husband. When she is old, she should still remain dependent – on the boys, her children, and be protected by her own children. For her whole life she has to be protected by somebody. If for thousands of years you protect somebody in this way, you are bound to create weakness, dependence, fear.

And it has been almost accepted as a scientific fact that man is the stronger sex. It is absolutely wrong! The woman is the stronger sex, and she has to be, because she has to produce children. She has to be pregnant and go through all the troubles of pregnancy.

Not a single man could stand one pregnancy. Just think of yourself being pregnant for nine months: You cannot eat, you vomit; you go on carrying a weight which is growing bigger and bigger within your belly. And then the final stage, the baby comes out of you. The passage is so small, the baby is big; it is painful. The woman passes almost through death when the child is born. And you think she is weaker than man?

Women live longer than men all over the world; the difference is of five years. If man lives on average seventy years, the woman lives on average seventy-five years. Strange, the weaker sex lives longer.

Man is more prone to sicknesses, diseases, infections, than woman. And the difference is not small, it is double. Women are prone to sickness in comparison to man just half as much; if they get sick, it is only fifty percent as often. If man has to be considered, he gets sick and is available to any infection twice as often as women, and more.

What is the cause of it? The woman has more resistance power. The man is very weak against small bugs – and yet he becomes Muhammed Ali the great! He cannot fight small bugs, he is incapable of doing any boxing against them. But the woman does.

It is a very strange thing that the suicide rate of the man is double that of the woman – and woman is the weaker sex? She suffers more, her whole life in the past has been of suffering. Women have been treated like cattle.

In China for thousands of years the woman has

not been believed to have a soul. So if the husband murders his wife, he commits no crime. The woman was a possession. Without a soul, so much resistance against diseases? And man has a soul, but the resistance is only half that which a woman has.

The man becomes frantic very soon, carries thousands of worries in his head, is almost on the verge of falling into anxiety, anguish, suicide. It starts even in the mother's womb.

An experienced woman who has given birth to one or two children can tell whether the child in her womb is male or female. How can she guess it? Very simple guesswork, which is absolutely certain. The boy starts kicking in her womb; the girl is calm and quiet. And the mother can feel that difference. The boy is becoming tense, worried already, already trying to learn boxing. The girl is very silent in the mother's womb – creates no movement, is more stable, more centered, more grounded.

Women threaten that they will commit suicide, but they do not do it. The difference is again the same: men commit suicide twice as often as women do. And it has to be understood that their suicides are also different. The woman commits suicide because the man forces her to commit suicide. Man commits suicide because of his own anguish, worry, despair.

If the woman were not forced by man to commit suicide, no woman would commit suicide. In fact, the woman's suicide is really a murder – murder by the man: man's society, man's rule, man's power. And the woman has survived all along without any complaint. That is strength. Man forcing the woman to commit suicide should be punished – it is a murder. But behind the word suicide he is completely free of any crime.

Your question is that women are becoming juicier here every day. They would become juicier all around the earth every day; they just have to be given the opportunity. It is their intrinsic nature to be juicier. The woman has to nourish the child – she needs the juice. The woman attracts the male – she

So just understand the natural way of things, and don't go against nature, because going against nature creates all sorts of problems. To be natural is to be unproblematic. And to be natural is so beautiful. To be natural is so at ease, at home.

has to be juicier. She is certainly more beautiful, more proportionate; her body is an artwork.

I do not believe in the bogus Christian story that God created man first. The story must have been created by a man, because what use is man? And then he created the woman, taking a rib out of the man. This is simply to insult women: "You are nothing but a rib taken out of man. You are not human beings."

If I have to write the story, I will say God first created Eve, not Adam – because the woman is creative, she is going to give birth. In fact, there was no need for Adam to be created by God. The story is, that God made love to the first woman he made. If that is true, then Adam is simply superfluous. The woman, and God making love to the woman…Adams will follow of their own accord. Adam need not be created, he will be born. But you need the woman *first*. Without her there is no possibility of anything getting born.

But for thousands of years, if you go on hammering the idea that woman is a weaker sex…. The woman has shrunk, she has accepted the idea. She has lived according to the male chauvinist's philosophy.

Here in this commune it is totally different. The woman finds herself absolutely free from all the jargon that man has been teaching her. And we have given all the opportunities to women that no society anywhere has been able to give them. All societies have taken away opportunities – and things need opportunities to grow, to reach to their potential.

The woman has somehow survived because she is so strong. But she has only survived – no nourishment. Here she is nourished, here she knows she is accepted on an equal basis. In fact, the women in the commune have more responsible posts than men. This is just a compensation – small, but it may become the model for the whole universe. And they are running the commune better than any society run by men.

In four years of the commune's existence there has not been a single crime, not a single murder, not a single suicide. Man has not been able to create a society where crimes are not growing. And as the woman becomes juicier, more powerful, stronger, takes her natural position, the man is bound to become lazier. That is his nature – he is bone lazy.

I have been in a few aboriginal communities in India. They are very primitive people; they live in the mountains, in the jungles. Somehow they are free from the stupidity the whole humanity lives under. Their small, primitive communities are matriarchal, not patriarchal. The woman rules, the woman is powerful. But I saw men almost shrunken, lazy, doing nothing. I was surprised. What happened to the strong sex?

The strong sex – the so-called strong sex – seeing that the woman is doing perfectly well, better than he can do, has done only one thing: he has married four, five women, and he sits in the house in the rocking chair, smoking, looking after the children. The woman works for everything – for food, for clothing, for all the necessities of life. Man's work has become confined just to looking after the children – which is not much of a job.

The woman takes all the responsibility of the outside world – farming the land, growing the gardens, weaving the clothes. And she also is responsible for the household: making food, making the house comfortable – and the man simply goes on becoming lazier and stupider. I would not like it to happen here. It is ugly.

Man should take the challenge. If women are becoming juicier, now is the time to prove…. And as far as laziness is concerned, I alone am enough. I am ready to take all your laziness upon myself. But remember that you have been for centuries lying, befooling. This is a great opportunity to prove that you are stronger – but every man deep down knows he is not.

Every man feels a deep inferiority complex, for the simple reason that he cannot produce children, he cannot give birth to life. His function in giving birth to children is only that of an injection. Any injection can do that. In fact, in the future, injections will be doing that; then man will be completely out of a job.

Don't be lazy…because it is easier to be lazy. Seeing that everything is going perfectly well, and women are doing perfectly well, the natural instinct is to fall into laziness; there is no need for you to do anything. But this is a wrong way of thinking. When women are doing so much, at least you have to prove your equality. You cannot prove that you are superior – forget it, that is completely out of the question – but you can at least prove yourself equal.

I know you cannot produce children. That inferiority in you is to be used as another opportunity. Down the centuries man has been using that, and you are not to forget it. Man has created great music, great art, great poetry, great drama, great sculpture. Women have not done anything.

In the first place they were not allowed. In the second place, to give birth to a child, a living child, is such a great creative act that they don't feel they have to make a dead statue. Michelangelo may make a beautiful statue of Jesus Christ, but it does not breathe. Mary, who gave birth to Jesus, is far superior. Howsoever beautiful the statue, it is just a dead stone. Jesus was an alive human being. So the woman has no inferiority complex in her.

I would like you to be creative. Man has to prove his equality, and he can prove his equality only by creating. And there is so much to create! We are in a desert, and we have to create a lush, green oasis. We are surrounded by all kinds of hostile forces. We have to be strong enough to face them.

It is a great encounter between the past and the future. We have to stand for the future; they are standing for the past. Those who stand for the past miss the present. Those who stand for the future have to take care of the present, because the present is going to become the future.

Don't get lazy because women are doing perfectly well, taking all the responsible jobs in the commune. Gather yourself together, take responsibility. Of course you cannot give birth to a child – there is no need – but you can give birth to many things which the woman may not be attracted to. Yes, beautiful paintings are needed, beautiful gardens are needed, beautiful lakes are needed; beautiful music, poetry, literature, are needed.

Perhaps the woman may not feel attracted. She is already a creator, a born creator. Man is not a born creator. Unless you make the effort to be a creator – that is, to be a painter, or a gardener, or a farmer – you are bound to fall into laziness. And laziness is a slow death. You cannot live life abundantly if you are lazy; life needs strength, overflowing energy. You cannot even love, because you don't have any juice to share. You are becoming a dry bone.

I have been receiving letters from the women sannyasins, asking, "What is happening? In the whole world, man chases the woman. Here we have to chase men – and they escape!" This is ugly. This is humiliating yourself – or have you become so lazy that you cannot even chase a woman? Do you want a rocking chair? The women can provide you with a rocking chair – so sit on the rocking chair. But you cannot even sit there, because women will be chasing you. They are full of juice and they want to share it, and it can be shared only with somebody who is equally overflowing.

Our commune is proving something significant. It is proving that if women are given the opportunity, they will prove far superior to men.

And if women are given the opportunity, the men will become lazier. They will not feel competent enough, so rather than joining in the race, it is safer for their egos to sit by the side of the road. But that is a kind of suicide. You have to take the challenge. Come out of your laziness! And you become juicier only when you are creative. That's why poets, painters, musicians, are more juicy than others – even if they are creating third-rate music.

The music of the Beatles cannot be called music, it is sheer madness. You cannot put the Beatles in the same company with Mozart, Wagner, Tansen. What the Beatles are doing is just something monkeyish, and naturally their music is finished; the Beatles are past already. Mozart is going to live forever. As long as humanity is there, and intelligent people are there, he will be alive. The Beatles were finished within ten years – came like a wind, and went away.

You have to create something in which your inner potentiality becomes actualized, materialized. And then you will be surprised that the more you create, the juicier you become. Poets have always attracted beautiful women, painters have always attracted beautiful women.

Any kind of creativity makes you juicier. The woman knows where the juice is; it is her natural instinct. And what is the point of falling in love with a lazy skeleton?

So stop escaping from women. Start chasing them, because it is absolutely unacceptable…for the simple reason that the natural phenomenon – not only in man, but all over in nature – is that the male chases the female, and the female tries to escape, although she does not want to escape. She goes very slowly, she goes on looking back. But it is a beautiful game of hide-and-seek. The woman, all over nature, is the one who hides. It is the man, the male who seeks. We cannot change nature, and if you try to change it you become something of a perversion. The game is so joyous….

Chase the woman, because that gives her strength, recognition; that makes her feel she is attractive, beautiful, wanted. And that is a great need in the feminine psychology: to be wanted. Don't take away something from my women here, because it is absolutely unnatural for them to chase men. It is unfeminine, it is not ladylike.

I don't know what this word "lady" means, but I figured out it means "a good lay." I don't know

English, so I can manage my own meanings. Now, a good lay has to be chased. The good lay is not going to chase you, that will look unfeminine.

Be a gentleman! And just as I think lady means a good lay, a gentleman means one who lays her gently. And you are chasing….

Chase the woman gently. And let her feel one of her greatest needs: that she is needed. That will make her juicier. And chasing her, you will come out of your laziness, so it is just the right thing to do.

If any man is not chasing a woman he is betraying me! I have chased women my whole life – of course, very gently. And you guys here are trying to destroy the whole natural balance!

A woman loves immensely to be chased, it is her inner necessity. Don't deprive the woman of her most basic need.

I was a lecturer in the university…just by coincidence I was sitting with the vice-chancellor – he had called me to discuss a few things about my behavior – and at that very moment a girl student came in. She was in tears. The vice-chancellor asked her, "What is the matter?"

She said, "Look at these letters! A few boys go on continuously writing me love letters. They even throw pebbles at me. They are harassing me!"

Naturally the vice-chancellor said, "You just name those people, they will be punished."

I said, "Wait. You don't understand psychology. Let me take the case in hand. I am teaching psychology – you don't know anything about it." He was shocked that a lecturer should say that. But it was absolutely certain that he had no idea of psychology. He had been the chief justice of a high court.

I said, "It is not a court. You know how to deal with criminals, but this is not a crime. In fact, if this woman receives *no* letters, if nobody pays any attention to her, nobody chases her, nobody throws pebbles at her, she will be in great despair."

The girl was shocked, but her tears disappeared. I said to her, "Just look within yourself. Don't you enjoy all those letters? Don't you enjoy all those people chasing you? Are you not creating jealousy in the other girls of your class?"

For a moment she was dumb. Then she said, "Of course, perhaps you are right. Perhaps I had come with these letters to show to the vice-chancellor just to make it known that I am the most chased girl in the whole university."

I said, "You are intelligent, you have understood the point." And I said to the vice-chancellor, "Never interfere in things which you don't know about."

It is an absolute need in feminine psychology, and it is a very complicated phenomenon. If she is not chased, she is in despair. That means she is worthless, nobody is paying attention to her, nobody writes love letters, nobody approaches her. Nobody tells her, in a roundabout way, that he loves her. She is waiting…. Don't let my women wait!

And out of despair a woman starts chasing men, because she sees time is passing – and time passes faster for the woman than it passes for the man. Because she is a beautiful flower, delicate in every way, her youth, her beauty will be soon gone. By the time she is forty-eight her menopause comes, and after that who bothers to chase her? She is in a hurry: youth will not be forever.

A man can be loved even when he is old. This is strange. You will find many young girls falling in love with an old poet, who is older than their fathers, an old painter, an old musician – young girls. I know twenty-year-old girls were falling in love with Picasso. And it has been always so, never the reverse.

I have never seen a young man falling in love with an old woman of seventy, eighty, ninety. And if any young man falls in love with a woman who is ninety, the motivation must be different. It must be money. The woman is just about to go into her grave – it is not difficult for a few days to pretend that he loves her, and then all her money is going to be his. But no young man is going to fall really in love with an old woman.

The woman's beauty, youth, is a very fleeting phenomenon. So she becomes despairing, afraid; time is running out and these lazy guys are not chasing her! Now, don't be so cruel, don't be so unkind. Be human, compassionate.

This word "compassion" is composed of passion. To be compassionate means to be in love. Compassion is just a dimension of love. Passion is hasty, hectic, a little violent. Compassion is gentle, nice, understanding – but it is passion after all.

It has to be remembered that when a woman out of despair chases a man, the man is bound to escape because something unnatural is happening. When the woman chases you, it simply means she is an unwanted woman, nobody is chasing her. The woman chasing the man becomes unattractive. The man cannot take it: she is not a woman, she is a monster.

Things are very much correlated. If women start chasing, men are bound to escape. The whole game has turned upside down. The chaser becomes the chased, and no man can love a woman who is chasing him. The very phenomenon of chasing makes the woman worthless, she is not a challenge. Man wants challenge. He wants to chase, he wants to be victorious. That's why nature has arranged it in such a way that in all the animals, man included, the males should chase the females.

Give great contentment to the woman. And don't be worried that you will have to chase her to the very end of the earth. She is willing, she is just giving you a little more chance to chase her, so it becomes a more attractive challenge. And once you start burning with the challenge, the woman becomes almost a fairy, not of this world. Your burning desire for her makes her a dream girl. You dream of her, you think of her, you write poetry, you play on the guitar. It is perfectly good.

And never be worried. She is not trying to escape you, she is just giving you a chance to chase. Take the challenge as a man, and soon she will allow you to be victorious. And that's what the man desires: victory.

But when a woman chases a man it is going to be defeat. If she catches hold of him, he is defeated. He will fall on his knees and beg her, "Please leave me, find someone else. I am not one to be defeated."

So just understand the natural way of things, and don't go against nature, because going against nature creates all sorts of problems. To be natural is to be unproblematic. And to be natural is so beautiful.

To be natural is so at ease, at home.

Beloved Bhagwan,

I am one of Your black sannyasins. My childhood was spent in Africa, my family lives there. I have been with you for ten years, and I've put aside my questions about Africa. Now I find that what You are saying about black people and Africa makes me feel raw and shaky. I feel ashamed as well. Can You explain what is happening? I am glad that it is happening, but it hurts.

Yes. I am also glad that it is happening. Go through the process. Something in your mind is still thinking in terms of white and black.

My commune has nothing to do with white and black. My commune is open to all with equal respect. Just look at me. I am neither black nor white, but it does not give me any trouble. I simply enjoy it. Not being black, not being white, with one hand I can chase a black woman, with another hand I can chase a white woman.

Of course, my ways of chasing are very subtle. I chase them sitting in my chair. I don't have to do all kinds of gymnastics. I don't have to take them to the cafe, to the restaurant, to the movie; I am simply sitting in my chair. But even if I look in their eyes, that is enough: cafes and restaurants and movies are nothing before it. Just waving my hand…and I see the woman becoming so happy. It makes me happy in return. And I have not done anything – just waved my hand!

When I see you laughing, it is a nourishment to me. When I see you singing and dancing with me, I become healthier. What medicines cannot do for me, my people, rejoicing, do.

Feel for everybody who is here. Don't think in terms of you being black. Black *is* beautiful – it has its own beauty, just as the white color has its own beauty. The black color is not to be condemned; the black color and the black people have to be discovered and welcomed. They are stronger than white people. White husbands are always afraid of black servants, chauffeurs, for the simple reason that their wives might find them more attractive. And certainly they are more powerful sexually – they are more primitive!

And they come from a world where only strong people can survive. Those who are weaker will not be able to take the sun of Africa; they will be finished.

In Tibet, for centuries there has been a tradition that when the child is born…. You cannot conceive what they do. They dip the child into ice-cold water nine times. A very strange thing! Nine children die; only one survives out of ten. But I know their reason. In Tibet, to survive you will need immense strength against the cold. It is icy cold all around. It is better to die in the very beginning, better to get out of the race. Otherwise, you will be continually sick, a burden on the society, on the parents, who are all poor, and you will carry a guilt within yourself your whole life – that you are of no use, worthless and unnecessarily existing like a parasite.

It looks cruel to dip the just-born child into ice-cold water, but I can see their point. It is better to retire from the very beginning, rather than suffer for seventy years. So only ten percent of children survive, ninety percent die in that ice-cold dipping. But those who survive are immensely strong.

The same is the situation in Africa. They have to be strong, the sun is too much. Their blackness is really a protection against the sun. Their strength has been always a point of jealousy in the white people's minds; in fact, the white man has always felt inferior. And just to destroy that inferiority within himself, he forced the black people to be inferior. He made them slaves, he sold them in the markets like a commodity. They were not given education, they were not economically free. They were always second-class citizens.

Even now, in the twentieth century, in the most modern country of the world – in America – the blacks are still fighting for their rights, and they are not receiving them. But in my commune, which is ahead of time…in my commune it is the twenty-first century! We have left the twentieth century far behind. Here, every color is respected.

You say you have been with me for ten years. Not really, if you had been really with me for ten years it would be impossible for this question to arise in your mind. Yes, I have never talked about Africa, because nobody ever asked about Africa, nobody ever asked about the African people.

I answer your questions – otherwise, I have nothing to say. I have found the answer, now no question arises in me.

If you want to drink out of my experience, you have to use your question as a bucket is used to draw water from a well. The well is not in any need of your bucket, he is perfectly contented. But he is happy to give you water, to fill your bucket, because he knows the more he gives, the more water – fresh, younger – flows in through hundreds of sources.

The same is my experience. You go on asking me and I will go on answering you. But if you don't ask, there is absolute silence in me. There is no question that has arisen in thirty-two years. Once you have found the answer, how can questions arise? But you have questions; use them as buckets. I am available, infinitely happy to give you all that I have, because the more I give, the fuller I am.

You have been with me physically for ten years, but somewhere lurking in your mind the idea has remained that you are a black person. And the white people have conditioned you to think that you are inferior. Just now, because somebody in the press conference asked me about Africans – why they are not coming here – the shadow that has been always lurking somewhere in your unconscious came into your conscious immediately. And my answer may have helped to bring it up.

There is no other way to get rid of things. If you go on keeping them deep in your unconscious, you may be unaware of them but they are there and growing their roots deeper and deeper. Underneath your unconscious mind there is a collective unconscious mind – which is far bigger. Underneath your collective unconscious mind is the cosmic unconscious mind – which is as big as the whole universe. So the deeper you repress something, the more you are giving it chances to survive. Bring it into the conscious mind.

It is good that somebody asked the question, and you have become disturbed, shaky. Don't repress it. Shake yourself perfectly well!

There used to be – there is still in some areas – a Christian sect called Shakers. I condemn their whole theology, but I accept their shaking. That's what they used to do in their churches: they would shake themselves as strongly as possible till they fell on the ground. I call it Dynamic Meditation!

There has been another Christian sect which was even better; they are called Quakers. Shaking is a little bit gentle, but quaking is as if an earthquake is happening. And that's what they used to do. I don't accept anything of their theology, but shaking and quaking are perfectly useful methods.

So if you are shaking inside, bring it out. And what has shaken you? – I said a truth. And I cannot say anything else. That's why I am against taking the oath in the courts. The oath in the courts means that if you don't take the oath you are liable to lie. That is accepting that you are a lying person. I am against the oaths in the courts, for the simple reason that they are already giving the judgment, without you asserting a single word. They have already judged: "You will lie, so take the oath."

But it is so stupid. If a person can lie, how can the oath prevent him? And particularly a person like me, who does not believe in God, who does not believe in heaven and hell – what oath can prevent me from lying? There is no fear of hell, there is no greed for heaven, and I don't want to meet your bogus God. I am completely fulfilled in myself. The oath can make superstitious people afraid; the oath can make a Christian, a Hindu, a Mohammedan afraid. The oath cannot make my people afraid – there is nothing to fear.

I am simply saying the truth as I see it. That's what has shaken you. But what can I do? If there are people who don't listen to Mozart, is Mozart responsible for that? If there are people who cannot understand the paintings of Van Gogh, is Van Gogh responsible for it? To understand Van Gogh you will have to grow more sensitive, more aesthetic; you will have to understand the mind of a creative painter.

Just the other day I saw a picture of Van Gogh's painting. Why has this picture suddenly been published? Van Gogh was condemned for this same painting for his whole life, and even after his life. And now suddenly the painting has become the most important of Van Gogh's paintings. I will have to tell you what the painting is and what happened.

The painting is of stars, but they are not the way you see them. They are more whirling, they are not static; they are more liquid than solid. Now who has seen a liquid star going round and round on its center? In Van Gogh's time, science itself condemned it as only imaginary. But now physicists have discovered that the stars are actually as they are painted by Van Gogh; they are liquid and whirling, they are not solid, static.

Something almost miraculous…Van Gogh could see something that science had to wait for one hundred years to discover. And now they are all paying respect to the genius of the man, to his unimaginable intuitive forces. How did he manage to see stars the way they are? If you want to understand Van Gogh, you will have to raise your consciousness. You cannot appreciate Van Gogh just the way you are; there is a gap.

If Africans are not coming to me, it is not my fault. There is a big gap, they cannot understand me. Their problems are not spiritual – why should they come to me? Their problems are very material, mundane. They need food, they need water, clean water. They need medicine, they need hospitals, they need schools. They need all kinds of things; and I am not distributing things here.

Only those who have *everything* and still find themselves discontented, who have all kinds of power and still feel they are empty; those who have been educated in the great universities of the world – Oxford, Cambridge, Harvard, Varanasi – and still they find, after all this long process of education, wasting one-third of their lives…. What have they got? A few papers certifying that they are an M.A., a Ph.D., a D.Litt., but their ignorance remains the same after all this knowledgeability.

They have not become knowers, they don't know even themselves. All these universities – Oxford, Cambridge, Harvard, Varanasi – they all have failed them, they have deceived them. They have not been true to their promise. Out of the university they come full of knowledgeability, but with no experience of their own: all knowledge borrowed, but no experience authentically their own. These are the people who will be coming to me.

Africans, I am sad to say, cannot come. But I am not responsible for it. It is not a question of their being black, it is a question of their poverty, their slavery. And as far as religion is concerned, I am condemning all the religions, because I find them pseudo, not true; mythological, not existential. The Africans are not even at that stage where they have a pseudo religion. They are far away, back in the world when there was no religion, only magical rituals.

I am condemning the religious people. What can I say to Africans who are five thousand years behind? They are still believing that a certain ritual can kill a man, that a certain ritual can save a man from dying, that a certain ritual can do miracles. There is such a gap! That's why they are not coming to me. You are fortunate that you have come and you have been here with me for ten years.

I don't ever discriminate between the black people and the white people. To me, anybody who is trying to seek, search inwards…. Inside nobody is black and nobody is white. Inside there are no colors. Inside it is luminous whiteness. Remember, white is not a color, just as black is not a color. It is strange that we say black people, white people; both are colorless, in different ways.

You can see…in the rainbow you will not find white and black. These two colors you will not find in the rainbow; all other colors are there. Why is the rainbow not interested in white and black? – because they are not colors. Black simply means that all colors have been absorbed.

You have to understand a little bit of scientific fact. When you see something black, that means none of the sunrays falling on it are reflected back. It absorbs them, it does not let any sunray escape. White does just the opposite. It reflects all the rays, and all the colors together create the illusion of white.

You can try it. Just on your ceiling fan, instead of three blades, put seven blades. Paint each blade in different colors – paint on it all seven rainbow colors. Then put the fan on, and you will be surprised: when those blades start moving fast, you only see white; all those colors have disappeared.

The reflection of all colors is white; rejecting all the colors is white. Absorbing all sunrays is black. The black people had to be black because they had to absorb the sunrays; otherwise they would be too much, they would kill them. They had to create a device, a simple device – to be black. It is not very costly, it is a very small amount of pigment. Things are becoming more and more costly, but still the black pigment is not more than half a dollar's worth. But it protects them from being burned by the sun, because the black immediately absorbs sunrays.

The white cannot accept all the sunrays; that is also simple. The white races live in colder countries where the sunrays are not so strong. To survive they don't need to be able to absorb all the sunrays. These are survival measures – don't make politics out of them!

And as far as your inside is concerned, there are no colors, just a luminosity, just pure light and utter silence. It is the same in the black, in the white, in the yellow, in the brown – it does not matter what kind of container you have, the content is the same.

You are fortunate, I say it again, to have been here for ten years. But do you remember anybody discriminating against you because you are black? In fact, I had to enquire who the questioner is, because I don't see you as black and white; I simply see you as red people! My concern is with the red people.

It is good that you got disturbed. But it is not your responsibility. It is nobody's responsibility, it just happens that the black people have not risen in consciousness, in intelligence. They have been struggling at the lowest level of survival.

The same is the situation in India. There was a time, twenty-five centuries ago when Gautam Buddha was alive, when the country was agog with arguments, philosophies, theologies. There were wandering masters all over the country discussing things of the beyond, searching for methods of meditation, contemplation, concentration. The country was not at the survival level; the country was perfectly happy, their basic needs were fulfilled. And when the basic needs are fulfilled, suddenly you find new needs of a higher order arising in you.

Do you think a hungry man should come to me to ask about meditation? A hungry man will come to ask about bread and butter. And if I start talking about meditation to him, he will say, "First give me something to eat so that I can at least hear you, what you are saying."

In India, there has been a great fall. After Gautam Buddha, India went down and down and down. Alexander the Great reached India three hundred years after Gautam Buddha, and after Alexander the Great, India became a constant target of invaders of all kinds, of all countries – whoever wanted to loot. India became a victim for two thousand years. It lost its glory, it lost its spiritual interest.

I was there for seven years in Poona, and people were asking why Indians don't come to me. When people from all over the world are coming, why are Indians not coming to me? Or even if they come, they are only few and far between, and they are all rich people who come.

I said, "It is so simple. The whole of India is struggling at the lowest level, trying somehow to manage to survive." When somebody is drowning in a river, do you think he will ask a question about meditation? He will say, "Save me! Take me out of the water!"

You can tell him, "The best way is meditation. Don't be worried about the water, everybody has to die someday. Die meditatively. Celebrate! And I will participate in celebration from the bank. I will dance and sing and play on the guitar, and you die joyously." That man is not going to forgive you. If somehow he comes out, he is going to break your guitar and your neck and teach you a lesson, that this is not the way to behave with a drowning man!

In India the poor people were not coming to me. Those who were coming were either the upper middle class people or the super-rich.

But it is not my fault that Indians are poor. It is their own responsibility.

What have Africans been doing for five thousand years? If Africa was not able to provide a higher standard of life, they should have moved. Who is preventing them? But they are clinging, just as in India the farmers go on clinging – and eighty percent of India consists of farmers. They go on clinging to their small pieces of land, which have been exploited by their crops for centuries: now the land doesn't have anything to give. But they are clinging, starving.

The gap is big…. I can tell them how to bridge the gap, but there were two African journalists in the world press conference, and I could see they could not understand what I was saying. And they were journalists, educated. In fact, they could not ask the question itself adequately.

One was standing in front of me, trying to make an effort to question me, but he was going in a strange round and round way. I could not see what he was trying to ask. And when I figured it out and I answered him, he did not listen – because my answer was finished and he was still standing there like a rock. Everybody else asked the question, received the answer, and immediately moved away to give place to somebody else. But this man was just standing there. He had not even enough intelligence to know that my answer was finished. He looked absolutely like an idiot.

The second African asked the question better than the first; it was perfectly clear. Perhaps he was preparing it, rehearsing it, cramming it, because I could see that he must have crammed the question. And I have reason to say that – because when I started answering him, he would not look at me. He was looking here, he was looking there. Except at me, he was looking everywhere.

In fact, he was cramming, inside, the second question. He did not want to get disturbed by my answer – he might forget the second question.

As my answer was finished…. If you have to ask a second question, it has to be related to my answer. But his second question was absolutely unrelated to my answer. Now what can I do?

You ask, "Why are Africans not coming?" in such a way – as if I am responsible for the fact that they are not coming. They cannot. They are not even contemporaries, what to say about the twenty-first century? They are five thousand years old – stuck, fossilized.

You are certainly blessed to be here, and any idea of black, of Africa – I am going to hammer all those things out of you.

It will be good if you drop them yourself, just to be compassionate to me.

Hammering is not for a lazy man like me – and I am not a blacksmith either!

Death
Never Happens

DISCOURSE 28,   July 26, 1985

Beloved Bhagwan,

A man like You comes along once in eternity. Whatever You are doing and saying is unique. I'm indeed fortunate to be here and I may never have this opportunity again. Yet every morning I come to discourse, I fall asleep. Am I missing? Should I also go and jump in Krishnamurti Lake?

It is just great – have a good sleep! Sleep is not contradictory to enlightenment. You will make history by becoming enlightened in your sleep. And there is no need to go to Krishnamurti Lake. I am here – your Krishnamurti Lake.

But don't say that what I am saying is unique. It is simply the truth. Anybody who is ready to relax in his ordinariness will realize it. And it is not that a man like me comes only once in an eternity. You all have the same potential.

Only men like me are born; there are no other kind. Just don't try to become somebody. That's why I am saying. Don't call me unique; otherwise you will start unconsciously trying to become unique. And the moment you go on the trip of becoming, you are going far away from the truth that you are.

Just be ordinary! It is beautiful and so relaxing. It is the most wondrous experience just to be nobody, not desiring to be somewhere else, not even thinking of the tomorrow. Can't you see this very moment the bliss that is descending upon you?

Can't you feel the silence that is beating in your very heart? It is here – and not unique, available to all. And it is not that you have to wait for an eternity, don't find excuses. I am not going to let you go without experiencing it. It is not something to be given to you; you have it already. Just go on relaxing, sleeping.

Sometimes *I* feel like sleeping; I can manage both to sleep and talk. Perhaps a few times I fall asleep and just out of habit I go on talking – you can ask Vivek. Once in a while when she comes to wake me up, she cannot believe it – I am addressing *you!* But the trouble for the poor girl is, when I speak in my sleep I speak my mother tongue. But I have promised her next time I will remember to speak in English.

Life in all its dimensions – awake or asleep – makes no difference to your enlightenment. So don't find any excuse. These are excuses: that it happens only in an eternity, how can it happen to you? It happens only to unique people, how can it happen to you? I am trying my best to destroy these tricks of the mind, so that nobody who is a sannyasin leaves this world unenlightened!

Beloved Bhagwan,

Recently You said that most people who become enlightened die shortly afterwards. What I want to know is how You have managed to stay with us so long? I am so grateful.

R eally I should be grateful to you. It is love for you, and the love that you go on pouring upon me that has helped me to remain with you. Love is a spiritual nourishment.

Those who died after their enlightenment died because they thought they had found it and now there was no reason to live. When I found it, I said to myself, "Now there is every reason to live." Before finding, there was no reason; I could have died easily. But after my finding it, my love would not let me die. I waited for you, and you started coming. I have not sent a message, not written a letter. Still, from faraway lands you started coming, as if you have always belonged to me.

Now I am part of you, you are part of me. It is going to be very difficult for death to take me away from so many people, from your love: I am protected.

Love is the antidote of death, not life.

Ordinarily you think that life and death are contraries. No, death and love are the contraries. Now it is going to be a great strain on death. I should be grateful to you. I have not given anything to you, there is nothing to give. You have already got it. At the most I go on shaking you, shocking you, hitting you. Do you think that is giving?

But you have loved me – a man who does not deserve anybody's love. I am immensely grateful to the sannyasins. You are my life! If you are with me, there is no death. If you are not with me, then this very moment I will be gone. It is your love which is keeping me breathing, living; it is your joy, your blissfulness, your songs, your dances.

In the night when I go to sleep, I tell death, "At least don't disturb my morning. My people would like me to be alive. Existence cannot go against so much love. Existence cannot do anything without the permission of so many people. Death has to wait!

It all depends on you. My work is done as far as I am concerned. There is nothing more to experience, nothing more to know. But I have become so much concerned with you that it does not matter that *my*

I have struggled with life, and I have been victorious. Death is a poor thing; if I can be victorious in life, I can easily keep death waiting outside the door. I will allow it in only when I see that you are awake, that your consciousness has arisen, that even if I am not here you will continue my work, you will go on spreading the fire around the world.

work is finished; there are so many people who love me whose work is not finished. I *have* to live, to find ways and means to postpone death.

And I am very stubborn. I have struggled with life, and I have been victorious. Death is a poor thing; if I can be victorious in life, I can easily keep death waiting outside the door. I will allow it in only when I see that you are awake, that your consciousness has arisen, that even if I am not here you will continue my work, you will go on spreading the fire around the world. But please, just to keep me alive don't go on sleeping

There are so many – eight hundred thousand – sannyasins around the world. It is going to be a difficult task for death to take me away from my people. I am not alone, I have penetrated into your beings. I have dispersed myself into so many beings that it is almost impossible for death to collect me unless I help.

Don't just feel grateful. If you are grateful, it is good, but not enough. Become what you are, *be* what you are. Let me rejoice! My only joy is to see somebody coming home.

I will wait till eternity. You can go on and on befooling yourself, but remember – I am waiting, and I want you to be enlightened. I want it to become the most important historical fact in human existence, that thousands of people relax into their ordinariness and become enlightened. Yes, in the past it was so that after thousands of years one person may become enlightened. I don't live in that bullock-cart age, I am a contemporary man. I want you to become enlightened with jet speed – and it is possible. I am not asking the impossible.

You have given so much to me.

You go on giving so much to me.

I wonder…what have I done? Where have I gone wrong? – that so many people for no reason go on pouring their love on one who deserves nothing. And your love goes on growing. As your love goes on growing, I become healthier and healthier.

Soon I am going to dance with you!

Beloved Bhagwan,

Hearing You talk about Your rebellious attitude in Your childhood, I feel connected to that, because I did the same. I struggled hard not to be repressed, but somehow they got me in the end. Half-heartedly I compromised. Why was Your rebellion not disturbed by anything?

The first thing to be remembered by all: never compare yourself with anybody, not even with me. Everybody is so different, and everybody passes through different phases, different paths. There is no similarity.

Don't deceive yourself by saying that you have been as rebellious as I was in my childhood. You were not rebellious, you were only reactionary. Yes, you fought against repression, but your fight was the fight of the ego.

My fight was not the fight of the ego. My family, my neighbors, my friends, my teachers, professors – it took a little time for them, but soon they realized that I was not struggling for my ego. Soon it became clear to them that my struggle had a totally different quality to it. I was struggling to find myself. I was struggling so that they could not create a false ego as a substitute for my self.

You say you have been struggling – but remember, your struggle was an ego fighting. That's where you failed. Your ego became strong, and remember, even the strongest ego is prone to compromise. It can fight if that fulfills it; it can fight if that fulfills it; it can compromise if *that* fulfills it. Why did you compromise? What can the world do to you? At the most they can kill you. The rebel from the very beginning decides, "I would prefer to accept death but I will not compromise."

You were not fighting, struggling, to destroy your ego. You were fighting to strengthen it, to make it more powerful. And then a moment came when you were powerful enough – now struggle was useless, unnecessary trouble; you could compromise. Your struggle has been reactionary and political; that's why you failed.

My struggle was totally different. I was continuously watching that my rebellion remained pure, that it was not polluted by reaction.

They look alike. When you don't follow an order from your father, your mother, it can be either reaction or rebellion. They look very similar; they are as far apart from each other as two things can be, but the appearance is very similar. And it is very easy to believe that you are a rebel. All reactionaries believe that they are rebellious spirits. In fact, that too fulfills their ego – that they are not ordinary people, they are rebellious people.

Reaction means your ego does not want to be dominated by anyone; on the contrary, you would like to dominate everybody. Once it becomes strong through struggle, once you are certain that now nobody can destroy your ego, you start compromising. There is no need to fight, you can manage things now through compromise – a far easier way. Compromise – the very word is not in my vocabulary.

Compromise is ugly.

Rebellion is either/or, it never compromises.

How can truth compromise with lies? Either the truth has to prevail, or death. And when you have a small taste of truth, who cares about death? because that very small taste of truth makes you immortal. Deep down you know death is a fallacy: nobody dies, so what is the fear? At the most you can get a new body instead of the old. So far, so good. Getting rid of the old model and finding the fresh, new, latest model of the body – it is a beautiful experience.

But to see that death is a fallacy, it never really happens, you never die, nobody dies, *nothing* dies…. Yes it can change forms, but life is eternal. Compromise means you have become a strong ego. Now you do not need to struggle; now you can manage through compromise to get whatsoever you want. Once the ego is certain, then compromise is bound to happen.

I have never compromised on anything with anybody, for the simple reason that I have made it plain to everybody who has come into my life: if you are true, I am with you; it is not a compromise. I am totally with you, I don't make any conditions. But if I am true, you have to remember that you will have to be with me without any conditions.

Neither I compromise with anybody, nor do I allow anybody else to compromise with me. I have never compromised and I have never allowed anybody to compromise with me. Compromise is not my game. This is possible only if you are not trying to strengthen your ego.

For ego, it makes no difference: struggle is okay if it is nourishment for the ego, compromise is okay if it is nourishment for the ego. The ego wants to remain – it can use any means. There is no question of deciding what is right, what is wrong. For the ego, anything that keeps it strong is right – might is right. So if you can get something through compromise, why should you bother to fight? Yes, if you cannot get it through compromise, you are ready to struggle, to fight, to do anything that you are capable of.

This must have been your situation – just look back. What I am saying, try to find out…be just a fair judge of your own past, because if you had been rebellious like me, I cannot conceive that there came a point where you compromised. In rebellion there never comes a point of compromise. Only in reaction is there a point of compromise.

Your word "compromise" makes me absolutely certain what it was – not rebellion but reaction. You say, "In the end they got me." Why? If you were so strong in the beginning, in the end you would have been even more strong, all the years of struggle would have sharpened your sword. But if in the end you compromise, that simply means now you have come to a higher position as far as ego is concerned.

Now there is no fear; you can compromise and still go on becoming bigger and bigger as an ego.

Nothing came in my way. You are asking, "Why did this happen to you and not to me?" We were working from totally different standpoints. I was not reactionary; hence, even the people with whom I fought had tremendous love for me, they never became my enemies. I fought with my father, I fought with my mother, but they both became sannyasins. It is a rare phenomenon. They knew that I was not fighting with them for my ego. Just the contrary: I was fighting so that they should not be able to create an ego in me.

I received their blessings always. It looks very strange that the people with whom I was fighting were always blessing me. What was the cause of it? They could see clearly that I was absolutely simple and humble. I was not trying my ego against their ego. My teachers loved me. My professors wept when I left the university. The same professors who were continually bothered by me, they wept.

I asked them, "What is the matter? You should be happy that you are getting rid of a great nuisance."

They said, "We will miss you."

One of my professors, S.S. Roy, said to me, "I don't expect to get another student of your type. For two years you have argued against me, but I could see that your argument was not an ego trip. You were sincerely searching for the truth. Students will come," he said. "I had students in the past; I will have students in the future. But I do not see that I will have a student like you, whose effort is not just to pass examinations, get degrees – in fact who is not interested in the examinations, not interested in the degrees, not interested in the gold medals – but is sincerely interested in knowing the truth about everything."

Nobody with whom I have struggled has ended in enmity with me. They all loved me, they still love me.

Professor S.S. Roy, with whom I fought the most, was one of the most intelligent people I have come across, and it was a joy to argue with him. Our arguments were never finished in the class, so I had to follow him to his home. By and by, his wife also became involved. And S.S. Roy said to his wife, "This is strange, you always seem to be on his side. He is enough! If you want to support somebody, support me! He will kill the arguments of both of us."

His wife said, "But he's so true and so sincere – not interested in defeating you. You are interested in defeating him. I have been watching the scene continuously. He is trying to figure out what is the truth, and you are trying somehow to prove that your argument is right. I am going to be on his side. And if you have guts. you should also be on his side."

S.S. Roy told me later on, "This is the first time my wife has been so strong. It must be your doing. She has adored me always, she has believed me to be one of the most intelligent people in the world. You destroyed everything. Now she thinks *you* are far better."

I asked S.S. Roy, "What do you think?"

He said, "My wife is right."

He is still alive. Anybody who is my sannyasin is received in his home in Allahabad with the same respect that he would give to me, with the same love. One of my sannyasins who lived in Allahabad said, "It is strange. He is a retired head of the department of philosophy of Allahabad University" – in India, Allahabad University has the best philosophical department – "and he is a dignified old man. But whenever I go to him, he simply asks, 'Have you received any new book, new magazine? Just say something to me, what is *he* doing now?'"

He is one of those rare people who can respect somebody who is not in any way equal to him. I was just a student; he was the head of the department and the dean of the faculty of arts – one of the most dignified persons in the university. He had every chance to become the vice-chancellor, he just did not want to become the vice-chancellor – for the simple reason, he said, "It is enough. I have always wanted to retire and relax and do something that one of my students has been continuously hammering on my head: meditate. Now I am old and I don't want to waste time in being the vice-chancellor."

Retired, he is doing my meditations. And once in a while somebody will come and tell me, "He has a picture of you in his room where he meditates. His wife thinks now he has gone crazy – doing dynamic meditation in his old age."

Revolution – reaction – and rebellion have a totally different flavor. Reaction is ugly. You simply react because you don't want anybody to have the upper hand. But one day when you find you can have the upper hand without struggle, you start compromising; that's why those people could get you in the end. It was your basic misunderstanding. Your reaction, your ego, helped you to fall into the trap.

I have never reacted to anything, I have rebelled against everything, and on the path of rebellion there is no compromise. Compromise is something Jewish! It is something that happens in the marketplace, in politics. It does not happen in the search for truth.

But nothing is lost. Get out of your compromises. Forget the past. Even if there is only one single moment available, one can drop the whole past and taste the beauty of rebellion. Just a single moment is needed, a moment of understanding, insight.

I am not just answering your questions, I am trying to help you to get an insight. And then your insight will show you the path. In India, we call that insight the third eye.

I am trying somehow…please open your third eye, so you can see clearly and straight.

It is a miracle to see something clearly. And if you find it is wrong there is no need to make any effort to drop it. Just in your seeing that it is wrong, your grip on it is finished, the thing drops out of your life of its own accord. It is miraculous. It is not that you become alert, aware, conscious, and then you have to drop this, stop that, do this, not do that – no. The moment you have the insight, that which is wrong falls away from you, that which is right you simply follow – no effort.

Insight is a miracle, it is magical.

So my answers are not just answers. My answers are really an effort to approach your third eye, and somehow make you aware. The moment you see it was a reaction, not rebellion, you are finished with it. The moment you see you compromised because you found now it is helpful to the ego, your compromise is finished. You come out of this imprisonment of your ego fresh, young, to start your life from the very first moment – as if you are born again.

Beloved Bhagwan,

After Your discourse about men and women, I felt that the men are afraid. They are saying, to reassure themselves, "Let's wait till tomorrow. Bhagwan will probably say the exact opposite." Could You comment?

I am not going to say anything that will be opposite, for the simple reason that what I said yesterday was not my opinion, it is the law of nature. If it was my opinion I could have said something opposite to it.

So please don't wait – don't wait uselessly. It is a law of nature. I cannot say anything against it. Start chasing the woman! Don't waste your time waiting, thinking perhaps I will say the very opposite, that the women have to chase men. Impossible! I contradict myself, but I cannot contradict existence.

I am perfectly a master of my own opinions, to keep them or to throw them out. But the law of existence can only be understood; you cannot add anything to it, you cannot deduct anything from it. And what I said yesterday was simply the law of nature: the feminine has to be chased. It is manly to chase the woman. To be chased by a woman is ugly.

You are not man enough! Women are chasing

you and you are escaping. It simply does not look graceful. On your part it is humiliation; on the part of the woman it is unnatural, ungraceful.

But why is it happening, that men are afraid? The reason is simple. In the ordinary society outside they are not afraid, they are chasing women because it is so difficult. The law is against it, their own wife, if she finds out, will kill them. The woman they are chasing is somebody else's wife – if he finds out, he will start cleaning his gun! It is difficult. Monogamy has made it very attractive to chase women.

This society, this commune is completely free from all rubbish of monogamy, of husbands, of wives; it is completely free. That's the trouble. In monogamy you are stuck with one woman, fed up with the woman; you start chasing another woman. Here the situation is different. Having a few love affairs…. New sannyasins chase, then after having a few love affairs, they feel spent, finished. Now they cannot fantasize a woman in their dreams. In their dreams women disappear. Now, on the contrary, they are afraid.

And you should remember one thing: that man is the weaker sex. A woman can have multiple orgasms, can make love many times in one night; the man is very poor, he can have only one orgasm. And the very phenomenon of lovemaking is such that the man loses energy in it, the woman is nourished. She does not lose energy in it, she is the gainer. And if a man knows many women, sooner or later he becomes aware that these women are killing him. Now he is not interested in women, he is interested in saving his life!

So please, be kind to poor men. They will not be afraid if lovemaking is not forced on them. They will enjoy cuddling you, they will enjoy the warmth only a feminine body releases; they will be nourished by it. But if they know that the woman is bent upon having sexual intercourse, any intelligent man will be afraid, because tomorrow he has to wake up and work twelve hours again. And he cannot manage so many women. Once in a while he may like to make love….

So leave men the freedom. When they want to make love to you, enjoy it. When they want just to lie down by your side, being nourished by your feminine energy, your warmth, enjoy it. Don't force them to go into sexual gymnastics. Then they will not be afraid if they are certain that when they have the energy they will make love and when they don't have the energy they will get warmth, love showered on them by the woman.

This has to be understood, because it is going to be a problem. The woman has to be a little more understanding. And sexual intercourse is a very ordinary thing – all the animals are doing it. It needs no intelligence. If you have intelligence – and you are supposed to have intelligence – then just be compassionate to the poor man.

And the man has also to understand, because for centuries he has been told that he is the stronger sex – that is absolutely wrong – so he tries to prove that he is the stronger sex. The moment he gets a woman, or a woman gets him, which is far more likely, immediately he is ready to make love, to prove that he is a strong man. If he does not make love to the woman, what will the woman think of him?

Forget this nonsense. If your body, if your energy is not ready to overflow, just be with the woman, hold her hand, hug her. She will understand.

You are the weaker sex; once you accept the fact, there is no trouble.

Just look at me. I am only fifty-four and I look so ancient. Do you know the reason? I went on chasing women all my life! They made me ancient. What has happened to me, please don't force on my sannyasins. Be loving to them, and they will be available, they will not be afraid. They will not escape and chicken out. They will be immensely happy to be with any woman who offers her love, her energy, her beauty. But the problem is sex.

Never force sex on a man, leave it up to him. If he feels that he has energy for it, he is free to make love.

But if he feels he is tired and would like simply to be showered with feminine energy, then help him. He *is* a weaker sex. Don't be hard on the poor man.

Just look at my white beard. This is what all the women have done to me. But I am the type of man who is never afraid. I said, "Even if I live twenty years less, it does not matter; I am not going to disappoint a woman."

For a few weeks I have been celibate, that does not mean I have taken a vow to remain celibate forever. I can take holidays once in a while. It is nothing spiritual with me.

Celibacy is every man's birthright. He needs to gather energy. As he becomes older, he needs longer periods to gather energy. When a man is young – I mean, when he is between fourteen and twenty-one – he has the greatest energy he will have ever in his life. And this society is so ugly; that is the time when he is not allowed. At that time, in one night he can make three women, four women, satisfied. But the society does not allow him. They teach him that he should remain celibate. They have spread such stupid nonsense about it – that if you are not celibate you will go crazy, you will become mad.

By the time he is back home from the university he is already on the decline. Twenty-five to thirty-five – between these ten tears he will be declining, he will not have the same energy that he had before. And after thirty-five it is a very steep fall.

After fifty he should not go on pretending that he is the same man that he was when he was twenty-one. He should declare to everybody, "Now I am fifty, now I am going to be celibate. Yes, once in a while I will take a holiday from celibacy, but that is going to happen only once in a while." That's why they are afraid. Please don't make them afraid.

The woman's situation is biologically very different. She loses nothing in making love, she is always the gainer. Secondly, as she grows old, she becomes more interested in lovemaking, particularly when she passes the period of menopause and there is no fear of getting pregnant. Now she is dangerous to any man; she wants to make love as many times as possible.

This was in the past. Now the situation has changed because of the great revolution: the pill. No woman is afraid of making love. In the past they were afraid before menopause. Menopause comes nearabout forty-eight; for forty-eight years they were continuously afraid of making love, because it meant getting pregnant. It was dangerous – dangerous to carry the child for nine months, dangerous to feed the child from your breast and destroy your beauty.

A woman who has given birth to one dozen children – do you see what happens to her breasts? They look like Jesus Christ hanging on the cross. Naturally, women were afraid, and they were not chasing men.

I am against breast-feeding, because the breast is one of the most beautiful things of the woman's body. The child should be given every chance to play with the mother's breasts, but as far as feeding is concerned, some other arrangement has to be made. The woman loses her youth, her beauty; she starts using bras, just to deceive people. This is ugly. There is no need for it; man is intelligent enough to give the child food in so many ways. But the child should be allowed to play with the mother's breasts. If he is not allowed that, then for his whole life he will think only of breasts and breasts and breasts.

That is what is happening in the world. Painters go on painting breasts, sculptors go on sculpting breasts. What is this breast mania? They have missed playing with their mothers' breasts, and now it is too late. And when they come in close contact with a woman of their age, the woman has breasts hanging – yes, just like Jesus Christ on the cross. They are no longer attractive, they have lost the beauty, the roundness, the fullness. They are just a memory, a faded memory.

Because of the pill, the woman is completely free of the fear of getting pregnant. And because she is capable of multiple orgasms, one man is not enough to fulfill her desire for love. It is the fault of a blind biology, I am not responsible for it. And I would like to improve on blind biological things, because you are now conscious, alert, intelligent.

The woman needs multiple orgasms, but the jealousy of the man prevents her. In my commune, we are going to live with understanding and awareness. If your woman finds that you alone cannot satisfy her, don't feel offended. She is simply stating a fact – it is not against you. If she keeps clinging to you unsatisfied, she is going to take revenge in every way, because it is you who are preventing her having as much joy as she is capable of.

In my commune, nobody should have even the slightest idea that he possesses the woman, or the woman possesses him. Things are possessed, not human beings. And if a woman is free, a man is free – to move with other men, to move with other woman – it is perfectly right, because joy is right, rejoicing is right. Having the freedom to not be a possession is right.

Just the other night, one beautiful girl was taking my interview for television. And you know I am mad…. She asked me – now, she was not aware what kind of man I am; she must have taken hundreds of interviews of politicians, priests, and all kind of dodos – she asked me, "You have loved so many women, but don't you have a stable relationship with one woman?"

I said, "That is impossible. I don't have any relationship – stable or unstable. I live in the moment."

She said, "At this time, who is the woman?"

I said, "*You* are the woman! I love you in this moment." And in the end, when I started singing and dancing with my sannyasins, I called her close to me: "Hold my hand and dance with me." And it was such a beautiful situation.

She told my secretary, "Now my boyfriend is going to freak out!" I have just said, "I love you," and was just holding her hand and just dancing with my people – why should her boyfriend freak out? And if he's a freaker, let him freak out. He's not worthy of being a boyfriend. Drop that worthless creature! Come to my commune where nobody freaks out, everybody freaks in.

Beloved Bhagwan,

I was really touched when I heard You talking about Your ordinariness. And in the same moment I realized that I don't want to see that You are ordinary. I see such a big distance between me and You. Please comment.

I am not! Who told you I am ordinary? I don't take care about yesterdays.

I am an extraordinary person! So rejoice…. You are right. I was wrong!

Beloved Bhagwan,

It seems to me that death enslaves us physically and psychologically. It allows us the illusion of freedom for so many years and then steps in to assert its claim on us and on those we care for. I feel at the mercy of an immense and whimsical phenomenon that makes a mockery of life, love and freedom. And it freaks me out.

So we have also one who freaks out? This is not allowed! If you enjoy freaking, why not freak in? Freak as much as you can, but always keep the direction inwards.

And the reason you are freaking out is absolutely stupid. You think death gives you the illusion of life, love, freedom, and then one day suddenly it comes in and everything is destroyed: life, love, freedom. Death is not a reality. It cannot step in or step out.

Death never happens.

The illusion is not given by death. How can death give the illusion? In fact, it *destroys* the illusion. If you are aware that death is *bound* to happen, how can you remain in the illusion that life is going to continue forever? For that you will need really a thick skull. Death is happening every day. All the cemeteries around the world, and the crematoriums – death has left its mark.

Death is not creating the illusion. It is your mind that creates the illusion that "It is always somebody else who dies, I never die." And in a way it looks logical: you always see somebody else dying, you cannot see yourself dying. The man who has died, he was also in the same illusion; he had also seen others dying, and deep down he must have been saying, "It is something that happens to others, it does not happen to me."

This is your mind. Certainly you will never see your death, because dead men don't see. Mind gives you the feeling that you are going to live forever. Drop that illusion, drop that mind! You cannot be certain even of the next moment.

And it is good that you cannot be certain of the next moment, and the tomorrow, and the day after tomorrow; it is good, tremendously good. Because the next moment is not certain, you are thrown back to the present. This is the only moment you have got of which you can be certain – enjoy it! Enjoy it as totally as possible. Squeeze the whole juice out of it, because who knows? – the next moment may never come.

Death is good – it keeps you alert.

It never gives you a warning of when it is coming; it comes suddenly out of nowhere. It is a great blessing. Just think: if you were allowed to be immortal in your body, do you think you would enjoy it? Even people who live for eighty years start praying for death. They are bored – the same routine, the same life. What more is there to live for? They are tired, exhausted, weak, old. Now death is their only hope.

I have heard about Alexander the Great, that when he was reaching India, passing the big desert of Saudi Arabia, he was informed that there is a well in Saudi Arabia – if you drink out of that well you become immortal. Naturally, anybody would have been attracted, and particularly a man like Alexander the Great, who was nothing but a big ego. He wanted to conquer the whole earth, and he was afraid – is there time enough or not? The earth is so big…. He wanted to become the first man in history who has conquered the whole earth.

This was a good chance; if he is immortal, then there is no problem. And if somebody is immortal, is not going to die, he is not going to be sick either. Sickness, illness, disease – they are just steps towards death. The immortal man will be young, healthy, with no possibility of any sickness or disease.

And Alexander was only thirty-three years old; this was a good time to become immortal. He was healthy, beautiful, strong – this was a good time to become immortal, that meant he would remain thirty-three forever.

He stopped his armies and he said, "I am going to the well. Nobody comes with me." He did not want anybody else to become immortal. If others also become immortal, his immortality would no longer be unique.

He went to the well – it is a beautiful story. In the East there are wells made in two ways. One is the ordinary way, a hole in the earth. To reach water level…you have to pull the water up in a bucket. There is also another type of well; only very rich people can afford it. On one side there is an arrangement where you can pull the water up in a bucket. On the side opposite to it there are steps going to the water itself. It is really cool there, silent.

I have been into many wells. When you sit there for hours, time seems to stop, the whole world seems to be so far away. The noise of the market, the people – nothing reaches there. Sixty feet deep in the earth, it is dark, cool, yet very fresh.

The well where Alexander went was this type of well. So he went in, step by step, immensely excited. And just as he was making a cup out of his hands, and filling his hands with the water to drink, a crow who was sitting just nearby on a tree by the side of the well, said, "Wait! Wait a minute!"

Alexander looked back. He could not believe that a crow – because there was nobody else – could speak, but he was speaking. The crow said, "Wait."

Alexander said, "Why did you stop me? Don't you know I am Alexander the Great? Nobody can stop me! And you are just a crow."

The crow said, "First listen to what I have to say to you, then do whatsoever you want. I have drunk from this well and I have become immortal. Now, for hundreds of years I have been trying to commit suicide – in this way, in that way. Nothing succeeds, and I am tired, utterly tired. And the very idea that I am going to live *forever* in this despair, in this anguish…even death is not going to relieve me.

"I have known everything, I have experienced everything. Now there is nothing in the future but a painful, miserable existence. That's why I said, wait a moment. Now, think it over, and then if you feel like drinking, drink. But I am sitting here only to prevent people, because I am suffering so much."

A moment of silence…Alexander's hands dropped the water back into the well, and he said to the crow, "Thank you, my friend. I am immensely grateful. I had never thought about it, that I would have to live forever and forever. My friends will be dying, my beloved will be dying, my parents will be dying, my teachers will be dying, my contemporaries will be dying – and I will remain stuck forever. No, I cannot drink this water, and I pray to you, please remain sitting here, because there are many fools like me. If they come to know about the well, stop them. It will be one of the greatest acts of compassion."

You say death creates the illusion of life, love? No. It is death that makes you aware that if you want to live, live now, because tomorrow is uncertain. If you want to love, love now, because you may be in the crematorium and sannyasins will be dancing, celebrating.

Death is a great reminder. If there were no death in the world, it would have been just hell. Just think: all those people who have died and are sleeping peacefully in the graveyard, all those people who have been burned in crematoriums and have been freed completely, have evaporated into thin air…. Just think, if all those people – your father, your father's father, and so on up to Adam and Eve – for millions of years, and nobody is dying…. Poison is useless, bullets are meaningless, swords cannot cut heads: what will be the situation? Do you think it will be very pleasant? It will be the worst that can happen.

Death makes life beautiful, because it makes you alert: don't miss the train, don't miss anything. Enjoy, relish everything possible to you, because tomorrow is death. Death is not your enemy, death is your greatest friend. Without death you will be just dead bodies moving around with no purpose, with no meaning, and no exit.

If there can be any hell, its name will be "No exit."

Jean-Paul Sartre has written a play titled *No Exit,* and it is the description of hell. The only trouble is there is no way out. And according to Christianity, you have to be there forever.

Death is your great friend, companion, which makes you love intensely, which makes you not want to miss anything. Religions have not told you the truth. They have been lying to you, telling you that beyond death there is paradise: all beautiful things, joys, blessings, freely available. These people are criminals, because they are destroying your present.

They are giving you a hope of a better, far more fulfilling life…after death, so why be bothered about this small time? Why be bothered about living intensely, totally? Just wait for death to come. Mean while you go on praying in the church, in the mosque, in the synagogue. You go on listening to all kinds of superstitions and stupidities – they call them sermons – and go on believing whatever the priest says to you. This is all that you have to do in life. And don't commit a sin; otherwise you may miss paradise.

And if you look deep into the word "sin," you

will be surprised. It means no joy, no laughter, no celebration, no love. Anything that makes you happy is condemned as sin by some religion or other. Remain serious, with long faces, dull, avoid living. Renounce life, love – renounce the world and move into some ugly caves in the mountains, and wait there chanting some mantra – transcendental meditation, or "Ave Maria, Ave Maria."

These religions have crippled you, destroyed you. They are really messengers of the devil. All the religions of the world are messengers of the devil, not of God. There is no God, but about the devil I am doubtful. Perhaps he exists; otherwise from where do all these theologians, religious preachers, monks, nuns, Mother Teresa, pope the Polack – from where do all these people come? Who sent them? There must be a devil. Or perhaps there is not a devil, but these people are in a conspiracy against human joy, pleasure, comfort, luxury.

There is no possibility of a devil. Without God, the devil cannot exist; he is only the shadow of God. The day I said to you, "There is no God," his shadow also disappeared. So it is a committee, not a devil, a committee of all your prophets, messengers, messiahs – all cheating, deceiving you, destroying your life in every possible way.

It is not death that destroys your life and keeps you in illusion. It is your religions that destroy your life and keep you in an illusion which will happen *after* death.

I say to you, never forget death. It is always there by your side. Before it grips you, do whatsoever you feel like doing. Dance, have a little champagne. Love, and don't be bothered about death, because that will be destroying your present. When it comes, if we have lived our life totally and intensely, we will be able to live our death too, with the same intensity, with the same totality.

Yes, in fact death is only a transmigration – changing your house which has become dilapidated, is almost in ruins, and moving into a new house, fresh, just made, made for you. Death is only a change.

You have changed many houses, many bodies, and you are still here. Only when you become enlightened, then the work of death is finished, because after enlightenment you will not be changing the house, you will not be entering into another body. After enlightenment you will be entering into absolute freedom, you will be becoming one with the whole existence. You will be in the flowers, in the birds, in the sun, in the moon, in the rain, in the wind. You will be all over the place.

To become enlightened means to live this moment without any hesitation, without being half-hearted. Put everything at stake. Be a gambler! Risk everything, because the next moment is not certain. So why bother? Why be concerned?

Live dangerously! Live joyously!

Live without fear, live without guilt; live without any fear of hell or any greed for heaven. Just live! Death is not creating any illusion for you, it is your mind. Put this mind aside, so that it cannot disturb your dance, your song, your music.

Freedom From
Blind Biology

DISCOURSE 29,   July 27, 1985

Beloved Bhagwan,

Yesterday You spoke of science and how we could produce a New Man – more intelligent, creative, healthier and freer. It sounds fascinating and at the same time it is scary because of the feeling of some sort of mass product. Can You say something about the fear I am feeling?

It is absolutely fascinating, and there is no need to feel any fear about it. In fact, what we have been doing for millions of years is mass production – accidental mass production.

Do you know to what kind of a child you are going to give birth to? Do you know if he will be blind, crippled, retarded, sick, weak, vulnerable to all kinds of diseases for his whole life? Does your lover know what he is doing? While you are making love you have no conception, not even a possibility of guessing.

You are giving birth to children just like animals, and you don't fell scared about it, you don't feel any fear about it. And you see the whole world full of retarded people, crippled, blind, deaf, dumb. All this rubbish! Who is responsible for it? And is it not mass production?

My conception of giving scientific birth to a child is that, conscious, alert, knowingly, we are bringing a visitor to the earth. We know who he is, what he is and what he is to become finally; how long he will live, how much intelligence he will have.

We are discarding all possibilities of having blind children, deaf children, dumb children, retarded in any way – physically, psychologically – and you are feeling fear? Don't be stupid.

The scientific birth of a child is not animalistic. You are transcending the animal by giving birth to a child scientifically. It is fascinating, the greatest, most fascinating thing around. We can manage it, it is already a scientific reality. We can manage healthier people, who will live as long as we want, and we can give them as much intelligence as is needed for their work.

A couple comes to a scientific lab and tells them that they want a child like Albert Einstein, but better than him, living two hundred years; and he should never suffer any disease, he should be strong. The scientific lab finds the right egg from the bank, the right semen from the bank, and the child is produced in a test-tube with all precautions.

You will have to adopt the child, you cannot produce the child. Production of children is animalistic. Adoption of children of your own imagination…. Everybody wants a Shakespeare to be born, wants their child to be a great poet, a great musician, a great dancer. Every mother thinks that her child is going to be in some way a superhuman being, and every mother is frustrated – the child turns out to be just rotten. He just gets lost in this whole crowd on an overpopulated planet. This is mass production.

But adopting a child, you can contemplate on all

the qualities that you need. You can ask the advice of the experts as to what other qualities will be helpful in his life, how much he will be capable of love.... You want a Romeo? – you can get a Romeo. It is only a question of chemistry. Romeo has more male hormones than anybody else – he is richer; that's why one woman is not enough for him.

You want a poet who will transcend all the poets of the past? A scientist in comparison to whom all the scientists of the past will look like pygmies? A musician who brings the unknown, the invisible, through sounds to you? A poet who sings songs of joy and celebration as nobody else has ever done? You can ask anything, and they have just to work out, calculate which female egg, which male semen will produce such a human being.

That semen is not yours, that egg is not your wife's; you adopt the child. In this way you can get what humanity has always dreamed about: the birth of the superman, a man who is made almost of steel. Your Muhammed Ali the Great will not be able to face him – just one punch on his nose and he will be finished. What makes you afraid? Don't you want to get above animals? The desire that it will be your semen, that it will be your wife's egg, is simply ugly.

Children belong to the universe.

What speciality has it got that it is your semen? What is the point of creating a crippled person, just because it is your semen? Science can manage to raise you above animality – and it is not mass production, it will be just the opposite. There is not going to be an assembly line the way cars are produced. It is going to be very individual because every couple has the choice and the freedom to decide what kind of child they want.

How has the idea of mass production come into your mind? Do you think everybody would like the same kind of child? You are wrong. Do you think science labs will go on producing children according to their own desire, and you have to adopt them? Then it will be mass production. I am not for it. You are

All depends on whether we have courage enough to rise over our fearful selves. We have to rise above the scary feeling. Be fascinated with the New Man! The New Man must have a new kind of birth. The New Man must have a new kind of life, a new kind of love, a new kind of death. He will be new in every possible way.

absolutely free to choose. Right now you are absolutely blind and doing whatsoever you are doing in utter darkness. You are simply a slave of blind biology.

Don't you want freedom from blind biology? Don't you want to go above this stupid attachment to the idea that the child is born out of your semen and your wife's egg? Those eggs don't know to whom they belong. And what is special about your semen? You don't know anything about it. You are completely unaware of what kind of people are struggling within you to be born. You have no choice, you are simply a slave.

What I am saying about scientific birth makes you go beyond slavery, blindness, darkness. It makes you in a certain way more spiritual, because you are no longer concerned that your semen, your wife's egg, are absolutely needed for your child. You give your requirements; you adopt the child. And you can ask experts what will be the best for the child. Would you not like your child to be a unique genius?

For futile attachments, you are satisfied with a crippled child. And giving birth to a crippled child, a blind child, are you doing any favor to the child? He will never forgive you! You are responsible. And he will have to live a life which is not life a all.

My vision gives total freedom to you, and of course, great responsibility. Right now you are producing children without any responsibility.

You have means available to determine what color the child should be, what kind of face – Greek, Roman? You can create children who will look like sculptures, utterly beautiful, with genius in some dimension of life, living a life of love, intelligent enough to discard all the priests and all the politicians. They will not become followers of a leader, they will be enough unto themselves.

Right now, what are you doing? First you create in blindness, darkness a child, not knowing what he is going to turn out like. Then you force him to become a slave by making him a Christian, Hindu, Mohammedan, or politically giving him a certain ideology – socialism, fascism, communism. And he is not intelligent enough to rebel against all these slaveries.

The child of my vision will be absolute freedom. He will not belong to any political party, he will not belong to any organized religion. He will have his own religion, he will have his own political ideology. What is the need for him to hang around Karl Marx and be a communist? He can think better than Karl Marx – and Karl Marx is not a great thinker. He can live so long that he is not in a hurry about anything; patient, ready to wait – he has time enough.

Just think of Albert Einstein living three hundred years. He would have given miracles to the world. But because he was living in an accidental body, he had to die.

We can discard disease, old age. We can program life in every way. We can even program the life of the child, so that when *he* wants to die only then will he die; otherwise he can go on living. If he feels that there are still juices that he has not tasted, if he feels there are still dimensions that he has not explored, if he feels that more time is needed, then he is the master, to decide how long to live.

Up to now, you have lived seventy years on average – that includes people who live one hundred and fifty years in some places of the world. In Russia there are people who have passed one hundred and fifty years, and they are still young. There are people in a certain part of Kashmir, which Pakistan has invaded, who live very easily to one hundred and fifty, sixty, seventy. And it is a surprising fact – I have been to those people – a one hundred and fifty-year-old person is just working in the field the same way he was working when he was fifty – with the same strength, with the same gusto.

All that is needed is better planning, better crossbreeding. It is a known and applied fact about animals. Do you see the many kinds of beautiful dogs around the earth? – small, big, powerful, or just beautiful. Just to see them jump around you is such a joy. Do you think they came out of blind nature? No, for centuries we have been crossbreeding dogs.

You know it as a fact – the whole world accepts it – that a man should not get married to his own sister. Why? That should be the most simple thing, to get married to your own sister. You love her already, you have been together since birth, you know each other. But why have all cultures prohibited it? All cultures have said that marriage should be with distant people, people who don't come from the same family tree, because the bigger the distance, the better the product.

If a white American marries a Negro, the child will be far better than a white American marrying another white American, or a Negro marrying another Negro, because the distance between those two is immense – different centuries. They have grown in different atmospheres, their programming is totally different from each other. So when these two totally different cultures, traditions, conventions, lifestyles meet, they give birth to a better man, who has a double heritage: the heritage of the Negroes and the heritage of the white Americans.

In a scientific lab it will be possible to find eggs and semen cells as distant as possible. And we can create through that crossbreeding a totally new man. There is nothing scary about it. It is not mass production. The couple has to say what kind of person they would like to have as their child. It avoids all accidents. And we will be creating the universal man – not the Chinese, not the Indian, not the English, but the universal man. So please, just feel fascinated, don't feel scared and afraid. There is nothing to be afraid of.

You have seen the way children have been produced in the past. For millions of years you have been doing the same thing – what is the outcome? The outcome decides the value of what you have been doing. Once in a while there is an Albert Einstein or a Bertrand Russell – once in a while!

This is not right. It should be the ordinary phenomenon, usual. Once in a while, perhaps there will be a person who is born out of some unawareness, unalertness on the part of the scientist; otherwise, everybody should be a genius. Just think: the whole world full of people like Rabindranath, Jean-Paul Sartre, Jaspers, Heidegger!

And we can prevent people like Adolf Hitler, Mussolini, Joseph Stalin from being born, because they have been calamities here. We can close the door completely on all Genghis Khans, Tamerlanes, Nadir Shahs – all those ugly monsters whose whole life consisted of killing people, destroying people, burning people.

The way we have lived has not proved right. We have only a crowd of pygmies all around – *this* is what you should be scared of! But having a garden of geniuses, creative people, a garden from where we have removed all fanatics, idiots, politicians – in short, we have taken out all that was poisonous, all pollution….

There is so much in the idea. Now, how many people are suffering because they have a snubbed nose? Their whole life they feel inferior. How many people are suffering because they have *only* nose? If you look at them, everything else is so small and the nose is so big….

I have heard…one millionaire had a very big nose and very small eyes, but he was the richest man in the community. People used to laugh behind him, but nobody ever dared…. He was invited by a family for dinner. The family was concerned about only one thing: their child, who was a born philosopher, asked about everything.

From the morning they were teaching him, "You can ask anything, but when the rich man comes, you are not to ask about his nose." They told him so many times that he became immensely interested, "What is so great about the nose?" They had never prevented him from asking any question. Why was this nose so important?

And he was really excited, eagerly waiting for the

man to come. When he came in, the child laughed. He said to his parents, "He has only nose, nothing else! And why were you preventing me…? He is a rare specimen!" He destroyed the whole effort.

But people…almost everyone is suffering from something or other. Somebody is suffering from his color, somebody is suffering from his tallness; somebody is too tall, somebody is too small. What have you produced? This is mass production – accidental, produced in darkness. At least human beings – who are the crown in existence – should not suffer anymore from an inferiority complex. The only way is scientific production of children. And there are immense possibilities in it.

For example, if the child is produced in a scientific lab, they can produce a similar child simultaneously. The other child will be kept in the lab growing simultaneously; exactly as the one who has gone out to be adopted by a family, the other will be growing in the scientific lab. Just the existence of the other gives great opportunities.

For example, you get a fractured leg. Now no need to bother to fix the fracture – the leg from the other fellow can be taken and given to you. Something goes wrong, berserk, in your head – now there is no need for all the psychologists, psychoanalysts, psychiatrists. Your head is just removed, you get a fresh head.

The other person will remain in anesthesia his whole life, in a deep freeze. He will not know anything of what is happening. He is just there in case something goes wrong with you – and many things go wrong in life, even with every precaution. Something can always go wrong; life is a long affair. You may have a car accident…now, that cannot be prevented by scientific reproduction of children.

In fact, those children will not believe in the fifty-five miles per hour limit; that will be sheer stupidity. The people who are going to live three hundred years will change everything around. Rather than keeping to fifty-five miles per hour for millions of people,

why not create better and straighter roads where you can move at two hundred miles per hour?

Your roads are just ugly, so many turns – their roads will be totally different. In fact, in Japan one scientist has proved that if a car moves at four hundred miles per hour – and a car can – at four hundred miles per hour the cars, just because of that great speed, rise one foot above the road. No bumps, no troubles from the road. There may be snow, and there may be ice; let it be there – you will be simply going one foot above.

In fact, that possibility makes it a great opportunity. If you can move four hundred miles per hour one foot above the road, the road is not really needed! You need only launching roads. The moment you pick up speed, then you can go anywhere; roads or no roads make no difference.

But all depends on whether we have courage enough to rise over our fearful selves. We have to rise above the scary feeling. Be fascinated with the New Man!

The New Man must have a new kind of birth. The New Man must have a new kind of life, a new kind of love, a new kind of death. He will be new in every possible way. He will replace the old models who are overcrowding the earth – junkyards. They are not needed.

It is a simple process of programming the first cell. And only the first cell can be programmed, because then it goes on reproducing itself – that is an autonomous process. You can program it for everything. Right now it is difficult; it is programmed for all kinds of diseases, it is programmed for death, old age. You can't have any control over it. There is no way to change the program now, because all the cells have the same program.

If they are programmed for a particular disease that you get by inheritance, you will suffer from that disease. It could have been changed, but only in the first meeting of the male and the female cells. Everything can be programmed, and an exact copy of you can be kept in the lab. If your heart is not functioning well, the new heart is available – which will fit you exactly, because it comes from your copy, your twin.

Any new thing scares, but it scares only cowards. Any new thing fascinates, but it fascinates only the brave ones. Be brave, because we need a new, brave world.

Beloved Bhagwan,

You spoke of transplanting the brain of geniuses like Einstein into the body of a young man. But if Einstein wanted to be a plumber instead of a scientist, and we transplanted his brain, have we not done something against his wishes? He could be stuck on earth for another seventy years, possibly against his choice. Can You say something about this?

It is so simple that I wonder, cannot you figure out small things yourself? The brain is a mechanism, it is not Einstein's soul. The brain is just a computer. We will transplant Einstein's brain; that does not make any difference to the journey of his soul. His soul will go on moving, and if he wants to be a plumber and really desires to be a plumber, he may become a plumber.

But this brain he has developed, which is unique…. You may not be aware that he himself donated his brain to Harvard University: "When I die, my brain should be studied as carefully as possible to find what the difference is between my brain and other people's brain." And there is a great distance. He himself was curious. He said, "Of course, I will not be able to know, because I will be dead, but it may help you, humanity, to know what the difference is."

After four years of research the difference has been found. It is very small. That small difference can be introduced into any brain and it will start functioning on a far higher level. But you will be again scared that science introduced something into your brain. It is just a little difference, but it makes a great difference: Einstein had proportionately more of certain cells than any other brain. Now, those cells can be cultivated and introduced into any brain.

But nobody is interested. The research is finished, the findings are at hand. Nobody is interested, because the whole world is interested in how to destroy each other. They are so much occupied with war, day in and day out, that many beautiful things that go on happening in scientific research are just lying by the side. Nobody is using them.

So don't be afraid that Einstein will be stuck for seventy years against his will, no. Einstein is a totally different phenomenon than the brain. The brain is just a thing attached to the soul of Einstein. The same brain can be attached to another soul. It will function the same, because it is an attachment; it has nothing to do with the soul. The soul will only supply the energy for the brain to function. If an idiot's brain is attached to you, your soul will supply energy to the idiot's brain; you will function like an idiot.

And you know small things change your behavior. You drink alcohol – although it is called spirits, it is not a spirit. Your spirit is absolutely unaffected by the alcohol. Alcohol goes into your brain, into your body, and creates all kinds of disturbances – pleasant, unpleasant. There are other drugs, such as LSD, which can change your whole mind at least for a few hours or a few days.

When Aldous Huxley for the first time – he was a pioneer in that sense – took LSD, he could not believe it: everything looked more beautiful, luminous. Even the chair in front of him was radiant, had an aura of light around it. What had happened?

The LSD had tricked his mind, influenced his mind. He saw the beauty of the flowers – those flowers he had seen before, but not the way they were appearing today. The fragrance was overpowering. His soul was the same, but the attached brain now had LSD in it, and was magnifying everything.

Aldous Huxley was a beautiful man of immense intelligence; hence, through LSD he saw only paradise. He started experimenting with other people. Then he became aware that it is not LSD that creates paradise; for some people it creates hell. It depends on the person's mind – LSD only magnifies, multiplies. If you are a miserable person, LSD will make you a million times more miserable. If you are a man of joy, LSD will magnify your joy a thousand times.

He became aware that it is not LSD that creates paradise. LSD does not create anything, it is simply a magnifying glass. So the same flower looks more beautiful, a thousand times more beautiful; the same fragrance is now so dense and overpowering. But a man who is miserable, a man who is continuously down in the dumps, will find himself in the darkest hole ever. That's why Aldous Huxley wrote a book and named it *Heaven and Hell*. It is a book about LSD.

Your soul remains unaffected. When LSD has run out of your physical system, you are back home, the same miserable person you have been before, or the same joyous person you have been before. But the experience of two or three days under LSD changes many of your ideas.

Aldous Huxley himself was so much impressed that he thought all the mystics who have experienced heaven must have been creating something like LSD by their exercises, prayer, meditation and other methods. That's not true. He was so much impressed that he thought this is the ultimate panacea. But soon he became aware that it not true, because a few people go into hell.

Your brain is a separate thing from your soul, so don't be worried about Einstein. His brain is already in the Harvard University, resting in alcohol. Do you think Albert Einstein is caged there in that bottle? Albert Einstein must be a plumber somewhere – perhaps here, because where else can he find a place where plumbers are as much respected as professors? where plumbers are not lower than presidents? This is the only place where nobody is higher or lower. Everybody is doing something essential, something which is needed.

I am reminded of a phenomenon that has happened in India. Jainism is the oldest religion in India. In one of the conferences of the Jainas, I challenged them. I told them, "If you are really a religion, you should create a commune consisting only of Jainas. And then you will know that you don't have a complete philosophy.

"Who is going to make the shoes? Jainas cannot do it. Who is going to be a plumber? Jainas cannot do that. Who is going to clean the toilets? Jainas cannot do it. Then what kind of religion is this?"

I told them – and made many enemies. That has been my life's work. I am going to write a book like Dale Carnegie: "How to Influence People and Make Enemies." I told them, "You are parasites. You are living amongst Hindus, exploiting Hindus; you are parasites. Why should anybody else clean your toilets?"

This is the first commune in the whole world which is not in any way parasitical. Here everybody is doing everything. In fact, there is so much movement – professors become plumbers. One day you see the professor teaching in the university and another day you find him plumbing. And you are surprised – what has happened? He says, "I got bored teaching, teaching, teaching. I am on holiday from teaching, and plumbing is beautiful."

In this commune we make holidays by changing your job, we don't have any other holidays. But changing the job, scientifically, is a holiday, because when you are functioning as a professor, a certain part of your brain functions – only a certain part, not the whole brain. When you are a plumber, another part of your brain functions; the professor is on holiday. This way we don't lose time, we don't lose days, and still we enjoy holidays as much as we want!

Don't be afraid about Einstein. Just remember, your body is not you.

Beloved Bhagwan,

When You talk about Christianity, You usually talk about Catholicism. Please, will You speak about Protestant churches? We do not acknowledge the pope.

I certainly have avoided speaking on Protestantism, for the simple reason that the man who created it, Martin Luther, is not worth considering at all. Jesus Christ may be crazy, nuts, but Martin Luther was just a politician.

There is no difference between the Catholic's basic doctrine and the Protestant's. Why did he create so much fuss and divide Christianity into two parts? — because he himself wanted to become the pope. Finding it difficult…and remember, he was a German, and Germans have something in them that drives them to become Adolf Hitlers; they want to be always on the top.

Just the other day one Germany journalist was asking me, "Why don't you use Mercedes-Benz?"

I asked, "Why should I use Mercedes-Benz? I have tried all the models of Mercedes-Benz, I have the latest Mercedes 500, but they don't come even close to a Rolls Royce."

He said, "This will make Germans feel very bad. The Mercedes-Benz has to be the topmost car."

Why? It is a good car; my secretary uses it. But the Rolls Royce is simply unique, no other car comes close to it. But to the Germans, it hurts. Strange, what kind of psychology is there?

It very much hurt Martin Luther that he was just a bishop. And no German has ever been chosen as a pope. Perhaps they were afraid that once a German becomes the pope, no one knows what he will do…. He tried hard in the beginning to be chosen a pope.

It is a good thing about popes, that by the time a person becomes a pope he is almost on his deathbed. Only this Polack who is now the pope has deceived — Polacks are Polacks. Perhaps he has forgotten to die! Otherwise, popes have been dying after one year,

two years, three years at the most. So it gave chances to other people.

Martin Luther tried many times, but he was never chosen. Then he rebelled. That's why his religion is called Protestantism. It is a protest — the protest of a politician, the protest of a German, the protest of a man who wanted to be on the top but could not be.

But there is no difference of any significance in their theologies. They both believe in Jesus Christ, they both believe in the virgin birth of Jesus Christ, and they both believe in his resurrection after the crucifixion. The only difference is that Catholics also worship Jesus' mother, Mary.

For this much difference, why should I bother about these people? I am hitting at the very roots. These small matters don't matter. So when I am speaking against Christianity, remember, I am not speaking only against Catholicism. I am speaking against all the sects and cults – and there are many. I am speaking against Christianity as a whole.

Martin Luther was against the pope because he could not become the pope. You can see he was not really against the pope; he himself wanted to be the pope. It was just the old story of Aesop….

A fox was trying to catch hold of beautiful grapes, ripe, inviting. But her jump was not enough to catch hold of the grapes. She tried many times. She was not aware that a small rabbit was watching, hiding in a bush. The moment she saw the rabbit, she walked away with dignity. The rabbit said, "Auntie, what is the matter?" The fox said, "The grapes are not ripe."

That's what Martin Luther said, "The grapes are sour." If he was really against the pope, then why did he want to become the pope?

I will not accept – even if all the Christians of the world ask me to become the pope, I will not accept it. I will not accept even if the whole world asks me to become God, the creator, the father who is… (A noise is heard on the roof of Rajneesh

Mandir)...above the roof of Rajneesh Mandir. Those are just two electricians! I will not accept it. Anything that is wrong, howsoever powerful it makes you, I am not going to accept. I am fulfilled, and I am absolutely contented with myself. I have no protest, no complaint, no grudge against anybody.

It was for this simple reason that I have not talked about the Protestant section of Christianity separately. There is nothing separate about it. It is just the German mind that makes it separate and I am not in favor of this kind of German mind.

I have more sannyasins in Germany than anywhere else, for the simple reason that they have seen the ugliness of Adolf Hitler and what he did. The younger generation does not want to carry that German mind any more, and this is the only place where we can deprogram them.

We have one dozen communes in Germany. It takes a little hard work to break down the German mind, but it is worth trying, because once it breaks down the breakthrough is not far away. And once a German drops the German mind – it takes longer for him to drop his mind, but once he drops it, he drops it forever.

Those people have guts. I love them. Sooner or later the whole of Germany is going to be red. We cannot leave Germany, for the simple reason that they are the strongest people in the world. If they can alone fight the whole world, and go on winning for five years under the leadership of a crackpot, these people are of immense value. If we can change Germany, we can change the whole world. That is the criterion: Germany in our hands, the whole world is in our hands, because nobody can have as much resistance as the Germans.

I have been experimenting, and I have been successful. Once a German has fallen in love with me, it is forever. You ask Haridas. He came to me somewhere around fifteen years ago; since then he has not left for a single moment. His old mother wanted to see him – she had to come, he would not go. He will not leave me for a single moment. And when his mother saw the flowering of her son, the transformation, she did not wait; she immediately became a sannyasin. I have given her the name Haridasi. She is old, but a beautiful woman, very loving.

Martin Luther was the same type as Adolf Hitler. He created this schism in Christianity, but he has not contributed anything to the world – that's why I don't criticize him. I simply ignore the fellow. He is just below me.

Beloved Bhagwan,

You say that we, Your disciples, are not followers but fellow travelers. It is true that we are wandering and seeking, but Your travelings came to an end long ago. You have nowhere to go, nothing to achieve; You are utterly fulfilled. So why don't You accept Your right position of being our guide? Why confuse and confound Your donkeys and camels?

I am going to confuse and confound all the Yankees, all the monkeys, all the donkeys, all the camels – because there is no other way to make them lions, and finally to create the child.

Yes, it is true that I have nowhere to go. I have got it, that which you are seeking and searching for. But still I will not accept the idea of being your leader, guide, because those words have very wrong connotations with them. The religious leaders and guides have exploited the whole humanity so much that I don't want to be associated with them in any way – and those words make me associated with them.

I am utterly contented, there is nothing more; but I go on walking, moving, just to destroy the idea that I am the leader and you are the follower. You are seeking; I have found it, but can't I play and seek with you just to help you feel that you are not followers but fellow travelers?

I do not want to insult you by calling you followers. I respect you. A small device I had to maintain: that is, just to go on seeking and searching with you, knowing perfectly well that there is nothing for me to seek. And there is nothing for you to seek either. It is just that I know it and you don't know it.

Just being your fellow traveler, I will infect you. I am contagious! Sooner or later you will realize my play, and you will be grateful, remember. You will be grateful that I never became your leader, never reduced you to be the led, never gave you any guidance – that is humiliating.

But just being with you – and I know you have got it, just the way I have got it – in some proper moment I will shake you and wake you up.

It is not guidance.

It is just shaking and waking.

Guidance is needed for a goal somewhere far away – what path to follow.

I want you to remember that it is not only you who respect me, I also respect you.

Buddha could not say that, Mohammed could not say that, Jesus could not say that. And I feel there is some weakness in these fellows. Somehow they are feeling a gratification from being the leader, the guide, the prophet, the messiah, the savior. Something of the ego is there – very subtle, sophisticated, refined, slippery, you cannot catch hold of it, but it is there in their declaration of being higher than you, better than you. They have arrived and you are miles away, with miles to travel, arduous miles.

Buddha and Mahavira say, "Where we are, you will take lives to reach." They are creating such a big distance between you and themselves. That's the way of the ego.

I am trying in every possible way to close any gap between me and you, knowing perfectly well that there is a *little* difference:

I am awake, you are asleep.

Playing with you, singing and dancing with you, I am certain I will make you awake without being your leader, without being your guide. Don't be worried, I am not renouncing you. When I say that I am not your leader, don't think that I am abandoning you. Don't think that if you are not my followers, then what the hell are you doing here? I take life very nonseriously. It is really a great joke!

I know more jokes than anybody in the whole world, and I can say with absolute certainty that there is no joke which is bigger than life itself. What a joke – that you are it, and you are seeking it! You are where you are meant to be, and you are running all around, searching for the right place.

Not only that, you are suggesting to me that I should take my right position as the guide. I am in my right position – not as the guide, but just as a playmate. Can't you accept it?

That means your ego comes in between. Your ego wants me to be the master of masters, the greatest master in the whole history of the world, because only then can you say, "I am the follower of the greatest master in history; certainly I am one of the greatest followers in the whole history."

I am not going to help you in strengthening your ego. I am perfectly aware what hurts you. You would like me to fulfill the image and all kinds of expectations so that you can feel, "This is the right guide, and I am the person who has found the right guide. All other leaders are pygmies, and their followers, of course, are even worse."

No, I am not going to help you in that way. I will play the role of being a very ordinary man. I know, and you know, that I am not an ordinary man, but what to do! I don't guide you, I help you. You don't need guidance, you need just a little help, a hit…just a little cold water thrown against your eyes so that you wake up.

You will be grateful one day that I never accepted the idea of the leader and the led, because once you accept the idea of the leader you free the led from all responsibility. Once you accept that the savior is here, it means you have nothing to do; you have just to be faithful, believing. And I am destroying all your beliefs and all your faiths – how can I be the leader? The leader needs believers.

I am something utterly different from the people you have known before: Jesus, Moses, Mahavir, Krishna, Buddha. I am not part of their company.

With me begins a new era in enlightenment, where the master will be just playing games with you, where the master will not allow you to be behind him, but drag you by his side. I can put you ahead of me, but I cannot put you behind. It is a subtle device.

So don't feel depressed, I am not abandoning you. I *am* your master, you *are* my follower. But don't tell it to anybody, keep it a secret!

Beloved Bhagwan,

Do only cowards drop sannyas?

Nobody ever drops sannyas. Yes, once in a while a coward takes sannyas. And I am just incapable of refusing, so even if a coward comes to take sannyas…I know perfectly well he will not be a sannyasin. He will wear the robe, he will make every effort, but sooner or later he will be gone.

I say nobody drops sannyas except those people who have never been sannyasins; they only looked as if they were sannyasins. I allow them to have the opportunity, because sometimes it happens that a person who takes sannyas without any understanding of what it is – perhaps already thinking, "Let us try it. There is nothing binding; when I go home, I will go home in the same dress as I had come, I will leave all these red clothes behind" – even such a person has the potential. So I don't refuse anybody.

It is unpredictable. The man becomes a sannyasin, already thinking that this is just to take part in the commune – it looks embarrassing not to be a sannyasin here, it is the "in" thing, so just as a fashion he enters. But he does not know that you cannot trick me. I allow him, and start playing the game with him. Ninety percent of these people turn out to be sannyasins. Ten percent, who were only pretending to be sannyasins, drop out.

That's why I say, no sannyasin drops sannyas. Only those who were not really sannyasins drop it. But what have they to drop? They were never sannyasins in the first place.

To have a taste of sannyas, to have a taste of me, to drink the wine I am making available to you, to laugh and to sing and to dance – then it is impossible that anybody can drop sannyas.

Yes, a few idiots will be there who will dance only because everybody else is dancing; it looks awkward not to dance. They will be in red clothes because everybody is in red clothes and they don't want to look like outsiders. Those few idiots will come and go. But my compassion for idiots is as much as for any genius – in fact, a little more. I try my hardest so that the idiot drops his camelhood, becomes a lion. And I have succeeded with many idiots, I have seen them transforming into lions. And a few idiots even have reached to the stage of the child.

So my sannyas is available for everybody – with no qualifications, with no conditions. I don't demand that you have to follow a certain discipline, then only can you become a sannyasin.

One day I said this and a few camels went to the office. They said, "Bhagwan says no qualifications, no conditions. We want to become sannyasins, but we will not wear the red clothes and we will not wear the mala." These camels don't understand that red clothes and mala are not qualifications, they are not conditions. They are your identification card – spread all over your body, so no need to pull it out of your pocket and show people. You will be seen anywhere from miles away.

The red color is really the color of danger. It is your identification card; it is not your quality, it is not your qualification.

It it has nothing to do with your discipline.

So remember, no camel should go to the office and ask for sannyas.... Then why are you asking for sannyas? Just *believe* you are sannyasins – because you will not be wearing the mala, you will not be wearing the red clothes. So what is the trouble? Why even *ask* for sannyas? Imagine, believe that you are a sannyasin.

But if you ask to become a sannyasin you will have to carry the identification card around the world, because this is how I have approached millions of people. Just think, if I had not given a particular uniform to you, you would have been lost in the world. I would not even be able to recognize you, you would not feel any connection with me. You would not even be able to drop sannyas, and your sannyas would not create any troubles for you in life.

And I want those troubles in your life, in your work, in your job.

I want you to be constantly in a state of challenge, surrounded by hostile forces, because this is the only way a real sannyasin grows – out of fire, burning all around.

My sannyasins have been thrown out of their jobs, they have been thrown out of the universities where they were teaching, where they were professors.

They are fighting in the courts. When you fight for your sannyas you have some respect for it, some love for it; you have some connection with me. When you are in trouble and you have to suffer many things, and you are ready to suffer but not to drop sannyas, that makes you stronger. It brings your capacities to their peak. You are ready to die, but you are not going to compromise.

Against me and the sannyasins, in Oregon, they have a slogan written on the trucks, buses – anywhere they can find a place. The slogan is: It is better to be dead than red.

I would like you to remember: It is certainly better to be dead than not to be red!

Everybody Wants Freedom, Nobody Wants Responsibility

DISCOURSE 30, July 28, 1985

Beloved Bhagwan,

I have heard You say that You would like to sever our relationships with all "isms."
Does this include Rajneeshism as well?

Certainly. But you don't understand one thing – Rajneeshism is not an "ism." It is just because of the poverty of language that we had to call it Rajneeshism. It is not an "ism" because it has no theology, no ideology, no philosophy – which are basic needs for an "ism" to exist.

You are absolutely free individuals. You don't belong to a certain concept about existence, about God, heaven and hell. You simply don't have any conceptualization.

We are existential: the "ism" is a mind thing. Our approach to reality is not a mind approach, it is a communion of heart to heart. All "isms" have belief systems: we don't have any belief system. You are not required to believe in anything unless you know it; and when you know something you don't believe, there is no need. You believe only things which you don't know.

Belief grows only in ignorance.

Knowing something is enough, there is no need to believe. We are seekers, searchers, not believers.

We don't have any idea beforehand about what we are going to get in the end, when the search is over. Hence, I say to you, it is just poverty of language that our approach to reality is called Rajneeshism.

But it is not an "ism" at all, because it does not fulfill the requirements to make it an "ism." Communism is, socialism is, fascism is; all religions are. They are not existential. They are not trying to discover individually, in a very intimate and personal way, what this life is all about. They have taken for granted words of others – and words are just words, containers without any content.

Words have a strange quality. You can go on and on building big palaces, castles in the air, through words, but there is no base to your castle in the air. The base is provided by your own experiencing. You can become a Christian just by believing in *The Bible*. You can become a Hindu just by believing in the *Vedas*.

You cannot become a Rajneeshee by believing in my words. You become a Rajneeshee when you also start feeling the same song I am feeling, you start the dance that is happening within me, you become full of the fragrance…. It is not wordy, it is existential.

To call it Rajneeshism was just a necessity enforced by poor language – it has no word for the existential approach. Even the philosophy of existence is called existentialism – the same stupid idea. Those philosophers are saying that there is no way to find the truth through argument, intellect.

Existence is available if you are silent, listening to it…. The sound of the running water, the wind blowing through the pine trees, the smell of a rose; the beauty of some face; the ecstasy of dropping all ideas, becoming a child – innocent, enchanted by everything life is made of. He knows nothing about it, but he feels it.

A just-born baby…. You bring the rose close to him, he will see it, he will certainly find fragrance. But he cannot have in his being, anywhere, words. He cannot say to himself, "What a beautiful red rose." He does not know that beautifulness has a name, that there are words which call this a flower, a rose.

He knows nothing about colors, he cannot say it is red, but he finds it redder than you find it. He finds it livelier than you find it. He discovers immense beauty, fragrance, fragileness – but he has no words. He does not say anything within himself, he is utterly silent, absorbing all that the roseflower can give to him.

Rajneeshism is basically a transformation of you to the child again.

The word "ism" is not really applicable, but what to do? Language is a kind of imprisonment. Some word has to be used and all words will be wrong. So I said, "Okay, call it Rajneeshism. But as far as the 'ism' idea is concerned, include Rajneeshism completely out of any other 'ism' that has existed before."

It would be easier to call it something totally new, but then nobody would understand what it is. So until we have enough people to understand, we will have to carry a wrong label on it. Once they have understood, the label will be removed. Once we have our own world around this earth, "ism" is not going to be part of our way of life. So if you think Rajneeshism is also an "ism," throw it away. You have not understood anything. Your approach is still intellectual;

God, fate, destiny – these are bogus words, mumbo jumbo, nothing more than that. Drop them completely, because dropping them will make you an individual, fully responsible for your acts. And unless you take the responsibility on yourself, you will never become strong, you will never become independent, you will never have the taste of freedom. You can have freedom. But the cost is to accept responsibility in its totality.

otherwise, such a question would not have arisen.

You can see – no dogma is preached, no belief system is given. You are not required to accept *anything*. The atheist can become part of my communes, the theist can become part, the communist can become part, the capitalist can become part. We don't discriminate against anybody. Our basic approach is such, that whosoever becomes part of us, we deprogram. And the process of deprogramming is the same; whether you deprogram a Communist or a Catholic or a Protestant does not matter.

It is just like surgery. If a communist has cancer, goes through surgery, do you think the surgery will be different than the surgery when a Catholic has cancer? Will there be a Catholic surgery? Hindu surgery? Mohammedan surgery? You can understand perfectly well that surgery doesn't take any account of who you are, but it knows how to remove the cancer. And I am continuously hammering on your cancer to destroy it.

All "isms" are nothing but spiritual cancer; and if you think of Rajneeshism also in the same intellectual terms, I am going to hammer on it too. But it is not an "ism," it is not a cancer: it is a surgical method. We just had to give it a wrong name, because no right name exists in any language.

Yes, the day will come when we will start creating new words, new languages. It is certainly foolish that in this world there are thousands of languages – all that it needs is one language. And these languages have grown haphazardly, unscientifically, but we go on carrying them – just junk, thousands of years old.

Just as I say one world is needed and one world government is needed, so one scientifically created language is needed, so that all men, wherever they are, are capable of understanding each other.

No old language should be accepted as the world language, for the simple reason that old languages are not capable of coping with the new reality that goes on changing. And the second reason: if you choose one language out of the old, all other languages which are not chosen will fight against it, naturally. If you just think of numbers, then Chinese will be the world language, because of every four people, one is a Chinese. And Chinese is the most difficult language, the most unscientific, because it is one of the most ancient languages.

It has no alphabet, it has only symbols. Just to be able to understand Chinese you have to understand at least ten thousand symbols – just to begin with! If you want to be a real scholar in the language, then one hundred thousand symbols you have to remember. It is an unnecessary burden, absolutely not needed. And even those symbols are not clear.

If in Chinese you want to write "war, conflict, struggle, fight," you have only one symbol – very true. The symbol is one tree and two women under it. That is, one husband and two women under one roof: the tree is the roof. But is is up to you whether to understand it as war, as fight, as struggle, as battle, or just a conflict, a debate, a discussion – because the symbol can represent all these things. You have to learn the context in which the symbol is used.

To learn Chinese, if you are not born Chinese, takes at least thirty years. As far as numbers are concerned, Chinese is the first language, and they will not be ready to give chances to any language which is far behind them.

No old language will do. But man is capable of creating a language like Esperanto and making it absolutely scientific so that no confusion arises. And because it will be a new language, there is nobody who will be privileged because it is his mother tongue. And nobody else will be disadvantaged because he has to learn a language for thirty years – almost half his life.

A new language will be equally acceptable to all. It will not be a competitor to any language. And only a new language can manage to be scientific; old languages cannot. Old languages go on adjusting to the new realities, but their adjustments make them silly. For example, horses are no longer important, but horsepower…strange, a car has so much horsepower, an airplane has so much horsepower. This is adjustment. Horses are gone, but horsepower will continue.

In English you have a word "daughter." You may not be aware that it is very ancient. It comes from the Sanskrit, *duhita*. Five or ten thousand years ago, it was the privilege of the daughter to milk the cow. *Duhita* means one who milks the cow. Now from *duhita* has arisen the word "daughter," because only daughters were doing that job ten thousand years ago in India.

The reason is that the cow is holy to the Hindus, and they would like it to be milked only by a virgin girl, to keep the milk holy. But what has it to do with daughter? There may be millions of daughters who have never touched a single cow, and they are still being called daughter.

If you look into the history of any word, you will make amazing discoveries. How has it arisen? Centuries have changed the word's color, its tone, its pronunciation – everything. New qualities have been given to it which are not applicable.

Words are dead things, and it is time that we have one language, scientifically arranged.

When the first American woman met me, it was nearly thirty years ago. She was interested in me – I was traveling, and she asked, "What is your schedule?"

I said, "Forgive me, I don't understand this word – skedual? What is a skedual?"

She was puzzled. She said, "This is a simple word, a common word."

I said, "You just explain it to me, perhaps I may be able to figure out what you mean."

And then I found out – because in India, English is spoken with the British pronunciation, not the American. Certainly the American pronunciation of the word is more accurate because of the spelling of the word. The British pronunciation is "shed-dule," not "skedual" – they are the same words. I was accustomed to hearing "shed-dule."

I said to her, "Forgive me, but there was no way to figure out that it is 'shed-dule' that you are using."

There is so much misunderstanding in the world, and one of the greatest reasons is that we have so many languages. It is a tower of Babel. You cannot understand what the communist is saying, because he has his own connotations of the word, his own meaning. The communist cannot understand what you are saying, he has different connotations of the same word.

Communists believe they have the real democracy, because how can a democracy exist where the society is divided into classes? – the poor and the rich and the middlers. If the society is divided and the gap is so big between the rich and the poor, the rich are going to dominate; so don't call it democracy, it is aristocracy. No communist is ready to believe that in America there is democracy, because the first basic thing is not to write in the constitution that "all men are equal," but to *make* them equal; then democracy is possible.

If there are so many poor people, their votes can be purchased. They *are* being purchased, because for the poor man democracy cannot give bread and butter. The word "democracy" is for those who have everything, it is not for him. If he can get something tangible just for giving a vote, he is ready.

I have seen it in India – India is a democracy, but not a single poor man becomes the prime minister, the governor, the chief minister. It is impossible for the poor man to reach there, because the expenses of election are so big. Yet in the constitution everybody has equal rights, and every vote has equal value. Communists cannot accept the idea.

America cannot accept Russia as a democracy, because only one party exists. There is no choice – how can you apply freedom? You have to choose the communists, there is nobody else. You have to choose the communists unanimously. What kind of democracy is this? Democracy according to the American mind needs two parties at least.

Russians go on declaring themselves the most democratic. Americans go on declaring they are the greatest democracy. Now, that word "democracy" is not scientific. It has different meanings to different people.

You know the English word "go." You cannot imagine, howsoever wild a dreamer you are, from where this word "go" comes. It comes again from the cow.

In Sanskrit, the cow is called *cav*. And the Hindus have been interested in the cow so much, they love the cow so much, they have called the cow their mother. And in fact, ten thousand years ago, when the hunting society was changing into an agricultural society, the cow became of immense importance. She was giving food, she was giving bulls to be used for bullock carts, to be used in farming. Everything that the cow gives is usable – even cow dung, because it is a very powerful fertilizer.

So they used to worship the cow. And it was a common thing that in the morning the cows would go to the grasslands, and in the evening at the time of sunset they would come back home. And the Hindus started saying, "The cow is going to the forest, the cow is going home." Going became associated with the cow.

The English word "go" or "going" has come from ten thousand-year-old Hindus, and it is associated with the cow, not with you. When you say, "I am going," you are saying, "I am a cow"! And that's what Sanskrit-speaking people will understand. And they will be amazed: "What are you saying?"

All the languages of the world create walls, very subtle transparent walls, which are far more difficult to remove than the wall that exists in Berlin. The world needs one language, and a new language – simple, accurate. The pronunciation has to be according to the spelling, so that there is now way to mis-pronounce a word.

Perhaps it is going to be our work sooner or later to create a new language which gives scope enough for all types of experiences. Right now, there is no way, so just out of compulsion we have called our approach to life, Rajneeshism. But if you think of it as an "ism," you don't understand it. If it is an "ism" for you, throw it. If you understand that this is only a label – out of compulsion we had to call it that, to use it – then you will not ask such a question.

We are not a religion in the same sense Christianity is, Judaism is, Hinduism is. But what to do with the American bureaucracy? Unless I am a religious leader, they cannot allow me to stay here. I am nobody's leader, and certainly not a religious leader. I am destroying all the roots of all the religions. But they won't understand it; I had to accept their stupidity and call myself a religious leader. They don't have any other category.

Just the other day my secretary was saying to me, "Somewhere you have said you are an anarchist. If the American government comes to know about it…. They have a basic rule that no anarchist should be allowed to become a resident of America." They do not understand. I am not an anarchist like Prince Kropotkin. Prince Kropotkin wanted governments to be dissolved immediately; he said there was no need of any government. I think he was a little bit crazy.

Governments in existence…. There is so much crime, so many murders, so many rapes, so many drugs, thefts. Just think, if for twenty-four hours the government stops functioning – just a holiday – for twenty-four hours there is no law, no government, what do you think will happen in America? Thousands will be murdered, thousands will commit suicide. Everywhere there will be stealing, everywhere there will be cheating. And it is only for twenty-four hours that the law is no more applicable, so you have to do it fast, whatever you always wanted to do.

Man has not come to the point where governments can be dissolved. Prince Kropotkin is against the government, the law. He wants to dissolve them.

I am also an anarchist, but in a totally opposite way to Prince Kropotkin.

I want to raise the consciousness of human beings to the point where government becomes futile, courts remain empty, nobody is murdered, nobody is raped, nobody is tortured or harassed. Do you see the difference? His emphasis is: dissolve the governments. My emphasis is: raise the consciousness of human beings to the point where governments become, of their own accord, useless; to the point that courts start closing, that police start disappearing because there is no work, judges are told, "Find some other job." I am an anarchist from a very different dimension. But my secretary was afraid that they would not understand. To them, anarchism means Prince Kropotkin.

I am against Prince Kropotkin and his anarchism because he is talking nonsense. First let people be ready – and governments will disappear on their own account. I am not in favor of destroying governments; they are fulfilling a certain need. Man is so barbarous, so ugly, that if he is not prevented by force, the whole society will be in a chaos. Prince Kropotkin is not an anarchist, he is in favor of chaos.

I am not in favor of chaos. I want human society to become a harmonious whole, a vast commune all around the world: people meditating, people without guilt, people with great serenity, silence; people rejoicing, dancing, singing; people who have no desire to compete with anybody; people who have dropped the very idea that they are special and have to prove it by becoming the president of America; people who are no longer suffering from any inferiority complex, so nobody wants to be superior, nobody brags about his greatness.

The governments will evaporate like dewdrops in the early morning sun. But that is a totally different story, a totally different approach. Till that moment comes, governments are needed.

It is a simple thing. If you are sick, medicines are needed. Prince Kropotkin wants to destroy the medicines. I want you to be healthy so you don't need medicines. Automatically you will throw them – what will you do with all those medicines? They are utterly useless, in fact, dangerous; most of the medicines are poisons. For what purpose will you go on accumulating them? See the difference of emphasis.

I am not against medicines, I am against the sickness of man which makes medicines necessary. I would like a healthier man – which is possible – a man who has no possibility of becoming sick, because we have programmed him from his very birth that he cannot be sick, we have made arrangements in his body to fight against any sickness. Certainly medicines will disappear, medical stores will disappear, doctors will disappear, medical colleges will be closed. But I am not against them! That will be simply a consequence of a healthy humanity.

Yes, I am an anarchist, and if the American government wants to bring in the question of anarchism, I am going to fight, because my anarchism is totally different. Perhaps they have never heard the distinction. They don't know that these are two totally different things; you cannot put them under one name. But that's how languages are, because we have not made languages scientifically. They have grown blindly, unconsciously, taken new colors, new meanings. As time changes, languages don't change. The words remain the same, they just acquire new meanings.

In India, there is a word "babu." It is thought to be very respectful to address somebody as babu. The great leaders of the country, like Subhash Chandra Bhose, are called Babu Subhash Chandra Bhose. Nobody bothers about where the word has come from. And it is not very ancient – only three hundred years old.

When the Britishers invaded India their capital was Calcutta, in Bengal. Only later on when they conquered the whole country and consolidated themselves did they move to the ancient capital of the country, Delhi. Before that Calcutta was their capital.

Bengalis, the people who live in Calcutta and around Calcutta, in the whole big state of Bengal, eat only rice and fish. They love fish so much that anybody who can afford it will have, just beyond the house, a big pond where he grows fish. Just as you see in other countries a beautiful lawn and trees and gardens, in Bengal you will see ponds, according to each one's capacity....

If you are rich you will have a big pond, surrounded by big trees, lawns. If you are a poor man, you will have just a naked pond, without trees, without lawns, but you will have a pond – dirty – and you will grow fish. And the people smell of fish. The word *bu* simply means stinking. The word *ba* simply means with.

The British people came in contact first with the Bengalis. Later they came to discover other people – India is a vast continent: so many cultures, so many different kinds of people – but their first acquaintance was with Bengalis. And they were smelling so badly of fish, all the Bengalis, that it was a word of condemnation to call them babu. Britishers started calling Bengalis, babus. It was sheer insult, humiliation. But to be close to the people who have the power...the word "babu" slowly became very respectable. It meant to be close to the throne, to be close to the hierarchy. And everybody forgot its basic meaning.

Now, the first president of India was called Babu Rajendra Prasad. He had nothing to do with fish, he was not a stinking man, but he never told people, "You should stop calling me babu," because he himself might not have been aware what the word means. And if the president is called babu, then anybody will feel joyous and grateful if he is called babu.

One of my vice-chancellors called me babu. I said, "Shut up! And take your words back immediately; otherwise I can be dangerous."

He said, "What are you doing? Have you gone suddenly insane? I have not said anything, I simply said, out of respect, babu."

I said, "It does not matter that you are ignorant about the meaning of babu. I know the meaning."

When I explained it to him, he said, "My God! I used to think this was a very respectful word, and I enjoyed being called babu. I used to use the word for people for whom I have a certain respect. But forgive me; I will never use that word again."

Old languages have become rotten. A new language is an absolute need – totally new, without any flaws, exact in its meaning. The older the language, the more meanings its words have. In Sanskrit, Arabic, Hebrew, Greek, Latin, one word has many meanings.

In Sanskrit one word can have one dozen meanings. Slowly, slowly a word got settled with one meaning, but those eleven meanings are there. Because of this, Indian philosophers and scholars were very much at ease; disputing, making new commentaries on the old scriptures was an easy job, because each word has ten, twelve meanings, so you can manage to make the scripture mean whatsoever you want it to mean. Another philosopher writes a treatise on the same scripture, and he gives it a totally different meaning.

The Hindu scripture, *Gita* – which is the bible of the Hindus – has one thousand commentaries. That is the number of famous commentaries. There may be many more, but they are not famous; they were written by people who never attained fame, who never attained the attention of the country. But one thousand commentaries on one book!

If you read one commentary, you will say, "Perfectly right." If you read a second commentary, you will be surprised – that too is perfectly right. And when you have read one thousand commentaries, as I have, you will say, "Crazy! Nuts! They are just playing with words." All the commentaries are contradicting each other. The game is very easy, the language allows it. This is an unscientific language.

I want one world, one language, one religious-ness, one humanity, and when humanity is really grown-up in consciousness, one government.

Government is not something to brag about. It is an insult. Its existence says to you that you are still barbarous, civilization has not happened; otherwise what is the need of a government to rule you?

If all the crimes disappear, if all the fears that others can exploit you, murder you, disappear, what will you do with this whole bureaucracy of govern-ment? You cannot continue it, because it is a burden on the economy of the nation, a big burden, and it goes on becoming bigger and bigger. The hierarchies have a tendency to become bigger and bigger, for the simple reason that everybody wants not to work, everybody hates work. So everybody needs more assistance; the work is growing.

You can see, in any government office, files just piled up on the tables. Unless you are able to bribe someone, your file may remain somewhere in the huge pile, it will never come to the top. And the bureaucrats enjoy many files there; that makes them big, special. They have power over so many people; all these files, to them contain their power over people. Files don't move unless you are after them. Bribe one table, the file moves to a higher table. Bribe again, it moves to a higher table. The moment you stop bribing, the file stops moving. Strange, it seems bribery is something like petrol: for the car to go on moving, you have to put petrol in. If you are out of gas, finished, the car has stopped.

I am an anarchist of a totally different category from all the anarchists who have existed on the earth. I am a category in myself, because my approach is totally different. I am not against government, I am against the *need* for government. I am not against the courts, I am against the *need* for the courts.

Someday, some time, I see the possibility that man will be able to live without any control – religi-ous or political – because he will be a discipline unto himself.

Beloved Bhagwan,

You say we are responsible for ourselves, and that there is no God. What part do fate and destiny have in our lives? Or are they just excuses to avoid our responsibilities by pinning hope on something outside ourselves?

They are just excuses and nothing more. There is no fate, no destiny. You are just trying to dump your responsibility on something which does not exist. And because it does not exist, it cannot resist you; it cannot say, Please don't dump your responsi-bility on me! God is silent, you can dump anything on him – no resistance, because there is nobody to resist.

Fate is again the same. You fail in love, you fail in other matters. It hurts, that "I have failed." You need some kind of ointment for your wounded heart. Fate is a beautiful ointment, and freely available, you don't have to pay for it. You say, "What can I do? – every-thing is decided by fate." Success or failure, richness or poverty, sickness or health, life or death – every-thing is in the hands of an unknown power called fate. "I am doing my best, still I go on failing. I am fol-lowing all the moral principles preached to me, still I am poor. And I see all kinds of immoral people be-coming richer, getting higher, becoming famous. It is all fate."

It gives you solace. It gives you solace that you are not reaching your goals. It also gives you solace that if others have reached, there is nothing much in it; it is just decided by fate. So on the one hand, you are saved from feeling inferior; on the other hand, your jealousy enjoys the idea that the successful is successful only because fate has determined it that way: "It has nothing to do with him, he's not superior to me."

God, fate, destiny – they all come in the same category: throwing your responsibility onto some-thing which does not exist.

If God existed he would not remain silent. I am continually saying he does not exist. If he existed, it is time – he should have appeared in Rajneeshpuram and announced, "I am here! Why do you go on saying that I don't exist?" But he will never come. There have always been people who have denied the existence of God, but he has never made any effort to prove himself.

Simple things…. Edmund Burke, one of the philosophers of the West, stood in the church and said to the priest, "This is my watch. If God exists – I don't want big proof, just a simple proof – my watch should stop moving. You pray, your congregation can pray, you do anything that you want to do. Persuade your God to stop my watch, and that will be enough to convert me."

They prayed – it was a question of the prestige of the whole of Christianity, a single man challenging God. And he was not asking for a big miracle, just a small miracle: "Stop my watch moving." And God could not do that. Edmund Burke has proved that there is no God. What an argument! – but simple, clear, relevant.

You go on dumping – all over the world – anything that you want to get rid of on God, on fate, on destiny. They are just different names of non-existential things. Certainly you cannot throw your garbage on somebody who is there. There is a limit to patience.

You just try throwing your garbage into the compound of your neighbor. Perhaps for one day he may not say anything; perhaps for two days he may wait – but how long? Sooner or later he is going to grab you by the neck and prove that "I exist. You cannot go on throwing your garbage in my compound." But if there is nobody in the house, you can continue to throw the garbage as long as you want. Nobody will resist, nobody will come out and say, "What is going on? Don't you have any sense of humanity in you?"

God, fate, destiny – these are bogus words, mumbo jumbo, nothing more than that. Drop them completely, because dropping them will make you an individual, fully responsible for your acts. And unless you take the responsibility on yourself, you will never become strong, you will never become independent, you will never have the taste of freedom.

You can have freedom. But the cost is to accept responsibility in its totality.

I have felt such immense freedom that looking at you I feel sad. You have the same opportunity, the same potentiality to blossom into a free individual, but you go on remaining a slave. And the way you manage it is by never being responsible. You think not being responsible makes you free? Not feeling responsible for your actions, for your thoughts, for your being, do you think you are freed from all the consequences? No, absolutely no.

It makes you a slave, it makes you something subhuman. It takes all glory away from you. You cannot walk straight, you become a hunchback. Your intelligence cannot grow because you have not accepted the challenge. You are waiting for fate, for destiny, for God. You are thinking, "When the time comes – the right time, God willing – I will be blissful too." There is no God who can will your blissfulness. You are alone in existence.

You come alone, you die alone. Between birth and death, of course you can deceive yourself that someone is with you – your wife, your father, your mother, your husband, your friend – but this is just make-believe. You come alone, you go alone; you are alone between birth and death.

And I am not saying that you cannot love a man or a woman. In fact, when two independent, free people, who take responsibility on their own shoulders, meet, there is immense beauty in it. Nobody is a burden to the other. Nobody is dumping anything onto the other – you have stopped the very idea of dumping anything.

You can be together, but your aloneness remains untouched, pure, crystal-clear, virgin. You never trespass each other's territories. You can enjoy each other just because you are separate.

The more separate you are – the more clearly it is

understood that you are alone, she is alone – the more there is a possibility of a great meeting of two alonenesses, two purities, two individuals.

Forget words like destiny, fate, kismet, God. And don't allow yourself to be cheated by astrologers, mind readers, palmists, predictors of your future. There is no future if you don't create it! And whatsoever is going to be tomorrow is going to be your creation. And it has to be done today, now – because out of today, today's womb, tomorrow will be born.

Take the responsibility totally on yourselves – that's my message to you. That's why I am continuously destroying the God in your mind. I have nothing against him. How can I have anything against him? – he does not exist! Do you think I am wasting my time fighting with something which does not exist? No, I am fighting with your conditionings; *they* exist. God does not exist, but an idea of God exists in you, and I am fighting with that idea, telling you to drop it, be clean, and take the whole responsibility.

This is my experience: the day I took my whole responsibility on myself, I found the doors of freedom opening to me. They go together.

Everybody wants freedom.

Nobody wants responsibility.

You will never have freedom, you will remain a slave. Remember, remaining a slave is also your responsibility. You have chosen it, it has not been forced upon you.

I am reminded of Diogenes, a beautiful Greek philosopher, mystic – and a mystic of a rare quality. He was a contemporary of Aristotle, and he was as much against Aristotle as I am, so I have a certain friendship with Diogenes.

Aristotle defined man as an animal who walks on two legs. What did Diogenes do? He caught one animal – and there are many animals who walk on two legs, but they have feathers also, they can fly also – a peacock. He took out all the feathers – because men have no feathers. Take out all the feathers of the peacock...the peacock walks on two legs. And he sent the peacock to Aristotle with the message: "Please receive the gift of a human being."

This man Diogenes used to live naked, because he said, "Man is born naked, and he becomes weaker because he is protected by clothes." All around the world no animal has clothes – except a few dogs in England. England is a mysterious country. Dogs have clothes because a naked dog is un-Christian. You will be surprised to know that in the Victorian Age in England even chair legs were covered with clothes, because they are legs and it is not gentlemanly to see naked legs.

Diogenes lived naked. He was a strong man. Four people who were doing the business of hijacking people and selling them as slaves in the market thought, "This is a great catch, this man can bring us great money. We have sold many slaves, but not so strong, beautiful, young. We can have as high a price as we demand; and there is going to be a great competition in the marketplace when we put this man on the pedestal for sale. But," they thought, "four are not enough to catch him. He alone could kill us all."

Diogenes was hearing what they were saying about him. He was sitting by the side of the river, just enjoying the cool breeze of the evening, underneath a tree; and behind the tree, those four were planning what to do. He said, "Don't be worried. Come here! You need not worry that I will kill you, I never kill anything. And you need not worry that I will fight, resist you – no. I don't fight anybody, I don't resist anything. You want to sell me as a slave?"

Embarrassed, afraid, those four people said, "That's what we were thinking. We are poor...if you are willing?"

He said, "Of course I am. If I can help you in your poverty in some way, it is beautiful."

So they brought out chains. He said, "Throw them in the river; you need not chain me. I will walk ahead of you. I don't believe in escaping from anything. In fact, I am getting excited about the idea of being sold, standing on a high pedestal, and hundreds of people trying to get me. I am excited about this auction – I am coming!"

Those four people became a little more afraid: this man is not only strong, beautiful, he seems to be mad also; he is dangerous. But now there was no way for them to escape. He said, "If you try to escape, you will be risking your own life. Just follow me, all four of you. Put me on the pedestal."

Unwillingly they followed him. They wanted to take him, but he *went*! You see the point? Even in such a situation, he was taking the responsibility on himself. He was a free man even in such a situation, where these people are conspiring and trying to sell him in the marketplace, which is the ugliest thing that can happen to a man – to be sold like a commodity, auctioned like a commodity.

But he told those people, "Don't be afraid, and don't try to escape. You have given me a great idea, I am grateful to you. This is my responsibility, I am going to the marketplace. You put me up for auction."

They could not believe…what type of man was this? But there was no way to escape, so they followed him. And when he was put on a high pedestal so that everybody could see, there was almost silence, pindrop silence. People had never seen such a proportionate body, so beautiful – as if made of steel, so strong.

Before the auctioneer said anything, Diogenes declared, "Listen, people! Here is a master to be sold to any slave, because these four poor people need money. So start the auction; but remember, you are purchasing a master."

A king purchased him. Of course, he could do it – more and more money he offered at the auction. Many people were interested, but finally a sum, larger than any which had ever been heard of, was given to those four people. Diogenes said to them, "Are you happy now? You can go, and I will go with this slave."

On the way, when they were moving to the palace in the chariot, the king said to Diogenes, "Are you crazy or something? You think yourself a master? I am a king, and you think me a slave?"

Diogenes said, "Yes, and I am not crazy, you are crazy. I can prove it right now." At the back of the chariot was the queen. Diogenes said, "Your queen is already interested in me, she is finished with you. It is dangerous to purchase a master."

The king was shocked. Of course, he was nothing in comparison to Diogenes. He took out his sword and asked his queen, "What he is saying, is it true? If you say the truth, your life will be saved – that is my promise. But if you say an untruth, and I find it out later on, I will behead you."

Fearful, afraid, still the queen said, "It is true. Before him, you are nothing. I am enchanted, allured; the man has some magic. You are just a poor guy compared to him. This is the truth."

Of course, the king stopped the chariot and told Diogenes, "Get out of the chariot. I make you free; I don't want to take such risks in my palace."

Diogenes said, "Thank you. I am a man who cannot be made a slave, for the simple reason that every responsibility I take on myself. I have not left those four people feeling guilty – they had not brought me there, I had come of my own accord. They must be feeling obliged. And it is your chariot, if you want me to get out, that is perfectly good. I am not accustomed to chariots at all, my legs are strong enough. And I am a naked man, a golden chariot does not fit with me."

Take responsibility! And then even in utter poverty, suffering, imprisoned in a jail, you will remain completely a master of yourself. You will have a freedom which comes with responsibility.

All these religions have been making you dependent on God, on fate, on destiny. Those are just different names of something non-existential. What is true is your slavery or your freedom. Choose. If you choose freedom, then you have to destroy all the strategies of religions which make you a slave. That's what I am doing here: cutting all your chains, making you free from everything, so that you can be yourself.

And the moment you are yourself, you start growing, you become greener.

Flowers start opening up, and there is great fragrance around you.

No Religions,
No Nations,
No Governments

DISCOURSE 31, July 29, 1985

Beloved Bhagwan,

Your way is the way of the heart, and the outside world is the way of the head. Will it ever be possible that man can function from a blend of both head and heart, or must the two always remain totally divorced? Will it always be essential to make a conscious choice for one way or the other?

The first thing to be understood is that there is no way, either of head or of heart. Every way leads you away, away from the truth that you are.

It would have been so easy if there were a truth somewhere. Howsoever difficult the way, people would have reached. The more difficult, the more far away the truth was, the more challenging to the ego. If man's ego challenges him to reach the highest peak in the Himalayas, Everest, where nothing is to be found; if man's ego gives him incentive to waste billions of dollars to reach the moon, risking lives…. But man has reached the moon. And the first man who walked on the moon must have looked silly to himself – there was nothing for which so much endeavor, technology, preparation was needed.

Remember, the ego wants challenges.

It lives through challenge.

Why have so few people been able to have a glimpse of the truth? – because it is not a challenge; it is not *there,* it is here within you. It does not need any way, you are already it.

But the question has one other implication too: Will it ever be possible for the head and heart to be married, or are they going to remain forever divorced? It all depends on you, because both are mechanisms. You are neither the head nor the heart. You can move through the head, you can move through the heart. Of course you will reach different places because the directions of the head and the heart are diametrically opposite.

The head will go round and round thinking, brooding, philosophizing; it knows only words, logic, argument. But it is very infertile; you cannot get anything out of the head as far as truth is concerned, because truth needs no logic, no argument, no philosophical research. Truth is so simple; the head makes it so complex. Down the centuries philosophers have been seeking and searching for the truth through the head. None of them has found anything, but they have created great systems of thought. I have looked into all those systems: there is no conclusion.

The heart is also a mechanism – different from the head. You can call the head the logical instrument; you can call the heart the emotional instrument. Out of the head all the philosophies, all the theologies are created; out of the heart, come all kinds of devotion, prayer, sentimentality. But the heart also goes round and round in emotions.

The word "emotion" is good. Watch...it consists of motion, movement. So the heart moves, but the heart is blind. It moves fast, quick, because there is no reason to wait. It does not have to think, so it jumps into anything. But truth is not to be found by any emotionality. Emotion is as much a barrier as logic.

The logic is the male in you, and the heart is the female in you. But truth has nothing to do with male and female. Truth is your consciousness. You can watch the head thinking, you can watch the heart throbbing with emotion. They can be in a certain relationship....

Ordinarily, the society has arranged that the head should be the master and the heart should be the servant, because society is the creation of man's mind, psychology, and the heart is feminine. Just as man has kept the woman a slave, the head has kept the heart a slave.

We can reverse the situation: the heart can become the master, the head can become the servant. If we have to choose between the two, if we are forced to choose between the two, then it is better that the heart becomes the master and the head becomes the servant.

There are things which the heart is incapable of. Exactly the same is true about the head. The head cannot love, it cannot feel, it is insensitive. The heart cannot be rational, reasonable. For the whole past they have been in conflict. That conflict only represents the conflict and struggle between men and women.

If you are talking to your wife, you must know it is impossible to talk, it is impossible to argue, it is impossible to come to a fair decision, because the woman functions through the heart. She jumps from one thing to another without bothering whether there is any relationship between the two. She cannot argue, but she can cry. She cannot be rational, but she

> My way has been described as that of the heart, but it is not true. The heart will give you all kinds of imaginings, hallucinations, illusions, sweet dreams – but it cannot give you the truth. The truth is behind both; it is in your consciousness, which is neither head nor heart.

can scream. She cannot be cooperative in coming to a conclusion. The heart cannot understand the language of the head.

The difference is not much as far as physiology is concerned, the heart and the head are just a few inches apart. But as far as their existential qualities are concerned, they are poles apart.

My way has been described as that of the heart, but it is not true. The heart will give you all kinds of imaginings, hallucinations, illusions, sweet dreams – but it cannot give you the truth. The truth is behind both; it is in your consciousness, which is neither head nor heart. Just because the consciousness is separate from both, it can use both in harmony. The head is dangerous in certain fields, because it has eyes but it has no legs – it is crippled.

The heart can function in certain dimensions. It has no eyes but it has legs; it is blind but it can move tremendously, with great speed – of course, not knowing where it is going. It is not just a coincidence that in all the languages of the world love is called blind. It is not love that is blind, it is the heart that has no eyes.

As your meditation becomes deeper, as your identification with the head and the heart starts falling, you find yourself becoming a triangle. And your reality is in the third force in you: the consciousness. Consciousness can manage very easily, because the heart and the head both belong to it.

You know the story of a blind beggar and a crippled beggar…. They both lived outside the village in the forest. Of course, they were competitors to each other, enemies – begging is a business. But one day the forest was on fire. The cripple had no way to escape, because he could not move on his own. He had eyes to see which way they could get out of the fire, but what use is that if you don't have legs? The blind man had legs, could move fast and get out of the fire, but how was he going to find the place where the fire had not reached yet?

Both were going to die in the forest, burned alive.

It was such an emergency that they forgot their competition. In such emergencies only a Jew can remain a businessman, and certainly those two beggars were not Jews. In fact, to be a beggar and a Jew is a contradiction in terms.

They immediately dropped their antagonism – that was the only way to survive. The blind man took the cripple on his shoulders, they found the way out of the fire. One was seeing, and the other was moving accordingly.

Something like this has to happen within you – of course, in reverse order. The head has the eyes, the heart has the guts to move into anything. You have to make a synthesis between the two. And the synthesis, I have to emphasize, should be that the heart remains the master, and the head becomes the servant.

You have as a servant a great asset – your reasoning. You cannot be befooled, you cannot be cheated and exploited. The heart has all feminine qualities: love, beauty, grace. The head is barbarous. The heart is far more civilized, far more innocent.

A conscious man uses his head as a servant, and his heart as the master – just the opposite of the story I told you.

And this is so simple for the man of consciousness to do. Once you are unidentified with head or heart, and you are simply a witness of both, you can see which qualities should be higher, which qualities should be the goal. And the head as a servant can bring those qualities, but it needs to be commanded and ordered. Right now, and for centuries, just the opposite has been happening: the servant has become the master. And the master is so polite, such a gentleman, that he has not fought back, he has accepted the slavery voluntarily. The madness on the earth is the result.

We have to change the very alchemy of man.

We have to rearrange the whole inside of man.

And the most basic revolution in man will come when the heart decides the values. It cannot decide for war, it cannot go for nuclear weapons; it cannot be death-oriented. The heart is life's juice. Once the head is in the service of the heart, it has to do what the heart decides. And the head is immensely capable of doing anything, just right guidance is needed; otherwise, it is going to go berserk, it is going to be mad. For the head there are no values. For the head there is no meaning in anything. For the head there is no love, no beauty, no grace – only reasoning.

But this miracle is possible only by disidentifying yourself from both. Watch the thoughts, because in your watching them, they disappear. Then watch your emotions, sentimentalities; by your watching, they also disappear. Then your heart is as innocent as that of a child, and your head is as great a genius as Albert Einstein, Bertrand Russell, Aristotle.

But the trouble is far bigger than you can conceive. It is a male-dominated society; man has been creating all the rules of the game, the woman has just been following. And the conditioning has gone so deep, because it has been going on for millions of years.

If in the individual the revolution happens and the heart is re-enthroned, given its right place as the master, and the head given the right place as a great servant, this will affect your whole social structure. You can see it happening in my commune.

The woman is the master; she is no longer mistress, and the man is no longer master. People go on asking me why, for all significant posts, I have chosen women? For the simple reason that the woman will not create the third world war.

It has been a historical fact that each war is created by the man, but the woman suffers most. Strange – the man is the criminal and the consequence happens to the woman! The woman loses her husband, the woman loses her children. The woman loses her dignity, because whenever a country is invaded, the soldiers are so much repressed – just like the monks…. Sexually they had no opportunity while the war was going on. When the opportunity arises – they invade a city and conquer it – their first attack is on the woman.

And the war has nothing to do with the woman, she is simply outside of the game – it is a male game, just like boxing – but she has to be raped.

Those soldiers are hankering not to be victorious for their nation's glory – that is a faraway thing – they are hankering to get the women of the enemies as quickly as possible.

I am putting women in all significant, powerful positions. It is symbolic. Man has a tremendous capacity to do things, but he should not be the guide anymore. He is hung up in his head. He can also become the master if he puts his heart above his head. That's why I said that all of my sannyasins are women – even those who biologically, physiologically, are men. The moment they become sannyasins they have accepted a new structure, they have put something above their head – their heart.

This is what I mean: that even men around me start learning feminine qualities. And feminine qualities are the only qualities worth having.

So there is a possibility, but the possibility has a basic condition to be fulfilled: you become more conscious, a witness, a watcher of all that goes on inside you. The watcher becomes immediately free from identification. Because he can see the emotions, it is an absolute certainty that "I am not the emotions." He can see the thoughts; the simple conclusion is, "I am not my thought process."

"Then who am I?" – a pure watcher, a witness. And you reach to the ultimate possibility of intelligence in you: You become a conscious man.

Amongst the whole world sleeping, you become awake, and once you are awake there is no problem. Your very awakening will start shifting things to their right places. The head has to be dethroned, and the heart has to be crowned again. This change amongst many people will bring a new society, a New Man in the world. It will change so many things, you cannot conceive.

Science will have a totally different flavor. It will

not serve death anymore, it will not make weapons that are going to kill the whole of life on the earth. It will make life richer, discover energies which can make man more fulfilled, which can make man live in comfort, in luxury, because the values will have completely changed. It will still be mind functioning, but under the direction of the heart.

My way is the way of meditation.

I have to use language, unfortunately, that's why I say may way is the way of meditation: Neither of head nor of heart, but of a growing consciousness which is above both mind and heart.

This is the key to open the doors for a New Man to arrive on the earth.

Beloved Bhagwan,

I was brought up as a Quaker, and we were told never to swear on a Bible in court, because as Quakers we could only speak the truth, and that the source of our truth was silence. This is so close to what You say, I am surprised when You say You don't agree with the theology of Quakerism.

I am also surprised.

The first thing: Quakerism is part of Christian theology. I have never said anything against Quakerism, but you are forcing me to now.

It is a by-product of Christian theology, and I am against all theologies. Quakerism is not an independent religion, but just a sect of Christianity. It accepts all kinds of stupidities that are propounded by Jesus and his theologians. It is not against *The Bible* – and *The Bible* is so full of rubbish, lies.

The basic lie is God, the holy ghost, Jesus the only begotten son of God. Lies upon lies – a virgin birth, resurrection after being crucified. Quakerism does not deny all these things, it accepts them.

Secondly, you are saying you have been told not to take oath upon the *Bible* in the court. I have also said that the oath is absolutely unnecessary. A man who is capable of lying – no oath can prevent him. And to take an oath placing your hand on *The Bible* is hilarious. *The Bible* is so full of lies, and you are taking an oath for truth – that you will not speak anything but truth!

My reason not to take an oath on any religious scripture is totally different from that of the Quakers. The Quakers believe – remember, they believe: I *know.* You have been told: I have *seen.*

And the difference is infinite between being told and experiencing it on your own.

Just by being told that because you are a Quaker whatsoever you speak will be truth…. This is strange. It is a belief, borrowed knowledge, conditioning. Just by your being a Quaker, it is not a certainty that whatsoever you speak will be the truth.

Yes, if you have experienced total silence, then nothing can come out of you which is not true.

But I know many Quakers. They sit in silence also in their congregations. I have been to their congregations, and I have asked them, "If you are really truthful, tell me: What were you doing in your silence?" And they have always said, "We were thinking – thinking of silence, trying to be silent, making efforts to be silent." Yes, it is true they are not speaking. If you mean just by not speaking you are silent, then you are just a fool.

Silence is such a deep experience, where thoughts, emotions, everything disappears. If you have attained to that silence you will not even call yourself a Quaker. You will not subscribe to any theology. You don't need one; you have found the very source of truth within yourself.

The Quakers have been defying the court; they will not take the oath. They have been punished for it, because it is an insult to the court, it is contempt of the court: they have been imprisoned, tortured. But the Quaker and my sannyasin are totally different.

I say the oath is useless. But I teach my sannyasins to be nonserious. To the Quakers it has become something of a dogmatic idea, a fanatic standpoint:

they will not take the oath. I tell my sannyasins, "You live in a society, you have to follow their rules – remembering that they are all man-made."

For example, in some countries you have to drive on the right side of the road, in some countries on the left side of the road. What is wrong with the right side? You can say that it makes no difference whether you drive on the right side or left side, it is simply a rule. Don't Quakers follow this simple rule? You don't take it seriously, there is no problem in it; it is simply a question of managing the traffic. It can be done in both ways, so there is nothing serious about it. It is not something like an ultimate law of existence, that if you drive on the right side you will go to hell.

Quakers have been going to jail. I will not tell my sannyasins to do that. It is not worth it. Take the oath, and say whatsoever you want to say. Oath or no oath, it makes no difference to your statements. Why unnecessarily enrage those poor judges and juries? Let them be satisfied. If they are feeling happy just by your taking an oath, and feeling that now whatever you say will be the truth, let them befool themselves. You have to say what you want to say. The oath is irrelevant to you, but why make so much fuss about it that you have to go for two years behind bars?

I am a nonserious man. Quakers are very serious about it. They will risk their life, but they will not take the oath. The oath has become more important than life itself.

It is just a game. You play cards: there is a king and there is a queen and there is a joker, and all sorts of people are there. You know that this is just a playing card, and this queen is just like the queen of England – absolutely meaningless, powerless. But while playing the game you have to accept that this is the queen, this is the king, this is the joker, and so on, so forth. You don't start going to jail because "I will not accept this card as the king!" It is up to you – don't play the game.

These are all games. That is the difference. You are asking me what the difference is, why I criticize Quaker theology. In fact, I have never done it before, but from now onwards I am going to do it unless you start quaking! To take games of life seriously shows only your stupidity, not your silence.

I have been in the courts. I have taken an oath, but before I take the oath I certainly make a statement telling the judge, "I will follow the rule, I will take the oath, but the oath cannot make any difference to me. I will speak only that which I want to speak.

"And your oath, in fact, frees me from telling the truth and only the truth, because the oath I am taking on *The Bible,* on the *Gita,* on the *Koran* – which are full of lies…naturally by taking the oath on *The Bible* I am completely freed. Now I can lie without any trouble. Without an oath I will only speak the truth; with an oath, there is no need because I have already lied by putting my hand on *The Bible*."

Quakers are not against *The Bible* – I am. In one court I refused to put my hand on *The Bible*. I said, "I will keep a little distance."

The judge asked, "Why?"

I said, "Because it is such garbage I don't want to touch it. It is your rule, so I will put my hand on top of it, but I will keep a little distance. I am very allergic." There is an immense difference between my criticism of this system of oath taking and the Quakers' criticism.

I am not saying that just because you are a sannyasin that's enough to guarantee that you will speak only the truth, no. Just being sannyasins does not mean that you will only speak the truth. And it is not so easy to decide what the truth is.

It happened that one of the great historians was writing the history of the whole world. It was an immense job to write the whole history of the whole world, of all the nations. He devoted almost fifty years, working almost twelve, fourteen hours a day. And the day he was coming to his last page, something happened and he burned his whole life's effort.

Somebody was murdered just in the neighborhood. Of course, so many people gathered there: the police were there, the journalists were there. The historian also went there. He asked one person who was an eyewitness, he asked another person who was an eyewitness – and he was amazed. The stories of all the eyewitnesses were different. And there was no reason for them to lie, they were not involved in it.

One eyewitness said he was killed inside the house. Another eyewitness said he was killed under the sky, the open sky. The truth was that he was killed in a house which was just being built, and the roof was not yet there. He was killed under the open sky – without the roof you can't call it a house. But it was a house in the process of being built. The roof is only a part of the house, so the other was not lying either, saying that he was killed inside the house.

Listening to other eyewitnesses, he became suddenly aware of one thing: "A murder happens in my neighborhood; within two minutes' time I am there, eyewitnesses are available – and it cannot be decided what actually happened. I have been wasting my whole life writing about Genghis Khan, Tamerlane, Nadir Shah – so much time has passed. Can I say truthfully that what I have written is factual? Perhaps many of these people never existed!"

George Gurdjieff had a theory about Jesus Christ: that he never existed, that it is only an ancient drama which was played amongst the Jews, there has never been a historical man Jesus. And he supported his idea that it is only a drama, just like the dramas of Shakespeare and Bernard Shaw. His first piece of evidence was that Jesus is not mentioned in any Jewish book.

Such a man, who could walk on water, do you think he would not create news? Would he not be mentioned somewhere in the contemporary literature? A man who can raise the dead back to life – if he is not mentioned, then who else will be mentioned? This man was doing all kinds of miracles: turning stones into bread, turning water into wine…. And the resurrection – he was crucified but God would not allow his only begotten Son to be dead, so he came back again.

These things make a man so significant that you cannot ignore him, yet in no Jewish history he is even mentioned, not even in the footnotes! George Gurdjieff has an argument there; he says it is simply a drama. Nobody has been able to criticize George Gurdjieff; you cannot find anything that can contradict what he is saying. So what is the truth?

Take the oath; if that is the rule of the game, play it accordingly. But make it clear that it makes no difference to you.

Perhaps it was making a difference to people in the past. And I say to you, it will make a difference to the Quakers too, because they believe in *The Bible,* they believe in the biblical God, they believe in the resurrection of Jesus Christ. The whole Christian theology is theirs.

If you believe in God, you feel afraid taking the oath in the name of God – the superstitious man will feel afraid: now it is not a question of the court, it is now a question of God and the holy book. To lie now will not only be a crime, it will be a sin also. Afraid of this, there is a possibility he will say the truth.

For my sannyasins there is no problem. There is no God, there is no holy book. My sannyasins can take an oath on any novel and it will be the same. They can take an oath on anything, it makes no difference at all; they will say what they want to say. The court cannot exploit their superstitions, because they have none.

The oath was significant, *is* significant, for the so-called religious people of the world. And that's why a Hindu is not given *The Bible* to take an oath on. He is given the *Gita,* because *The Bible* he can spit on without any trouble. But the *Gita*? If by accident the *Gita* falls from his hands, or his feet by accident touch the *Gita,* he is in tremendous anguish. He has to fast, and go to the holy Ganges river to take a bath: he has committed a great sin.

Now, this man can be exploited. The court can manipulate this man to tell the truth. But no court in the whole world can manipulate my people. We don't have any holy book, we don't have any God to be afraid of. Once you are free of superstitions, laughingly you can take the oath and say whatsoever you always wanted to say – oath or no oath.

So remember, there *is* a difference.

And if the court is stubborn, don't take it seriously. It is stupid to suffer two years in jail just for not taking the oath. And why are you so afraid? Are you afraid because you were going to lie, and now after the oath you cannot lie? What is the fear?

You say, "I have been told that the Quaker only speaks the truth." You have been told – and the man who has told you was lying! Just being a Quaker makes no difference. How can it make any difference? Yes, Quakers sit in silence, but I know their silence is bogus, because they don't have the method to enter into silence. They just say, "We sit in silence." Yes, they are not talking, but they are thinking, they are feeling – emotions are there.

Silence means you are a witness, and that word "witness" has no place in the Quaker theology. And without being a witness you cannot be silent; there is no other way. You will have to go through the whole process of witnessing; only then, slowly, slowly, things will start dropping away.

My people know that unless they succeed in meditation – which is another name of witnessing – they will remain unconscious, and an unconscious man is asleep. Can you say to a man who is just getting ready to fall into bed and go to sleep, can you tell the man, "Please take an oath that you will not dream about wrong things"? He may take the oath, but he will be dreaming in the same way as he was dreaming before.

The oath will not make any difference, because the oath is taken by the conscious mind, and there are deeper layers which know nothing about it. The unconscious mind has no idea about the oath, and the collective unconscious mind is far deeper, and the cosmic unconscious mind is deeper than the Pacific. They know nothing about your oath, and in sleep *they* will be functioning, not your conscious mind. Your conscious mind, which has taken the oath, will be asleep.

Sleepy people, unconscious people, can believe in anything, but their belief makes no difference to their inner reality.

So please, forget the idea that my opposition to the oath is the same as the Quakers' opposition to the oath. Their opposition has different arguments for it. They say, "Because a Quaker always speaks the truth, that's why we will not take the oath."

I say to my sannyasins, "Make the statement in the court: 'The oath is a very ancient superstition. I will take it, if this is the game that I have to play, but I cannot be serious about it. It does not matter – you can give me *The Bible* or you can give me *Playboy* magazine, it won't make any difference; I will simply say what I have to say. Your oath cannot make any difference to my statements.'"

And we are not ready to go for two years to jail for such a stupid thing. If those judges and juries and the courts are behaving stupidly, have you also to behave the same? Make them a laughingstock, make their idea of oath taking foolish.

My reasoning against the oath is totally different. It has nothing to do with your Quakerism.

Beloved Bhagwan,

My fear around Your vision of the birth of the New Man through test-tubes and genetic engineering comes not from the technology itself, but from fear of who might control the technology. How can we guarantee that this knowledge will be used by conscious human beings, rather than the idiot politicians who would turn our brave new world into Orwell's 1984?

Who controls the technology today? Who controls all your nuclear weapons? Who controls all your scientific discoveries?

Have you raised your voice against it? Have you even thought that the whole life on the earth is now in the hands of idiotic politicians?

And it has been always so. Anything discovered is immediately captured by the governments, so why is the question only about genetic engineering? Are you not afraid that the politicians have nuclear weapons which can destroy you seven hundred times? Although destroyed once, you will not need to be destroyed again – because you are not the only begotten son of God, you will not resurrect; and messiahs are not around who will bring you back to life.

But you are afraid – I can understand – that if this genetic engineering is in the hands of politicians, certainly they are not going to produce the man of beauty, love, silence, intelligence, grace. They are going to create steel robots, to make all of them soldiers to fight, to kill. I know it. That's why I have proposed there should not be nations, the world should have only one functional government. All boundaries have to be removed, all passports and green cards have to be burned. That you are a human being is enough to enter any country.

It is a very strange thing. You don't ask the birds, "Where is your passport? How did you dare to enter America? – you need a visa. And if you want to remain permanently here you will need a green card." Animals seem to be more free than you, because animals don't know anything about the boundaries that you have drawn on your map. They go on moving from one place to another place. Sometimes they travel thousands of miles.

There are a few birds who live at the North Pole, but when it becomes absolutely impossible to live there because of the cold, they start moving towards warmer places. Three thousand miles they will travel – and they don't care about your nations. In a new place...for example, they will travel and come to a warmer place, and when it it the time, there is the season of mating. So they give birth to eggs, but they don't have enough time to take care of the eggs; three thousand miles have taken so much time.

They have to go back, because now the climate at the North Pole is again ready to welcome them. So they leave their eggs and fly three thousand miles again. The eggs grow on their own, the children are born. And it is something mysterious – science has not been able to figure it out: there is no guide, there is no school to teach them, there is nobody even to tell them where their parents have gone, but these newly-born birds start moving towards the North Pole three thousand miles away. Existence is really mysterious.

Nobody asks about them, when they cross the borders. Even if you ask, they will not understand your language. And even if you try to keep them out, it will be almost impossible. Man is not as free as birds, animals, fish. What a degradation!

Hence, whenever I say anything, remember the whole context of it; otherwise you will misunderstand me. I want one world, so that there is no war and no need of soldiers. I want one world government. I want the president of the world government only to be president for six months, so that he cannot do any harm. And I want one person to be chosen only once. These are all precautions.

Genetic engineering, to give birth to children in scientific labs, will be in the hands of the scientists.

We have tried religion and it failed. We have tried politics and it has failed. Now we have to try science. Give it a chance, because in three hundred years it has made more progress than man has made in his whole history of millions of years.

And I have proposed to you that the world should have one academy of sciences, so there is no Russian scientist, no American scientist, no Hindu scientist, no Christian scientist – all that is past. That academy will have all the geniuses of the world. And all other efforts have failed; science should be given a chance. There is no harm. At the most it can fail – the worst possibility is that science also will fail – but I don't think it can fail.

We have to prepare a new kind of man. Out of that new kind of man – meditative, silent, loving – will be coming scientists.

And I am not a pessimist; nor am I an optimist. I am very much a realist. As I conceive it, all these things are possible. In fact, without them life will become impossible. The choice is yours. Give science a chance, and prepare the ground so that there are no governments – only one government, which has no desire to fight because there is nobody to fight.

Even the politician's character will change, because there will be no political parties. People will be choosing individually, there will be no political vested interest. Because of political parties the politician is bound to be cunning, exploiting, doing all kinds of things.

Just a few days ago they imprisoned the Reverend Moon, because all the Christians were against him – he is a Christian, he comes from Korea – and he was attracting young people. The churches were against him because they were losing their sheep. And he is a perfect businessman, he has industries in Korea; he is a great salesman. He has been selling other things, but there is no better business than selling God. You don't have to produce, you don't need any factory; you don't have to do anything. All that you need is to provoke people's fear and greed. And he was collecting enormous amounts of money.

All the Christian churches were against him, parents were against him. They found a small flaw; that over three years' time he has not paid seven thousand dollars of taxes. He is jailed. He fought in many courts, but finally the Supreme Court refused to consider the case.

The vice president of America has not paid fifty thousand dollars in taxes – no punishment! The government simply said it was an "oversight." Fifty thousand dollars is an oversight – seven thousand dollars, and you are in prison for eighteen months!

It amazes me. It is a beautiful thing to look around…. The same churches who were against Reverend Moon – in fact, these churches forced the tax department and the government: "This man should be punished. He is putting the money given to the church into his own account." Now he is punished, and he is punished only because he is not an American. Otherwise American law provides that if a man fails to pay two thousand dollars per year he can be forgiven; he can be given a chance. There is no need to punish him, he should just give the money to the tax department.

Over three years' time, seven thousand dollars is not much of a crime. He should be given a chance to give the money – and he was ready to. These churches forced the government, because they wanted him to be punished, so that his congregation disperses. Now the same churches are making an appeal; they have made a protest that his case should be reconsidered.

I have seen the whole list. All kinds of churches, Christian associations, have signed it. They are all religious organizations with one exception: it has been signed by the state of Oregon also! That is something really great. What has the state to do with it?

The State is fighting against us, saying that we are mixing state and religion. In fact, there is no state here, no religion here, just individuals, utterly independent, living together because they feel a certain affinity. Just because of their experiences, they find it easier to be with people who are peaceful, silent, meditative. It helps them also in return to become more meditative. I call this the Buddhafield. A certain energy is created by so many people, which can trigger anybody into going inwards.

The state of Oregon is in favor of Reverend Moon; it says that he should not be punished. This is not in any way the concern of the state. It means that the state does not believe the federal courts, does not believe that those courts are fair. It is a contempt of the federal courts to protest.

And why with all those churches? Is the state of Oregon a church? And what authority have they got? We are also part of the state of Oregon. We have not been asked – how can they sign it on our behalf? They should have asked the whole state.

They did not protest when Scientologists were punished, because they were not Christians. Other religious groups have been punished, forced, harassed; the state of Oregon has never signed a protest. And they are protesting because the man is a Christian – one thing.

The second thing: Why are all these churches protesting? These were the people who forced the government in every possible way, so that Reverend Moon should be either imprisoned or deported. They are protesting now because if Reverend Moon is a criminal by not giving seven thousand dollars to the tax department, is a criminal because he was putting the church money, corporate money, in the banks under his own name…all these churches and their bishops are doing the same!

After this decision of the courts that Reverend Moon should be punished, sent to jail, they must have freaked out, because they have been doing the same thing on a larger scale. Bishops have bank accounts through which church money moves. Seeing the possibility that this may create a trouble for all the church leaders, now they are protesting on behalf of the same man they were trying to have punished.

Do you see the cunningness?

And only Christian churches have signed it. No Jews have signed it, no Mohammedans have signed it. And amongst those churches, the state of Oregon looks simply odd. Is it a church? And they are saying to us that we are mixing church and state! In fact, that's what *they* are doing. Because they are basically Christian, they don't want some Christian leader to be punished.

And a state trying to save someone who has committed a crime is strange. The state government of Oregon seems to be a Christian state. Their hostility to us has no other base except that we don't belong to any religion, that we have dropped all kinds of superstitions.

I have the whole vision of the New Man: No religions, no nations, no governments – only one functional government, and a powerful world academy of scientists. And science should be the decisive factor.

Don't be afraid. Scientists are not monsters, scientists are very humane. And if meditation goes on flowering and sannyasins go on growing, scientists will be the first people to be interested in the inner journey. They need it; otherwise their lives are unbalanced. They are only going out, out, out. They need certain methods so they can go inwards and keep a certain balance. And a meditative scientist cannot conceive of creating monsters, murderers.

Science has been a blessing to man. It can be a greater blessing if there is only one world.

God:
The Need Of
The Old Man

Beloved Bhagwan,

My memory of my parents when I was young is so alive. My father painted and wrote poetry. My mother taught me dancing. Both of them were agnostic, and never taught me religion. Now divorced, they each live in quiet desperation, unwilling to take chances. For me they have died and are just shells of fear. This makes me sad, because once they flowed with juice. What has happened to them?

It is a complicated question. In the first place, you do not know the meaning of agnosticism. Just not to teach you religion is not agnosticism. Just not to believe in religion is not agnosticism. If you call it agnosticism, you will have to use the word "negative"; it is negative agnosticism.

The positive agnostic is a seeker, and he goes on seeking, risking everything to find the truth, the life.

It is so easy to be a negative agnostic; not much intelligence is needed for that. All religions are so full of rubbish that any man of average intelligence can see it. And seeing it, he becomes non-religious. Your parents must have been of the same kind. Religions were wrong – that was their intellectual standpoint. But they never tried to fill the vacuum that religion was occupying.

They threw the baby out with the bath water.

To be an agnostic means tremendous search. You have not to believe, and you have not to disbelieve either. The negative agnostic disbelieves; and there is not much difference between belief and disbelief. The religious person believes in God, the irreligious person does not believe in God, but their beliefs and their disbeliefs are only mental games. Neither of them has searched, meditated, gone deeper into his own center. To be an agnostic needs tremendous courage, immense energy and patience.

And when the agnostic comes to the center of his being, certainly he finds there is no God, because the moment you know your center, you have known the center of the whole existence. On the periphery we are separate, but our separation is only at the circumference. As you go on moving towards your own self, you are coming closer and closer to other people's selves. Ultimately when you reach to the center, you are amazed: there is no God, but there is tremendous beauty, incalculable silence.

If their agnosticism were what I am defining it to be, they would not have been in desperation. The agnostic can never live in desperation. Either he is involved in the great search of what it is all about.... He has no energy for desperation, he is pouring his whole effort into one single dimension: he wants to know.

The agnostic is not the end of the search.

It is just the beginning.

The agnostic cannot say there is no God, there is no heaven, no hell. That is what the atheist goes on doing. Perhaps your parents were atheists. The atheists are bound to come someday to deep despair. As death comes close by, they start trembling. They have not believed in God, they have disbelieved in religion. It was good when they were young, but before death almost all atheists become theists, they start believing. A simple arithmetic....

Death is there. What is beyond they don't know. They don't know themselves. It was easier when they were young, hot. They enjoyed criticizing, they enjoyed destroying arguments of those who believe. And it is very easy to destroy their arguments. God is not an argument. At the moment of death, as they become older and the gap between them and death is becoming less and less, they freak out. Now they are no longer young, no longer hot. They have become just cold, shrunken, and death scares them.

Now the only way is to accept religion, because religion is a kind of opium. It helps you to forget your despair, your anguish. It helps you to hallucinate whatsoever you want. And the reasoning is: "If there is no God, there is no harm. By becoming a theist, if there is a God, then we can say, 'Forgive us, we were too young, inexperienced. Knowing nothing, we started disbelieving in you.'" And all the religions teach that God forgives those who ask for it.

It is simple. Whether he is or not, is not the question. The person is going to die and has to face the reality – if he survives death, with what face is he going to encounter God? This is the despair of your parents. Young, they were painters and poets and dancers. It is easy, when you are young, to do all kinds of foolishnesses. And when you do not believe in the religion people all around you are believing in, you have a certain satisfaction that you are unique, individual. You assert your uniqueness. It is nothing but an ego number.

If you meditate you will come to a space of godliness, but you won't find an old man with a long beard, sitting on a golden throne, saying to you, "Hi! So at last you have come. How do you do?" No meditator in the whole of history has found any person. Yes, every meditator has found a tremendous experience of awakening, enlightenment, liberation.

In youth, everybody thinks he is a great painter, a great poet, a great musician. Youth is blind – it is just the energy of nature which is overflowing in you. And you are not even concerned with death, it is too far away. There is a certain limit beyond which you cannot be worried. You can worry for tomorrow, you can worry for the day after tomorrow, but are you going to worry about the coming year? Are you going to be worried about the coming century? You will say, "Today is so much, tomorrow is close by – who cares about the coming century?"

One person has asked, "Bhagwan, is it not enough to be with You and enjoy, rather than thinking of the future of humanity?"

He himself is in doubt; otherwise from where does the question arise? Who is telling you to be worried about the future of humanity? It is enough if you can manage your life; the future will come out of it. Tomorrow is going to be born out of today. Whatever you are doing today will create your tomorrow. Once you know the secret, you are not only enjoying here, you are also creating the future.

The way the question is asked it seems you must be worried about the future of humanity. You want my approval: that it is perfectly okay, don't feel guilty, just enjoy this day with me. Your question does not need an answer, your question needs approval.

But in youth, death is almost non-existential. You cannot disregard it when you get older. Your parents must be getting older. Their youth is finished, the love between your mother and father is finished – that too was there because they were young. In old age everybody would like to be divorced, not only from his wife, but from womankind as such.

Youth is the time of romance. That's why young people have never been taken seriously. The elders, the old people who have passed through all experiences of life, have been respected throughout history. You will not find a single civilization where the young man was respected – just tolerated; he was only a

nuisance and nothing else. But the old people knew – they were also young once, they have also befooled themselves in many ways: "There is nothing to worry about, these young people will also get over their romantic ideas, ideas of revolution, of the future of mankind."

As death comes, you will shrink to a single question: What is beyond death, what is going to happen? If there is a God, then I am doomed – my whole life I denied him.

If there is no God, that too is scary. Then you will become a ghost, without a body, a consciousness who wants things but cannot get them, because things are material and the ghost is not material, he has no material body. This is one possibility, which is not very appealing.

And ghosts have never been known to paint, or to compose poetry, music. They have never been known to dance and enjoy. Ghosts don't fall in love, for the simple reason that the ghost has lost the body, the biology, the physiology; he is just a shadow.

It is not appealing to become a ghost and wander around hungry for all the things that he had desired in life. He would like to have a woman, but in ghosts I have never heard that there is any sexual difference. They are all alike. There is no beautiful ghost, and there is no ugly ghost; there is no male ghost, there is no female ghost. And they are stuck with all kinds of desires.

No, no old man would like to live like that; it is better to die completely. Death should be total, not only of the body but of the soul too. That will be a great relaxation, because if you are not, who is going to worry?

Just think back: when you were not born, do you remember that you were very much concerned about things – nuclear weapons, world war, Ethiopia? And do you think that before your birth, when you were non-existential, there was any problem? There was no problem. Not to be is the end of all problems, all sufferings, all misery.

But if there is a God, the old man who has denied him all his life is in despair. He cannot say now that God exists. It goes against his ego which he has cultivated for seventy, eighty years. And now he cannot stand up so strongly for his disbelief either.

It is my experience that any atheist I have come across is always young. I have never come across an old man who is an atheist. It is a similar case: you never come across an old man who is a hippie. To be a hippie you need to be between twenty-five and thirty-five. For those ten years you have strength to fight the society, to go against its morality, to do things which are not allowed – to take drugs…. It is a challenge.

But as you go on growing, nearabout between thirty-five and forty the hippie disappears. Suddenly thousands of hippies simply disappear. Now that youthful, romantic ideology of free love, drugs, not caring about anything, is not possible. You are becoming older; you need a home, you need a wife to look after you. You need children, because they will be, in a subtle way, tremendously satisfying. You know that you will die, but at least you will live in your child. The child is part of you. Even if a part is saved, it gives consolation.

Your parents in your childhood were young, full of romantic ideas. In fact, the young man wants to be recognized, his greatest need is attention. If you are a theist, who is going to give you any attention? There are millions of theists, it is a very common thing. But to be an atheist – you immediately start getting attention. That fulfills the ego.

And the trouble is that the atheist can always defeat any other kind of believers. The atheist can win in argument with any theist, because the theist has no evidence, no eyewitness about what happens after death, because nobody comes back after death and tells you stories about what is beyond death. So it is left up to your imagination. Of course, older people start imagining a God; otherwise they will be so helpless without the body – wandering like a cloud with no direction, no purpose. They need God. God is the need of the old man.

Children don't care; they are forced to believe in God. The old man is again in a similar situation, but far more difficult and complex. A child can easily be molded; he is soft, vulnerable, imitative. The old man feels for seventy, eighty years he has been a certain kind of person. His personality has become consolidated, and now at the moment of death it is very difficult for him to undo himself. That is why the old are in despair.

Why did they get divorced? As youth leaves you one day, it takes many things from you; it does not go alone. It takes all your paintings, all your poetries, all your music, all your dances. It takes all your love, and leaves behind something utterly empty, dark, nobody to take care of. Children must have been grown up by now, they must be passing through revolutionary, rebellious stages – perhaps they may be hippies. They don't care about you; you have lived your life, they want to live their life.

They may be somewhere in Kabul, in Kulu Manali, in Kathmandu, in Goa – they are enjoying their youthfulness and its freedom, and they have energy to waste. They must be taking marijuana, hashish, opium, LSD. They don't care even if they are imprisoned – I have known many people who have been imprisoned for using drugs which governments declare illegal. But imprisonment does not help. Out of the prison, they are again on the same track: Kabul, Kulu Manali, Kathmandu, Goa. Goa is their destination. These are just stopping, resting places; Goa is the final goal.

By the way, just a little drifting…. All the Christian countries are against marijuana, LSD, hashish, but they are not against alcohol, which is far more dangerous to health. Why? – because Jesus himself was a drunkard, his apostles were all drinking. So alcohol has some religious significance for the Christians.

The Christian community or the Christian

country cannot prohibit it. Prohibiting it, making it illegal, means you are raising questions against Christ and his behavior, you are doubting the great twelve apostles. And if Jesus can drink wine – not only that, if he changed water into wine – how can you say wine is illegal? If wine is illegal, then Christ was not doing a miracle but was committing a crime by turning water into wine.

Christians accept alcohol – it is strange – and they deny LSD, for the simple reason that LSD was not available to Jesus Christ. Otherwise, I can say with certainty that Jesus Christ and all his apostles would have been taking LSD and real grass. They had to confine themselves only to alcohol; that was the only drug available.

You ask me what went wrong with your parents? Everything. First, they got married. If they were not married, at least they would have saved you from this life! And they were so much involved with painting, poetry, dances…. I have never heard their name as a great painter, or as a great poet, or as a great dancer. But in youth the balloon of the ego is big. You write a third-rate letter and you call it a love letter. Most probably you have copied it from a third-rate novel, or from a movie.

You perform the act of love – it is some kind of exercise, it is not love. Real love is possible only to the meditator, that is his reward. A man who does not know himself, a woman who does not know herself – these two ignorant people fall in love with each other, and out of this ignorance you are born. And sooner or later, those two ignorant people become fed up with each other.

Now your parents are living separately, alone, in despair, in desperation. What is their desperation? Now your father knows that his paintings are just stupid, these same paintings that looked as if a new Picasso is born. His poems look like rubbish. There is nothing in them, he was just putting words together in a certain order. These poems are created, composed, they have not been given birth.

The real poet gives birth to his poetry. He breathes it, his heart beats in it. In the moment he is pouring forth his poetry, his music, his dance, he is not there. If he is there, then the poetry and the dance and the music will remain mediocre. One has to disappear, one has to disappear in the act so totally that nothing is left behind.

One of the great poets, Coleridge, was asked by a professor, "I want to come and see you, because I am in trouble. Your poetry I have to teach to the students. There are a few lines, statements in your poetry, which I find difficult to explain. And the students are asking me. I feel embarrassed to say that I don't know, and I am a D.Litt in literature! I thought it better I come to you and ask the meaning of those lines."

Coleridge said, "You can come, but remember, I am also in great difficulty."

The professor said, "About your poetry you are in difficulty?"

He said, "Yes. When I wrote them, two persons knew the meaning of what I was writing: God and I. Now only God knows! I cannot figure out myself what the hell I have done."

An authentic poet is not present, he gives way for the poetry to flow from him. And the same is true about music and dance, sculpture and architecture, about everything that is beautiful. If they come out of a meditative state, then they are not ego products. Ego products are going to be very ordinary.

Now, let me come back.

Why have your parents divorced? You are asking me what has gone wrong. The romance is over. Romance is nothing permanent. It is just like the wind: it comes, you feel the coolness, the breeze, and then it is gone. It is like the flowers blossoming in the early morning sun – so beautiful, so colorful, so magical that even dewdrops on their petals look like pearls. But by the evening the petals are falling, the flower is disappearing.

Romance is just a flower. It is not a coincidence

that the hippies and their type of people were called flower people. They will blossom and they will disappear, there is no need to bother about them. It happens, this disease, to every young person.

And if your mother was also a dancer, then certainly both were artists. It happens more to the artistic people. They are against the whole world, against everything, because they think they can create a new world. The old poetry, the old paintings are nothing to them, and their very ordinary painting is just the greatest piece of art.

In youth you can believe in anything. And when you can believe in your creativity, poetry, music, it is easy to drop believing in God, in religion, because you have found your own opium. You don't need pope the Polack to supply opium to you. You grow your marijuana in your own garden; there is no need to get it from all kinds of peddlers. But one day youth is going to disappear. And the day youth disappears, you have entered into the arena of death. Old age is only a preparation for death.

Now they must be feeling empty. Their art has failed, their love has failed, their revolution has failed, but their ego is still there. The ego cannot go against itself. If it has been atheist all its life, it cannot become suddenly theist. That is the desperation. Otherwise, just as youth has its opium, old age has its own opium: believe in God, believe in Jesus Christ, believe in the messiah – he will save you, he will take you into the kingdom of God.

Reverend Jim Jones managed to convince one thousand people that if they died with him, he would take all of them into paradise. He went a little farther than Jesus Christ. Jesus was saying, "At the time of judgment, the final day of judgment, I will choose my sheep and take them into paradise."

Reverend Jim Jones is more progressive, more speedy, more American. "Why wait for the day of judgment? I am going, come along with me." And all those people – most of them black, uneducated, uncultured, knowing nothing about existence, its

experiences – they had heard only this fool, Reverend Jim Jones. They had followed him out of the country; then finally they followed him out of life.

And it is a surprise that nobody criticized Christianity for it. Nobody could see a simple connection: that what Jesus was saying, this poor fellow, Reverend Jim Jones, was practicing, of course with more modern techniques. The people who died in Jonestown, they were given Kool-Aid to drink which was full of poison. Really contemporary! Jesus cannot be thought to have known anything about Kool-Aid.

It was tasty, and death was not a fear because the leader, the shepherd, was going with them, and he knew the way, he had a direct communication line with God.

On the contrary, Christians criticize me; they say that I am creating another Jonestown. They are responsible for Jonestown. They are responsible for so much violence... in history that it would have been a great blessing if the holy ghost had missed his target. The world would have been in a better condition without Christians. It will be, one day, in a better condition without all religions. In some way or other, they are all suicidal. A few, like Reverend Jones and his followers, do it quickly.

Jainas in India have followed the same idea for the thousand years at least: their monks fast unto death. It takes sometimes seventy days, eighty days, ninety days. The man goes on becoming a skeleton. His eyes go on deepening, becoming dark. He cannot move, he cannot speak. I don't think after seventy days' fast he recognizes anybody, or even knows what is happening, what he is doing. They have given it a beautiful name, *santhara,* and they think this is the greatest ascetic practice. It is a crime, but the Indian government cannot stop it: it is a religious crime and you are not supposed to interfere in religion.

Your parents are feeling empty, trembling before death. All that was meaningful is no longer there. They are simply hollow. It is right that you say, for you they are dead. They are really living a ghostly life.

On the one hand, their whole past does not allow them to change their minds. On the other hand, death, the darkening night. Death says it is better to change your ideology; perhaps there is a God, who knows?

If they were real agnostics, by this time they would have found what the truth is. The truth is godliness. Yes, there is no God, but there is a quality so high, so pure, so innocent, so fragrant, that once you have known it, you have known all that is worth knowing.

It is a quality. That's why I emphasize again and again that if you meditate you will come to a space of godliness, but you won't find an old man with a long beard, sitting on a golden throne, saying to you, "Hi! So at last you have come. How do you do?" No meditator in the whole of history has found any person. Yes, every meditator has found a tremendous experience of awakening, enlightenment, liberation.

Your parents need meditation, otherwise they will die in tremendous despair and frustration. And meditation needs no belief system, so they need not drop their belief systems. Meditation does not require you to believe in God, heaven and hell. It requires nothing. It simply gives you a method which you can work easily.

You say that they are afraid to take any chances. Of course, they had lived with a certain disbelief for so long, and that disbelief and the philosophy they had woven around it have failed. And there is not much time left. Now to try anything new, naturally, they will feel afraid. They tried one thing their whole life, and it failed. Their paintings failed, their poetry failed, their philosophy failed, their music, their dance – they are bankrupt, spiritually bankrupt.

If you love them, if you have any feeling for them…and you must have, otherwise the question would not be raised. You may think they are dead, but you know they are not dead; they are dying. Then it becomes a responsibility for you.

At least they have done one favor to you – you have to accept the obligation – they never taught you any religion. It is time to help them. It is a great opportunity for paying back all the love that they have given to you when they were young. Teach them how they can meditate. And the way of meditation I am teaching you is very simple. If they can just watch their minds – and we are not asking much – if they can become just a witness, a watcher, the mind will slowly melt away as ice melts when the sun rises.

Meditation is the only medicine for them now. If they can die meditatively, silently, blissfully – which is simple and possible – you will feel also relieved of a burden; otherwise, you will carry some burden on your soul, that you could not help them when they needed it.

You are asking, "They were so juicy – what has happened?" Everybody is juicy when they are young, youth brings all your juices to their peak. But youth is a fleeting phenomenon.

I have heard about three old men: one was seventy, another was seventy-five, and the third was eighty-five. They were sitting in a park – and that was their routine, every day they would come. They had no work the whole day, so by the evening they would come and sit and talk about the past.

The old man has no future, he has only a long past. The child has no past, he has only a long future; hence children want to grow fast. Old people cling to the past: perhaps that will help against the oncoming death.

So they used to talk about beautiful moments in their life, difficult times in their life, successful moments in their life – most of which was exaggerated. It was their imagination that they were a great success when they were young, that they were this and that.

This evening when they met, the first old man, seventy, said, "One thing has been bothering me, and I would like to say it to you – it is almost a confession – so that I am relieved of it. I cannot go to the priest, he is just a young fellow – what does he know about religion? You are older than me, you have lived more, known more. I would like to confess to you."

The other two became very excited. They said, "What is the thing that is bothering you? Tell it, get rid of it."

He was very embarrassed, but he said, "The problem is that I was caught red-handed peeping through the keyhole of the bathroom, because a beautiful woman was the guest and I could not take myself away from the keyhole. And my grandmother caught me red-handed. I am ashamed."

The two old people started laughing. One said, "You are a fool! Everybody does it, it is not a problem. In fact, why are keyholes made? This is their purpose, and we all have done it, so don't be worried. And it is our experience, that from the keyhole of the bathroom, an ordinary, homely woman also looks like Cleopatra, because you cannot see exactly. It is vague. You can make it seem, through your imagination, as if a fairy has descended in the bathroom. We all have done it," those two said, "you don't be worried."

He said, "You don't understand me at all. It happened this morning!"

Then they were a little shocked. *This* morning? At the age of seventy?

They said, "Naturally, it is understandable why you are feeling so much in the dumps. But, boy, get out of it. What has happened has happened. Next time, be careful. First watch about your grandmother, whether she is around or not; all that is needed is that little awareness. And find some excuse – drop your handkerchief on the floor. The moment your grandmother comes, start looking for the handkerchief, so you have an excuse: 'The handkerchief had fallen and I was just picking it up. I have nothing to do with the keyhole.'"

The seventy-year-old man was very happy. He said, "Great idea! I never thought that some way I can manage an excuse to be there. This is great! I am completely unburdened. Now I will really be waiting for tomorrow morning. It will be difficult to sleep tonight. That woman is really great!"

Because he had opened a certain subject, the second man said, "I also have something to confess to you. For almost five years I have been making love to my wife in a special way."

They said, "What special way? You should have told us. Don't you think we are your friends? You have found a special way, and you are keeping us in the dark? Tell us! What is the special way?"

He said, "It is nothing much. Before going to sleep I hold her hand, and press her hand two or three times, and then we go to sleep."

The other two said, "This is a way of making love?"

He said, "What else to do? The trouble has arisen because once in a while I forget to press her hand, and she immediately starts nagging me, 'It seems you are pressing some other woman's hand! I will not allow this! You have to give an explanation. With whom are you making love nowadays?'"

The third man said, "You both are idiots – you think these are difficulties? I am eighty-five. I am feeling a real difficulty, and when you know about my difficulty you will forget all this nonsense of pressing hands, being nagged by the wife, becoming a Peeping Tom, finding some excuse…." He said, "I never thought that you are so stupid.

"The real trouble is with me. This morning when I started preparing to make love to my wife, she said, 'Have you gone mad? – because two times in the night you have done the same thing. And it does not suit you – an eighty-five-year-old man making love three times? You disturbed my sleep and I am fed up with you! I was hoping that now that we are getting old, this animal game will finish. You are getting older, and you are doing more and more the same thing that I was thinking would be finished!'"

The two were really amazed. They said, "You think this is trouble? This is great!"

He said, "It is a great trouble. In fact, my memory

is failing – I didn't have any idea that I had made love two times, I was thinking this is the first time. Your problems are nothing – my memory is just disappearing!"

Your parents are old. They must be having many kinds of problems which only old people have. Help them to meditate a little bit. Perhaps they can get back the memory of those juicier days. Perhaps they can start painting again, and now it will be far better. Perhaps they can start music and dance, and now it will be better because it will be coming out of their meditation.

Everything changes its quality the moment the meditator touches it. I say it to you on my own experience. I never quote the scriptures unless something is my own experience. For these thirty-two years or more, I have enjoyed food as I had never enjoyed before. Since enlightenment I have enjoyed everything so profoundly, so deeply that I feel sorry for the whole humanity. They also eat, but they go on doing many other things in their mind while their mouth is chewing. Their mind is engaged – how can they know the taste?

That's why people eat too much. That's why it is one of the biggest problems in rich countries. Women are dieting, men are dieting, doing exercises to make the body slim, because a fat man is declaring by his fatness that he is empty and filling that emptiness with food.

After enlightenment, when you are eating you are simply eating. You are not there, there is only a process of eating. Then it becomes exactly like painting, when the painter is not there. It becomes like dancing, when the dancer disappears in the dance.

I want to teach you that it is not only painters and dancers and singers that have the prerogative to enjoy life. It is everybody's birthright – it has nothing to do with special talents. Cooking can be a joy, cleaning the house can be a joy.

It is all the same. What you are doing is not the point; the doer must be lost in doing, you should not remain separate. If you are separate, then of course, there is going to be boredom. Every day cleaning the house…. All housewives are bored, utterly bored. All men are bored: the same job, the same stupid customers, the same wife at home.

To a meditator, everything is beautiful.

He lives life in its abundance.

I say to you, only the enlightened person can live luxuriously. Whether he has luxurious things around him or not does not matter. He has some inner change. His vision, his attitude, his approach to things is totally different from the average man or woman.

Help your parents. Pay the debt. And if you can see them again painting, dancing, perhaps they may fall again in love. Perhaps they will come closer to each other. My feeling is that people get divorced only because they both become too much to each other. It becomes simply impossible to live together, it becomes a constant harassment to both.

If you can introduce meditation…and I am certain they will welcome it, because they are in desperation. They need some help from somewhere. And if you cannot do it for them, who is gong to do it for them? And remember, meditation is not something that happens while you are young. It is not something like love, romance, great ideas about revolution.

I was also young, and while I was studying, I had many friends. Somebody was a communist, somebody was a socialist, somebody was a fanatic Christian, somebody was a Hindu chauvinist, and they all were full of great ideas.

They used to ask me, "You don't seem excited about the great problems the world is facing."

I said, "You leave me alone. I am working in a totally different dimension – you cannot understand it. Be a communist!"

Now they all have disappeared in the crowd.

Once in a while, if, by accident I met somebody, I would ask him, "What happened to your communism?"

He would say, "Forget all about it! My wife is pregnant, four children I have already. Prices are going up, the rupee is shrinking smaller and smaller, and I am just a clerk. There is no time for me to think of communism. Those days are gone when I was trying to reach to the moon."

None of the students – and there were thousands of students in the university – *none,* not a single one, has remained what he was in the university. Perhaps I am the only one amongst that whole crowd of socialists, communists, who has remained in the same dimension, going on and on; I have found the way to infinity.

Remember, enlightenment is not something that happens as an incident and there comes a full stop, no. Enlightenment begins, but it never ends. It is an ongoing process. It becomes juicier and juicier.

And when things go on becoming juicier and juicier, how are you going to go back? Who remembers the way back, the past? – because every day you are facing a new revelation, a new light, a new joy. Every day it is so fresh that there is no need to look backwards.

The enlightened man is a child forever.

He has only the future, and there is no limit to his growth. Perhaps even the sky has some limit, but enlightenment knows no limit.

Beloved Bhagwan,

All the news media are talking about the sixth of August, the unfortunate day forty years ago when Hiroshima and Nagasaki were bombed with the first atom bombs. After all these years, governments are still spending most of their money making these nuclear weapons. Can You please comment?

The sixth of August can never be forgotten. That day we proved that civilization has not happened to humanity yet, that we are barbarians, that we are cannibals, that we are still animals. Darwin is wrong; the whole idea of evolution is just imagination.

Instead of believing in Darwin, I believe in the monkeys, because monkeys also have their idea: they think man has fallen – and certainly he has fallen – from the trees. Falling from the height, you call that evolution?

The sixth of August proved the monkeys are right, because to drop atom bombs on Hiroshima and Nagasaki was the ugliest thing that man has done in the whole of history. Everything else paled before it. And the wonder of wonders is that it was not needed at all. Germany had already surrendered; the Japanese forces were almost finished. Perhaps without the dropping of the atom bombs the war may have continued one week more.

That would not have been a great calamity – people had been fighting for five years; for seven days more…. But that was the reason for dropping the atom bomb on Nagasaki and Hiroshima, because if the war ended then you would never be able to drop the atomic weapons that you had. It was the time to make the world feel how much power and strength you had. America wanted it to be remembered that if Nagasaki and Hiroshima can disappear in smoke, then there is no problem: Moscow, New Delhi, London, Paris – any place can be evaporated within seconds.

America was trying to prove itself the greatest power in the world. It had nothing to do with the war, they were winning. Now, dropping atom bombs on people who are already losing every day – there cannot be any other reason.

President Truman – and what a name he has got. Certainly he was a true-man. We should change his name to President True-monkey; that's where he belongs. Even his military experts were not willing. They told him, "It is absolutely unnecessary, the war has really ended. It is only just a week's work and Japan will surrender. Now that Germany has surrendered, Japan cannot survive; the basic power was

Germany. And we are winning every day, so just wait seven days more. And if after seven days the war is not finished, you can drop atom bombs."

But he did not listen, because there was some other motivation in dropping the atom bombs. It was not to win, they were winning already. The motivation was to make it clear to the whole world that now America is by far the biggest power. And just to prove this, two big cities, throbbing with life, were just destroyed.

Obviously, Japan surrendered immediately; otherwise Tokyo would go the same way as Hiroshima and Nagasaki had gone. And President True-monkey told his military experts, "See? The war is finished immediately. We don't have to wait."

Hiroshima and Nagasaki are wounds which have not healed yet. And rather than healing those wounds, America is piling up nuclear weapons. Naturally, afraid of America, Russia is doing the same; they are piling up nuclear weapons. In fact, it is now difficult to say who is more powerful, because about American things are known, how much power America has, but about Russia everything is secret. She may be more powerful, she may have more nuclear weapons. She may have new methods which are even superior.

For example, they have been trying, and perhaps they have succeeded, in creating death rays. No bomb is needed, certain rays are just directed towards the country. You will not see them, so you cannot protect yourself. When somebody is bombing, there is time – Russia cannot destroy the whole of America in a day, nor can America destroy Russia in a day. But death rays will kill people and nobody will be able to know what is happening. Suddenly the death ray hits your heart, you fall dead. It is an invisible way of killing, and as far as I know, there is as yet no way found to protect people against death rays.

And because these two biggest powers in the world are continuing to create more and more destructive weapons, even small countries – just out of fear, the whole humanity is living in fear – countries which are starving, cannot manage even to survive, which perhaps will not be there to see the third world war at all, they are also trying to make atomic plants, nuclear plants. Their people are already dying and starving, and they are preparing death for others, knowing perfectly well that now there is no time to become in any way a great world power.

Russia and America are so far ahead that by the time you reach that point, they would have moved again, miles further ahead. Now there is no way for them to catch up. It is sheer stupidity on the part of other countries to waste their money on nuclear weapons, for the simple reason that they can never be the top power. That is impossible; they don't have the means, they don't have the time.

And it is stupid for America and Russia too, because they have already so much destructive energy in their hands that they can kill all living beings on the earth, from trees to man – everything that breathes. They both are ready enough to destroy life seven times over. Can you see any intelligence in making more weapons? Are not these enough? A man dies only once! And you are not the begotten son of God, that after death you will be resurrected with glory, so they will have to kill you again.

But I think the whole idea of resurrection of Jesus is a fiction. Yes, I know he did not die on the cross. It was a Friday, and that was chosen specially by Pontius Pilate. He was not a Jew, he had nothing against Jesus. He was simply worried that a young man, only thirty-three, innocent in every way – he has never committed any crime, he has never harmed anybody – is being crucified. And Pontius Pilate will be remembered always as the person who gave orders for the crucifixion.

Judea was under the rule of the Romans and Pontius Pilate was the Roman governor general of Judea. He tried in many ways to free Jesus; first he tried to persuade the chief priest of the Jews, but they were adamant. Then he tried…. Three people were being crucified: two were criminals, murderers, and it was a custom that if the chief rabbi and the people wanted, one person could be forgiven. Pontius Pilate was hoping that the people would ask that Jesus be forgiven. He had not done anything wrong. But people asked that Barabbas should be forgiven. He was a confirmed criminal who had been to jail again and again many times. They asked that Barabbas should be released. So that second idea also failed.

Then he tried a third method. On Friday Jesus was to be crucified. Pontius Pilate managed to delay the process as long as possible. Jesus was to be prosecuted and crucified in the morning, but Pontius Pilate was able to postpone it a little bit more: he had to ask the emperor, the message was coming, all the papers had to be filled in.

Jesus was crucified in the afternoon; this was a strategy – because the Roman way of crucifying a man is really barbarous, utterly inhuman. They nail the person's hands on the cross, his feet on the cross; then slowly blood starts oozing out. It takes at least forty-eight hours of immense suffering for the man, and only then does he die.

Crucifixion is not an electric chair, where before you know you are dead, you are dead – just a switch and you are finished. Even Adolf Hitler was more human, although he killed millions of Jews; but he had created gas chambers. People would go into the chamber, and within a minute you would see smoke rising above the roof: the people were gone. Thousands of people together, within a single minute, just evaporated.

But to hang a person and keep him hanging for forty-eight hours at least…. He will be hungry, he will be thirsty – more so because blood is oozing out, there will be dehydration….

Pontius Pilate managed to crucify Jesus in the afternoon. It was a custom of the Jews that on Saturday – that is their sabbath, their holy day – all work should stop, everything should stop. On the day of sabbath nothing is to be done. Pontius Pilate took advantage of this. He said, "If it is so, then Jesus should be brought down" – he was still alive, because blood was still oozing; when a man is dead, blood does not come out of the body. "So he should be brought down, and after three days, we will crucify him again."

He was put in a cave with a big rock that single-handedly he could not remove. And after three days, the cave was found empty. This was not resurrection. This was Pontius Pilate and one of Jesus' sympathizers who managed the whole strategy. First, you bring him down – he is still alive – put ointments on him, give him enough to drink, and then remove his body.

Jesus died in India in Kashmir. Naturally, those six hours on the cross gave him a great lesson. And he had seen that there is no God, he had seen that there is no miracle, he had seen that: "I was just crazy proclaiming myself as the only begotten son of God." In India he lived really a long life – one hundred and twelve years, but in India he never said again, "I am the messiah, the prophet." Those six hours took away all his fanatic ideas; those six hours brought him to his senses.

He was thirty-three when he was crucified. In India he lived to one hundred and twelve years. He escaped Judea, because if he was in Judea he would be crucified again. The experience of six hours on the cross was enough. He did not want to do any more teaching, preaching. He did not want anymore to be the savior. In fact, he saved *himself,* just in time. He remained there with a small group of followers, but no promises of the kingdom of God. He had promised that, and he had seen the result.

That's why the world does not know what happened to Jesus after crucifixion. And Christians took the opportunity to claim that he was resurrected, because the cave was found empty. But his grave exists in Kashmir.

I have been to his grave, and it is an absolute proof, because on the grave the writing is in Hebrew. Nobody knows Hebrew in India. Mohammedans also make graves, but their graves always point towards Mecca, their holy city. There are only two graves in India – one of Moses and the other of Jesus – which are not pointing towards Mecca. And on both the inscriptions are in Hebrew.

Of course, Jesus Christ is not named on that grave, because in Hebrew his name was Joshua, not Jesus. Jesus is a Greek translation of Joshua. And Christ is not used, because Christ is also a Greek word for messiah. So on the grave you will not find the name of Jesus Christ, you will find the name Joshua, the messiah. But that is the Hebrew name by which he was known to his people.

Hiroshima and Nagasaki create a division in history. And now, to go on piling up more and more weapons of destruction, just out of fear.... Even India wants a nuclear plant. The difficulty is that one of the most important things needed to make nuclear weapons is uranium, and uranium is found only in Russia and America. So anybody who wants to create a nuclear plant has to depend on these two powers.

America has bigger resources for uranium, so although India deep down condemns America, it cannot declare openly that "We are not with America," because from where are they going to get the uranium? Russia has only enough for itself; otherwise Russia would have provided the uranium for India.

And the situation is absurd. When you have already enough to destroy every man seven hundred times, then stop everything!

All the energy should move to provide people with more comfort, more education, more health, more medicine. And this is so simple.

People go on asking me, "Don't you have any compassion for Ethiopia? What are your people doing for Ethiopia?" I am not so unintelligent as to send you to Ethiopia to serve the poor people there who are starving. The crisis has been going on for four years, because for four years there have been no rains. I don't feel responsible at all for Ethiopia, or India.

There are two kinds of people who are responsible, and on this sixth of August, those two categories should take the responsibility to see that things like Hiroshima and Nagasaki never happen again.

Who are these two categories? One is the politicians. They should stop – not a semicolon, a full stop. No more money goes into making destructive things, no money goes into the service of death. And you should remember, seventy-five percent of the energy of all the nations is going into the service of death. This seventy-five percent of the energy should become available to the poor, the downtrodden. And can you imagine? Seventy-five percent of the finances, if released from the service of death, can make this earth a paradise.

This sixth of August.... The second category is that of priests of all religions, who are teaching people that birth control is against God, that abortion is a crime, is a sin. These are the people who are helping the population grow faster and faster. These people should be behind bars: the pope, his bishops, the *shankaracharya,* the *imam,* Mother Teresa – certainly at least one woman should be included with these criminals. They all should be in prison. Leaving them out is leaving ferocious animals without chains in the society. They go on helping the population to grow, and the population goes on creating more poverty.

I am not responsible. For thirty years I have been continuously teaching that the pill is the greatest revolution after the discovery of fire. Nothing else in between is of any importance. Birth control is your birthright. It is up to you to decide, because there is no God who is deciding. You have to take the responsibility upon yourself.

We are in our own ways trying to raise the consciousness around the world to prevent the politicians from creating more destructive weapons. And whatever nuclear energy, atomic energy, is available should be used for creative purposes. The same energy can bring clouds over Ethiopia; the same energy can stop floods in India. Energy is always neutral. It depends on you for what purpose you are going to use it.

The politicians are responsible – and the religious leaders. I am not responsible at all, because for thirty years I have been teaching in favor of birth control, the pill and other methods. And I have been teaching against atomic energy. But if people don't listen then it is their responsibility.

If Ethiopia dies, it is not my responsibility; it is the responsibility of Ethiopia itself. If India dies, it is not my responsibility. They should hang their *shan-karacharyas* who are responsible for poverty in India. They should tell their politicians, "We don't need nuclear plants." India is dying, half of India is starving, and the wheat is being exported, because only by exporting wheat and other things which their *own* people need, can India arrange finances enough to make nuclear plants.

These politicians should be forced: "Either stop all efforts for war, or get down from your seats. We will find other presidents, other prime ministers."

The sixth of August should be a day of declaration against the politicians and the priests.

You Are My
Fellow Travelers

DISCOURSE 33, July 31, 1985

Beloved Bhagwan

Never have You seemed so human, dancing, laughing and celebrating with us. But never have You told it to us quite so straight, without catering to our unenlightened mortal stupidities. Is this the twenty-first century vibe?

You got it! This is the twenty-first century for me, and I am trying to push you towards it.
Sannyasins should live ahead of time. The people who are burdened with the past live five thousand years ago, ten thousand years ago, and they are stuck there.

You cannot live with the past. The past is dead, and to live with the past is to be dead. The only life possible is in the present, and the future is always changing into the present. It is always making the twenty-first century in the twentieth century. The farther ahead you can live in the moment, the more alive you will feel. And remember, it is better to be red than dead!

I had to wait for you to behave humanly. I was waiting for my people, because only they will understand that to be human is the highest value there is.

I was talking to the Christians, to the Hindus, to the Mohammedans, to the Jainas, to the Buddhists, and it was a difficult job. I could not behave humanly with them. They wanted me to be their messiah, their prophet, their messenger.

Just the other day I received two letters. One was from a woman in California. She said, "I have loved you for many years. I have been reading all your books – how beautiful it was when you spoke on Jesus! And now after three years of silence, what you are saying has enraged me so much that I have burned all your books. I will pray to Jesus Christ and God to forgive you. Perhaps you should go into silence again. And if you don't go into silence, then there is only one possibility for you to be saved: that is, when you expire the silence will descend on your grave."

Now this woman had all my literature, had loved me, she thinks. But do you think she loved me? She loved Jesus Christ, and because I had spoken on Jesus Christ, putting myself behind him. putting my gun on his shoulder, she was happy, immensely happy and grateful. The poor woman is not aware of the fact that she had never been in tune with me. Because I was speaking on Jesus as no one had spoken before, I was supporting her mind, her tradition, and she was feeling immensely happy. I was fulfilling her ego.

Now she is so against me, she has burned all the books, and she is praying to Jesus Christ, the God, to forgive me. She should also burn the house in which my books have been. They have already infected the air and the house.

Whenever you feel that you are supported in some way, you are happy. Hindus were happy, Mohammedans were happy, Christians were happy – everybody was happy.
And I am not here to make you happy.

I want you to be blissful. I want you to know

yourself, to know this vast existence. And you cannot know it being a Christian or a Hindu. Your eyes are covered with layers of dust that centuries have poured over you.

Now she is feeling very offended, but still she cannot see the point. I had to speak on Jesus, Buddha, Mahavira, and hundreds of other prophets, messiahs, saviors. But that speaking was very difficult for me, it broke my back, because I was doing something which was against my own nature. I was sorting out sentences from Jesus; those which I could not support I never mentioned. Those which I could support, I supported them with all the growth of the twenty centuries after him.

Naturally many Christians, priests, bishops, were influenced. They could not believe that a man who is not a Christian has such great insight into Jesus, his words, his implications. It was not like that. I was using Jesus only to catch fish in the big ocean of Christianity; I have done that with all the religions. And then for three years I became silent, just to know how many people were hanging around my words because they supported their belief system.

In my silence this woman was happy. She said, "While you were silent, I loved you. Since you have started speaking again you have destroyed my love." So those who were here for their own ego fulfillment.... And the ego cannot be fulfilled by my silence; the ego need words, theologies, philosophy. She wants me to become silent again. She is furious. She wants me to be dead, but to be silent.

So in these three years I have sorted out my people, who can be with my silence. That means it does not matter to them whether I speak or not. It does not matter to them whether I say something which is against their conditioning or favoring their conditioning. They love *me,* not my words. Their communion is heart to heart.

And when I saw all the camels have moved towards Santa Fe – Santa Fe has become a great camel camp – I thought that the moment has come to speak

Now I can be human to you. I always wanted to be an authentic human being. There was never a desire to be a prophet, a messiah, an avatar, a godman. To me, all these words are four-letter words. I wanted just to be simple, ordinary – the way I am. I wanted to expose my heart to you without thinking what is going to be the consequence. This was possible only when I had found my own people, who can understand.

directly to you. And now I will be speaking directly to you. There will be no Jesus between me and you, no Buddha between me and you, just a pure communion. Only then can I reach to your heart; otherwise, I can reach only to your mind – and mind has no function in bringing you blissfulness, ecstasy, enlightenment. Mind can give you better technology, but it cannot give you the New Man.

I feel sorry for the woman, but she should understand that it is all her doing. I don't know her even, she is not a sannyasin. And her love was false; she was still a Christian, and she was being supported by my meanings that I had put through Jesus' mouth.

I know I have been doing a very risky job. If ever Jesus, Buddha, Mahavira meet me, they are all going to attack me and kill me. They will forget all their messages of love, their messages of peace. And it will not be only Mohammed, it will be all those whom I have used. But there is no possibility of meeting these guys again.

Now I can be human to you. I always wanted to be an authentic human being. There was never a desire to be a prophet, a messiah, an avatar, a godman. To me, all these words are four-letter words. I wanted just to be simple, ordinary – the way I am. I wanted to expose my heart to you without thinking what is going to be the consequence. This was possible only when I had found my own people, who can understand.

You are fortunate that you have remained. All the sannyasins around the earth are fortunate, because what they have listened to before was not the truth. I tried hard to put the truth…I interpreted those people, who were just crackpots – but it was compulsory. In this vast world, it is very difficult to find your own people. They are already belonging to some group, some theology, some religion. They have their own church, their own mosque, their own temple, and they have great investments there. They are hoping to attain paradise; they are afraid of falling into hell.

We are not interested in heaven and hell or God. There is no need to go to hell to experience it – you can just go driving on the county road and you will know what kind of roads exist in hell. You need not travel long to heaven – you can be just here, dancing, singing, rejoicing, and you know heaven has come to you.

I emphasize the fact that nobody ever goes to heaven or hell. It is just vice versa: Hell comes to you, heaven comes to you. It is your doing, it is your heart that attracts it.

Hell is your misery, your suffering.

Heaven is your rejoicing.

I have also received another letter, one from a Zen master who wants to come and see me. And you will see the difference between a Christian, Mohammedan, Hindu, and a Zen monk.

The Zen monks have emphasized that they do not belong to Buddhism. In fact, Zen is a revolt against Buddhism. Buddha would not approve of these people, they are too human. They are so simple: chopping wood, drawing water from the well – you cannot conceive Buddha doing that.

This Zen master gives you a totally different vision. He is happy that I am here. He is immensely rejoiced that somebody is here who can even prevent the third world war. He just wants to sit by my side, to feel the vibe. He also knows what I am saying. He is also reading my books and he had read my old books too. But now he has decided that the time has come, that he should come here, because now I am speaking on my own authority. Now it is worth being close to a man who is not a commentator, but is an enlightened soul.

He says in his letter that Buddha had declared that he would be coming again after five thousand years. Twenty-five centuries have passed. The Zen monk declares, "We are exactly in the middle: twenty-five centuries back there was a Buddha, and perhaps twenty-five centuries ahead there will be a Buddha. And you seem to be the bridge, just exactly in the middle – twenty-five centuries." He says he has not seen Buddha, but he would like to meet me, to have some taste of buddhahood, awakenedness.

This man has a totally different approach. He is a man of understanding, meditation. If he ever wants to burn, he will burn the old books and save the new ones, because the old books were commentaries, which I had to make under compulsion. Now it is no longer a commentary, I am telling you my experience. If Jesus or Buddha or Zarathustra agrees with me, good; if they don't agree, they can go to hell.

They had all pretended to be higher than you, holier than you, more special than you. They fulfilled a great need in you: you wanted to follow somebody who was the only begotten son of God. By following the son of God you were also participating in something divine. I have dissolved the very idea of following. You are my fellow travelers.

I want it to be declared throughout the earth, to all the corners of the earth, that someone has transcended, for the first time, even the experience of enlightenment – because that too is a way of creating distance, great distance: I am enlightened, you are not enlightened; I am always right, you are always wrong.

You are right as much as I am right. Accept the responsibility of your actions, of your thoughts, of your being, and fight every kind of trespass. You have to be yourself. If you cannot accept me being as human as you are just because I am enlightened, then I throw that enlightenment away. But I cannot allow you to be humiliated in a subtle way; I cannot allow you to go on becoming bigger egos.

To hell with enlightenment!

And I will do everything that will destroy it. No Buddha has laughed. What kind of miserable creatures…? No Buddha has danced. No Buddha has sung.

You just wait! You will be the first ones to see a buddha dancing. As your laughter and your love are making me stronger, soon I am going to dance. You should not be surprised when someday I appear in your disco or your playing cards room!

I want to erase all kinds of stupidities that have arisen in the past, and have become bigger and bigger as time has passed.

My sannyasins and I are not different. Your faults are my faults, your errors are my errors. I accept you as you are; remember it, because if I come to your disco perhaps you will not be ready to accept me. I am preparing you for that, I don't want you freaking out. It has been a long and hard struggle for me to find my people, I am not going in any way to freak them out.

Slowly, slowly you will get accustomed to the idea that an enlightened man can come to a disco, dance with you, play cards with you, drink a little champagne with you. You should be immensely happy that you are with a man who claims no holier-than-thou attitude. It is ugly. There is nobody above human beings.

I have always loved one statement of Chandidas. He was thought to be mad, because he declared: *Sabar uppe manu sut, tahar uppe nain* – "Above all is the truth of man, and there is nothing above it."

Although he was in the past, I can recognize him as belonging to us, he is a contemporary. And he is courageous enough to enter the twenty-first century with us. What a great statement! *Sabar uppe manu sut…* "Above all is the truth of man, and there is nothing above it." He dissolved all gods, all angels. He recognized that man's consciousness is the highest.

You don't see it because you are asleep, but there is not much difference between the man who is asleep and the man who is awake. The man who is awake was asleep just few moments ago, the man who is asleep may be awakened just in a few moments, but there is no basic difference.

I would like you to accept me as an ordinary human being. I don't want to be a leader, I don't want you to be led. I simply want to dance amongst you, completely lost.

You need not be afraid of me. All the followers of Jesus Christ were afraid of him, Buddha's followers were afraid of him – because these people have been continuously nagging their disciples. I think if Mohammed, Buddha, Mahavira, Zarathustra, Krishna had been housewives, the world would have been far better. They would have nagged only one man, not the whole of humanity. I *hate* nagging!

When I was a child and lived in a very small village where no train passes, no buses reach, my grandfather had a beautiful white horse. I used that white horse for roaming around the town, going along the river, going around the big lake. Slowly, slowly the horse started feeling some synchronicity with me. He started feeling when I wanted to return. But I never nagged even that horse. If he wanted to go north, I said, "Okay." If he wanted to go around the lake, I said, "Okay, you decide, but I am not going to nag you against your wishes."

And it was a strange thing, that he always went to the place where I wanted to go. Between his consciousness and mine, something must have been transpiring. There was a communion without words. And if a horse can go to the place where I want, without my nagging and forcing him to go there, certainly…even if I am amongst you, don't be afraid. All that is needed is not a superman to lead you, but a man with whom you can have a synchronicity.

A subtle vibe of love joins you and me, and it will do miracles.

I have been receiving letters from sannyasins: "It feels tremendously beautiful to see you as a human being just like us, but still somewhere I want you to be extraordinary, not ordinary. I want you to be higher than your disciples." Why?

My being higher simply makes it difficult to communicate. That's why all these people have failed. Jesus, Moses, Mohammed, Confucius, Lao Tzu – they all have failed, for a simple reason: they were there sitting on the clouds, and you were crawling on the earth. What communication is possible? They maintained the distance; it was the fulfillment of their egos. And you stupidly wanted your prophet's cloud to be higher than those of other prophets. But do you know what it means? It means your communication with your leader, prophet, messiah, is even more difficult.

All the religions have been trying to prove they are higher. Buddhists say, "Buddha is higher than Jesus, than Moses, then Mahavira." And the other people are doing the same.

I am starting a new history as far as enlightenment is concerned. The closer I am to you, holding your hand and dancing, the more is the possibility of communication.

I am going to wake you, because I am so close to you. If I can dance with you, you cannot remain asleep long; it is risky for you and your sleep! If I can drink a little champagne with you, then our hearts can melt into each other.

You need not look above to God the father, who is always above the roofs – I don't know what he is doing there! You can see me, look into my eyes, because I am standing on the same ground as you are. There is no distance, only a little difference – so little that I don't care much about it.

You will be awakened. When I am so close to you, it is impossible for you to go on sleeping. I can shake you, I can hit you – I am so close. I can throw cold water in your eyes – I am so close. Buddha cannot do it; he is sitting on a white cloud far away.

But that has been the conspiracy between the masters and the disciples. The disciple really loves the master to be far away. That gives him a satisfaction: "I am no ordinary man's follower, I follow an extraordinary master. Naturally, I am an extraordinary disciple."

If you are with me, a man who says that he is an ordinary human being, I am destroying your ego. You cannot be an extraordinary disciple, you have to be ordinary. If your master himself is ordinary, what can you do? You have to be ordinary.

And this is my basic experience, that to be ordinary is the most beautiful thing in existence. To be ordinary means to be relaxed. There is nowhere to go, nothing has to be found; you have it already. It was your ego that was blocking the way. Now the ego has disappeared, and you can see to your innermost being, crystal clear.

Seeing it, you are going to laugh – what a joke life has played upon you! Life has put the kohinoor inside you, and given you the desire to search for the kohinoor. And you are running all over the world – to the churches, to the synagogues, to the monasteries, and doing all kinds of stupidities to find that which you have never lost, to find that which even if you want to lose, you cannot. It is your very being.

I have heard about a man who was walking in the desert all alone…desert as far as he could see. It was his own shoes making noise – that was the only noise – but it appeared as if somebody was following him. It takes a little time; sound travels six hundred miles per hour, so when your shoe makes some sound you don't hear it instantly, there is a gap. By the time you hear it your shoe has moved.

He was a logical, philosophic man. Certainly it was not the sound of *his* shoes; somebody was following him. He looked behind, saw his own shadow and figured out that this shadow seemed to be some kind of ghost, because shadows are not known to make noise. He started running and the sound became louder. He looked back – the shadow was also running faster. He said, "My God! It means I am not running fast enough!"

He did his best, till he was almost spent and fell under a tree near an oasis. Now he was even more afraid, but he looked around: there was no noise, and the shadow was not there, for the simple reason that he was under the shadow of the tree. His shadow was so clear-cut under the sun on the sand, and here, when he was sitting under the tree, the shadow had left. He laughed. He understood that he had been making the noise himself, and the faster he ran, the louder the noise became – and it was his own shadow.

The moment you become enlightened, the first thing will be a mad laughter – that this is the thing you have been searching for for many lives, and you had it always in your pocket! All that is needed is just a little shaking. And I have found many ways to shaking you, to help you open your eyes. And it is not a difficult job, in fact it is a great joy.

Try with some sleeping man just brushing his cheeks with a toothbrush slowly, and see what happens to him – how he tries to throw it away. Just tickle his feet, and he pulls up his leg. Just start playing with his belly, and he is bound to open his eyes – how long can he keep them shut? How long can he remain asleep? What is going on? And he will also join in your laughter.

I want you to live abundantly, with great laughter, rejoicing, and the only possibility is if your ego is destroyed. And the best way I have found is that I should be *amongst* you, not leading you, so that you forget completely that you are followers of a great master. I am perfectly ready to be your follower: you can walk ahead and I can follow you and do all kinds of tricks from the back – which is easier!

Beloved Bhagwan,

A long time ago I replaced the word God with simply "It." It is about as vast as I can go with my mind. Do I need to abolish It as well? – because It is alive and all around me.

The first thing to be understood is that changing names does not change anything. You can call it God, you can call it Allah, you can call it Ishwar – there are three hundred languages on the earth. There are three hundred ways to call God, or you can invent your own private name for God.

You say, "I have replaced God with the word 'It'." What does it mean? You have only changed the label. Perhaps you can change even the container, but the question is of the content. And the content is there, I can see from your question, because you say, " *It* is alive and all around me." Now, "it" is used for things. You have changed just the word; you are giving him a new name, but "It" is all alike.

And the second thing you say is, "This is as far as my mind can go." That's true. Mind can play with words, that's as far as it can go. It can never attain to the state of wordlessness. Your "It" will dominate you, will keep you in slavery just as God has done for so long.

And the third thing…you ask me, "Should I drop 'It' also?" No, because then you will replace it by another word.

The women's liberation movement uses for God, "She." And I think it is a better word than "he," because in "she," "he" is present, but in "he," the "she" is absent. "She" is a bigger word. It is symbolic: in "woman" the man is there, but in the word "man," the woman is not there. But basically it does not make any difference – you can call God "she." So I will not tell you to drop calling God "It." It is not going to help in any way.

I would like you to drop the mind which is playing this game of changing one word for another. Drop the mind! Nothing else can help. Forget about God. You don't know him, you have not met him – how can you change his name, his address?

You are not to trespass the boundary. You cannot take it into your own hands, how God should be called. You don't know anything about God, and you will never know, because God does not exist at all. So you are changing the name of something non-existential.

If you are so good at dropping from "he" to "It," if you can even drop God from "he" to "It"…. *He* stands for something, someone alive. *It* is used for things. If you can do such a great job, pulling down God from his golden throne, and making him a commodity in the market, then you can do a far easier

thing: drop the mind.

It is a mind game, and the mind can play thousands of games. You reduce God to It, but from the back door the "It" becomes alive all around you. So what is the point? God is back. And it will give you great ego satisfaction that you managed something of immense importance: you have changed the name of God. It is not going to help. Your question is simply indicative of it. God has come from the back door, and is alive all around you.

Drop the mind. That is meditation.

In meditation we don't change the names of God. We don't allow ourselves in meditation to be identified with the mind. We are the witness, and all games the mind plays are in front of the witness. The witness is separate from all games.

You can be a Christian; then, fed up with being a Christian, for a few years you can become a Hindu – "Hare Krishna, Hare Rama…" – anything new gives a certain excitement. But soon Hare Krishna or Hare Rama is found in scientology – and you will not find him there long. If you go on following these people, perhaps now he is in EST. By the time you reach EST, the seeker has moved to Esalen. He will elude you, unless by some accident he ends up here. From here there is no way out.

We open the doors of inwardness, and the method is: just be watchful of your mind, how it fabricates philosophies, theologies, religions. Just watch. I am not telling you to *do* anything. In the beginning it is difficult, because you have never watched your mind. You have always thought you *are* the mind, you have always remained identified with the mind. So in the beginning it is going to be a little difficult, but it is not impossible. In fact, what you have done – identifying yourself with the mind – *is* something of the impossible. You have even managed that!

What I am saying to you is simple, natural, possible. You are not the mind. And when mind stops, who is going to change the name of God? And who cares? When the mind is silent, not even a ripple of thought, that serenity, that silence will give you the first taste of godliness – not of God, because to taste God will reduce you to a cannibal.

Please, don't try to eat God! But religions have been telling you to. Jesus, before departing from his company of fools, said to them, "Eat me, drink me." Don't do anything like that with me. I am an ordinary man, please – if you start eating me and drinking me, I will be finished soon. I will not last even one day.

The taste is not of God, but of godliness.

That too, you simply experience and feel.

It is a quality, a quality that makes you aware of your immortality, that makes you aware of the infinity of existence, that makes you aware of utter beauty, grace, peace, blissfulness.

But there is no person like God. There is nobody, there is pure emptiness. And only pure emptiness or nothingness is what I have been calling enlightenment.

Beloved Bhagwan,

You said recently that women's liberation would be men's liberation also.
Would You please comment on men's liberation?

This is one of the fundamental laws of life, that if you make anybody a slave, in return, unknowingly, you become a slave to your slave. Slavery is a double-edged sword. You cannot simply remain the master and the other a slave. You start becoming dependent on the slave. And to make somebody a slave is to create troubles for yourself, because the slave cannot love you, cannot respect you.

The slave will always hate you, the slave would like to kill you. He may not be able to, but these will be the thoughts moving around him. He may be bowing down to you, but deep in his heart he wants to destroy you, because freedom is an intrinsic necessity of every human being. Nobody can like slavery. One

can pretend, just to save one's neck, but one goes on gathering fire against the master.

Jesus was crucified…one never thinks about Judas – there are so many implications in it. Why did he sell Jesus for thirty pieces of silver? Certainly he was more valuable a man – crazy, but beautiful; harmless, but with a charismatic personality. A little bit off his head, but that is not a crime. And Judas had been with him for years as a disciple. Why did he betray him?

My understanding is that being a disciple is a kind of slavery, and there is a limit to how long one can tolerate it. And it is not only with Jesus that it has happened; otherwise, it would be an exception, not the rule. But it is the rule, not the exception.

Mahavira's own son-in-law tried to kill him. He had taken initiation and become a disciple. He was hoping that because he was the son-in-law…. And Mahavira had only one daughter; she was also initiated, they both were disciples. You can imagine, it is simple, that the son-in-law was hoping that Mahavira would declare him his successor. And when Mahavira declared that Gautam Gantha – a far more intelligent person – was going to be his successor, the son-in-law tried to kill him. And the son-in-law revolted against Mahavira, taking five hundred other disciples with him.

Now, these five hundred disciples had also been with Mahavira for years. What was boiling within them, that rather than remaining with Mahavira they went with an idiot who had nothing to offer? And they all disappeared, evaporated, because he had nothing to offer. But they also must have been angry at the slavery that Mahavira was imposing on them.

In Jainism, things are really very strict. It is the most ascetic religion in the world. The Jaina monk has to remain naked in all the seasons around the year. It is difficult. The Jaina monk has to eat only one meal, begging. The Jaina monk cannot drink water in the night – even in the hot summers of Bihar where Mahavira was. As the sun sets, the Jaina monk cannot take anything in his mouth, not even water.

The Jaina monk, naked, with one meal a day, has to walk on hot days, on cold days, without any shoes – a naked man in shoes will look awkward. I have seen Jaina monks and nuns – their feet show the story of their asceticism: in the hot summer days they start bleeding, cracking.

These people who have had all these disciplines imposed on them are boiling within. They are following Mahavira because he is giving them the promise of *moksha*. You will be surprised that *moksha* is higher than what you know as paradise. So in Jainism there are three things: hell, the lowest; heaven, in the middle; and *moksha,* the ultimate.

From heaven you are going to fall back again into life. It is a kind of spiritual holiday, a holiday place on a beautiful beach. You earn virtue – that is a bank balance of good deeds. When you have enough bank balance, you are born in heaven. But no bank balance can last forever; once your bank balance is finished you are thrown back to the earth again to be human beings. Moksha is liberation forever.

These poor people who had gathered around Mahavira were torturing themselves in every possible way, because this life is not long enough. So much time has passed…somebody is fifty; perhaps twenty years more, and then the eternal moksha, blissfulness forever, freedom forever.

So on the one hand they were doing all the austerities. But when you torture yourself, you cannot love the man really who has somehow manipulated you to torture yourself. When in the hot night you start feeling thirsty, you will curse this man – silently, of course. Even if you are sick, you cannot take medicine, because that is materialistic. You want to live in the body – that is materialistic. So if the body is falling apart, so far so good: the sooner you reach moksha.

But one thing is certain and simple, that these people will be gathering anger against the so-called *tirthankara,* Mahavira. So when his son-in-law left

the fold, five hundred followed him.

The same is the case with Gautam Buddha. His own cousin-brother had taken initiation. The same mind, the same ego…. He was older than Buddha, he had renounced his own kingdom – he had had his own kingdom. He was hoping that he was going to be the successor. But slowly, slowly he became aware that there were people like Sariputta, Mahakashyap, Moggalayan, who were very intimate with Gautam Buddha; there was not much chance for him. And he was not even worthy!

He left Gautam Buddha, and he also was followed by hundreds of monks. And this man tried in every way to kill Gautam Buddha. When Buddha was meditating one day under a tree in the valley by the side of a mountain, the cousin rolled a huge rock at him. The story is that the rock, seeing Buddha there, changed her route; Buddha was saved.

I don't think rocks can change routes – what is more possible is that Buddha's cousin-brother missed the target. And it is difficult to calculate…. If from the high top of a mountain you roll a rock, the target will not be necessarily hit, because the rock will come against other rocks, trees, and will be going this way and that way until it reaches the valley. So I don't think that the rock was very compassionate.

Buddha's cousin used a mad elephant who was always kept in chains because he was very dangerous, he used to kill people. He brought the elephant near Gautam Buddha when he was sitting with closed eyes, and released the elephant.

The story is – but it is just a story – that the elephant, who was mad, came rushing, roaring towards Buddha. But as he saw Gautam Buddha he knelt down and touched Buddha's feet. I don't think that elephants are wiser than man. If the cousin-brother is not changed, what possibility is there for a mad elephant to change? Perhaps it was just out of his madness that he was doing it. You can expect from mad people anything.

The mad elephant may have seen so many people

bowing down before Buddha and touching his feet. His screws were loose, but it is a well-known fact that elephants are very imitative. That's why they are used in circuses; they learn to imitate very easily. You will not have seen camels in the circuses, for the simple reason that camels are just idiots. Elephants are imitative. So if this mad elephant did it, it simply shows imitation. He had seen so many people every day doing it to Buddha. He was mad enough not to bother about the cousin-brother who had released him — and he was not aware of the purpose either.

What I am pointing at is that the moment you claim to be higher, stronger, better in comparison to someone else, you are creating an enemy.

Man for centuries has been repressing the woman. Calling her the weaker sex, which is absolutely wrong: man is the weaker sex. But he has deprived the woman of education, deprived the woman of any financial independence, deprived the woman of the right to move in society freely, just as he moves. The woman is carrying immense anger accumulated for centuries, and she takes revenge in her own way. She nags the husband, she screams at him, she throws pillows at him. She turns the husband into a henpecked husband.

Slavery is always mutual.

Freedom is always mutual.

So I don't make any distinction between women's liberation and men's liberation. These are two sides of the same coin. If the woman is liberated, man's liberation follows automatically. If man wants not to be nagged, not to be screamed at, not to be a target of all kinds of things that the woman throws at him…. And this is an everyday scene in every family.

The man has reduced the woman to a slave; the woman has her own ways to reduce him to a slave. If you see a couple walking on the road, you can decide without asking them whether they are married or not, whether the woman is a wife or a girlfriend. With the girlfriend the man is so happy — you can see it. With the wife he is so bored, so utterly sad, for the simple reason that this woman has made his life a hell. But who is responsible?

First, you have made her a slave, now she is returning it to you in the same coins. Of course, the feminine way of taking revenge is different — her psychology is different. But no woman gives freedom to the husband. She keeps an eye on him — with whom he is talking, where he is going. She goes on looking at his coat to see if there is any woman's hair on it. She goes on looking into his diary for phone numbers, and through phone numbers she easily can figure out with whom he is flirting.

It is an ugly relationship. Marriage is madness, because both are trying to overpower each other. The women can never forgive the man for what he has done to her: deprived her of education, deprived her of financial freedom, deprived her of her human dignity.

So if the woman has liberation, man automatically becomes liberated. There is no need for a man's liberation movement, one movement is enough. That will help the man immensely. His joy will come back, he will be again chasing women, and that is the greatest game in the world. The poor man has to play tennis, football, volleyball, hockey — but nothing is a substitute! Chasing a woman is simply the most beautiful game.

Once marriage is dissolved completely and people are free to be with whomsoever they want to be — no barrier, no legality, no government, no society interfering — you will see this whole world smiling, happier, healthier, because you cannot get nourishment when you are in a state of slavery. Although you go on proclaiming to the world that you are the master of the house, you know perfectly well the moment you enter the house who is the master and who is the mistress. Certainly you are not the master.

This creates a strange split in you, it makes you a hypocrite. It makes you hurt, but that is an outcome of your own stupidity.

Give freedom if you want freedom.

Just one movement is enough. The woman's liberation movement is enough, but it is not going in the right direction. It is not becoming a rebellion, it is becoming a reaction. The woman declares she is equal to man, so if the man is smoking she has to smoke; she is equal. If the man is drinking, she has to drink; she is equal.

This is not rebellion, this is reaction.

Women are turning into lesbians. They feel so much hatred for men that millions of women don't want to have any love relationship with men, they would prefer an unnatural and perverted relationship with a woman. And it is easier, because a man will never be able to suspect that his wife has a girlfriend. Even if the two women go on making love in the house, the husband will never suspect. But if a man comes on the scene and makes the triangle of all the stories and the films and the novels, it cannot be long before the husband discovers it.

It is the slavery of women that is turning the women towards lesbianism, but she thinks this is liberation from men. Dropping love for men is not liberation, you are becoming perverted.

Drop the marriage contract, drop the license which has been issued by the court. Make your man free. Tell him, "It is up to you if you want to have any love relationships – I have no jealousy, no argument about it. But I demand the same for myself." And if there is no slavery, no bondage between man and woman, perhaps there will be great love happening – as it happens in my commune.

I don't think so much love is happening anywhere else in the whole world, because nobody is jealous. People change their partners very easily. It is just a game: you get tired of playing tennis with one partner, you find another partner. And nobody is harmed, everybody is happy.

You will not find in my commune people who are sad, with long faces. Even Britishers in my commune are no more British.

Even Proper Sagar is becoming improper!

It's Better To be Red Than Dead!

DISCOURSE 34,   August 1, 1985

Beloved Bhagwan,

On the fortieth anniversary of the U.N., the one-cent American postal stamp has the message,
"We the peoples of the United Nations determine to save succeeding generations from the scourge of war." Can the U.N. save humanity from war?

The U.N. has proved in these forty years only one thing: that it is as impotent as its predecessor, the League of Nations.

The members of the U.N. are the people who are going to create the third world war. The U.N. has no power to prevent it; it is only a debating club, and not of the best kind. It is not even democratic. The big powers like America and the Soviet Union have the capacity to veto any resolution. Just one nation, America or Russia, can stop any resolution which is being passed by the whole world. Is this democratic? Every nation, small or big, poor or rich, must have equal rights! In forty years the U.N. has not been able even to do that.

It is just keeping people consoled: "Don't be afraid, we are going to save you." In fact, from whom are they going to save us? They are the people we have to be saved from!

The U.N. has not been able to stop the increasing amount of nuclear weapons. That should be the first step if you don't want the third world war. Why wait for the last moment? Why not start it now? And the basic step will be that no war preparations are made. When everybody is prepared to fight...in fact they will be forced to fight, just because each country has invested so much energy and power, and it has piled up nuclear weapons sky high: what are the nations going to do with those weapons? And they have poured such immense amounts of money into them. At what point will the U.N. stop them? And the Soviet Union can just veto it, America can veto it.

But this is how politicians have been cheating humanity all along, throughout the whole history of man. They say one thing and they do just the opposite. It is very easy to publish a postal stamp that says, "We the peoples of the United Nations are determined to save humanity from the scourge of war." Who are these "we"? Have you asked the people of the world?

Nobody wants war around the world except these idiotic politicians, because without war they have no job. War keeps politicians powerful. People have to depend on politicians because the war is coming.

Adolf Hitler wrote in his autobiography, *My Struggle*...he has a few very important points to make. The first thing he says is that never in history has a great leader been born unless there is war.

That's true. If there had been no second world war you would have never heard of Adolf Hitler, Benito Mussolini, Winston Churchill, Roosevelt – they all became stars high in the sky. Of course, millions of people died to make them great leaders.

The same has been the case all along, throughout history. The politician wants to be on the top, as high as possible. If there is peace, no fight, no war, no preparation for war, he is just ordinary – perhaps a little bit less intelligent than the average person. His intelligence is not better than the average person's; it can be worse.

Before the second world war, the same promise was given by the League of Nations: "We are going to save the world from war." But those were the same people who fought the second world war. And I say to you, these same people who constitute the U.N. are going to create the third world war.

These stamps are cheap. You can go on befooling humanity, but for how long? It is time that humanity understands the politician and his cunningness. Even in the U.N. you cannot be peaceful, discussing in a friendly way. I said it is only a debating club and not the best one, because nobody is listening to anybody else. It is a tower of Babel: everybody is speaking for *his* government, *his* nation, *his* politics, and is not ready to listen to anything else.

Do you know what Khrushchev did in the U.N.? He was the premier of the Soviet Union…and this kind of behavior and the people who behave in this way, can they prevent the second world war? Then who is going to start it? Do they think I am going to start the third world war, that the red people around the world are going to start the third world war?

Khrushchev was delivering his talk to the U.N., and he became so angry that he took his shoe off and started beating on the table with the shoe! A great history of forty years, not an ordinary history. They could not prevent even Khrushchev beating their

Make people aware of their gratitude towards life, and make people love, sing, dance. If we can spread this at-ease around the world, the third world war will be prevented. We need not bother about it. Joyous people don't want war; it is only those who are already dead who would like everybody else to be dead.

their faces with his shoe, shouting and screaming at the whole U.N.

In forty years they have not been able to do anything at all. This is a sheer wastage of time. The fortieth anniversary should be declared as the death of the U.N.! Finished! There is no point, they cannot agree. But the existence of U.N. gives consolation to people: "We don't need to be worried, the U.N. is taking care of us." And the U.N. consists of warring nations who have nuclear weapons. They have been talking about putting a stop to it, but it is just pure talk; nobody stops.

I think it is time that the people of the world start understanding the politician and his hypocrisy, his double personality, because if the third world war happens, then there will be no life on this beautiful planet. I don't believe at all in this declaration of the U.N., but I have another program for the people:

First, don't trust your politicians. Don't be consoled by their cunning strategies.

Second, remember that you are going to be destroyed with your children, with your wife, with your parents, with your trees, with your animals – everything that is alive on the earth.

If the people of the whole earth simply refuse and say, "We are not going to fight, there is no point in it," if they refuse and say, "We don't want boundaries of nations. If there is going to be no war, why keep these boundaries? What purpose do these boundaries serve?".... If the people of the world force their governments and say, "Disperse all your armies. Let those people be *creative*...."

Millions of people around the earth, in the army, are just doing nothing. In fact, they are hankering for war. They are not meditators who can just sit silently, doing nothing, and the grass grows by itself. They are very ordinary people. To keep them holding their guns, watching their nuclear missiles.... How long can you keep them in this situation? Sooner or later, they will find it is better now to start – "We are tired and bored...."

This is an established fact, that during the war people are less sad, more excited, happier than they are in peaceful times, because so much is going on. Every moment brings new news; excitement is natural.

Human history can be divided in two parts: first when there is war; second, when they are preparing for a new war. There has never been a period of real peace. Preparing for war is cold war – getting ready, because the last has taken so much, destroyed so much, that you have to prepare again. Within ten to twenty years' time they are again ready, the weapons are ready, the enemies are there.

If really they mean what they say, then take the preliminary steps. The first is to dissolve boundaries, dissolve passports and green cards. The world, the whole earth is ours. Wherever we want to be, it is nobody's business to prevent us. Let there be freedom of movement. Let all the races, all the nations get mixed. And once the boundaries are not there, they will get mixed, they will spread all over the world – all kinds of races – and it will be a great experiment in crossbreeding. We will have better generations to come.

It is not enough to save the coming generations from war, if they are simply carbon copies of you. What is the point? If they are carbon copies of you, they will do the same as you have been doing. A new man is needed, a new man who feels the whole earth is his mother – not small segments of it.

Do you see? You call your land your motherland, and you have cut the mother into so many pieces – is your mother alive still? You are carrying only limbs of your mother. Somebody has taken the leg, somebody has taken the head....

I am reminded of a religious master. He had two disciples – just as every democracy has two political parties. Those disciples were competing in every way to get more attention from the master. And the question basically was, who is going to succeed the master? – he was getting old. So both were trying their best to serve the master, to follow the master, to practice the discipline that he has given.

But the motivation was neither the discipline nor the principles. They were not concerned with the master at all.

One summer day the master was sleeping, and they were not going to lose any opportunity. So they both were massaging the legs of the master. He was tired, naturally – he had come from a long journey. One was working on the left leg, the other was working on the right leg. The master was asleep.

The man who was working on the right leg told the other, "Remember, if your leg comes on top of my leg, I am not going to tolerate it." The other said, "And what do you think? – *I* am going to tolerate it? I will cut off your leg if it comes on my leg!" And they both had their swords ready.

The master was not really asleep, no master ever is. He opened his eyes and said, "Boys, those legs are both mine! Who told you that the right leg is owned by one and the left leg is owned by the other?"

But this is the situation of the world. The mother earth has been cut into thousands of pieces. People have to be awakened to the fact, to stop calling America your motherland, stop calling Germany your fatherland. You see the difference? The whole world calls its country the motherland, except Germany! Their land is the fatherland. It is not a coincidence; they are more male chauvinistic than anybody else. Stop all this nonsense! – and people can do it.

I am preparing you to spread the fire around the world, that the whole earth belongs to us.

And let the U.N. go on discussing. If they want to wrestle against each other in the U.N. building, they can have good boxing matches. It is better than throwing shoes at each other. And it will be really great entertainment, seeing your great politicians wrestling. But that will not be decisive as far as the earth is concerned.

The people of the earth have to take the responsibility from the hands of the politicians. And this will be a first step: to erase all the boundaries. And see how many people they can put in jails; you cannot put a whole nation in jail.

All the constitutions of democratic countries accept in their list of birthrights the right of movement. But where is it? You can move only within the country. They have given you a little rope to feel that you are free, but an authentic freedom of movement will mean that anybody can go anywhere on the earth. Wherever he feels to live, he can live; no hindrance should be there. Removal of the boundaries will bring one world and one world functional government.

The U.N. has no power over anything. I know it…. In India, in 1947 after independence, Pakistan invaded Kashmir, which was part of India, and took over a large chunk of land. India fought against Pakistan. It could have been the beginning of a third world war, because the land that Pakistan had taken was very significant; it joined Pakistan with China.

Pakistan now could have a road – now they do have a road – going over the Himalayas to Peking. And China is not on speaking terms with Russia anymore. China is going to be with America, so that small piece of land is of immense significance.

And what did the U.N. do? It did not force Pakistan, because America would not like that land to be lost, it is a key point in any war in Asia. So the U.N. did something futile. They said, "First stop the war, have a cease-fire line." On one side Indian armies have been standing for forty years, on the other side Pakistani armies have been standing for forty years. Between the two is the camp of the U.N. observers to make sure that the cease-fire line is not crossed till the matter is settled.

Who is going to settle it? And if you cannot settle such a small matter in forty years, how many centuries will you take to settle the third world war?

They cannot settle the matter, because if they settle in favor of Pakistan, Russia will veto it; the settlement is finished. If they settle it in favor of India,

America will veto it, and the matter is finished. So it is in limbo, and it is going to be in limbo perhaps forever, unless my people succeed in dissolving all boundaries; then that cease-fire line will also dissolve.

And this is a sheer wastage! – thousands of people unnecessarily standing there with their guns ready, on alert, on both sides. Just a single crackpot can start shooting, just out of boredom. Forty years…! He was young, now he is old, getting senile. Just for the sake of fun, if one man starts firing from the other side, then immediately both the armies will jump up – and nobody will care about the observers. Perhaps they will be the first ones to be killed.

What has the U.N. to its credit? Nothing at all. Without any credibility, to claim that they are going to stop the third world war is simply befooling the people. They cannot stop the war between India and Pakistan, between Pakistan and Bangladesh. They cannot stop the war between Israel and the surrounding Mohammedan countries, because everywhere these two great powers are involved.

Israel is supported by the Americans, because the American political parties cannot survive without Jews' donations to their parties. If they want donations from Jews, they have to stand by Israel. And Russia is behind the Mohammedan countries, which are bigger, surrounding the small Israel from all sides. And since the birth of Israel, the child has been in bed, almost dead. But America is keeping it alive by artificial breathing. If American steps out, Israel will be finished within a day.

America cannot step out, Russia cannot step out. In fact, it is a good opportunity; America has created it. They have a vast majority of Mohammedan countries of the whole Middle East sympathetic towards them, because in any case, these countries will need support. They are all oil countries, that's why America is hesitating, is now in a fix: if it does too much, goes a little more towards support of Israel, then all the oil countries are in the hands of Soviet Russia. And oil is now far more precious than gold.

The U.N. in forty years has not been able to do anything – and still these people have the nerve to say they are going to save the world from a third world war. Even in small wars they have not been able…. What did the U.N. do in Vietnam? Poor people were being killed unnecessarily by Americans. It was none of America's business. Vietnam belongs to the people who live there, and if they want to be communist, who are you to prevent them? What right have you got? The same was the situation in Korea. The U.N. has failed utterly, and I am amazed that they are not even ashamed, and are declaring that they will save the coming generations from the third world war.

Only one thing can save the world from the coming war – which will be a total war, for the first time; all other wars were child's play. This is going to destroy the whole of life on the earth. Trees, birds, animals, man – anything living will simply be gone.

I say there is one way only, and that is to spread to people more meditativeness, more love, more friendliness, more rejoicing. If we can make the earth sing songs and dance in joy, in gratitude because existence has given so much – otherwise, it would have been impossible even to purchase one sunrise. The whole wealth of the earth would not be able to purchase one sunrise.

And a sunrise is a big thing – the whole wealth of the earth would not be able to produce a single rose-flower. And all this is given to man without his asking. You don't deserve it, you are not worthy of it! It is out of the compassion of existence, the overflowing joy of existence, the continuous creativity of existence that you are so rich. Millions of stars in the night….

Make people aware of their gratitude towards life, and make people love, sing, dance. If we can spread this at-ease around the world, the third world war will be prevented. We need not bother about it. Joyous people don't want war; it is only those who are already dead who would like everybody else to be dead. They are really suffering because they are dead. They cannot laugh, they cannot enjoy, they cannot love, they cannot feel. They don't have any heart, and others have. It is making them so jealous! It will be far better that everything is finished. At least there will be no grounds for their jealousy – they will also be finished in it.

So I don't say that there is any *direct* way to prevent the third world war. That is what the pacifists of the world say: "Protest. Have protest marches to Washington, to Moscow" – but nobody listens to those protest marches. And I have seen those pacifists shouting and screaming against the war – I could not see any difference between them and the people who are getting ready to fight. Their screaming was enough proof that they belonged to the same category.

If those pacifists had weapons and missiles, they would create a war to prevent the third world war! The way they are shouting and screaming and throwing stones, simply shows that they are of the same species as the politicians against whom they are throwing stones. The difference is just that the politicians have the power, and they don't have the power.

Remember, the husband does not scream at the wife, the wife screams at the husband. When he gets tired of her nagging and screaming, he hits the wife, he beats her. And strangely, the wife simply becomes silent. If she is not beaten, then she is going to drive the man nuts.

In old countries like India and China, it was told to the newly-married couple by their elders – the husband was told, "Remember, once in a while a wife needs beating; otherwise, you will not be able to live peacefully." But why does the wife scream? – because the husband has the muscular strength she cannot beat the husband. There are a few exceptions, but exceptions only prove the rule. She would like to beat him, but as far as muscular strength is concerned, she cannot compete with the husband. So the moment the husband starts beating her she becomes peaceful.

The weak, the powerless, scream. The powerful takes his gun, puts his army on alert. The pacifists continually go on protesting. This helps nobody. Nobody listens to their protest.

I used to know a man…. My house in one city was just near the high court of the state, so all protest marches, all kinds of pacifists were passing in front of my door. And I watched them – their behavior did not seem to be peaceful. They looked more ugly than the people in the high court. But I was amazed that one man was always there, whether the communist party was protesting, or the socialist party was protesting, or the people's party was protesting. And in India there are so many parties…. He was always there, with every party.

One day I got hold of him, and I asked him, "You are an amazing man – to what party do you belong?"

He said, "Who cares? I am a member of all the parties." I said, "But how it is possible? Communists are against the socialists, socialists are against the communists. How can you be?"

He said, "I am not concerned with their politics – I enjoy screaming! It is such a healthy thing, that whenever there is a protest I close my shop; and whoever is protesting, I am always ahead holding the flag." He said, "It is really healthy."

I said, "I know. My people are doing it every morning, but they don't protest about anybody." I said to him, "It is better that you start dynamic meditation, because these protests happen only once in a while, and you have to be dependent on these political parties. There is no need, you can do it on your own."

He said, "On my own? Alone?"

"No," I said, "don't be worried." I had a meditation hall there. I said, "Every morning many people come there." And he started coming. Now he is a sannyasin – I don't think for any other reason, just every day, early in the morning, it is healthy to scream. It gives you stronger lungs, a better heart, more strength. And moreover, he need not close his shop anymore; financially it is good.

I am not a pacifist, and I don't want my people to be pacifists. That is fighting with those who are preparing for war – but you are doing the same on a small scale, in a feminine way. No, that won't help. We want to create our own movement which has nothing to do with the third world war.

Do you see my point? If we can make humanity happier, more loving, more silent, more peaceful, we will create a real barrier against the third world war. The leaders cannot go without their people. If the people refuse, the armies refuse, if everybody refuses and says, "I am so happy, I don't want to die. And I love humanity, so I don't want to kill. If you can manage on your own, you do it." A peaceful and happy man does not want to die, and does not want to kill.

So spread the message far and wide:
It's better to be red than dead!

Beloved Bhagwan,

The other day You said that women create children, and men create arts and other material things. Is it unnatural or neurotic for a woman not to desire a child, and to prefer to be an artist? I never wanted to have a child. Dance, music, poetry, theater and painting were my passion and expression. Could You comment?

There is nothing unnatural in it. If you don't want to have a child, you have the right not to have one. If you want to put your creativity into painting, into art, into music, it is perfectly good – far better than creating a child who is bound to be a burden on the earth. And who knows what kind of child will come out of you?

Adolf Hitler can come out of you. He is waiting, searching for a womb. Joseph Stalin can come out of you. Beware! – that greasy Italian, Mussolini, is waiting. All these people are standing in line, in a queue. This is not the time to give birth to a child!

A painting is harmless. Music is beautiful, dancing will do. No, there is nothing unnatural in it. It has been said by men again and again that it is women's natural duty to give birth to children. That's how they have been able to keep the woman in slavery, because if a woman goes on giving birth to children, where is the time for her to paint? Where is the time for her to create music, poetry, drama?

So on the one hand they have been forcing the woman to remain continually pregnant. Just a hundred years ago, every woman around the world was continually pregnant. One child takes nine months of her life, then she has to raise the child. And when the child is not even six months old, she is again pregnant. It is like chain-smoking. And even a single child is such a nuisance....

I agree with you. I have been asked many times, "Wouldn't you like to have a child?"

I said, "*Me?* Either I would kill the child or I would kill myself; we could not coexist! A child in my room? Impossible!" Just to be alert, I have never married, because who knows? – the woman I marry may want a child. Then trouble will arise.

There is no problem, unless you feel there is. Don't listen to anybody, what they say – that it is unnatural. It may be unnatural to them, so they can give birth to as many children as they want. If you feel good in painting, in writing poetry, in composing music, you are giving better children to the world – children who are harmless, who will make many rejoice. Nothing can go wrong. At the most, your poetry will not be worth anything, your music just a noise, your painting just a copy of some other painter, your literature.... Reading ten books anybody can write the eleventh book. That's how books go on increasing.

There are very few books which are original. Other books are simply creations of average minds. You can see it in the films: the same story. Yes, a little bit different in details, but almost the same triangle. One woman and two men, or two women and one man – which is a little more exciting – but this triangle is the whole story of all the stories that have been written, of all the films that have been created. I sometimes wonder whether this is literature or geometry! And in geometry there are many other things, not just a triangle.

Details you can fit very easily, but this is not creativity. This is sheer theft, you are stealing. But that is not a harm to anybody; you are just wasting your time. And if you enjoy wasting it, why should anybody prevent you? But please, don't give birth to a child. At the most he will be just an average idiot. And the world is so full of idiots that it is time that the woman refused to give idiots to the world.

That's why I am for bio-engineering. It is not your birthright to go on giving birth to as many children as you want, because those children are going to live on this earth, and they will do something or other.

Only a medical board should decide about a couple. Unless you have a clearance from the medical board, you cannot produce a child. And since the pill it is so simple. Nobody is preventing you from making love; make love as much as you want, or as much as you can manage! But as far as children are concerned, you are doing something to the whole world. Making love you are not doing anything to anybody – just a little fun between two individuals; the world is not involved in it.

Children should be born only if a couple gets permission from the medical board. Still, that is not the best way to do it, because while he is making love a man releases millions of living beings, millions of living cells; and it is just chance in that race who will reach the female egg first. You cannot decide it, you cannot even know it. So this is not the best way. The medical board may feel that the woman is healthy, the man is healthy; they can look at your heritage – three, four generations back – and they can allow you. But this is not the best way.

The best way will be for intelligent people to do-nate their semen to the hospital, to donate the female eggs to the hospital, so the hospitals have banks – just like they have blood banks. And they can figure out which female egg and which male sperm are going to create a tremendously great, loving genius.

You can make a condition: "We are donating our sperm and our eggs; if you find that some combination can create a beautiful human being, we would like to adopt. If it is not possible, then from other eggs…." What is the problem? You can't recognize your own sperm, your sperm has no seal on it; no egg has any seal on it. The medical board can find those of some other woman, some other man, and you can adopt the child.

It will be healthier for the society, it will be a beautiful experience for you to raise a child who is going to be an Albert Einstein, or a Bertrand Russell, or a Jean-Paul Sartre. What a joy, that your child is not going to be pope the Polack! that your daughter is not going to be Mother Teresa!

It is sheer joy. And knowing what your child is going to be…because the medical, the biological study of the sperm and the egg can give you all the predictions: how long he will live, what kind of man he will be – or woman; how he should be brought up so that his potential flowers and he is not distracted from his potential. It will be really a work of art, far more precious than any painting, because you will be giving to the world a treasure.

So I am all for bio-engineering. And this stupid way of producing children has done enough harm. The whole history is full of it. Don't you ever think that if a gardener plants thousands of trees, and only once in a while one tree flowers – would you call that gardener a gardener?

Thousands of children are born, and rarely will someone become a Mozart or a Gautam Buddha. Most of them will be clerks, postmasters, stationmasters. Your son being a clerk, even if he becomes the head clerk, is not going to bring you the rejoicing that I would like. And these jobs soon will be transferred to the machines, to the computers. The clerks are going to be out of employment very soon.

Don't produce clerks! Don't produce station-masters, postmasters. We have had enough. Now machines can take the place of all ordinary jobs. But the machine cannot become a Bertrand Russell, a Wittgenstein, a Martin Heidegger; that is beyond the computer.

You have to create a child which will be needed, and cannot be replaced by any machine. otherwise, everybody is going to be unemployed, hungry, starving. It will not be only in Ethiopia, it will be all over the world. And the machine is more reliable than your beloved son who has become the clerk.

Just now I got the information that they have made a computer specially for Mohammedans, because the Mohammedan has to pray facing towards Mecca, his holy land. But it is really a difficult job to be absolutely accurate. Most probably you are wrong, there is only a small chance that you are exactly facing towards Mecca. A computer has come onto the market: you just put the machine on, move the machine, and when it starts giving an alarm that means this is the place; you are absolutely accurate.

Perhaps my sannyasins will also need it. Where you face while you are doing your *gachchhamis* is just approximate. A computer can make it a hundred percent certain. The same computer that Mohammedans are using, with a little change, will be able to do your work too. Then around the earth, wherever you are, you can do the *gachchhamis* directed towards me!

Please give birth to a child who cannot be replaced by machines, by computers. And that is possible only if you drop that old jealous idea that the semen has to be yours, that the egg has to be your wife's. I don't see what is so special about your semen and your wife's egg. Why bother about it? And you have practiced that thing for thousands of years – just look at the world, what you have done! Such a mediocre lot. And if this mediocre lot is there, it is very difficult to get rid of politicians.

If you can give birth to children which have the highest possibility of intelligence, I don't think they will vote for any chimpanzee to be the president of America. In fact, all political parties will disappear, because every individual will have enough intelligence to decide on his own. He does not need any political propaganda, he does not need to be persuaded. It is an insult.

I have never voted in my life, for anything, but when there were elections politicians would come, not knowing. And then they would get into trouble, because I would ask them questions.

They said, "We have not come here to take an examination."

I said, "But first, I have to examine your mind. How can I vote for an idiot? You have to prove that you have some genius in you."

They said, "This is strange. Nobody asks whether you have genius in you or not."

I said, "Unless you prove that you have genius in you, I cannot give my support to you to be in power. You can be dangerous to humanity." I would criticize their political line, their ideology, and say, "You have to defend it." They wanted to escape, they wanted to find some excuse. I would say, "This is not going to do. And remember, if you fail with me, I am going to tell all the neighbors, all the professors around, that this is not the man to vote for."

I have seen tears in their eyes: why in the first place did they get caught with this man? Slowly it became known, and for years no politician has approached me in election time to vote. I have been waiting for them, I enjoyed the game.

No, these mediocre people are not needed. They are accidental. The children that you think are yours are only accidents. Because you are not giving birth consciously, you are groping in the dark; you don't know what the result is going to be.

With bio-engineering, for the first time you can have guidelines for the child's whole future. You can even tell the medical board what kind of child you would like, how long he should live, that you would not like him to have AIDS, that you don't want him to be a homosexual, that you don't want him to be a Catholic or a communist. You want him to be simply human and absolutely free from all ideology. You would like him to have the sharpest intelligence that has ever happened on the earth. You would like something better than Socrates.

And this is possible. When you can have Socrates as your child, then why go for Tom, Dick and Harry?

Just leave *my* Harry out of it!

Beloved Bhagwan,

Sannyasins who are dying in Your presence discover their enlightenment. Why is it so difficult for those of us who are still alive? Is it that life comes so close to death, and we are afraid of dying yet still not capable of being alive in this precious moment?

It is an important question. It may have arisen in many people's mind: "Why, when a person dies, is it easy to become enlightened? The same person when he was alive was not capable of becoming enlightened."

The reason is very simple. When you are alive you cannot drop your ego, you cannot drop your jealousy. You cannot drop your hatred, anger, greed, because you think these are all that life consists of. If you drop all these, what is there to live for? You cannot drop your ambition; otherwise your life will be simply meaningless. That is your reasoning. And enlightenment requires as a basic condition that all this luggage should be thrown. You should stand absolutely in purity, without any luggage, without even any clothes, just naked.

Those who can gather that much courage can become enlightened any moment. But when a sannyasin is dying it is easy for him. Now he knows that he is dying: what use is ambition? What use is hatred?

What use is jealousy? What use is greed? What use is the ego?

Death standing in front of his eyes makes it clear that now he can drop all that unnecessary luggage: anyway, death is going to take all that away. It happens in a single moment – the whole idea, the revelation that now there is nothing to be lost – so why not try? "Bhagwan has been saying, 'Drop this, drop that.' I could not do it while I was alive, but now there is no problem. Take a chance – see whether he was right or wrong."

And this is not a long process of thinking. It is a simple experience in a single moment before death. And the person simply slips out of the old, rotten bag in which he has been living; now he can feel the stink and everything.

Death immediately becomes enlightenment.

Then death is no longer ordinary death, then death is a door to the divine. You can do it while you are living, there is no problem. In fact, to do it when you are dying is not of much use: you never got to enjoy it. While you are alive, if you can do what I say, you will have time to enjoy enlightenment.

And enlightenment is not something that is given to you, handed over to you. Enlightenment is a growing process in you. The man who becomes enlightened at the moment of death has missed much. He has missed all the joys of life, which are available only to the enlightened consciousness.

He had loved, but that love was simply phony, American. If he had had the chance to love after enlightenment, he would have known the tremendous beauty of it, the ecstasy of it. He has been eating tasteful, delicious food all his life, but he was asleep, he had no sensitivity. He was never in the moment; while he was eating, he was somewhere else faraway – perhaps on the moon.

The enlightened man is always in the moment; hence, every experience becomes intense, enjoyed to the fullest.

It is better to die enlightened than to die unenlightened. At least there is one thing left for you to experience as an enlightened man: that is death. But much more you have missed.

So I will not suggest to you to wait for death. Certainly those who are with me are going to become enlightened at the moment of death, but why wait for it when you are young and alive and full of juice? Becoming enlightened at the time of death, you are just a dry bone, there is no juice left; otherwise why should you die? When you are full of juice, full of life, with all the dimensions available, become enlightened.

And the process is so simple that even a dying man can manage it. It is really a shame that you are alive and you cannot manage it. Perhaps you only think you are alive. Perhaps you only dream you are alive, and death is such a shock that you wake up.

But I am here to give you any kind of shock you need. I am giving you them already without asking your permission, because the moment you become a sannyasin I take it for granted that now I do not need any permission to give this man a shock – any kind of shock.

Drop all that nonsense which is holding you back from experiencing life in its totality. Drop all that which is keeping you in a narcotic sleep. And what I am asking you to drop is worthless, perhaps *worse* than worthless.

It is poison that you are not dropping, that you are holding on to: Jealousy is poison, hate is poison, greed is poison. The ego is perhaps the most dangerous poison.

Just the other night I was talking to a woman journalist. She had come directly from Billy Graham – she had been covering Billy Graham for three weeks, and of course she asked about him. And I said, "He is a worthless man. None of my sannyasins will be impressed with that idiot, and none of his audience is going to understand me. His audience consists of retarded people. His face itself looks retarded. Whenever I see his photograph I simply close my eyes. He looks like a chimpanzee, well shaved."

I told her, "My work and his work are totally opposite, diametrically opposite. He is giving consolation to people so they can sleep better. He is telling them, 'Have faith in Jesus Christ, he is the savior. He can do anything, he is the only begotten son of God. If things are not happening to you, if miracles are not happening to you, that only shows your faith is not enough. Have more faith and your life will be filled with miracles.'"

This is consoling people, helping them to go into deeper sleep.

My work is totally different.

If you are asleep and snoring perfectly, I will do everything that can be done so that you have to jump out of bed. I know you will try every possible way…. I will tickle your nose, and you will throw my hand away. I will tickle your feet, and you will pull them in. I may tickle with a hair in your ear, and you will turn to the other side. To protect yourself you will pull the blanket over yourself. But nothing is going to help, no blanket can save you.

And sooner or later you are going to get tired of all these things that I am doing to you. You will have to open your eyes and see what is happening. Those who are not courageous enough to wake up, those camels start moving on the county road which goes to Santa Fe, with all their blankets, with their sleeping bags.

Only courageous people can remain with me, because I may throw ice-cold water over you. And if nothing else works, then some electric shock.

But I am determined to wake you!

Beloved Bhagwan,

Do enlightened masters lie out of compassion?

I do not know about other enlightened people, but I certainly lie!

WORLDWIDE DISTRIBUTION CENTERS
FOR THE WORKS OF BHAGWAN SHREE RAJNEESH

Books by Bhagwan Shree Rajneesh are available **AT COST PRICE** in many languages throughout the world. Bhagwan's discourses have been recorded live on audiotape and videotape. There are many recordings of Rajneesh meditation music and celebration music played in His presence, as well as beautiful photographs of Bhagwan. For further information contact one of the distribution centers below:

EUROPE

Denmark
Anwar Distribution
Carl Johansgade 8, 5
2100 Copenhagen
Tel. 01/420218

Italy
Rajneesh Services Corporation
Via XX Settembre 12
28041 Arona (NO)
Tel. 02/8392 194 (Milan office)

Netherlands
Rajneesh Distributie Centrum
Cornelis Troostplein 23
1072 JJ Amsterdam
Tel. 020/5732 130

Norway
Devananda
Rajneesh Meditation Center
P.O. Box 177 Vinderen
0386 Oslo 3
Tel. 02/123373

Sweden
Madhur Rajneesh Meditation Center
Hag Tornsv. 30
12235 Enskede (Stockholm)
Tel. 08/394946

Switzerland
Mingus AG
Asylstrasse 11
8032 Zurich
Tel. 01/2522 012

United Kingdom
Purnima Rajneesh Publications
95A Northview Road
London N8 7LRa
Tel. 01/341 4317

West Germany
The Rebel Publishing House GmbH
Venloer Strasse 5-7
5000 Cologne 1
Tel. 0221/57407 42

Rajneesh Verlags GmbH
Venloer Strasse 5-7
5000 Cologne 1
Tel. 0221/57407 43

Also available from nationwide bookshop distributor VVA Vereinigte Verlagsauslieferung GmbH
An der Autobahn - Postf. 7777
4830 Guetersloh

ASIA

India
Rajneeshdham
17 Koregaon Park
Poona 411001 M.S.
Tel. 0212/60963

Japan
Eer Rajneesh
Neo-Sannyas Commune
Mimura Building 6-21-34
Kikuna, Kohoku-ku
Yokohama, 222
Tel. 045/434 1981

AUSTRALIA

Rajneesh Meditation &
Healing Center
P.O. Box 1097
160 High Street
Fremantle, WA 6160
Tel. 09/430 4047

AMERICA

United States
Chidvilas
P.O. Box 17550
Boulder, CO 80308
Tel. 303/665 6611
Order Dept. 800/777 7743

Also available in bookstores nationwide at
Walden Books and B. Dalton

BOOKS BY BHAGWAN SHREE RAJNEESH

ENGLISH LANGUAGE EDITIONS

RAJNEESH PUBLISHERS

Early Discourses and Writings

A Cup of Tea *Letters to Disciples*
From Sex to Superconsciousness
I Am the Gate
The Long and the Short and the All
The Silent Explosion

Meditation

And Now, and Here (Volumes 1&2)
The Book of the Secrets (Volumes 1-5)
    Vigyana Bhairava Tantra
Dimensions Beyond the Known
In Search of the Miraculous (Volume 1)
Meditation: the Art of Ecstasy
The Orange Book
    The Meditation Techniques of
    Bhagwan Shree Rajneesh
The Perfect Way
The Psychology of the Esoteric

Buddha and Buddhist Masters

The Book of the Books (Volumes 1-4) *The Dhammapada*
The Diamond Sutra *The Vajrachchedika Prajnaparamita Sutra*
The Discipline of Transcendence (Volumes 1-4)
    On the Sutra of 42 Chapters
The Heart Sutra *The Prajnaparamita Hridayam Sutra*
The Book of Wisdom (Volumes 1&2)
    Atisha's Seven Points of Mind Training

Indian Mystics:

The Bauls

The Beloved (Volumes 1&2)

Kabir

The Divine Melody
Ecstasy – The Forgotten Language
The Fish in the Sea is Not Thirsty
The Guest
The Path of Love
The Revolution

Krishna

Krishna: The Man and His Philosophy

Jesus and Christian Mystics

Come Follow Me (Volumes 1-4) *The Sayings of Jesus*
I Say Unto You (Volumes 1&2) *The Sayings of Jesus*
The Mustard Seed *The Gospel of Thomas*
Theologia Mystica *The Treatise of St. Dionysius*

Jewish Mystics

The Art of Dying
The True Sage

Sufism

Just Like That
The Perfect Master (Volumes 1&2)
The Secret
Sufis: The People of the Path (Volumes 1&2)
Unio Mystica (Volumes 1&2) *The Hadiqa of Hakim Sanai*
Until You Die
The Wisdom of the Sands (Volumes 1&2)

Tantra

Tantra, Spirituality and Sex
    Excerpts from The Book of the Secrets
Tantra: The Supreme Understanding
    Tilopa's Song of Mahamudra
The Tantra Vision (Volumes 1&2)
    The Royal Song of Saraha

Tao

The Empty Boat *The Stories of Chuang Tzu*
The Secret of Secrets (Volumes 1&2)
    The Secret of the Golden Flower
Tao: The Golden Gate (Volumes 1&2)
Tao: The Pathless Path (Volumes 1&2)
    The Stories of Lieh Tzu
Tao: The Three Treasures (Volumes 1-4)
    The Tao Te Ching of Lao Tzu
When the Shoe Fits *The Stories of Chuang Tzu*

The Upanishads

I Am That *Isa Upanishad*
Philosophia Ultima *Mandukya Upanishad*
The Supreme Doctrine *Kenopanishad*
That Art Thou *Sarvasar Upanishad,*
    Kaivalya Upanishad, Adhyatma Upanishad
The Ultimate Alchemy (Volumes 1&2) *Atma Pooja Upanishad*
Vedanta: Seven Steps to Samadhi *Akshya Upanishad*

Western Mystics

Guida Spirituale *On the Desiderata*
The Hidden Harmony *The Fragments of Heraclitus*
The Messiah (Volumes 1&2)
    Commentaries on Kahlil Gibran's The Prophet
The New Alchemy: To Turn You On
    Mabel Collins' Light on the Path
Philosophia Perennis (Volumes 1&2)
    The Golden Verses of Pythagoras
Zarathustra: A God That Can Dance
Zarathustra: The Laughing Prophet

Yoga

Yoga: The Alpha and the Omega (Volumes 1-10)
    The Yoga Sutras of Patanjali
Yoga: The Science of the Soul (Volumes 1-3)
    Originally titled Yoga: The Alpha and the Omega
    (Volumes 1-3)

Zen and Zen Masters

Ah, This!
Ancient Music in the Pines
And the Flowers Showered
Bodhidharma The Greatest Zen Master
    Commentaries on the Teachings of the
    Messenger of Zen from India to China
Dang Dang Doko Dang
The First Principle
The Grass Grows By Itself
The Great Zen Master Ta Hui
    Reflections on the Transformation of
    an Intellectual to Enlightenment
Hsin Hsin Ming: The Book of Nothing
    Discourses on the Faith-Mind of Sosan
Nirvana: The Last Nightmare
No Water, No Moon
Returning to the Source

Roots and Wings
The Search *The Ten Bulls of Zen*
A Sudden Clash of Thunder
The Sun Rises in the Evening
Take it Easy (Volumes 1&2) *Poems of Ikkyu*
This Very Body the Buddha
    Hakuin's Song of Meditation
Walking in Zen, Sitting in Zen
The White Lotus *The Sayings of Bodhidharma*
Zen: The Path of Paradox (Volumes 1-3)
Zen: The Special Transmission

Responses to Questions:

Poona 1974-1981

Be Still and Know
The Goose is Out!
My Way: The Way of the White Clouds
Walk Without Feet, Fly Without Wings
    and Think Without Mind
The Wild Geese and the Water
Zen: Zest, Zip, Zap and Zing

Rajneeshpuram

From Darkness to Light
From the False to the Truth
The Rajneesh Bible (Volumes 1-4)

The World Tour

Beyond Psychology *Talks in Uruguay*
Light on the Path *Talks in the Himalayas*
The Path of the Mystic *Talks in Uruguay*
Socrates Poisoned Again After 25 Centuries
    Talks in Greece
The Transmission of the Lamp *Talks in Uruguay*

The Mystery School 1986 - present

Beyond Enlightenment
The Golden Future
The Great Pilgrimage: From Here to Here
The Hidden Splendor
The Rajneesh Upanishad
The Razor's Edge
The Rebellious Spirit
Satyam-Shivam-Sundram *Truth-Godliness-Beauty*
Sermons in Stones

Personal Glimpses

Books I Have Loved
Glimpses of a Golden Childhood
Notes of a Madman

Interviews with the World Press

The Last Testament (Volume 1)

Intimate Talks between Master and Disciple – Darshan Diaries

Hammer on the Rock
    (December 10, 1975 - January 15, 1976)
Above All Don't Wobble
    (January 16 - February 12, 1976)
Nothing to Lose But Your Head
    (February 13 - March 12, 1976)
Be Realistic: Plan For a Miracle
    (March 13 - April 6, 1976)
Get Out of Your Own Way *(April 7 - May 2, 1976)*
Beloved of My Heart *(May 3 - 28, 1976)*
The Cypress in the Courtyard *(May 29 - June 27, 1976)*
A Rose is a Rose is a Rose *(June 28 - July 27, 1976)*
Dance Your Way to God *(July 28 - August 20, 1976)*
The Passion for the Impossible
    (August 21 - September 18, 1976)
The Great Nothing *(September 19 - October 11, 1976)*
God is Not for Sale *(October 12 - November 7, 1976)*
The Shadow of the Whip *(November 8 - December 3, 1976)*
Blessed are the Ignorant *(December 4 - 31, 1976)*
The Buddha Disease *(January 1977)*
What Is, Is, What Ain't, Ain't *(February 1977)*
The Zero Experience *(March 1977)*
For Madmen Only (Price of Admission: Your Mind)
    (April 1977)
This is It *(May 1977)*
The Further Shore *(June 1977)*
Far Beyond the Stars *(July 1977)*
The No Book (No Buddha, No Teaching, No Discipline)
    (August 1977)
Don't Just Do Something, Sit There *(September 1977)*
Only Losers Can Win in This Game *(October 1977)*
The Open Secret *(November 1977)*
The Open Door *(December 1977)*
The Sun Behind the Sun Behind the Sun *(January 1978)*
Believing the Impossible Before Breakfast
    (February 1978)
Don't Bite My Finger, Look Where I'm Pointing *(March 1978)*

Let Go! *(April 1978)*
The 99 Names of Nothingness *(May 1978)*
The Madman's Guide to Enlightenment *(June 1978)*
Don't Look Before You Leap *(July 1978)*
Hallelujah! *(August 1978)*
God's Got a Thing About You *(September 1978)*
The Tongue-Tip Taste of Tao *(October 1978)*
The Sacred Yes *(November 1978)*
Turn On, Tune In, and Drop the Lot *(December 1978)*
Zorba the Buddha *(January 1979)*
Won't You Join the Dance? *February 1979)*
You Ain't Seen Nothin' Yet *(March 1979)*
The Shadow of the Bamboo *(April 1979)*
Just Around the Corner *(May 1979)*
Snap Your Fingers, Slap Your Face & Wake Up! *(June 1979)*
The Rainbow Bridge *(July 1979)*
Don't Let Yourself Be Upset by the Sutra,
    Rather Upset the Sutra Yourself *(August/September 1979)*
The Sound of One Hand Clapping *(March 1981)*

Compilations

Beyond the Frontiers of the Mind
Bhagwan Shree Rajneesh On Basic Human Rights
The Book *An Introduction to the Teachings of*
    Bhagwan Shree Rajneesh
    Series I from A - H
    Series II from I - Q
    Series III from R - Z
Death: The Greatest Fiction
Gold Nuggets
I Teach Religiousness Not Religion
Life, Love, Laughter
Meditation: The First and Last Freedom
The New Child
The New Man: The Only Hope for the Future
A New Vision of Women's Liberation
Priests and Politicians: The Mafia of the Soul
The Rebel: The Very Salt of the Earth
Rebelliousness, Religion and Revolution
Sex: Quotations from Bhagwan Shree Rajneesh

Photobiographies

The Sound of Running Water
    Bhagwan Shree Rajneesh and His Work 1974-1978
This Very Place The Lotus Paradise
    Bhagwan Shree Rajneesh and His Work 1978-1984

Books about Bhagwan Shree Rajneesh

Bhagwan Shree Rajneesh: Crucifixion and Resurrection
   Was Bhagwan Shree Rajneesh poisoned by the United States of America under Ronald Reagan's fascist, fanatic regime? (by Sue Appleton, LL.B., M.A.B.A.)
Bhagwan Shree Rajneesh:
   The Most Dangerous Man Since Jesus Christ
   (by Sue Appleton, LL.B., M.A.B.A.)
Bhagwan: The Buddha For The Future
   (by Juliet Forman, S.R.N., S.C.M., R.M.N.)
Bhagwan: The Most Godless Yet The Most Godly Man
   (by Dr. George Meredith M.D. M.B.,B.S. M.R.C.P.)
Bhagwan: Twelve Days that Shook the World
   (by Juliet Forman, S.R.N., S.C.M., R.M.N.)

OTHER PUBLISHERS

UNITED KINGDOM

The Art of Dying *(Sheldon Press)*
The Book of the Secrets *(Volume 1, Thames & Hudson)*
No Water, No Moon *(Sheldon Press)*
Roots and Wings *(Routledge & Kegan Paul)*
Straight to Freedom *(Sheldon Press)*
The Supreme Doctrine *(Routledge & Kegan Paul)*
Tao: The Three Treasures *(Volume 1, Wildwood House)*

Books about Bhagwan Shree Rajneesh

The Way of the Heart: the Rajneesh Movement
   by Judith Thompson and Paul Heelas, Department of Religious Studies, University of Lancaster (Aquarian Press)

UNITED STATES OF AMERICA

The Book of the Secrets *(Volumes 1-3, Harper & Row)*
Dimensions Beyond the Known *(Wisdom Garden Books)*
The Great Challenge *(Grove Press)*
Hammer on the Rock *(Grove Press)*
I Am the Gate *(Harper & Row)*
Journey Toward the Heart
   (Original title: Until You Die, Harper & Row)
Meditation: The Art of Ecstasy
   (Original title: Dynamics of Meditation, Harper & Row)
The Mustard Seed *(Harper & Row)*
My Way: The Way of the White Clouds *(Grove Press)*
The Psychology of the Esoteric *(Harper & Row)*
Roots and Wings *(Routledge & Kegan Paul)*
The Supreme Doctrine *(Routledge & Kegan Paul)*
Words Like Fire *(Original title: Come Follow Me, Volume 1, Harper & Row)*

Books about Bhagwan Shree Rajneesh

The Awakened One: The Life and Work of
   Bhagwan Shree Rajneesh *by Vasant Joshi (Harper & Row)*
Dying for Enlightenment *by Bernard Gunther (Harper & Row)*
Rajneeshpuram and the Abuse of Power
   by Ted Shay, Ph.D. (Scout Creek Press)
Rajneeshpuram, the Unwelcome Society
   by Kirk Braun (Scout Creek Press)
The Rajneesh Story: The Bhagwan's Garden
   by Dell Murphy (Linwood Press, Oregon)

FOREIGN LANGUAGE EDITIONS

Chinese
I am the Gate (Woolin)

Danish
Bhagwan Shree Rajneesh Om Grundlaeggende
  Menneskerettigheder (Premo)
  Bhagwan Shree Rajneesh On Basic Human Rights
Hu-Meditation Og Kosmik Orgasme (Borgens)
  Hu-Meditation and Cosmic Orgasm
Hemmelighedernes Bog (Borgens)
  The Book of the Secrets (Volume 1)

Dutch
Bhagwan Shree Rajneesh Over de Rechten van de Mens
  (Rajneesh Publikaties Nederland)
  Bhagwan Shree Rajneesh On Basic Human Rights
Volg Mij (Ankh-Hermes) *Come Follow Me (Volume 1)*
Gezaaid in Goede Aarde (Ankh-Hermes)
  Come Follow Me (Volume 2)
Drink Mij (Ankh-Hermes) *Come Follow Me (Volume 3)*
Ik Ben de Zee Die Je Zoekt (Ankh-Hermes)
  Come Follow Me (Volume 4)
Ik Ben de Poort (Ankh-Hermes) *I am the Gate*
Heel Eenvoudig (Mirananda) *Just Like That*
Meditatie: De Kunst van Innerlijke Extase (Mirananda)
  Meditation: The Art of Inner Ecstasy
Mijn Weg, De Weg van de Witte Wolk (Arcanum)
  My Way: The Way of the White Clouds
Geen Water, Geen Maan (Mirananda)
  No Water, No Moon (Volumes 1&2)
Tantra, Spiritualiteit en Seks (Ankh-Hermes)
  Tantra, Spirituality & Sex
Tantra: Het Allerhoogste Inzicht (Ankh-Hermes)
  Tantra: The Supreme Understanding
Tau (Ankh-Hermes) *Tao: The Three Treasures (Volume 1)*
Het Boek der Geheimen (Mirananda)
  The Book of Secrets (Volumes 1-5)
De Verborgen Harmonie (Mirananda)
  The Hidden Harmony
Het Mosterdzaad (Mirananda)
  The Mustard Seed (Volumes 1&2)
De Nieuwe Mens (Volume 1) (Zorn) *Compilation on
  The New Man, Relationships, Education, Health,
  Dutch edition only*

De Nieuwe Mens (Volume 2) (Altamira) *Excerpts from
  The Last Testament (Volume 1), Dutch edition only*
Het Oranje Meditatieboek (Ankh-Hermes)
  The Orange Book
Psychologie en Evolutie (Ankh-Hermes)
  The Psychology of the Esoteric
De Tantra Visie (Arcanum)
  The Tantra Vision (Volumes 1&2)
Zoeken naar de Stier (Ankh-Hermes) *10 Zen Stories*
Totdat Je Sterft (Ankh-Hermes) *Until You Die*
Priesters & Politici: De Maffia van de Ziel
  (Rajneesh Publikaties Nederland)
  Priests & Politicians: The Mafia of the Soul

Books about Bhagwan Shree Rajneesh
Een Tuin der Lusten? Het rebelse tantrisme van
  Bhagwan en het nieuwe tijdperk *by Sietse Visser*
  (Mirananda) *A Garden of Earthly Delights?*
Oorspronkelijk Gezicht *by Dr. J. Foudraine* (Ambo)
  Original Face
Bhagwan, Notities van een Discipel *by Dr. J. Foudraine*
  (Ankh-Hermes) *Bhagwan, Notes of a Disciple*
Bhagwan, een Introductie *by Dr. J. Foudraine*
  (Ankh-Hermes) *Bhagwan, an Introduction*

French
Je Suis la Porte (EPI) *I am the Gate*
La Meditation Dynamique (Dangles)
  Meditation: The Art of Inner Ecstasy
L'Eveil a la Conscience Cosmique (Dangles)
  The Psychology of the Esoteric
Le Livre des Secrets (Soleil Orange)
  The Book of Secrets (Volume 1)

German
Und vor Allem: Nicht Wackeln (Fachbuchhandlung fuer
  Psychologie) *Above All Don't Wobble*
Der Freund (Sannyas Verlag) *A Cup of Tea*
Vorsicht Sozialismus (Rajneesh Verlag)
  Beware of Socialism
Bhagwan Shree Rajneesh: Ueber die Grundrechte des
  Menschen (Rajneesh Verlag)
  Bhagwan Shree Rajneesh On Basic Human Rights

Komm und folge mir (Sannyas/Droemer Knaur)
  Come Follow Me (Volume 1)
Jesus aber schwieg (Sannyas) *Come Follow Me (Volume 2)*
Jesus – der Menschensohn (Sannyas)
  Come Follow Me (Volume 3)
Sprung ins Unbekannte (Sannyas)
  Dimensions Beyond the Known
Ekstase: Die vergessene Sprache (Herzschlag)
  Ecstasy: The Forgotten Language
Vom Sex zum kosmischen Bewusstsein) (New Age/
  Thomas Martin)
  From Sex to Superconsciousness
Goldene Augenblicke:
  Portrait einer Jugend in Indien (Goldmann)
  Glimpses of a Golden Childhood
Sprengt den Fels der Unbewusstheit (Fischer)
  Hammer on the Rock
Ich bin der Weg (Sannyas) *I am the Gate*
Meditation: Die Kunst, zu sich selbst zu finden
  (Heyne) *Meditation: The Art of Inner Ecstasy*
Mein Weg: Der Weg der weissen Wolke (Herzschlag)
  My Way: The Way of the White Clouds
Nirvana: Die letzte Huerde auf dem Weg
  (Rajneesh Verlag/NSI) *Nirvana: The Last Nightmare*
Kein Wasser, Kein Mond (Herzschlag)
  No Water, No Moon
Mit Wurzeln und Fluegeln (Lotos)
  Roots and Wings (Volume 1)
Die Schuhe auf dem Kopf (Lotos)
  Roots and Wings (Volume 2)
Spirituelle Entwicklung und Sexualitaet (Fischer)
  Spiritual Development & Sexuality
Tantra, Spiritualitaet und Sex (Rajneesh Verlag)
  Tantra, Spirituality & Sex
Tantrische Liebeskunst (Sannyas)
  Tantra, Spirituality & Sex
Tantra: Die hoechste Einsicht (Sannyas)
  Tantra: The Supreme Understanding
Das Buch der Geheimnisse (Heyne)
  The Book of the Secrets (Volume 1)
Die Gans ist raus! (Rajneesh Verlag)
  The Goose Is Out!
Rebellion der Seele (Sannyas) *The Great Challenge*
Die verborgene Harmonie (Sannyas) *The Hidden Harmony*
Die verbotene Wahrheit (Rajneesh Verlag/Heyne)
  The Mustard Seed
Das Orangene Buch (Rajneesh Verlag/NSI) *The Orange Book*
Esoterische Psychologie (Sannyas)
  The Psychology of the Esoteric

Auf der Suche (Sambuddha) *The Search*
Das Klatschen der einen Hand (Gyandip)
  The Sound of One Hand Clapping
Tantrische Vision (Heyne)
  The Tantra Vision (Volume 1)
Alchemie der Verwandlung (Lotos)
  The True Sage
Nicht bevor du stirbst (Gyandip) *Until You Die*
Was ist Meditation? (Sannyas)
  Compilation about meditation,
  German edition only
Yoga: Alpha und Omega (Gyandip)
  Yoga: The Alpha and the Omega (Volume 1)
Der Hoehepunkt des Lebens (Rajneesh Verlag)
  Compilation on death, German edition only
Intelligenz des Herzens (Herzschlag)
  Compilation, German edition only
Kunst kommt nicht vom Koennen (Rajneesh Verlag)
  Compilation about creativity, German edition only
Liebe beginnt nach den Flitterwochen (Rajneesh Verlag)
  Compilation about love, German edition only
Sexualitaet und Aids (Rajneesh Verlag)
  Compilation about Aids, German edition only
Die Zukunft gehoert den Frauen – Neue Dimensionen der
  Frauenbefreiung (Rajneesh Verlag)
  A New Vision of Women's Liberation
Priester & Politiker – Die Mafia der Seele (Rajneesh Verlag)
  Priests & Politicians: The Mafia of the Soul
Das Ultimatum: Der Neue Mensch oder globaler Selbstmord
  (Rajneesh Verlag) *The New Man:*
  The Only Hope for the Future
Mein Rezept: Leben Liebe Lachen (Rajneesh Verlag)
  Life, Love, Laughter

Greek

Bhagwan Shree Rajneesh Gia Ta Vasika
  Anthropina Dikeomata (Swami Anand Ram)
  Bhagwan Shree Rajneesh on Basic Human Rights
I Krifi Armonia (PIGI/Rassoulis)
  The Hidden Harmony

Hebrew

Tantra: Ha'havana Ha'eelaeet (Massada)
  Tantra: The Supreme Understanding

Italian

Bhagwan Shree Rajneesh parla Sui Diritti dell'Uomo
(Rajneesh Services Corporation)
Bhagwan Shree Rajneesh On Basic Human Rights
Dimensioni Oltre il Conosciuto (Mediterranee)
Dimensions Beyond the Known
Estasi: Il Linguaggio Dimenticato (Riza Libri)
Ecstasy: The Forgotten Language
Dal Sesso all'Eros Cosmico (Basaia)
From Sex to Superconsciousness
Guida Spirituale (Mondadori) *Guida Spirituale*
Io Sono La Soglia (Mediterranee) *I am the Gate*
Meditazione Dinamica: L'Arte dell'Estasi Interiore
(Mediterranee) *Meditation: The Art of Inner Ecstasy*
La Mia Via: La Via delle Nuvole Bianche
(Mediterranee) *My Way: The Way of the White Clouds*
Nirvana: L'Ultimo Incubo (Basaia) *Nirvana: The Last Nightmare*
Dieci Storie Zen di Bhagwan Shree Rajneesh:
Ne Acqua, Ne Luna (Mediterranee) *No Water, No Moon*
Philosofia Perennis (ECIG) *Philosphia Perennis (Volumes 1&2)*
Semi di Saggezza (Sugarco) *Seeds of Revolution*
Tantra, Spiritualita e Sesso (Rajneesh Foundation Italy)
Tantra, Spirituality & Sex
Tantra: La Comprensione Suprema (Bompiani)
Tantra: The Supreme Understanding
Tao: I Tre Tesori (Re Nudo)
Tao: The Three Treasures (Volumes 1-3)
Tecniche di Liberazione (La Salamandra)
Techniques of Liberation
Il Libro dei Segreti (Bompiani)
The Book of The Secrets (Volume 1)
L'Armonia Nascosta (ECIG)
The Hidden Harmony (Volumes 1&2)
Il Seme della Ribellione (Rajneesh Foundation Italy)
The Mustard Seed (Volume 1)
La Nuova Alchimia (Psiche)
The New Alchemy To Turn You On (Volumes 1&2)
Il Libro Arancione (Mediterranee) *The Orange Book*
La Rivoluzione Interiore (Mediterranee)
The Psychology of the Esoteric
La Bibbia di Rajneesh (Bompiani)
The Rajneesh Bible (Volume 1)
La Ricerca (La Salamandra) *The Search*
La Dottrina Suprema (Rizzoli) *The Supreme Doctrine*
La Visione Tantrica (Riza) *The Tantra Vision*

Japanese

Shin Jinkensengen (Meisosha Ltd.)
Bhagwan Shree Rajneesh On Basic Human Rights
Seimeino Kanki – Darshan Nisshi (Rajneesh Publications)
Dance Your Way to God
Sex kara Choishiki e (Rajneesh Publications)
From Sex to Superconsciousness
Meiso – Shukusai no Art (Merkmal)
Meditation: The Art of Inner Ecstasy
My Way – Nagareyuku Shirakumo no Michi
(Rajneesh Publications)
My Way: The Way of the White Clouds
Ikkyu Doka (Merkmal) *Take it Easy (Volume 1)*
Sonzai no Uta (Merkmal)
Tantra: The Supreme Understanding
Tao – Eien no Taiga (Merkmal)
Tao: The Three Treasures (Volumes 1-4)
Baul no Ai no Uta (Merkmal) *The Beloved (Volumes 1&2)*
Diamond Sutra – Bhagwan Shree Rajneesh
Kongohannyakyo o Kataru (Meisosha Ltd./LAF Mitsuya)
The Diamond Sutra
Koku no Fune (Rajneesh Publications)
The Empty Boat (Volumes 1&2)
Kusa wa hitorideni haeru (Fumikura)
The Grass Grows by Itself
Hannya Shinkyo (Merkmal) *The Heart Sutra*
Ai no Renkinjutsu (Merkmal)
The Mustard Seed (Volumes 1&2)
Orange Book (Wholistic Therapy Institute)
The Orange Book
Kyukyoku no Tabi – Bhagwan Shree Rajneesh
Zen no Jugyuzu o Kataru (Merkmal)
The Search
Anataga Shinumadewa (Fumikura) *Until You Die*

Korean

Giromnun Gil Il (Chung Ha)
Giromnun Gil Ih (Chung Ha)
Tao: The Pathless Path (Volume 1)
Haeng Bongron Il
Haeng Bongron Ih
Tao: The Pathless Path (Volume 2)
Joogumui Yesool (Chung Ha) *The Art of Dying*
The Divine Melody (Chung Ha)
The Divine Melody (Sung Jung)
Salmuigil Hingurumui Gil (Chung Ha) *The Empty Boat*
Seon (Chung Ha) *The Grass Grows by Itself*
Upanishad (Chung Ha) *Vedanta: Seven Steps to Samadhi*
Sesoggwa Chowol (Chung Ha) *Roots and Wings*
Sinbijuijaui Norae (Chung Ha) *The Revolution*

Mahamudraui Norae (Il Ghi Sa) *The Supreme Understanding*
Sarahaui Norae (Il Ghi Sa) *The Tantra Vision*
Meongsang Bibob (Il Ghi Sa) *The Book of the Secrets*
Banya Simgeong (Il Ghi Sa) *The Heart Sutra*
Kabir Meongsangsi (Il Ghi Sa) *The Path of Love*
Salmui Choom Chimmoogui Choom, Il (Kha Chee)
  Tao: The Three Treasures (Volume 1)
Salmui Choom Chimmoogui Choom, Ih (Kha Chee)
  Tao: The Three Treasures (Volume 2)
Salmui Choom Chimmoogui Choom, Sam (Kha Chee)
  Tao: The Three Treasures (Volume 3)
Sarangui Yeongum Sool (Kim Young Sa) *The Mustard Seed*
Yeogieh Sala (Kim Young Sa) *I am the Gate*
The Psychology of the Esoteric (Han Bat)
Soomun Johwa (Hong Sung Sa) *The Hidden Harmony*
I Say Unto You (Hong Sung Sa)
Sunggwa Meongsang (Sim Sul Dnag)
  From Sex to Superconsciousness
From Sex to Superconsciousness (Ul Ghi)
The White Lotus (Jin Young)
Beshakaui Achim (Je Il)
  My Way: The Way of the White Clouds
Iroke Nanun Durotda (Je Il) *The Diamond Sutra*
Meong Sang (Han Ma Um Sa)
  Meditation: The Art of Ecstasy
The Orange Book (Gum Moon Dang)
Jameso Khaeonara (Bum Woo Sa)
The Search – The Ten Bulls of Zen
The Teaching of the Soul (compilation) (Jeong-Um)
Alpha Grigo Omega (Jeong-Um)
  Yoga: The Alpha and the Omega (Volume 1)
Come Follow Me (Chung-Ha)
Philosophia Perennis (Chung-Ha)
Sinsim Meong (Hong-Bub)
  Hsin Hsin Ming: The Book of Nothing
Maumuro Ganungil (Moon Hak Sa Sang Sa)
  Journey towards the Heart
Saeroun Inganui Heong Meong *Neo Tantra*
Hayan Yeonkhot *The White Lotus*

Books about Bhagwan Shree Rajneesh
Jigum Yeogiyeso (Je Il) *The Awakened One*

Portuguese
Sobre Os Direitos Humanos Basicos (Editora Naim)
  Bhagwan Shree Rajneesh on Basic Human Rights
Palavras De Fogo (Global/Ground)
  Come Follow Me (Volume 1)

Dimensoes Alem do Conhecido (Cultrix)
  Dimensions Beyond the Known
Extase: A Linguagem Esquecida (Global)
  Ecstasy: The Forgotten Language
Do Sexo A Superconsciencia (Cultrix)
  From Sex to Superconsciousness
Eu Sou A Porta (Pensamento) *I am the Gate*
Meditacao: A Arte Do Extase (Cultrix)
  Meditation: The Art of Inner Ecstasy
Meu Caminho: O Caminho Das Nuvens Brancas (Tao)
  My Way: The Way of the White Clouds
Nem Agua, Nem Lua (Pensamento) *No Water, No Moon*
Notas De Um Homem Louco (NAIM) *Notes of a Madman*
Raizes E Asas (Cultrix) *Roots and Wings*
Sufis: O Povo do Caminho (Maha Lakshmi Editora)
  Sufis: The People of the Path
Tantra: Sexo E Espiritualidade (Agora)
  Tantra, Spirituality & Sex
Tantra: A Suprema Compreensao (Cultrix)
  Tantra: The Supreme Understanding
Arte de Morrer (Global) *The Art of Dying*
O Livro Dos Segredos (Maha Lakshmi)
  The Book of the Secrets (Volumes 1&2)
Cipreste No Jardim (Cultrix)
  The Cypress in the Courtyard
A Divina Melodia (Cultrix) *The Divine Melody*
A Harmonia Oculta (Pensamento) *The Hidden Harmony*
A Semente De Mostarda (Tao)
  The Mustard Seed (Volumes 1&2)
A Nova Alquirnia (Cultrix)
  The New Alchemy To Turn You On
O Livro Orange (Pensamento) *The Orange Book*
A Psicologia Do Esoterico (Tao)
  The Psychology of the Esoteric
Unio Mystica (Maha Lakshmi) *Unio Mystica*

Russian
Bhagwan Shree Rajneesh On Basic Human Rights
  (Neo-Sannyas International)

Serbo-Croat
Bhagwan Shree Rajneesh (Swami Mahavira)
  (Compilation of various quotations)
Bhagwan Shree Rajneesh O Osnovnim Pravima Covjeka
  Bhagwan Shree Rajneesh on Basic Human Rights
The Ultimate Pilgrimage
Vrovno Hodocasce *A Rajneesh Reader*

Spanish

Sobre Los Derechos Humanos Basicos (Futonia, Spain)
Bhagwan Shree Rajneesh on Basic Human Rights
Ven, Sigueme (Sagaro, Chile) *Come Follow Me (Volume 1)*
Yo Soy La Puerta (Diana, Mexico) *I am The Gate*
Meditacion: El Arte del Extasis (Rosello Impresiones)
Meditation: The Art of Inner Ecstasy
El Camino de las Nubes Blancas (Cuatro Vientos)
My Way: The Way of the White Clouds
Solo Un Cielo (Collection Tantra) *Only One Sky*
Introduccion al Mundo del Tantra (Rosello Impresiones)
Tantra: The Supreme Understanding (Volumes 1&2)
Tao: Los Tres Tesoros (Sirio, Espana)
Tao: The Three Treasures

El Sutra del Corazon (Sarvogeet, Espana) *The Heart Sutra*
El Libro Naranja (Bhagwatam, Puerto Rico)
The Orange Book
Psicologia de lo Esoterico: La Nueva Evolucion del Hombre
(Cuatro Vientos, Chile) *The Psychology of the Esoteric*
¿Que Es Meditacion? (Koan/Rosello Pastanaga)
What Is Meditation?

Swedish

Den Vaeldiga Utmaningen (Livskraft)
The Great Challenge

RAJNEESH MEDITATION CENTERS
ASHRAMS AND COMMUNES

There are many Rajneesh Meditation Centers throughout the world which can be contacted for information about the teachings of Bhagwan Shree Rajneesh and which have His books available as well as audio and video tapes of His discourses. Centers exist in practically every country.

For further information about Bhagwan Shree Rajneesh please contact:

Rajneeshdham Neo-Sannyas Commune
17 Koregaon Park
Poona 411 001, MS
India